Innovation Paradox in Merger Control

Professor Gönenç Gürkaynak

Foreword by Professor Frederic Jenny
Introduction by Professor William E. Kovacic

Copyright © 2023 by Institute of Competition Law
106 West 32nd Street, Suite 144 New York, NY, 10001, USA
www.concurrences.com
book@concurrences.com

First Printing, November 2023
978-1-939007-75-9 (Hardcover)
Library of Congress Control Number: 2023947859

Cover Design: Yves Buliard, www.yvesbuliard.fr
Book Design and Layout implementation: Nord Compo

Concurrences Books

Tributes

Eleanor M. Fox – Antitrust Ambassador to the World, *2021*

Herbert Hovenkamp – The Dean of American Antitrust Law, *2021*

Frédéric Jenny – Standing Up for Convergence and Relevance in Antitrust, (Vol. I & II), *2019 & 2021*

Albert Foer – A Consumer Voice in the Antitrust Arena, *2020*

Richard Whish – Taking Competition Law Outside the Box, *2020*

Douglas H. Ginsburg – An Antitrust Professor on the Bench (Vol. I & II), *2018 & 2020*

Wang Xiaoye – The Pioneer of Competition Law in China, *A. Emch, W. Ng (eds.), 2019*

Ian S. Forrester – A Scot without Borders (Vol. I & II), *A. Komninos (eds.), 2015*

William E. Kovacic – An Antitrust Tribute (Vol. I & II), *2013 & 2014*

Practical Books

Global Dictionary of Competition Law, *D. Healey, W. Kovacic, P. Trevisan, R. Whish, 2023*

Antitrust in Life Sciences, *M. Cowie, G. Gordon, M. Thill-Tayara, 2023*

State Aid & the Energy Transition, *D. Buschle, L. Hancher, M.-T. Richter-Kuhnert (eds.), 2023 (in collaboration with the Energy Community)*

State Aid & National Enforcement, *J. Derenne, D. Jouve, C. Lemaire, F. Martucci (eds.), 2023*

Antitrust and the Digital Economy, *Y. Katsoulacos (ed.), 2023 (in collaboration with CRESSE)*

Judicial Review of Competition Cases, *D. Ginsburg, T. Eicke (eds.), 2023*

Competition Law Treatment of Joint Ventures, *B. Bleicher, N. Campbell, A. Hamilton, N. Hukkinen, A. Khan, A. Mordaunt (eds.), 2022 (in collaboration with the IBA)*

Information Exchange & Related Risks, *Z. Marosi, M. Soares (eds.), 2022 (in collaboration with the IBA)*

Rulemaking Authority of the US Federal Trade Commission, *D. Crane (ed.), 2022*

The International Competition Network at Twenty, *D. Anderson & P. Lugard (eds.), 2022*

Competition Case Law Digest – 5th Edition, *F. Jenny, N. Charbit (eds.), 2022*

Competition Inspections in 21 Jurisdictions – A Practitioner's Guide, *N. Jalabert-Doury (ed.), 2022*

Perspectives on Antitrust Compliance, *A. Riley, A. Stephan, A. Tubbs (eds.), 2022 (in collaboration with the ICC)*

Turkish Competition Law, *G. Gürkaynak, 2021*

Competition Law – Climate Change & Environmental Sustainability, *S. Holmes, D. Middelschulte, M. Snoep (eds.), 2021*

Merger Control in Latin America – A Jurisdictional Guide, *P. Burnier da Silveira, P. Sittenfeld (eds.), 2020*

Competition Inspections under EU Law – A Practitioner's Guide, *N. Jalabert-Doury, 2020*

Gun Jumping in Merger Control – A Jurisdictional Guide, *C. Hatton, Y. Comtois, A. Hamilton (eds.), 2019 (in collaboration with the IBA)*

Choice – A New Standard for Competition Analysis? *P. Nihoul (ed.), 2016*

PhD Theses

Abuse of Platform Power, *F. Bostoen, 2023*

Reform of Chinese State-Owned Enterprises, *X. Bai, 2023*

Competition & Regulation in Network Industries – Essays in Industrial Organization, *J-M. Zogheib, 2021*

The Role of Media Pluralism in the Enforcement of EU Competition Law, *K. Bania, 2019*

Buyer Power, *I. Herrera Anchustegui, 2017*

General Interest

Women and Antitrust – Voices from the Field (Vol I & II), *E. Kurgonaite & K. Nordlander, 2020*

Conference Proceedings

Antitrust in Emerging and Developing Countries – (Vol I & II), *E. Fox, H. First, 2015 & 2016*

Global Antitrust Law – Current Issues in Antitrust Law and Economics, *D. Ginsburg, J. Wright, (eds.) 2015*

Competition Law on the Global Stage – David Gerber's Global Competition Law in Perspective, *D. Gerber, 2014*

> **e-Book versions** available for **Concurrences+** subscribers

*To my father, Prof. Dr. Mehmet Rüştü Gürkaynak,
with love, admiration, and gratitude, for teaching me to stay
hungry for knowledge and towards life, through his elastic
strings of questions and joyful morning whistle tunes.*

AUTHOR BIOGRAPHY

Dr. Gönenç Gürkaynak is the founding partner of ELIG Gürkaynak Attorneys-at-Law, a leading law firm of 95 lawyers based in Istanbul, Turkey. He is also an academician, teaching law & economics and competition law at undergraduate and graduate levels at the University College London (UCL) Faculty of Laws as an honorary professor and at Bilkent University Faculty of Law in Turkey as a visiting professor.

Dr. Gürkaynak graduated from Ankara University Faculty of Law in 1997 and was called to the Istanbul Bar in 1998. Dr. Gürkaynak received his LL.M. degree from Harvard Law School and his Doctor of Philosophy in Law (Ph.D.) degree from UCL Faculty of Laws. Before founding ELIG Gürkaynak Attorneys-at-Law in 2005, Dr. Gürkaynak worked as an attorney at the Istanbul, New York and Brussels offices of a global law firm for more than eight years. In addition to his membership to the Istanbul Bar since 1998, he was admitted to the American Bar Association in 2002; New York Bar in 2002 (currently non-practicing; registered); Brussels Bar in 2003–2004 (B List; not maintained); Law Society of England & Wales in 2004 (currently non-practicing; registered).

In addition to his continuing private practice as an attorney, primarily through ELIG Gürkaynak Attorneys-at-Law in Istanbul, Dr. Gürkaynak is an honorary professor of practice at UCL Faculty of Laws in London. In addition to his academic role at University College London, he also teaches competition law at Bilkent University Faculty of Law in Ankara since 2005, and he has taught competition law in more than ten universities in Turkey, the EU, the UK, and the US in the last eighteen years.

Dr. Gürkaynak is also a senior research fellow at the Centre for Law, Economics and Society (CLES) at UCL Faculty of Laws.

Dr. Gürkaynak frequently speaks at international conferences and symposia on competition law matters. He has authored four books, and over 80 academic articles published in refereed international law journals.

FOREWORD

PROFESSOR FRÉDÉRIC JENNY
ESSEC Business School, Paris

This book explores the ways and the extent to which competition authorities analyze the effects of mergers on innovation. As one would expect, a substantial part of the book is devoted to the specific case of the digital sector. However, the author places his discussion in a broader context, analyzing economic theory, commenting on the relevant legal and economic literature, and reviewing a large number of merger decisions given by competition authorities in three important jurisdictions, i.e., the United States, United Kingdom, and European Union.

Although we know that dynamic efficiencies are more important than static efficiencies for the future of our economies, until fairly recently, authorities in charge of competition law enforcement and merger control have paid relatively little attention to the effects of anti-competitive mergers or practices on innovation.

This timely book is important for the future development of competition law, because it is a balanced and excellent source of information on the jurisprudence of major jurisdictions on theories of harm relating to innovation.

It is timely because, as is clear from the case law examined, competition authorities are more and more concerned with the dynamic implications of mergers and, in particular, with the impact of these mergers on innovation. This concern first arose due to the importance of a number of mergers in the highly innovative pharmaceutical and chemical sectors. This concern was further enhanced by the rapid development of the digital sector, and a growing number of concentrations in that sector, where competition, differentiation, and innovation are closely linked.

This book is important for the future development of competition law, first, because it very clearly shows the complexity of the relationship between competition and innovation, both from a theoretical point of view and from a practical one (in particular because we do not have a good metric to measure innovation). Second, by commenting on the jurisprudence of a number of competition authorities, Dr. Gönenç Gürkaynak analyzes the changes in their perspective that have taken place with respect to the analysis of the effects of innovation on mergers (for example, in the EU), and he also presents his opinion on the direction competition authorities should be taking in the future.

The approach of this book is balanced, because the author, recognizing the complexity of the relationship between competition and innovation, analyzes the jurisprudence of different competition authorities with a view to assessing whether, in each case, the authority has been thorough in its analysis of the expected effects of mergers not only on the innovation of the merging parties but also on the possible indirect effects of the mergers on the innovation of non-merging firms in the market. In his analysis,

Dr. Gürkaynak also criticizes simplistic or dogmatic models of the relationship between competition and innovation, and insufficiently motivated decisions. A convincing theme that permeates the book is the necessity for competition authorities to engage in a thorough analysis on a case-by-case basis.

Dr. Gönenç Gürkaynak also provides a thorough commentary on some 80 merger decisions in cases raising issues related to innovation and taken by the EU Commission, the UK CMA, and US competition authorities. He also comments on the academic literature concerning these cases. The wealth of information provided by the author on these decisions, the commentaries presented and discussed, and the author's personal notes on these cases, make this book an invaluable source for anyone interested in the issue of "concentration and innovation."

Finally, it takes courage for an eminent lawyer to publish a book on innovation in merger control, when one is aware of the ferocity of the theoretical debate on this issue among economists, of the fact that economists lack a robust theory of the relationship between these two variables, that competition authorities have a well-known restrictive approach to efficiencies whether they be static or dynamic, that competition authorities, lacking a compass, have had to pragmatically try to deal with this issue, and lastly that we are in the middle of a technological competition for innovation between nations and regions in the world. Dr. Gönenç Gürkaynak has done an excellent job of navigating these treacherous waters, with this book.

Dr. Gönenç Gürkaynak's book is a must-read for those interested in the relationship between competition and innovation in merger enforcement, a topic that undoubtedly will be more and more crucial in the years to come.

INTRODUCTION

PROFESSOR WILLIAM E. KOVACIC
The George Washington University Law School

Since the development of national competition laws in North America in the late Nineteenth Century, enforcement agencies and courts have struggled to account for innovation – in products and services, industrial processes, and business organization – in determining the competitive significance of various commercial practices. The outcome of this struggle has enormous significance given the paramount role that innovation plays as a stimulant to economic progress.

The treatment of innovation-related issues has proven to be especially difficult in the evaluation of mergers that pose questions about whether specific transactions will boost or retard innovation. The predictive judgments required by merger review generally present challenging tasks in forecasting, and these challenges often become more daunting where the merging parties contend that their proposed consolidation will yield valuable innovation efficiencies.

The evaluation of innovation effects has acquired increasing importance in contemporary practice. In a number of widely reported transactions, the central issue for resolution for competition agencies and courts has been the likely impact of the merger on innovation. Concerns about consolidation in technologically dynamic sectors such as information services have drawn attention, among other issues, to the acquisition by larger enterprises of "nascent competitors" – smaller start-ups that threaten to disrupt sectors through the introduction of new products or services.

Amid a modern avalanche of new literature on innovation as a core concern of competition policy, Dr. Gönenç Gürkaynak has provided a uniquely informative analysis of innovation considerations in merger control. This volume stands out in several respects. It begins by providing valuable perspective by situating the modern debate in a larger context by tracing the historical development of thought about innovation and commerce and defining the core issues relating to the analysis of innovation effects and the formulation of efficiency arguments to support specific mergers.

The core of the volume is a masterful comparative examination of practice in the three jurisdictions whose enforcement programs and jurisprudence figure most prominently in contemporary policy debates: the European Union, the United Kingdom, and the United States. The comparative chapters provide a comprehensive examination of relevant merger policy experience, offers superb summaries of the most significant enforcement events, and uses the discussion of recent decisions and pending cases to illuminate the most pressing modern issues. The volume applies the insights from the comparative survey to the arena of greatest concern today to digital markets, the commercial setting that provides the main focal point for current debate. A final chapter takes on theories of harm associated with "killer acquisitions" in the three featured jurisdictions.

Introduction

As one of its most enduring contribution, the volume concludes with suggestions about how to take innovation analysis forward in future merger reviews. In particular, the author makes a powerful case for competition agencies to accept the cost of a more intensive examination of innovation efficiency arguments as necessary to determine when intervention to block or qualify proposed transactions is appropriate. These proposals stand upon an impressive foundation of conceptual analysis and the practical insights about merger control. This reflects the author's enviable accomplishments as a scholar and practitioner. Theory meets practice in the best way possible.

TABLE OF CONTENTS

Chapter 3 – The Innovation Effects of Mergers: The Concepts and Theoretical Background

LIST OF ABBREVIATIONS

1995 Licensing Guidelines	The 1995 Antitrust Guidelines for the Licensing of Intellectual Property
2010 Guidelines	FTC Horizontal Merger Guidelines in 2010
ALJ	Administrative law judge
AOSP	Android Open Source Project
API	Application programming interface
AAC	Augmentative and assistive communication
CAT	Competition Appeal Tribunal
CC	Competition Commission
CES	Constant elasticity of substitution
CFA	Consumer Federation of America
CIS	Central infrastructural services
CMA	The UK Competition and Markets Authority
CMA Guidelines	CMA Merger Guidelines
Commission	The European Commission
COPD	Chronic obstructive pulmonary disease
CPU	Central processing unit
DCF	Discounted cash flow
DIP	Downward innovation pressure
DOJ	The United States Department of Justice
EA	The UK Enterprise Act 2022
ECJ	European Court of Justice
EDM	Elimination of pre-merger double marginalization
EEA	European Economic Area
EU	The European Union
EUMR	The EU Merger Regulation
Fempop	Femoropopliteal
FDA	Food and Drug Administration
FTC	The Federal Trade Commission
FTC	The Federal Trade Commission Bureau of Competition
GDP	Gross domestic product
GDS	Global distribution system
GPT	General-purpose technologies
HSR Act	The Hart-Scott-Rodino Antitrust Improvements Act of 1976
IoT	Internet of things
IP	Intellectual property
IRMS	Isotope ratio mass spectrometers
Kill zone effect	Evidence indicating that when a big platform buys out a start-up, the venture capital investment in the market where the start-up is active decreases
LBOs	Licensed betting offices
MC-ICP-MS	Multi-collector-inductively coupled plasma MS

List of Abbreviations

MNOs	Mobile network operators
MS	Mass spectrometers
MSS	Meta-search site
NHMG	Commission's Non-Horizontal Merger Guidelines
NRA	National regulatory authority
NSA	National Security Agency
OECD	Organisation for Economic Co-operation and Development
OFT	Office of Fair Trading
OS	Operating system
OTAs	Online travel agencies
OVDs	Online video distributors
PCS	Price comparison site
PSBs	Public service broadcasters
PSS	Core and non-core passenger service system
RCBs	Relevant customer benefits
Replacement effect	If the innovation of the entrant is a close substitute to the products or services of the acquirer, the latter would not have sufficient incentive to develop it, given that the incremental profits to be gained as a result of the innovation would be small due to cannibalization.
Revised Merger Guidelines	CMA Merger Assessment Guidelines
RMS	Relevant merger situation
SIEC	Significant impediment of effective competition
SLC	Substantial lessening of competition
SoC	Systems-on-chip
Strategy Report	The CMA's Digital Markets Strategy (July 2019)
Study	The CMA – Online platforms and digital advertising (July 2020)
Supreme Court	The US Supreme Court
TFEU	Treaty on the Functioning of the European Union
TFP	Total factor productivity
The Report	Non-HSR Reported Acquisitions by Select Technology Platforms, 2010–2019
TIMS	Thermal ionization mass spectrometers
Transfer Guidelines	Commission's Transfer of Technology Guidelines
TSPs	Travel service providers
UK	The United Kingdom
UPP	Upward Price Pressure
US	The United States
VOD	Video-on-demand

Chapter 1
Introduction

1.1 Defining the Question

This book is based on the exploration of the principles for the proper assessment of innovation considerations in merger control analysis. In this context, the discussion focuses on the discrepancy in the approach followed by competition authorities, that is, how and why innovation is seen as calculable, concrete and predictable when the competition law enforcer examines its anti-competitive effects, but as speculative and mystical when the concept of innovation is used as a defense by undertakings to counterbalance the substantive competition law concerns expressed by the competition law enforcer; which I will call the innovation paradox. In parallel, the book also investigates if the standards of proof of innovative efficiencies in merger control could be set in a way to better protect and foster innovation, especially in the discovery phase. Accordingly, the target is identifying the principles and analytical tools when reviewing innovation matters in the merger control context.

The reason for this study stems from the recognition that enforcement agencies have begun to increasingly distinguish "innovation" as a significant and specific concern in merger control. Clear signals of this approach have culminated in *Dow/DuPont*[1] and have been demonstrated most recently in *Illumina/Grail*[2] (or, perhaps, *Microsoft/Activision*, as will be discussed in a separate chapter in this book). Having said that, the enforcement agencies adopted this approach as a means to protect the competitive structure of the markets, specifically those innovation-intensive sectors such as the digital or pharmaceutical/agrochemical markets, and not for the sake of innovation itself. That would be an intermediate rather than primary objective, considering the European Commission's Arrowian view that innovation flourishes in a competitive market. The enforcement agencies' focus in the control of concentrations (be they joint ventures, mergers or acquisitions) is now more visibly directed towards assessing the future effects of the transaction on the innovation spheres and pipeline products, and the language in their reasoned decisions touches upon innovative efficiency. Here, the discussion is whether the agencies are able to protect innovation by merely flagging the concerns they have or if they could and should do more, e.g., by allowing the transaction parties more room to maneuver by "hearing" their defenses on innovative efficiency and perhaps going the extra mile of their own accord and taking on some of the evidentiary burden to more objectively assess the status of and effects on innovation. The analysis is therefore focused on this very interesting point of debate.

---

[1]   Dow/DuPont, European Commission Decision case M.7932 (Mar. 27, 2017).
[2]   Illumina/GRAIL, European Commission Decision case M.10188 (Sept. 6, 2022).

To that end, this book will set out the "state of play." First, it will explore the path dependencies with the way the concept of innovation has been theorized throughout history. This analysis is the key to understanding the reluctance and inherent difficulties in fully integrating innovation goals and concerns in the traditionally static microeconomic framework and, more broadly, the legal system. It will then turn to assess innovation in competition law and in particular merger control as it currently stands. This is aimed at being a normative work in that sense, i.e., it does not claim to have discovered the ultimate solution or method to the innovation assessment that should be adopted by competition law enforcers, but shows the asymmetry in the way innovation is assessed as a sword and as a shield for competition law enforcement, despite claims otherwise. It is imperative that we realize that although innovation seems to be recognized as a crucial factor, this is neither sufficient nor unbiased; which runs the risk of perverse enforcement and actually hindering innovation efforts, instead of protecting them.

1.2 Scope and Methodology

Taking into account the above objectives, this book examines and evaluates cases, primarily from the European Union ("EU"), the United Kingdom ("UK") and the United States ("US"), to demonstrate the extent innovation considerations have become, either in the form of a concern or a defense, a central topic of discussion by competition authorities as well as competition law practitioners. Having said this, the aim is not to perform a comparative study of these three jurisdictions in the traditional sense; thus, the discussion will not touch upon their institutional structures or how these affect the decisions of the respective authorities or shape the underlying policies. As the three most developed competition law jurisdictions, the focus shall be on how they approach innovation under their regulatory and enforcement roles; and to demonstrate that currently, even these jurisdictions have not been able to fully embrace innovation; that they remain satisfied with merely paying lip service to its importance and dismissive of the distinctive character of innovative industries in particular in the digital economy, by still using traditional tools to assess competitive concerns.

Furthermore, again in light of this approach, policy papers of international and national authorities and organizations are reviewed, and extensive research of academic literature is conducted to test and support the analyses, conclusions, and proposals. They will be gateways to relevant and critical cases and academic works in some jurisdictions other than the EU, the UK and the US, as far as they relate to the tension between the dynamism of innovative markets and the inherent static and speculative nature of *ex ante* merger control analysis, based on snapshots and projections.

The book has been designed to set out the above premise in the following structure:

The introductory chapter will address the roots and the historical connotations of the word "innovation" and how it has been a difficult journey for it to gain its positive connotation. This setting is crucial as one of the most important premises of this work is that innovation still has not actually been fully embraced and is almost treated with suspicion by competition authorities. This indicates that innovation's negative historical trajectory still continues and falls short of full integration, contrary to what the authorities would have us think. The following chapters will demonstrate that the competition authorities approach innovation one-sidedly, i.e., as a theory of potential harm and not as a countervailing factor, demonstrating that the historical pejorative connotation that innovation carries still casts a shadow on their perceptions. This is not to say that enforcement agencies wholly eschew innovation; on the contrary, it is evident that they see it as their duty to protect and promote innovation. However, their perceptions do not yet appear to go as far as fully appreciating it as a countervailing factor and remain limited to the sphere of protective concern. Once enforcement agencies make heavy inroads into adopting dynamic efficiency defenses, they will have fully shaken off the effects of this historical pejorative connotation.

Chapter 2 will focus on the role of innovation in economic growth, in order to demonstrate that the purpose of competition law is parallel to that of economic development and total welfare, similar to innovation and its journey. Part of the problem is that competition authorities fail to grasp (or acknowledge and embrace) the importance of innovation in economic growth, and therefore, they underappreciate the role innovation plays in furthering total welfare. This, in turn, causes competition authorities to restrict their analyses and views to only traditional methods, getting stuck at rote arguments, thereby failing to maximize the real potential that the undertakings could contribute. The aim of this chapter is to demonstrate that innovation is crucial for economic development and therefore should be taken more seriously as a plausible argument when brought up as a defense and not just dismissed outright. Chapter 3 then concentrates on the innovation effects of mergers themselves, i.e., what are the concerns of the competition authorities in the selected jurisdictions and what defenses are brought forward by the undertakings that are trying to convince the authorities that the proposed transactions will not harm the existing innovative drive of the parties. These will be addressed in existing arguments in real cases as well as potential arguments that could also have been put forward, showing that what the authorities dismiss as being speculative are, in fact, sound theories and defenses that should be taken into consideration for a comprehensive analysis.

The book then brings the EU, US and UK competition authorities' practices into the spotlight in the next three chapters and discusses the cases that have presented complex innovation considerations. The purpose here is to analyze their approaches and to determine whether they were able to assess the innovation aspects of the particular transactions in a way that could balance the authority's concerns with countervailing arguments and thereby bestow the due importance on the defenses brought by the undertakings.

The final substantive chapter shall focus on a particular aspect that seems to be emphasized by authorities when evaluating transactions, i.e., killer acquisitions that allegedly put an end to or materially reduce potential innovation following completion. Here, the author will present that despite the perception that killer acquisitions are always harmful, there are studies indicating these may still be beneficial, whether in providing an exit for unicorn investors or incentivizing start-ups and innovations in the first place. Therefore, the hesitant approach of competition authorities and scaremongering may actually be giving rise to further harm, even if their stated intention is to prevent any restrictions to innovation.

The discussions in these chapters will all be wrapped up in the conclusion chapter.

1.3 Reasoning

The number of merger control analyses putting an emphasis on the concept of innovation is growing all around the world at an increasing speed. We are now at that stage where even principles are being introduced by enforcers. In merger control analyses relating to dynamic and innovative markets, the European Commission has recently started using a "significant impediment to effective innovation competition" test,[3] which clearly indicates that there is a growing need for research and scholarly work in the field of proper integration of innovation goals in merger control, as principles are being devised already. Having said that, the asymmetry is revealed in the practice: the Commission has been excluding all innovation arguments of the parties' defenses as speculative, despite readily embracing scaremongering or merely theoretical constructs of potential harm to innovation. It seems the elusive nature of the innovation concept makes it prone to being used unilaterally to feed anxieties about anti-competitive effects, but never as a countervailing factor for theories of potential harm to competition. Furthermore, although the Commission is eager to rely on stochastic models in terms of its theory of harm on innovation competition, when it comes to parties' reliance on general and hypothetical grounds (e.g., that regulatory pressure on existing products would foster future innovation and competition), it is dismissive of such arguments on the grounds that the parties have provided no evidence in support of their statements.

Although cognizant of the need to use alternative tools and assessments, the Commission has been relying heavily on economic literature and theory in its assessment of a theory of harm in innovative markets. When the traditional worries about increasing market power take the lead, and innovation concerns are given a supportive role to provide depth to such existing anxieties, it is difficult to provide the independent and neutral focus that innovation goals deserve. This necessitates conducting counterfactual analyses; the authority would need to weigh up what new undertakings, innovations, technological creations it is preventing in prohibiting the transaction at hand, and consider whether the seller would have actually invested in that particular industry or product had it known that in the future the transaction would not be permitted: would they have expanded the business no matter what, or did they always have an exit strategy in mind? This is one of the questions the discussion on killer acquisitions in Chapter 7 aims to address.

It is also seen that the authorities have a somewhat cynical approach as they tend to resort to speculative scaremongering with respect to the undertakings' intentions behind the mergers. This is apparent in how they focus on the products in the pipeline in the pharmaceutical industry and their theories of harm, arguing that the undertakings would scale back or even drop some of the research post-merger, resulting in a loss of innovation. However, for those sectors that lack pipelines or similar visible/demonstrable routes regarding their innovative progress, the authorities should at least try to identify and conduct a similar innovation analysis without outright dismissal. The half-hearted approach results in missing those opportunities that may have contributed to economic

---

[3] Mario Todino, Geoffroy van de Walle & Lucia Stoican, *EU Merger Control and Harm to Innovation – A Long Walk to Freedom (from the Chains of Causation)*, 64 ANTITRUST BULL. 11 (2019).

development and total welfare. Furthermore, if competition authorities are indeed sincere about integrating innovation into competitive theory of harm, then they should consider whether the parties have been able to sufficiently and credibly demonstrate their innovative progress and plans post-merger. Hence, the enforcers should accept that a way to protect innovation is also respecting it as a defense on the part of the undertakings. This is a necessary component if they want to sincerely claim that their innovation assessments have fully integrated and reached some level of maturity. As will be explained in the following section, although the concept of innovation was vilified or feared centuries ago, this asymmetry in treating the concept of innovation becomes even less acceptable now that we live in a period where innovation is ostensibly lauded, but still remains not fully integrated or embraced due to unfounded anxieties or a lack of understanding that prevents any leaps of faith or the courage to take even the smallest step towards a more symmetrical approach.

When innovation concerns are raised purely on theoretical grounds in the absence of factual economic modeling, there would be many unanswered questions, the answers of which would be germane to properly defining and protecting innovation. Innovation has always been seen as a stochastic concept, which may also explain the myriad of definitions and connotations it has carried throughout history, as the following sections set out in painstaking detail. Nevertheless, now that enforcers are increasingly claiming that they can more concretely assess these innovation concerns during the merger control review, they should also be invited to show the same appetite to recognize innovation gains and defenses.

In summary, this book explores the principles and tools of a functioning and feasible trade-off when reviewing innovation matters in the merger control context. While principles in this field are newly emerging, the author contends that they are flawed and are characterized by different biases that will be explored in this book. They are designed to allow for speculative assessments when innovation considerations are presented as a concern, but they are not designed to allow for innovation considerations to be recognized as a redeeming virtue when they are presented as a defense. This book will focus on how and why this happens, and then will propose ways of developing a holistic innovation analysis in merger control, with the aim of truly serving the goal of fostering innovation, also aiming at limiting the risk that innovative efficiency concepts are appropriated to serve more traditionally understood concerns in merger control enforcement.

1.4 The Multiple Meanings of "Innovation": An Introduction to the Concept in a Historical Perspective

Innovation is one of the main drivers of the economy, as it not only contributes to facilitating people's daily activities but also results in heightened economic growth and competitiveness, as witnessed in various industries. In this context, it should be noted that the term "innovation" does not merely refer to assorted technological developments but also encompasses concepts such as the invention of a new product, the improvement of already existing products, cultural transformations, the introduction of new ways of providing services, as well as the establishment of new industries. The products of innovation, in turn, further contribute to the well-being of people, mainly through the increases in benefits to consumers. The term, in fact, has been laden with so many connotations and roles since its conception that even now, it is proving difficult to delineate and find a proper measurement to do it justice.

Innovation also leads to massive shifts in traditional industries through the introduction of "breakthroughs," which either alter existing industries significantly or demolish such long-established industries and create new ones. Recognizing this type of innovation, more aptly described as drastic or disruptive innovation,[4] is significant as businesses need to distinguish whether a technology will disrupt their organization and carefully consider any actions they may need to take before the drastic innovation affects the market.[5] Is this not one of the reasons why the world was deemed to have experienced an industrial "revolution" in the first place? Starting in England in the 18th century and spreading all around the world, the global transformative influence of the first industrial revolution and the next ones pushed scholars to seek its causes and variables.[6] Some focused on the increase in the savings rate due to economic activities, technological inventions and innovations leading to mass production by machines, some on the rise of capitalism with competitive markets (rather than state-controlled ones) in ascent, as well as the growth of the market due to the increase in demand caused by a growing population.[7] Some like Mokyr, however, considered the actual dissemination of "useful knowledge" to the masses, particularly during the Enlightenment, as being vital and attributed Western economic development to the accumulation of useful knowledge in society and the increasing ability to put that useful knowledge into practice.[8]

The subsequent industrial revolutions also comprised of breakthroughs, in the use of electric power and electronics to increase efficiency and automation, breaking from traditional industries or amalgamating different business spheres. Some of the most illustrative examples of these shifts were provided by the well-known technology firms that have introduced breakthrough concepts into traditional industries in the past few decades, which led to the demolition of the existing industries and contributed to the establishment of new, highly innovative industries, such as the music-recording industry and its recent moves towards streaming services and live concerts, away from physical album and CD sales. The pace of the change has been gaining speed; now we are in the "Fourth Industrial Revolution" with the emergence of technologies such as artificial intelligence, the Internet of things, blockchain, and virtual reality, among others. As Klaus Schwab,

---

[4]   *See* Chapter 4 for a discussion on what constitutes a drastic or disruptive innovation, as opposed to an incremental or sustaining innovation.

[5]   Delmer Nagy, Joseph Schuessler & Alan Dubinsky, *Defining and Identifying Disruptive Innovations*, 57 INDUS. MKTG. MGMT. 119, 120 (2016).

[6]   R. M. Hartwell, *The Causes of the Industrial Revolution: An Essay in Methodology*, 18 ECON. HIST. REV. 164 (1965).

[7]   *Id.*

[8]   Joel Mokyr, *The Intellectual Origins of Modern Economic Growth*, 65 J. ECON. HIST. 285, 287–95 (2005).

the executive chairman of the World Economic Forum, puts it, the current revolution "is characterized by a fusion of technologies that is blurring the lines between physical, digital and biological spheres."[9] The borders between different industries increasingly seem to disappear; new ecosystems have appeared in the business world through the merging of various markets and value chains, in order to meet the consumers' constantly evolving needs and wants. In this new economic model of "ecosystems," consumers are offered an ecosystem that amalgamates different industries, which are integrated in such a way that the consumers are able to fulfill their needs without ever leaving it.[10] These "ecosystem orchestrators" garner unique characteristics that challenge the regulators, so the traditional approaches to defining the relevant market and assessing market power through product substitutability are no longer sufficient for dynamic markets and ecosystems.[11] New methods to infer market power emerge,[12] based on concepts such as multi-sided[13] and zero-price markets,[14] and taking into account the impact of network effects, multi-homing, the role of user data, and switching costs.[15] As the characteristics of the market change, so should the tools of the regulators. Nevertheless, the Fourth Industrial Revolution still fundamentally shares common traits with the first three, such as being founded on innovation, astonishing enhancements in efficiency, and increased production that results in higher levels of earnings.[16]

In light of these trends, the following sections aim first to provide a broad overview of the historical development of the innovation concept. Chapter 2 will then focus more specifically on innovation effects in economic growth, market structures, mergers, and competition law.

---

[9] Klaus Schwab, *The Fourth Industrial Revolution: What It Means, How to Respond*, WORLD ECONOMIC FORUM (Jan. 14, 2016), https://www.weforum.org/agenda/2016/01/the-fourth-industrial-revolution-what-it-means-and-how-to-respond.

[10] Venkat Atluri, Miklós Dietz & Nicolaus Henke, *Competing in a World of Sectors without Borders*, MCKINSEY QUARTERLY (July 12, 2017), https://www.mckinsey.com/business-functions/mckinsey-analytics/our-insights/competing-in-a-world-of-sectors-without-borders.

[11] Michael G. Jacobides & Ioannis Lianos, *Regulating Platforms and Ecosystems: An Introduction*, 30 IND. CORP. CHANGE 1131 (2021), https://doi.org/10.1093/icc/dtab060.

[12] For detailed discussions on the next steps to be taken towards a competition policy in keeping with digital platforms and ecosystems, *see* Ioannis Lianos & Bruno Carballa-Smichowski, *A Coat of Many Colours – New Concepts and Metrics of Economic Power in Competition Law and Economics*, 18 J. COMPETITION L. & ECON. 795 (2022), https://doi.org/10.1093/joclec/nhac002, and JACQUES CRÉMER, YVES-ALEXANDRE DE MONTJOYE & HEIKE SCHWEITZER, COMPETITION POLICY FOR THE DIGITAL ERA (Report commissioned by the European Commission, Publications Office of the European Union 2019), http://ec.europa.eu/competition/publications/reports/kd0419345enn.pdf.

[13] For detailed discussions on multi-sided markets, *see, e.g.*, OECD, *Rethinking Antitrust Tools for Multi-Sided Platforms* (2018), https://www.oecd.org/competition/rethinking-antitrust-tools-for-multi-sided-platforms.htm.

[14] For detailed discussions on zero-price markets, *see* GSMA, *Resetting Competition Policy Frameworks for the Digital Ecosystem* (2016), https://www.gsma.com/publicpolicy/wp-content/uploads/2016/10/GSMA_Resetting-Competition_Report_Oct-2016_60pp_WEBv2.pdf; John M. Newman, *Regulating Attention Markets* (University of Miami Legal Studies Research Paper, 2020), https://papers.ssrn.com/sol3/papers.cfm?abstract_id=3423487; OECD, *OECD Handbook on Competition Policy in the Digital Age* (2022), https://www.oecd.org/daf/competition-policy-in-the-digital-age.

[15] OECD, *The Evolving Concept of Market Power in the Digital Economy*, OECD Competition Policy Roundtable Background Note 8–18 (2022), https://www.oecd.org/daf/competition/the-evolving-concept-of-market-power-in-the-digital-economy-2022.pdf.

[16] Min Xu, Jeanne M. David & Suk Hi Kim, *The Fourth Industrial Revolution: Opportunities and Challenges*, 9 INT'L J. FIN. RSCH. 90 (2018).

1.4.1 Innovation in a Static Social and Economic Paradigm: Ancient Western World until the Renaissance

Today, the term "innovation" has become one of the most widely used concepts in modern economic and legal discussions, and is usually employed to demonstrate (or indicate) "development." Nevertheless, the word itself has developed and transformed throughout the centuries, encompassing various meanings and connotations.

As languages reflect the cultures that they inhabit, the social values and cultures of a particular society have a palpable influence on the transformation of its language(s). Indeed, the earliest indications found regarding the term "innovation" reveal a different conception of this term (in both its usage and meaning) than the one we are familiar with today. Thus, the linguistic transformation of the term "innovation," not surprisingly, uncovers and demonstrates the changing views of various societies during the periods in question. However, it is also true that the term "innovation" has been primarily used within the context of "novelty,"[17] since the early ages.

The first appearance of innovation as a standalone concept dates back to Ancient Greece, where the term "καινοτομία" (*kainotomia*) was used to express this basic concept, starting from about the fifth century BC. The actual meaning of καινοτομία was "making new cuttings," which was made up from the combination of two words: "καινός" (*kainos*, "new") and "τομ" (*tom*, "cutting"). With this term, innovation was initially used as a metaphor for "introducing change to the established order."[18] We also note that the use of the term "καινοτομία" in ancient times was mainly related to politics, philosophy, and history.[19]

Turning to Ancient Rome, one can see that the Romans did not have a specific term to represent the idea of "innovation"; however, they used *novitas* (or *res nove* and *novare* in different forms) to embody the meaning of novelty.[20] *Novitas* was also used within the context of religion, philosophy, law, and poetry.[21]

Taking a closer look at the period, while we are familiar with Archimedes and the advances in agricultural productivity, mining, and the improvements to ships and maritime transport in these ancient civilizations,[22] we now understand that they were far more observant of the workings of nature and the universe, had a scientific understanding and created such technological novelties that were almost unfathomable in their

---

[17]   Benoît Godin, *Innovation: History of a Category* 8–9 (Project on the Intellectual History of Innovation, Working Paper No. 1, 2008), http://www.csiic.ca/PDF/IntellectualNo1.pdf.

[18]   Benoît Godin, *Innovation and Conceptual Innovation in Ancient Greece* (Project on the Intellectual History of Innovation, Working Paper No. 12, 2012), http://www.csiic.ca/PDF/Antiquity.pdf.

[19]   *Id.*

[20]   Benoît Godin, καινοτομία: *An Old Word for a New World, or, The De-Contestation of a Political and Contested Concept* (Project on the Intellectual History of Innovation, Working Paper No. 9, 2011), http://www.csiic.ca/PDF/Old-New.pdf.

[21]   Benoît Godin, Innovation Contested: The Idea of Innovation Over the Centuries 36–37 (Routledge 2014).

[22]   Alain Bresson, The Making of the Ancient Greek Economy 205–11 (Princeton Univ. Press 2016).

complexity.[23] Interestingly, however, the dominant view in both Ancient Greek and Ancient Roman civilizations used the term "innovation" in its various forms in a pejorative connotation, although earlier sources do indicate that some positive connotations existed as well. For instance, Plato once wrote, "Either it's some war that violently overturns regimes and transforms laws, or it's the baffling impasse of harsh poverty that does it. Diseases, too, make many innovations necessary, when epidemics occur, or bad weather comes and frequently lasts many years,"[24] where he calls attention to the fact that even negative experiences may trigger constructive and positive changes. Yet, according to Benoît Godin, that statement was the only positive utterance that Plato had on the topic of innovation.[25] Did this mean innovation was acceptable only when necessary, incremental, or a mere practical improvement with visible benefits in the short run? Indeed, Plato maintained an oppositional stance against innovation (i.e., καινοτομία), since he considered it to constitute a degeneration of the original and of "pure culture," as well as a threat to states, asserting that "there is no greater punishment for all cities."[26] Plato further expressed his critical opinions on the adverse effects of innovation within the context of the influence of children's games on social stability in *The Laws*:

> I assert that in all the cities, everyone is unaware that the character of the games played is decisive for the establishment of the laws, since it determines whether or not the established laws will persist. Where this is arranged, and provides that the same persons always play at the same things, with the same things, and in the same way, and have their spirits gladdened by the same toys, there the serious customs are also allowed to remain undisturbed; but where the games change, and are always infected with innovation and other sorts of transformations, where the young never call the same things dear, where good form and bad form – in the postures of their own bodies or in other things they use – are not always agreed upon, where instead they honor especially the man who continually innovates with something new and carries in shapes and colors and all such things that are different from the usual, we would be speaking in an entirely correct way if we were to assert this of such a man: there is no greater ruin than this that can come to a city. For, escaping notice, this man transforms the characters of the young, and makes them dishonor what is ancient and honor what is new. Of this man and his talk and dogma I say once again: there is no greater punishment for all cities. Hear how much evil I assert this is.[27]

The above quotation clearly illustrates that Plato believed that innovation would be the worst thing that could happen to a state, in terms of disrespecting its past and the accumulated wisdom of the ages. Even providing children with an environment in which they could play their games in novel and "*innovative*" ways would be sufficient to raise a new generation that would diverge from the customs and practices of the older (yet honored) generations.[28]

[23]   Jo Marchant, *Decoding the Antikythera Mechanism, the First Computer*, SMITHSONIAN MAG. (Feb. 2015), https://www.smithsonianmag.com/history/decoding-antikythera-mechanism-first-computer-180953979.
[24]   THE LAWS OF PLATO bk. IV, at 709A (Thomas L. Pangle ed. & trans., Basic Books 1980).
[25]   Godin, *supra* note 18, at 11.
[26]   THE LAWS OF PLATO, *supra* note 24, at 797.
[27]   *Id.*
[28]   Godin, *supra* note 18, at 11–13.

At first glance, it is surprising to see a philosopher who has immersed himself in the search for the Idea and "liberation from the cave," vehemently opposing change, or what we would now call progressive theory. However, upon examining Plato's life, we see that he was a close witness to war (many assume this to be the Peloponnesian War) from very early on, and throughout his life, the norm was a continuous conflict rather than peace, which naturally influenced his understanding of politics and thus his works.[29] As a result of multiple elements, the conflicts in Greece changed nature during his lifetime, from fighting foreign tribes and peoples to a battle of cultures within the society itself. The political instability and the constant shift of the political actors led Plato to word the following: "And the corruption of our written laws and our customs was proceeding at such amazing speed that whereas at first I had been full of zeal for public life, when I noted these changes and saw how unstable everything was, I became in the end quite dizzy…"[30]

In this excerpt from the Seventh Letter, Plato's writing illustrates that due to the ongoing turmoil, the connotations of change and the word "καινοτομία" were often negative. Having said that, it must also be noted that Platonic theory does not wish to entirely reject the new and reinstate the old. The goal is to establish "a continuum between ancient and contemporary times."[31] Plato outlined his ideal of an everlasting state by way of creating an educated group of people, or a philosophical ruling class[32] that would ensure this continuum, and as seen previously, his approach to education, music and culture rejects any innovative thinking that could endanger the stability.[33]

Somewhat contrary opinion from Ancient Greece is found in the teachings and philosophy of Aristotle, reflecting on the dilemma of the efficiency of the innovation process. Aristotle believed that, even though the cultural needs and laws of a society may be modified and adapted to minor changes in time, it is nevertheless quite difficult to cope or deal with innovative activities.[34] Aristotle supported the view that innovative behavior requires the alteration of the applicable laws and must be approached cautiously:[35]

> These considerations then do seem to show that it is proper for some laws sometimes to be altered. But if we consider the matter in another way, it would seem to be a thing that needs much caution. For in cases when the improvement would be small, while it is a bad thing to accustom men to repeal the laws lightly, it is clear that some mistakes both of the legislator and of the magistrate should be passed over; for the people will not be as much benefited by making an alteration as they will be harmed by becoming accustomed to distrust their rulers. Also, the example from the case of the arts is fallacious, as to change the practice of an art is a different thing from altering a law; for the law has no power to compel obedience beside the force of custom, and custom only grows up in long lapse

---

[29]   Joan-Antoine Mallet, *War and Peace in Plato's Political Thought*, 1 PHILOSOPHICAL J. CONFLICT & VIOLENCE 87 (2017).

[30]   PLATO, THE SEVENTH LETTER (George Burges trans., 1851) (c. 385 BC).

[31]   Mallet, *supra* note 29.

[32]   M. O. Olatunji, *Plato on Political Stability: Some Lessons for Nigeria*, 17 SABARAGAMUWA U. J. 38 (2019).

[33]   Godin, *supra* note 18.

[34]   ARISTOTLE, POLITICS bk. II, at 1269A (H. Rackham trans., Harvard Univ. Press 1932).

[35]   *Id.* at 1269A.

of time, so that lightly to change from the existing laws to other new laws is to weaken the power of the law. Again, even if alteration of the laws is proper, are all the laws to be open to alteration and in every form of constitution, or not? And is any chance person to be competent to introduce alterations or only certain people? For there is a great difference between these alternatives...[36]

To that end, Godin concludes, concerning the abovementioned approaches and stances taken by Plato and Aristotle, that one suggests that change was not acknowledged during the time of Ancient Greece, while the other indicates that change had impressed the Ancient Greeks.[37] According to Godin, the key to resolving this apparent contradiction is to properly define and delineate the distinction between the concepts of "change" and "innovation." As explained above, in Ancient Greece, the prevalent attitude towards the idea of novelty in terms of innovation had clearly been negative. Nevertheless, the "change" is a process that has been bequeathed to us from antiquity, when we consider that social change occurs, in most cases, continuously, gradually, and gently.[38] On the contrary, "innovation" referred to a change in an established order that was not welcomed, as illustrated by the above quotations from Plato and Aristotle. When the acceptable changes in a society are those that materialize slowly over time, innovation stands out as a man-made disruption; therefore, the process of its harmonization and integration into the existing economic, legal and political structures of society requires increased time and effort. This certainly proved to be a more uphill battle in societies that crave continuity and stability.

1.4.2   The Influence of Renaissance and Reformation

The term "innovation," meaning "to introduce as new" (transitive), comes from the Latin term "*innovatus*," which is the past participle of "*innovare*," which can be defined as "to renew, restore."[39] *Innovare* is composed of the prefix "in," meaning *into*, and the word "*novare*," meaning *novelty*, and it was first used in 13th-century law texts concerning the concept of "renewing."[40] Innovation, as a term, had become more and more prevalent in social, legal, and conomic contexts, especially since the Renaissance (approximately from 1300 to 1600) and the Reformation (1517–1648) periods. Both the Renaissance and the Reformation them-selves can be separately deemed as seminal epochs of innovation, especially in light of their impact in reshaping societies and the modern world. Since those eras, the frequency of the practice and demonstration of innovation has increased gradually over the years.

The term "Renaissance" means "rebirth," which implies admiration and praise for ancient times/societies and suggests a desire for the revival of the heritage of ancient cultures.[41]

---

[36]   *Id.*
[37]   Godin, *supra* note 18, at 25–27.
[38]   *Id.*
[39]   *See* ONLINE ETYMOLOGY DICTIONARY, https://www.etymonline.com/word/innovate.
[40]   Godin, *supra* note 20, at 12.
[41]   Brian Vickers, *The Idea of the Renaissance* 74–90 (2019), https://www.researchgate.net/publication/268396324_THE_IDEA_OF_THE_RENAISSANCE_REVISITED.

The central idea underlying the Renaissance was an opposition to the driving force of society – namely, curiosity. In fact, the idea of "novelty" was constantly being protested during this time, animated by a wish to go back to the days of antiquity, as described by the art historian Erwin Panofsky: "From the fourteenth and through the sixteenth century, then, and from one end of Europe to the other, the men of Renaissance were convinced that the period in which they lived was a 'new age' as sharply different from the medieval past as the medieval past had been from classical antiquity."[42] The main objective of the Renaissance was to regenerate the classics. The effects of the Renaissance regarding the term "innovation" were reflected in numerous different fields, especially those requiring human ingenuity, such as the visual arts, literature, music, and architecture. The use of the term "innovation" in politics maintained its well-established meaning as "the introduction of change into the established order." Thus, innovation was viewed quite differently than today, not as an agent of progressive change but rather as a means to return to a pure, past state by means of renewal.

Nonetheless, in the late Reformation, innovation would come to mean "unorthodoxy."[43] During the Reformation, "Kings and Churches forbade innovation; bishops supported these instructions with sermons, and followers (pamphleteers) developed arguments to this end – normative, legal and cultural."[44] Protestants had, in fact, wanted to restore Christianity to its original state, which they viewed as pure and faultless. They claimed they wanted reform, not innovation. "They strove for a reformation in the sense of a restoration of the original form of the true congregation of Jesus Christ… renovation, nor innovation. The Church of the Roman papacy accused them of being too innovative in a fatal way."[45] Reformation and innovation were distinguished by a difference in degree: the former implied a more fundamental and expansive change, the latter less so. The Catholic Church saw innovation as a problem because during the Middle Ages and the Reformation era, novelty was considered the essence of heresy.[46] To be more precise, novelty was only seen as dangerous in the context of innovation, when this was intentional, systematic, and teleological: "[N]ovelty (something new) itself is not the issue… Innovation is action: 'introducing' something new into the world, new ideas (doctrine) or activities (worship) into practice."[47] Moreover, "The innovator has a purpose, a scheme or design to 'overthrow' the social order. He is never alone. He creates a whole 'sect' that follows him."[48] Therefore, innovation was seen as a deliberate action leading to different practices and ideologies that could endanger the status quo. It was perceived as a sudden and violent force that would destroy the social order, thus something to be feared:[49] an "unorthodox"[50] and dangerous deviation.

---

[42]   ERWIN PANOFSKY, RENAISSANCE AND RENASCENCES IN WESTERN ART 36 (Harper & Row 1969).

[43]   Benoît Godin, *The Spirit of Innovation* 3 (Annual meeting of the Canadian Economics Association, Session on Innovation organized by The Centre for the Study of Living Standards and the Institute for Research in Public Policy, McGill University, June 1–3, 2018), http://www.csiic.ca/wp-content/uploads/2018/06/Spirit.pdf.

[44]   *Id.*

[45]   Berndt Hamm, *How Innovative was the Reformation? in* ARCHÄOLOGIE DER REFORMATION: STUDIEN ZU DEN AUSWIRKUNGEN DES KONFESSIONSWECHSELS AUF DIE MATERIELLE KULTUR 26 (Carola Jäggi & Jörn Staecker eds., De Gruyter 2007).

[46]   *Id.*

[47]   Godin, *supra* note 43, at 3.

[48]   *Id.*

[49]   *Id.*

[50]   *Id.* at 5.

Especially after the Reformation, "innovation" maintained its position as a useful concept mostly in the fields of politics and religion, which reached its climax in the 17th century.[51] With the influence and impact of the Renaissance, the debates and controversies over the corruption of the Church and its abuses led to a new structure in official Christendom.[52] The intensity of the religious controversies with regard to the renewal of the structure of Christianity was reflected in the established connotations of the term "innovation." According to Godin, the period between the Reformation and the 19th century was thus described as a time when innovation was most unwelcome.[53]

As a reflection of the spirit of the Renaissance, "innovation" already had a negative implication, but the term adopted a more derogatory meaning in the following years due to the influence of the Reformation: the connotation gained religious undertone, as in the sense of "heretic."[54] As innovation garnered such a heated meaning in those decades, "innovating" became the subject and focus of accusations. The public authorities of that period, such as royal houses and churches, began to prohibit innovations of any kind whatsoever. According to Godin,[55] two of the earliest instances of such actions taken by the authorities from the earlier years of Reformation were: (i) when Edward VI, King of England from 1547 to 1553, issued the *Proclamation against those that doeth innouate* in 1548, concerning a caveat on not to innovate and the punishments to be imposed in case of its breach, and (ii) the publication of the *Book of Common Prayer*, a liturgical book first authorized for use in the Church of England in 1549,[56] counseling its readers not to get involved in innovations.

Another prominent argument against innovation had been the idea of protecting the natural order. Indeed, "[I]nnovation… was frequently meant to imply that the changes were unwanted, unnatural (apart from the natural order of things), revolutionary, and/or dangerous, as in '*introducing change into the established order.*'"[57] Philosophers, as well as rulers, considered natural order and innovation to be in conflict; innovation was considered to be potentially violent and dangerous.[58] Such a deviation from the natural order, which is divinely ordained and therefore peaceful, could turn people away from God. Innovation could even be considered "revolutionary:"[59] "The association between revolution and innovation has made of innovation a sudden and violent affair. Revolution is an overall or total change, often with a violent overtone."[60] This was perceived as a grave threat as revolutions were much likelier to be violent. Since natural order

---

[51]   Godin, *supra* note 20, at 8–9.
[52]   Philip Schaff, History of the Christian Church, vol. VII: Modern Christianity: The German Reformation 3–6, 12 (Christian Classics Ethereal Library 2nd ed. 1882).
[53]   Benoît Godin, *The Vocabulary of Innovation: A Lexicon* (Project on the Intellectual History of Innovation, Working Paper No. 20, 2014), http://www.csiic.ca/PDF/LexiconPaperNo20.pdf.
[54]   Godin, *supra* note 18.
[55]   *Id.* at 8–13.
[56]   *Book of Common Prayer*, Encyclopaedia Britannica, https://www.britannica.com/topic/Book-of-Common-Prayer.
[57]   Laurier L. Schramm, Innovation Technology: A Dictionary 1 (De Gruyter 2017).
[58]   *Id.*
[59]   Benoît Godin, *Innovation: A Conceptual History of an Anonymous Concept* (Project on the Intellectual History of Innovation, Working Paper, No. 21, 2015), http://www.csiic.ca/PDF/WorkingPaper21.pdf.
[60]   Godin, *supra* note 53, at 16.

was considered so important, Protestant reformers appealed to this idea by highlighting their moderation. In contrast with innovation, the terms "reformation" or "restoration" were frequently used to describe positive, moderate, natural-order-restoring changes by the Protestant reformers.[61]

In light of all these views, the term took on such a pejorative meaning during this era that people started accusing each other of "being an innovator" or of "innovating," and such accusations became powerful and compelling arguments that could be used against one's enemies during this era – "a polemical weapon used against those who attempt to change things."[62] As a counter-argument, people accused of being innovators defended themselves by contending that they were not inventing but merely imitating. They used the prevailing indulgence for earlier and primitive ages in their societies and turned it to their advantage.[63]

As a linguistic term, innovation has become especially ubiquitous and widely used since the Renaissance and the Reformation. The propagation of the concept of innovation started slowly at first, and then extended towards its climax, in parallel with the increasing influence of such eras. As a result of the royal and church authorities' dominance over their societies in this period, innovation was still considered to have ill repute and continued to be used with derogatory meaning. However, the controversies over the concept and practice of "innovation" made the term more popular than it had ever been.

1.4.3 Constructing the Modern Concept of Innovation

Following the Renaissance and the Reformation, the connotation of the term "innovation" gradually evolved over the coming decades of the second half of the 18th century, which encompassed the eras of the Enlightenment (1715–1789) and the French Revolution (1789–1799). After the strict and censorious views of the Renaissance and the Reformation periods, innovation regained its positive meaning following the French Revolution.[64] The concept gained a constructive perspective, especially since the 19th century, and, following the increasingly favorable social attitudes towards the concept of "novelty," it has reached the zenith in popularity in the modern era. At the time, the term "innovation" encompassed politics and religion, as well as economics and any other field that can show progress, whereas in the more recent years, it has been mainly used in the context of technology and technological advancements.

The paradigm shift brought about by the French Revolution was also reflected in the term "innovation," which regained the political sense it had had in Ancient Greece, but positively and constructively. "[B]y the nineteenth century, a third kind of argument

---

61   SCHRAMM, *supra* note 57.
62   Godin, *supra* note 38, at 8.
63   Godin, *supra* note 20, at 8–9, 23.
64   *Id.*

enters the discourses on innovation: *logos*... Innovation is rational, in many ways. It brings benefits, if introduced correctly... This rehabilitation occurred between c. 1750 and c. 1850, that period Koselleck designates as *Satellzeit*, when many words changed meanings due to a 'shift in the conception of time and reorientation towards the future.'"[65] The connotative transformation of innovation was not an isolated incident but rather part of the paradigm shift, precipitated by changes in philosophy, politics, science, and technology at the time.

As discussed, the ancient civilizations had not yet adopted the notion that efficiency and productivity are intrinsically beneficial, which is more typical of recent times.[66] The abundant supply of manpower – provided by the enslaved people in the empires – reduced the need for technical processes for the most part. Those who had ideas that could lead to technical development lacked the resources, and those who had resources lacked the interest and desire for novelty and efficiency.[67] All these led to a dearth of technical progress or, if nothing else, reduced its momentum. However, as the world's population dramatically increased in the following centuries, technical progress became a means to increase efficiency, and satisfy the needs of the growing population with scarce resources available. Along with this, especially during the Industrial Revolution and the Enlightenment, society embraced the positive value of innovation and its contribution to the economy.

In parallel, the change in how innovation was viewed was primarily aided by an appeal to rationality and progress. Seeing certain kinds of change as "progress" rather than prioritizing tradition and classical works was an important step. Theorists began to provide direct counter-arguments to those who opposed innovation, which would, in time, become even more overt: "To the opponents of innovation, the age of innovation is subversive to social order, being too radical. The modern writer praises this same spirit, precisely because it changes things in a revolutionary way."[68]

Thus, the term "innovation" was aligned with the term "revolution" in this era. However, the main difference is that, where innovation is a term that denotes "private liberty" (as pointed out by Godin),[69] revolutions are experienced collectively. Another favorable impact of the French Revolution on innovation was that the term itself became more and more commonly used in the everyday vernacular, starting in France.[70] The novelties and innovative changes caught the public's attention more quickly than before, as, at the time, purposeful and essential changes were being made in various areas, such as politics, economics, science, industry, technology, and social order.

At this time, research gained particular focus and importance. Back in the 11th century, the first universities in Paris, Oxford and Bologna had been hierarchically tied to the

---

[65]   GODIN, *supra* note 21.

[66]   M. I. Finley, *Technical Innovation and Economic Progress in the Ancient World*, 18 ECON. HISTORY REV. 29, 31 (1965).

[67]   *Id.*

[68]   GODIN, *supra* note 21

[69]   Godin, *supra* note 59, at 18 (referring to the Scottish philosopher Thomas Reid).

[70]   Godin, *supra* note 53

Church, lacking autonomy and academic freedom.[71] The unsecular and dogmatic nature of the curriculum was not ideally suitable for research and innovative activities. In the 19th century, many modern universities were established all over Europe, with German universities becoming renowned for their excellence in organizational structure. These modern universities had two main activities: teaching and researching. While the professors could initially take part in both, as the research methods became more complex and workload increased over time, the assistants alone conducted research in the additional units of the universities called *Institutes*.[72] The establishment of modern universities led to the emergence of a new profession: education and research activities performed by specifically trained individuals in their fields, known as academicians today.[73] By then, the value of research and technological progress was clear – so much so that governments, such as the United States federal government, directly funded universities that specialized in research. In the last decades of the 19th century, industrial research laboratories were commonly found within public and private investments, where companies conducted research and development activities for their products.[74] The systematic research methods, as well as the advent of a field solely focused on researching, paved the way for scientific development and carried innovation one step forward.

Innovation became the positive, ubiquitous concept it is today with technological and economic developments: "It then became an inclusive term that covers both religion and politics, then the social, giving to a secular term for heresy. In the nineteenth century, innovation was reconceptualized to serve modern society... Religion is not the whole story of course. Technology is a major source of concepts that define the semantic field of innovation and the discourses in the twentieth century, through economics and market ideology (Godin, forthcoming)."[75]

The First Industrial Revolution, which took place in Europe and especially in Great Britain between the 17th and 18th centuries, is rightly considered to be the economic and technological milestone of its era. Therefore, the concept of innovation within this specific timeframe featured and emphasized the aspects of technology, institution, and product development.[76] The increasing use of technology and its impact on the general public came to be a topic of heated intellectual discussion,[77] and consequently, it could be seen that the economic dimensions of the concept of innovation could not (and would not) be ignored from that time on.

---

[71]   Kimberly Georgedes, *Religion, Education and the Role of Government in Medieval Universities: Lessons Learned or Lost?* 2 F. Pub. Pol'y 21 (2006).

[72]   Joseph Ben-David & Awraham Zloczower, *Universities and Academic Systems in Modern Societies* 3 Eur. J. Socio. 45 (1962).

[73]   Henry Etzkowitz & Loet Leydesdorff, *Universities and the Global Knowledge Economy: A Triple Helix of University-Industry-Government Relations* (Jan. 2002), https://www.researchgate.net/publication/239066835_Universities_and_the_global_knowledge_economy_A_triple_helix_of_university-industry-government_relations.

[74]   David Mowery, *Technological Change and the Evolution of the U.S. National Innovation System 1880–1990, in* Innovation: Perspectives for the 21st Century (BBVA 2011), https://www.bbvaopenmind.com/en/articles/technological-change-and-the-evolution-of-the-u-s-national-innovation-system-1880-1990.

[75]   Godin, *supra* note 43, at 5.

[76]   Kristine Bruland & David Mowery, *Innovation Through Time* 2–11 (Feb. 22, 2004), http://hdl.handle.net/1853/43162.

[77]   Godin, *supra* note 17, at 18–21.

1.4.4 Innovation and History of Intellectual Property Rights

In terms of philosophy of knowledge, from ancient times and in many civilizations, the question was whether philosophers should be compensated for teaching their knowledge and wisdom.[78] At the time, the knowledge and ideas of the philosophers or poems of the poets were considered divine wisdom and not creations of a person's mind. Confucius did not receive payments as he considered that his teaching was not a creation but a way of conveying the wisdom of the ancients.[79] The Biblical verse "Freely ye have received, freely give," defining knowledge to be God-given and thus freely transmitted, dominated the early Judeo-Christian doctrine[80] and continued in the medieval age. In the 15th century, this conviction came to an end, as the invention of the printing press changed the way information circulated, made reading accessible for larger groups with limited education, and famously contributed to the spread of the thoughts behind the Reformation.[81] Due to the rise in demand for reading material, writing became extremely popular, and the writers wanted their profit.

First, in Venice, a primitive form of intellectual property emerged as privileges granted on demand.[82] In England, the birthplace of the Industrial Revolution, Queen Elizabeth I used her right to grant royal monopolies for political maneuvers and as a source of income at the end of the 1500s. However, her arbitrary decisions and the wide nature of monopolies granted dissatisfied the public,[83] which led Elizabeth's successor, James, to pass the Statute of Monopolies in 1623, prohibiting all monopolies with a few exceptions for limited rights: "[F]or the term of 14 years or under hereafter to be made of the sole working or making of any manner of new manufactures within this Realm to the true and first inventor…"[84] Subsequently, the rapidly expanding publishing industry and the high demand for written content also required a regulation. Accordingly in 1710, the Statute of Anne (also known as the Copyright Act) was passed, which granted a fourteen-year protection period (renewable once) to existing written works, and twenty-one years for the works to be written henceforth. Although its purpose is a subject of debate among scholars, the Statute of Anne was certainly progressive as it recognized the author as the main subject and owner of the intellectual property rights.[85]

It is therefore no surprise that patent rights flourished particularly in the 17th and 18th centuries, the time of the Industrial Revolution. The French Revolution brought

---

[78]   David L. Blank, *Socratics versus Sophists on Payment for Teaching*, 4 CLASSICAL ANTIQUITY 1 (1985).

[79]   *Id.*

[80]   Carla Hesse, *The Rise of Intellectual Property, 700 B.C.-A.D. 2000: An Idea in the Balance*, 131 DAEDALUS 26 (Spring 2002), and DAVID VAVER, INTELLECTUAL PROPERTY RIGHTS: CRITICAL CONCEPTS IN LAW 53 (Taylor & Francis 2006).

[81]   Louise W. Holborn, *Printing and the Growth of a Protestant Movement in Germany from 1517 to 1524*, 11 CHURCH HIST. 123 (1942).

[82]   Christopher May, *Venise: aux origines de la propriété intellectuelle*, 14 L'ÉCONOMIE POLITIQUE 6 (2002) (Fr.).

[83]   Ronana Deazley, *Commentary on the Statute of Monopolies 1624*, in PRIMARY SOURCES ON COPYRIGHT (1450–1900) (L. Bently & M. Kretschmer eds., 2008), www.copyrighthistory.org.

[84]   Statute of Monopolies of 1623 § VI.

[85]   Oren Bracha, *The Adventures of the Statute of Anne in the Land of Unlimited Possibilities: The Life of a Legal Transplant*, 25 BERKELEY TECH. L. J. 1427 (2010).

the notion of a property right in knowledge, whereas the United States based intellectual property rights directly on individual rights.[86] Economic historians believe that the incentives provided by patents, along with the Industrial Revolution, led to an era that was more productive and faster to develop than ever before.[87] At the time, despite the initial costs, it was profitable for one to make an invention, as the eventual returns during the Industrial Revolution were superior, and the patents provided sufficient security for the initial costs to be recovered.[88] Furthermore, an incentive patent system also ensured that innovations were continuous, with benefits being invested back into innovative processes.

Since the First Industrial Revolution, the process of creating and registering "patents" has become crucial to economic growth, together with the developments in technology, science, and industry.[89] There was a reciprocal link between the advent of "patenting" and industrialization, each having substantial positive effects on the other.[90] Increasing technological and industrial developments offered consumers a more extensive range of goods, whereas improvements in the quality and durability of the goods also raised the productivity of a given society.[91] Before these developments, inventors had not preferred to patent their inventions due to the high costs of patenting and the limited access to patent attorneys. With the increased pace of technological developments and economic gains, patenting started to seem quite beneficial, and the patent system became one of the most popular economic tools of its time.[92]

1.4.5 Historical Progress of Development Economics and R&D

With the economic and technological progress made in the Second Industrial Revolution of 1870–1914, which took place primarily in Europe and the United States, entirely new industrial sectors emerged in the economic landscape. Accordingly, the need for innovations, inventions, and improvements expanded significantly, especially in the field of technology.[93] At the time, however, the classical and, later, the neoclassical economic approaches were prevalent, characterized by a static model. Their views focused on economic growth and determined that development resulted from the multiplication of markets, free trade, and specialization/division of labor, but failed to address the

---

[86] CHRISTOPHER MAY & SUSAN K. SELL, INTELLECTUAL PROPERTY RIGHTS: A CRITICAL HISTORY 101 (Lynne Rienner Publishers Inc. 2006).

[87] Sean Bottomley, *Patents and the First Industrial Revolution in the United States, France and Britain, 1700–1850* 7–8 (Institute for Advanced Study in Toulouse (IAST) Working Papers 14-14, 2014), https://ideas.repec.org/p/tse/iastwp/28752.html.

[88] *Id.*

[89] Bruland & Mowery, *supra* note 76, at 2–6.

[90] Christine MacLeod & Alessandro Nuvolari, *Patents and Industrialization: An Historical Overview of the British Case* 2–3 (Laboratory of Economics and Management (LEM), Working Paper Series No. 1624–1907, 2010).

[91] *Id.* at 11–13.

[92] Bruland & Mowery, *supra* note 76, at 4–5.

[93] *Id.* at 12–13.

dynamic element.[94] According to Schumpeter, the economic models and concepts that had been developed by John Maynard Keynes and David Ricardo were highly abstract and incapable of providing an opportunity to conduct a precise and accurate evaluation, as they would "freeze" most of the interdependent variables when analyzing factors in their models.[95] Such an approach, which aimed to bring a formula-based relationship to economic variables at the cost of disregarding interdependencies, and totally ignoring various factors such as innovation or the possibility of "multiple equilibria,"[96] was deemed unsuitable, thus necessitating more comprehensive approaches.[97]

Meanwhile, from the mid-20th century onwards, mainly due to the impact of the two World Wars and the economic depression periods witnessed in their aftermaths, a transformation was observed in the structure of innovations. This change in the concept of innovation was realized through the system known as "research and development," commonly abbreviated as "R&D." R&D became a vital part of the process of production in various new and existing industries.

Faced with economic and military challenges, the governments were aware that an innovation strategy was essential. In the US, the first attempt to create an innovation strategy in the 1930s as a response to the Great Depression[98] failed and faced public antagonism as the public strongly believed that it was the creation of new technologies that hindered their opportunities for employment.[99] Nevertheless, the Second World War and the imminent need for new technologies changed their perspective and, subsequently, the outcome of the war, as it is considered that the US victory was a result of new technologies like radars and nuclear energy.[100] This led the US President, Franklin Roosevelt, to ask his scientific advisor, Vannevar Bush, to come up with a new innovation-based strategy for the post-WW2 period.[101]

According to Bush in his report *Science: The Endless Frontier*, basic research (what he calls "science") that creates fundamental knowledge supports the establishment of applied research, contributing to development and innovation.[102] It is widely accepted that Bush's strategy serves as the foundation of the "*linear model*" theory of the modern economy.[103] Bush knew that the creation of fundamental knowledge had to be constant; otherwise, it would lose traction. Therefore, he recommended government intervention through the funding of universities and non-profit organizations, in order to assure an

---

[94]   Ioannis Lianos, Abel Mateus & Azza Raslan, *Development Economics and Competition: A Parallel Intellectual History* 5–8 (CLES Working Paper Series 1/2012, 2012), https://discovery.ucl.ac.uk/id/eprint/10045074.

[95]   *See* JOSEPH A. SCHUMPETER, HISTORY OF ECONOMIC ANALYSIS (Routledge 2nd ed. 1954).

[96]   Lianos, Mateus & Raslan, *supra* note 94.

[97]   *See* PAUL BELLEFLAMME & MARTIN PEITZ, INDUSTRIAL ORGANIZATION (Cambridge Univ. Press 2nd ed. 2015).

[98]   Henry Etzkowitz, *An Innovation Strategy to End the Second Great Depression*, 20 EUR. PLAN. STUD. 1439, 1440 (2012).

[99]   *Id.*

[100]   *Id.* at 1445.

[101]   Ioannis Lianos & Rochelle C. Dreyfuss, *New Challenges in the Intersection of Intellectual Property Rights with Competition Law: A View from Europe and the United States* 6 (CLES Working Paper Series 4/2013, 2013), https://discovery.ucl.ac.uk/id/eprint/10045063.

[102]   Dennis Patrick Leyden & Matthias Menter, *The Legacy and Promise of Vannevar Bush: Rethinking the Model of Innovation and the Role of Public Policy*, 27 ECON. INNOV. NEW TECH. 225, 228 (2018).

[103]   *Id.*

efficient and perpetual creation process of innovation.[104] By this recommendation, Bush clearly desired to connect the relevant entities of the private sector and the government, intending to increase competition in the private sector and enhance economic growth.[105] The expansion of R&D also necessitated protection of the results: the Bayh-Dole Act of 1980 in the US allowed universities to own patent rights for their government-funded innovations and incentivized R&D.[106] Having said this, the exclusive nature of these intellectual property rights might have also resulted in creating abusive monopolies or anti-competitive rights for the IP rights owners, which made competition law crucial in order to maintain effective competition in markets.[107]

The markets most affected by the introduction of the R&D system to the production processes of such industries have been the pharmaceutical and biotechnology, electronics, information, and communications technology ("ICT") markets.[108] Richard Gordon describes the period of 1870–1970 as the "special century," as it heralded these great inventions that transformed living standards and enabled a faster economic (labor productivity) growth compared to any decade that came before. Inventions of the Second Industrial Revolution, electricity, internal combustion engine, and running water were instrumental for the life boom in this period, much more so than those of the third revolution, in entertainment, communication, and IT.[109] This is also in parallel with Godin's description of the progress of innovation in the period from the mid-19th to the early 20th century: "[T]he use of the concept exploded and permeated the scientific literature, above all in medicine, chemistry, engineering, and instrumentation. One thing is certain: as titles of the time attest, to the scientists, 'innovation' was novelty in *methods* – not technology."[110]

When seen in this light, the term "innovation" is indeed more encompassing than just technological developments, no matter what the general public perception may be today. Distinguished scholars have highlighted a wide range of sub-categories, such as the invention of new methods and cultural developments. Economist Joseph A. Schumpeter simplified the definition of innovation as "setting up of a new production function" with respect to both the improvement of the current outputs and the development of new products.[111] Following this, the anthropologist H. G. Barnett approached innovation as a cultural development issue, and defined it as "any thought, behavior, or thing that is new because it is qualitatively different from existing forms."[112] A broader definition of innovation was offered by sociologist Everett M. Rogers as "an idea, practice, or object that is perceived as new by an individual or another unit of adoption."[113]

---

[104]   *Id.*

[105]   Lianos & Dreyfuss, *supra* note 101, at 7.

[106]   *Id.* at 8.

[107]   THE INTERFACE BETWEEN INTELLECTUAL PROPERTY RIGHTS AND COMPETITION POLICY 1–5 (Steven D. Anderman ed., Cambridge Univ. Press 2007).

[108]   *Id.* at 22–31.

[109]   ROBERT GORDON, THE RISE AND FALL OF AMERICAN GROWTH 438 (Princeton Univ. Press 2016).

[110]   Godin, *supra* note 77, at 16.

[111]   Simon Mee, *Joseph Schumpeter and the Business Cycle: An Historical Synthesis* 87 (2015), https://www.tcd.ie/Economics/assets/pdf/SER/2009/simon_mee.pdf.

[112]   Nigel B. Cook, *Review of H. G. Barnett's Book, Innovation: The Basis of Cultural Change* (2014), http://rxiv.org/pdf/1405.0301v1.pdf.

[113]   EVERETT M. ROGERS, DIFFUSION OF INNOVATIONS (Free Press 3d ed. 1983), https://teddykw2.files.wordpress.com/2012/07/everett-m-rogers-diffusion-of-innovations.pdf.

Focusing our attention on the modern era, we note that the financial world of the 21st century has been built on the idea of innovation. Despite the scholars, the public perception of the concept of innovation, together with the influence of R&D in various industries, is now linked with technology. Godin criticized the general myopia of this position by declaring: "Today, the concept of innovation is wedded to an economic ideology, so much that we forget it has mainly been a political – and contested – concept for the last five hundred years."[114]As technology continues to develop, and companies seek to achieve further innovations, the term "innovation" has ultimately turned into a buzzword, and the era we live in has come to be called the "technology era." Furthermore, the global economy relies on innovation; thus, being an "innovator" is now a title to be proud of. This is a total reversal of the perception as it was during the Renaissance and the Reformation.

Innovation, in addition to contributing to economic growth, is also being seen as providing economic value even by its potential existence. This is linked to the concept of futurity, which measures business value in terms of anticipated future profits.[115] The clearest appearance of this approach is in valuations for blockchain technology projects or digital platforms: due to the market's expectation of very significant future profits, their current cash flow is not deemed to be indicative of what the market expects their actual value to be; it is the innovative potential that is being put in the center of the economic game. Furthermore, especially for digital platforms, the reason the giants are valued so high is again based on a forecast of "their monopolistic potential as they control important bottlenecks in the attention and prediction economy."[116] Thus, futurity (and therefore, innovative potential, including analyses based on future market value) also grabs the attention of competition authorities.

There is a growing awareness for the centrality of innovation and considerable effort by competition authorities to build stronger foundations and human resources that will diagnose and track the market phenomena related to innovation.[117] The concern here is how they employ this awareness within their enforcement practices.

1.5 Conclusion

Despite the controversies surrounding the concept of innovation in the old days, the term has eventually and perhaps inevitably taken on a more positive connotation. Considering the fact that economic growth stems primarily from innovation, there is not much room left for such skepticism or controversy in the modern global economy; economic theorists have been consistently demonstrating the role and driving force

---

[114] Godin, *supra* note 59.

[115] JOHN R. COMMONS, INSTITUTIONAL ECONOMICS: ITS PLACE IN POLITICAL ECONOMY (Univ. Wisconsin Press 1934) as mentioned in Ioannis Lianos, *Competition Law for the Digital Era: A Complex Systems' Perspective* 10 (CLES Research Paper Series 6/2019, 2019),https://www.ucl.ac.uk/cles/sites/cles/files/cles_6-2019_final.pdf.

[116] Lianos, *supra* note 115, at 54.

[117] The Legal 500, *The Legal 500 Webinars: A Contemporary Analysis of the Prime Objective(s) of Competition Law*, YouTube (Sept. 29, 2022), https://www.youtube.com/watch?v=S3RuEJFOUkk (last visited Feb. 26, 2023).

of innovation behind economic growth, as discussed in more detail in Chapter 2. The introduction of the concept to competition law itself has been admittedly delayed and relatively recent; however, as argued, it is still yet to be fully embraced. To break the historical trajectory of the term, it is imperative that the role of innovation in economic development is recognized and thus fully integrated and immersed in assessments by the competition authorities.

Chapter 2
Understanding the Role of Innovation
in Economic Growth and Competition Law

2.1 Introduction

Picking up the concept of innovation from its historical progression, this chapter focuses on how innovation has been incorporated into and assessed within the framework of economics and growth. It is crucial to demonstrate the strong link between innovation and economic growth, as failing to recognize this may lead competition authorities to underappreciate its role. If the main purpose of competition authorities is to promote total welfare and economic growth, there is no doubt that a too cautious, self-restricting approach to innovation will be a hindrance to that goal.

One important issue here is with regard to how (and if) innovation can be measured. The book will also explore the forms innovation has evolved into, its interlink with intellectual property rights, the diffusion of innovation in general-purpose technologies, and the effect of trade between countries, among others. With this background and demonstrated link with economic growth, a discussion on the role of innovation in various aspects of competition law sets the scene, before delving into the practices of the enforcers in developed jurisdictions in the coming chapters.

2.2 The Broad Role of Innovation in Economic Growth

2.2.1 Schumpeter's Innovation Theory

Even though the meaning of the term "innovation" has been the subject of much controversy and debate, Joseph A. Schumpeter (1883–1950) is widely considered to be the most influential economist in advancing the concept of innovation and establishing its impact on economic growth.[118]

---

[118] Joseph A. Schumpeter, *Business Cycles: A Theoretical, Historical, and Statistical Analysis of the Capitalist Process*, 6 Can. J. Econ. Pol. & Sci. 90 (1940).

Fundamentally, Schumpeter believed that economic changes were not directly brought about by consumer preferences,[119] and maintained that consumers do not actually play an active role in economic development. In this regard, he identified five essential phases in terms of the historical development of structural changes, driven by the results of innovation,[120] and which may be categorized as follows:[121]

–   Invention of a new product of the new species of an already existing product

–   Introduction of new methods of manufacturing and selling a specific product

–   Establishment of a new market that has not existed before

–   Acquisition of new sources for the supply of raw materials used in the manu-facturing phase

–   Change in the industry structure which usually occurs through destruction of monopolization.

To that end, Schumpeter believed that any company or individual who wishes to generate profits would innovate in order to achieve such a goal.[122] For this fundamental reason, he described *innovation as the primary driver* of both competitiveness and the development of economic dynamics.[123] In this regard, he puts innovation at the center of the process of structural economic change, which is often described as *"creative destruction."*[124] Accordingly, he defines the term "innovation" as the "process of industrial mutation that incessantly revolutionizes the economic structure from within, incessantly destroying the old one, incessantly creating a new one."[125]

Moreover, Schumpeter depicted the economic development occurring as a result of innovation leading to the historical progress of structural changes.[126] In this regard, Schumpeter divided the innovation process into four main categories – namely, invention, innovation, diffusion, and imitation.[127] According to Schumpeter's theory, entrepreneur-ship occurs at the center of innovation.[128] In other words, entrepreneurship activities, such as the discoveries made by scientists and inventors, lead to the creation of new investment opportunities, as well as economic and technical growth and employment opportunities.[129] (This is also why it is crucial that overregulation does not disincentiv-ize entrepreneurs, as it would cripple, or at least significantly hinder, any meaningful impetus in innovation.) He further believed that the invention phase and the fundamental

---

[119]   JOSEPH A. SCHUMPETER, THE THEORY OF ECONOMIC DEVELOPMENT: AN INQUIRY INTO PROFITS, CAPITAL, CREDIT, INTEREST AND THE BUSINESS CYCLE (Redvers Opie trans., Harvard Univ. Press 1934).

[120]   Schumpeter, *supra* note 118, at 90–96.

[121]   SCHUMPETER, *supra* note 119.

[122]   *Id.*

[123]   MICHAEL E. PORTER & SCOTT STERN, THE NEW CHALLENGE TO AMERICA'S PROSPERITY: FINDINGS FROM THE INNOVATION INDEX (Council on Competitiveness 1999).

[124]   JOSEPH A. SCHUMPETER, CAPITALISM, SOCIALISM AND DEMOCRACY 132–45 (Harper and Brothers 1942).

[125]   *Id.*

[126]   SCHUMPETER, *supra* note 119.

[127]   ALAN BURTON-JONES, KNOWLEDGE CAPITALISM: BUSINESS, WORK, AND LEARNING IN THE NEW ECONOMY (Oxford Univ. Press 1999).

[128]   SCHUMPETER, *supra* note 119.

[129]   *Id.*

underlying innovation have a smaller impact on the innovative process, whereas the diffusion and imitation phases have a more extensive impact on the economic well-being of societies and economic growth.[130] In other words, what matters for economic growth is often the diffusion of the necessary innovation to the rest of the economy, where the imitators of the innovator recognize the potential for profits offered by the new products or processes.[131]

Schumpeter thus rejected the prevailing static neoclassical model of the time and instead argued that the economy is a dynamic entity. More precisely, he contended that there are also changes in the economy that are caused endogenously,[132] giving rise to emergent entities and development intrinsically generated from within itself.[133] According to this framework, entrepreneurs, who take risks and try new things, create new combinations[134] – "that is the innovative reallocation of economic resources and changes in organizational forms,"[135] are the spine of evolutionary, endogenous growth. With entrepreneurs helping to connect innovation and economy, as Schumpeterian suggests, the entry of new combinations of products and markets that provide more preferable prices for better quality becomes possible, and entrepreneurs create optimally efficient production lines and new markets, which result in "a creative destruction" by simultaneously driving poorly performing companies out of the market.[136]

Schumpeter was opposed to the so-called static economic models because they relied on the optimization of certain variables in static models instead of taking into account the dynamic, non-linear nature of economics. "He challenged the neoclassical assumption that normality is an economic system in an equilibrium state constituted by prices where the quantity supplied equals the amount of commodities demanded, and that disequilibrium must come from forces outside the economic system."[137] He was much more concerned about "development" than optimizing for equilibrium. More specifically, his framework development was achieved by discrete steps and the observation that economic development is chaotic, where one could only correlate a specific input with a specific output after the fact. "The kind of 'novelty' constitutes what we here understand as 'development,' which can now be exactly defined as: transition from one norm of the economic system to another norm in such a way that this transition cannot be decomposed into infinitesimal steps."[138] Indeed, this is very different from neoclassical economics, where outcomes can be deterministically determined based on input, without needing non-linear equations. Such a transition is orchestrated by the entrepreneur, who does not

---

130   *Id.*

131   *Id.*

132   JOSEPH A. SCHUMPETER, THE THEORY OF ECONOMIC DEVELOPMENT (New Jersey Transaction Publishers 1912).

133   Ulrich Witt, *How Evolutionary Is Schumpeter's Theory of Economic Development?* 9 INDUS. & INNOVATION 7 (2002).

134   SCHUMPETER, *supra* note 132.

135   Witt, *supra* note 133

136   Joao Ferreira, Cristina I. Fernandes & Vanessa Ratten, *Entrepreneurship, Innovation and Competitiveness: What is the Connection?* 18 INT'L J. BUS. & GLOBALISATION 73, 73 (2017).

137   Stefan Hauptmann, Empirical Research in Evolutionary Economics. The Potential of the "Social World Perspective" (2004) (M.Sc. thesis, University of Manchester) (on file with the University of Manchester), https://epub.uni-regensburg.de/25312/1/Hauptmann_MSc_Empirical_Research_in_Evolutionary_Economics.pdf.

138   SCHUMPETER, *supra* note 124, at 132–45.

desire to fit into the existing "perfect competition equilibrium," which was perfected in theory by the marginalist school, with compatible products in terms of substitutability and price, but rather seeks novelty in production, functioning and technological aspects, and therefore revolutionizes the whole industry ultimately in favor of the customer. Thus, some commentators have argued that, as the change and revolution were the essence, rather than pursuing the assessment of competition on the basis of prevailing conditions, an inclusive examination should be made of the components that constitute the competitive framework among players to truly understand the "perpetual disequilibrium."[139]

Schumpeter's definition of innovation had also been different from the past in that he concentrated on "technological innovation."[140] The historical development of innovation eventually led to the digital revolution that we witness all around us in the modern global economy. The technological and economic revolutions of the past are the two crucial aspects (indeed, the twin pillars) that comprise the digital revolution. Various technological terms that have recently entered our lexicon, such as "digitization," "analytics," "artificial intelligence," "algorithms," and "big data," are all fruits of the digital revolution and innovation.[141] Perhaps it would not be far-fetched to say that such terms have entered into our lives as a direct result of the Schumpeterian innovation process of creative destruction, a structural change that has demolished the traditional monopolistic market structures of earlier periods and replaced them with innovative, creative, and dynamic business models.[142]

2.2.2 Innovation Forms and Evolution

The most prevalent modern definition of innovation as "new products and processes that are introduced to the market" basically has locked the concept into two forms: product and process. As seen in the section above, Schumpeter's description of the five phases during which innovation affects the market actually incorporates them as the first two steps. Having said this, according to him, the internal phases, i.e., the invention and the underlying innovation, actually have less impact than the external phases of diffusion and imitation. As the result of the innovation, be it a product or a process, is getting a wider audience and clientele, its effect is spread from the individual innovator/company to the sector, to the economy, which was also denoted in his "creative destruction" terminology. The companies were the instigators of change, as well as the imitators.

Recently, however, the idea is that innovation sources and forms have changed, displacing the market from its traditional position of guiding demand and supply.[143] While

---

[139] David J. Teece, *Next Generation Competition: New Concepts for Understanding How Innovation Shapes Competition and Policy in the Digital Economy*, 9 J.L. Econ. & Pol'y 97, 100 (2012).

[140] Witt, *supra* note 133.

[141] Wolfgang Kerber, *Competition, Innovation, and Competition Law: Dissecting the Interplay* (MAGKS Joint Discussion Paper Series in Economics, No. 42-2017, 2017).

[142] Schumpeter, *supra* note 119.

[143] Karl-Heinz Leitner, *Innovation Futures: New Forms of Innovation and their Implications for Innovation Policy*, 9 Int'l J. Foresight and Innovation Pol'y 269 (2013).

Schumpeter focused on the entrepreneur and the R&D lab, today we also see some new models such as open, user-based, or crowdsourced innovation, which indicates a collaborative and open approach that is not driven by the companies but by a network of public organizations, universities, and customers who wish to be a part of the process.[144]

Nevertheless, one cannot say economic development and innovation alone led to the digital revolution. Competition law policies also had a significant impact on the advent of the digital revolution and the alteration in the market dynamics, especially by prohibiting undertakings' anti-competitive conduct.[145]

It is undoubtedly true that new products and the provision of novel services do generate reasonably higher profits compared to traditional ones, and this economic fact encourages companies to invest vast amounts of money in the innovation process – namely, their research and development activities.[146] This state of affairs amply illustrates the close link between competition and innovation in the case of newly emerged industries, as well as traditional business models.[147] Since innovation's starting point and *raison d'être*, in current times, is to improve the company's business model and to meet its customers' needs, innovation may lead to entirely novel business models and introduce new product markets. As a result of establishing new products and product markets, as well as improving business models in order to benefit consumers, companies can stand out and distinguish themselves from their competitors, and this makes innovation a crucial tool for competition between businesses. In other words, innovation is one of the critical features of robust competition throughout the world and directly contributes to the economic growth of companies, nation-states, and the global economy. With such direct and demonstrable economic welfare and consumer benefits, it is therefore very disheartening that the competition authorities still fail to fully embrace innovation, despite being formally entrusted with promoting consumer welfare.

In the modern world, technological developments are considered to be the main engine of economic growth. This may be illustrated with the data shared by the US Department of Commerce in 2010, where it was stated that three quarters of the growth rate witnessed in the US since World War II resulted from technological innovations.[148] It was not possible to provide particular examples of these innovations leading to economic growth since they were so diverse; however, it was emphasized that by helping decrease the prices of many existing products as well as improving their quality and efficiency, innovation has enhanced the investment desirability in capital goods such as computers, telecommunications equipment and machinery and venture in new areas such as robotics, e-commerce, and online advertising.

---

144 *Id.* at 270.
145 Bundeskartellamt, *Innovations – Challenges for Competition Law Practice, Series of Papers on Competition and Consumer Protection in the Digital Economy* 8–29 (2017), https://www.bundeskartellamt.de/SharedDocs/Publikation/EN/Schriftenreihe_Digitales_II.pdf?__blob=publicationFile&v=3.
146 Igor Dubina & Elias G. Carayannis, *Potentials of Game Theory for Analysis and Improvement of Innovation Policy and Practice in a Dynamic Socio-Economic Environment*, 3 J. INNOVATION ECON. & MGMT. 165 (2015).
147 Kerber, *supra* note 141.
148 Arti Rai, Stuart Graham & Mark Doms, *Patent Reform: Unleashing Innovation, Promoting Economic Growth & Producing High-Paying Jobs* (A White Paper from the US Department of Commerce, Apr. 13, 2010), https://www.commerce.gov/sites/default/files/migrated/reports/patentreform_0.pdf.

Another significant feature of innovation is its positive impact on labor compensation. It is clearly illustrated by the fact that the average salary per employee in innovation-supported industries in the US has increased by 50% in the ten-year period between 1990 and 2000.[149] This 50% increase in average compensation corresponds to almost two and a half times the increase in the national compensation average.[150] In this regard, any hurdles to innovation are highly likely to harm society. These are mainly economic impacts, where impediments to innovation would prove costly for the society in question.[151] Commentators have pointed out that any delay and/or lack of certainty in patent applications may set back national economies by costing billions of dollars and undermining economic growth and job creation opportunities.[152]

Since innovation fosters consumer welfare and promotes economic efficiency by introducing and spreading technological developments throughout an economy, it would not be an overstatement to say that it is the most crucial feature supporting economic growth. This is due to innovation's contribution to reducing costs, as a result of finding more creative and economically efficient ways for manufacturing and distribution.[153] Moreover, innovation also introduces new and/or improved products that benefit consumers, who eventually prefer these new products over older or more traditional ones. The following example briefly mentioned above may illustrate one such improvement: The recorded music industry got its start when innovative entrepreneurs invented a method for storing recorded music on the phonographic cylinder.[154] Later on, this phonographic cylinder was replaced by gramophone discs, and then by vinyl records.[155] After the introduction of compact audio cassettes, consumer preferences shifted from vinyl records to these new products.[156] Through ensuing technological developments, compact discs and later MP3 players were invented, after which consumer preferences once again shifted.[157] Nowadays, the number of people using MP3 players has decreased considerably from its peak in the mid-2000s. Instead, consumers have started to prefer using streaming companies, which offer access to recorded music through their cloud databases, such as Apple Music, SoundCloud, and Spotify.[158]

In this regard, former US Attorney General Christine Varney has defined the relationship between economic growth and innovation as follows: "Progress in technology and production processes drives prices down and quality up while expanding the range of consumer choices.... [I]nnovation is an essential element not only of economic growth

---

[149]   Id.
[150]   Id.
[151]   Id.
[152]   Id.
[153]   Nathan Rosenberg, *Innovation and Economic Growth* (OECD, 2004), https://www.oecd.org/cfe/tourism/34267902.pdf.
[154]   Amandine Pras, Catherine Guastavino & Maryse Lavoie, *The Impact of Technological Advances on Recording Studio Practices*, 64 J. AM. SOC'Y INFO. SCI. & TECH. 612 (2013).
[155]   Id.
[156]   Id.
[157]   Id.
[158]   Id.

but of human progress as well. We thus have a vital interest in seeing it flourish."[159] Nevertheless, innovation does not suddenly materialize out of nowhere or come into being on its own. Instead, vigorous competition between companies provides an incentive to innovate and produce new products and technologies, in order to make their products stand out from the rest of the crowd. Accordingly, underappreciating the importance and role of innovation in economic growth by sticking to a constrained view frame with rote arguments is actually creating a problem for the current and future welfare of consumers. Considering that the purpose of competition law is parallel to that of economic development, when the authorities' approach to innovation remains one-sided, these benefits cannot be maximized.

2.2.3 Economics of Innovation and Intellectual Property Rights

It seems, therefore, that a competitive market structure and the protection of intellectual property ("IP") rights are essential in order to promote fruitful and productive innovation.[160] These two aspects, in turn, support innovation and incentivize companies to promote new features linked to existing products or to invent new products, in order to become the most successful undertakings within their markets.[161] On the other hand, if such inventions are not bestowed with (and protected by) intellectual property rights, there will be no incentive for companies to promote their innovations, as every other competitor in the market will be entitled to copy and use such inventions, without financially compensating the inventor, which has invested significant amounts of time and money through its research and development activities. Thus, IP rights bring with them the incentive to innovate by financially rewarding companies for their success in the innovation process.[162] They do so by enabling the owners of IP rights to exclude others from using such products or processes for a limited time.[163] Moreover, IP rights also entitle the owner to disclose such inventions to the public and to allow others to build onto them, as in the recorded music industry example mentioned above. Finally, healthy competition, in conjunction with IP rights, also encourages companies to innovate, especially in cases where they strive to be the first to introduce a new product or process into the market and thereby increase their market shares.[164]

---

[159] Christine A. Varney, Promoting Innovation Through Patent and Antitrust Law and Policy. Remarks as Prepared for the Joint Workshop of the United States Patent and Trademark Office, the Federal Trade Commission, and the Department of Justice on the Intersection of Patent Policy and Competition Policy: Implications for Promoting Innovation, Alexandria, Virginia (May 26, 2010), https://www.justice.gov/atr/speech/promoting-innovation-through-patent-and-antitrust-law-and-policy.

[160] Rosenberg, *supra* note 153.

[161] Kerber, *supra* note 141.

[162] Lee Branstetter, *Intellectual Property Rights, Innovation and Development: Is Asia Different?* 8 MILLENNIAL ASIA 5 (2017).

[163] *Id.*

[164] Partha Dasgupta & Joseph Stiglitz, *Industrial Structure and the Nature of Innovative Activity*, 90 ECON. J. 266 (1980).

Having said all this, IP rights are also under fire for actually failing to promote innovation. According to the above, IP is supposed to be "the currency of open innovation."[165] However, the current IP regimes are also found to impose detrimental effects both on innovators and on customers due to their being "rigid, static, and unresponsive."[166] Some commentators have taken extreme hardline views by proposing the complete abolition of patents and copyrights in order to prevent the hindering effects of IP rights on innovation.[167] Patents are almost anathematized by some groups, as they are perceived as anti-competitive and anti-innovative, due to the fact that some sectors are solely controlled by the dominant players, but also due to the emergence and rising nuisance of "patent trolls."[168] Especially from the software and information sectors' perspective, patents seem weak, overarching and uncertain within their scope.[169] According to these arguments, increasing prices, distorted resource allocations, welfare losses and inefficiencies all occur because of the monopolies created through IP rights.[170]

When examining the rationale behind the IP opponents' criticisms, we observe that most commentators try to assert that IP rights do not provide any financial advantages to innovators; instead, they might even impose further financial burdens.[171] Furthermore, the transaction costs associated with "bundling rights" is deemed another strain on innovation. Especially in certain specific sectors where such costs are quite oppressive (such as the music, automobile, or aircraft manufacturing industries),[172] rightsholders have created common institutions or patent pools in order to cut down the transaction costs of multiple licenses.[173] However, as this practice carries a very high potential of creating anti-competitive effects,[174] patent pools cannot be easily and frequently used. Moreover, it has been observed over the years that when patent pools give rise to numerous litigation risks favoring the rightsholder firm's members, these pools end up actually discouraging and altering innovative research projects.[175]

---

[165]   Oliver Alexy, Paola Criscuolo & Ammon Salter, *Does IP Strategy Have to Cripple Open Innovation?* 51 SLOAN MGMT. REV. 71 (2009).

[166]   Michael Schrage & Marshall Van Alstyne, *Life of IP*, 58 COMMC'N ACM 20, 2 (2015), https://cacm.acm.org/magazines/2015/5/186009-life-of-ip/fulltext.

[167]   MICHELE BOLDRIN & DAVID K. LEVINE, AGAINST INTELLECTUAL MONOPOLY (Cambridge Univ. Press 2008).

[168]   "Patent trolling" occurs when a party acquires an inactive patent and, following that, with the sole purpose of receiving a licensing income, threatens the counterparty by filing a lawsuit. *See* Michael Risch, *Patent Troll Myths*, 42 SETON HALL L. REV. 457, 462–66 (2012); *see also* Jason Schultz & Jennifer Urban, *Protecting Open Innovation: The Defensive Patent License as a New Approach to Patent Threats, Transaction Costs, and Tactical Disarmament*, 26 HARV. J.L. & TECH. 1, 3 (2012).

[169]   JAMES BESSEN & MICHAEL J. MEURER, PATENT FAILURE: HOW JUDGES, BUREAUCRATS, AND LAWYERS PUT INNOVATORS AT RISK (Princeton Univ. Press 2008).

[170]   Michele Boldrin & David K. Levine, *The Case Against Patents*, 27 J. ECON. PERSP. 3 (2013). *See also* Joseph Stiglitz, *Economic Foundations of Intellectual Property Rights*, 57 DUKE L.J. 1693 (2008).

[171]   Schrage & Van Alstyne, *supra* note 166.

[172]   Michael A. Heller & Rebecca S. Eisenberg, *Can Patents Deter Innovation? The Anticommons in Biomedical Research*, 280 SCIENCE 698 (1998).

[173]   Robert P. Merges, *Contracting into Liability Rules: Intellectual Property Rights and Collective Rights Organizations*, 84 CAL. L. REV. 1293 (1996).

[174]   George Bittlingmayer, *Property Rights, Progress, and the Aircraft Patent Agreement*, 31 J. L. & ECON. 227 (1988).

[175]   Petra Moser, *Patents and Innovation: Evidence from Economic History*, 27 J. ECON. PERSP. 23 (2013).

The ultimate aim of the IP protection regime, which is to incentivize inventions, is fulfilled by providing strong protections; however, that protection paradoxically prevents the emergence of inventions in further stages (i.e., in the future) by increasing the costs.[176] However, despite these robust challenges to the necessity of IP rights, the critical aspect of this *IP vs. Innovation* debate does not always come up with an extreme solution, such as the total abolition of IP rights. It should also be underlined that there is not adequate empirical data on the current economic aspects of the hindering effect of IP in terms of innovation; therefore, making such severe and far-reaching changes to the IP regime should not be embraced as the first or most suitable policy option, at least not without conducting further research.[177] These suggestions mainly highlight that IP rights must be fairly balanced without granting too much monopoly power to any single party[178] that and any change should be incremental in order to reach an efficient solution.[179]

2.2.4 Innovation – How to Measure It?

The prevalent message from all of the above is that economic growth highly depends on the development of new ideas and innovations, among other vital ingredients. Thus, societies have employed a number of tools to *encourage* the development of new ideas, with IP rights being one of them. It is therefore fair to say that an increase in intellectual property may also denote an increase in innovation, such as an increase in the number of patents, references to patent analyses, and research paper citations. However, considering that most of the R&D 100 innovations were not actually patented (and conversely, those that were patented were not actually all valuable, useful, or profitable inventions), this measure is not an accurate one.[180] Smith & Funk argue that a true measure of innovation, away from the illusions created by patent numbers, would necessitate databases and studies that focus on the actual value of the new technology, its origins (novel or derivative), the extent of research funding as well as looking deep into knowledge flows and intermediate linkages.[181]

Other alternative parameters that are empirically evaluated could be R&D, total factor productivity ("TFP") and individual measurements. It must be noted that "research productivity," described as the proportion of patents to R&D, has dramatically declined over the last decade across various sectors and countries. Scholars and global organizations such as the Organisation for Economic Co-operation and Development ("OECD")

---

[176] WILLIAM M. LANDES & RICHARD A. POSNER, THE ECONOMIC STRUCTURE OF INTELLECTUAL PROPERTY LAW (Harvard Univ. Press 2009).

[177] Liza A. Vertinsky, *Responding to the Challenges of "Against Intellectual Monopoly"*, 5 REV. L. & ECON. 1115 (2009).

[178] Schrage & Van Alstyne, *supra* note 166.

[179] David J. Kappos & Christopher P. Davis, *Functional Claiming and the Patent Balance*, 18 STAN. TECH. L. REV. 365 (2015).

[180] Gary N. Smith & Jeffrey Funk, *Why We Need to Stop Relying on Patents to Measure Innovation*, PROMARKET (Mar. 19, 2021), https://www.promarket.org/2021/03/19/patents-bad-measure-innovation-new-metric.

[181] *Id.*

attributed these facts to a particular slowdown in TFP[182] since the mid-1960s.[183] With this in mind, research conducted using industry-level data for the US and other countries clearly showed that market size is important. Nevertheless, a significant rise in growth is not sufficient to describe the whole extent of the fall in R&D productivity. One potential diagnosis was technical exhaustion, with the remedy proposed as government policies.[184] Private investments are also a crucial incentive for technological advances, which in turn lead to increased efficiency and profits on tangible capital investment. Grossman and Helpman underlined the fact that the TFP can be observed in countries with a higher rate of private investment.[185] This variable includes changes in the productive use of land, the procurement of new equipment, the development of new highways, schools, hospitals, and other public infrastructure, as well as the net change in the stock of products held by businesses to deal with unforeseen fluctuations in sales revenue and developed technology.[186]

It is also considered that the more radical an innovation, the more drastic the economic results due to new methods, with higher productivity rates and growth effectiveness.[187] Radical innovation has the potential to create fresh demand by introducing completely new applications.[188] Nevertheless, it must not be forgotten that if radical inventions did ultimately produce superior economic results, measuring innovation outcomes would have to rely on identifying the degree of creativity in the innovations, which is challenging to do. With this in mind, individualized tests to measure innovation have been around for many years. Significant empirical studies conducted by innovation scholars such as Fred Gault and Eric von Hippel have indicated that many of the innovative products that customers eagerly buy from the producers are significantly tested and developed by "lead users."[189] For Gault and von Hippel, this user-oriented innovation model has been adopted to "hold both in the case of innovating user firms developing processes and equipment and software for in-house use, and in the case of innovative products developed for individual end-users, like novel sports equipment and foods."[190]

An accurate measurement of innovation is undoubtedly beneficial as well as indispensable for assessing the well-being of advanced economies in today's world.[191] In reality, quantification of innovations can make it easier to trade this intangible asset, using

---

[182]   Total factor productivity (TFP) is the output level based on a calculation assessing the efficiency of the inputs used during production (instead of making a calculation based on the input quantities).

[183]   Jean O. Lanjouw & Mark Schankerman, *Patent Quality and Research Productivity: Measuring Innovation with Multiple Indicators*, 114 ECON. J. 441 (2004).

[184]   *Id.*

[185]   GENE M. GROSSMAN & ELHANAN HELPMAN, INNOVATION AND GROWTH IN THE GLOBAL ECONOMY (MIT Press 1993).

[186]   Anthony Arundel & Dorothea Huber, *From Too Little to Too Much Innovation? Issues in Measuring Innovation in the Public Sector*, 27 STRUCTURAL CHANGE & ECON. DYNAMICS 146 (2013).

[187]   Giovanni Dosi, *Technological Paradigms and Technological Trajectories: A Suggested Interpretation of the Determinants and Directions of Technical Change*, 11 RSCH. POL'Y 147 (1982).

[188]   *Id.*

[189]   Fred Gault & Eric A. von Hippel, *The Prevalence of User Innovation and Free Innovation Transfers: Implications for Statistical Indicators and Innovation Policy* (MIT Sloan School Working Paper No. 4722-09, 2009), https://papers.ssrn.com/sol3/papers.cfm?abstract_id=1337232.

[190]   *Id.*

[191]   Balkrishna C. Rao, *Economic Recognition of Innovation*, SINGAPORE ECON. REV. CONF. (SERC) (2007).

adequate derivative securities. The pressure to measure innovations has peaked recently, with the US Department of Commerce providing incentives in a wide range of aspects to encourage innovation measurement in the economy. In addition to the US, the EU, the United Kingdom, and the OECD are all making progress to measure this intangible attribute.[192] The European Innovation Scoreboard is an example that showcases country-based efforts. It uses R&D spending, availability of possible investments and number of students willing to pursue science degrees as some of its indexes to conclude the total innovation performance score.[193] The Summary Innovation Index ("SII") attributes balanced weight to the entire index used for receiving the score.[194] In contrast to an equally balanced index such as SII, individual innovation scores calculated in the EU use such sources as surveys of individuals and different business sectors, the strength of R&D within various sectors, and data from journals. Scholars' research efforts have also focused on the measurement of innovations using financial statements submitted to various databases for patents as a benchmark to quantify innovation success and innovation metrics for conventional industries.[195] Although this again incorporates the patent element that has been so criticized, the indexes show that the ideal measure, when found, may turn out to be composed of many variables, including intellectual property.

The discussions around the "measurability" of innovation are therefore very significant in terms of antitrust enforcement. As will be demonstrated later, the one-sided approach of the competition authorities seems to indicate that when innovation is a concern that they point out in a particular transaction, it is deemed to be objectively measurable. However, if the innovative efficiency gains arising from a transaction are being brought forward by the undertakings as a defense to other competitive concerns of the authorities, then "innovation" somehow becomes non-measurable – a fluid, non-verifiable or speculative concept that takes us right back to the pejorative and threatening connotations that it carried not so long ago. The best method to measure innovation may still be contested, but it seems that even the available methods do not hold water when used as a defense by the parties.

2.2.5 Effect of Innovations from an Economic Perspective

The introduction of the America Competes Reauthorization Act of 2010[196] in 2011 stemmed from America's objective of increasing innovation, through research and development activities, and eventually boosting economic growth in the United States. This development is viewed as the practical reflection of the theory linking economic growth

---

[192]   *Id.*

[193]   Jürgen Janger, Torben Schubert, Petra Andries, Christian Rammer & Machteld Hoskens, *The EU 2020 Innovation Indicator: A Step Forward in Measuring Innovation Outputs and Outcomes?* 30–41 (ZEW Discussion Papers, No. 16-072, 2016).

[194]   MINISTRY OF ECONOMIC AFFAIRS, SCIENCE, TECHNOLOGY AND INNOVATION IN THE NETHERLANDS (The Hague 2006).

[195]   Fernando Henrique Taques, Manuel G. López, Leonardo Fernando Cruz Basso, Nelson Areal, *Indicators Used to Measure Service Innovation and Manufacturing Innovation*, 6 J. INNOVATION & KNOWLEDGE 11 (2021).

[196]   America Competes Reauthorization Act of 2010 Pub L. No. 111–358

and innovation, and the fact that enhanced innovation results in the economic growth of any given country.[197]

According to Nathan Rosenberg, there are essentially two fundamental ways to increase economic development: either by (i) increasing the number of inputs used in the production process or by (ii) inventing improved and/or entirely new products or processes, which result in the production of a higher number of outputs by using the same number of inputs.[198] There have been several studies conducted by various economists since the late 1800s in order to determine which method mentioned above is more important and useful in terms of economic development.[199] In this regard, one of the pioneer studies was carried out by Moses Abramovitz and Pierre Dieterlen, in which he tried to measure the growth of the American economy between 1870 and 1950.[200] The study first measured the growth in the output of the American economy and then the growth of the input, which is often the amount of capital and labor.[201] The results showed that the growth of capital and labor (i.e., the inputs) only amounted to 15% of the real output of the American economy.[202] Rosenberg commented that this proved the existence of an unexplained residual of no less than 85%.[203]

After Abramovitz, various economists have also conducted studies on this matter. Indeed, as a result of a similar study at a different time, Robert M. Solow has found a large residual,[204] which was again calculated as 85%.[205] Such studies have revealed that innovation was indeed the main underlying reason for the growth observed in the output.[206] This was the turning point that impelled economists to start conducting research studies on innovation rather than just focusing on capital and labor.[207]

Solow's growth model had replaced an older one, which was and still is subject to criticism: the Harrod–Domar growth model.[208] The Harrod–Domar growth model aimed to discover whether economies can grow continuously at a constant rate, or whether certain sectors would stumble, creating fluctuations in economic growth ratios.[209] The basic idea behind the Harrod–Domar model is that output is the direct reflection of the capital.[210]

---

[197]   Beñat Bilbao-Osorio & Andrés Rodríguez-Pose, *From R&D to Innovation and Economic Growth in the EU*, 35 Growth & Change 434 (2004).

[198]   Rosenberg, *supra* note 153.

[199]   Philippe Aghion & Peter Howitt, The Economics of Growth (MIT Press 2008).

[200]   Pierre Dieterlen, *Abramovitz (Moses), Resource and Output Trends in the United States Since 1870. Occasional Paper 1952*, 9 Revue économique 164 (1958).

[201]   *Id.*

[202]   *Id.*

[203]   Rosenberg, *supra* note 153.

[204]   Robert M. Solow, *Technical Change and the Aggregate Production Function*, 39 Rev. Econ. & Stat. 312 (1957).

[205]   *Id.*

[206]   *Id.*

[207]   *Id.*

[208]   William Easterly, *The Ghost of Financing Gap: How the Harrod-Domar Growth Model Still Haunts Development Economics* (World Bank Policy Research Working Paper No. 1807, 1997), https://ssrn.com/abstract=11020.

[209]   A Dictionary of Economics and Commerce (Stella E. Stiegeler & Glyn Thomas eds., Pan Reference Books 1976).

[210]   Easterly, *supra* note 208.

In other words, the capital and output ratio is fixed.[211] As a result, the model did not account for a number of things, such as labor and other substitutions of production factors,[212] and lacked flexibility in the long run. However, it should be noted that Domar himself had disowned his model, stating that it was not accurate in the long run, and endorsed the model created by Solow.[213]

Solow changed the game and updated the approach of its predecessors by first establishing that, contrary to the popular belief that growth can only be achieved by population growth, increase in labor or equipment, growth is achieved with technological progress. He managed to mathematically explain that sustainable growth lies with the "ability to create, absorb and use new technology"[214] and reached the conclusion that steady economic growth can only be achieved when all of the elements – output, capital, and labor – grow hand in hand.[215]

Although Solow's starting point and conclusion were more advanced than what was accomplished by both Abramovitz and Harrod–Domar, it has also been criticized. Initially, Solow's assumptions were deemed "unrealistic" by some, since the model was built around the idea of perfect competition, neutral economic policy-making and continuous production.

Solow's criticism begins with a "perfect flexible market" where "frictionless matching of an unfilled job and an unemployed worker with the appropriate skills" is possible, not taking into account that this match could ultimately be broken by governmental unemployment policies. Furthermore, the Solow model does not account for pricing elements and fails to consider that the only method savings could be directed to investment is through forced mechanisms.[216] Solow has also been criticized for illustrating innovation and technological progress as a singular, stable growth factor. Yet, it has been established that innovative thought is unpredictable, whether it is timing or the actual effect innovation would bear on any given sector.[217] Likewise, while establishing that technological progress plays a critical role in growth, Solow fell short of establishing a link between capital and technology. As with his predecessors, Solow's limitations were addressed by another Nobel laureate, Paul Romer, who examined technology as an economic element on its own.[218] Romer approached technology in abstract form; to him, "it is the 'ideas' or knowledge to produce goods or deliver services, different from the tools and machines that embody the ideas."[219] Nevertheless, a better formulation for an unpredictability like

---

[211] *Id.*

[212] Kevin D. Hoover, *Was Harrod Right?* (CHOPE Working Paper No. 2012-01, 2012), https://ssrn.com/abstract=2001452.

[213] Easterly, *supra* note 208.

[214] Paul Donovan, *Why Do Some Economies Grow Faster Than Others*, UBS NOBEL PERSPECTIVES (2020), https://www.ubs.com/microsites/nobel-perspectives/en/laureates/robert-solow.html.

[215] Daniele Schilirò, *A Glance at Solow's Growth Theory* (MPRA Paper No. 84531, Feb. 13, 2018), https://mpra.ub.uni-muenchen.de/84531/1/MPRA_paper_84531.pdf.

[216] Dicle Ozdemir, *A Post-Keynesian Criticism of the Solow Growth Model*, 5 J. ECON. BUS. & MGMT. 134 (2017).

[217] *Id.*

[218] Rui Zhao, *Technology and Economic Growth: From Robert Solow to Paul Romer*, 1 HUM. BEHAV. & EMERGING TECH. 62 (2019).

[219] *Id.*

technological progress was and remains a challenge for modern economists who are trying to analyze growth in economies dominated by technology. The unpredictability of innovation makes it almost impossible to be used as an efficiency defense, as long as Horizontal Merger Guidelines discount such claims for "being vague, speculative or otherwise cannot be verified by reasonable means."[220] As long as the imbalance between the standards of proof of harms and efficiencies exists, it is impossible for competition authorities to fully recognize the significance of competition, with all its facets.

2.2.6 General-Purpose Technologies and Diffusion of Innovation

Innovative developments, aside from their transformative effect on their own, can also have spillover effects and trigger changes and technological advances in other seemingly unrelated areas. The water wheel showed how to convert and use the water's energy first in agriculture, but it was crucial in the development of a wide variety of mechanical systems that saved in labor and increased productivity until steam engine power came along.[221] Due to their positive effects on overall technological development, these advances such as the water wheel are known as general-purpose technologies ("GPT"). They are characterized by being extremely pervasive in many sectors of the economy, leading to continuous technical advances and requiring complementary investments.[222] These features establish a mechanism that can be considered an "engine of economic growth." As a GPT becomes more attainable, it is adopted by larger portions of society, constantly fostering complementary developments and raising the attractiveness of its adoption. Therefore, when the demand for a GPT increases, it prompts and stimulates new rounds of downstream advances.[223] Thus, according to many industrial economists, GPTs are the driving force of technological development and economic progress.[224] In other words, GPTs might foster the innovation process and, by doing so, might pave the way for the diffusion of technological products as well as other GPTs.

Rogers defines diffusion as the social process by which an innovation is communicated through certain channels over time, among members of the social system.[225] In this context, James Watt's steam engine can be viewed as one of the early examples of a GPT that fulfilled its duty in the larger economy, since it gave rise to the industrial factory production system, and together, they played a substantial role in the diffusion of

---

[220] US Dep't of Just. & Fed. Trade Comm'n, Horizontal Merger Guidelines (2010), https://www.ftc.gov/sites/default/files/attachments/merger-review/100819hmg.pdf

[221] ALAIN BRESSON, THE MAKING OF THE ANCIENT GREEK ECONOMY 293–300 (Princeton Univ. Press 2016).

[222] Elhanan Helpman & Manuel Trajtenberg, *Diffusion of General Purpose Technologies* (NBER Working Paper Series, 117, 1998) also in GENERAL PURPOSE TECHNOLOGIES AND ECONOMIC GROWTH 85–119 (Elhanan Helpman ed., MIT Press 1998).

[223] *Id.*

[224] *Id.* at 99.

[225] EVERETT M. ROGERS, DIFFUSION OF INNOVATIONS (Free Press 3d ed. 1983), https://teddykw2.files.wordpress.com/2012/07/everett-m-rogers-diffusion-of-innovations.pdf.

various other emerging technologies, such as automobiles. Starting with Ford Model T, the production and diffusion of affordable cars offered and enabled an unprecedented level of social mobility, while providing consumers with the high level of freedom of choice that they enjoy today. Indeed, many families started to discover the blessings of suburban dwelling, and the suburbanization of American society paved the way to the current geographic allocation of the US population and contributed to the emergence and development of America's unmatched intra- and interstate highway systems. The invention and development of airplanes showed a similar trajectory. At first glance, the invention of the airplane had not been considered a commercially profitable invention or even an invention that attracted much public or media attention.[226] Even though the first-ever flight occurred in 1903, it took until the 1930s for airplanes to become widely accepted and used by the public in general.[227]

The same cumulative process was also on display in the diffusion of electricity. The Gramme dynamo was the first commercially successful electric power generator. First built in New York in 1876, it was initially developed for the goal of conducting scientific research, then Thomas Edison perfected it and made it suitable for daily use.[228] At the time, the generator had been so costly to use that one of the first two generators was installed in a naval vessel and the other was used for scientific research. These distinct phases of the development of electricity make it a process whereby incremental innovation can be easily observed.

Television is another major subject of global diffusion.[229] Unfortunately, once again, the innovation itself had not garnered much attention in the early 1900s.[230] For instance, a news article published in the *New York Times* in 1939 introducing the television (which was a new invention at that time) revealed that people never imagined that it could have a substantial impact on their daily lives.[231] The main reason for this seemingly blinkered outlook was that people thought that they would not have any free time left over from their daily activities to watch the screen.[232] First commercially introduced in 1929 as the "Baird Televisor," it was initially sold for the average annual salary of an American worker, which made it a high-luxury item that only the rich could afford. Every television set producer (including HMV, Motorola, and others) innovated on this device throughout the first half of the 20th century, and by the 1950s, more than a hundred thousand TVs were being sold weekly in America. Companies kept introducing new technologies, such as the electronic remote control, and ultimately, color TVs. The launch of the color TV sparked a drastic decline in the price of black-and-white televisions, and suddenly, TVs became more attainable than ever before. Despite its slow beginnings, television

---

[226] Rosenberg, *supra* note 153.

[227] *Id.*

[228] James E. Brittain, *The International Diffusion of Electrical Power Technology, 1870-1920*, 34 J. Econ. His. 108 (1974).

[229] Michael Gurevitch & Zipora Loevy, *The Diffusion of Television as an Innovation: The Case of the Kibbutz*, 25 Hum. Rel. 181 (1972).

[230] National Research Council, The Positive Sum Strategy: Harnessing Technology for Economic Growth (Ralph Landau & Nathan Rosenberg eds., The National Academies Press 1986)

[231] *Id.*

[232] Solow *supra* note 204.

has undoubtedly become one of the main household products among the technological developments of the 20th century, which is still widely used in the 21st century.

Another technological development that has experienced rapid diffusion is the Internet. In 1993, there were fewer than 150 Internet domains; by December 1996, there were 258,000.[233] The Internet is perhaps the fastest-spreading major technology in human history. Being a stand-alone innovation, the Internet sets itself apart from other rapidly spreading technologies. It is so radical and disruptive a technology that it would be accurate to say that survival is nearly impossible for any business that fails to adopt and adapt to it. It started as a research project in 1968, and it was first opened for commercial use in 1991. Since then, the residential access speed has been on a steep climb, while the price tag has gone significantly down, which has made widespread diffusion possible.[234] The diffusion rate of the new technologies strongly depends on two factors: the embodiment effect and the variety effect. The embodiment effect reflects how much the new technology is better than the old technology, while the variety effect reflects potential gains from varieties induced by the introduction of the new technologies.[235] For the Internet, the variety effect is virtually infinite. That is why it is so disruptive and also the biggest invention of our age.[236]

Mobile phones are undoubtedly one of the most important technological innovations of the 20th century.Indeed, in 1983, after the AT&T competition lawsuit,[237] AT&T worked with a consulting company to assess whether it wanted to enter into the mobile phone market and retain the frequencies that would be required for this operation, during its divestment. The consulting firm forecast that the number of people using mobile phones in 1999 would be almost one million, whereas, in actuality, it surpassed seventy million, merely twenty years after their invention.[238] This example also clearly illustrates the role that invention plays in terms of economic growth, by showing how it can help develop an entirely new industry worth billions of dollars and involving millions of customers in a short time. Innovation looks not at the past but at the future and targets the demands of that future.[239] Nevertheless, this does not mean that innovation is an easy or straightforward process; on the contrary, it requires a lot of time and capital, as well as patience and perseverance. In this sense, mobile phones are also another conclusive proof that innovation has an enormous impact on the reduction of costs,[240] mainly due to the increased efficiencies and performance improvements achieved through new technologies. The first mobile phone was sold for $3,000 in 1983, whereas now, the average basic mobile phone is sold for approximately $100, despite vast improvements to mobile phone technology.[241]

---

[233] *See* Agha Ali, *How Many Websites Are There?* DIGITAL INFORMATION WORLD (2019), https://www.digitalinformation-world.com/2019/09/how-many-websites-exist-today-on-the-internet.html.

[234] Andrew Odlyzko, *Internet Pricing and the History of Communications*, 36 COMPUT. NETWORKS 493 (2001).

[235] Diego Comin & Bart Hobijn, *An Exploration of Technology Diffusion*, 100 AM. ECON. REV. 2031 (2010).

[236] Per Botolf Maurseth, *The Effect of the Internet on Economic Growth: Counter-Evidence from Cross-Country Panel Data*, 172 ECON. LETTERS 74 (2018).

[237] *AT&T* case, United States v. Am. Tel. & Tel. Co., 552 F. Supp. 131, 195 (D.D.C. 1982), aff'd sub nom. Maryland v. United States, 460 US 1001, 103 S. Ct. 1240, 75 L. Ed. 2d 472 (1983).

[238] Rosenberg, *supra* note 153.

[239] *Id.*

[240] Ioan Radu Petrariu, Robert Bumbac & Radu Ciobanu, *Innovation: A Path to Competitiveness and Economic Growth: The Case of CEE Countries*, XX THEORETICAL & APPLIED ECON. 15 (2013).

[241] NATIONAL RESEARCH COUNCIL, *supra* note 230.

Again a slow starter, despite its invention in the 1960s, laser technology had no practical areas of use in those years.[242] Nevertheless, due to the fierce competitive pressures in free-market economies, and the incentives and willingness of competing undertakings to manufacture new products in order to obtain more significant market shares and generate increased profits, businesses have later discovered areas of use for laser technology. Specifically, laser technology attracted much attention and interest in the chemical industry.[243] Later on, it started to be used as a surgical tool by dermatologists, ophthalmologists, and surgeons.[244] This has accelerated the development of the healthcare sector and generated millions of dollars in revenues. Similarly, lasers were eventually adapted for use in the music industry with the introduction of compact discs.[245] Finally, another field that introduced laser technology into its operations (and thereby benefited both businesses and consumers) was supermarkets. Indeed, at market checkouts, lasers are now widely used to scan the products' barcodes.[246] Today, laser technology is also widely used in printers, telecommunications, and dentistry operations, among others.

Last but not least, the computer had monumental effects not only on companies but also on people's daily lives. The first computer (known as ENIAC) was used in 1945 at the University of Pennsylvania,[247] and by 1950, various companies had become engaged in the manufacturing and sales of computers.[248] In 1956, most scientists still considered the computer to be only a scientific instrument, instead of a tool that would facilitate (indeed, revolutionize) people's daily activities. In this regard, Howard Aiken stated the following in 1956 in his deliberations on the future use of computers: "[I]f it should ever turn out that the basic logic of a machine designed for the numerical solution of differential equations coincide with the logistics of a machine intended to make bills for a department store, I would regard this as the most amazing coincidence that I have ever encountered."[249] Today, after more than 75 years of use, the true nature and world-changing potential of this transformative invention have been fully recognized, and the vital importance of computers in every industry and to the everyday lives of most of the world's population has unquestionably been established. Computers have become attainable for all middle-class households in developed countries. This unprecedented diffusion rate has also sparked huge levels of user co-invention, giving rise to numerous new technologies, such as artificial intelligence, the Internet of things, blockchains, and cryptocurrencies, among others. Taken together, these new technologies have led to an astonishing leap in the living standards of humanity and produced widespread economic welfare. The computer is a unique stand-alone innovation that fundamentally changed both the structure of the business world and its processes, creating an everlasting chain of innovation, improvement and enhanced economic welfare.

---

[242]   *Id.*
[243]   *Id.*
[244]   *Id.*
[245]   Pras, Guastavino & Lavoie, *supra* note 154.
[246]   Rosenberg, *supra* note 153.
[247]   *Id.*
[248]   *Id.*
[249]   Howard Aiken, *The Future of Automatic Computing Machinery*, *in* ELEKTRONISCHE RECHENMASCHINEN UND INFORMATIONSVERARBEITUNG [ELECTRONIC DIGITAL COMPUTERS AND INFORMATION PROCESSING] (Alwin Walther & Walter Hoffmann eds., F. Vieweg 1957).

Most GPTs are stand-alone innovations that are "disruptive." At the outset, the adoption of these technologies might be very costly, or may require significant changes in the functioning of the societies. However, once embedded, their spillover effects give rise to new innovation and increase in total welfare. Thus, the diffusion of general-purpose technologies is critical for both continuing innovation and economic welfare.[250] It therefore remains a surprise that although economic welfare is the purpose of competition law, the pro-competitive effects of innovation in dynamic efficiencies are still being held to impossible burdens of proof.

Innovation as Improvement of Existing Technologies

Even though computers, televisions, lasers, and mobile phones are clear-cut examples of the products of innovation, people often hesitate to use a broader definition for "innovation" that would encompass the improvement of certain existing products and processes. However, it would be a mistake to consider that only high-tech inventions fall under the definition of "innovation." Some well-known scholars have suggested that, aside from a few exceptions, most economic activities would fall within the scope of innovation.[251] To be more specific, developments in the fields of logistics, distribution channels or marketing should also be considered as products of innovation, even though they are not among the first items that come to one's mind when one hears the term.[252]

To that end, Hartmut Hirsch-Kreinsen et al., citing Tunzelmann and Acha, suggest that innovation has a considerable impact even in low-tech industries and that this process eventually leads to significant economic efficiencies, just as in the high-tech industries.[253] Even though innovative activities in high-tech industries attract more attention from the public and in the media, innovations that occur in low-tech industries also create considerable economic and social impacts, as pointed out by Fagerberg.[254]

2.2.7 Factors Encouraging Innovation

The significant impact of innovation in everyday life and economic growth did not arise only out of the hard work of inventors; in fact, it was also associated with and spurred by the rising incentives to innovate as a result of the competitive pressures in the free market, the creativity of end users, and the diverse needs of society.[255]

---

[250] Rainer Andergassen, Franco Nardini & Massimo Ricottilli, *Innovation Diffusion, General Purpose Technologies and Economic Growth*, 40 STRUCTURAL CHANGE & ECON. DYNAMICS 72 (2017).

[251] Martin Bell & Keith Pavitt, *Technological Accumulation and Industrial Growth: Contrasts Between Developed and Developing Countries*, 2 INDUS. & CORP. CHANGE 157 (1993).

[252] *Id.*

[253] Hartmut Hirsch-Kreinsen, David Jacobson & Paul L. Robertson, *'Low-tech' Industries: Innovativeness and Development Perspectives – A Summary of a European Research Project*, 24 PROMETHEUS 3 (2006) (citing Nick von Tunzelmann & Virginia Acha, *Innovation in "Low-Tech" Industries*, in THE OXFORD HANDBOOK OF INNOVATION 407–32 (Jan Fagerberg, David C. Mowery & Richard R. Nelson eds. Oxford 2005)).

[254] Jan Fagerberg, Martin Srholec & Bart Verspagen, *Innovation and Economic Development*, in 2 HANDBOOK OF ECONOMICS OF INNOVATION 833 (Bronwyn H. Hall & Nathan Rosenberg eds., Elsevier 2010).

[255] Rosenberg, *supra* note 153.

For example, the use of steam power in factories adversely affected manufacturing efficiency when compared with the use of electricity as a power source.[256] In the early years, during which steam was used as a power source, leather belts and pulleys led to a relatively slow production process, resulting in a low daily manufacturing output.[257] However, by introducing electricity to the factory floor and inserting electrical motors into each machine, the production process was accelerated to a remarkable extent,[258] and the hazardous waste resulting from the use of steam and leather was also reduced. An American study spanning the sixty years between the 1920s and the 1980s has revealed that the introduction of electricity into the manufacturing process has materially increased overall productivity.[259]

Another factor is the state. It is the most powerful economic actor of modern times as well as one of the most prominent actors in innovative progress. According to the OECD, there are many methods available to the state to foster an innovative environment. These vary from ensuring access to financing and unwavering macroeconomic conditions, to a free economy where both foreign investment and pro-competitive market environment are promoted.[260] It is within the state's power to increase the levels of R&D, by putting in place a regulative framework targeted to attract entrepreneurs, approving the necessary educational spending and encouraging private funding.[261] Despite the criticisms discussed earlier, proper protection of intellectual property rights is also another incentive to drive R&D, as intellectual property is still the number one protector of the financial interests of those who innovate.[262] Another practical method would be the tax incentives.[263] Direct state investment in innovation also plays an important role. Yet, the inclusion of the state directly into the innovative process is also a matter of policy making.[264]

Since the Industrial Revolution, national performance of innovation has played a crucial role in capital growth.[265] But is there a specific environment in which innovation is fostered and motivated more than usual? where innovation is promoted, financed by the state that diligently keeps time and oversight on the process? The evident answer would be times of conflict. The connection between modern technology and warfare is more than obvious. However, whether war times enable private enterprises to pursue their capacity to innovate and invent is another topic of debate.[266]

---

[256]   *Id.*

[257]   Sukkoo Kim, *Industrialization and Urbanization: Did the Steam Engine Contribute to the Growth of Cities in the United States?* 42 EXPL. ECON. HIS. 586 (2005).

[258]   *Id.*

[259]   *Id.*

[260]   OECD, *Innovation and Growth: Rationale for an Innovation Strategy* (2007), https://www.oecd.org/science/inno/39374789.pdf.

[261]   *How Does Innovation Lead to Growth?* EUROPEAN CENTRAL BANK (June 27, 2017), https://www.ecb.europa.eu/explainers/tell-me-more/html/growth.en.html.

[262]   Hasa Torun & Cumhur Çiçekçi, *Innovation: Is the Engine for the Economic Growth* (Ege University, Faculty of Economics and Administrative Sciences 2007), http://citeseerx.ist.psu.edu/viewdoc/download?doi=10.1.1.452.4897&rep=rep1&type=pdf.

[263]   Dirk Czarnitzki & Otto Toivanen, *Innovation Policy and Economic Growth*, 483 ECON. PAPERS (2013).

[264]   OECD, *supra* note 260.

[265]   *Id.*

[266]   GEORGE BASALLA, TEKNOLOJININ EVRIMI [THE EVOLUTION OF TECHNOLOGY] (Cen Soydemir trans., Tübitak Publications 2000).

The most striking evidence of innovative progress fueled by war or international conflict is destructively illustrated by the technological advancements of the 20th century. Starting with World War I, developing new techniques has become a focal point, as it enhanced profit and productivity and provided advantages on the field of war, – an area in which innovation was now correlated with efficiency and value for money.[267] At that stage, there were many government-funded institutions, which led to a network of organizations, not only enhancing their military capacity[268] but also working on the advancement of matters of mass production and healthcare.

It is accepted that World War I's legacy has led to the foundation of maybe the most prominent governmental science organizations, such as the National Aeronautics and Space Administration ("NASA") of the United States, the French National Centre for Scientific Research ("CNRS"), and the Commission for the Study of the Natural Productive Forces ("KEPS") of Russia.[269] Furthermore, in order to deal with starvation and famine, states in conflict resorted to scientific and technological cooperation.[270] Maybe one of the most obvious examples of technological advancement resulting from warfare is the nuclear reactor. The nuclear energy industry would not have been what it is if the military methods of utilizing it had not been developed during World War II in scope of the infamous Manhattan Project, bringing together the brightest minds of the century.[271] The sort of technological advancement that created the atomic bomb also brought along many ethical, societal and environmental debates, dividing the literature as to whether its existence was necessary to begin with. DARPA (Defense Advanced Research Projects Agency) had a greater role to play in the US innovation system. We have already touched upon innovation policies fostered by Vannevar Bush, who was instrumental in bringing together talent and R&D under a technological "connected" and "challenge" model, although it was dismantled after the war and replaced with a decentralized and science-focused network of organizations afterward. DARPA was a unique bridging model that combined the research groups and embodied the connected system. It had expanded its scope into non-defense organizations, realizing that advances needed to encompass the whole economy.[272]

Many economists, including Solow,[273] Romer,[274] and Mansfield,[275] agree that techno-logical innovation (which has led to the digital revolution) is one of the main drivers of humanity's economic growth and well-being. Correspondingly, the close link between

---

[267] Benoît Godin, *Innovation: History of a Category* (Project on the Intellectual History of Innovation, Working Paper No. 1, 2008), http://www.csiic.ca/PDF/IntellectualNo1.pdf.

[268] Examples of warfare technology introduced or enhanced for utilization during this period could be tanks, submarines, machine guns, etc.

[269] Jörg Lehmann & Francesca Morselli, *Science and Technology in the First World War* (CENDARI Archival Research Guide, 2016).

[270] Giuditta Parolini, 'The Commission Would Have Been Definitely Appointed If the War Had Not Supervened': The International Meteorological Organisation and Its Commission for Agricultural Meteorology after WWI, The First World War: The Aftermath, The Royal Society, London (Sept. 13, 2018).

[271] BASALLA, *supra* note 266.

[272] NATIONAL RESEARCH COUNCIL, 21ST CENTURY INNOVATION SYSTEMS FOR JAPAN AND THE UNITED STATES: LESSONS FROM A DECADE OF CHANGE: REPORT OF A SYMPOSIUM 206–23 (The National Academies Press 2009) https://doi.org/10.17226/12194.

[273] Robert M. Solow, *A Contribution to the Theory of Economic Growth*, 70 Q. J. ECON. 70 65 (1956).

[274] Paul M. Romer, *Increasing Returns and Long-Run Growth*, 94 J. POL. ECON. 1002 (1986).

[275] Edwin Mansfield, *Contribution of R&D to Economic Growth in the United States*, 175 SCIENCE 477 (1972).

innovation and economic growth has been emphasized in various empirical and theoretical studies conducted in the US, Europe, and Japan, as well as many other countries.[276] Moreover, scholars such as Agénor and Neanidis have also revealed that innovation and economic growth often trigger and spur each other on in the development process.[277] In this regard, patents, R&D expenditures and activities, and high-technology exports have come to play key roles in terms of economic growth across the globe.

2.2.8 GDP as the Link Between Innovation and Economic Growth

One of the measures that best demonstrates the relationship between economic growth and innovation is the gross domestic product ("GDP").[278] GDP is a monetary measure of the market value of all the final goods and services produced in a country during a specific time (often annually), and it is known as the value used to measure the growth rate of an economy year-to-year.[279] This measure is quite useful in economic studies when considered as a proxy representing the overall economic well-being of a country.[280] Indeed, "GDP per capita" is considered to represent the financial resources of a country and its knowledge stock (e.g., human capital).[281] In this regard, Furman, Porter, and Stern believe GDP per capita directly represents the technological development of any given country.[282] This view is in line with the earlier discussions, which demonstrated that technological development is directly linked with a country's capability to innovate, and therefore, with its economic growth. Having said this, GDP per capita has also been criticized as a suitable measure for economic growth, for being a short-term measure that omits certain externalities like the cost of environmental matters or depletion of resources and is unable to portray a true picture of long-term economic welfare – although a more acceptable alternative measure is yet to be proposed.[283]

Moreover (notwithstanding some exceptions) innovation generally finds its final expression in a patent form, where an inventor is often eager to obtain patent protection for its invention due to the patent system's economic and personal advantages.[284] On the other hand, since an invention under patent protection must be disclosed to the public after the patent is granted, it also enables others to improve upon such models and gain financial

---

[276] Rosenberg, *supra* note 153.

[277] Pierre-Richard Agénor & Kyriakos C. Neanidis, *Innovation, Public Capital, and Growth*, J. MACROECONOMICS 252 (2015).

[278] Edward Ang, *The Positive Effects of Education, Research and Innovation on GDP per Capita* (2012) https://www.researchgate.net/publication/270418934_The_Positive_Effects_of_Education_Research_ and_Innovation_ on_GDP_Per_Capita.

[279] *Id.*

[280] *Id.*

[281] *Id.*

[282] Jeffrey L. Furman, Michael E. Porter & Scott Stern, *Understanding the Drivers of National Innovative Capacity*, ACAD. MGMT. BEST PAPER PROC. A1 (2000).

[283] Diane Coyle, *Rethinking GDP*, 54 FIN. & DEV. 16 (2017), https://www.imf.org/external/pubs/ft/fandd/2017/03/coyle.htm.

[284] Prabuddha Ganguli, *Intellectual Property Rights: Mothering Innovations to Markets*, 22 WORLD PAT. INFO. 43 (2000).

returns from their efforts.[285] In this regard, even though it is difficult to explicitly prove or establish the link between the number of patents obtained in a country and its GDP trends, it is clear that there is an inherent and foreseeable relationship between them. Devinney's study implicitly revealed that there was a positive correlation between the number of patents and GDP growth in 1994.[286] Moreover, Crosby's study (conducted in 2000) also discovered that patenting activities had a positive impact on labor efficiency and productivity, and eventually established its link to economic growth, as a result of the study on the relationship between innovative activities in particular countries and their GDP growth rates.[287] Similarly, Yang's study in 2006 revealed the positive impact of innovative activities on GDP growth rates.[288]

Considering that the foremost purpose is economic growth, in light of such strong links between GDP growth and innovation, we should also agree that we do not have the luxury of merely paying lip service to the concept of innovation. Unfortunately, at this time, it is nearly impossible to get competition authorities to truly focus on innovation and exhaust all aspects of potential dynamic efficiencies without jumping through all the hoops of prerequisites, conditions of admissibility, asymmetrical and improbable standards of proof. Parties claiming dynamic efficiencies in a proposed acquisition find it very difficult to get the authority to give them the benefit of the doubt and conduct a sincere and exhaustive innovation analysis. On the other hand, if the authority has concerns related to innovation, then it is surprisingly enthusiastic to take a deep dive into the acquisition's potential adverse effects on innovation. Because the burden of proof is reversed when dynamic efficiencies are flagged up as points of defense, the authorities are comfortable with sitting back and letting counsel struggle to "prove" their claims. Considering that parties' counsel do not enjoy the same accessibility to market or data from third parties as the competition authorities, and furthermore, their considerable disadvantage due to restrictions on transaction parties' sharing strategic data before closing, any studies that the defense teams are able to present to demonstrate their claims will fall short of what the authority could have established, had it taken on this burden itself.

2.2.9 Expanding Competition, Innovation, and Economic Growth Through International Trade

There is a long-standing school of thought that believes that a greater R&D specialization is more likely to elevate innovation.[289] This perspective may be illustrated with the following example: if one computer company invests in improving memory chips, its

---

[285]   *Id.*

[286]   Changtao Wang, The Long-Run Effect of Innovations on Economic Growth, Paper Prepared for the IARIW-UNSW Conference on Productivity: Measurement, Drivers and Trends, Sydney, Australia 4 (Nov. 26–27, 2013), http://www.iariw.org/papers/2013/WangPaper.pdf.

[287]   *Id.*

[288]   *Id.*

[289]   Jason Furman, Trade, Innovation, and Economic Growth, Remarks at The Brookings Institution (Apr. 8, 2015), https://obamawhitehouse.archives.gov/sites/default/files/docs/20150408_trade_innovation_growth_brookings.pdf.

competitors will also be incentivized to begin to conduct innovative activities, which, in turn, will help consumers to access better and cheaper products as a result of this augmented activity of R&D.[290]

A study connected with Branstetter, Fisman, and Foley has shown that if foreign IP rights are strengthened in a country, this automatically leads to "more outward licensing from the US."[291] As a result, companies that are innovatively prolific would also license and allow others to use their ideas and innovations, in return for royalty payments, which benefits both parties.[292] Moreover, the authors contend that, since the reforms on the protection of intellectual property rights, the number of US companies that allow foreign companies to use their innovative products and ideas has increased by up to 16.6% due to their increased confidence that their ownership rights and royalty payments would be adequately protected.

As numerous commentators have noted, "[r]elatively free trade has the advantage that the possibility of increasing market share in world markets is a constant incentive for innovative activity."[293] In this regard, free trade not only provides an incentive for innovative activities in a broader sense but also enables businesses to become more productive, as a result of the acceleration witnessed in the global flow of ideas from one country to another.[294] Importers, as well as exporters, come across various fresh and innovative ideas, and new products shaped in light of these ideas, in other parts of the world. Eventually, such companies become more productive and creative. Similarly, exporting activities also enable local companies to learn about international industries and may even allow them to acquire technical expertise from foreign buyers.[295]

This international diffusion of ideas and technologies is also linked to "learning by doing." This is an economic concept first used by Kenneth Arrow, where he claims that productive efficiency is ensured through practice, experience and the transfer of cumulative knowledge.[296] It is thought that, in practice, much of the technological development we see all around us stems from the accumulation of small modifications, amendments, and adjustments.[297] This definition paves the way to the idea that, while technological development itself (i.e., discovery, invention or innovation) is clearly important, the perfect implementation achieved through the accumulation of experiences is accountable for

---

[290]   *Id.*

[291]   Robert M. Solow, On Macroeconomic Models of Free-Market Innovation and Growth 15–20 (Princeton Univ. Press, 2007).

[292]   Lee G. Branstetter, Raymond Fisman & C. Fritz Foley, *Do Stronger Intellectual Property Rights Increase International Technology Transfer? Empirical Evidence from the United States Firm-Level Panel Data,* 121 Q. J. Econ. 321 (2006).

[293]   Entrepreneurship, Innovation, and the Growth Mechanism of the Free-Enterprise Economies (Eytan Sheshinski, Robert J. Strom, and William J. Baumol eds., Princeton Univ. Press 2007).

[294]   Furman, *supra* note 289.

[295]   Jan De Loecker, *Detecting Learning by Exporting,* 5 Am. Econ. J.: Microeconomics 1 (2013).

[296]   Peter Thompson, *Learning by Doing, in* Handbook of the Economics of Innovation 220–29 (Bronwyn H. Hall & Nathan Rosenberg eds., Elsevier 2010).

[297]   Hillard G. Huntington & John P. Weyant, *Modeling Energy Markets and Climate Change Policy, in* Encyclopaedia of Energy 41 (Cutler J. Cleveland ed., Elsevier Science 2004).

the bulk of the resulting economic welfare.[298] For instance, when power looms were first introduced, workers were able to produce 2.5 times more clothes than they had produced while working with handlooms; but after 80 years of experience in working with power looms, workers were able to increase their production to an astonishing 80 times more than they had with the handlooms.[299] Past experience shows that while it is usually very expensive to adopt new technologies in the initial stage, the costs decline drastically when such technologies are used more widely and further lessons are extracted from it in time. Therefore, in terms of an economic approach, *learning by doing* rationalizes the early investments in new technologies that are currently inefficient but promising, if they succeed in moving the learning curve downwards.[300]

Learning by doing also connects international trade and competition policy through governmental protection of infant industries.[301] For instance, if foreign actors are competitive and refrain from further learning and improvement, and a domestic monopolist is unable to offer long-term contracts, then import bans in favor of a domestic infant industry might culminate in greater welfare compared to free trade.[302] As another example, in circumstances where a domestic production is too costly and a given commodity has to be imported, if learning effects are strong enough and the importing country is able to offer reasonable subsidies on imports, then future prices might decrease significantly, and thus promote and enhance the consumer welfare.[303]

2.3 The Role of Innovation in Competition Law

Innovation manifests in the daily life of consumers in the form of improved products and services, and innovation-driven companies compete to become the market leader or the most preferred choice for consumers in a given market. Thanks to innovative steps in technology, as consumers, we now have access to many different products that have become integral to the daily lives of everyone around the world. In this regard, the vital importance of innovation for consumer benefit is undeniable. However, this demand for innovation is associated with the risk of exploitation by dominant undertakings. Hence, the importance of competition law for the protection of the competitive process and innovation.

Competition law principles throughout the world share the same fundamental goal, which is to preserve the competitive market structure by preventing anti-competitive conduct that

---

[298] JAMES BESSEN, LEARNING BY DOING: THE REAL CONNECTION BETWEEN INNOVATION, WAGES, AND WEALTH 62 (Yale Univ. Press 2015).

[299] *Id.* at 24.

[300] William Nordhaus, *Integrated Economic and Climate Modeling, in* HANDBOOK OF COMPUTABLE GENERAL EQUILIBRIUM MODELING 1069 (Elsevier 2013).

[301] Partha Dasgupta & Joseph Stiglitz, *Learning-by-Doing, Market Structure and Industrial and Trade Policies,* 40 OXFORD ECON. PAPERS 247 (1998).

[302] *Id.* at 264.

[303] *Id.* at 265.

hinders competition, impedes innovation, and harms consumers.[304] In this regard, competition law also safeguards and preserves the innovation incentives within the market. In fact, the European Commission's Guidelines on the Assessment of Horizontal Mergers[305] manifestly point out that one of the Commission's roles is to prevent mergers that may culminate in harm to consumer welfare and deprive the consumer of the benefits of competition, including innovation, by significantly increasing the market power of firms. In this context, "increased market power" means the "ability of one or more firms to profitably increase prices, reduce output, choice or quality of goods and services, diminish innovation, or otherwise influence parameters of competition."[306] Three particular categories of behavior can be identified that might cause this decline in innovation: exclusionary practices (exclusionary innovation), exploitation, and harm to the innovation process.

Exclusionary practices are actions taken by dominant firms to deter new competitors from entering an industry, force rivals to exit, confine them to fringe markets, or prevent them from expanding, which ultimately causes consumer harm.[307] The theory relies on the assumption that exclusionary practices strengthen the position of monopolists, and thus, the monopolist loses its motivation to innovate since there is no effective competitor in the market; therefore, once devoid of innovation, the quality of products decreases, the production costs increase, ultimately resulting in the productive inefficiency and harm to the consumer interests. Nevertheless, there is no consensus over whether all exclusionary practices stifle innovation. In the two-firm model, antitrust prohibitions over exclusionary conducts regarding innovation are found to be effective in different strategic settings:[308] banning the exclusionary conduct of the dominant firm contributes to the total potential of industry innovation, as long as the dominant firm's best response function slopes upward and it is sufficiently steep, or if its rival's best response function slopes downward and it is sufficiently steep. Banning the exclusionary conducts of a dominant firm increases the overall chance of industry innovation if the dominant firm considers the rivals' R&D investment as a strategic complement.[309]

Another potentially harmful behavior, from a competition policy perspective, is that the knowledge produced by innovators can be exploited either directly by having the innovators themselves produce and sell goods and services that embody the newly created knowledge or indirectly through a transfer of new knowledge by licensing it to others who undertake the production.[310] This exploitation damages the innovation process

---

[304]   Eleanor M. Fox & Deborah Healey, *When the State Harms Competition – The Role for Competition Law* 31 (NYU Law and Economics Research Paper No. 13-11, UNSW Law Research Paper No. 2013-312013), https://ssrn.com/abstract=2248059.

[305]   European Commission, Guidelines on the Assessment of Horizontal Mergers Under the Council Regulation on the Control of Concentrations Between Undertakings (2004/C31/03) 2004 OJ (C 31) 5 ("Horizontal Merger Control Guidelines"), https://eur-lex.europa.eu/legal-content/EN/TXT/HTML/?uri=CELEX:52004X-C0205(02)&from=EN.

[306]   *See id.*, para. 8.

[307]   Chiara Fumagalli, Massimo Motta & Claudio Calcagno, *Introduction, in* Exclusionary Practices: The Economics of Monopolisation and Abuse of Dominance 1–13 (Cambridge Univ. Press 2018).

[308]   Jonathan B. Baker, *Exclusionary Conduct of Dominant Firms, R&D Competition, and Innovation*, 48 Rev. Indus. Org. 269 (2016).

[309]   *See* Fumagalli et al., *supra* note 307.

[310]   David Encaoua & Abraham Hollander, *Competition Policy and Innovation*, 18 Oxford Rev. Econ. Pol'y 63 (2002), https://doi.org/10.1093/oxrep/18.1.63.

and consumer welfare since it decreases the rate of diffusion to end customers. When exploitation is on the scene, it might raise other competition law concerns. Practically, if the exploitation level is high, the outsider must possess superior know-how and innovation not yet exploited in the relevant product market. This practically means that a high level of exploitation raises barriers to entry, ultimately decreasing the overall level of competition, innovation, and thus, welfare. In *Microsoft*,[311] Judge Jackson and the Consumer Federation of America ("CFA") both asserted that Microsoft's monopoly had harmed the consumer. In its report, CFA identified dozens of ways in which Microsoft harmed the public welfare, stating that "Microsoft retarded innovation by preventing specific products from being developed and deterring other software companies from devoting developer time and money to new products."[312] This harm might emerge in the forms of price increases, inefficiency in production, and deprivation of consumers from better product offers.

Horizontal mergers might also have a stifling effect on the innovation process, even though their initial effects may seem benign. Alongside digitalization, industrial consolidation appears to be an irreversible trend of modern times: 10% of the world's public companies generate 80% of all profits. The annual number of mergers and acquisitions is more than twice what it was in the 1990s.[313] According to the Horizontal Merger Guidelines,[314] effective competition may be significantly impeded by a merger between two important innovators, for instance between two companies with "pipeline" products related to a specific product market, in which case the transaction can eliminate an important competitive force and thus lead to a significant impediment of effective competition. When these two important innovators merge, so does the big innovation know-how, which might increase the innovative power of the merging parties in the short term; however, in the long run, they will not feel as much incentive to innovate.[315] Their merger would decrease costs by combining the development assets needed for innovation, and after a while, other firms in the industry would fall behind in know-how or development assets to innovate, which would, in turn, decrease the innovation motivation of the merging parties.[316] Thus, cumulative innovation in the industry would decrease, and this would be reflected to the consumers in increasing prices, fewer innovative products, and fewer product choices. The basic problem in competition law enforcement for the innovation assessment is that competition and innovation are analyzed separately in mainstream neoclassical economics.[317] There is a strict split between the (i) competition policy dealing with the market failure "competition problems" in existing markets and thus for the existing products by mainly focusing on price competition, and (ii) innovation policy

---

[311] United States v. Microsoft, State of New York v. Microsoft, Civil Action Nos. 98-1232, 1233 (1998).

[312] Consumer Federation of America, *Microsoft Monopoly Caused Consumer Harm*, https://consumerfed.org/pdfs/antitrustpr.pdf.

[313] Tommaso M. Valletti & Hans Zenger, *Should Profit Margins Play a More Decisive Role in Merger Control?* 9 J. EUR. COMPETITION L. 336 (2018).

[314] Horizontal Merger Control Guidelines, para.31

[315] Vincenzo Denicolò & Michele Polo, *The Innovation Theory of Harm: An Appraisal* (2018), https://ssrn.com/abstract=3146731.

[316] Bruno Jullien & Yassine Lefouili, *Horizontal Mergers and Innovation* 8–15 (Aug. 1, 2018), https://papers.ssrn.com/sol3/papers.cfm?abstract_id=3135177.

[317] Harry Bloch & Stan Metcalfe, *Innovation, Creative Destruction and Price Theory*, 27 INDUS. & CORP. CHANGE 1 (2018), https://www.researchgate.net/publication/319479740_Innovation_creative_destruction_and_price_theory.

dealing mainly with the market failure problems of insufficient innovation incentives.[318] As a natural outcome, innovation has always been seen in competition economics as more of an "additional" issue that does not really fit into this basic theoretical concept of (static) competition.[319] Scholars agree that a more dynamic approach is necessary, and one suggestion was improving the interaction between competition law and IP law.[320] On the other hand, the greater challenge for taking into account innovation in the application of competition is that the static concept of competition has already affected the basic categories and the approaches in competition law. One of the most important examples is the methodology for defining the relevant market, which is the hypothetical monopoly test (small but significant and non-transitory increase in price (SSNIP)-test). The reason is that it only looks at the currently existing products, and analyses in this step-by-step process of including products in the market whether profitable price increases of 5–10% are possible, which basically requires an analysis of the substitutability between all current products.[321] However, future products whose characteristics remain unknown at that stage cannot be taken into account. Therefore, the SSNIP test only leads to a product market definition that entirely comprises existing products in a static perspective where competitors that regularly develop new products and services by their innovative risks and thus change demand and cost functions, which disregards the substitutability between the products. Another consequence of this static concept is that the authorities, in their competitive assessment, deem that the only possibility of consumer welfare being affected negatively is through higher prices.[322] Despite a broad consensus that competition law should not only protect price competition but also competition with regard to quality, variety and innovation, these other non-price parameters usually play no role in competitive assessments even though they may be brought up as points of defense by the undertakings, as long as they submit solid evidence on that front.[323]

The new concept of "ecosystems," which was briefly introduced earlier, and how these are formed are also relevant with respect to competition analyses. Jacobides states that digital platforms use two distinct types of ecosystems: (i) multi-actor ecosystems and (ii) multi-product ecosystems. Multi-actor ecosystems refer to ecosystems in which independent firms contribute to the value creation, while multi-product ecosystems denote the supply of a collection of different, but typically linked, services and products by a single firm.[324] The different services or products in these ecosystems may be substitutes (e.g., Facebook and WhatsApp) or complements (e.g., Apple devices and iCloud).[325]

---

[318]   Kerber, *supra* note 141, at 3.

[319]   *Id.*

[320]   Frederic Jenny, Ioannis Lianos, Herbert Hovenkamp, Frances E. Marshall & Sivaramjani Thambisetty Ramakrishna, Competition Law, Intellectual Property Rights and Dynamic Analysis: Towards a New Institutional "Equilibrium?" CONCURRENCES No. 4-2013, art. No. 58808, para. 8.

[321]   Commission Notice on the Definition of the Relevant Market for the Purposes of Community Competition Law, 1997 OJ (C 372) 5.

[322]   Gregory J. Sidak & David J. Teece, *Dynamic Competition in Antitrust Law*, 5 J. COMPETITION L. & ECON. 581 (2009).

[323]   MAURICE E. STUCKE & ALLEN P. GRUNES, BIG DATA AND COMPETITION POLICY (Oxford Univ. Press 2016).

[324]   Michael G. Jacobides, *Regulating Big Tech in Europe: Why, so WHAT, and How Understanding Their Business Models and Ecosystems Can Make a Difference* 25 (2020), http://dx.doi.org/10.2139/ssrn.3765324.

[325]   OECD, *Digital Competition Policy: Are Ecosystems Different? – Note by Amelia Fletcher* 2 (DAF/COMP/WD(2020)96, Nov. 9, 2020), https://one.oecd.org/document/DAF/COMP/WD(2020)96/En/pdf.

In this context, multi-product ecosystems are characterized by: (i) strong economies of scale and scope resulting from the efficiencies on the supply side of different markets; (ii) data synergies across markets (i.e., data may be used to develop products and services in a different market); (iii) interoperability between different markets; (iv) across-market network effects; (v) barriers to multi-homing, as users may tend to use a single provider for different services due to, for instance, consumer trust and the possibility of using the same digital ID; (vi) barriers to switching to another provider, especially if the customer has to switch for all services provided by a single ecosystem, and (vii) gateway role arising from the fact that consumers' subsequent choices may nest within their initial choices.[326]

These characteristics of ecosystems may raise a number of competitive concerns. First, they may create barriers to entry and expansion, thus restricting the potential for future disruptive innovations or reducing the innovation incentives of the firm operating the platform.[327] Furthermore, contacts through different markets may facilitate coordination among digital platforms. Also, the firm operating the ecosystem may "lock in" its customers[328] and leverage its market power stemming from the possession of vast quantities of data and other characteristics of ecosystems in complementary or adjacent markets[329] – e.g., through (i) limiting interoperability to third parties in order to direct them to its own interoperable products; (ii) self-preferencing;[330] (iii) tying its services supplied in the market in which it possesses market power, with its other services;[331] (iv) using the data gathered through providing platform services to customers that compete with the firm in the supply of other products and services when competing against them.[332] In this way, such characteristics are claimed to restrict consumer choice and innovation.[333]

Accordingly, Jacobides and Lianos argue that the traditional tools for competition analysis are not sufficient to assess the market power of ecosystems, nor to address the concerns associated with them. First, the relevant market definition does not fully take into account all related markets where the dominant platform might leverage (and abuse) its market power (e.g., charging prices below cost for the sale of printers but imposing excessive prices for ink cartridges).[334] Secondly, given the multi-sided nature of these platforms, if one focuses on one side of the platform that is a distinct "relevant market," it may not accurately capture the whole dynamics surrounding the service in question. For example, general search services and the sale of inferences from data to advertisers

---

[326]   *Id.* at 5–6.

[327]   *Id.* at 8–11.

[328]   Michael G. Jacobides & Ioannis Lianos, *Ecosystems and Competition Law in Theory and Practice* 5 (2021) http://dx.doi.org/10.2139/ssrn.3772366.

[329]   OECD, *supra* note 325, at 8–11.

[330]   Google Search (Shopping), European Commission Decision case AT.39740 (June 27, 2017).

[331]   *See* Doh-Shin Jeon & Jay Pil Choi, A Leverage Theory of Tying in Two-Sided Markets with Non-Negative Price Constraints, 13 AM. ECON. J. MICROECONOMICS 283 (2021).

[332]   *See, e.g.*, European Commission Press Release IP/20/2077, Antitrust: Commission Sends Statement of Objections to Amazon for the Use of Non-Public Independent Seller Data and Opens Second Investigation into its E-commerce Business Practices (Nov. 10, 2020), https://ec.europa.eu/commission/presscorner/detail/en/ip_20_2077 (last visited on May 10, 2021).

[333]   Jacobides & Lianos, *supra* note 328, at 16.

[334]   Case T-83/91, Tetra Pak International SA v. Commission, 1994 ECR II-755; case C-333/94 P, Tetra Pak International SA v. Commission, 1996 ECR I-5951, paras. 21–23.

are complementary services that cannot be considered in isolation.[335] The authors argue that the issue about ecosystems is related to intra-ecosystem competition and innovation competition.[336] Hence, the competitive analysis should not focus on substitutability through horizontal rivalry. Rather, it should concentrate on competition from rents emerging from complementarities. That is why the traditional market definition based on the consideration of substitutability and the analysis of market power and market share based on such a market definition fall short of addressing the competitive concerns.[337]

In line with this approach, the EU Competition Policy Report argues that mergers involving ecosystems may cause competitive harm despite the lack of overlapping activities between parties.[338] Accordingly, it proposes that if merging parties are active in the same "technological space," competition authorities should analyze whether the target may be deemed an actual or potential competitor in the broader ecosystem.[339]

On the effect of blurring the boundaries of sectors and markets, although there may be cases where the consideration of wider ecosystem competition may not lead to an increase in intervention in mergers (e.g., in case of a merger where there are horizontal concerns due to the substitutability of the products of merging firms, but these concerns are eliminated because there is an intense competition between the parties and non-horizontally related firms that are active in the same ecosystem),[340] it seems that the arguments in favor of the approach of considering the wider sector mostly aim to address the potential competitive concerns by lowering the threshold for intervention. Hence, even though this approach may help identify the effects that restrict competition, since there is no empirical evidence showing that sticking to the consideration of substitutability has led to a decrease in innovation,[341] and there is empirical research demonstrating that these mergers may cause efficiencies outweighing any anti-competitive impact,[342] it is not possible to conclude that more intervention on the grounds of anti-competitive impact on markets other than the relevant market would follow an increase in innovation. Innovations could be a decisive factor in competition law in many ways. For competition law authorities, innovations could lead to significant changes in (i) the market definition and structure, as well as (ii) market power and dominance.[343] In terms of market definition, we observe

---

[335]   Jacobides & Lianos, *supra* note 328at 12.

[336]   *Id.* at 17, table 2.

[337]   *Id.* at 21.

[338]   JACQUES CRÉMER, YVES-ALEXANDRE DE MONTJOYE & HEIKE SCHWEITZER, COMPETITION POLICY FOR THE DIGITAL ERA 116–17 (Report commissioned by the European Commission, Publications Office of the European Union 2019), http://ec.europa.eu/competition/publications/reports/kd0419345enn.pdf.

[339]   *Id.*

[340]   Daniel A. Crane, *Ecosystem Competition and the Antitrust Laws*, 95 NEB. L. REV. 412, 423–24 (2019).

[341]   *See* Axel Gautier & Joe Lamesch, *Mergers in the Digital Economy* 25–26 (CESifo Working Paper No. 8056, 2020) (finding that only a few of the digital mergers may be considered to have caused ceasing the innovation of the target).

[342]   *See* ELENA ARGENTESI, PAOLO BUCCIROSSI, EMILIO CALVANO, TOMASO DUSO, ALESSIA MARRAZZO & SALVATORE NAVA, EX-POST ASSESSMENT OF MERGER CONTROL DECISIONS IN DIGITAL MARKETS 71 (Final Report prepared by Lear for the Competition Markets Authority, May 9, 2019), https://assets.publishing.service.gov.uk/government/uploads/system/uploads/attachment_data/file/803576/CMA_past_digital_mergers_GOV.UK_version.pdf.

[343]   Gönenç Gürkaynak, Taking the Lead in Antitrust Enforcement Evaluating Innovation and Technology, 19th Loyola Antitrust Colloquium, Institute for Consumer Antitrust Studies at Loyola University Chicago School of Law 2 (Apr. 26, 2019).

that as innovations pave the way for improved goods and services, the market structure is changed, existing markets become subject to alterations, and even new market definitions may emerge.[344] As such, traditional market definitions could become obsolete in "innovation-driven markets,"[345] and appropriate analyses of the innovative effects become imperative for conducting an accurate competition law review.[346] Moreover, for two-sided or multi-sided markets, a simple analysis of the market power of the undertakings concerned may fail to deliver a sufficient and accurate analysis or results, mainly if one or more of the relevant undertakings are two-sided or multi-sided platforms.[347]

2.3.1 The Role of Innovation in Merger Control Regimes

For merger control regimes, jurisdictions such as the EU and the US demonstrate a sophisticated level of understanding of the relationship between innovations and their possible effects in relevant markets. In this regard, paragraph 38 of the EU Guidelines on the Assessment of Horizontal Mergers Under the Council Regulation on the Control of Concentrations Between Undertakings states that "in markets where innovation is an important competitive force, a merger may increase the firms' ability and incentive to bring new innovations to the market and, thereby, the competitive pressure on rivals to innovate in that market. Alternatively, effective competition may be significantly impeded by a merger between two important innovators, for instance, between two companies with 'pipeline' products related to a specific product-market." Accordingly, paragraph 38 acknowledges the fact that innovations deliver pro-competitive effects and essential benefits to consumers but also realizes that mergers and acquisitions between innovation-driven companies could also have the opposite effect on the relevant market. In a 2016 speech, EU's Competition Commissioner Margrethe Vestager stated that "when [they] look at high-tech mergers, [they] do not just look at whether they might raise prices. [They] also assess whether they could be bad for innovation."[348]

The deliberations of the European Commission in various cases, discussed in detail in Chapter 4, support and reinforce the viewpoint of paragraph 38, evaluating that mergers

---

[344]   This is described by the OECD as "disruptive innovation." According to the OECD, disruptive innovations "have the potential to drastically alter markets and their functioning; and they not only involve a new product or process, but can also involve the emergence of a new business model."

[345]   The OECD describes the characteristics of innovation-driven markets as (i) high R&D intensity and dependence on IP rights; (ii) a high degree of technical complexity; (iii) rapid technological change and short product cycles; (iv) increasing returns to scale; (v) important network effects and (vi) significant compatibility and standards issues. *See* OECD, *Merger Review in Emerging High Innovation Markets* (Policy Roundtable, DAFFE/COMP(2002)20, Jan. 24, 2003), http://www.oecd.org/daf/competition/mergers/2492253.pdf.

[346]   Christopher Pleatsikas & David Teece, *The Analysis of Market Definition and Market Power in the Context of Rapid Innovation*, 19 INT'L J. INDUS. ORG. 665 (2001).

[347]   David S. Evans, *The Antitrust Economics of Multi-Sided Platform Markets*, 20 YALE J. ON REGUL. 325 (2003), https://openyls.law.yale.edu/bitstream/handle/20.500.13051/8032/12_20YaleJonReg325_2003_.pdf?sequence=2&isAllowed=y.

[348]   Margrethe Vestager, Competition: The Mother of Invention, European Competition and Consumer Day (Apr. 18, 2016), https://ec.europa.eu/competition/publications/weekly_news_summary/2016_04_22.html

and acquisitions could potentially have adverse effects on the undertakings' incentives to innovate, or to enter into a given market due to "innovation competition." In other words, if, in a given relevant market, the number of players decreases due to mergers and acquisitions, this might eventually lead to a decrease in the incentive to innovate. In this context, the phrase *innovation competition* is explained by the OECD as the restriction of innovation-based competition due to the changes in market structure that create more concentration.[349] Examples of significant Commission decisions on this issue include the *Dow/DuPont* and *GE/Alstom* cases, which will be discussed in detail below.

Parallel to paragraph 38 of the EU Horizontal Merger Guidelines, section 6.4 of the US Horizontal Merger Guidelines delves into the subject of innovation in merger control. The US Department of Justice and the Federal Trade Commission have recognized the possibility of "a merger to diminish innovation competition by encouraging the merged firm to curtail its innovative efforts below the level that would prevail in the absence of the merger." Thus, a merger could reduce the incentive to innovate, as the merged entity could maintain its market presence with an "existing product-development effort." Furthermore, the US Horizontal Merger Guidelines also analyze the short-term and long-term effects of mergers on the market players' incentives to innovate, stating that a merger that would combine two entities out of a small number of firms with the most substantial capabilities to innovate could also have the potential to diminish innovation competition in the market.[350] The *Bayer/Monsanto* transaction and its reflection in the US approach to innovation in antitrust law will be discussed in the relevant chapter.

Based on the preceding discussion, the competition authorities do evaluate whether a merger or acquisition could have adverse effects on any incentives to innovate or lead to difficulties for small-scale, innovative undertakings to compete effectively in the relevant market.

2.3.2 The Role of Innovation in Cartel and Abuse of Dominance Investigations: *Ex Ante* and *Ex Post* Control

Innovations are also crucially significant for determining the market position and dominance of undertakings in a given relevant market. As the market shares of incumbent players can change rapidly, and as new entrants are continually observed to be coming into innovation-driven markets, the power balance between the players is also subject to constant fluctuation. Furthermore, in innovation-driven markets, profitability is neither the main nor the accurate criterion for determining market power. In innovation-driven markets, potential future profits are more important than past or current profits – but

---

[349]   OECD, *Key Points of the Hearing on Disruptive Innovation* (DAF/COMP/M(2015)1/ANN8/FINAL, May 11, 2017), https://one.oecd.org/document/DAF/COMP/M(2015)1/ANN8/FINAL/en/pdf.

[350]   US Dep't of Just. & Fed. Trade Comm'n, Horizontal Merger Guidelines (1992, revised 1997), https://www.ftc.gov/sites/default/files/attachments/merger-review/hmg.pdf.

these cannot be easily determined.[351] Accordingly, the evaluation of the current status or past profits of an undertaking does not provide an accurate assessment of its market power, and the risks arising from the constantly changing structure of innovation-driven markets must also be taken into consideration.

Moreover, the viability of new entrants to innovative markets depends on the possibility of achieving profitability and acquiring market share in a short time.[352] Accordingly, competition enforcement authorities should also analyze whether the leading player in an innovation-driven market prevents such entries to the market, and focus on the cartel and abuse of dominance aspects of competition law that may hinder innovative progress. Antitrust law has dealt with innovation primarily in terms of market structure until now, believing that market dominance enables firms to evade economic pressures, even those that spur innovation.[353] The dispute between government and industry on this subject has devolved into a disagreement about the nature and timing of government action.[354] One school of thought advocates for maintaining a suspicious approach towards bad behavior and hence argues for the need to resort to preventative government action (i.e., *ex ante* competition law enforcement or anticipatory government intervention). Alternatively, other commentators advocate for governmental restraint and propose that government interference should only be implemented as harmful behavior manifests (i.e., *ex post* competition law enforcement or remedial government intervention).[355]

Historically, the common consensus has held that it is preferable to keep *ex post* and *ex ante* disciplines completely independent and governed by distinct departments; however, there has recently been an increase in lawmakers' demands for hybrid entities that can regulate all professions while still exercising consumer protection authority, which brings together the *ex ante* and *ex post* disciplines.[356] It is also important to emphasize that the *ex ante* and *ex post* disciplines have distinctive features. *Ex post* competition regulations are backward-looking, aimed at determining a narrow product market definition, fact-specific, focused on strategic behavior, and they provide remedies that are declaratory in nature.[357] On the other hand, *ex ante* competition regulations are forward-looking, define markets in broader terms, and focus on addressing market failures and providing detailed and specific remedies.[358] Therefore, *ex ante* discipline is referred to as "impact assessment," and it aims to use evidence to forecast the impact of a specific enforcement action, spending programs or other measures and to determine if the action is justified

---

351 Encaoua & Hollander, *supra* note 310, at 64.

352 *Id.* at 69.

353 Francisco Costa-Cabral, *Innovation in EU Competition Law: The Resource-based View and Disruption* (NYU School of Law, Jean Monnet Working Paper 2/17, 2018).

354 *Ex Post v. Ex Ante Regulatory Remedies Must Consider Consumer Benefits and Costs*, ACI (May 14, 2008), https://www.theamericanconsumer.org/2008/05/ex-post-v-ex-Ante-regulatory-remedies-must-consider-consumer-benefits-and-costs/ (last visited May 10, 2021).

355 *Id.*

356 *Id.*

357 Peter Alexiadis, *Balancing the Application of Ex Post and Ex Ante Disciplines under Community Law in Electronic Communications Markets: Square Pegs in Round Holes?* in RIGHTS AND REMEDIES IN A LIBERALISED AND COMPETITIVE INTERNAL MARKET (Eugène Buttigieg ed., University of Malta 2012).

358 *Id.*

and how it can be implemented to accomplish those goals; however, *ex post* discipline is described as a critical, evidence-based assessment.[359]

Most countries follow an *ex ante* model of government supervision, relying on sector-specific legislation to address expected and real tensions in the markets, especially digital ones. However, the EU has recently formulated a system for transitioning from *ex ante* to *ex post* regulation, where a particular business sector exhibits adequate competitiveness to exclude a single venture or party from operating discriminatory networks that pursue anti-competitive goals.[360] Furthermore, the Commission has stated that the existing system is fundamentally deregulatory in nature, as it envisions a gradual rollback of *ex ante* regulation, to be supplemented by general competition law enforcement (i.e., *ex post* regulation), and its plans include national regulatory authorities ("NRAs") to facilitate effective investment and competition.[361] Only after a comprehensive business analysis may NRAs enforce *ex ante* legislation, and additionally, *ex ante* regulation can be abandoned only after sustained competition has been established.[362] In other countries, such as the United States, the NRAs must examine the legality of implementing *ex ante* rules using legislatively drafted service definitions.[363] The proponents of less intrusive government regulation advocate for the rapid or incremental substitution of expert organizations conducting supervision with adjudication and compliance remedies, which would be implemented as and where disputes and issues occur, as well as when it is clear that *ex post* remedies would not be sufficient.[364] On the other hand, the proponents of *ex ante* regulations argue that an expert institution is essential to effective regulation, considering the critical role of digital platforms in the lives of consumers and nations. They further conclude that, amid the ongoing technical advancements, the industry is clearly incapable of self-regulating and preventing anti-competitive behavior, and add that if a dominant company abuses its market position and engages in anti-competitive behavior, *ex post* solutions only become accessible and operational well after competitors and consumers suffer damage.[365]

Ex post competition law enforcement is claimed to be much better suited to dynamic industries (such as digital platforms) with a significant risk of regulatory uncertainty, as competition law is, in fact, much more pragmatic than *ex ante* regulations, since it does not prescribe what companies can do, but rather what they should not do.[366] Thus, competition regulation enables companies to set the terms and conditions across a theoretically

---

[359] FABIENNE ILZKOVITZ & ADRIAAN DIERX, EX-POST ECONOMIC EVALUATION OF COMPETITION POLICY ENFORCEMENT: A REVIEW OF THE LITERATURE (Publications Office of the European Union 2015),https://ec.europa.eu/competition/publications/reports/expost_evaluation_competition_policy_en.pdf.

[360] *Open Internet Policy*, EUROPEAN COMMISSION (2021), https://ec.europa.eu/digital-single-market/en/open-internet (last visited May 10, 2021).

[361] European Commission, Commission Staff Working Document, SEC(2007) 1472 (Nov. 12, 2007), https://ec.europa.eu/transparency/documents-register/detail?ref=SEC(2007)1472&lang=en.

[362] *Id.*

[363] Rob Frieden, *Ex Ante Versus Ex Post Approaches to Network Neutrality: A Cost Benefit Analysis*, 30 BERKELEY TECH. L.J. 1561 (2015).

[364] *Id.* at 1611.

[365] *Id.* at 1570.

[366] GSMA, *Resetting Competition Policy Frameworks for the Digital Ecosystem* (2016), https://www.gsma.com/publicpolicy/wp-content/uploads/2016/10/GSMA_Resetting-Competition_Report_Oct-2016_60pp_WEBv2.pdf.

broad spectrum of permissible behavior, which is critical in digital environments, where companies may wish and aim to deliver a range of differentiated offerings, with varying prices, product characteristics, and service quality; and where consumer conditions may shift rapidly.[367] In light of the fast-paced nature of the markets for digital media and considering the scope of the problems that arise within them, it has also been argued that *ex post* compliance alone is insufficient to safeguard competition and that stricter and more transparent *ex ante* regulations are needed.[368] Therefore, according to this view, a hybrid model would raise the competitiveness in the market, and hence spur innovation, thereby providing a positive impact on consumer welfare and the economy.

In terms of the effects of innovation in abuse of dominance cases, *Microsoft/Sun Microsystems*[369] was an influential precedent, where the Commission investigated the allegations that Microsoft had abused its dominant position in the PC operating systems market through product-tying (i.e., by tying the Windows Media Player program with its operating system), and by preventing interoperability (i.e., by not allowing competitors to obtain the necessary information for interoperability in the workgroup server operating system market).[370] The Commission concluded that Microsoft had indeed abused its dominant position, as interoperability was imperative to increase the levels of competition and boost the incentives to innovate.[371] Similarly, in another *Microsoft* tying case,[372] Microsoft's refusal to grant access to its operating system was also deemed to be a factor that limited the competitors' incentives to innovate in the relevant market.[373]

Furthermore, in its *Motorola* decision, the Commission reviewed the allegations that Motorola had infringed article 102 of the Treaty on the Functioning of the European Union ("TFEU") by seeking an injunction against Apple regarding the enforcement of GPRS (i.e., "general packet radio service") standard essential patents. In its analysis, the Commission considered that the GPRS standard was also crucial for "follow-on innovation as it paved the way for the development of complex communication networks and sophisticated mobile devices"[374] and ultimately concluded that (i) for Motorola to seek an injunction while claiming that Apple was an unwilling licensee was erroneous, and in this regard (ii) causing a halt in Apple's activities was harmful to innovation and ultimately to consumers.[375]

The foregoing decisions demonstrate that, in line with the stance of the Commission in its Guidance on the Commission's enforcement priorities in applying article 82 of the EC

---

[367] *Id.*

[368] UK CMA, ONLINE PLATFORMS AND DIGITAL ADVERTISING: MARKET STUDY INTERIM REPORT (2019), https://assets.publishing.service.gov.uk/media/5ed0f75bd3bf7f4602e98330/Interim_report_---_web.pdf.

[369] Microsoft Corporation, European Commission Decision case C–3/37.792 (Mar. 24, 2004).

[370] The group server operating systems are described by the Commission as operating systems that are designed and marketed to deliver collectively to PC users the core tasks of file and print sharing and group and user administration within a corporate/administrative network.

[371] *Microsoft Corporation*, para. 627.

[372] Microsoft, European Commission Decision case COMP/C–3/39.530 (Dec. 16, 2009).

[373] Bundeskartellamt, *supra* note 145, at 17.

[374] *Microsoft Corporation*.

[375] European Commission Press Release IP/14/489, Antitrust: Commission Finds that Motorola Mobility infringed EU Competition Rules by Misusing Standard Essential Patents (Apr. 29, 2014), http://europa.eu/rapid/press-release_IP-14-489_en.htm.

Treaty to Abusive Exclusionary Conduct by Dominant Undertakings, (i) an innovation-driven undertaking could constitute serious competition for a dominant undertaking, and (ii) a dominant undertaking's conduct which is aimed at hindering the innovation incentives in the relevant market could lead to consumer harm. In this regard, competition authorities need not only to strive to ensure the continuity of innovative incentives but also to prevent any dominant undertaking from impeding innovation in order for consumers to have access to improved goods and services.

At this juncture, a brief analysis of the differences in institutional structures, especially between the US and EU competition enforcers (whose substantive approach is discussed in the following chapters), may also shed some light. Werden and Froeb discuss this in light of antitrust cases of tech giants and note the structural differences of the EU approach from the US in a number of (admittedly simplistic) headings, pointing out that the European system is (i) driven by competitor complaints, (ii) run by politicians (iii) designed as a regulatory structure and not law enforcement, (iv) grounded in skepticism of markets; (v) lacked the process and burden of proof of US court proceedings; (vi) failing to disregard unsound theories and (vii) maintains a low threshold for anti-competitive effects, (viii) is receptive to leveraging theories and (ix) does not recognize competition on the merits.[376] Coppola and Nazzini, in reply, dissect all of these points and provide more context to reflect the whole picture.[377] They contend that while the complainant is important, it is not the sole driver as the Commission goes beyond the claims set forth by the complainant, explaining that many of the tech cases have actually been initiated *ex officio*. The differences between the US and EU antitrust law are explained as different perceptions regarding Type 1 versus Type 2 errors, and not a separation of "law enforcement" versus "regulation," as Werden and Froeb claim. It is also emphasized that under EU law, both the Commission and the national competition authorities are enforcing the legislature, not regulating the markets, and that courts are also obliged to comply with the same, regardless of what the initial decision of the administrative authority may be. Since a complainant has the option to bring an abuse of dominance case to the Commission or go straight to court, the outcome of the case should be the same as the assessment will be done on the same legal rules. In any case, decisions of the Commission or the national competition authorities are open to appeal and review by the authorized and independent court, in both factual and legal matters. It is agreed, though, that US and EU procedures are not identical, and regardless of the competition matter involved, the EU process appears to take more time to conclude, which may affect a defendant's stance as to legal strategy and cost practicalities.[378] It is noted, however, that despite their differences, especially the US highlighting more the self-correcting power of the market, in order to steer away from an overly regulatory approach, in the last decades, the EU is seen to be moving more towards a focus on "effects on the market," and closer to the US stance.[379]

---

[376] Gregory J. Werden & Luke M. Froeb, *Antitrust and Tech: Europe and the United States Differ, and It Matters*, ANTITRUST CHRON. (2019).

[377] Maria Coppola & Renato Nazzini, *The European and US Approaches to Antitrust and Tech: Setting the Record Straight – A Reply to Gregory J. Werden and Luke M. Froeb's, Antitrust and Tech: Europe and the United States Differ, and It Matters*, ANTITRUST CHRON. (2020).

[378] *Id.* at 7–8.

[379] *Id.* at 12.

Another notable structural difference is that the private enforcement of antitrust law had a more deterrent and encompassing role in the US (the triple damages rule), although the Commission has also tried to incentivize this in the EU.[380] Having said this, based on factors like access to information, detection skills, quality and capacity of competition authorities and courts, available legal remedies, etc., there are pros and cons to each mode of enforcement depending on the type of infringement at hand. Hüschelrath and Peyer argue that private litigants may have difficulty with sufficient access to information on the market or the infringer(s) in *horizontal agreements* and are likely to opt for a follow-on legislation after a decision has been rendered by a competition authority, which may unfortunately delay damage recovery and lower the deterrence factor of private claims. This is in contrast to *vertical agreements*, where they believe the private parties may have more of an advantage and insider knowledge; nevertheless, future potential cooperation opportunities may play a role in a firm hesitating to go down a private enforcement route. As for *abuse of dominance*, here again, sufficient access to information, especially the detailed cost and price structures of the alleged infringer, was found to make public enforcement more viable for efficient competition and consumer welfare.[381]

Private enforcement also brings with it the risk of forum shopping, for those complainants to choose the jurisdiction that will provide them with the best possible remedy, e.g., in cases with an EU component or in matters that have cross-border implications, as would be the case in tech giants, or undertakings that span the digital markets of multiple countries. From the point of view of individuals/consumers, going outside of their own legal regime may be daunting due to costs and uncertainty. Nevertheless, the digital markets/ tech giants touch the lives of thousands of people; therefore, "[w]hile the loss suffered by an individual end-consumer following a breach of EU competition law may be de minimis, the aggregate harm can amount to a significant sum. In the absence of effective private enforcement, infringing undertakings will retain the profit from their conduct."[382] A more efficient and perhaps unified system enabling the end consumers who suffered losses to bring a collective claim to the infringer would be a high deterrent indeed.

Be they national competition authorities with different structures or specialized courts, different institutional structures must provide decisions and enforcement actions that are not contradictory to each other.[383] Moreover, the duration of these procedures/actions is crucial for the most efficient way to pursue these cases through different institutions, for adequate and timely access to justice and remedies, and civil courts should be taking into consideration the decisions delivered by competition authorities in order to provide and sustain consistent precedents.[384] Ultimately, competition policy as a whole must demonstrate a credible commitment to awarding the reward to the effective competitor.[385]

---

[380] Kai Hüschelrath & Sebastian Peyer, *Public and Private Enforcement of Competition Law: A Differentiated Approach* (Centre for Competition Policy (CCP) Working Paper 13-5, Apr. 2013).

[381] *Id.* at 23.

[382] Robert Thomas Currie Telfer, Forum Shopping and the Private Enforcement of EU Competition Law: Is Forum Shopping a Dead Letter? 264 (2017) (Ph.D. thesis, University of Glasgow) (on file with the University of Glasgow).

[383] David McGowan, *Innovation, Uncertainty, and Stability in Antitrust Law*, 16 BERKELEY TECH. L.J. 729 (2001).

[384] *Id.*

[385] Tim Wu, *Taking Innovation Seriously: Antitrust Enforcement If Innovation Mattered Most*, 78 ANTITRUST L.J. 313, 327 (2012).

2.3.3 The Role of Innovation in the Digital Era

Innovations in technology have also paved the way for dynamic markets in which digital platforms, such as Google or Amazon, have become forces to be reckoned with. In online platforms, the ultimate service provider offers different services based on its customer groups,[386] such as a medium for third-party sellers to provide goods and services, while also acting as an intermediary for the end-user customers. Accordingly, the business models of various online platforms differ from one another according to their functions, and each has its own levels of complexity. As such, competition authorities nowadays seem inclined to scrutinize online platforms' activities in more detail.

The concepts of killer, creeping and defensive acquisitions in digital markets and the effects on competition for pre-emptive acquisitions are assessed in detail under Chapter 7 below. Having said this, it is also worthwhile to note that the effect of digital mergers on innovation may arise in several different ways.[387] First, acquisitions may actually motivate innovative entries as the firms anticipate that they will be acquired by an incumbent,[388] although this may also cause inefficient entries into the markets, which create little value for customers.[389] On the other hand, Kamepalli et al. argue that if consumers foresee that a new platform will be acquired by an incumbent, they have a tendency not to use the platform in order to avoid unnecessary switching costs.[390] Also, there is some evidence indicating that when a big platform buys out a start-up, the venture capital investment in the market where the start-up is active decreases (*kill zone effect*).[391] One of the reasons for this might be that start-ups may be losing their ultimate motivation for growth, which is to be acquired by a tech giant.[392] Moreover, start-ups may direct their R&D efforts towards improving the incumbent's technology in order to maximize their chances of being acquired, which may not be optimal in terms of the quality of the innovation.[393]

As to another effect of digital mergers on innovation, if the innovation of the entrant is a close substitute to the products or services of the acquirer, the latter would not have sufficient incentive to develop it, given that the incremental profits to be gained as a result of the innovation would be small due to cannibalization (*replacement effect*).[394]

---

[386] PHILIP SCHAFF, HISTORY OF THE CHRISTIAN CHURCH, vol. VII: MODERN CHRISTIANITY: THE GERMAN REFORMATION 22 (Christian Classics Ethereal Library 2nd ed. 1882).

[387] Marc Bourreau & Alexandre de Streel, *Big Tech Acquisitions: Competition and Innovation Effects and EU Merger Control* 3 (CERRE Issue Paper, Feb. 2020), https://cerre.eu/publications/big-tech-acquisitions-competition-and-innovation-effects-eu-merger-control.

[388] Joshua S. Gans, David D. Hsu & Scott Stern, *When Does Start-Up Innovation Spur the Gale of Creative Destruction?* 33 RAND J. ECON. 571 (2002).

[389] Bourreau & de Streel, *supra* note 387, at 5.

[390] Sai Krishna Kamepalli, Raghuram Rajan & Luigi Zingales, *Kill Zone* 3 (NBER Working Paper 27146, 2019).

[391] Heli Koski, Otto Kässi & Fabian Braesemann, *Killers on the Road of Emerging Start-ups – Implications for Market Entry and Venture Capital Financing* 2 (ETLA Working Papers 81, 2020).

[392] Geoffrey Parker, Georgios Petropoulos & Marshall W. Van Alstyne, *Platform Mergers and Antitrust* 26–27 (Boston University Questrom School of Business Research Paper No. 376351, 2021).

[393] Bourreau & de Streel, *supra* note 387, at 7–8.

[394] RICHARD R. NELSON, THE RATE AND DIRECTION OF INVENTIVE ACTIVITIES: ECONOMIC AND SOCIAL FACTORS (Princeton Univ. Press 2016), and Kenneth Arrow, *Economic Welfare and the Allocation of Resources for Invention, in* NATIONAL BUREAU OF ECONOMIC RESEARCH, THE RATE AND DIRECTION OF INVENTIVE ACTIVITY: ECONOMIC AND SOCIAL FACTORS 609 (Princeton Univ. Press 1962).

Hence, the incumbent will acquire the target to kill its innovation. Nevertheless, Gautier and Lamesch find that only one of the 175 acquisitions that Google, Amazon, Facebook, Apple and Microsoft have made between 2015 and 2017 might be regarded as a "killer acquisition."[395] On the other hand, there is the possibility that the incumbent's incentive to develop the acquiring firm's product may be higher due to the synergies that may arise as a result of the relationship between the new product and the incumbent's existing products,[396] or the incumbent may have higher innovation capabilities that may accelerate the development of innovations.[397]

Therefore, neither the theories nor the empirical studies are conclusive on whether digital mergers create a systemic positive effect on innovation by way of motivating innovative entries, while theory and empirical evidence show that killer acquisitions are not likely to be prevalent in the digital sector, and it is possible that digital mergers may increase both the incentive and the ability to innovate.

Going back to the "ecosystems" concept, there are also arguments that digital mergers may lead to competitive harm when parties' activities overlap in a technological space, even if they do not overlap in the relevant product market. That is because digital ecosystems may use mergers as a strategy to isolate their core service from competition by acquiring firms providing complementary or adjacent services.[398] Having said that, the competition authorities' analysis of the effects of innovation of digital mergers remains rather limited[399] and currently does not include such an analysis of the wider ecosystem.[400]

Even in non-ecosystem structures, for digital platforms that are constantly changing with the emergence of new products and services, a turnover-based approach to defining market power would be unjustified and lack a sound basis, as turnover figures do not accurately reflect an undertaking's current or future market power in the digital realm.[401] The fate of Yahoo!, with its astronomic rise and swift fall from grace, could be considered an illustrative example of this fact. In the 1990s, Yahoo! was one of the world's biggest, if not *the* biggest, online platforms, and none could have predicted its subsequent downfall during its prime. However, upon the launch of Google and many other search engines, Yahoo! could not keep up with its innovation-driven competitors, and what once was a company valued at $125 billion was eventually sold to Verizon for $4.8 billion in 2016.[402] Even if not specifically relevant to competition law, the example of Yahoo! provides a valuable lesson for a better understanding of how digital markets can change

---

[395] Gautier & Lamesch, *supra* note 341, at 25–26.

[396] Marc Bourreau & Alexandre de Streel, *Digital Conglomerates and EU Competition Policy* 7–11 (2019), https://dx.doi.org/10.2139/ssrn.3350512

[397] Chiara Fumagalli, Massimo Motta & Emanuele Tarantino, *Shelving or Developing? The Acquisition of Potential Competitors under Financial Constraints* (Universitat Pompeu Fabra, Department of Economics and Business, Economics Working Papers No. 1735, 2020).

[398] CRÉMER ET AL., *supra* note 338.

[399] OECD, *Summary of the Roundtable Discussion on the Non-Price Effects of Mergers* 10 (DAF/COMP/M(2018)1/ANN2/FINAL, May 14, 2019) (Susan Creighton noting, the lack of analysis about non-price effects of mergers).

[400] Jacobides & Lianos, *supra* note 328, at 21.

[401] *Id.*

[402] Brian Solomon, *Yahoo Sells to Verizon in Saddest $5 Billion Deal in Tech History*, FORBES (July 25, 2016), https://www.forbes.com/sites/briansolomon/2016/07/25/yahoo-sells-to-verizon-for-5-billion-marissa-mayer/#46fc9051450f.

rapidly, sometimes with unforeseeable results, and thus, why a turnover-based approach might not provide the most accurate method for assessing market power, particularly when making a projection into the future.

In this context, the network effects that are observed in online platforms and related markets fail to offer a reliable indication of market power, as consumers can easily switch their preferences among online platform services, and thus, the network effect of an undertaking could easily be negated by any innovative goods and services that are launched by one of its competitors.

Therefore, the main issues to be considered when it comes to innovation-driven digital markets are: (i) the shift in the market power of undertakings and (ii) the delicate counterbalance between consumer benefit and hindering the competition in the relevant market.[403] For instance, in the Commission's *Google Shopping* investigation, the Commission determined that Google had abused its dominant position in the market for search engines by providing advantages to its own comparison-shopping service, thereby foreclosing the market for comparison-shopping services and thus hindering the competition in the market for its competitors. In a similar case, the Commission also focused on whether the obligations imposed by Amazon on its dealers would hinder its competitors' incentives to create new business models and effectively compete in the relevant market.[404] In that decision, the Commission evaluated whether Amazon had abused its dominant position by obliging its dealers to (i) inform Amazon about new business models available to other retailers and (ii) provide the lowest price to Amazon rather than to any other e-book retailers. In its assessment, the Commission underlined that the obligation to inform Amazon about new business models would indeed hinder its competitors' incentives to create new business models and to compete effectively in the market, as discussed in more detail in Chapter 4.

The foregoing cases demonstrate that, in the case of online platforms, the conduct under investigation does not relate only to the prices of goods and services. Instead, the competition authorities consider possible anti-competitive conduct's effects on the undertaking's competitors and on their incentives to innovate. This approach rightly recognizes that decreasing the incentives to innovate will ultimately lead to consumer harm, as consumers will be deprived of the opportunity to receive improved products and services.

2.4 Conclusion

Despite innovation's various (pejorative) connotations in history, Schumpeter's views on innovation as the primary driver of competitiveness and its vital role in the development of economic dynamics maintain their validity today.[405] As for the determination of the role of innovation in competition law, the abovementioned precedents indicate that a uniform

---

[403]   Gürkaynak, *supra* note 343, at 13.

[404]   Amazon.com Inc., European Commission Decision case AT.40153 (May 4, 2017).

[405]   PORTER & STERN, *supra* note 123.

approach cannot be adopted as it would not be sufficient for the goals of competition rules since innovations lead to different market structures. Therefore, careful analyses must be conducted on a case-by-case basis. Accordingly, competition authorities should analyze when it would be appropriate to intervene, in order to protect the incentives to innovate in the relevant market, while also ensuring that the undertakings do not exploit the emphasis put on the concept of innovation.[406] A case-by-case analysis will also ensure that any pro-competitive effects of innovation are not disregarded, i.e., the competition authorities should not dismiss out of hand the dynamic efficiencies claimed by the parties and should (notwithstanding where the burden of proof lies) conduct full analyses to ascertain what innovative efficiencies could be achieved by the transaction.

It is, admittedly, difficult to ascertain where the point of no return for intervention lies – especially in dynamic markets where the circumstances change rapidly – while aggressive actions of a firstcomer in a new market can be tolerable to enhance consumer benefit and promote innovation, if that entity resorts to abusive behavior to new entrants down the line, an intervention may already be too little, too late.[407] That is also why the correct assessment of harm and quantification of the detriment creates an important challenge to the authorities in how to put their increased advocacy in support of preserving and promoting innovation into actual practice.

As will be demonstrated, the precedents of the Commission, the US Department of Justice, and those in the UK, indicate that the competition authorities in these jurisdictions are fairly well acquainted with a link between innovation and competition in a relevant market. Having said this, they still have to fine-tune their approaches, especially where innovation is being used as a defense, and recognize the opportunities offered with the transaction as a counterbalance to any threats they perceive. While the need to move away from static analyses for dynamic markets is getting more apparent, the competition authorities (as well as the appeal courts/bodies) still require convincing to embrace and give weight to what may be less concise economic analyses and estimations in terms of dynamic benefits.[408] There has been extensive work by the competition authorities themselves, independent experts that they have appointed and scholars to assess the competitive and regulatory needs of dynamic markets, especially in the context of digital markets. What the recommendations are, whether they are applicable and how they are being implemented are analyzed in the coming sections.

---

[406] Gürkaynak, *supra* note 343, at 29.

[407] David Currie, On the Role of Competition in Stimulating Innovation, Speech at the Concurrences Innovation Economics Conference (Feb. 3, 2017), https://www.gov.uk/government/speeches/david-currie-on-the-role-of-competition-in-stimulating-innovation.

[408] *Id.*

Chapter 3
The Innovation Effects of Mergers: The Concepts and Theoretical Background

3.1 Introduction

Having introduced the historical journey of the term "*innovation*" and how it may relate to the concept of "*competition*," we now shift our focus to the theoretical and empirical academic research in competition law and economics regarding the effects of mergers on the innovation incentives of undertakings. This chapter will first outline various competition law concepts that underlie the authorities' assessments in merger control, and touch upon certain novel concepts that have arisen to address innovation concerns. Following this, we will then develop the ideas and findings that constitute the theoretical basis for the concerns that competition authorities have with regard to innovation in merger control enforcement and then proceed to an analysis of the literature that supports the arguments of merging parties concerning such transactions. The ultimate aim is to lay the grounds to demonstrate that the practices of the competition authorities have remained rather too cautious and restrictive in mergers, despite their intentions to protect innovation as stated or implied in their own guidelines. Perhaps it is a more fundamental question: Should that protection be geared towards only what has already been achieved in terms of innovative success, or also support and foster the means to potential new innovations? Would consumer welfare benefit from disregarding future innovations that may be pro-competitive, just because it is not verifiable under strict standards of proof at this time?

3.2 Certain Competition Law Concepts in Merger Control

In the US, Europe, and many other jurisdictions that follow their decisional practices, the merger control system is based on the evaluation of two effects: (i) *unilateral effects* and (ii) *coordination effects*. *Unilateral effects* occur when a merger eliminates competition between the transaction parties, enhances market power or reduces competition significantly, *even if it does not change the behavior of other firms*. If a merger enhances market power also by increasing the risk of coordinated, accommodating, or interdependent behavior among rivals, the adverse competitive effects arising in this manner are called *coordinated effects*.[409]

Unilateral effects can emerge with regard to changes in the various competition parameters in the post-merger market, such as (i) increase in price, (ii) reduction in output or capacity, and (iii) diminished innovation or reduced product variety. In the Horizontal Merger Guidelines issued by the US Department of Justice and the Federal Trade Commission in 2010 (hereafter, "Horizontal Merger Guidelines"), it is recognized and acknowledged that a merger might result in different unilateral effects along various dimensions of competition. For example, a merger may increase prices in the short term but not raise longer-term concerns about innovation, either because rivals in the relevant market will provide sufficient innovation competition or because the merger will generate *"cognizable"* research and development efficiencies.[410]

The relationship between competition and innovation is theoretically and empirically ambiguous. Nonetheless, the Horizontal Merger Guidelines take the position that competition "often spurs firms to innovate" and state that competition enforcement agencies will consider whether a merger is likely to diminish "innovation competition" by encouraging the merged undertaking to curtail its innovative efforts below the level that would prevail in the absence of the merger.[411] Section 6.4 provides that curtailment of innovation can take the form of "reduced incentive to continue with an existing product-development effort or reduced incentive to initiate the development of new products."

According to the Horizontal Merger Guidelines, the reduction in the incentive to continue with an existing product-development effort is most likely to occur when at least one of the merging firms is engaged in efforts to introduce new products to consumers that would capture substantial revenues from the other merging firm. The reduction in the incentive to initiate the development of new products is most likely to arise if at least one of the merging firms possesses capabilities that are likely to lead it to develop new products in the future that would capture substantial revenues from the other merging firm. Along with these principles, the Horizontal Merger Guidelines state that competition enforcement authorities will consider whether a merger will diminish "innovation competition" by combining two small number of firms with the most substantial capabilities to successfully innovate in a specific direction.[412]

As in the assessment of unilateral price effects, the Horizontal Merger Guidelines suggest that the competition authorities should evaluate the extent to which successful innovation by one merging firm is likely to take away sales from the other, and investigate the extent to which post-merger incentives for future innovation will be diminished compared to those that would have prevailed in the absence of the merger.[413] Competition enforcement authorities should also consider whether the merger is likely to enable innovation by

---

[409]   US Dep't of Just. & Fed. Trade Comm'n, Horizontal Merger Guidelines (2010) ("Horizontal Merger Guidelines"), https://www.ftc.gov/sites/default/files/attachments/merger-review/100819hmg.pdf.

[410]   *Id*. at 20.

[411]   *Id*. at 23.

[412]   *Id*.

[413]   *Id*.

bringing together complementary capabilities of the merging undertakings.[414] However, in the actual assessment, the weight accorded to the innovation enabled may be much less than that accorded to the potential reduction of innovation in the market.

The merger control enforcement regime in Europe generally follows similar principles as the enforcement system in the United States. The European Commission ("Commission") has put forth its principles on the horizontal merger control in its Guidelines on the Assessment of Horizontal Mergers Under the Council Regulation on the Control of Concentrations Between Undertakings, which was issued in 2004 (hereafter, "EU Horizontal Merger Guidelines"). The Commission assesses whether or not a proposed concentration would significantly impede effective competition, as a result of the creation of a dominant position, in a particular market.

The Commission examines and assesses the anti-competitive effects of a merger by using the SIEC test and seeks to answer the fundamental question of whether the merger would "significantly impede effective competition." In general, competition is considered to be harmed (i) if the merged party obtains market power, (ii) if the merger would eliminate a competitive constraint on the merging parties (e.g., a close competitor or a potential competitor), or (iii) if the merger would significantly increase the likelihood of coordination among the competitors.[415,416]

The Commission accepts and acknowledges that innovation is one of the benefits that effective competition brings to consumers.[417] In the EU Horizontal Merger Guidelines, it is stated that, in markets where innovation is an essential competitive force, a merger may increase the firm's "ability and incentive to bring new innovations" to the relevant market and, thereby, boost the competitive pressure on rivals to innovate in that market.

---

[414] *Id.* at 23–24.

[415] European Commission, Guidelines on the Assessment of Horizontal Mergers Under the Council Regulation on the Control of Concentrations Between Undertakings, 2004 OJ (C 31) 5 See note 305: "Horizontal Merger Control Guidelines", recital 22.

[416] In horizontal mergers, when assessing whether the unilateral merger effects are significant, the European Commission analyzes whether the merging firms have large market shares, whether they are close competitors, whether the customers have limited possibilities of switching suppliers (i.e., the existence of few alternative suppliers or high switching costs), whether the competitors are unlikely to increase supply if prices increase (e.g., capacity constraints, costly capacity expansion), whether the merged entity would be able to hinder expansion by competitors (e.g., through control over patents or other intellectual properties), and whether the merger would eliminate an essential competitive force (e.g., by removing a particularly innovative competitor) (EU Horizontal Merger Guidelines, recitals 27–38). A merger with a potential competitor can have the same significant anti-competitive effect as a merger between two competitors if there is a *significant likelihood* that the potential competitor would become an effective competitor, and if there were none or not enough other potential competitors remaining in the market to exert sufficient competitive pressure (*id.*, recitals 58–60). A merger is unlikely to cause a significant impediment to active competition if entering into a market is sufficiently easy. In this regard, a new entrant must be able to exert a sufficient competitive constraint, and an entry must be likely, timely, and of sufficient scope to counter the anti-competitive effects of a merger (*id.*, recitals 68–75). Incumbents' preferential access to intellectual property rights, innovation or R&D, or economies of scale can constitute entry barriers in this respect (*id.*, recital 71). In addition, while assessing the effects of a merger, the European Commission also considers whether customers have countervailing buyer power (*id.*, recitals 64–65). Even a supplier with a high market share cannot act independently and is constrained by its customers. Finally, the European Commission assesses whether a "failing firm defense" is applicable (*id.*, recital 89).

[417] *Id.*, recital 8.

On the other hand, effective competition may be significantly impeded by a merger between two talented innovators, for instance, between two companies with *pipeline products* related to a specific product market. The EU Horizontal Merger Guidelines also consider the possibility that a firm with a relatively small market share may, nevertheless, be a principal competitive force if it has promising pipeline products.[418]

The Commission is likely to challenge a merger if one of the merging parties is a recent entrant with a small market share or a potential entrant, even if the level of concentration in the relevant market and the expected increase in the concentration level in the market after the merger are small. In such a case, the Commission will consider whether one of the merging parties holds a market share above 50% or if one or both parties are *important innovators*, even if their importance as innovators is not reflected in their market shares.[419]

As for the coordinated effects, the EU Horizontal Merger Guidelines assert that, in markets where innovation is essential, coordination may be more difficult since innovations (particularly significant ones) may allow one firm to gain a major advantage over its rivals.[420] Therefore, the Commission considers that coordinated effects are unlikely to cause innovation competition concerns in mergers because the complex and uncertain nature of R&D activities, the ability/potential to keep innovations secret, and the long-time period that it would take for competitors to find out if one party breaches coordination would make the monitoring of tacit and explicit coordination quite tricky with respect to innovation and R&D activities.[421] If coordination effects in merger control are unlikely, why then are these reasons not – at least sometimes – acknowledged in other capacities?

In merger analysis, competition authorities also take into account the fact that mergers may generate significant *efficiencies*, which are likely to reduce or reverse adverse unilateral effects. It is generally accepted that mergers that create efficiencies may enhance the merged firm's ability and incentive to compete, which may subsequently result in lower prices, improved product quality, enhanced services, or new products. Moreover, efficiencies may also lead to new or improved products, even if they do not immediately and directly affect the price.[422] The US Horizontal Merger Guidelines declare that, when evaluating the effects of a merger on innovation, competition authorities will consider the ability of the merged firm to conduct R&D activities more effectively. Such efficiency may indeed spur innovation without affecting short-term pricing.

According to the US Horizontal Merger Guidelines, competition authorities "also consider the ability of the merged firm to appropriate a greater fraction of the benefits resulting from its innovations. Licensing and intellectual property conditions may be important to this enquiry, as they affect the ability of a firm to appropriate the benefits of its innovation."[423]

---

[418] *Id.*, recital 38.
[419] *Id.*, recital 20.
[420] *Id.*, recital 45.
[421] Michael L. Katz & Howard A. Shelanski, *Mergers and Innovation*, 74 ANTITRUST L.J. 1, 8 (2007).
[422] Horizontal Merger Guidelines at 29.
[423] *Id.* at 31.

On the other hand, it is pointed out that cost savings in research and development may not be *"cognizable"* efficiencies, because they are difficult to verify or they may result from anti-competitive reductions in innovative activities. This is an example of the unduly strict standard of proof that the entities are faced with when trying to rely on the efficiency defense.

More recently, competition authorities have created novel innovation-based concepts or repurposed traditional ones to address the effect of mergers on innovation,[424] although these also have their shortcomings and fall short of addressing the whole. One such example is *potential competition*, which has been traditionally applied not only in merger control but also in the assessment of other competition law concerns. This focuses on a competitive constraint that may potentially arise (but has not yet actually arisen)[425] and considers entry by potential competitors (i.e., undertakings that have real and concrete possibilities of entering an existing relevant product market).[426] However, this concept may still be inadequate to address innovation-based R&D-related matters where no comparable product markets are yet in existence.[427] There is also an asymmetry in the proof issue: cost savings in research and development are not deemed cognizable because they are difficult to verify, but how verifiable is the potential competition that may take place in a future product market?

The *future market* concept is considered to be an extension of potential competition as it seeks to evaluate potential competition that may take place in a future product market that does not exist at the time of evaluation.[428] Since it is not linked to an existing product market, it can be applied when the undertakings are currently or possibly competing with one another (i.e., future entry) in the same actual product market. In other words, this concept helps the authorities evaluate innovation competition, independent of the respective undertaking's role in the current relevant market.[429] Even though the future market concept is not linked to an existing product, it requires the evaluation of real and observable R&D efforts. Therefore, as this concept places heavy reliance on the success of R&D projects of the undertakings and concentrates on the future product

---

[424] Such as Dow/DuPont, European Commission Decision case M.7932 (Mar. 27, 2017), https://ec.europa.eu/competition/mergers/cases/decisions/m7932_13668_3.pdf, BMS/Celgene, European Commission Decision case M.9294 (July 29, 2019), AbbVie/Allergan, European Commission Decision case COMP/M.9461 (2020).

[425] OECD, *The Concept of Potential Competition – Note by the EU* 9 (DAF/COMP/WD(2021)21, May 25, 2021), https://one.oecd.org/document/DAF/COMP/WD(2021)21/en/pdf.

[426] Sandra Marco Colino, Knut Fournier, Sofia Pais, Derek Ritzmann & Niamh Dunne, *The Lundbeck Case and the Concept of Potential Competition*, CONCURRENCES No. 2-2017, art. No. 83827, 24.; European Night Services and others v. Commission (1998); Merck and Generics UK v. CMA (2021; Novartis/Glaxo Smith Kline's Oncology Business, European Commission Decision case COMP/M.7275 (Jan. 28, 2015); Pfizer/Hospira European Commission Decision case COMP/M.7559 (Aug. 4, 2015), GE/Alstom European Commission Decision case COMP/M.7278(2015)

[427] Genzyme/Novazyme, FTC File No. 021-0026 (2004); Benjamin R. Kern, *Innovation Markets, Future Markets, or Potential Competition: How Should Competition Authorities Account for Innovation Competition in Merger Reviews?* 37 WORLD COMPETITION 173 (2014), https://ssrn.com/abstract=2380130.

[428] *Id.* at 6.

[429] Nielsen Holding/Arbitron, FTC Matter No. 131 0058 (2014). It concerns a conditional approval of a merger between two undertakings that are active in audience measurement services. The FTC stated that the elimination of future competition between Nielsen and Arbitron would likely cause advertisers, ad agencies, and programmers to pay more for national syndicated cross-platform audience measurement services and lead to the decrease of future competition in relation to an innovative product.

market rather than innovation competition in general, it could fall short of safeguarding innovation as a whole.[430]

As another novel concept, *innovation market analysis* focuses on innovation itself and not the relevant market. It is believed to have been developed to eliminate the deficiencies that arise from the application of the concepts of future markets and potential competition. Rarely applied until now, in the *iRobot/Amazon* case, the FTC is considering whether the takeover would boost Amazon's market share in the market for connected devices and the retail market, and whether the home maps created by the iRobot vacuum could help Amazon in suggesting particular furniture customers are looking to buy and innovation regarding this issue would effect.[431] This analysis includes a step in defining the interdependencies between "market structure" and innovation. However, since it is not always possible to define the interdependencies due to uncertainty in innovation-heavy markets, this could fail to capture all types of innovation concerns.

The *cannibalization effect* was first adopted in *Novartis/GSK Oncology* and the assessment was considered close to a unilateral effects approach. The Commission noted in its decision that the merged entity would internalize that investing in one of the clinical research programs for colorectal cancer could be expected to cannibalize future sales of its other clinical research program.[432] As the cannibalization effect concerns clearly identified existing products, the theory may fall short when authorities attempt to account for products that do not yet exist (like in *Dow/DuPont*, where the Commission introduced the *innovation space* concept, discussed in detail below). This is indeed the main challenge in assessing potential innovation. Evolving from the cannibalization effect, *killer acquisitions* is a theory where the incumbent firm acquires the innovating firm to eliminate its innovative efforts and any future competition it may have brought.[433] Discussed widely in the doctrine, this theory was also expanded into the concept of "*reverse killer acquisitions,*" where the acquiring entity shuts down the development of its own product line post-merger.[434]

---

[430]   *Genzyme/Novazyme*; Kern, *supra* note 427, at 21; Johnson & Johnson/Tachosil, European Commission case M.9547, in which the parties have abandoned the transaction due to the competition concern.

[431]   iRobot/Amazon, FTC File No. 001-36414 (2022). It concerns the potential acquisition of iRobot by Amazon, which is currently under investigation by the FTC.

[432]   *Novartis/Glaxo Smith Kline's Oncology Business* at 104.

[433]   *See* Colleen Cunningham, Florian Ederer & Song Ma, *Killer Acquisitions*, 129 J. POLITICAL ECON. 649 (2021), http://dx.doi.org/10.2139/ssrn.3241707, JACQUES CRÉMER, YVES-ALEXANDRE DE MONTJOYE & HEIKE SCHWEITZER, COMPETITION POLICY FOR THE DIGITAL ERA (Report commissioned by the European Commission, Publications Office of the European Union 2019), http://ec.europa.eu/competition/publications/reports/kd0419345enn.pdf, where the authors state that "killer acquisitions" are observed in the pharmaceutical industry in which an incumbent acquires a potential competitor with an innovative project that is still at an early stage of development and subsequently terminates the development of the target's innovation in order to avoid a replacement effect. *See also* Chapter 7 below for further discussion on killer acquisitions.

[434]   *See* Gregory Crawford, Tommaso Valletti & Cristina Caffarra, *"How Tech Rolls": Potential Competition and "Reverse" Killer Acquisitions*, VoxEU (May 11, 2020), https://cepr.org/voxeu/blogs-and-reviews/how-tech-rolls-potential-competition-and-reverse-killer-acquisitions. The authors explain that in cases of "buys instead of builds," the incumbent acquires an already-well-established product and shuts down the development of its own product, or never starts developing a competing product – which they call the "*reverse killer acquisitions*" (as opposed to "*killer acquisitions,*" in which the incumbent firm acquires the innovating firm and terminates the innovative efforts of the latter, post-merger).

Closely linked with the above, the *concept of nascent potential competition*[435] refers to an acquisition that would control the innovation while eliminating the competitive danger for a firm, whose potential innovation offers a serious threat to an established competitor yet may not be considered as such, given the financial resources and breadth of the new entrant.[436] Overall, it requires a link between the future market and nascent competitors. However, the acquisition of a nascent competitor is nearly impossible to challenge, given the difficulty in establishing with sufficient precision and certainty whether there is really a potential competition, as it requires a presumption that a certain actor will turn into a competitor based on some vague circumstantial evidence.[437]

In line with the above, safeguarding innovation incentives and finding the proper tools for that is widely recognized as a concern and challenge for competition enforcement authorities. In recent times, several high-profile mergers have been scrutinized, especially concerning their potential effects on innovation. However, the relationship between competition and innovation is still far from clear, and the findings and conclusions of academic research on the relationship between market structure and innovation are by no means unambiguous.[438] In this regard, Richard Gilbert states that "we remain far from a general theory of innovation competition."[439] According to Gilbert, the available literature has amply demonstrated that competition may be either good or bad for innovation, depending on the circumstances.

3.3 Basic Theoretical and Empirical Background on the Relationship Between Competition and Innovation

As discussed in the previous chapters, the theoretical debate on the relationship between competition and innovation goes back to the works of Joseph A. Schumpeter (1942) and Kenneth Arrow (1962), who reached opposing conclusions on this fundamental issue.[440]

According to the Schumpeterian approach, the reduced competition will lead to more innovation, as long as "competition for the market" remains in effect.[441] Schumpeter

---

[435]   C. Scott Hemphill & Tim Wu, *Nascent Competitors*, 168 U. PA. L. REV. 1879 (2020).

[436]   *Id.*

[437]   OECD, *supra* note 425, at 9.

[438]   Justus Haucap, *Merger Effects on Innovation: A Rationale for Stricter Merger Control?* 3 (University of Düsseldorf, Düsseldorf Institute for Competition Economics, Discussion Paper No. 268, Sep. 2017), http://www.dice.hhu.de/fileadmin/redaktion/Fakultaeten/Wirtschaftswissenschaftliche_Fakultaet/DICE/Discussion_Paper/268_Haucap.pdf.

[439]   Richard Gilbert, *Looking for Mr. Schumpeter: Where Are We in the Competition-Innovation Debate?* in 6 INNOVATION POLICY AND THE ECONOMY 159, 206 (Adam B. Jaffe, Josh Lerner & Scott Stern eds, MIT Press 2006), http://www.nber.org/chapters/c0208.pdf.

[440]   [440] Matthew Johnson, *Mergers and Innovation: Fewer Players, More Ideas?* OXERA (Feb. 27, 2017), https://www.oxera.com/agenda/mergers-and-innovation-fewer-players-more-ideas.

[441]   *Id.* at 1.

emphasized that a significant portion of innovation is generated by large firms operating in oligopoly markets, not by small firms in atomistic (i.e., highly competitive) markets. Schumpeter's position was summarized by Shapiro in simple terms as follows: "The prospect of market power and large scale spurs innovation."[442] In the Schumpeterian view, large firms and concentrated market structures promote innovation,[443] and less competition leads to more innovation, because the profits that can be generated as a result of innovative activities will be higher in such markets.[444] Schumpeter's theory of *"creative destruction"* has been described as a never-ending process.[445] The innovation brought by competitors will drive even the most efficient firms out of the market unless the latter can come up with its own innovations in order to continue to compete in the market.

On the opposite side, Kenneth Arrow concluded that the incentive to innovate is diminished under monopoly market conditions compared to competitive markets due to the monopolist's financial interest in maintaining the status quo.[446,447] For instance, Arrow compares an unchallenged monopolist that considers implementing a cost-reducing innovation in a market with exclusive IP rights with a firm operating in a perfectly competitive market that considers the same innovation. In Arrow's view, the incentive to innovate can be measured by the difference in profits a firm can expect to earn by either investing or not investing in R&D activities. According to this analysis, the result is that the competitive situation provides higher incentives to innovate for the firms in question. This is because the monopolist would be replacing an already high level of profit with an even higher one, while the competitive firm would be able to replace and supplant a low level of profit with a substantially higher one.[448]

Arrow's fundamental idea is that a company that is already earning substantial profits has a vested interest in protecting the status quo and is thus less likely to be the initiator or pioneer of disruptive new technologies. In other words, the secure monopolist's incentive to launch or achieve a process innovation is lower than that of a competitive firm because the monopolist with lower costs will merely replace itself in the relevant market, while the competitive firm will (by assumption) conquer the market, in which it previously earned little or no economic profits. Tirole called this "the replacement effect."[449] In other words, Arrow emphasized that "[t]he pre-invention monopoly power acts as a strong

---

[442]   Carl Shapiro, *Competition and Innovation: Did Arrow Hit the Bull's Eye?* in THE RATE AND DIRECTION OF INVENTIVE ACTIVITY REVISITED 361, 363 (Josh Lerner & Scott Stern eds., Univ. of Chicago Press 2012), https://www.nber.org/chapters/c12360.pdf.

[443]   Gilbert, *supra* note 439, at 160.

[444]   European Commission, *EU Merger Control and Innovation*, COMPETITION POLICY BRIEF (Apr. 2016), http://ec.europa.eu/competition/publications/cpb/2016/2016_001_en.pdf.

[445]   Markus Seiler, Innovation Competition in EU Merger Control 9–10 (2018) (on file with the University of St. Gallen)

[446]   Kenneth Arrow, Economic Welfare and the Allocation of Resources for Invention, *in* NATIONAL BUREAU OF ECONOMIC RESEARCH, THE RATE AND DIRECTION OF INVENTIVE ACTIVITY: ECONOMIC AND SOCIAL FACTORS 609 (Princeton Univ. Press 1962).

[447]   Shapiro, *supra* note 442, at 362.

[448]   Norbert Schulz, *Review of the Literature on the Impact of Mergers on Innovation* 8 (ZEW Discussion Paper No. 07-061, 2007), https://www.econstor.eu/bitstream/10419/24635/1/dp07061.pdf.

[449]   Shapiro, *supra* note 442. *See also* JEAN TIROLE, THE THEORY OF INDUSTRIAL ORGANIZATION 392 (MIT Press 1997).

disincentive to further innovation,"[450] and Carl Shapiro condensed Arrow's position into its most succinct summarization: "Product-market competition the spurs innovation."[451]

Numerous authors have empirically tested the different conclusions of Schumpeter and Arrow. For example, Stephen Nickell, by using data obtained from 680 firms in the UK, has presented evidence that competition, as measured by increased numbers of competitors or by lower levels of rents, is associated with a significantly higher rate of total factor productivity growth.[452] Moreover, Blundell, Griffith, and Van Reenen have investigated the statistical robustness of the effect of market structure on innovation and its economic interpretation.[453] As a result, they have come up with an estimated innovation equation and a value equation on a "firm panel level data source" and found that "*less competitive*" industries (i.e., those with lower import penetration levels and higher concentration levels) had fewer aggregate innovations. Nevertheless, within industries, it was the large market share firms that tended to commercialize a higher number of innovations, even though increased product-market competition in the industry tended to stimulate innovative activity. The authors also determined that there was a direct effect of innovation in the stock market value model (in terms of levels or differences). In other words, higher market share firms tended to benefit the most from innovations. Thus, Blundell, Griffith, and Van Reenen argue that their results are in line with models in which large market share firms have more significant incentives to innovate pre-emptively.

The works of both Nickell and Blundell et al. have purported to estimate a positive "linear" effect of competition on innovation. However, other authors have discovered a "non-linear" relationship between innovation and competition.

In this regard, Aghion and Griffith have surveyed the theoretical and empirical literature on competition, entry, and growth, and examined the relevance of distance to the technology frontier.[454] In their book, the authors systematically challenged theoretical models about the relationship between competition and innovation with empirical data, which either invalidated the investigated models or suggested useful changes in the modeling strategy. On the theoretical side, they have built upon Schumpeterian growth models, in which economic growth results from entrepreneurial innovations. In this theoretical paradigm, innovative activities are induced and stimulated by the economic environment, and each new innovation destroys the monopoly rents that had been generated by the previous innovators. The authors conclude that existing theoretical models in an industrial organization and new growth economics all predict a negative effect of competition on innovation and growth, asserting that competition is bad for growth because it reduces the monopoly rents that reward successful innovators.

Practically, Aghion and Griffith illustrate the use of novel techniques that have been implemented by applied micro econometricians to analyze the random process of

---

[450] Arrow, *supra* note 446, at 620.

[451] *Id.* at 362.

[452] Stephen J. Nickell, *Competition and Corporate Performance*, 104 J. POL. ECON. 724 (1996).

[453] Richard Blundell, Rachel Griffith & John Van Reenen, *Market Share, Market Value and Innovation in a Panel of British Manufacturing Firms*, 66 REV. ECON. STUD. 529 (1999).

[454] PHILIPPE AGHION & RACHEL GRIFFITH, COMPETITION AND GROWTH: RECONCILING THEORY AND EVIDENCE (MIT Press 2005).

innovation and patenting, in order to develop adequate measures and instruments for competition and entry. To reconcile theory and empirical evidence, they distinguish between pre- and post-innovation rents and propose that innovation may be a way to "escape competition." Furthermore, they test this idea by using microeconomic data, hypothesizing that more intense competition may potentially lead to more innovation because it reduces pre-innovation rents by more than it reduces post-innovation rents. The authors assert that whether the "escape competition" effect or the "rent dissipation" effect dominates will depend on the technological distance between firms in that industry. Ultimately, the balance between these two effects will depend upon the distribution of technological characteristics across sectors.

Aghion et al.[455] predict that there is an inverted-U relationship between competition and innovation and demonstrate that this prediction is entirely consistent with the empirical evidence. This means that, for low levels of competition, innovation initially increases as competition becomes more intense; however, after reaching its peak, innovation declines as competition intensifies further.[456] The authors develop a *duopoly model* where, at each point in time, the industry can be either in a *"neck-and-neck"* state or in a *"leader-laggard"* state. In the former state, both firms have the same marginal costs, while in the latter, one of them (i.e., the leader) is more efficient than the other (i.e., the laggard).[457] Focusing on cost-reducing innovations, it is shown that, in the *"neck-and-neck"* scenario, firms have stronger incentives to innovate if the competition is more intense. This is what Aghion et al. call the *"escape competition"* effect. In this scenario, competition may increase the incremental profits for firms from innovating and thereby encourage R&D investments aimed at escaping competition. This incentive is particularly valid in sectors where the incumbent firms are operating at similar technological levels. However, in sectors where laggard firms generate innovations with already low initial profits, product-market competition will mainly affect post-innovation rents. This means that an increase in competition gives a laggard firm a lower incentive to innovate.[458]

It is the Schumpeterian effect that the rents that can be captured by the laggard firm that succeeds in catching up with its rivals by innovating have been reduced. By combining these two effects, Aghion et al. arrive at an inverted-U-shaped relationship between competition and innovation.[459,460] A similar inverted-U-shaped relationship was also found between competition and patent counts in Aghion et al.[461] When the level of competition

---

[455]   *Id.* at 701–28.

[456]   Johnson, *supra* note 440, at 1.

[457]   Philippe Aghion, Nick Bloom, Richard Blundell, Rachel Griffith & Peter Howitt, *Competition and Innovation: An Inverted-U Relationship*, 120 Q. J. ECON. 701 (2005). *See* below in 4.4.3.

[458]   The assumptions of the model are such that a leader does not have incentives to innovate in Aghion et al.

[459]   Gilbert, Riis & Riis extend the stepwise models in Aghion et al. (2005) to (symmetric) oligopolies and demonstrate that the predictions of the effects of competition on innovation from the duopoly models do not generalize to oligopolies. Richard Gilbert, Christian Riis & Erlend S. Riis, *Stepwise Innovation by an Oligopoly*, 61 INT'L J. INDUS. ORG. 413 (2018), https://eml.berkeley.edu/~gilbert/Selected%20Papers/Stepwise%20innovation%20by%20oligopoly_IJIO.pdf.

[460]   Bruno Jullien & Yassine Lefouili, *Horizontal Mergers and Innovation* 5 (Toulouse School of Economics, Working Papers No. 18-892, 2018) https://www.tse-fr.eu/sites/default/files/TSE/documents/doc/wp/2018/wp_tse_892.pdf.

[461]   Philippe Aghion, Richard Blundell, Rachel Griffith, Peter Howitt & Susanne Prantl, *The Effects of Entry on Incumbent Innovation and Productivity*, 91 REV. ECON. & STAT. 20 (2009).

is low, a substantial equilibrium fraction of sectors involve *neck-and-neck* competing incumbents, so that, taken as a whole, the *escape competition effect* is more likely to dominate the *Schumpeterian effect*. On the other hand, when the level of competition is high (i.e., in conditions of fierce competition), the Schumpeterian effect is more likely to dominate because a more significant fraction of sectors in equilibrium will have innovation being generated and created by laggard firms with low initial profits.

Moreover, Carl Shapiro aimed to develop a more specific framework to address the role of *competition policy* in promoting innovation, instead of addressing broader questions regarding innovation policy or competitive strategy.[462] Therefore, Shapiro chose to focus his efforts on the possible effects of a proposed merger on innovation. As a result, he argues that the approaches of Schumpeter and Arrow are not as entirely incompatible as they seem and that they are actually mutually reinforcing, at least as far as competition policy is concerned. Shapiro reasons that, in order to understand the relationship between innovation and competition in a specific market, one should focus on the "*incentive*" and "*ability*" of firms to engage in innovative activities. According to Shapiro, the incentives to innovate can be assessed using three fundamental guiding principles: (i) *contestability*, (ii) *appropriability*, and (iii) *synergy*.[463] Contestability relates to the nature of *ex post* product-market competition. Appropriability concerns the possibilities for the successful inventor to capture the social benefits of its invention. Moreover, synergies are linked with the capabilities of enhancing innovation by combining complementary assets. In other words, the contestability and appropriability factors relate to the *incentive* to innovate, while the synergy factor relates to the *ability* to innovate.[464]

In more recent literature, Petit and Teece argue that Schumpeterian and Arrowian theories are largely irrelevant to real-world circumstances.[465] They point out that if monopolistic firms are not willing to allocate some of their revenue for innovation, as suggested by Arrow, they potentially offer an advantageous entry point for new market players. Thus, according to them, maintaining a certain level of market contestability would protect the relevant firm. Also, they note that Schumpeter's hypothesis that only monopolies can take the risk of innovation due to their supra-competitive profits may not be accurate in the modern world, where investment resources from multi-product firms or venture capital are typically available for raising finance.[466] They underline that today, technology opportunities with breakthrough potential may affect the incentives of potential entrants and produce results that differ from the expectations based on current assumptions about the relationship between innovation and market power.[467] Therefore, they suggest that new models developed in the field of (technology) management may better shed light on the policy discussion when compared to Arrowian and

---

[462]   Shapiro, *supra* note 442.

[463]   Johnson, *supra* note 440, at 2.

[464]   OECD, *Disruptive Innovation and Competition Policy Enforcement – Note by Alexandre de Streel and Pierre Larouche* (DAF/COMP/GF(2015)7, Oct. 20, 2015), recital 41.

[465]   Nicolas Petit & David J. Teece, *Innovating Big Tech Firms and Competition Policy: Favouring Dynamic over Static Competition* 9 (DCI Working Paper, 2021), https://www.dynamiccompetition.com/wp-content/uploads/2022/08/DCI-WP2-Petit-and-Teece-2021.pdf.

[466]   *Id.*

[467]   *Id.*

Schumpeterian views.[468] In a similar vein, Petit analyses the US Department of Justice ("DOJ") approach in the proposed acquisition of General Motors' Allison Division by ZF Friedrichshafen and questions (i) whether the decrease in the number of competitors would necessarily mean reduced competition and (ii) even if it is true, whether the restriction of short-term competition would necessarily reduce long-term innovation.[469] Therefore, Petit seems to question and criticize the applicability of Arrowian theory to the case at hand.

In his book on competition policy for the high-technology economy, Richard Gilbert explores the impact of antitrust lawsuits filed by the DOJ and the challenges presented by the Commission against Microsoft's practices. In Gilbert's view, such antitrust actions have favorably influenced software innovation, curtailed Microsoft's behavior, which could otherwise stifle competition, and prompted the tech giant to support interoperable software products.[470] He notes there is a case for intervention to prevent exclusionary conduct by dominant firms that diminishes innovation because (i) the monopolist firm's profit would decrease its incentives to invest in a new product, as suggested by Arrow, and (ii) in the absence of intervention, the relevant profit deterring from intervention would increase.[471] While Gilbert's above views on the *Microsoft* case appear to be in line with the Arrowian theory, he does criticize both Arrowian and Schumpeterian principles in another chapter for not addressing the intricate relationship between the drive to innovate, the generation of these innovations, and the condition of market competition.[472] According to Gilbert, Arrow does not take into account the motivations driving a monopolist to innovate in order to safeguard its profits by preventing competition from competitors; rather, he focuses solely on innovations that reduce costs.[473]

Similar to Gilbert, Thatchenkery and Katila examine the *Microsoft* case and delve into the consequences of Microsoft's intervention on the innovation and profitability landscape within the undertaking infrastructure applications sphere.[474] Their primary focus is on how the enforcement against Microsoft, the leading server platform, influenced future innovation endeavors and profitability for those who complement their platform – namely, the creators of infrastructure applications. The researchers discovered that the innovation rate among these complementors escalated post-intervention, implying that innovating becomes a more enticing option when the reigning platform has limited capacity to hinder the competition from its complementors.[475] Their discovery can be considered to support the Arrowian theory, where increased competition stimulated innovation. There are also certain studies that focus on the market players' influences on public policy and how, if any, this affects

---

[468]   *Id.*

[469]   Nicolas Petit, *A Framework for Antitrust Retrospectives: Illustrated by the 1993 Antitrust Case Against General Motors' Sale of Allison Transmission Roundtable Takeaways* (DCI Roundtable Takeaways, 2022), https://www.dynamiccompetition.com/wp-content/uploads/2022/11/DCI-RT2-GM-ZF-Complaint-FINAL-1.pdf.

[470]   RICHARD J. GILBERT, INNOVATION MATTERS: COMPETITION POLICY FOR THE HIGH-TECHNOLOGY ECONOMY 170–71 (MIT Press 2022).

[471]   *Id.* at 189.

[472]   *Id.* at 42.

[473]   *Id.*

[474]   Sruthi Thatchenkery & Riitta Katila, *Innovation and Profitability Following Antitrust Intervention Against a Dominant Platform: The Wild, Wild West?* 44 STRATEGIC MGMT. J. 943 (2023).

[475]   *Id.*

the regulators and their approach to concentration and innovation in the market. Research indicates that lobbying and campaign contributions are strong determinants of public policy outcomes,[476] although large-scale data on the subject is very difficult to collect considering that such activities are not transparently exercised, and the interpretation of the data is even more challenging.[477] Philippon notes that lobbying and campaign contributions' effects on policymaking, free market, competition and innovation are a key problem of the American economy.[478] High campaign contributions are found to be correlated with notable decreases in terms of non-merger enforcement, signaling the strategic nature of contributions by the corporate players to guard themselves against future antitrust scrutiny.[479] While lobbying comes in handy for policy-makers to keep the pulse of sectors by receiving useful information on the fast-evolving technological changes and innovations,[480] a contrasting view suggests that lobbying is a means to rent-seeking rather than beneficial sharing of information, as businesses often attempt to protect their rents by way of suppressing the new entrants, or even blocking entry entirely by way of lobbying.[481] Accordingly, although lobbying and overall participation in the process of policy-making are vital elements of democracy, the rent-seeking and blocking of market entry aspects can be problematic and harm the economy, competition and innovation[482] and manipulate free-market dynamics.

3.4 Innovation Concerns by Competition Enforcement Authorities in Merger Control

Although the literature so far provides useful insights for understanding the relationship between competition and innovation, it does not directly address the assessment of the impact of a particular merger on the incentives to innovate of firms in the relevant market.

In his literature survey on the economic studies focusing on the link between mergers and innovation, Norbert Schulz concluded that at an aggregated level, the effect of mergers

---

[476] OECD, *Lobbyists, Governments and Public Trust, Volume 3: Implementing the OECD Principles for Transparency and Integrity in Lobbying* (2014), https://www.oecd.org/gov/ethics/lobbyists-governments-trust-vol-3-highlights.pdf.

[477] Konstantinos Dellis & David Sondermann, *Lobbying in Europe: New Firm-Level Evidence* 2 (European Central Bank, Working Paper No. 2071, 2017); Lynda W. Powell & Clyde Wilcox, *Money and American Elections*, in THE OXFORD HANDBOOK OF AMERICAN ELECTIONS AND POLITICAL BEHAVIOR (Jan E. Leighley ed., Oxford Univ. Press 2010).

[478] THOMAS PHILIPPON, THE GREAT REVERSAL: HOW AMERICA GAVE UP ON FREE MARKETS 151 (Belknap Press 2019).

[479] Germán Gutiérrez & Thomas Philippon, *How EU Markets Became More Competitive Than US Markets: A Study of Institutional Drift* 25–29 (NBER Working Paper No. 24700, 2018).

[480] Martin Gregor, *Corporate Lobbying: A Review of the Recent Literature* 29 (Charles University, Inst. of Econ. Stud. Working Paper, No. 32/2011, 2011).

[481] Gene M. Grossman & Elhanan Helpman, *Protection for Sale*, 84 AM. ECON. REV. 833 (1994); GENE M. GROSSMAN & ELHANAN HELPMAN, SPECIAL INTEREST POLITICS (MIT Press 2002); PHILIPPON, *supra* note 478, at 160–61.

[482] PHILIPPON, *supra* note 478, at 161.

and acquisitions on innovation was *negligible* or *negative*.[483] However, putting aside the aggregate view, he noted that when a more disaggregated strategy is taken, the positive effect of innovation could be evidenced. Importantly, he observed that there was a distinction between process and product innovation cases and also that innovation activities increased when the merging partners had complementary technologies.[484] Most of the studies included in the survey did not consider a specialized industry but rather used data that encompassed many diverse industries. He also pointed out that these studies had shown the importance of heterogeneity and that a balanced view was imperative as the impact of mergers on innovation could be thoroughly assessed only if the study also focused on the effect of innovation on mergers.[485]

With this in mind, the following sections will address how competition authorities assess mergers that have the potential to affect innovation incentives, and the ideas and factors shaping the relevant merger control enforcement systems.

3.4.1 The Presumption that Horizontal Mergers Reduce Innovation Incentives

Carles Esteva Mosso, then deputy director-general for mergers at the Directorate-General for Competition of the European Commission, has declared that the economic principles related to the effects of mergers on innovation (e.g., internalization of the competitive effects of innovation, effects of appropriability, complementarity of innovation efforts, and synergies, among others) do not establish an economic (nor legal) presumption that mergers necessarily reduce innovation and harm future market competition in the absence of efficiencies. However, Mosso has also expressed the view that these economic principles nevertheless provide useful guidance for merger control and establish a solid economic foundation for the concern that, under certain conditions, a merger may reduce innovation competition to the detriment of consumers.[486] Mosso adds that to understand whether a horizontal merger will have a negative impact on innovation, it is necessary to conduct a detailed examination of the available evidence in each case, in particular, with respect to (i) the overlaps between the parties' R&D capabilities and projects, (ii) the importance of the rival innovators, and (iii) the barriers to entry.[487]

Despite this cautious approach regarding a presumption of harm to innovation, Shapiro argues that

> we *do* know enough to warrant a presumption that a merger between the only two firms pursing [*sic*] a specific line of research to serve a particular need is likely

---

[483] Schulz, *supra* note 448.

[484] *Id*. at 4.

[485] *Id*. at 2–3.

[486] Carles Esteva Mosso, *Innovation in EU Merger Control*, 66th ABA Section of Antitrust Law Spring Meeting 5 (Apr. 12, 2018), http://ec.europa.eu/competition/speeches/text/sp2018_05_en.pdf.

[487] *Id*. at 8.

to diminish innovation rivalry, absent a showing that the merger will increase appropriability or generate R&D synergies that will enhance the incentive or ability of the merged firm to innovate.[488]

RBB Economics, referring to a more recent theoretical paper co-authored by the European Commission's Chief Economist Tommaso Valletti and his colleagues, Giulio Federico and Gregor Langus, from the same department,[489] has argued that the Commission holds a presumption that horizontal mergers can be expected to reduce innovation incentives as a result of a standard unilateral effect.[490] They believe this is unjustified and that innovation incentives may depend on various co-existing factors (without one factor necessarily dominating).

Although they take a multitude of factors into consideration, the fundamental factor underlying the innovation concerns of competition enforcement authorities in the assessment of horizontal mergers is that the merging parties can internalize the constraint between the rival products and that this may give the merged entity an incentive to reduce its innovation efforts. In the extreme scenario, the merged entity might even discontinue one of the products in order to avoid "*cannibalizing*" the other product's sales. The analysis of competition authorities relies not only on the closeness assessment of competition between the two products but also on the competitive constraint exerted by the rivals' products.[491]

However, various authors have criticized this finding of harm by arguing that the assessment of the impact of a merger on R&D investments requires a complex balancing act, which involves many different factors that can affect the incentives to innovate.[492] Accordingly, innovation incentives cannot be limited to a supporting role in a standard unilateral effects analysis.

3.4.2 The (Changing) Presumption that Non-Horizontal Mergers Do Not Reduce Innovation Incentives

Authorities analyze various factors while assessing the innovation effects of a merger, which are usually discussed under horizontal merger cases, as non-horizontal mergers[493] have generally been deemed to give less cause for concern. Considering that a

---

[488]   Shapiro, *supra* note 442, at 368.

[489]   Giulio Federico, Gregor Langus & Tommaso Valletti, *A Simple Model of Mergers and Innovation* (CESifo Working Paper No. 6539, June 2017), https://papers.ssrn.com/sol3/papers.cfm?abstract_id=3005163.

[490]   RBB Economics, *An Innovative Leap Into the Theoretical Abyss: Dow/DuPont and the Commission's Novel Theory of Harm* 1 (2017), https://www.datocms-assets.com/79198/1667304872-rbb-brief-54.pdf.

[491]   *Id.*

[492]   *Id. See* Sections V and VII below for further discussion on the various applicable factors.

[493]   In non-horizontal mergers, *vertical integrations* can be defined as mergers between non-competing companies that are positioned at different levels of the production chain, whereas *conglomerate mergers* involve the merging of undertakings that operate in unrelated markets.

non-horizontal merger does not eliminate a rival or an innovation process from the market, but can also potentially create various efficiencies through integrated product portfolios, there has been less scrutiny.[494] These transactions raise two types of anti-competitive concerns: (i) unilateral effects, such as tying, bundling and other similar *foreclosure* practices, and (ii) coordinated effects, such as increased risk of coordination among the remaining competitors.[495] In such mergers, the products of the merging parties do not directly compete, nor are they crucially important in the parties' supply chains. Thus, vertical and conglomerate mergers have been generally considered not to raise anti-competitive concerns, except for unilateral effects of foreclosure practices.[496] However, authorities have recently been focusing more on the anti-competitive effects of non-horizontal concentrations and the need for stricter enforcement.[497] In particular, in the sectors where significant amounts of innovation are involved (e.g., digital sectors), the merging parties' capability to innovate similar products in an ecosystem could result in certain anti-competitive concerns in terms of creating innovation, even in conglomerate mergers.[498] FTC Chair Lina Khan noted that business strategies adopted by the digital market necessitate enforcers to move beyond ideas like foreclosure and exclusion and signaled that non-horizontal integrations in the digital market might raise new theories of harm.[499] Occasionally, even without bundling concerns, the innovation

---

[494]   *Id.*

[495]   EUROPEAN COMMISSION, DIRECTORATE-GENERAL FOR COMPETITION, THE IMPACT OF VERTICAL AND CONGLO-MERATE MERGERS ON COMPETITION 2 (Publications Office of the European Union 2004).

[496]   Eliana Garcés & Daniel Gaynor, *Conglomerate Mergers: Developments and a Call for Caution*, 10 J. EUR. COMPETITION L. & PRAC. 457, 457–58 (2019); *see, e.g.*, European Commission, Guidelines on the Assessment of Non-Horizontal Mergers Under the Council Regulation on the Control of Concentrations Between Undertakings, 2008 OJ (C 265) 6, 20.

[497]   *See* Chapter 6 on the US 2020 Vertical Merger Guidelines and next steps for further discussion. The FTC withdrew the 2020 Vertical Merger Guidelines on the grounds that they featured a "flawed discussion of the purported procompetitive benefits" and old guidelines "adopted a particularly flawed economic theory regarding purported pro-competitive benefits of mergers, despite having no basis of support in the law or market reality." (FTC Press Release, Federal Trade Commission Withdraws Vertical Merger Guidelines and Commentary (Sept. 15, 2021), https://www.ftc.gov/news-events/news/press-releases/2021/09/federal-trade-commission-with-draws-vertical-merger-guidelines-commentary) In the US, lawsuits brought by the agencies recently encompass vertical theories of harm. For example, the DOJ filed a complaint to the court regarding the acquisition of Change Healthcare by an insurer, UnitedHealth Group, on the grounds that the acquirer (i) would have access to competitor data enabling it to co-opt its rivals' innovations, which may reduce competitors' incentives to pursue innovations, and (ii) would deny competitors' access to the targets' services. (DOJ's administrative complaint against UnitedHealth Group and Change Healthcare 2 (Feb. 24, 2022).)Nevertheless, the court denied the challenge by the DOJ, and although the DOJ appealed the case, it then dismissed its own appeal. (*See* Reuters, *US Drops Appeal of UnitedHealth Acquisition of Change Healthcare* (Mar. 21, 2023), https://www.reuters.com/legal/us-drops-appeal-unitedhealth-acquisition-change-healthcare-2023-03-21). The FTC's administrative complaint regarding Illumina's proposed acquisition of GRAIL is another example where the FTC claimed that Illumina might prevent GRAIL's multi-cancer testing competitors' access to Illumina's technology that is necessary to develop and commercialize their tests, which they expect to compete closely with GRAIL's products. (FTC's administrative complaint, In re Illumina and GRAIL (Mar. 30, 2021), paras. 12–13, https://www.ftc.gov/system/files/documents/cases/redacted_administrative_part_3_complaint_redacted.pdf.)

[498]   Pierre Régibeau & Ioannis Lianos, *Digital Mergers: A Primer* 12 (2020), https://papers.ssrn.com/sol3/papers.cfm?abstract_id=3837281.

[499]   Remarks of Chair Lina Khan at the Charles River Associates Conference, Competition & Regulation in Disrupted Times in Brussels, Belgium (Mar. 31, 2022), https://www.ftc.gov/news-events/news/speeches/remarks-chair-lina-m-khan-charles-river-associates-conference-competition-regulation-disrupted-times. In line with this statement, the FTC scrutinized several digital transactions in detail, e.g., Meta (Facebook) alleging that it violated section 2 of the Sherman Act through conducting acquisitions of companies that might become a competitive threat

theories of harm regarding conglomerate mergers might emerge in numerous ways, such as reduced research and development incentives of the entrants, especially in cases where the merging parties produce complementary products.[500] These rising concerns and the EU and UK competition authorities' changing approach towards vertical transactions[501] are clearly apparent in recent cases, such as Illumina/GRAIL[502] and *Microsoft/Activision*.[503]

3.4.3 Main Factors Analyzed in Assessing Innovation Competition in Merger Control

The Commission builds its assessment of the effects of mergers on innovation competition mainly on the analysis of the following factors: (i) the market characteristics and market structure; (ii) the importance of the merging parties as innovators; (iii) the intensity of the innovation rivalry between the merging parties in innovation spaces;[504] (iv) the impact on

---

against Meta in the absence of acquisitions and requesting the divestitures of Meta's assets, including Instagram and WhatsApp. Therefore, the FTC alleged that transactions that do not give rise to horizontal overlaps lead to a restriction of nascent competition, which constitutes a new theory of harm. (*See* FTC's administrative complaint, FTC v. Facebook, Inc., Case No. 1:20-cv-03590 (Dec. 9. 2020), https://www.ftc.gov/system/files/documents/cases/051_2021.01.21_revised_partially_redacted_complaint.pdf). The judicial process before the district court is still ongoing. *See* FTC v. Facebook, Memorandum Opinion Civil Action No. 20-3590 (JEB), at 2, https://s3.documentcloud.org/documents/21177063/memorandum-opinion.pdf.

[500] Frederico Etro, *Conglomerate Mergers and Entry in Innovative Industries* 2–3 (Univ. Ca' Foscari of Venice, Dep't of Econ. Resch., Working Paper Series No. 19/WP/2018, 2018).

[501] Stéphane Dewulf, Timo Klein, Andrew Mell & Anastasia Shchepetova, *EU and UK Vertical Merger Control: What's the State of Play?* 14 J. EUR. COMPETITION L. & PRAC. 113 (2023).

[502] Similar to the FTC, the Commission blocked the acquisition of GRAIL by Illumina on the grounds that Illumina would have the ability and incentive to foreclose GRAIL's competitors' access to Illumina's technology, putting forth an innovation theory of harm stating that GRAIL and its competitors are engaging in an innovation race on the development of cancer tests and that it is crucial to protect this innovation competition. *See* European Commission Press Release IP/22/5364, Mergers: Commission prohibits acquisition of GRAIL by Illumina (Sept. 6, 2022), https://ec.europa.eu/commission/presscorner/detail/en/ip_22_5364. Please refer to Chapter 7 for a detailed discussion of the case.

[503] The CMA updated its Merger Assessment Guidelines in 2021 and no longer characterizes vertical mergers as typically harmless. In line with this amendment, the CMA had initially prohibited the acquisition of Activision by Microsoft, finding that the transaction would likely result in a substantial lessening of competition in cloud gaming services in the UK primarily because, post-transaction, Microsoft would have the ability and incentive to limit access to Activision's games and some of Activision's games are likely to be an important input for the success of rival cloud gaming services. The CMA had also initially noted that the likely future growth, competitive dynamism and innovation in the cloud gaming market would be substantially reduced as a result of the transaction (CMA, ANTICIPATED ACQUISITION BY MICROSOFT OF ACTIVISION BLIZZARD, INC. (Final Report) (Apr. 26, 2023), https://assets.publishing.service.gov.uk/media/644939aa529eda000c3b0525/Microsoft_Activision_Final_Report_.pdf (*"Microsoft/Activision* (Final Report)"), paras. 8.314, 8.346, 8.347 & 10). With a view to eliminating the said concerns, Microsoft submitted in August a restructured transaction. Under the restructured transaction, Microsoft will not purchase the cloud gaming rights of Activision, which will instead be sold to Ubisoft Entertainment SA ("Ubisoft"), before the deal is completed. Accordingly, the CMA considered that there are reasonable grounds that the restructured transaction (or a modified version of it) might be accepted by the CMA (CMA, Anticipated acquisition by Microsoft Corporation of Activision Blizzard (excluding Activision Blizzard's non-EEA cloud streaming rights) (ME/7068/23, Sept. 22, 2023), paras. 8–13.)

[504] The "innovation spaces" concept introduced by the Commission in *Dow/DuPont* (4.4)refers to an abstract potential of future innovation that is not related to any specific/pipeline products or technology markets. Thus, it is "a current, dynamic, and forward-looking assessment of the competition in innovation," which would allow

the incentive to innovate and evidence concerning the effects of innovation; and (v) the capacity of the remaining competitors to offset the loss in innovation competition. This type of analysis was mentioned in the Commission's *Dow/DuPont* decision, as well as other recent cases.[505]

3.4.3.1 Market Characteristics and Market Structure

Regarding the market characteristics and structure, the Commission aims to identify and analyze the following aspects: (i) the key drivers for innovation in a given industry; (ii) whether the concern is about *product* innovation or *process* innovation; (iii) the degree of uncertainty with respect to innovation; (iv) whether entry or expansion barriers are present in the relevant market; (v) whether customers are likely to switch to innovative products (i.e., contestable environment); (vi) the strength of intellectual property rights (i.e., appropriability); (vii) the time-to-market of an innovation; (viii) other industry-specific features, such as regulatory pressure; (ix) whether other relevant innovation competitors are present in the market (i.e., concentration at the industry level and in innovation spaces); and (x) if the innovation capabilities of the other players are comparable with those of the merging parties (e.g., similar assets, expertise, and financial strengths/resources). The Commission also takes into account how past mergers have affected innovation competition in the industry.[506,507]

In this regard, it is worth noting that the Commission assesses the level of concentration as regards innovation both at the *industry* level and at the level of *innovation spaces*.[508]

The UK's Competition and Markets Authority ("CMA") adopts a stricter approach to assessing mergers that might affect innovation negatively. The analysis of the innovation effects of mergers is parallel to that of price changes in the market, given that innovation may lead to offering more innovative products with lower prices.[509] On the other hand, the CMA notes that the traditional assessment based on the impact of price changes may not be sufficient to establish other competitive parameters, such as quality and innovation.[510] According to the CMA's Merger Assessment Guidelines (hereinafter "CMA Guidelines"), "innovation will play a key role in some merger investigations" and "innovation is a key aspect of competition between the merger firms and the level or pace of future innovation or product development is threatened by a merger."[511] The Guidelines refer to quantity sold, service quality, product range, product quality, and innovation. The extent to which each of the parameters are assessed in an individual case will depend on the aspects of

---

competition authorities to assess the effect of a merger where a product may not yet exist. Ioannis Kokkoris & Tommaso Valletti, *Innovation Considerations in Horizontal Merger Control*, 16 J. COMPETITION L. & ECON. 220 (2020).

[505] Mosso, *supra* note 486 at 8.

[506] *Dow/DuPont*, §§ V.8.4–V.8.6, recitals 2039–2395.

[507] Seiler, *supra* note 445, at 40.

[508] *Dow/DuPont*, § V.8.6.

[509] Julie Bon, San Sau Fung, Alan Reilly, Terry Ridout, Robert Ryan & Mike Walker, *Recent Developments at the CMA: 2020-2021*, 59 REV. INDUS. ORG. 665 (2021), doi: 10.1007/s11151-021-09848-5.

[510] CMA, Digital Competition Expert Panel Recommendations (2019).

[511] CMA, Merger Assessment Guidelines (CMA129) (Mar. 18, 2021), https://assets.publishing.service.gov.uk/government/uploads/system/uploads/attachment_data/file/1051823/MAGs_for_publication_2021_--_.pdf.

the merging firms' competitive offers to customers over which the firms compete, and which may be harmed as a result of the merger.[512] Thus, the CMA favors a strategy that focuses more on non-price effects whereby the CMA assesses whether the actions of the undertakings may have a detrimental impact on innovation or reduce the amount of funds that will be invested in R&D projects and product quality.[513]

The EU Horizontal Merger Guidelines also refer to non-price effects that a merger or an acquisition may bring about and note that the Commission prevents mergers that would lead to price increases and reduction in output, choice or quality of goods and services, or decrease in innovation.[514] In addition to the innovation cases such as *Bayer/Monsanto*[515] and *Dow/DuPont*,[516] the Commission had noted in *Microsoft/LinkedIn* that privacy may be taken into account in the competition assessment to the extent that consumers see it as a significant factor of quality, and the merging parties compete with each other on this factor. The Commission found that privacy drives consumer choice for professional social networks and decided that data privacy (as a parameter of competition) may be negatively affected by the transaction.[517] Accordingly, just like the CMA, the Commission seems to increasingly take into account non-price effects in merger control cases, in particular, decreased innovation and product quality. Nevertheless, in terms of comparing the two authorities, it is worth noting their differing views on the recent *Microsoft/Activision* case. Although both authorities articulated their concerns under similar traditional vertical theories of harm and made some references to innovation competition in their assessments, the Commission deemed that the commitments offered by Microsoft would fully address the competition concerns and unlock significant benefits for competition and consumers, making the games available on new platforms and more devices than before. The CMA, however, found these commitments to be insufficient. Microsoft then submitted a restructured transaction to the CMA, where Microsoft will not purchase the cloud gaming rights of Activision, which will instead be sold to Ubisoft, before the deal is completed. After the submission of the restructured transaction, the CMA considered that there are reasonable grounds that the restructured transaction (or a modified version of it) might be accepted by the CMA.[518] In the US, similar to the EU approach, both price and innovation effects are important due to their effects on consumers in the assessment of mergers, and the value of innovation is well recognized and emphasized by the DOJ officials.[519] Indeed, one of the main issues specifically

---

[512] *Id.* Based on the evidence before it, the CMA will consider whether a merger would lead to the merged entity being able to profitably and unilaterally raise its prices, worsen its quality or service and non-price factors of competition, or reduce innovation efforts at one or more of the pre-merger businesses.

[513] CMA, Submission from the Competition and Markets Authority to the Business, Innovation and Skills Committee's inquiry into the Government's industrial strategy (Sept. 28, 2016), https://www.gov.uk/government/publications/governments-industrial-strategy-cma-submission-to-bis-committee.

[514] Horizontal Merger Control Guidelines, para. 9.

[515] Bayer/Monsanto, European Commission Decision case M.8084 (Mar. 21, 2018).

[516] Dow/DuPont, European Commission Decision case M.7932 (Mar. 27, 2017).

[517] Microsoft/LinkedIn, European Commission Decision case M.8124 (Dec. 6, 2016). The Commission ultimately conditionally approved the transaction.

[518] *See* Chapter 5, Section 4.2, for a more detailed analysis of the CMA's approach to *Microsoft/Activision*.

[519] Robert Kramer, Chief, Litigation II Section, Antitrust Div., US Dep't of Jus., Antitrust Considerations in International Defense Mergers, Address before the American Institute of Aeronautics and Astronautics, Arlington, Virginia (May 4, 1999) (the more important that innovation becomes to society, the more important it is to

addressed by the new US Horizontal Merger Guidelines issued jointly by the FTC and the DOJ is "restraints on innovation" along with the other substantive merger concerns that are classified as (i) exclusion, (ii) unilateral effects and (iii) coordinated effects.[520] The US Horizontal Merger Guidelines also specifically regulate mergers limiting innovation and product variety.[521]

For the sake of completeness, the DOJ's approach differs from the FTC's approach to innovation in that the DOJ uses a traditional approach, whereas the FTC uses the innovation markets approach. Overall, traditional merger policy in the US is mainly conducted with static analysis that basically focuses on the impact of the transaction over prices and generally disregards dynamic considerations like research and development.[522] Nevertheless, the reference to innovation as "a force that could make static measures of market structure unreliable or irrelevant"[523] plays a significant role in the US merger control assessments.

The *Sabre/Farelogix* case provides a comparative outlook regarding the significance of the nature of the competitive constraints over formalistic market definitions in merger control regimes in the US and the UK. Accordingly, the market definition appears to have a substantial role in the US district court's decision in Sabre's favor by overruling the DOJ's decision concluding that Sabre's platform does not compete with Farelogix's distribution product in a relevant market definition under the US merger control regime.[524] On the other hand, the CMA's approach[525] emphasized the assessment of competitive constraints irrespective of the markets whereby the merging parties operate and yet focused more on the impact of the transaction. To that end, it may be argued that the CMA Guidelines underline the growing significance of competitive assessment over mere and strict market definition.

3.4.3.2 The Importance of the Merging Parties as Innovators

The Commission holds the view that a merger between two talented innovators may significantly impede innovation competition in the relevant market.[526] A party's importance as an innovator may not correspond directly to its overall size, its overall investment in R&D activities, or its market share at the industry level – as Seiler has observed, the impediment to innovation competition is most significant and pronounced if the merging parties are important innovators in the same innovation space.[527] Thus, the Commission suggests employing data on the quality-rated patent share of the undertakings or the

---

preserve economic incentives to innovate and "[a]s important as price competition is to us, a second major and possibly even greater concern is maintaining competition for innovation"); *see* M. L. & Shelanski, H. A., "Mergers *and Innovation*" *Antitrust Law Journal* 74 1 (2007): 1-85.

[520]   Herbert Hovenkamp, *Harm to Competition Under the 2010 Horizontal Merger Guidelines*, 39 REV. INDUS. ORG. 3, 3 (2011).

[521]   *Id.*

[522]   *Id.*

[523]   *Id.* at 111.

[524]   United States v. Sabre Corp. et al., case 19-1548 (D. Del. 2020) (Stark, J., opinion).

[525]   Sabre Corporation v. CMA [2021] CAT 11.

[526]   *Id.*, recital 2599.

[527]   Seiler, *supra* note 445, at 44.

firms' share in successfully launched new innovative products or active ingredients (based on turnover in downstream markets), if market share or other similar measures are considered to be inadequate for reflecting the innovation strength of the merging parties.[528]

3.4.3.3 The Intensity of Innovation Rivalry Between the Merging Parties in Innovation Spaces

To analyze the intensity of innovation rivalry between the merging parties in innovation spaces, the Commission examines whether the two merging parties are close innovation competitors and evaluates whether they have overlapping lines of research and/or overlapping early pipeline products. Closeness is an essential factor in assessing the extent of the *"cannibalization effect,"* e.g., how much sales the two merging parties would take away from one other in the absence of the merger.

3.4.3.4 The Impact on the Incentive to Innovate and Evidence Regarding the Effects of Innovation

The assessment of a merger's impact on the incentive to innovate is mainly based on the extent of the cannibalization effect. The term "cannibalization" is used for the negative externality that rival firms exert on each other through their innovation efforts in the same innovation spaces. A merger offers the merging parties the opportunity to internalize these negative externalities and is, therefore, likely to cause a reduction in their innovation efforts in overlapping lines of research and pipeline products. As a result, one of the overlapping projects of the merging parties may be discontinued or delayed after the merger. Product variety may be reduced, or the future competitive pressure between the merging firms may be eliminated. The overall probability that an innovative product will be brought to the market may, therefore, be diminished too.[529]

In its analysis of the transformation of the incentives to innovate in the post-merger market, the Commission takes into account evidence from documents obtained from the merging parties about their future R&D plans and their projected reductions in innovation efforts.[530]

3.4.3.5 The Capacity of Remaining Competitors to Offset the Loss in Innovation Competition

The Commission evaluates whether the remaining competitors are able and willing to compensate or offset the reduction in innovation competition as a result of the merger, in the innovation spaces targeted by the merging parties and at the industry level.[531]

---

[528]   *Dow/DuPont*, recitals 2426 *et seq.*
[529]   Seiler, *supra* note 445, at 41.
[530]   *Dow/DuPont*, §§ V.8.4–V.8.6. recitals 2039–2395.
[531]   *Id.*, recitals 3225 *et seq.*

3.4.4 Theoretical Literature Influencing the Innovation Concerns of Competition Authorities

The primary concern of competition authorities regarding the innovation effects of mergers is that a merger between two out of a limited number of innovators is likely to reduce competition in innovation, thus limiting the overall rate of innovation in the relevant market. In this regard, Shapiro's proposal is that the antitrust agencies should determine (i) whether the proposed merger significantly reduces contestability (e.g., the future rivalry between the merging parties, which is based on the calculation of an *innovation diversion ratio*) and (ii) whether the merger nonetheless enhances innovation by increasing appropriability or enabling merger-specific synergies.[532] Accordingly, the recent economics literature supporting the innovation concerns of competition enforcement authorities will be summarized and discussed below, on the basis of such "effects" that are taken into account in the assessment of impacts of mergers on innovation competition – namely, (i) cannibalization, (ii) contestability, and (iii) appropriability.

3.4.4.1 *Cannibalization*

Cannibalization occurs when the introduction of innovative new products to a market can divert sales from existing products in that market. When an innovating firm merges with a rival, it may internalize the diverted sales of its rival. In other words, the post-merger firm will take into account the degree to which its innovations will cannibalize its sales.[533]

Therefore, the basic idea for merger control systems is that a merger can reduce the overlapping innovation efforts of the merging parties.[534] Since, in the post-merger period, the future products and the overlapping products developed by a merging party will "cannibalize" the merged entity's future products, the merged company would have a clear incentive to reduce this innovation competition in these overlapping areas. Thus, one consequence of such a merger would be a reduction in product variety and a loss in innovation rivalry between the merging innovators.[535] Before the merger, each party had an incentive to engage in R&D activities in order to develop new products, which, if successfully brought to market, would compete against the products of its competitors, but in the post-merger world, the incentive to innovate would be reduced, as the cannibalization effect is internalized.[536]

---

[532] OECD, *supra* note 464, recital 41.
[533] OECD, *Considering Non-Price Effects in Merger Control – Background Note by the Secretariat* (DAF/COMP(2018)2, May 4, 2018), https://one.oecd.org/document/DAF/COMP(2018)2/en/pdf.
[534] Seiler, *supra* note 445, at 40–41.
[535] *Id.* at 42–43.
[536] RBB Economics, *supra* note 490, at 1.

RBB Economics has clearly explained and illustrated the cannibalization effect with a straightforward numerical example, as follows:[537]

> A simple example can be used to illustrate the logic behind the cannibalisation concern. Suppose that firm A is contemplating an R&D investment of €50 in a new product that would deliver sales of €100. €20 of these sales would come from cannibalising firm A's own existing products, €40 would take place at the expense of firm B and €40 at the expense of firm C. Once the R&D cost (€50) and cannibalisation of its existing products (€20) are taken into account, firm A would find it profitable to undertake the investment since it would deliver a profit of €30 (= €100 − €50 − €20). Following a merger between firms A and B, however, the decision would be different. The new product would still deliver sales of €100, but it would now cannibalise €60 of its products (€20 from firm A and €40 from firm B). Due to this higher level of cannibalisation, the merged entity would no longer have an incentive to proceed with the R&D investment since it would obtain a negative profit (€100 − €50 − €60 = −€10).

I disagree with the above that the merged entity would not invest in R&D, such firms do not have the luxury to refrain from engaging in R&D. Cannibalization effect analysis should not be done as a snapshot analysis, assuming the behavior and circumstances of the merged entity will be the same throughout. The escape effect, the need and potential to drive profits up though innovation might be higher for the merged entity in the Schumpeterian sense. They could switch from one singular stochastic product innovation to acquiring the means and incentive to engage in process innovation. The question to ask is whether the merger *could* increase the *potential* for post-innovation process innovation profits to a greater extent than it increases pre-innovation product specific profits; "could" and "potential" make this question invisible today; which is a part of the very asymmetry and paradox I discuss in this book.

Shelanski provides an alternative explanation as to how the cannibalization effect leads to "*downward innovation pressure.*" He notes that, as mentioned before, cannibalization occurs when an incumbent introduces a new product that competes with its pre-existing product, and some customers choose to abandon the incumbent's pre-existing product for this new product. This cannibalization effect naturally discourages incumbents from developing or introducing new products.[538] He describes this cannibalization effect and downward innovation pressure by using a simple mathematical relationship, as follows:

> Suppose that Firm 1 produces product A and that a rival, Firm 2, is developing innovation B, which will compete with A. If introduced, product B will draw a fraction d of its sales from customers who would otherwise buy A (thus d is the diversion ratio). Let MA be the profit margin that Firm 1 earns on incremental sales of A, and let MB be the profit margin that (for simplicity) either firm would earn on sales of B once introduced. Firm 2's profit from introducing B

---

537   *Id.* at 2.
538   Howard Shelanski, *Information, Innovation, and Competition Policy for the Internet*, 161 U. Pa. L. Rev. 1663, 1703 (2013), http://scholarship.law.upenn.edu/cgi/viewcontent.cgi?article=1025&context=penn_law_review.

and selling Q units exceeds its cost, C2, of product introduction if MB.Q ≥ C2. But, if the firms have merged and no other entry is imminent, the merged firm will find it profitable to introduce B only if [MB – d.MA]Q ≥ CM, where CM is the merged firm's cost of product introduction. If d.MA is not much less than MB; then the merged firm may well find the introduction much less profitable than would an independent Firm 2, even if the merged firm's cost of introduction is considerably lower. This example illustrates how a merger can dramatically affect the incentives to introduce an innovative product – what we might call downward innovation pressure (DIP).

Farrell and Shapiro, on the other hand, have developed a measure known as *upward price pressure* ("UPP") to analyze and handle this issue.[539] The UPP method is referred to in the US Horizontal Merger Guidelines,[540] and it is also one of the most well-known and widely used indicators employed by competition enforcement authorities to evaluate the unilateral price effects of horizontal mergers.[541] Farrell and Shapiro illustrate how the UPP method can be generalized to non-price dimensions of competition, such as product selection, product variety, and innovation competition. The authors state that the direction of the effects of a merger depends upon the relative strength of cannibalization effects and merger-specific efficiencies.[542]

However, they also declare that the impact of a merger on pricing incentives might not match up very closely with its impact on innovation incentives. For example, the two merging undertakings might not currently offer directly competing products in the relevant market, but they could both be working on and developing new products that will compete more directly in the future, either with each other or with the firms' current offerings.

At this point, Farrell and Shapiro introduce the concept of "*innovation diversion ratio*" as the key parameter of their analytical framework. According to their definition, the innovation diversion ratio of Firm A from Firm B is the fraction IAB of the extra gross profits earned by Firm A when it devotes more resources to innovation that come at the expense of Firm B. For example, "Firm A is considering a risky R&D investment that, if it succeeds, will yield $100 million in profits for Firm A and reduce Firm B's profits by $30 million. Since 30% of the extra profits to Firm A come at the expense of Firm B, I_{AB} is 30%."[543] The authors provide the following simple example to explain the unilateral innovation effects: In an oligopoly where firms A and B are Bertrand price-setting firms with two single products, if the merger between A and B yields R&D

---

[539] In an oligopoly where players *i* and *j* are Bertrand price-setting firms with two single products, suppose $\bar{P}_i$ and $\bar{C}_i$ are the pre-merger price and marginal cost of firm "i". When firm i merges with firm *j*, the marginal cost of *i* decreases to $C_i = (1 - E_i\bar{C}_i)$ post-merger. E_i stands for the efficiency gains in percentage. The merger will cause an upward price pressure (UPP) for firm *i*, if $D_{ij}\bar{M}_j \frac{\bar{P}_j}{\bar{P}_i} > E_i(1 = \bar{M}_i)$, where $\bar{M}_i = \frac{\bar{P}_i - \bar{C}_i}{\bar{P}_i}$ is the margin for product *i*. (*See* Joseph Farrell & Carl Shapiro, *Antitrust Evaluation of Horizontal Mergers: An Economic Alternative to Market Definition*, 10 B.E. J. THEORETICAL ECON. POLICIES & PERSP. 1, 12 (2010), art. 9, https://faculty.haas.berkeley.edu/shapiro/alternative.pdf.)

[540] Horizontal Merger Guidelines at 21.

[541] Farrell & Shapiro, *supra* note 539, at 33.

[542] *Id.*

[543] *Id.*

efficiencies such that the cost of R&D falls by a factor $(1 - E_R)$, this merger will tend to retard innovation on Firm A's products if $I_{AB} > E_R$. Thus, we observe that the impact of the proposed merger on innovation incentives does depend on the extent to which Firm A's pre-merger rewards from innovation come at the expense of Firm B, and on merger efficiencies relating to innovation. On the other hand, the authors also note that it may not be easy to estimate the actual *innovation diversion ratio* in any given case.

Process innovation reduces the cost of production. This is what drives a merged entity to innovate, especially if price competition is lessened. But even cost savings in R&D are not recognized as cognizable efficiencies.

The reduction in the intensity of price competition following a merger might enhance and provide capability for innovation. But can this be heard when innovation only has a supportive role in articulating unilateral effects concerns?

Federico et al. have also analyzed the effects of horizontal mergers on innovation with the help of a theoretical two-stage game model. By using this model, they found that the negative impact of the cannibalization effect on innovation incentives dominates any other innovation effect, and will generally reduce the post-merger firm's innovation efforts.[544] In this regard, Jullien and Lefouili report that[545] Federico, Langus and Valletti, who are employed as economists at the Chief Economist Team at the European Commission, have formalized the arguments that the Commission had used in the *Dow/DuPont* case, in their papers.[546] These economists set up a highly stylized model of merger in an industry where innovation plays a vital role, incorporating the two main channels for merger-induced innovation effects: (i) internalization of the negative externality of innovation that the merging parties impose on each other, and (ii) product-market channel. That type of model provides some essential insights into the likely net effect of merger's innovation and consumer welfare.

In their 2017 paper, Federico, Langus, and Valletti assume that the firms in their model do not make any profits in the absence of innovation. This assumption implies that innovation does not actually cannibalize any pre-existing profits and that the product-market competition channel can only serve to promote and enhance innovation. The authors further assume that there are no merger-induced efficiencies and that the effects on innovation are based solely on changes to the competition between the merging parties. Finally, their model focuses on the case of stochastic product innovation (as opposed to process innovation), which means that research is assumed to be an uncertain activity and that the number of labs that succeed in finding a treatment is random.

In the first stage of the game, the firms engage in some costly R&D efforts, which determine the probability of discovering/inventing a new homogenous product (i.e., successful innovation).[547] In the second stage, the firms observe the outcome of

---

[544] Federico et al., *supra* note 489.

[545] Jullien & Lefouili, *supra* note 460, at 3.

[546] Federico et al., *supra* note 489; *See also* Giulio Federico, Gregor Langus & Tommaso Valletti, *Horizontal Mergers and Product Innovation*, 59 Int'l J. Indus. Org. 1 (2018), https://www.researchgate.net/publication/318392882_Horizontal_Mergers_and_Product_Innovation.

[547] Federico et al. (2018), *supra* note 546.

the first stage and receive their payoffs. In this sense, their model is an illustration of the *innovation diversion effect* in merger analysis. In their 2017 paper, the authors consider N (identical) research labs that compete to invent a product to serve a new market, e.g., pharmaceutical labs trying to develop a new treatment for a disease. When several new products made available to consumers in the market, and competition erodes the firms' profits, the innovations of the undertakings divert each other's sales. In this model, the authors assume that competition between three or more products erodes all profits. Therefore, an investor can expect to gain profits only if it is the sole successful inventor in the relevant market or if there is only one other successful inventor.[548]

Federico, Langus, and Valletti then analyze the effects of a merger between two research labs. In this scenario, they assume that the two research units remain separate, but the merged entity coordinates the research efforts exerted in each research lab. If the merged entity continues to invest (the same amount) in R&D activities at both research units, the authors conclude that a merged entity controlling both research labs would invest less in R&D than two independent research labs. The fundamental idea behind their argument is that, when determining its investment level in one research lab, the merged entity discounts the fact that a successful innovation at that lab would divert (i.e., cannibalize) sales from the product(s) discovered by the other research lab, if both labs succeeded simultaneously at their research efforts. Thus, the authors claim that the merged entity would then decide to invest less in R&D because it internalizes the sales externality. They also contend that, for concentrated industries, the reaction of non-merging firms regarding R&D will not be sufficient to offset the reduction of innovation by the merging firms.[549]

The same authors have chosen to examine the innovation effects of horizontal mergers in another paper (published in 2018), by considering the interaction of two separate and competitive channels: (i) the channel of price coordination and (ii) the channel of innovation externality.[550]

Price coordination relates to the elimination of price competition between the merging firms. The authors admit that the effect of price coordination on innovation incentives remains ambiguous. Moreover, they state that if the merger increases pre-innovation profits in the product market to a greater extent than it increases post-innovation profits, then price coordination will introduce downward pressure on the merging firms' incentive to innovate. If the converse is true, price coordination will exert upward pressure on the merged entity's incentive to innovate. Which of the two directions will prevail would be determined depending on the specific assumptions made on the nature of the competition. According to the model put forth by the authors, the reduction in the intensity of price competition following a merger tends to favor and enhance innovation.

The authors above believe that innovative activities by one party cause a reduction in profit to the second party – whether or not the latter has innovated – the first merging

---

[548]   Jullien & Lefouili, *supra* note 460, at 11.
[549]   *Id.* at 11–12.
[550]   Federico et al. (2018), *supra* note 546.

firm must divert profitable post-innovation sales to the other party. However, if the second party to the merger has not innovated, then innovation by the first merging firm cannibalizes the pre-innovation sales. Ultimately, the merged firm internalizes the negative externality caused by the innovation effort. In the model set forth by Federico et al. (2018), a merger, therefore, exerts downward pressure on the innovation incentives of the merging firms via the innovation externality channel.[551]

The authors analyze the interaction of the price coordination and innovation externality channels in the context of a merger by considering symmetric oligopoly where firms invest in improving the quality of their products and assume that an innovation replaces an old product with a new, better (i.e., higher quality) product. The authors then examine the effects of a merger between two firms on the incentives to innovate, assuming away any spillover effects or efficiencies. For this purpose, they separate the impact of a merger into two terms: one term summing up the consequences of unilateral effects in prices on innovation, and another one measuring the innovation diversion effect. The authors do not attempt to solve the model analytically but rather discuss the effects at work and perform some numerical simulations. As a result, they reach two conclusions:

a) Their simulations indicate that there are conflicting effects in the models they consider: the effect of the merger on the pre- and post-innovation price equilibrium increases the incentives to innovate, while the innovation diversion effect reduces these incentives.

b) In their simulations, the innovation externality channel overcomes the countervailing effect of the price coordination channel. The innovation diversion effect dominates so that the overall impact of a merger on the merging firms' innovation efforts is *negative*, and so is the ultimate effect of the merger on consumers.

Therefore, the authors determine that the innovation effort of the merging parties decreases following the merger. Moreover, the negative effect on innovation incentives tends to be more pronounced when the merging parties are close competitors. The non-merging firms increase their innovation efforts following a merger, but this increase does not compensate for the reduction of innovation efforts by the merging firms, which implies that the total amount of innovation in the relevant market falls after the merger. Thus, the authors find that the merger has a welfare-reducing effect on consumers.[552]

Federico, Langus, and Valletti also consider the innovation-related efficiencies that a merger may bring forth, including reductions in R&D costs and merger-specific enhancements in innovation effectiveness. They do not, however, proceed to model involuntary knowledge spillovers. The authors admit that both the findings on innovation incentives and consumer welfare can be overturned and invalidated if there are sufficiently large R&D efficiencies.[553]

---

[551]   *Id.* at 2.
[552]   *Id.* at 14.
[553]   *Id.* at 2.

Both of the studies conducted by Federico, Langus and Valletti were based on innovation at the *"product"* level. Motta and Tarantino,[554] on the other hand, focus on the effects of mergers on *"process"* innovation (which reduces the cost of production) in their baseline model. They also analyze the effects of a merger on quality-improving innovations in an extension of their model.

In their analysis, Motta and Tarantino assume that firms simultaneously set both cost-reducing investment levels and prices. Therefore, investment decisions are presumed to be unobservable. Pre-merger firms sell one differentiated product, and the merger creates a new multi-product firm that offers two product varieties. In this way, the merger breaks the symmetry in the industry. Subsequently, the authors demonstrate that, under no (or weak enough) efficiency savings, a merger will reduce aggregate investments and harm consumers. This net effect will be the result of the decrease in investments and rise in prices on the part of the merging parties (i.e., insiders), and the increase in investments, with prices that may either increase or decrease, on the part of the non-merging parties (i.e., outsiders).[555]

The authors find that the merger will have pro-competitive effects only if the merger-driven cost savings in investments are sufficiently high. Under weak or no efficiency gains, the authors suggest that the merger will always result in the insiders raising their prices and reducing their investments, because the merged entity internalizes that a price decrease for one of its products will reduce the consumer demand for the other product it sells, and this dynamic leads to an upward pressure in prices compared to the pre-merger case. In turn, higher prices will lead to lower quantities of the product being sold by the insiders, and to lower marginal revenues from investing for the insiders, the insiders' investments will be reduced.[556]

In the standard models of mergers concerning price-setting firms, without considering investments, outsiders' prices will also increase due to strategic complementarity. However, this is not always the case in Motta and Tarantino's model. According to their model, when the insiders increase their prices, the prices of the outsiders increase, too. The outsiders, however, use lower prices, and therefore demand and market shares tend to rise, ultimately will increase their (cost-reducing) investment levels. The authors demonstrate that, at equilibrium, depending on the particular assumptions made about the type of demand function, the prices of outsiders may either increase or decrease.[557]

Motta and Tarantino admit that the net effects of a merger are not apparent a priori, since a merger may have different effects on insiders' and outsiders' prices and investments, and since undertakings sell differentiated products. In an alternative model, the authors assume that each firm chooses to determine either price or investment. They analyze the

---

[554]   Massimo Motta & Emanuele Tarantino, *The Effect of Horizontal Mergers, When Firms Compete in Prices and Investments* (University of Mannheim, Department of Economics, Working Paper No. 17-01, Sept. 2017), https://ub-madoc.bib.uni-mannheim.de/42805/1/17-01_Motta%2C%20Tarantino.pdf.

[555]   *Id.* at 2.

[556]   *Id.*

[557]   *Id.*

outcome of this model using an aggregative game theory formulation, where the payoff received by a player depends on its own actions and an additively separable aggregate of all the players' actions.[558]

With this alternative modeling, the authors can show that – absent efficiency gains – the merger hurts consumer surplus. Moreover, this result holds for classes of demand functions, such as the constant elasticity of substitution ("CES") demand and the logit demand, and for the standard parametric product differentiation models – such as the Shubik – Levitan model and the Salop circle models. The authors demonstrate that the merger will be pro-competitive and boost investments if it allows and enables the firms to benefit from strong enough efficiency gains in terms of R&D.[559] Unfortunately, these are not heard by competition authorities as a sufficient defense and are generally overlooked through focus on effect on innovation incentives.

Motta and Tarantino also extend their analysis in several new directions, by considering the scenario in which the firms in the relevant market offer asymmetric goods. As a result, a merger between any two firms will reduce consumer welfare because they identify sufficient conditions for the merger to reduce aggregate investments.[560] If a merger allows for incentives and conditions to increase aggregate investments, would R&D investments be exempt from this trend? A merger potentially raising prices would also increase the marginal profitability of investments.

The authors also analyze the effects of a merger in which the firms undertake quality-enhancing investments. Within a general model, the results of this assumption are a priori ambiguous: on the one hand, the merger will raise prices, and this, in turn, will increase the marginal profitability of investments; on the other hand, the merged entity will internalize the fact that increasing the quality of one product reduces the attractiveness (and profits) of its other product, and this will reduce its incentives to invest. However, Motta and Tarantino illustrate that the merger harms consumers under some broad classes of models with quality-enhancing investments (e.g., vertical product differentiation models).[561]

Motta and Tarantino have also modified the "*simultaneous game*" assumption, and they have analyzed the case of a *sequential game*, where the firms invest first, all observe their choice, and they then choose prices. They have concluded that the presence of strategic effects makes it difficult to establish propositions of general validity about the effects of a merger in this scenario. The authors also note that an aggregative game theory formulation for the sequential game is not possible. Nonetheless, the analysis of parametric models confirms the qualitative results that were reached for the *simultaneous moves* case: (i) the merger harms consumers; (ii) it increases the prices and decreases the investments of the insiders; (iii) it increases the investments of the outsiders; and (iv) it may either decrease or increase the prices of the outsiders.

---

[558]   *Id.*
[559]   *Id.* at 3.
[560]   *Id.*
[561]   *Id.*

3.4.4.2 Contestability

According to Shapiro, one of the three fundamental principles that should be taken into account in assessing the effects of mergers on innovation is *contestability*. Contestability refers to the situation in which rivals can challenge the incumbent position(s) in a particular market. For innovation to flourish, the market needs to remain contestable. Shapiro explains this principle briefly as follows: "The prospect of gaining or protecting profitable sales by providing greater value to customers spurs innovation."[562]

The contestability principle focuses on the extent to which a firm can take away profitable sales from its rivals by offering greater value to the customers. Sales are characterized as *contestable* if profitable sales shift towards the successful innovator, depending on the nature of *ex post* product-market competition.

If market shares are sticky, for example, because consumers have strong brand preferences or face high switching costs, relatively few sales will be contestable, and innovation incentives will be muted. If customers are tied to their existing suppliers, relatively few customers will be able to switch to the new product. In such a case, a limited amount of the sales will be contestable, and a company's incentive to innovate will be lower than in a market where customers can switch products often and market shares are not sticky.[563]

According to Shapiro, the Arrow effect fits well with the contestability principle: for a given level of *ex post* sales, a firm with scant *ex ante* sales has more to gain from innovation. To put it differently, a firm that will make substantial sales even if it does not innovate (such as Arrow's incumbent monopolist that faces no competitive threat) would have muted/lower incentives to innovate.[564]

Shapiro argues that the Schumpeter effect also fits well with the contestability principle: companies generating major innovations are often rewarded with large market shares, leading to high *ex post* market concentration. Conversely, a small firm that will not be able to grow much, even if it successfully innovates, has lower incentives to invest in R&D than a larger firm.[565]

The Commission agrees with Shapiro, in that it considers contestability to be in line with both Schumpeter's and Arrow's theories. The Commission expresses the view that Arrow and Schumpeter both accept and recognize that markets need to remain contestable for innovation to flourish.[566] In the Schumpeterian sense, though, the sheer *ex post* market concentration or *ex post* growth potential of the merged entity should not, in and of itself, be seen as negating contestability, and this might actually be the very reason why the merger might stimulate innovation in the mid-term. If, for example, a "trickling of future profits into innovation" argument is introduced by the

---

[562] Shapiro, *supra* note 442, at 364.
[563] *Id.*
[564] *Id.*
[565] *Id.*
[566] European Commission, *supra* note 444, at 2.

merging parties, the antitrust agency should not dismiss this offhand for being "not case-specific and quantifiable" but should rather see it as a sign that they should do a thorough and case-specific analysis of whether there are demonstrable reasons in the market (such as the innovation dependency and vulnerability of market power in that particular market) before placing parties under a burden of proof of efficiencies and synergies, especially if there are also countervailing appropriability gains through the merger. When antitrust agencies put too much emphasis on concentration levels and market shares in the innovation effects analysis, they miss the true core of contestability issues, as contestability revolves around the nature of consumer preferences and the content of the specific innovation at stake rather than market shares and concentration.

3.4.4.3 Product-Market Rivalry

Aghion et al. have shown that innovation efforts depend on the particular structure of the product market and that the rate of patent development increases with competition up until a certain point, after which it starts to decrease (i.e., exhibiting an inverted-U-shaped relationship).[567] Their model shows that between high levels and low levels of competition, the balance points between two effects change, and this creates an "inverted U" shape. According to them, if competition increases, neck-and-neck firms may engage in more innovation to distinguish themselves from competitors because competition may increase the incremental profit of more innovation and getting ahead (the "escape competition effect").[568] On the other hand, competition may reduce the prospective returns of innovation because of the rapid imitation of the innovation by competitors (the "Schumpeterian effect").[569]

Their model reveals that if there is a low degree of competition, there is not sufficient incentive for neck-and-neck firms to innovate, and thus, the innovation rate increases where the industry is in an unleveled state. Accordingly, in such cases, the predominant influence is the "escape competition effect," where the innovation rate increases with an increase in competition. However, in industries where the starting level of competition is very high, laggard firms will have little incentive to innovate in an unleveled state under the "Schumpeterian effect" since their profit would not be large enough to incentivize them to innovate, and the leader firm will not innovate. Hence, if the competition level is already high, an increase in competition will reduce the average innovation rate. Therefore, the overall effect draws an inverted U where industries are distributed across the increasing and decreasing sections of the U-shape. This "inverted U-shaped relationship" is illustrated below:

---

[567] AGHION & GRIFFITH, *supra* note 454, at 701–28.
[568] *Id.* at 714.
[569] *Id.* at 714, 720.

**Figure 1: The inverted U-shaped relationship
between patent development and competition**

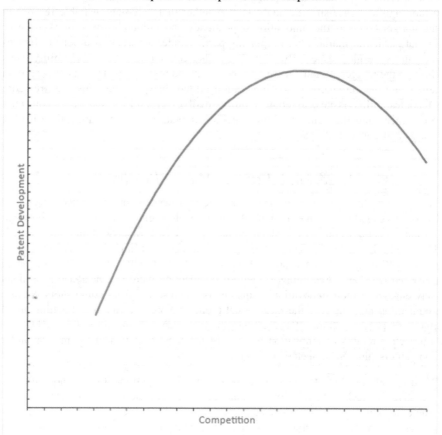

However, Federico, Langus and Valletti argue that the inverted-U relationship between innovation and some measure of competition does not have an immediate counterpart in a merger setting, at least insofar as the innovation output of the merged firm is concerned.[570]

According to Federico et al., one of the channels through which horizontal mergers affect the incentive to innovate is the *product-market competition channel*. They state that, through the product-market competition channel, a merger internalizes the negative price externality, which leads to an ambiguous result regarding innovation: lower price competition increases the profits of the merging parties, whether or not they innovate. Moreover, a price increase in the post-innovation period reduces the benefit that the consumers receive. The effect of the *innovation competition* channel

---

[570]   Federico et al., *supra* note 489, at 8.

(where a merger internalizes the negative innovation externality),[571] combined with the *product-market* channel, could result in a reduction in innovation efforts and an increase in post-innovation prices.[572] They conclude that (i) a merger always decreases the competitive drive for innovation among merging parties; (ii) although the outsider firms respond by increasing their innovation efforts, mergers are likely to reduce overall innovation.[573] In more detail, according to the model set out in the paper, the decrease in the innovation efforts of the merging parties always dominates the increase in the efforts of the outsiders in a concentrated industry, whereas the rise of innovation by outsiders prevails in a fragmented industry where (i) the merged entity continued innovation in both labs of the transaction party and (ii) the prize that the merged party gets in case labs of each transaction party succeed in innovation and only one rival makes the same discovery is close to zero.[574] Finally, the authors argue that mergers always decrease consumer welfare because not only of the change in innovation efforts but also of the price coordination effect.[575] The relevant conclusions are illustrated thus:

Figure 2: Difference between post- and pre-merger innovation effort

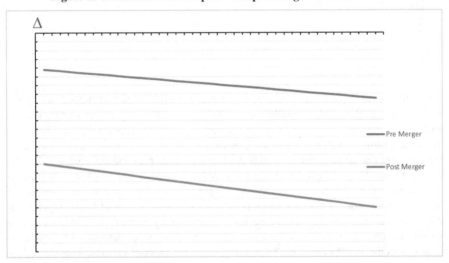

---

[571] This refers to the negative effect that innovation by one of the merging parties may have on the profits of the other merging party.

[572] Giulio Federico, *Horizontal Mergers, Innovation and the Competitive Process*, 8 J. Eur. Competition L. & Prac. 668 (2017).

[573] Federico et al., *supra* note 489, at 1.

[574] *Id*. at. 4, 5, 6.

[575] *Id*. at 7, 8.

Figure 3: Difference between post- and pre-merger consumer surplus

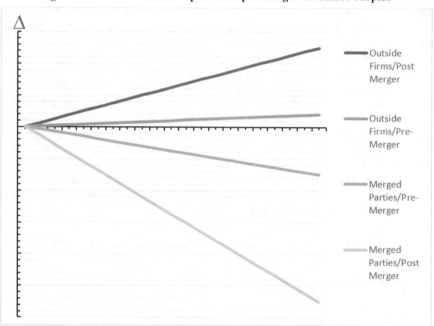

On Aghion et al.'s study, it should be noted that even if the relationship set out by the authors is true, it would be challenging to use this relationship in the merger control analysis setting since, in order to create a theory of harm/or approval decision based on this relationship, one should know the exact shape of the curve of the market subject to the case and the graph point on which the market stands pre- and post-merger.[576] With respect to the study of Federico, Langus and Valletti, as also noted by the authors, they explore the effect of only two channels on merging parties' incentive to innovate. Nevertheless, they do not consider the situation where the transactions lead to efficiencies that may increase the merging parties' incentive to innovate post-merger.[577] Moreover, it is worth exploring in more detail the cases where the increase of innovation by outsiders may overcome the decrease in the innovation of the merged entities. Therefore, it is difficult to formulate assumptions that could be used in specific merger analyses based on the foregoing studies.

3.4.4.4 Appropriability

According to Shapiro, appropriability is one of the factors that should be taken into account as an essential determinant of post-merger incentives to invest. Appropriability refers to the ability of an innovator to benefit from its investments. It is "the extent to

---

[576]   OECD, *Dynamic Efficiencies in Merger Analysis* 28 (Policy Roundtables, DAF/COMP(2007)41, May 15, 2008), https://www.oecd.org/daf/competition/mergers/40623561.pdf.
[577]   *Id.* at. 8.

which a firm can capture the value created by its innovation and protect the competitive advantage associated with it."[578]

Shapiro contends that increased appropriability increases the incentive to innovate.[579] Intellectual property rights (such as patents) can offer adequate protection for innovations. If competitors can easily imitate or "patent around" an invention, the successful innovator will not be able to differentiate its products or maintain cost advantages, and it will not be able to increase its profit margins through innovation. Therefore, the incentive of such a firm to innovate will be minimal. If imitation occurs quickly, an innovator can hardly offer more value to the customers than its rivals, and the principle of contestability, as discussed above, loses its importance and becomes insignificant.[580,581]

A firm that can appropriate the benefits of its innovations will have stronger incentives to invest in the first place than a firm whose innovations can be rapidly copied and reproduced.[582] Appropriability can be a factor that balances the negative effects of a merger on innovation caused by the internalization of the cannibalization effect.[583,584]

The degree of appropriability depends on the effectiveness of IP rights and whether rival firms are innovating (or are perceived to be innovating) in the same area.[585] If a firm that plans to invest in the development of a new product faces a risk that numerous rivals may also invest in developing new competing products, which can take sales away from it, then the firm may be discouraged from investing in the development of the product in question. As the number of potential rival innovators increases, the expected returns that a firm can hope to obtain from its R&D investment decreases, and it may reach the point where the firm may choose to refrain from investing in the project in the first place.[586]

Scale helps with appropriability. Scale being scarce, an R&D investment that is enabled by scale will also contain a built-in defense against rapid imitation. Especially if IP rights are not strong, and if certain companies are in the same innovation space, their merger might bring about a dynamism in terms of innovation through new prospects of higher profits protected by the sale demanded for such investments. Today, this defense would be found speculative in merger control, and appropriability being low would always be seen as a reason to believe innovation is vulnerable pre-merger, and not a candidate for efficiencies post-merger.

According to Shapiro, the Schumpeter effect fits well with the appropriability principle: one cannot expect substantial innovative efforts from undertakings if rapid imitation causes *ex post* competition to be so severe in the relevant market that even a successful

---

[578]   European Commission, *supra* note 444, at 1.

[579]   Shapiro, *supra* note 442, at 364.

[580]   *Id.*

[581]   Seiler, *supra* note 445, at 6.

[582]   Johnson, *supra* note 440.

[583]   RBB Economics, *supra* note 490, at 1.

[584]   Shapiro explains this principle succinctly as follows: "Increased appropriability spurs innovation." *See* Shapiro, *supra* note 442, at 364.

[585]   RBB Economics, *supra* note 490, at 2.

[586]   *Id.*

innovator earns little in profits.[587] However, Seiler has pointed out that when appropriability is already high (for instance, because of strong IP rights for product innovations), a merger does not further increase the incentive to innovate.[588]

Baker, Shapiro, Gilbert, and Greene have all posited in their studies that a merger between two out of a few rival innovators is likely to reduce product innovation incentives in the relevant market if (i) pre-merger appropriability is high (resulting from the fact that innovators acquire an effective exclusive right to their innovation, with limited knowledge spillovers), and (ii) there are no merger-related efficiencies.[589] Similarly, the results of Arrow, as well as Greenstein and Ramey, suggest that a secure product-market monopolist has fewer incentives to innovate than a firm facing product-market competition.[590]

In this regard, Gilbert concludes that, for process innovations that reduce marginal production costs, innovation incentives are lower for a monopoly protected from both product and R&D competition than for a competitive firm, provided that the innovator maintains exclusive rights to the innovation. However, it is worth noting that allowing for competition in R&D can reverse this effect. With non-exclusive intellectual property rights, competition can lower incentives to invest in process R&D by reducing each firm's output, and hence, its return from attaining lower costs. Incentives are more complicated for new products because profits depend on a firm's product portfolio, and even competitive firms are likely to earn profits if they offer and supply differentiated products to their customers. Nonetheless, the results for product innovations are similar to those for process innovations if the new product is sufficiently attractive to make the existing products obsolete.[591]

Kwoka, in his examination of the effects of mergers on innovation, focused on the R&D in the US pharmaceutical sector based on various studies that analyzed the significant mergers that took place since 1998 in the sector. He notes that studies have actually shown that mergers in this sector have not resulted in increases in innovation output or in R&D expenditure, and in fact, "various metrics for innovation on average decline by several percentage points in the first few years after the merger" under certain circumstances.[592] Kwoka emphasizes that these studies have empirically tested and found no support for the proposition that innovation (R&D) has benefited from mergers in the pharmaceutical sector. On the contrary, despite changing the sector's structure significantly, these mergers have failed to produce new molecules and drug therapies and even seem to have adversely affected R&D.[593]

In the *Dow/DuPont* merger, although the Commission did acknowledge that appropriability was a factor that could positively affect post-merger incentives to innovate, it

---

587   Shapiro, *supra* note 442

588   Seiler, *supra* note 445, at 17.

589   Federico et al. (2018), *supra* note 546, at 3.

590   *Id.*

591   Gilbert, *supra* note 439 at 204.

592   John Kwoka, *The Effects of Mergers on Innovation: Economic Framework and Empirical Evidence, in* THE ROLES OF INNOVATION IN COMPETITION LAW ANALYSIS 13, 23–24 (Paul Nihoul & Pieter Van Cleynenbreugel eds., Edward Elgar Publishing 2008).

593   *Id.* at 32.

did not find it necessary to engage in a balancing exercise between the cannibalization and appropriability effects. Instead, the Commission primarily relied on the theoretical economics papers, claiming that these provided a rational basis and support for the conclusion that cannibalization is inherently likely to outweigh appropriability and that horizontal mergers can, therefore, be expected to impact innovation incentives negatively.[594] The assumption that cannibalization is inherently likely to outweigh appropriability in *Dow/DuPont* is also a part of the asymmetry and paradox we discuss here. The Commission's reliance on theoretical economic papers is allowed, but this is not the case for the transaction parties' defenses. A complex balancing analysis is needed between cannibalization and appropriability without assumptions as to one dominating the other.

Although the Commission relies upon economic theories in its assessments, it is imperative that merger control is conducted on a case-by-case basis, especially where innovation-centric industries are concerned, where a one-size-fits-all method can hardly be deemed valid. Let alone responding to case-specific parameters and fact-based defenses with reliance on theoretical economic papers, it should be recognized as the duty of the antitrust agencies to engage in specific concrete economic analysis to exclude the possibility of relevance of theoretical arguments presented by defense counsel. Mergers with a significant innovation dimension require significant and specific analysis of concrete facts and parameters without resorting to reliance on assumptions of general theoretical economic papers, as a case-specific balancing act can only be undertaken with concrete analysis to exclude the possibility of relevance of theoretical arguments, facts and parameters of that case, which, in turn, requires adequate weight to be given to the case-specific defenses, even if they are to be dismissed on concrete case-specific grounds. This reinforces the need for a flexible approach and analysis of the relevant effects for each particular case *in concreto*, which may merit a more lenient look to those mergers in dynamic sectors that can give rise to specific efficiencies.[595] Moreover, Régibeau et al. argue that (assuming that the authorities will be correctly addressing the conventional, static competition issues of the transaction) the effect of a merger on innovation should also be assessed on the *additional factors* it gives rise to, not just the efficiencies that may arise due to economies of scale or scope, or the sharing of R&D resources.[596] They list these additional efficiency factors under (i) knowledge diffusion within the merged entity, (ii) spillovers, (iii) appropriability, (iv) coordination of R&D investments, (v) sequential innovation, and (vi) legal certainty issues regarding IP rights.[597] Through these factors, as well as any significant overlaps in the merging parties' product lines, or the availability of licensing in the technology markets, the authors provide a "policy-algorithm" framework and flow charts for competition authorities to follow where innovation factors play a material role in the merger. Their policy algorithm demonstrates that while novel theories of harm are not sector-specific, mergers with a significant innovation dimension require extensive analysis by the relevant authority, on a case-by-case basis. Appropriability effects and prospects of sequential innovation, and positive spillover effects for future innovations are underrated components of case-specific analysis by antitrust agencies.

---

[594]   RBB Economics, *supra* note 490, at 2.
[595]   Pierre Régibeau & Katharine E. Rockett, *Mergers and Innovation*, 64 ANTITRUST BULL. 31 (2019).
[596]   *Id.*
[597]   *Id.* at 38.

3.5 Innovation Defenses by Applicant Entities in Merger Control: A Survey on Existing Arguments

3.5.1 Incentives to Innovate

The merger control regimes in both the EU and the US adopt a consumer welfare approach. It clearly defines the scope and the extent of innovation defenses that could be raised by the merging parties.

In the *Dow/DuPont* merger, the submissions of the merging parties to the Commission put forth the various innovation defenses currently in use.[598] The applicants presented various theoretical arguments to demonstrate that the *Dow/DuPont* merger could lead to higher incentives to innovate, even in the absence of efficiencies. On that note, the parties offered two economic submissions that identified six separate channels through which the merger could lead to higher incentives to innovate.[599] Having said this, the Commission pointed out within its decision that some of the arguments offered in the parties' submissions on why a merger could positively affect innovation incentives in general had not been specific to the *Dow/DuPont* merger.[600]

According to the merging parties, the channels that could lead to higher incentives to innovate were as follows:[601]

1. Higher returns to R&D investment when firms compete in R&D: A reduction in the number of independent competitors in R&D may increase the return to R&D efforts and thereby increase innovation.

2. Reduced uncertainty in R&D competition: The possible reduction of uncertainty in R&D competition as a result of the merger can also stimulate innovation.

3. Reduction of imitation: A merger may increase the rewards to innovation by lessening information spillovers to competing firms and thus reduce imitation.

4. Higher scale: A merger may increase the return to innovation by allowing the merged entity to attain higher sales and, hence, enable it to appropriate more of the value of innovation if this is proportional to sales.

---

[598] Some other cases discussing incentives to innovate are Medtronic/Covidien, European Commission Decision case COMP/M.7326 (Nov. 28, 2014); *BMS/Celgene*; CMA, Acquisition by Mastercard UK Holdco Limited of VocaLink Holdings (2017; CMA, BT Group plc and EE Limited: A Report on the Anticipated Acquisition by BT Group plc of EE Limited (Jan. 15, 2016); CMA, Completed Acquisition by Tobii AB of Smartbox Assistive Technologies Limited and Sensory Software International Ltd (Final Report) (Aug. 15, 2019); In re Danaher Corp., No. C-4710 (F.T.C. 2021).

[599] The European Commission has declared that they assume that "all of theoretical arguments raised are in principle applicable to the Transaction according to the two economic submissions."

[600] *Dow/DuPont*, annex 4, recital 25, n. 7.

[601] *Id.*, annex 4, recital 25.

5. Product complementarities: A merger may allow a firm to capture a greater value of its innovation by combining it with complementary products offered by the other merging party (and vice versa), in ways that had not been feasible prior to the merger.

6. Cost synergies: A merger may reduce the cost of R&D activities via merger-specific synergies, and therefore stimulate innovation.

In the *Dow/DuPont* case, the merging parties argued that only the *"cost synergies"* channel should be assessed as a merger-specific efficiency. According to the undertakings, the other alleged pro-innovation effects should be considered within the overall competitive assessment of the transaction.[602] Therefore, these arguments can be interpreted as possible defenses in a typical horizontal merger. However, do arguments offered on why a merger could potentially affect innovation incentives in general need to be specific to that merger? Does not such a submission, if credible, still drive the standards of proof of the Commission on the point of potential loss of innovation incentives in the future?

Incumbent position and market power might not mean the same thing in innovation-dependent markets; for example, when there is low ecosystem emergence challenge and low ecosystem expansion opportunity, the expanding borders of the products and the cannibalization by the more innovative versions of the same product would make the market extremely innovation dependent. The innovation incentive consequences of a proposed concentration might not be subject to the easy Arrowian formula of "more competitive market structures result in more innovation incentives" if the particular market at hand imposes innovation as a condition of market power even in the short term. If innovation is deterministic and indispensable for the continuation of market power in a given market, the proof of this point by defense counsel should move antitrust agencies away from the assumptions of Arrow's prediction that a more competitive market structure will always necessarily lead to stronger incentives to innovate.

The existence of potential competition, the vulnerability of the incumbent to competitive threats, whether innovation has become the main parameter of competition in that market, whether innovation of new products might address new and different customers (leading to innovation diversion effects) and whether innovation of new processes might lead to cost efficiencies should all be analyzed before submitting the case to Arrow's predictions. Otherwise, in innovation-dependent markets, we would always be starting from an initial assumption point that a merger will always be likely to impede incentives to innovate, and this would, in turn, lead to an undue placement of the burden of proof of case-specific and quantifiable efficiencies and case-specific synergies and proof of innovation incentives on the merging parties. This, in turn, feeds the innovation paradox and asymmetry in merger control analysis, while leading to erroneous rejection decisions, and therefore inefficient commitments by the transaction parties. For the parties to be placed under a burden of proof of case-specific and quantifiable efficiencies and synergies, the antitrust agencies should first prove beyond reasonable doubt that, in the particular case at hand, Arrow's predictions do apply.

---

[602]   *Id.*, recitals 25, 26.

The Commission reported that both submissions of the merging parties in the *Dow/DuPont* case claimed that the well-known prediction of Arrow that firms in a competitive market structure are likely to face stronger incentives to innovate than firms in a more concentrated market is not always valid. According to the merging parties, Arrow's prediction may not hold if the parties compete in R&D, since, in this scenario, an incumbent firm may face stronger incentives to invest than a new entrant to the market. This stems from the fact that the incumbent may be investing in protecting its existing monopoly profits, while the latter would only be able to realize (lower) competitive profits after a successful innovation and its subsequent entry to the market. The economic submissions of the merging parties noted that Arrow's conclusion could be reversed in the case of an insecure monopolist threatened by competition. In that case (assuming that innovation is deterministic), the vulnerable monopolist may face incentives to pre-empt entry in order to protect its existing market power.[603] The European Commission noted that this result relies on the Gilbert and Newbery study, discussed below.[604,605]

When analyzing the relationship between competition and innovation, Gilbert and Newbery developed a simple alternative model in which a potential entrant threatens the monopolist in the relevant market.[606] In this model, the monopolist possesses an old technology (or product) and considers investing in R&D activities to develop and introduce new technology. Gilbert and Newberry assume that if the monopolist innovates, then the potential entrant will not enter the relevant market. In other words, the entrant will only enter the market if it possesses new technology. Hence, there are two distinct scenarios: either the monopolist innovates and remains a monopolist in the relevant market, or the entrant innovates, and a duopoly emerges. In this context of firm-level innovation, Arrow's prediction about the incentives to innovate will be reversed. In this model, the profit level of the monopolist using the old technology does not matter to the analysis because the entrant will enter the market with the new technology if the monopolist does not innovate. Therefore, the monopolist will compare its *ex post* monopoly profits after successful innovation with its profits to be gained under the duopoly condition if it does not innovate. The monopolist may even consider adopting some sort of fast defensive measure in the meantime and create barriers to entry, e.g., by way of pseudo-innovation mimicking the new technology, which could slow down new entrants and buy the monopolist time to assess the future of the market before investing.

On the other hand, the incentive of the entrant to innovate is measured simply by its duopoly profits. The monopolist's incentive to innovate will be at least as high as the entrant's incentive, as the *ex post* monopoly profit will always be at least as large as the sum of both duopoly profits. Indeed, both incentives will only be equal if the old technology becomes obsolete. This model explains the "*efficiency effect*" and the "*competitive threat*" by others. A dominant firm has more to lose in profits if it is a competitor (rather than the monopolist) that innovates in the relevant market. Thus, it is clear that the underlying factor behind

---

[603]   *Id.* at recital 75.
[604]   *Id.* at 72, 514–26.
[605]   Richard Gilbert & David Newbery, *Preemptive Patenting and the Persistence of Monopoly*, 72 AM. ECON. REV. 514 (1982).
[606]   *Id.*

this effect is a competitive threat.[607] On the other hand, Jullien and Lefouili have asserted that the "*innovation diversion effect*," which had been analyzed by Federico et al. in a simple model of mergers, can be viewed as providing only one of the factors that should be considered when evaluating the innovation effects in merger assessments. They believe it would be misleading to conclude that mergers are always likely to impede incentives to innovate (in the absence of efficiency gains) due to the innovation diversion effect.[608] An innovation that results in a product enhancement would divert sales from competing firms, whereas innovation of new products, which address different customers, may benefit the competing firms as it relaxes price competition.[609] Since the firm's innovation increases the demand for competitors' products, the innovation diversion effect would be positive. This would mean that merging firms would be more willing to invest in R&D to invent new products, compared to the situation without merger.[610]

Arrow's conclusion depends on the assumption that the competitive situation is modeled in the context of a homogenous commodity under perfect competition. In an oligopolistic market with product differentiation, Arrow's prediction would not hold in general, and the monopolist may have a higher incentive to innovate. If a monopolist could sell its old product and the new product simultaneously and use both products to divide its customers into different segments, then the monopolist may have a more significant incentive to innovate, considering that a firm under perfect competition could only gain a positive profit with the new product. In this context, Schulz reports that Greenstein and Ramey provide an example in a vertically differentiated product context and that Gilbert offers an example in a horizontally differentiated product model.[611] Therefore, the conclusions from Arrow's analysis are not universally applicable.

According to the merging parties, an incumbent firm may also face stronger incentives to innovate than a competitive firm if it can capture greater market value by combining the new product with its existing product. The European Commission observed that this claim relies on the study conducted by Chen and Schwartz.[612] The submissions of the merging parties also noted that Arrow's conclusion does not apply to non-drastic product innovations that allow a (secure) incumbent to horizontally differentiate its product offers to its customers, as Chen and Schwartz have shown in their work. In that case, the incumbent would be able to extract more value from a new product than a new entrant that faces (perfect) competition from the old product.[613]

607　Schulz, *supra* note 448. Although most studies have focused on firm-level innovation, the effect of mergers on industry-level innovation was also brought into focus by the authorities, as described further below. Research on public companies has shown that innovation at the industry or country level, although depending on the business environment and dynamism of the relevant sector, will have a significant effect at the organization level, through agglomeration benefits or spillover effects. *See* Yufei Zhang, G. Tomas M. Hult, David J. Ketchen Jr. & Roger J. Calantone, *Effects of Firm-, Industry-, and Country-Level Innovation on Firm Performance*, 31 Mktg. Letters 231 (2020), https://doi.org/10.1007/s11002-020-09530-y.

608　Jullien & Lefouili, *supra* note 460, at 12.

609　*Id*. at 13.

610　*Id*.

611　*Id*. at 9.

612　*Dow/DuPont*, 513–28, Annex 4, recital 25, n. 7.

613　The Commission mentioned that this result depends on the nature of product differentiation and does not apply in the case of vertical product differentiation. The authors also showed that a monopolist would have stronger incentives to introduce a high-quality product in comparison to a duopolist.

By relying on the findings of the two articles, it appears that the merging parties in *Dow/DuPont* intended to argue that a merger that reduces product-market competition may nevertheless stimulate innovation by either increasing the scope for price differentiation by incumbent firms (on the basis of the economic mechanism highlighted by Chen and Schwartz) and/or by strengthening the pre-emption incentives faced by incumbent firms (relying on the results of Gilbert and Newbery's study). However, the Commission rebuffed the submissions of the merging parties by asserting that these economic reports had failed to explain how exactly their results should have been interpreted and applied to the Commission's assessment of the case and concluded that it would, therefore, be difficult for the Commission to assess the reports' arguments accurately.[614]

The merging parties in *Dow/DuPont* argued that, under certain conditions, a less competitive product-market structure might lead to an increase in innovation, generating an inverted-U relationship between product-market competition and innovation by each firm, as described in several studies in the economics literature.[615] They also put forth the following framework for the proper assessment of merger effects on innovation incentives: (i) the incentive to invest in R&D activities is driven by the difference between the expected profits if a firm invests in R&D and the profits that it can earn if it does not invest in R&D; (ii) competition reduces the profits that a firm can earn if it does not invest in R&D – in that sense, a merger, by reducing competition, decreases the incentive to invest in R&D – however (iii) competition also reduces the profits that a firm can earn after it innovates – in that sense, a merger increases incentives to innovate.[616] The merging parties explained that because (ii) and (iii) generate opposing effects, depending on the particular assumptions and facts of the case, a merger could ultimately either positively or negatively impact the innovation incentives in a post-merger market.

The merging parties' submission also referred to the work of Xavier Vives,[617] in order to support their defense argument that a reduction in product-market competition may stimulate innovation. In that regard, the merging parties presented a simple numerical example that demonstrated that a reduction in the number of firms active in the market (e.g., as a result of a merger) could indeed lead to higher industrywide innovation in the framework supplied by Vives.[618] The Commission observed that the merging parties, depending on Vives's work, had argued that "too much competition harms consumers by reducing the incentives for firms to engage in cost-reducing innovation." In this context, it is essential to note that Vives examines process innovation by using several assumptions regarding the competition. For instance, he models a change in competition as a change in the number of firms active in the relevant market. However, the Commission objected to the use of Vives's results as a defense argument because whilst Vives found that process innovation efforts *per firm* tended to decrease with the number of competing firms, he also concluded that total R&D intensity (for example, the amount of cost-reduction expenditures over total sales) typically increased with

---

[614]   *Dow/DuPont*, 513–28, recital 76.
[615]   *Id.*, recital 82.
[616]   *Id.*, recital 115.
[617]   *Id.* at 419–69.
[618]   *Id.*, recital 57.

an increase in the number of firms.[619] The Commission asserted that the underlying reason for this finding was similar to the one from the patent-race literature: while the presence of fewer innovators in the market may make innovation efforts more attractive for each firm, the loss of an independent innovator typically reduces overall innovation. According to the Commission, Vives's results do not support the assertion advanced in the merging parties' submissions that an increase in competition can reduce innovation and harm consumers.[620]

In *Dow/DuPont*, the merging parties claimed that cannibalization considerations did not play a significant role in the investment decisions of crop-protection companies, due to two key market features: (i) biological resistance (i.e., products become obsolete once the targeted pests mutate and develop a resistance to them), and (ii) regulation (i.e., the fact that many pesticides have had their application restricted or banned outright as a result of tightened regulations about toxicity tolerance levels). Biological resistance and regulation considerations have limited the growth of future profits that could be expected to flow from existing products. Dow and DuPont provided evidence to show that the cannibalization effect was not a significant factor in their business decisions since they had largely disregarded over time any effect that new products may have on sales of their existing products when launching new pesticides.[621]

Dow and DuPont also submitted specific evidence highlighting the importance of appropriability considerations in their investment decisions. For example, they showed that the perceived threat of rival innovation in the same product space was a key negative factor in considering the commercial prospects of new active ingredients.[622]

3.5.2 Synergies and Efficiency Gains

In competition law, efficiency is considered in two separate categories: (i) static efficiencies and (ii) dynamic efficiencies. Static efficiencies arise in the short term. Alternatively, dynamic efficiencies are seen as occurring in the more distant future. Furthermore, static efficiencies focus mostly on reductions in marginal costs that might arise from the merger, whereas dynamic efficiencies include (i) the diffusion of know-how, (ii) more efficient use of IP rights, and (iii) increased R&D activities and investment. Dynamic efficiencies might enable firms to improve their business performance potentially in a continuous manner, and they might provide a much more significant benefit than static efficiencies. For instance, mergers may encourage the development of new products or

---

[619] Vives states that in the model with the restricted entry (which is more suitable for merger assessments): "[I]t is still possible, and indeed likely, that increasing the number of firms increases R&D intensity (i.e., cost reduction expenditure over sales)" (at 423). The paper also notes, in relation to models of differentiated pricing, that "a usual measure of the firm's R&D intensity as well as the total R&D intensity is in fact increasing in [the number of firms] *n* in the examples." Xavier Vives, *Innovation and Competitive Pressure*, 56 J. INDUS. ECON. 419, 430 (2008).

[620] *Dow/DuPont.*

[621] RBB Economics, *supra* note 490, at 2.

[622] *Id.* at 3.

help to reduce costs by combining assets and expertise that are not easily transferred between separate companies. Moreover, a merger might also eliminate the duplication of R&D efforts or make it easier to obtain financing for R&D or investment projects. Furthermore, a merger could lead to an increase in investments and improve the existing infrastructure.[623]

According to Shapiro, one of the three principles that should be taken into account in assessing the effects of mergers on innovation is *synergies*. The *"synergies principle"* is about the extent to which combining complementary assets will produce incentives to increase innovation. In some cases, firms are not able to innovate in isolation, especially in industries where value is created by systems that incorporate multiple components and where alternative methods of cooperation are not viable (such as patent pools or joint R&D agreements). In these cases, a merger that leads to the combination of complementary assets can create synergies and thus spur innovation.[624] Shapiro has explained this principle succinctly as: "Combining complementary assets enhances innovation capabilities and thus spurs innovation."[625]

The EU merger control regime recognizes and acknowledges that some mergers may result in synergies arising from innovation, which can offset the anti-competitive effects of the transaction.[626] There have been many cases in which the merging parties have offered arguments regarding the possible efficiency gains of the relevant transaction.[627]

---

[623]   Johnson, *supra* note 440, at 3.

[624]   *Id.* at 2.

[625]   Shapiro, *supra* note 442, at 365.

[626]   European Commission, *supra* note 444, at 1.

[627]   There have been efficiency claims relating to investments in mobile telecommunication networks, which raise similar issues to innovation-related efficiency claims. For instance, in the mobile telecommunication mergers in Ireland and Germany, the Commission analyzed whether the mergers would bring additional material benefits in terms of network coverage, speed, and quality. In both cases, it concluded that any improvements would be limited and could not outweigh the consumer harm and/or would not be merger-specific. *See* Hutchison 3G UK/Telefónica Ireland, European Commission Decision case M.6992 (May 28, 2014), § 7.10, and Telefónica Deutschland/E-Plus, European Commission Decision case M.7018 (July 2, 2014), §§ 6.9, 6.10. There was a similar approach in Ryanair/Aer Lingus III, European Commission Decision case COMP/M.6663 (Feb. 27, 2013), paras. 1649, 1659, 1664, where the Commission noted efficiencies such as a decrease in staff costs could also be achieved independently of the transaction, and given the high market share of the combined entity, the efficiencies were unlikely to be passed on to customers. In UPS/TNT Express, European Commission Decision case M.6570 (Jan. 1, 2013), the Commission prohibited the acquisition of TNT Express by UPS on the grounds that the transaction would significantly impede effective competition in the market for the international express deliveries of small packages in fifteen EU Member Statesand determined that the possible efficiency gains alleged by the parties would not outweigh the price increases. The General Court annulled the Commission's decision, finding that the Commission had infringed UPS' rights of defense by using an econometric analysis that had not been discussed in its final form during the procedure, but did not discuss UPS' other pleas that the Commission erred in law (i) "by setting an arbitrary standard for verifiability of efficiencies" and (ii) "committed a manifest error of assessment in assigning insufficient or zero weight to efficiencies that it accepted in principle." The Court of Justice upheld the decision of the General Court (UPS v. Commission, case T –194/13 (2013), https://eur-lex.europa.eu/legal-content/en/TXT/PDF/?uri=uriserv%3AOJ.C_.2013.147.01.0030.01.ENG). More recently, in 2019, the Commission prohibited Siemens's proposed acquisition of Alstom on the grounds that the transaction would have had a substantial impact on competition in markets for railway signaling systems and very high-speed trains, despite Siemens' arguments that the transaction was expected to result in several synergies over a four-year period, including cost savings in various areas such as procurement and R&D. In addition to its concerns about verifiability and merger specificity of the synergies set out by the parties, the Commission also stated that the claimed savings from the elimination of overlapping R&D projects which

Efficiency gains are theoretically expected to balance the negative effects of mergers on innovation. On the other hand, in the merger enforcement regimes of the EU and the US, the standards required for accepting an efficiency defense are high. Competition enforcement authorities ask the merging parties to demonstrate that the relevant efficiency gain is *merger-specific* and also *quantifiable*.

Dynamic efficiencies can occur in the form of fixed-cost reductions, quality improvements, service improvements, or new product development. However, some of these dynamic efficiencies might emerge over a long period of time, and their occurrence may sometimes be perceived as speculative and not easily verifiable. Therefore, it may be difficult to predict or forecast their implications at the time of the proposed merger. Moreover, even if such efficiencies are quantified, it is often difficult to provide clear evidence that the benefits will be both merger-specific and passed on to consumers.[628] Finally, even if some benefits do occur, it is difficult to weigh the efficiencies against a potential price increase accurately.[629] All these restrictions, as discussed throughout this book, demonstrate that despite all their concerns voiced to protect it, the authorities have not wholly embraced innovation and are still uncomfortable with looking into the future and taking into account those potentialities where innovation could thrive. Would antitrust agencies ever sincerely weigh dynamic efficiency and synergies arguments – even if they are case-specific and quantifiable against a potential likelihood of price increase due to the transaction? If they do not do this (and I contend that they currently don't), are they not sacrificing the true engine of economic growth – dynamic efficiency – to their ingrained reflexes about protecting distributive efficiency in the short term? Would not the antitrust agency then be moving away from a target of procuring consumer welfare in the mid-to-long term on a more sustainable basis and larger scale to short-term snapshots of worries of harm to consumers? Consider an instance where the antitrust agency finds correspondence regarding the possibility of a shutdown of a research unit post-merger. Would not the antitrust authority see this as having done its homework of finding evidence for a concern? What if the research unit is not being closed for pre-emptive reasons but to render R&D activities more efficient (for example, by reducing R&D duplication)? I fear that discussion would currently be dismissed as speculative the moment there is a material risk of research unit closure observed. This, again, is the innovation paradox of focusing on concerns rather than starting from a neutral point and computing all pros and cons with a complex balancing analysis of facts and data-intensive nature.

The finding that mergers reduce innovation incentives in the theoretical models of the economics studies summarized above (i.e., Federico et al. 2017 and 2018; Motta and Tarantino, 2017) is based on the assumption that the merger in question does not generate any efficiency gains. Therefore, this finding could be reversed if the synergies resulting

---

both parties would have independently pursued could actually indicate a decline in innovation competition between the parties and ultimately limit customers' options. Overall, the Commission decided that the claimed efficiencies would not counterbalance the detrimental impact on competition (Siemens/Alstom, European Commission Decision case M.8677 (Feb. 6, 2019)).

[628] Johnson, *supra* note 440, at 3.
[629] *Id.*

from a merger are taken into account. In Motta and Tarantino (2016),[630] the authors can illustrate that, under specific scenarios (where decisions on investment and prices are taken simultaneously, sequentially, or with quality-enhancing investments), if the synergies in the form of economies of scope are substantial enough, the merging firms will increase their investments and that this effect may outweigh the detrimental effect on prices.[631] Moreover, they focus on involuntary spillovers that share similarities with efficiency gains, and note that similar to economies of scale, merger allows internalizing spillovers, and higher spillovers incentivize merging parties to invest further.[632] Having said that, the authors emphasize that the mergers' effects on firms' incentives to inno-vate will develop over time, typically years, as is the case for dynamic efficiencies.[633] This complicates the balance between short-term harms to consumers and procuring consumer welfare in the long term.[634] On the other hand, their analysis still leaves room for other scenarios: according to Loertscher and Max, in a merger to monopoly, the impact of incentives for cost-reducing investment depends on buyer power and produces different results for the merging parties and its rivals.[635] In case of no buyer power, the merger will increase the incentives of the merging parties but not impact the rivals.[636] In case of buyer power, the merger will increase the incentives of rivals, but the case for merging parties is ambiguous and can either decrease or increase.[637] Loertscher and Max contradict Motta and Tarantino's model showing a merger will decrease merging parties' incentives while increasing their rivals'.[638] There may also be additional efficiency factors, as well as the "hard to measure" efficiencies as discussed under Régibeau et Rockett's policy algorithm framework, which may have a significant role in specific merger cases and scenarios.[639]

3.5.3 Treatment of Demand-Side Efficiencies

With respect to demand-side efficiencies, the parties in *Inco/Falconbridge*[640] argued that due to the intense global competition in the nickel supply industry, any efficiencies achieved by the merged entity that lead to increased output are expected to be transferred to consumers, resulting in direct benefits.[641] However, the Commission stated that this claim solely relies

---

[630] Massimo Motta & Emanuele Tarantino, *The Effect of a Merger on Investments* (Centre for Economic Policy Research (CEPR) Discussion Paper Series No. DP11550, 2016), https://papers.ssrn.com/sol3/papers.cfm?abstract_id=2850392.

[631] *Id.* at 4.

[632] Massimo & Tarantino, *supra* note 554, at 3.

[633] Massimo & Tarantino, *supra* note 630, at 29.

[634] *Id.*

[635] Simon Loertscher & Leslie M. Marx, *Merger Review for Markets with Buyer Power*, 127 J. Pol. Econ. 2967, 2970 (2019), https://people.duke.edu/~marx/bio/papers/BuyerPower.pdf.

[636] *Id.*

[637] *Id.*

[638] *Id.* at 2997.

[639] Régibeau & Rockett, *supra* note 595.

[640] Inco/Falconbridge, European Commission Decision case COMP/M.4000 (July 4, 2006), https://ec.europa.eu/competition/mergers/cases/decisions/m4000_20060704_20600_en.pdf.

[641] *Id.*, para. 535.

on the assumption that competition in the nickel supply market would naturally result in such benefits, and that the parties have not specifically addressed or substantiated how these efficiencies would directly benefit the end customers operating in the three identified product markets where competition concerns have been raised.[642] The Commission acknowledged that the proposed transaction is likely to decrease the new entity's costs through synergies in mining and processing, but also found that these efficiencies would primarily be achieved at the upstream mining and processing level rather than at the final stage of the nickel production chain. Therefore, the Commission considered that these efficiencies would not benefit customers for the end-nickel products in the relevant markets – any potential benefits would be directed to markets other than those identified.[643] Also, the Commission doubted that the new entity would be motivated to transfer the efficiency gains to the relevant end customers in light of the specific market characteristics that give rise to competition concerns and the fact that the transaction would result in the new entity having a near-monopoly in certain markets.[644] It was deemed that the parties have not sufficiently shown that the claimed demand-side efficiencies would meaningfully benefit the end customers in the markets where competition concerns have been raised, and thereby fall short of offsetting the identified competition issues.[645] Additionally, although the supply-side efficiencies (where the benefit accrues directly to the merging entities) put forward by the parties were documented and supported by various studies conducted by Inco, the Commission concluded that the parties failed to demonstrate these efficiencies could not have been attained through alternative means.[646] Despite acknowledging there would be supply-side efficiencies to be generated by the transaction, the Commission seemed to focus more on whether the efficiencies would be passed on to consumers in the downstream market. Accordingly, the Commission decided that the transaction would significantly impede effective competition in the market, and ultimately cleared the merger subject to commitments.

In the *Deutsche Börse/NYSE* case, a discussion was raised as to whether demand-side efficiencies (where the claimed benefit accrues directly to the customer) should be treated differently than supply-side efficiencies. The transaction parties argued that demand-side efficiencies, such as reduced collateral requirements, arise directly on the customer's side and thus do not need to be "passed on" by the combined entity through price reductions (as is often the case for supply-side efficiencies). However, in its decision on *Deutsche Börse/NYSE*, the Commission outlined that, even though consumers may directly save costs as a consequence of reduced collateral requirements, the merged entity could nevertheless raise prices and therefore "*claw back*" at least some part of the savings.[647]

The Commission's reasoning in this decision was based on a standard economic argument. If the value of goods for the consumers increases, it is typically rational for

---

[642]   *Id.*, para. 543.
[643]   *Id.*, para. 544.
[644]   *Id.*, para. 545.
[645]   *Id.*, para. 547.
[646]   *Id.*, para. 550.
[647]   Deutsche Börse/NYSE Euronext, European Commission Decision case COMP/M.6166, paras. 1235–42 (Feb. 1, 2012).

sellers to increase their price since consumers will have a higher willingness to pay (more) for goods. Assuming that the economic models can predict the unilateral effects of mergers, the part of the benefits that resides with the customers after "*clawback*" is similar to the part of the supply-side benefits (such as cost savings of the merging firms) that would be expected to be passed on to the customers. However, the General Court upheld the reasoning of the Commission regarding the potential clawback of demand-side efficiencies.[648] Also, it confirmed that, even if benefits arise directly for the benefit of consumers (such as the alleged benefits of reduced collateral requirements), the Commission is entitled to assess whether some of these benefits could be clawed back by the merged entity.[649]

It is perhaps worth discussing whether, after eleven years since this decision, particularly in the sphere of dynamic efficiencies in merger control, the time has come to make sure that a passing-on of these efficiencies is not a requirement for the merging parties, since (combined with the efficiencies being merger specific and quantifiable) this would basically mean that there will be very little articulable redeeming virtues of a transaction in the innovation sphere, once concerns are flagged through a liberal use of assumptions of general economic theory. Especially as this, in turn, results in the innovation paradox highlighted here by feeding the asymmetry and lack of equal footing that will only employ innovation as a sword and never as a shield.

3.5.4 Vertical Efficiencies

The *TomTom/Tele Atlas*[650] deal was a vertical merger between a leading producer of navigation systems and a digital map developer. The Commission unconditionally cleared the merger in 2008 and partly recognized the efficiency claims of the merging parties in its decision. This was important because this was the only case where the Commission acknowledged some of the efficiencies for being merger-specific despite finding the quantification studies insufficient.[651]

Firstly, the Commission recognized and acknowledged that the removal of specific double markups met the legal test for efficiencies. Secondly, the parties claimed the merger would lead to substantial innovation efficiencies.[652] Accordingly, depending on an economic analysis provided by the merging parties, the Commission predicted that the merger would result in a decrease in the average prices for personal navigation devices, provided that the efficiency gains in the form of the elimination of double marginalization were taken into account. The Commission also accepted that the merger would create individual efficiency gains in the form of better cooperation regarding the use of

---

[648]   *Id.*, paras. 267–80.
[649]   Benno Buehler & Giulio Federico, *Recent Developments in the Assessment of Efficiencies of Mergers in the EU*, 2 COMPETITION L. & POL'Y DEBATE 64 (2016).
[650]   TomTom/Tele Atlas, European Commission Decision case M.4854 (May 14, 2008).
[651]   Raphaël De Coninck, *Innovation in EU Merger Control: In Need of a Consistent Framework*, 2 COMPETITION L. & POL'Y DEBATE 41 (2016).
[652]   European Commission, *supra* note 444, at 7.

TomTom's customer database in improving Tele Atlas's digital maps.[653] Therefore, in its decision, the Commission acknowledged innovation efficiencies that were at least partly merger-specific and beneficial to consumers.[654] Having said this, the Commission also found that the two studies submitted by the parties to quantify these efficiencies were not particularly convincing.[655] At any rate, it was unnecessary in this particular case to estimate precisely the magnitude of likely efficiencies, given the proposed transaction's lack of anti-competitive effects, irrespective of efficiencies.[656]

Similarly, in the *Western Digital Ireland/Vivity Technologies* case,[657] the transaction parties also claimed that innovation efficiencies would arise in terms of higher and faster product development through the combination of the merging firms' R&D resources. However, the European Commission found that these claims were not verifiable, because no specific quantitative or other types of evidence had been put forward that would allow their credibility to be assessed and verified in the Commission's examination.[658]

All in all, we observe that if the anti-competitive effects of a merger have been established, the EC Merger Regulation[659] also recognizes that efficiencies – including synergies arising from innovation – can offset the anti-competitive harm, provided that the efficiencies put forward by the merging parties are (i) beneficial for consumers, (ii) merger-specific, and (iii) verifiable.[660] Unfortunately, it is very challenging for the parties to demonstrate with verifiable results that future innovation potential shall be beneficial for the consumer in a given merger case; therefore, they are almost always disregarded by the authorities for being speculative. Considering innovation's crucial role in economic development, increase in GDP, and consumer welfare, there are certainly strong arguments, such as the ones listed below, for the authorities to adopt a more flexible and welfare-based approach.

3.6 Potential Arguments for Innovation Defenses

In addition to the above, certain other potential arguments may be raised or employed in more cases by transaction entities against the competition authorities.

---

[653] Ekrem Kalkan, *Role of the Economics in the EU's New Vertical Merger Policy: Thoughts on the Merger between Tomtom and Tele Atlas*, 25 EKONOMIK YAKLAŞIM 55 (2014), https://www.ejmanager.com/mnstemps/94/94-1398808973.pdf?t=1561106271.

[654] European Commission, *supra* note 444, at 1.

[655] *TomTom/Tele Atlas*, recitals 244–50.

[656] European Commission, *supra* note 654, at 7.

[657] Western Digital Ireland/Vivity Technologies, European Commission Decision case M.6203, recitals 996–1007 (Nov. 23, 2011).

[658] European Commission, *supra* note 654, at 7.

[659] Council Regulation (EC) No. 139/2004 of Jan. 20, 2004, on the Control of Concentrations Between Undertakings (the "EC Merger Regulation" or "EUMR"), 2004 OJ (L 24) 1, https://eur-lex.europa.eu/legal-content/EN/ALL/?uri=CELEX%3A32004R0139.

[660] European Commission, *supra* note 654, at 3.

3.6.1 No Presumption Should Be Accepted About the Effects of Mergers on Innovation Incentives

Competition authorities may presume that horizontal mergers can reduce innovation incentives as a result of a standard unilateral effect.

RBB Economics has argued that no such presumption is justified, except in cases of mergers to monopolies, and even then under certain parameter values.[661] The assessment of a merger's impact on R&D investments requires a complex balancing exercise involving several factors that affect the incentives to innovate, most notably *cannibalization* and *appropriability*. The fact that these factors exert opposing influences on incentives to innovate implies that one effect cannot be presumed to dominate the other.

Katz and Shelanski also suggest that, where innovation is at stake, there should not be a presumption about the harm imposed by mergers on innovation, and they recommend that merger reviews should be carried out on a more fact-intensive, case-by-case basis. In their view, the correct presumption would be that a merger's effects on innovation are neutral, except in the case of a merger to monopoly, where there would be a rebuttable presumption of harm.[662]

Jullien and Lefouili state that the academic literature on mergers and innovation does not support the presumption that mergers have a negative impact on innovation. They reach this conclusion by considering the existence of potential positive effects of mergers on innovation, even in the absence of spillovers and R&D complementarities.[663] Therefore, they suggest that competition enforcement authorities adopt a neutral perspective when assessing the impact of a merger on innovation and that they should balance the various effects at work in a particular transaction. They also argue that various effects, such as the "*demand expansion*" effect, the "*margin expansion*" effect, and "*spillover*" effects, should be part of the main competitive assessment carried out by competition authorities in assessing the effects of a merger on the incentives to innovate.[664]

With regard to the *Dow/DuPont* merger, Nicolas Petit has argued that it is not possible to apply the "*significant impediment of effective innovation competition*" ("SIEIC") model of unilateral effects in its current form to predict post-innovation competition to merger innovation effects.[665] Petit notes that in *Tetra Laval*,[666] the European Court of Justice

---

[661]   RBB Economics, *supra* note 490.

[662]   Michael L. Katz & Howard A. Shelanski, *Merger Policy and Innovation: Must Enforcement Change to Account for Technological Change?* in 5 INNOVATION POLICY AND THE ECONOMY 109 (Adam B. Jaffe, Josh Lerner & Scott Stern eds, MIT Press 2006).

[663]   Jullien & Lefouili, *supra* note 460, at 26.

[664]   *Id.*

[665]   Nicolas Petit, *Innovation Competition, Unilateral Effects and Merger Control Policy*, ICLE Antitrust & Consumer Protection Research Program, White Paper 2018-03), https://laweconcenter.org/wp-content/uploads/2018/06/ICLE-Petit-Innovation-Competition-Merger-Control-Policy-ICLE-2018.pdf

[666]   Case C-12/03 P, Commission v. Tetra Laval, 2005 ECR I-987.

("ECJ") had laid down four conditions – namely accuracy, reliability, consistency, and completeness – that must be satisfied by the Commission for the lawful use of economic models in merger assessments, and indicates that the Commission had failed to achieve the required standard in *Dow/DuPont* for all four conditions.[667] First, with respect to accuracy, Petit criticizes the Commission for not considering all factors that may be key to innovation incentives (e.g., regulatory pressure, biological resistance) but solely considering rivalry as the main source of innovation.[668] Regarding reliability, Petit notes, among others, that the argument that *dissipation of rivalry post-merger will always result in lower innovation and, as a result, consumers will always be worse off* is not embedded in mainstream economic analysis.[669] Petit also notes several inconsistencies in the decision. For example, he notes that even though the SIEIC model predicts a reduction in relation to R&D inputs, which mainly consists of R&D expenditure, the decision measured R&D outputs instead of measuring R&D inputs;[670] however, R&D output produced may be affected by factors that may arise after the decision.[671] Finally, as for the completeness, Petit states that the Commission should have considered both supportive and unsupportive evidence, but it completely ignored research stating that new agrochemicals continue to enter the market and that regulation and resistance are key drivers of innovation, and statistics showing that the firms that are active in the market increased their R&D expenditure.[672] All in all, in Petit's view, the *Dow/DuPont* decision does not meet the four conditions set out in *Tetra Laval*, so it does not exhaust the burden of persuasion,[673] and the discussion under Annex 4 of the decision was mainly to lend credence to the Commission's decision from an academic point.[674] (This is parallel to what Petit had argued even before the Commission had concluded its investigation on the *Dow/DuPont* merger: that the Commission's intervention seemed to be based on a novel theory of harm, which he called "Significant impediment to industry innovation," which did not comply with the standard of proof set out in *Tetra Laval*.)[675] In this regard, Petit contends that "the dispositive value of Annex 4 of the *Dow/DuPont* decision is

---

[667]   Petit, Nicolas, *Innovation Competition, Unilateral Effects, and Merger Policy*, 82 ANTITRUST L.J. 873, 906 (2019), https://papers.ssrn.com/sol3/papers.cfm?abstract_id=3113077.

[668]   *Id.* at. 911–12. Petit also states that while the decision addresses how resistance and regulatory pressure are unlikely to affect the existing products, it does not provide any view on the effects on future products.

[669]   *Id.* at 913.

[670]   *Id.* at 914–15.

[671]   *Id.*

[672]   *Id.* at 910, 916.

[673]   This term is used to explain the Commission's burden of proof in economic assessments. *See* Ioannis Lianos & Christos Genakos, *Econometric Evidence in EU Competition Law: An Empirical and Theoretical Analysis* HANDBOOK ON EUROPEAN COMPETITION LAW 64, 75 (Edward Elgar Publishing 2013), https://EconPapers. repec.org/RePEc:elg:eechap:15373_1.

[674]   Petit, *supra* note 667, at 906.

[675]   *See* Nicolas Petit, *Significant Impediment to Industry Innovation: A Novel Theory of Harm in EU Merger Control?* (ICLE Antitrust & Consumer Protection Research Program, White Paper 2017-1, 2017), https://orbi. uliege.be/bitstream/2268/207345/1/SSRN-id2911597.pdf, where the author contends that, under this theory, the Commission may prohibit a merger by stating that the merger restricts R&D incentives in the concerned industry as a whole, without proving harm in relation to specific product market/pipeline. According to Petit, the underlying presumption is that the removal of a "parallel path R&D" of the target itself calls for intervention, as it will diminish innovation in the industry. He points out that such an approach does not comply with the standard of proof set out in *Tetra Laval*, which requires a detailed market search on the effect on the innovation incentive of the acquired firm and the market.

challenging to assess since it is not entirely clear to what extent the selected models influenced the Commission's decision to intervene in the merger."[676]

On the other hand, it should be pointed out that Lianos et al. disagree with Petit's criticisms, stating that when determining the effect of the merger on the innovation incentives in the industry, the Commission is not necessarily required to define a specific "innovation market" on which the merger may have an impact. On this front, they refer to the Commission's Transfer of Technology Guidelines ("Transfer Guidelines")[677] and state that when providing the cases where competitive concerns may arise, the Transfer Guidelines did not require an analysis of the market shares; therefore, it was not tethered to a specific product market as long as there exists "at least four independent technologies that may constitute a commercially viable alternative, in addition to the licensed technology controlled by the parties to the agreement."[678] According to them, this shows that the Commission's main concern is whether there is a sufficient number of independent technologies that may constitute competitive alternatives. They remark that competition law should concern itself not only with high market shares but also with firms that use different technologies that may challenge those used by the incumbent; hence, the Commission should not limit its innovation competition assessment to the delineation of an innovation market.[679] Accordingly, they assert that the Commission is entitled to assess innovation incentives in the industry without necessarily defining a specific "innovation market."

Denicolò and Polo have asserted that competition agencies and the courts should keep in mind that the effects of mergers on innovation can be either negative or positive and that they are more likely to be favorable for mergers that pass the traditional static tests. A presumption that horizontal mergers always hamper innovation risks prohibiting many pro-competitive mergers. According to Denicolò and Polo, if any presumption is to be adopted, it must be that mergers are *innovation neutral*. A neutral starting point guarantees that arbitrary a priori beliefs do not bias the assessment of the impact of mergers on innovation and that it can be open-minded and grounded on the facts of each specific case.[680]

3.6.2 Market Definition and Innovation Spaces

Katz and Shelanski recommend that antitrust authorities reduce their reliance on defining bright-line (but often illusory) market boundaries and instead focus more on direct evidence of the likely effects of a transaction on price competition and

---

[676] Petit, *supra* note 667, n. 156.

[677] European Commission, Guidelines on the Application of Article 101 of the Treaty on the Functioning of the European Union to Technology Transfer Agreements, 2014 OJ (C 89) 3.

[678] IOANNIS LIANOS, VALENTINE KORAH & PAOLO SICILIANI, COMPETITION LAW: ANALYSIS, CASES & MATERIALS 1516 (Oxford Univ. Press 2019). In the Guidelines, it is stated that where there exist four commercially viable alternatives, it is unlikely that article 101 TFEU will be infringed, outside the areas of hardcore restrictions. *See* European Commission, Guidelines on the Applicability of Article 101 of the Treaty on the Functioning of the European Union to Horizontal Co-operation Agreements, 2011 OJ (C 11) 1, para. 157.

[679] *Id.*

[680] Vincenzo Denicolò & Michele Polo, *The Innovation Theory of Harm: An Appraisal* 27–28 (2018), https://ssrn.com/abstract=3146731.

innovation.[681] They argue that even the "innovation market" concept developed by Gilbert and Sunshine[682] (which requires identifying overlapping R&D activities of the merging firms, alternative sources of R&D, actual and potential downstream competitors of the parties, the effect of the increased concentration on R&D and the transaction's impact on the efficiency of R&D)[683] would not be sufficient to identify the innovation concerns as it does not address, among others, (i) how innovation that is not connected to any current or future product can be analyzed, (ii) how an increase in concentration affects innovation, and (iii) what welfare presumptions should be used after determining the innovation markets.[684]

Other scholars have also noted the shortcomings of considering product market definition as a prerequisite for competitive assessment. The traditional method of market definition relies on identifying the relevant competitors prior to the competitive assessment of the market where customers may be harmed due to changes in prices, innovation, barriers to entry, etc.[685] Kern, Dewenter, and Kerber criticize this approach and state that the innovation dimension can only be taken into consideration during the competitive assessment phase of the merger review.[686] They explain the primary problem with such an approach is that all incumbents may also not be competitors in terms of innovation under the defined product market, or those undertakings competing for innovation by investing in R&D may not be active under the product market at the time of the merger assessment.[687] According to Kern, Dewenter, and Kerber, the foregoing would lead to a flawed market definition since "the innovation competition might be different from the relevant competitors in the current product market."[688]

Hassid also agrees with Katz and Shelanski, and states that defining markets with clear boundaries may be erroneous in evaluating unilateral effects cases, as well as those involving differentiated products, and prevent an accurate analysis of the anti-competitive harm.[689]

In line with the above, Baker suggests that antitrust should not spend much time on market definition in cases where the direct harm to competition can clearly be shown, since "there exists a market where harm will occur, but there is little need to specify

---

[681]   Katz & Shelanski, *supra* note 421, at 6.

[682]   Richard J. Gilbert & Steven C. Sunshine, *Incorporating Dynamic Efficiency Concerns in Merger Analysis: The Use of Innovation Markets*, 63 ANTITRUST L.J. 569 (1995).

[683]   *Id.* at 43.

[684]   Katz & Shelanski, *supra* note 421.

[685]   Horizontal Merger Guidelines 7–13.

[686]   Benjamin R. Kern, Ralf Dewenter & Wolfgang Kerber, *Empirical Analysis of the Assessment of Innovation Effects in U.S. Merger Cases*, 16 J. INDUS. COMPETITION & TRADE 373 (2016).

[687]   *Id.*

[688]   *Id.*

[689]   Amanda J. Parkison Hassid, *An Oracle Without Foresight - Plaintiffs' Arduous Burdens under U.S. v. Oracle*, 58 HASTINGS L.J. 891, 904–05 (2007), https://repository.uchastings.edu/hastings_law_journal/vol58/iss4/6. In the same vein, *see* Jonathan B. Baker, *Product Differentiation Through Space and Time: Some Antitrust Policy Issues*, 42 ANTITRUST BULL. 177 (1997); Jonathan B. Baker, *Stepping Out in an Old Brown Shoe: In Qualified Praise of Submarkets*, 68 ANTITRUST L.J. 203 (2000); Marc G. Schildkraut, *Oracle and the Future of Unilateral Effects*, 19 ANTITRUST 20 (2005) (arguing that a bright-line product market definition would not be plausible for differentiated products and unilateral effects cases).

the market's precise boundaries."[690] Also, Cameron, Glick and Mangum agree that since bright-line definitions provide single, conclusive and stricter outcomes, the real-world complexity of certain cases is frustrated.[691] In a similar vein, Kaplow argues that (i) the only role of market definition is to enable the authorities to calculate the market shares, but (ii) market shares are insufficient to indicate market power and (iii) market power should be determined based on other indicators such as residual-demand curves.[692]

Nevertheless, there are also scholars who contend that market definition has an essential role in competitive assessment, for example, for the analysis of future entries and the durability of the market power, both of which require a market concept.[693] Also, in cases concerning coordinated effects, it may still hold some importance to determine the active firms and concentration ratios in the market.[694]

3.6.3 Cannibalization Effects Should Be Balanced by Other Effects

The role of the *"cannibalization effect"* in assessing the impact of mergers on innovation is similar to the standard unilateral price effects in a horizontal merger. It is argued, however, that cannibalization captures only part of the competitive assessment of the likely impact on competition of a horizontal merger with regard to the incentive to innovate. Other effects can balance the negative impact of the internalization of cannibalization. According to RBB Economics, for example, a reduction in the number of competitors in an industry can also have positive influences on the firms' incentives to invest in R&D. Indeed, *appropriation* is one of these alternative effects. RBB Economics argues that the cannibalization effect will only be strong enough to reduce overall innovation in the case of a merger to monopoly.[695]

According to Shelanski, in order to minimize the cannibalization effect, the merged firm could, in some cases, coordinate the introduction of new products to the market alongside the established product lines of the pre-merger firms. For example, a firm's new and existing products could be repositioned in the relevant market to minimize any potential sales cannibalization between them. This could allow a post-merger firm to protect its profit margins in a manner that would not have been possible prior to the merger.[696] Thus, a firm's innovation incentives would be preserved, while the overall impact on consumer welfare would depend on the effects of the product repositioning.

---

[690]   Jonathan B. Baker, *Contemporary Empirical Merger Analysis*, 5 GEO. MASON L. REV. 347 (1997).
[691]   Duncan Cameron, Mark Glick & David Mangum, *Good Riddance to Market Definition?* 57 ANTITRUST BULL. 719 (2012).
[692]   Louis Kaplow, *Market Definition and the Merger Guidelines*, 39 REV. INDUS. ORG. 107 (2011).
[693]   Gregory Werden, *Why (Ever) Define Markets? An Answer to Professor Kaplow*, 18 ANTITRUST L.J. 729 (2013).
[694]   Herbert Hovenkamp & Carl Shapiro, *Horizontal Mergers, Market Structure, and Burdens of Proof*, 127 YALE L.J. 1742, 1996 & 2000 (2018).
[695]   RBB Economics, *supra* note 490, at 2.
[696]   Shelanski, *supra* note 538, at 1703.

In addition to arguing against the presumption that mergers impede the incentive to innovate (in the absence of efficiency gains) due to the innovation diversion effect, Jullien and Lefouili have introduced the *"demand expansion effect"* into the analysis of the innovation effects of mergers.[697] According to their study, increased prices in the post-merger market enhance the incentives to invest in innovation for next-generation products, and increased margins enhance the incentives to invest in innovation and to boost demand by offering a wider variety of differentiated products to the consumers. As a result, the positive effects on innovation may be stronger than the negative effects of the internalization of each other's profit reductions when the merging parties can differentiate their products and increase demand in the post-merger market. Thus, a merger can still be beneficial to innovation if the innovators are able to expand demand for their rivals through uninternalized positive externalities and spillovers.[698] The authors conclude by recommending that competition enforcement authorities adopt a neutral perspective when assessing the effects of mergers on innovation. Furthermore, they suggest that all merger effects, including positive spillover effects for future innovations and other efficiencies, should be incorporated into the central part of the competitive assessment by the Commission, and that the Commission should consider the theory of benefits together with the theory of harm.[699]

At this time, most of the innovation in the digital economy (as well as some of the non-digital industries) is conducted in ecosystems that have a continuous cycle and balance within, akin to the more widely recognized system of ecology.[700] The fast progression of innovation inevitably creates management issues in case of strong substitution relations between the interchangeable products of the same undertaking rather than with its competitors (i.e., cannibalization) and requires careful management.[701] Novelli notes the case of the substitution relationship between Apple's iPod and iPhone products, which demonstrates that cannibalization could lead to a situation where an innovative product, either a new model or a different product, could be perceived as a substitution in the customers' eyes, and lead to a decrease in the sales of the preceding product.[702]

---

[697]   Jullien & Lefouili, *supra* note 460, at 21.

[698]   Kokkoris & Valletti, *supra* note 504, at 257. The authors, however, contend it is very unlikely that mergers could prove to be good for innovation in the absence of efficiencies.

[699]   Jullien & Lefouili, *supra* note 460, at 26. A theory of harm is a claim that puts forward why the investigated action (such as an acquisition) should be prohibited as it breaches competition law rules.

[700]   The concept of innovation ecosystem has gained rapid ground over the last decade. For digital sectors, innovation ecosystems do not refer to an individual undertaking operating in the digital sectors in particular, but comprise the entire innovative environment in which such undertakings operate. Therefore, the concept of digital innovation ecosystem refers to the set of actors working collectively with resources to create value and promote innovation in digital sectors. These undertakings in different parts of an industry operate autonomously but work interdependently to create valuable outputs through innovation. *See* Deog-Seong Oh, Fred Phillips, Sehee Park & Eunghyun Lee, *Innovation Ecosystems: A Critical Examination*, 54 TECHNOVATION 1, 1 (2016); Yuliani Suseno, Christofer Laurell & Nathalie Sick, *Assessing Value Creation in Digital Innovation Ecosystems: A Social Media Analytics Approach*, 27 J. STRATEGIC INFO. SYS. 335, 337(2018); Ping Wang, *Theorizing Digital Innovation Ecosystems: A Multilevel Ecological Framework*, *in* PROCEEDINGS OF THE 27TH EUROPEAN CONFERENCE ON INFORMATION SYSTEMS (ECIS) 6 (Stockholm & Uppsala, Sweden, June 8–14, 2019).

[701]   Francesco Novelli, *Platform Substitution and Cannibalization: The Case of Portable Navigation Devices*, SOFTWARE BUS. ICSOB 141, 141 (2012).

[702]   Francesco Novelli, *Detection and Measurement of Sales Cannibalization in Information Technology Markets*, *Publications of Darmstadt Technical University* (Institute for Business Studies (BWL), 2015).

This is similar to the decreasing effect that the launch of GPS-enabled smartphones in 2008 had on the sales of portable navigation devices,[703] when they were substituted by an ecosystem output, in other words, cannibalized by the expanding borders of digital platforms. Depending on the industry that the innovation ecosystem affects, as the innovation in this ecosystem led to new technology, the old technology was substituted in terms of the consumer preferences, but at different speeds depending on both the emergence challenges and extension opportunities.[704] Empirical studies on the S-curve (representing the product's growth over time) and the link between the activities of the undertaking support that, in an innovation ecosystem, when there is low ecosystem emergence challenge and low ecosystem extension opportunity, the more innovative generations of a product swiftly gain a strong place in the market, while the innovative products facing high ecosystem emergence challenge and high ecosystem extension opportunity take considerably longer time to reach that level.[705]

Innovation ecosystems are also observed in non-digital markets; however, the pace of substitution and, hence, cannibalization may prove to be much slower. For example, in the pharmaceutical market, do-it-yourself laboratories, contract research organizations, and pharmaceutical firms collaborated to form an innovation ecosystem in terms of the research and development phase for new medicines.[706] Their interdependency with pharmaceutical companies formed a *biopharma ecosystem* where the actors generate commercial returns via different innovation models.[707] In the aerospace and defense sector, the ecosystem consists of different actors such as suppliers, vendors, operators, and competitors, similar to digital innovation ecosystems, along with other key and leading elements, including governmental agencies and international regulatory bodies.[708] However, the pace of substitution might be relatively slower than those in the digital sectors due to the sectoral necessity for a longer product life span.[709] Due to such differences, the innovation characteristics in non-digital sectors are more risk-reducing, slow-paced and collaborative, which might change the management perspectives as cannibalization might not be as direct or common as in digital markets.

3.6.4 Appropriability

If appropriability is high (for example, through robust patent protection), a successful innovator is more likely to be able to turn its innovations into profits (e.g., through sales or licensing) in a competitive market than in a stable market (with low switching rates).

---

[703]   Novelli, *supra* note 701, at 152.

[704]   Ron Adner & Rahul Kapoor, *Innovation Ecosystems and the Pace of Substitution: Re-examining Technology S-curves*, 37 STRATEGIC MGMT. J. 625, 5–22(2016).

[705]   *Id*. at 24–28.

[706]   Qiang Wu & Qile He, *DIY Laboratories and Business Innovation Ecosystems: The Case of Pharmaceutical Industry*, 161 TECH. FORECASTING & SOC. CHANGE 1, 4 (2020).

[707]   *Id*. at 7–8.

[708]   Paavo Ritala, Vassilis Agouridas, Dimitris Assimakopoulos & Otto Gies, *Value Creation and Capture Mechanisms in Innovation Ecosystems: A Comparative Case Study*, 63 INT'L J. TECH. MGMT. 244, 254 (2013).

[709]   *Id*. 254–60.

According to Shapiro, this finding is in line with Arrow's basic theory that product-market competition increases innovation. Shapiro also argues that with high appropriability, a successful innovator has an increased incentive to innovate because it can obtain temporary market power, which provides a big incentive to innovate, according to Schumpeter.[710]

When the level of appropriability is high, a merger will increase the incentive to invest in innovation for the merged entity. The reduction in the number of firms in the relevant market brought about by a merger between a given firm and one of its rivals would also increase the benefits that the new entity could expect to gain (appropriability), furnishing it with an incentive to invest where it may have chosen not to do so in the pre-merger market environment.[711]

Although appropriability is not directly related to the number of innovation players in a market, concentration can increase appropriability because of the scale effects of cost-reducing process innovations and the reduction of adverse spillover effects.[712]

Motta and Tarantino have also analyzed the situation in which investments give rise to involuntary spillovers (whereas, in the base model, they assume instead that firms can fully appropriate their investments), and they have shown that the existence of such spillovers shares certain similarities with efficiency gains: since the merger allows the merging firms to internalize them, higher spillovers lead to stronger incentives to invest by the merged entity.[713]

3.6.5 Product-Market Competition and Contestability

The incentive and ability of firms to undertake innovation efforts will depend on the competition they face in the current product markets.

A company would have an incentive to invest in innovation (and to develop new products) to the extent that it can replace its competitors' products with its own new products in the market, and thereby gain sales from those competitors. Moreover, a firm will have an incentive to innovate in order to protect its sales. The extent to which customers are willing to switch products depends on the dynamics of product-market competition.[714]

As mentioned before, according to Shapiro, the contestability principle is in line with Schumpeter's theory of innovation. If a company can gain substantial market shares through innovation, that will provide a significant incentive to innovate for that firm. This process is at the core of Schumpeter's *"creative destruction"* theory: the innovative firm may be rewarded with temporary market power as a result of its innovation. If, on

---

[710]   Shapiro, *supra* note 442, at 363. *See also* Seiler, *supra* note 445.
[711]   RBB Economics, *supra* note 490.
[712]   Seiler, *supra* note 445, at 16–17.
[713]   Massimo & Tarantino, *supra* note 554, at 3.
[714]   Johnson, *supra* note 440, at 2.

the other hand, the market dynamics are such that a small company cannot grow even if it develops an innovation, such a small company will have less incentive to invest in innovation compared with a large company.[715]

Shapiro advocates considering the degree to which a firm's innovation efforts would make a market contestable, e.g., cause consumers to switch their purchases to the innovating firm or to continue purchasing from the innovating firm. The answer to this question turns less on the current concentration level or market share(s) in a particular sector since both large and small firms would have an incentive to make investments in contestable markets in order to maintain or gain market share, respectively. Instead, the question of contestability relates more to the nature of consumer preferences, the innovation at stake, and specific transaction characteristics (such as switching costs in the relevant market). Contestability will also depend on the ability of firms in other markets with innovation capacities to redirect their efforts to the market in question, which provides a challenging dynamic analysis.

The research conducted by Aghion et al. demonstrates that innovation efforts exhibit a specific, if not unidirectional, pattern that depends on the structure of the product market. The authors have shown that the relationship between industry markup and innovation (as measured by citation-weighted patent counts) takes the shape of an inverted U; in other words, patent development increases with competition up until a certain point, after which it decreases.[716]

Its effect on product-market competition may partially determine a merger's impact on innovation. According to Jullien and Lefouili, the incentives of merging firms to innovate may be affected by higher post-merger margins and lower post-merger volumes. Under the *demand expansion* effect, the margin increase induced by a merger provides the merging firms with higher incentives to innovate in order to increase their demand.[717] Thus, higher post-merger margins raise the incentive to invest in demand-enhancing innovations.[718]

Bourreau, Jullien, and Lefouili have constructed a model to investigate the effects of a merger on demand-enhancing innovations.[719] They have studied the merged entity's incentives to increase its innovation efforts for a given behavior by its rivals. In other words, they have focused on the *"initial impetus"* by referring to studies by Farrell and Shapiro, and Federico, Langus and Valletti. They have investigated the effects on innovation of a merger to monopoly (where the initial impetus is the only effect at work) in a symmetric context, assuming that (i) the outcome of innovation is deterministic, and (ii) investment levels are not observed by competitors prior to price competition taking place. In this regard, they first derived a necessary and sufficient condition for a merger to reduce the equilibrium level of innovation, allowing for (potential) small synergies in production. They then proposed a breakdown of the overall impact of a merger on the

---

[715]   Shapiro, *supra* note 442, at 368. *See also* Seiler, *supra* note 445, at 19.

[716]   AGHION & GRIFFITH, *supra* note 454, at 701–28.

[717]   Jullien & Lefouili, *supra* note 460, at 3.

[718]   *Id.* at 18.

[719]   Marc Bourreau, Bruno Jullien & Yassine Lefouili, *Mergers and Demand-Enhancing Innovation* (Toulouse School of Economics, Working Paper No. 18-907, Mar. 2018, Revised July 2018), https://www.tse-fr.eu/sites/default/files/TSE/documents/doc/wp/2018/wp_tse_907.pdf.

incentives to innovate. This analysis shows that a merger's impact is a combination of potentially opposite effects and that it can be either positive or negative, depending on the context. More specifically, in the baseline model, they have identified the following effects of a merger on the merging firms' incentives to innovate:

First, the merger affects the merging firms' output, and therefore, their incentives to innovate in order to increase their margin. This "*margin expansion*" effect is negative if the synergies in production are small (or absent) because the merger leads to lower output by the merging firms for a given innovation level.

Second, the merger affects the merged firm's margin, and therefore, its incentives to innovate in order to increase demand. This "*demand expansion*" effect is positive, as a merger tends to increase margins.

Third, a merger induces an "*innovation diversion*" effect, leading to the internalization of the impact that each merging firm's innovation investment has. The direction of this externality depends on the impact of an increase in one merging firm's investment based on the other merging firm's demand and can be either positive or negative, depending on the nature of the innovation. The innovation diversion effect is negative when this externality is negative, and it is positive when this externality is positive.

A final element of their analysis accounts for the effect of the merger on the return to innovation per unit of output, which is an effect that may mitigate or exacerbate the demand expansion effect. By applying the breakdown analysis to some of the specific models commonly used in the relevant literature, they illustrate that the overall impact of the merger can be either positive or negative and that the direction of this effect is partially driven by the "horizontal" or "vertical" nature of innovation.

The authors have also developed a simple model in which innovation has both a horizontal dimension and a vertical one, showing that the overall effect of a merger can be either positive or negative, depending on which dimension matters more in a particular case.

Finally, they extend their baseline model to account for technological spillovers, synergies in R&D, and significant synergies in production. A key insight from their analysis is that non-R&D synergies in production are essential not only for the effect of a merger on prices but also for its effect on the incentives to invest in R&D. In particular, they conclude that the fact that synergies in production may lead to an increase in output (for a given innovation level) implies that the margin expansion effect may become positive.

3.6.6 Efficiencies

3.6.6.1 Combining Complementary R&D Assets and Knowledge

It is widely accepted, both in the economics literature and by competition enforcement authorities, that a merger that can combine complementary R&D assets and knowledge will be able to increase the merged entity's ability to innovate.[720] One important example concerning the combination of the complementary R&D assets of two pharmaceutical companies is the FTC's *Genzyme/Novazyme* decision.[721] The companies were the only two companies conducting research for a certain drug, and the concern was whether the merger would negatively affect the R&D process. The parties claimed that as a result of the combination of their expertise and skills, the merged entity would be able to accelerate the development of the drug, and that Genzyme has unique technologies and capabilities that it could use for the development of Novazyme's drug. The FTC did not challenge the decision in part due to the synergies arising from complementing the R&D activities. The FTC's then Chairman Muris noted that the merger "made possible comparative experiments and provided information that enabled the Novazyme program to avoid drilling dry holes. By accelerating the Novazyme program, the merger may have increased its odds of success. Moreover, the merger made possible synergies that will help avoid a delay in the Novazyme program."[722] On the other hand, Commissioner Thompson dissented and stated that eliminating competition between these two rivals would reduce incentives to innovate.[723] Other examples to note: the competition authorities of the Czech Republic and Turkey have highlighted that combining knowledge and resources may benefit consumers and lead to increased R&D and investment.[724]

It should be noted that while the Commission considers the possibility that combining complementary R&D activities may result in an increase in innovation incentives, it also imposes a heavy burden of proof on the parties to show that such an effect of the merger outweighs any anti-competitive effect. For instance, in the *TomTom/Tele Atlas* decision, although the Commission noted that a vertical integration between two undertakings might benefit customers by way of combining the parties' complementary databases used for the creation of maps, it found that such efficiencies are difficult to quantify.[725] Similarly, in its *Dow/DuPont* decision,[726] the Commission rejected the parties' argument that the transaction would allow them to combine complementary strengths (R&D information) on the grounds that the parties did not submit sufficient proof enabling the Commission to analyze whether the claimed efficiencies are likely, verifiable, merger-specific and beneficial to consumers.[727] This approach of the Commission is also noted by Laskowska, who highlights that although many economists consider complementary

---

[720] Mosso, *supra* note 486, at 4; *See also* Schulz, *supra* note 448.

[721] FTC File no. 021-0026 (2004).

[722] Statement of Chairman Timothy J. Muris in the matter of Genzyme Corporation / Novazyme Pharmaceuticals, Inc. 17 (2004), https://www.ftc.gov/system/files/attachments/press-releases/ftc-closes-its-investigation-genzyme-corporations-2001-acquisition-novazyme-pharmaceuticals-inc./murisgenzymestmt.pdf.

[723] Dissenting Statement of Commissioner Mozelle W. Thompson Genzyme Corporation's Acquisition of Novazyme Pharmaceuticals Inc., https://www.ftc.gov/system/files/attachments/press-releases/ftc-closes-its-investigation-genzyme-corporations-2001-acquisition-novazyme-pharmaceuticals-inc./thompsongenzymestmt.pdf.

[724] *See* OECD, *supra* note 576, at 126 &129 for a discussion of the Czech competition authority approach; Legrand/Schneider, Turkish Competition Board Decision No. 01-48/486-121 (Oct. 8, 2001) and Gemplus/Exalto, Turkish Competition Board Decision No. 06-33/410-107 (May 11, 2006).

[725] *TomTom/Tele Atlas*, para. 248. For completeness, the EU Commission ultimately decided that the transaction would not lead to anti-competitive effects irrespective of the efficiencies (para. 250)

[726] Petit, *supra* note 667 at 876-77.

[727] *Dow/DuPont*, paras. 3272–84.

strengths of merging parties may lead to significant synergies, the Commission usually does not examine these efficiencies and considers the competitive advantage that would arise from the complementary nature of the parties' activities as a basis for its anti-competitive theory of harm.[728] This again bolsters our argument for the existence of an innovation paradox.

3.6.6.2 Reduction in R&D Duplication

Denicolò and Polo have argued that the analysis of Federico et al. fails to consider that a merger can increase the probability of successful innovation. This is because a horizontal merger allows the merged entity to reduce R&D duplication and to allocate its research resources to the most promising project(s). That, in turn, increases the probability of innovation success, which directly translates into higher consumer welfare.[729]

Denicolò and Polo's second paper[730] focused on mergers between firms that had to compete for projects at the development stage prior to the merger (e.g., the development of a similar drug) and examined the impact of a merger on the merging firms' R&D efforts. In particular, they analyzed the incentive of the merging firms to discontinue one of the projects after the merger to avoid cannibalization between their projects. The authors show that whether the merged entity keeps both research units active or, conversely, shuts down one of the research units depends on the shape of the curve representing the probability of success as a function of R&D efforts. In this framework, the merged entity closes one of the research units not due to pre-emptive motives but for reasons that pertain to the efficiency of its R&D activities.[731]

3.6.7 Broadened Application of R&D Projects and Innovation Sharing

Denicolò and Polo also emphasized the positive effects of sharing innovation among the merging parties and pointed out that broader applicability of research results (e.g., basic innovations) may increase the incentive to invest in basic innovations.[732] They argue that the analysis in Motta and Tarantino's study relies on a restrictive assumption (at least in the baseline model, from which the sharpest results were derived), which is that the innovations achieved by one firm can only be applied to that firm's production plants or products, both before and after the merger. Denicolò and Polo assert that, in many cases, this assumption appears to be unrealistic. Very often, new technologies developed

---

[728] Magdalena Laskowska, *A Global View of Innovation Analysis in EC Merger Control* 7 (2013), http://dx.doi.org/10.2139/ssrn.2337174 (citing General Electric/Honeywell, European Commission Decision case COMP/M.2220 (2001))

[729] Denicolò & Polo, *supra* note 680, at 11.

[730] Vincenzo Denicolò & Michele Polo, *Duplicative Research, Mergers and Innovation*, 166 ECON. LETTERS 56 (2018).

[731] Marc Bourreau & Alexandre de Streel, *Digital Conglomerates and EU Competition Policy* 20 (2019), https://dx.doi.org/10.2139/ssrn.3350512.

[732] Denicolò & Polo, *supra* note 680, at 26.

by a firm can (in principle) also be used by others.[733] Therefore, when innovation is not firm-specific, mergers may spur innovation by facilitating the sharing of innovative technological knowledge among the merging firms. In this regard, sharing innovation expands the scope of application of new technologies, increasing their value, and hence enhances the merged entity's incentive to innovate. Denicolò and Polo contend that this effect may be so strong that a merger may increase total output and reduce prices, thereby benefiting consumers, even in the absence of static production synergies.[734]

The authors' premise is that innovation sharing may take place even among independent firms, via voluntary disclosures or through contractual licensing agreements. Although there may be various factors that impede the sharing of innovations among competitors, mergers eliminate the economic barriers to innovation sharing among the merging firms.[735] Accordingly, after the merger, the merging parties can share their fundamental discoveries and then apply them to a broader set of applied research projects. This possibility substantially increases the innovations' value for the merged entity and hence raises its incentive to invest in more research.[736]

Denicolò and Polo have elaborated and developed these insights further in another joint article, and thereby expanded them into a formal economic model. Their model is an extension of the setting of Federico et al., where they add a more basic "*research*" stage to the "*development*" stage, the output of which is a new product. The successful completion of the research stage guarantees higher productivity of the R&D expenditure that had been undertaken at the development stage. This productivity increase is not firm-specific or product-specific; the research stage produces innovative knowledge that can be used to facilitate the invention and development of a range of new products.[737]

In a duopoly where both firms complete the second stage, the firm that succeeds in the first stage has no incentive to share its intermediate innovation with its rival. Doing so would increase the probability that the rival would realize the final innovation, reducing the original firm's expected profits. In contrast, when the two firms merge, they would share the basic innovation. This would raise the R&D investment both in the research stage and development stage. The investment in the research stage increases as the basic innovation can be applied to the research projects of both divisions of the merged firm and hence becomes more valuable. The investment in the development stage increases, on average, as it is more likely that the R&D expenditure will be more productive due to the basic innovation.[738]

As a result, the merger increases the probability that new products will eventually be brought to the market. Even if the merger leads to a reduction in product-market competition, the positive effect on innovation may be substantial that the merger may increase overall

---

[733]   *Id.* at 4.
[734]   *Id.*
[735]   *Id.*
[736]   *Id.* at 26.
[737]   *Id.*
[738]   *Id.*

social welfare and consumer surplus.[739] This study indicates that the *"innovation theory of harm"* claims can be reversed. A merger that would decrease output and increase prices for a given technological state may become pro-competitive because it spurs innovation.

There are cases where European competition authorities, taking into account the innovation efficiencies that would result from the merger, cleared mergers that would lead to an increase in prices, such as the Portuguese competition authority's *Sonaecom/Portugal Telecom* decision in 2006. The acquisition of Portugal Telecom by Sonaecom had raised significant competition concerns, in particular because of the creation of a dominant position in the mobile communications market, which the authority considered would lead to a price increase. The notifying party argued that the transaction would result in certain efficiencies, which included avoiding duplication of investments (especially for a new technology – 3G), enabling the launch of new innovative products and reducing operational and fixed costs. The authority decided that the claimed efficiencies were merger-specific (considering the economies of scale to be achieved post-transaction) and verifiable. Nevertheless, the authority found that an important part of the synergies was fixed cost savings and that it was unlikely that (i) these savings (that would increase the merged entity's profits) would result in reductions in price that could benefit consumers in the short-run, and thus (ii) they were not likely to outweigh the effect of restriction of competition. However, the authority cleared the acquisition by considering the efficiencies, in addition to the remedies proposed. The authority underlined that technological innovation plays a crucial role in the sector and that launching new technologies requires a wide network and huge investments in marketing, which could be provided with the acquisition at hand. Moreover, it considered the technological convergence between mobile and fixed communications in this case and the fact that market shares may not reflect market power in these dynamic sectors.[740] Accordingly, the authority cleared the merger, taking into account its positive impact on innovation and the launch of new (3G) technologies, despite the possibility that the merger may lead to higher prices.

In the same year, the *UPC/Karneval* decision rendered by the Office for the Protection of Competition of the Czech Republic also noted that the merger between the two most important cable operators in the country would lead to a significant restriction of competition in the market for services consisting of pay-per-view signals due to the increase in market power of the merged entity, but the authority approved the merger with remedies, by taking into account the efficiencies related to innovation. The authority found that the merged entity would use its increased financial power to finance the launch of new services such as telephony over the internet (with advanced technology for digital broadcasting), interactive services and unified technology elements, and that these investments in innovation would lead the merged entity to become an effective competitor in the market for broadband access to the internet and the fixed-line telephony market, thus exerting competitive pressure on the main player in the market, i.e., Telefonica O2.[741]

---

[739]   *Id.*
[740]   OECD, *supra* note 576, at 199–200.
[741]   *Id.* at 128–29 (citing Decision of the Office S 271/06-22601/2006/720 (Nov. 22, 2006)).

3.6.8 Overcoming the Methodological Barriers

One of the main challenges faced by competition authorities has been to identify the proper tools to assess competition in innovative industries, as long-term changes to entities or sectors that comprise innovative dynamics are considered to be difficult to foresee and calculate, particularly via the static instruments at hand.[742]

Some methods for calculating efficiencies could still be applicable to innovation efficiencies; for instance, certain critics support a laissez-faire strategy, arguing that the authorities should not take into account efficiency in certain situations. Instead, they should simply trust that the safe harbors incorporated into the concentration levels of merger rules would, in most instances, answer the efficiency question correctly,[743] which could mean that if a merger does not lead to a certain level of concentration, it is unlikely that the efficiencies would outweigh the effect of restriction of competition. Nevertheless, this suggestion may not fly true in every case: When dealing with innovation issues, authorities are expected to identify which firms may become a viable competitor to the merging parties (or whether merging parties would compete in certain products absent the transaction) in the future.[744] This requires an advanced understanding of the innovative process in the market and the ability to forecast the prospects of success of the products that are being developed. Although authorities may request information from third parties and experts, they may receive inconsistent data from different market players and experts. At this point, Padilla notes how economic assumptions may not be useful in the assessment of the transaction's impact on innovation and how market tests may be misleading – and transaction parties may well be too optimistic about the success of their R&D programs and the possibility of entering into a certain market.[745] Therefore, it seems important that authorities equip themselves with the necessary tools to better analyze any inconsistency in the data provided. Furthermore, finding the best appropriate analytical timescale that can capture the dynamic consequences of a merger beyond the very short term is also crucial for authorities to properly assess innovation in the market.[746] Petit and Schrepel also argue that rendering decisions about innovation questions is difficult when there are unclear data or inadequate facts. They claim that the decisions about innovation questions are frequently driven by opportunism, ideology, or experience because they are unrelated to the most recent information in the policymaking field that is based on empirical research.[747] They suggest that

---

[742] See Linus J. Hoffmann, Anouk van der Veer, Friso Bostoen, Bowman Heiden & Nicolas Petit, *Dell – A Case Study of Dynamic Competition* 6 (DCI Case Study, Oct. 27, 2022), https://www.dynamiccompetition.com/wp-content/uploads/2022/10/DCI-CS2-Hoffmann-et-al-compressed.pdf.

[743] See OECD, *supra* note 576, at 19.

[744] See the discussions about the EU Commission's decisions in Mario Todino, Geoffroy van de Walle & Lucia Stoican, *EU Merger Control and Harm to Innovation – A Long Walk to Freedom (from the Chains of Causation)*, 64 ANTITRUST BULL. 11 (2019).

[745] The Legal 500, *Innovation and Competition Law* (webinar moderated by Jorge Padilla, Rachel Brandenburger and Gönenç Gürkaynak (June 15, 2023)), YOUTUBE, https://www.youtube.com/watch?v=Dw23C-7UYoM (last visited Aug. 19, 2023).

[746] See OECD, *Theories of Harm for Digital Mergers: OECD Competition Policy Roundtable Background Note* 10 (2023), https://www.oecd.org/daf/competition/theories-of-harm-for-digital-mergers-2023.pdf.

[747] Nicolas Petit & Thibault Schrepel, *Complexity-Minded Antitrust*, 33 J. EVOLUTIONARY ECON. 541 (2023), https://ssrn.com/abstract=4050536.

a complexity-minded antitrust would provide a solution to this problem and recommend using information revealed by complexity research, where fundamental concepts such as feedback loops and the significance of uncertainty provide new understandings that can be utilized by the authorities.[748]

In addition to the above suggestions on improving authorities' understanding of innovation considerations, to prevent any Type I error in the future (i.e., prohibiting a transaction that does not impede innovation), the authorities may require undertakings to acknowledge a certain set of commitments that can be monitored after the approval of the transaction. In the UK, the Lear Report commissioned to conduct *ex post* assessments of digital mergers was utilized to ascertain the gaps in UK authorities' assessments and later served as a basis for revising the CMA's merger guidelines and theories of harm.[749] Accordingly, conducting more case studies in the long run would also improve the authorities' awareness of any methodology shortcomings.[750]

3.7 Conclusion

In merger control, the analysis on the part of competition authorities relies on various factors and an assessment of the closeness of competition between the two products and the competitive constraint exerted by the rivals' products. Innovation concerns of competition enforcement authorities in the assessment of horizontal mergers are mainly related to whether the merging parties can internalize the constraint between the rival products and whether this may give the merged entity an incentive to reduce its innovation efforts. In extreme cases, the merged entity can even discontinue one of the products in order to avoid cannibalization of the other product's sales.

is the key parameter in evaluating the cannibalization effect. On the other hand, it may be quite difficult to estimate or determine the innovation diversion ratio in a given case.

The assessment of the impact of a merger on R&D investments requires a complex balancing exercise involving several factors that affect the incentives to innovate, most notably *cannibalization* and *appropriability*. The fact that these factors exert opposing influences on the merged entity's incentives to innovate implies that it would not be accurate to presume that one effect dominates the other.

The finding in the theoretical models that a horizontal merger reduces innovation incentives is mostly based on the assumption that the merger does not create any efficiency gains. This finding could be reversed if the synergies resulting from mergers are taken into account properly. Besides, the results can differ when other factors (such as the *demand expansion effect* and *margin expansion effect*) are considered as well. Competition authorities are also advised to contemplate and incorporate the welfare-increasing effects of

---

748   *Id.* § 3.3.1.
749   *Id.*
750   *See* Hoffman et al., *supra* note 742.

information sharing and R&D cooperation between merging firms into their merger assessments. As the traditional methods fall short of proper assessment of dynamic efficiencies, the need to find and utilize the appropriate tools and methodologies is apparent at every turn.

In summary, there is not a single overarching general theory on the effects of mergers on innovation, and the findings of current theoretical research papers should be read and interpreted in light of the assumptions underlying a particular study. As for applying the conclusions of a given theoretical research study to a real-life/tangible merger case, one should carefully consider how the assumptions of the relevant research study match up with the particular facts and circumstances of the merger under examination.

Chapter 4
Innovation Considerations
in Merger Control in the European Union

*"The progressive development of man is vitally dependent on invention.
Invention is the most important product of man's creative brain.
The ultimate purpose is the complete mastery of mind over the material world,
the harnessing of human nature to human needs."*– Nikola Tesla[751]

4.1 Introduction

The digital revolution and globalization, as they extend their roots deep within the societies, have changed how concepts such as prosperity, competition, and development are perceived around the world. It is now evident that innovation and progress are phenomena that can inescapably alter the competitive landscapes of markets, production chains, utilities, advertising, and prices, as well as bringing along the ability to create new markets, products, and efficiencies. Naturally, as a result, technological advancements have now become the driving force of economic growth, and innovation`s dynamic reflection bears more and more significance for the assessment of the competition in a given sector.

The milieu bridging the innovative technological leaps and the competitive theories of harm has multiple aspects and brings up an array of thorny questions. For instance, what happens to the R&D department of Company X when it merges with a stronger Company Y, which is active in the same innovation space? Will one of the two R&D departments lose its significance or simply not be prioritized as much, considering cost and efficiency? What happens if Company X's product is removed from the market, once again due to cost considerations, and the merged entity continues its operations solely with Company Y's product? Will Company X's innovative efforts be redirected into another field or product? Will Company Y lower its total innovative budget now that it no longer has to compete with Company X?[752] Alternatively, on the flip side of the coin, could Company X and Y merging actually lead to the compilation or synthesis of diverse and harmonized know-how, thus creating "complementary products or firms that have complementary skills"?[753]

---

[751]   Nikola Tesla, "My inventions", in Electrical Experimenter Science and Innovation (1919).
[752]   Nicolas Petit, *Innovation Competition, Unilateral Effects and Merger Control Policy*, (ICLE Antitrust & Consumer Protection Research Program, White Paper 2018-03), https://laweconcenter.org/wp-content/uploads/2018/06/ICLE-Petit-Innovation-Competition-Merger-Control-Policy-ICLE-2018.pdf.
[753]   Mengmeng Shi, The Divestiture Remedies Under Merger Control in the US, the EU and China: A Comparative Law and Economics Perspective (2019) (doctoral thesis, Maastricht University) (on file with the Maastricht University).

Competition law scrutinizes each link of the industrial chain, and the competition authorities around the world act as guardians of consumer welfare. Maintaining the delicate balance between innovation and competitiveness of markets has become a significant part of the antitrust enforcers' duties. Against this background, as the EU's competition overseer, the Commission's outlook on the assessment of innovation has become the leading voice and most influential force for other competition authorities. In this regard, the Commission's perspective on this issue provides a word of caution for tech-driven companies and innovators. The Commission, which is known to focus primarily on traditional parameters such as "price, quality, and output,"[754] also conducts detailed innovation analyses in its decisions[755] – now more so than ever, becoming more apparent with the highly debated *Dow/DuPont*,[756] and the subsequent *Bayer/Monsanto* decisions,[757] demonstrating its novel approach towards innovation assessments. However, the changeability of the methodology for assessing innovation-focused cases and the vague wording of the legislative framework have combined to make the task at hand quite tricky. This could also be observed in the zigzagging course that the Commission's decisions have taken in its case law. It is also important to note that certain sectors are more vulnerable than others to the changing winds of competition law assessment, such as the digital, pharmaceutical, telecommunications, and aerospace industries, where innovative advances constitute a considerable competitive advantage for undertakings.

Because of the nature of these types of markets, the Commission applies much stricter scrutiny in its competition assessments.[758] Moreover, the innovation assessment becomes even more intricate when it comes to the merger control aspect of competition law, where the Commission needs to conduct a successful *ex ante* analysis of the innovative force of a concentration, during which the traditional tools of merger control assessment might fail to hit the mark.

All in all, this chapter aims to assess the innovation concerns and efficiencies derived from the Commission's merger cases, as well as the legal framework of the EU and the economic tools for innovation assessment, in order to provide an overview of the gradual transition of the Commission's approach pertaining to innovation considerations in EU merger control.

---

[754] Pablo Ibáñez Colomo, *Restrictions on Innovation in EU Competition Law* (LSE Law, Society and Economy Working Papers 22/2015, 2015), http://ssrn.com/abstract=2699395.

[755] *See, e.g.*, cases discussed in more detail under Section V below.

[756] Dow/DuPont, European Commission Decision case M.7932 (Mar. 27, 2017).

[757] Bayer/Monsanto, European Commission Decision case M.8084 (Mar. 21, 2018).

[758] European Commission, Study for DG Enterprise and Industry, *Impact of EU Competition Legislation on Innovation* (2000).

4.2 An Innovation-Centric Overview of European Merger Control Legislation

The EU merger control regime, although brought under detailed regulation with the Merger Regulation,[759] is primarily sourced from the concept of protection of competition in the internal market, as embedded in articles 101–109 of the Treaty on the Functioning of the European Union ("TFEU"). The infrastructure built by the TFEU for the protection and monitoring of competition has tasked the Commission with overseeing transactions with an EU dimension. The Commission is authorized to reject a transaction because it would "impede effective competition in the common market or in a substantial part of it, in particular through the creation or strengthening of a dominant position,"[760] thus declaring such a transaction to be incompatible with the stock market of the EU. It should be highlighted that article 101(3) TFEU also provides that the retributive section of article 101 shall not be applied in cases where the anti-competitive behavior "contributes to improving the production or distribution of goods or to promoting technical or economic progress, while allowing consumers a fair share of the resulting benefit" – as long as it does not impose indispensable restrictions or eliminate competition in a substantial part of the products in question. Accordingly, innovation has become a focal point for the Commission within different stages of its competition assessments, as discussed below.

The Relevant Market

The Commission has previously considered innovation when designating the relevant market in its competition assessments. The Commission Notice on the definition of the relevant market[761] does not directly refer to innovation, and although the Commission's focus on innovation is revealed through the precedents and other supporting secondary legislation, the results of the evaluation study on the Commission notice indicate that there are market realities, such as innovation-intensive sectors, where market definition still requires careful application.[762] In this context, it could be said that the Commission exhibits a dual approach when integrating innovative power and market consideration: innovation which is or could be.[763] By way of connecting the dots, this approach is reflected in the Horizontal Co-operation Guidelines of the EU,[764] which states that "R&D

---

[759]   European Union, Council Regulation (EC) No. 139/2004 of Jan. 20, 2004, on the Control of Concentrations Between Undertakings (the "EC Merger Regulation" or "EUMR"), 2004 OJ (I 24) 1, https://eur-lex.europa.eu/legal-content/EN/TXT/PDF/?uri=CELEX:32004R0139&from=EN.

[760]   *Id.*

[761]   European Commission, Commission Notice on the Definition of the Relevant Market for the Purposes of Community Competition Law, 1997 OJ (C 372) 5.

[762]   European Commission, Commission Staff Working Document, *Evaluation of the Commission Notice on the Definition of Relevant Market for the Purposes of Community Competition Law of 9 December 1997* 62, SWD(2021) 199 final (July 12, 2021), https://competition-policy.ec.europa.eu/system/files/2021-07/evaluation_market-definition-notice_en.pdf.

[763]   Magdalena Laskowska, *A Global View of Innovation Analysis in EC Merger Control* 7 (2013), http://dx.doi.org/10.2139/ssrn.2337174.

[764]   European Commission, Guidelines on the Applicability of Article 101 of the Treaty on the Functioning of the European Union to Horizontal Co-operation Agreements, 2011 OJ (C 11) 1.

co-operation concerns the development of new products or technology which either may – if emerging – one day replace existing ones or which are being developed for a new intended use and will therefore not replace existing products but create a completely new demand."[765]

Delineating the borders of the relevant product market remains a key aspect for the Commission's assessment of many merger cases, simply because it also coincides with outlining the borders of the competitive analysis, where elements such as market share and position, competitors and buyer power, amongst others, are identified from this initial deduction.[766] In innovation-centric sectors, the approach towards the relevant market carries significant weight, as it is easy to overlook that innovation occurring outside the borders of the relevant market may also have the power to drastically alter the relevant market.[767] (Hence, the Commission's move away from traditional approaches and introduction of the concept of innovation spaces in *Dow/DuPont* and *Bayer/Monsanto* for their herbicides, insecticides and fungicides, discussed in detail below.)[768]

In this context, the Horizontal Co-operation Guidelines have examined the question of an innovation market under research and development agreements. Although the application of article 101 and competition restrictive agreements is an altogether different branch of the overall European competition law regime, the following excerpt clearly outlines the primary method in determining a market based on a product that remains unknown at the time:

> [A]t one end of the spectrum of possible situations, innovation may result in a product (or technology) which competes in an existing product (or technology) market. This is, for example, the case with R&D directed towards slight improvements or variations, such as new models of certain products. Here possible effects concern the market for existing products. *At the other end of the spectrum, innovation may result in an entirely new product which creates its own new product-market (for example, a new vaccine for a previously incurable disease).* However, many cases concern situations in between those two extremes, that is to say, situations in which innovation efforts may create products (or technology)

---

[765]   *Id.*, para. 119.

[766]   European Commission, *supra* note 761.

[767]   Also known as "disruptive innovation." European Commission, *EU Merger Control and Innovation*, COMPETITION POLICY BRIEF (Apr. 2016), http://ec.europa.eu/competition/publications/cpb/2016/2016_001_en.pdf.

[768]   This approach is different in the UK, where the CMA aims to focus more on competitive assessment rather than a strict market definition (CMA, Merger Assessment Guidelines (CMA129) (Mar. 18, 2021), para. 9.2, https://assets.publishing.service.gov.uk/government/uploads/system/uploads/attachment_data/file/1051823/MAGs_for_publication_2021_--_.pdf). As per the CMA Guidelines, market definition provides a framework for assessing the competitive effects of a merger and involves an element of judgment; however, the boundaries of the market do not determine the outcome of the analysis of the merger's competitive effects, recognizing that the CMA will assess the constraints on merging parties from outside the relevant market, segmentation within the relevant market, or other material constraints, if any (para. 9.4). Accordingly, in *Roche/Spark Therapeutics*, the CMA focused its assessment on the likely impact of the merger with regard to (i) innovation, (ii) price and (iii) product quality and market expenditure, and evaluated that the prevailing conditions of competition are associated with both merging parties, along with other market players' continuation of investment and innovation compatible in terms of their pre-merger business plans (Roche/Spark Therapeutics, case ME/6831/19 (Dec. 16, 2019)). *See also* Chapter 2 above for a brief comparison of the EU, UK and US approaches.

which, over time, replace existing ones (for example, CDs which have replaced records). A careful analysis of those situations may have to cover both existing markets and the impact of the agreement on innovation.[769]

Moreover, there are examples of cases where the Commission approached the relevant product market solely based on the R&D aspect, thus creating a distinction between the assessments of *"competition in the existing markets"* and *"competition in innovation."*[770] Herein, it should be noted that the concept of *"innovation markets"* alone creates discord and debate; some commentators have criticized this concept as nebulous and borderless, and pointed out that economic and competitive analyses cannot be conducted with regard to such "innovation markets" due to the unpredictability and limited foresight of *ex ante* assessments when it comes to unknown players and market parameters.[771]

Significant Impediment of Effective Competition

The second and principal innovation consideration in the European merger control regime is the reflection of innovation in the substantive competitive case analysis. Under the EU's Merger Regulation, the substantive test applied in merger control cases by the Commission involves the assessment of whether a transaction results in *"significant impediment of effective competition"* ("SIEC").[772] The Merger Regulation nods to the concept of dominance therein, by stating that SIEC generally occurs by the creation or strengthening of a dominant position. As a result, a bridge between the possibility of SIEC and innovative analysis is built during the Commission's assessment, as detailed in the below analyses of precedents. Furthermore, in the primary legislation, the Merger Regulation leaves the framework for the assessment of theories of harm and efficiencies to the guidelines that will be published by the Commission.[773] In the scope of the guidelines, the Commission makes a distinction between horizontal and non-horizontal mergers.

Horizontal Mergers

The EU Horizontal Merger Guidelines recount the benefits of effective competition as "low prices, high-quality products, a wide selection of goods and services, and innovation."[774] It should, however, be noted that the EU Horizontal Merger Guidelines do not give a concrete definition for the concept of "innovation" despite subsequently referring to it multiple times. Therefore, it is evident that the legislative position of the Commission leaves the door open to a case-by-case analysis, in order to identify and demarcate innovation by considering the facts of the case at hand in any given

---

[769] European Commission, *supra* note 764, para. 112 (emphasis added).

[770] Eline Vancraybex, *Innovation in the EU Merger Control Battlefield: In Search for Best Practices* (Maastricht Centre for European Law, Working Paper No. 1, 2018).

[771] Michael A. Carrier, *Two Puzzles Resolved: Of the Schumpeter–Arrow Stalemate and Pharmaceutical Innovation Markets*, 93 Iowa L. Rev. 393 (2008).

[772] This test was introduced in the scope of the new Merger Regulation (in force today), which was drafted and adopted to replace the Merger Regulation of 1990.

[773] EC Merger Regulation, paras. 28, 29.

[774] European Commission, Guidelines on the Assessment of Horizontal Mergers Under the Council Regulation on the Control of Concentrations Between Undertakings, 2004 OJ (C 031) 5, https://eur-lex.europa.eu/legal-content/EN/TXT/HTML/?uri=CELEX:52004XC0205(02)&from=EN ("EU Horizontal Merger Guidelines").

assessment. In any event, any diminishments in innovation, along with price, reduction of output, choice or quality of goods (amongst others), have been listed as an element that would indicate *"increased market power,"* which undertakings may achieve by way of a horizontal merger.[775,776]

However, acknowledging innovation as a market element that could be diminished or reduced post-merger does not, by itself, establish how innovation-centric theories of harm are structured within the legislative framework. The EU Horizontal Merger Guidelines also refer to the gray area in between by stating that "a merger may increase the firms' ability and incentive to bring new innovations to the market and, thereby, the competitive pressure on rivals to innovate in that market," whereas "effective competition may be significantly impeded by a merger between two important innovators, for instance between two companies with 'pipeline' products related to a specific product-market."[777] In addition to the foregoing, the EU Horizontal Merger Guidelines also put forth and explicate the possible competition law concerns arising from a merger between two companies where one is already active in a particular market, and the other could easily enter without having to endure significant sunk costs or "is very likely to incur the necessary sunk costs to enter the market in a relatively short period of time."[778]

The guidelines go on to explain that two conditions would cause a red flag to be raised when assessing the proposed merger of potential competitors. Firstly, the potential competitor should already constitute a competitive pressure or demonstrate the likelihood of doing so in the future. Secondly, the number of remaining potential competitors should be insufficient.[779] The fulfillment of these two conditions would lead the Commission to assess the transaction for any *"significant anti-competitive effects."* It should also be noted that the assessment of the market entry period of the potential competitors (which may be deemed to lead to an anti-competitive effects assessment if anticipated to be within a *"relatively short period"*) is also determined on a case-by-case basis. Therefore, the market specifics, such as the product cycle and the aptitude of the potential competitor, would be taken into consideration.[780,781]

As acknowledged by the EU Horizontal Merger Guidelines, innovation considerations also present other difficulties when it comes to the technical assessment of a proposed merger. The market share calculation constitutes "ground zero" for most concentration analyses. In a "mature" market, a new entrant would be expected to grow its market share

---

[775]   *Id.*

[776]   Similar to the structure in the EU Horizontal Merger Guidelines, the word "merger" is used to cover all types of concentrations within the meaning of the EU merger control regime, e.g., acquisitions, joint ventures, takeovers, etc.

[777]   EU Horizontal Merger Guidelines, para. 38.

[778]   *Id.*, para. 59.

[779]   European Commission, Competition Merger Brief (May 1, 2017), http://ec.europa.eu/competition/publications/cmb/2017/kdal17001enn.pdf.

[780]   *Id.*

[781]   Para. 74 of the EU Horizontal Merger Guidelines stipulates that entry within two years, under normal circumstances, would be regarded as "timely," with the caveat that such assessment would be based on the facts of the case.

gradually, and any dramatic changes in market shares would be regarded as uncommon and unusual.[782] However, in fast-moving and innovative sectors, the market shares of an undertaking may not be sufficient to accurately depict the market reality, due to a number of factors. Firstly, the ability for a new player to step into the relevant market and create a whole new portion/source of supply would be deemed more likely in such a sector.[783] Secondly, an existing competitor may also alter the distribution of demand in a market by offering a new/enhanced product,[784] and this possibility is explicitly referenced in the EU Horizontal Merger Guidelines by: "[A] firm with a relatively small market share may nevertheless be an important competitive force if it has promising pipeline products." Therefore, rapid changes in the market structure would lower the predictive power of a market share assessment for competition law purposes. A similar conclusion can also be reached with respect to the Herfindahl–Hirschman Index ("HHI"),[785] where the standard conclusions attained via HHI would be deemed inapplicable if "one or more merging parties are important innovators in ways not reflected in market shares."[786] As a result of the foregoing considerations, the question that must be asked at this juncture is whether the legislative framework relating to assessment methods, such as the HHI, the definition of a relevant market and market shares (and thus, the utilization of static analysis tools), would correspond to the realities of dynamic and innovative markets, and whether they would be adequate for competition law assessments in such markets. There is a real and underappreciated risk that the utilization of stagnant methodologies in such a scenario may even cause consumer welfare to diminish[787] due to over-intrusive and counterproductive competitive analyses.

Non-Horizontal Mergers

An innovation-oriented competition law assessment is certainly not exclusive to horizontal mergers. Non-horizontal mergers are also scrutinized with innovation considerations in mind, as indicated in the legislative framework and the relevant case law of the Commission.[788] Non-horizontal mergers occur when undertakings at different levels of the production chain come together and join forces.[789] A competitor is not

---

[782]   David Encaoua & Abraham Hollander, *Competition Policy and Innovation*, 18 Oxford Rev. Econ. Pol'y 63 (2002), https://doi.org/10.1093/oxrep/18.1.63.

[783]   OECD, *Merger Review in Emerging High Innovation Markets* (Policy Roundtable, DAFFE/COMP(2002)20, Jan. 24, 2003), http://www.oecd.org/daf/competition/mergers/2492253.pdf.

[784]   *Id.*

[785]   EU Horizontal Merger Guidelines, para. 16: "In order to measure concentration levels, the Commission often applies the Herfindahl-Hirschman Index (HHI). The HHI is calculated by summing the squares of the individual market shares of all the firms in the market. The HHI gives proportionately greater weight to the market shares of the larger firms. Although it is best to include all firms in the calculation, lack of information about very small firms may not be important because such firms do not affect the HHI significantly. While the absolute level of the HHI can give an initial indication of the competitive pressure in the market post-merger, the change in the HHI (known as the 'delta') is a useful proxy for the change in concentration directly brought about by the merger."

[786]   *Id.*, para. 20(1).

[787]   Gregory J. Sidak & David J. Teece, *Dynamic Competition in Antitrust Law*, 5 J. Competition L. & Econ. 581 (2009).

[788]   The Commission assessed the possibility of vertical input foreclosure in the scope of the merger of *Intel/McAfee* (European Commission Decision case COMP/M.5984 (Jan. 26, 2011)).

[789]   A "vertical merger" is used here as an umbrella term for vertical and conglomerate transactions in the scope of the EU merger control regime.

removed from the market in question as a result of a non-horizontal merger; instead, a non-horizontal merger paves the way for an integrated vertical portfolio, which has the potential to create a number of efficiencies.[790] Nevertheless, as vertical mergers do not commonly result in the elimination of an innovator/innovation process from the market, the strict scrutiny applied to horizontal mergers in this regard is not expected to be reflected in the assessments of non-horizontal mergers, at least not at the same level of intensity.[791]

The competitive analysis of the vertical integration of two or more undertakings would focus on whether the undertakings in question can limit output or increase prices in the post-merger market, thereby shutting downstream rivals out of the market. This could occur by the foreclosure of rival undertakings, which is required to innovate in that particular market. The Commission's Non-Horizontal Merger Guidelines ("NHMG") define effective competition in parallel with the EU Horizontal Merger Guidelines. Conversely, a vertical or conglomerate merger is seen as less of a threat to effective competition and is known to give rise to multiple efficiencies, including service improvements or *"stepping up innovation."*[792] In correlation, the NHMG set out that it is less likely for a non-horizontal merger to create coordinated effects unless the post-merger assessment of HHI or market shares are below certain thresholds. Nevertheless, the NHMG stipulate some exceptional circumstances in which the Commission will apply greater scrutiny to a non-horizontal merger, one of which clearly articulates the following circumstances: "[A] merger involves a company that is likely to expand significantly in the near future, e.g., because of a recent innovation."[793]

Thresholds and Article 22

Concerned by a perceived rise in "killer acquisitions" and their effects on innovation, the Commission conducted a study regarding the effectiveness of thresholds in mergers,[794] which concluded that while the mechanisms in place were able to capture most of the transactions that had a significant impact on competition in the EU internal market, there were still a few transactions, especially in the digital and pharma sectors, that were able to evade the review mechanism of the Commission and Member States. Accordingly, the Commission published guidance[795] regarding the "referral mechanism" set out in article 22 of the EU Merger Regulation. Initially designed for Member States without a merger

---

[790] Markus Seiler, Innovation Competition in EU Merger Control 9–10 (2018) (on file with the University of St. Gallen).

[791] Id.

[792] European Commission, Guidelines on the Assessment of Non-Horizontal Mergers Under the Council Regulation on the Control of Concentrations Between Undertakings, 2008 OJ (C 265) 6.

[793] Id., para. 26.

[794] European Commission, Commission Staff Working Document, *Evaluation of Procedural and Jurisdictional Aspects of EU Merger Control*, SWD(202) 66 final (Mar. 26, 2021), https://ec.europa.eu/competition/consultations/2021_merger_control/SWD_findings_of_evaluation.pdf.

[795] European Commission, *Commission Guidance on the Application of the Referral Mechanism Set out in Article 22 of the Merger Regulation to Certain Categories of Cases*, C(2021) 1959 final (Mar. 26, 2021) ("Article 22 Guidance"), https://ec.europa.eu/competition/consultations/2021_merger_control/guidance_article_22_referrals.pdf.

control regime to refer cases to the Commission,[796] this article had only been used for cases where the referring Member States had jurisdiction.[797] Now, article 22 has been reappraised as a tool to catch transactions that do not meet the jurisdictional turnover thresholds but are otherwise deemed "competitively significant." The first application of this reappraised article 22 referral was used in the proposed *Illumina/Grail* transaction (explained further below).

Efficiencies

It is important to note that the Merger Regulation also accommodates the possibility that the efficiencies that a transaction gives rise to might also mitigate the competition law concerns that it has the potential to cause,[798] so long as these efficiencies are "beneficial for consumers, merger-specific and verifiable."[799] However, verifying such efficiencies creates a challenge in practice, as the innovative force and potential of a company are often difficult to foresee and, more importantly, to quantify through qualitative economic assessments. Additionally, the requirement that the efficiencies must be merger-specific would mean that the transaction parties would have to prove that the efficiencies that they claim to counterbalance the anti-competitive effects of the transaction could not be achieved by less anti-competitive alternatives (such as licensing agreements, joint ventures, or a differently structured transaction).[800] In other words, the efficiencies must be in a "direct causality" relationship with the transaction itself.[801] As a result, in practice, the "efficiency escape route" is claimed, but not preferred, due to the difficulties that the transaction parties may run into when attempting to demonstrate, validate and prove the three conditions listed above.[802]

Nevertheless, the demonstration of consumer-benefiting efficiencies is not the only exit route in the context of merger control. The parties to a transaction are also entitled to offer solutions, such as divestitures or behavioral commitments, to remedy the anti-competitive effects of a merger transaction. Such commitments will be market-tested by the Commission, in order not only to assess their applicability but also to consider the views of market participants concerning the potential remedying effects.[803]

---

[796] *See* Sophie Lawrance & Sean-Paul Brankin, *Illumina/GRAIL: Bio-Tech Companies in the Firing Line as the European Commission Expands the Limits of European Merger Control*, BRISTOWS (Oct. 13, 2021), https://www.bristows.com/news/illumina-grail-bio-tech-companies-in-the-firing-line-as-the-european-commission-expands-the-limits-of-european-merger-control.

[797] Van Bael & Bellis, *Commission Issues Statement of Objections in Illumina/GRAIL Gun-Jumping Investigation as Parties Argue Jurisdictional Overreach*, 2021 VBB ON COMPETITION L. 3 (Sept. 2021), https://www.vbb.com/media/Insights_Newsletters/VBB_on_Competition_Law_Volume_2021_No_8-9.pdf.

[798] European Union, Council Regulation (EC) No. 139/2004 of Jan. 20, 2004, on the Control of Concentrations Between Undertakings (the "EC Merger Regulation" or "EUMR"), 2004 OJ (L 24) 1, https://eur-lex.europa.eu/legal-content/EN/TXT/PDF/?uri=CELEX:32004R0139&from=EN.

[799] European Commission, *supra* note 767.

[800] Gönenç Gürkaynak & Naz Topaloglu, *Turkey: Innovation Based Analysis of Mergers*, CONCURRENCES No. 1-2019, art. No. 88891.

[801] OECD, *The Role of Efficiency Claims in Antitrust Proceedings* (Policy Roundtables, DAF/COMP(2012)23, May 2, 2013), https://www.oecd.org/competition/EfficiencyClaims2012.pdf.

[802] *Id.*

[803] European Commission, Commission Notice on Remedies Acceptable under Council Regulation (EC) No. 139/2004 and under Commission Regulation (EC) No. 802/2004, 2008 OJ (C 267) 1.

4.3 Approaching Innovation in EU Merger Control: The Debate, the Progress and the Focus Areas

Although the legislative framework of the European merger control regime refers to the concept of "innovation" on several occasions, it is also sufficiently vague to allow the case law of the Commission to fill in the blanks and to enable the Commission to try various approaches in its application. The Commission's approach and oversight are explained in detail below through a case-by-case analysis. However, it is essential to note at the outset that the intricate structure of economic innovation theory comprises numerous segments, which also alters and affects the legal theory and assessment of innovation. In addition, the development of a sound legal theory for assessing the link between competition and innovation has been accelerated as the topic has gained currency and relevance due to rapid technological advancements in recent years. In specific sectors, both the policies of competition authorities and the economic doctrine applied in such assessments have varied substantially over time.

4.3.1 Chasing Innovation: Definitions and Classifications

> "INVENTION is here interpreted broadly as the production of knowledge."
> – Kenneth J. Arrow[804]

For competition law, defining the precise meaning of "innovation"[805] has proved to be a difficult challenge, both within case law and in doctrine. A business-oriented definition is found in the Oslo Manual of the OECD, which defines innovation as "a new or improved product or process (or combination thereof) that differs significantly from the unit's previous products or processes and that has been made available to potential users (product) or brought into use by the unit (process)."[806] There are other (and vaguer) definitions in the doctrine, where the focus shifts to the notion of a novel "idea," such as "a multistage process of transforming ideas into new products/services or processes."[807] Other approaches have added in the value of consumer welfare, and describe innovation

---

[804] Kenneth Arrow, Economic Welfare and the Allocation of Resources for Invention, *in* National Bureau of Economic Research, The Rate and Direction of Inventive Activity: Economic and Social Factors 609 (Princeton Univ. Press 1962).

[805] Derived from the word "*innovatus*" in Latin, which is traced to "*innovo*," meaning "to renew or restore." The connotations this concept has carried throughout history are discussed in detail in Chapter 1.

[806] OECD/Eurostat, Oslo Manual 2018: Guidelines for Collecting, Reporting and Using Data on Innovation, 4th edition (The Measurement of Scientific, Technological and Innovation Activities, OECD Publishing/Eurostat 2018).

[807] E. J. A. Vincent, The Impact of Regulation on Innovation: A Case Study on Small Biscuit Producers in The Netherlands (2017) (bachelor thesis, University of Twente) (on file with the University of Twente).

as "the ability to apply new ideas and transform them into commercial or social outcomes that enhance consumer welfare by using new processes, products, or services."[808]

The various types of innovation and how they correspond and interact with the market competition are based on a few different characteristics. In this regard, the historical context of innovation theory cannot be communicated without acknowledging the previously introduced Schumpeterian view of innovation.

The Schumpeterian perspective on innovation correlates the five sub-categories of innovation to what he calls "*creative destruction,*" in which novel units of production replace dated or outmoded products. The Commission's policy brief on innovation, however, refrains from defining the concept itself and instead focuses on the distinctions between different types of innovation.[809] It is unclear whether the Commission's categorizations nod to Schumpeter in any way; however, one can still recognize the similarities.

When defining innovation in its discussion paper on EU merger control and innovation[810], the Commission makes the initial distinction to the end result of innovation – namely, a distinction is drawn between (i) product innovation and (ii) process innovation. In simple terms, product innovation is the introduction of a new product to the market. Herein, the Commission also takes into account significant changes "to [the product's] characteristics or intended uses."[811] In the doctrine, product innovation is commonly deemed to give birth to a patentable outcome.[812] As for process innovation, it refers to the application of a new method or the improvement of an existing method of production or delivery.[813,814] Process innovation does not usually result in a patent; therefore, the ability to invest in process innovation is often found in undertakings with higher market power, since a prominent market player would be better able to reflect the costs of the improvements/changes to the price of the product itself.[815] Therefore, the incentive to invest in and to intensify the undertaking's focus on a specific type of innovation would be based on a financial appropriation assessment by any market player, which would lead to different results depending on numerous elements, including market power.[816]

The Commission's second categorization focuses on the length of the "innovative leap," or in other words, the significance of the change occurring as a result of the

---

[808] Sofia Ranchordás, *Innovation Experimentalism in the Age of the Sharing Economy*, 19 Lewis & Clark L. Rev. 871 (2015).

[809] European Commission, *supra* note 767.

[810] *Id.* at 2.

[811] *Id.*

[812] Carrier, *supra* note 771.

[813] *Id.*

[814] In summary, it is important to note that the OECD's Oslo Manual, assuming a more business management outlook on the topic, specifies process innovation as "business process innovation" and defines it as "a new or improved business process for one or more business functions that differs significantly from the firm's previous business processes and that has been brought into use by the firm." OECD/Eurostat, *supra* note 806.

[815] Carrier, *supra* note 771.

[816] Ólafur Páll Torfason, Appropriability Mechanisms and Strategies for Innovations: The Case of Rotulus (2011) (master thesis, Copenhagen Business School) (on file with the Copenhagen Business School), https://research. cbs.dk/files/58427580/olafur_pall_torfason.pdf.

innovation. The first type of such innovative leap is known as "incremental" innovation. This self-explanatory term refers to changes or improvements on an existing product or process, which the Commission refers to as "a small step forward."[817] Conversely, a major innovative leap is required for an innovation to be described and categorized as a "breakthrough innovation."

The final classification of the Commission's policy brief is based on the "game-changing" ability of the innovation. In this context, improving on what is readily available is defined as *"sustaining innovation,"* whereas displacing the old by implementing a novel "value network" is defined as *"disruptive innovation."*[818] Therefore, a disruptive innovation could have the power to create an entirely new market, making it the most difficult type of innovation to analyze or foresee by competition policymakers.[819]

The doctrine has also made additional categorizations, with a special focus on, for instance, the market power/position of the innovator firm, the source of the innovation initiative, the availability of the innovation,[820] or the freedom that the innovation gives the innovator not to be limited or constrained by competitive pressures (i.e., drastic vs. non-drastic innovation).[821,822]

All in all, it is crucial to recognize that innovation itself is a dynamic concept in law and economic theory. Therefore, it is reasonable to assume that the approaches, definitions

---

[817] European Commission, *supra* note 767. *See also* Peter Thomond & Fiona Lettice, Disruptive Innovation Explored, 9th IPSE International Conference on Concurrent Engineering: Research and Applications (CE2002) (July 2002).

[818] *Id.* In literature, there are also different definitions of disruptive innovations from different perspectives (Steven Si & Hui Chen, *A Literature Review of Disruptive Innovation: What It Is, How It Works and Where It Goes*, 56 J. ENG'G & TECH. MGMT. (2020)). These take into account (i) specific domain and effects, (ii) process, (iii) effects, and (iv) characteristics. In terms of "specific domain and effects" a new technology that outperforms an existing one disrupts the market (Mohammad Hajhashem & Amir Khorasani, *Demystifying the Dynamic of Disruptive Innovations in Markets with Complex Adoption Networks: From Encroachment to Disruption*, 12 INT'L J. INNOVATION & TECH. MGMT. (2015); Ariel K. H. Lui, Eric W. T. Ngai & Kwan Yu Lo, *Disruptive Information Technology Innovations and the Cost of Equity Capital: The Moderating Effect of CEO Incentives and Institutional Pressures*, 53 INFO. & MGMT. 345 (2016)). In terms of "process," existing competitors do not appear in the market due to disruptive innovation (Marina Levina, *Disrupt or Die: Mobile Health and Disruptive Innovation as Body Politics*, 18 TELEVISION & NEW MEDIA 548, 18 (2017)). In terms of "effects," new demands, new competitors and new ways of operating are created as a result of disruptive innovation (Yuliani Suseno, *Disruptive Innovation and the Creation of Social Capital in Indonesia's Urban Communities*, 24 ASIA PACIFIC BUS. REV. 174 (2018)). In terms of "characteristics," disruptive innovation brings radical new functionality and changes consumer expectations (Delmer Nagy, Joseph Schuessler & Alan Dubinsky, *Defining and Identifying Disruptive Innovations*, 57 INDUS. MKTG. MGMT. 119, 120 (2016); Ronny Reinhardt & Sebastian Gurtner, *Differences between Early Adopters of Disruptive and Sustaining Innovations*, 68 J. BUS. RSCH. 137 (2015)).

[819] Inge Graef, Sih Yuliana Wahyuningtyas & Peggy Valcke, How Google and Others Upset Competition Analysis: Disruptive Innovation and European Competition Law, 25th European Regional Conference of the International Telecommunications Society (ITS), Brussels, Belgium, June 22–25 (2014), https://www.econstor.eu/handle/10419/101378.

[820] Paul Lugard & David Cardwell, *Innovation is King. Or is it? Summary Observations on the Application of EU Antitrust and Merger Control Law to Innovation-related Transaction*, ANTITRUST CHRON. 2 (Sep. 2012). Edwin Mansfield, *Contribution of R&D to Economic Growth in the United States*, 175 SCIENCE 477 (1972)

[821] Carrier, *supra* note 771.

[822] PAUL BELLEFLAMME & MARTIN PEITZ, INDUSTRIAL ORGANIZATION: MARKETS AND STRATEGIES (Cambridge Univ. Press 2009).

and categorizations will vary, as will the practical application of competition law policies. In this context, it is perfectly understandable that policymakers may choose to refrain from drawing the borders of the concept of "innovation" too strictly with a definition that is set in stone, as they may prefer to leave room for nimble maneuvering regarding considerations of unknown market dynamics that the future might hold, and thereby enable the Commission's outlook and approach to innovation to progress from the traditional to the novel.

4.3.2 The Debate and its Reflection on the Enforcement Approach to Interactions of Innovation and Competition

"The first thing to go is the traditional conception of the modus operandi of competition. Economists are at long last emerging from the stage in which price competition was all they saw." – Joseph A. Schumpeter[823]

The puzzle of the interplay between innovation and competition is this: does competition nurture or weaken innovation? This fundamental question has led to numerous debates between economists and policymakers, as discussed in Chapter 3. Nevertheless, as economists attempt to analyze whether a concentrated market would create an incentive to innovate and excel,[824] it falls on the policymakers to try and establish a middle ground between innovation and competition and to strike a delicate balance in order to foster innovation without being artificially intrusive on the competitive parameters of a given relevant market.

In this respect, the divisions among the proponents of economic innovation theory regarding the market environment that is most capable and conducive to fostering innovation have led to the infamous debate between the two opposing schools of thought: in support of Schumpeter vs. in support of Arrow. Simply put, the Schumpeterian view stipulates that, in a more highly concentrated market, a strong market player or a monopolist would have less to fear from competitors, and therefore, more to spend and more to gain from engaging in innovative processes. For the sake of clearly communicating Schumpeter's idea of "monopolists as innovators," the process can be separated into three basic sections: incentive, application, and outcome. Schumpeter stipulates that a monopolist would have an incentive to stay ahead of its competitors,[825] while enjoying a head start. Therefore, the said incentive would not be hampered by a fear of competitive pressures; rather, it would be further enhanced by experience

---

[823] JOSEPH A. SCHUMPETER, CAPITALISM, SOCIALISM AND DEMOCRACY (Harper and Brothers 1942), https://periferiaactiva.files.wordpress.com/2015/08/joseph-schumpeter-capitalism-socialism-and-democracy-2006.pdf.

[824] Carl Shapiro, *Competition and Innovation: Did Arrow Hit the Bull's Eye?* in THE RATE AND DIRECTION OF INVENTIVE ACTIVITY REVISITED 361 (Josh Lerner & Scott Stern eds., Univ. of Chicago Press 2012), https://www.nber.org/chapters/c12360.pdf.

[825] European Commission, *supra* note 767.

and by the ability to convey the innovation to investors and share it with customers by virtue of effective marketing from a position of strength.[826] When it comes to the application of this view in practice, Schumpeterians contend that a strong undertaking could implement a better infrastructure for R&D and innovative funding.[827] The financial outcome or appropriation of this process could be higher for a firm with strong market presence, high production capacity, and powerful marketing, thus making it even more profitable for such market leaders to innovate.[828] To complete the full circle of this economic philosophy by returning to the initial debate, Schumpeter stipulates that "only the large firms are induced to seek innovation to increase and strengthen its market power, which is why the monopoly is more rewarding for the purpose of economic growth compared to the competitive market."[829] As for Kenneth Arrow, he claimed, in contrast to Schumpeter, that a monopolist would gain more by the preservation of the status quo[830] and would thus have no incentive for novelty that would shake up the market structure and protect itself from innovation "cannibalizing"[831] the profits of the existing products or services.[832]

The two diverging opinions were consolidated and synthesized by Carl Shapiro, who claimed that they did not contradict each other and that they had the potential to be integrated, based on three fundamental principles: contestability, appropriability, and synergies, as set out in Chapter 3.[833] The Commission's policy brief touches upon these concepts and points out that these are in line with the EU's legal framework.[834]

Competition policymakers can assess each side of these arguments to arrive at their own conclusions or try to integrate these views in order to adopt their own. The European Commission's policy paper on innovation and merger control also recognizes the existence and significance of this debate and acknowledges the split in the literature. Although the Commission does not take a strong position in this respect, the different approaches evinced by the Commission's case law demonstrate that, during the assessment of an actual concentration situation, the inclinations of the Commission may shift. In this respect, the Commission has set out its stance within the scope of its policy paper, stating that "As long as competition policy promotes contestability (i.e., by keeping markets competitive) and does not unduly negatively affect appropriability, it will be compatible with both Arrow and Schumpeter, and therefore will encourage innovation."[835] In a more recent policy brief on industry concentration, the Commission contends that in light of the trend of increasing concentration and profits, competition enforcement cannot afford to loosen the reins and deems that (referring to the current economic

---

[826] Jonathan B. Baker, *Beyond Schumpeter vs. Arrow: How Antitrust Fosters Innovation*, 74 ANTITRUST L.J. 575 (2007), http://dx.doi.org/10.2139/ssrn.962261.

[827] *Id.*

[828] European Commission, *supra* note 767.

[829] SCHUMPETER, *supra* note 823.

[830] Shapiro, *supra* note 824.

[831] European Commission, *supra* note 767.

[832] Also known as the "Arrow effect" or the "replacement effect." *See* FREDERICO ETRO, COMPETITION, INNOVATION, AND ANTITRUST: A THEORY OF MARKET LEADERS AND ITS POLICY IMPLICATIONS (Springer 2007).

[833] Shapiro, *supra* note 442.

[834] European Commission, *supra* note 767.

[835] *Id.*

climate post-Covid) strong enforcement of EU competition policy "promotes efficiency and encourages innovation."[836]

Such intricate and layered outlooks in theory and the framework of the relevant legislation leave ample elbow room for the Commission to assume different approaches as it applies and implements the principle ideas in its case law. Following an investigation, the Commission is known to make progress in its methodology and policy, obviously depending on the particular facts of the concentration transaction. This progress is visible most clearly in the Commission's transition from a traditional approach to a novel approach in merger control assessments, which was a gradual and incremental process, as demonstrated below. It may be fair to say that the Commission's views lean closer to the Arrowian stance with respect to the effect of these transactions on innovation: the burden remains asymmetrically high for efficiency defenses that can be employed by the entities, which means any uncertainty regarding the future of innovation is deemed to perpetuate the presumption of harm and distrust against concentrations.

4.4 The Commission's Traditional Approach to Innovation in Merger Control

4.4.1 Ground Zero for Innovation Assessments: The Traditional Approach

Under the EU Horizontal Merger Guidelines[837] – since the mid-1990s – innovation is considered a competitive parameter. The Commission can assess mergers' impact on innovation[838] in order to preserve or even foster innovation in the marketplace. In fact, back in 1992, in the Commission's *DuPont/ICI* decision,[839] the threat to innovation was treated as a competitive concern within the framework of the transaction between the leading firms in the relevant product market (i.e., nylon carpet fiber), since the competition took place between ICI and DuPont specifically in terms of innovation and product development. In this respect, the Commission ultimately decided to approve the transaction conditionally, whereby the parties undertook to enter into good faith negotiations with third parties in order to eliminate the potential threat towards innovation through the loss of competition between the leading firms in the relevant market.[840] Therefore, it can be stipulated that the Commission had already started, almost thirty years ago, to

---

[836]   European Commission, *Industry Concentration and Competition Policy*, COMPETITION POLICY BRIEF (Nov. 2021), https://op.europa.eu/en/publication-detail/-/publication/e2e54d72-5cbf-11ec-91ac-01aa75ed71a1/language-en.

[837]   EU Horizontal Merger Guidelines, paras. 8, 38.

[838]   Petit, *supra* note 752, at 9.

[839]   DuPont/ICI, European Commission Decision case IV/M.214 (1992).

[840]   *Id.*, para. 48.

evaluate the effects of mergers on innovation, by way of assessing the transactions in which the parties' product development activities play an important role in supply and where the dynamics of the relevant market are largely determined by innovation competition. However, even though innovation was accepted as a competitive parameter, there were no specific comprehensive regulations to determine how the effects on innovation should be analyzed in merger reviews,[841] and even today, no such regulations exist.

In the traditional merger control approach, the assessment of the impact of mergers on innovation for transactions in which the parties were current or potential competitors to one another was limited to the principles outlined under paragraph 38 of the Horizontal Merger Guidelines.[842] As per the guideline, a proposed transaction may give rise to a significant impediment of effective competition in the relevant market in cases where there are competing undertakings with innovation capabilities and pipeline products. In fact, due to the lack of an established framework of analysis for harm to innovation, the example provided under the EU Horizontal Merger Guidelines has played a determinant role in shaping the Commission's approach towards innovation in its merger control reviews.[843] Therefore, in line with paragraph 38 of the EU Horizontal Merger Guidelines, transactions in which pipeline products of a merging party overlap with the existing ("pipeline-to-existing overlap") or pipeline products of the other merging party ("pipeline-to-pipeline overlap") are the cases in which the Commission has traditionally set forth theories of harm related to innovation.[844] In this sense, the product markets where the companies that are not yet present in a given sector, but are nevertheless potential competitors due to their pipeline products, have been carefully examined by the Commission. Therefore, the Commission had effectively evaluated the impacts on innovation within the framework of potential competition, as regulated under paragraph 60 of the EU Horizontal Merger Guidelines.[845]

According to paragraph 60 of the EU Horizontal Merger Guidelines, in order for a merger with a potential competitor with a pipeline product to have anti-competitive effects in a relevant product market, the following two conditions must be fulfilled: (i) the potential competitor should either already exert a significant competitive constraint over the existing product of the other party, or there should be a significant likelihood that it will enter into the market in a relatively short period of time, which would result in the relevant competitor being able to constrain other existing companies in the relevant market, and (ii) there should not be a sufficient number of other potential competitors that could ensure the maintenance of competitive pressure over the merged company.[846]

In this context, while reviewing the harm to innovation in mergers, the Commission has looked into and evaluated certain vital features, which are mainly related to the other conditions set forth for the assessment of the potential competition.

---

[841] Mario Todino, Geoffroy van de Walle & Lucia Stoican, *EU Merger Control and Harm to Innovation – A Long Walk to Freedom (from the Chains of Causation)*, 64 ANTITRUST BULL. 11, 5 (2019).

[842] *Id.*

[843] *Id.*

[844] Carles Esteva Mosso, Innovation in EU Merger Control, 66th ABA Section of Antitrust Law Spring Meeting 6 (Apr. 12, 2018), http://ec.europa.eu/competition/speeches/text/sp2018_05_en.pdf.

[845] *Id.*

[846] Raphaël De Coninck, *Innovation in EU Merger Control: In Need of a Consistent Framework*, 2 COMPETITION L. & POL'Y DEBATE 41 (2016).

4.4.2 Key Features of the Traditional Approach to Innovation in the Commission's Precedents

4.4.2.1 The Commission's Theories of Harm Related to Innovation Were Traditionally Tied to a Specific Product Market

Paragraph 38 of the EU Horizontal Merger Guidelines refers to a specific product market for assessing the merger's impact on effective competition through innovation. In this regard, the Commission has traditionally analyzed the harm to innovation about a clearly defined product market in order to determine whether a merger with a potential competitor would give rise to a significant anti-competitive effect.[847] In EU competition law, above all else, defining the borders of the relevant market is utilized as a crucial instrument for understanding the anti-competitive effects of a merger, including the potential harm to innovation.[848]

Therefore, the Commission's traditional approach to innovation is founded on the analysis of a clearly delineated relevant market.[849] The relevant market definition is deemed as a crucial step for analyzing the scope of the competitive landscape and for identifying the relevant (potential) competitors.[850] Even though innovation is not a static competitive parameter (like price, quality, and output), innovation competition has been assessed by reference to R&D activities specifically tied to well-defined current or future product markets, in terms of the Commission's traditional approach.

For instance, in its *Pasteur Mérieux/Merck*[851] decision, the Commission evaluated the anti-competitive concerns related to innovation based on a product market that was defined according to the parties' overlapping late-stage pipeline vaccine products. The decision was related to the establishment of a joint venture between two pharmaceutical companies, Pasteur and Merck, which operated in the research and development of a series of vaccines. The transaction was envisaged and structured in a way to ensure that the parties would remain autonomous in their R&D decisions; however, as the joint venture would establish a development committee, the Commission considered that this committee could potentially lead to the diminishment of the parties' R&D activities for future pipeline products related to the vaccine market, through coordination.[852] Therefore, the Commission focused its competitive assessment in this case on a specific (future) product market – namely, the pipeline products in monovalent vaccines – and evaluated the parties' positions therein.[853] Nevertheless, even though the Commission mentioned its concerns regarding the possibility of a decline in the parties' R&D activities in the post-merger market, it eventually approved the transaction in question after analyzing

---

847   Petit, *supra* note 752, at 12.
848   L. I. M. Suijkerbuijk, Innovation, Competition in EU Merger Control 10 (2018) (on file with the Tilburg University), http://arno.uvt.nl/show.cgi?fid=145944.
849   Petit, *supra* note 752, at 12.
850   Suijkerbuijk, *supra* note 848, at 10.
851   Pasteur Mérieux/Merck, European Commission Decision 94/770/EC, case IV/34.776 (Oct. 6, 1994).
852   *Id.*, para. 64.
853   *Id.*

the particular dynamics of the vaccine market. In this regard, the Commission found that coordination would require significant investment and time for research and that it involved certain risks stemming from the difficulty of launching successful products into the market, and also took into account the efficiencies that the merger would bring.[854]

In its *Ciba/Sandoz* decision, the Commission once again defined (future) product markets for the assessment of concerns related to R&D potential and innovation, in the merger between Ciba and Sandoz, which would result in the formation of a new undertaking called Novartis.[855] Ciba and Sandoz were two companies that operated in the research, development, and production of active chemical substances, as well as the production and marketing of pharmaceutical products.[856] Before assessing the merger's potential effects on innovation, under its decisional practice, the Commission first determined the parties' overlapping activities as follows: healthcare products, crop protection products, animal health products, and seeds.[857] Because the affected markets were all related to the pharmaceutical industry, the decision was "a full assessment of the competitive situation requires examination of the products which are not yet on the market but which are at an advanced stage of development."[858] Therefore, the (future) relevant product markets were defined by taking into account the innovation progress of the parties' overlapping activities. Most importantly, in order to assess the anti-competitive concerns arising from the future competitive advantage that would be attained from the current R&D and innovation potential of the parties in the future markets, it was indicated in the decision that "as research and development must be assessed in terms of its importance for future markets, the relevant product-market must, by its very nature, be defined in a less clear-cut manner than in the case of existing markets."[859]

In this regard, in terms of the theories of harm related to innovation in future markets, the Commission's traditional assessment in this decision suggests that the transaction could not lead to the creation or strengthening of a dominant position, considering that the products in future markets contain uncertainties related to the process of patent applications.[860] In addition, the dynamics of the clearly defined market that were taken into account by the Commission, in this case, were as follows: (i) rapid successions of new products; (ii) market share fluctuations; (iii) a large number of competitors with significant R&D capacities; (iv) a large number of product launches; (v) the convenience of entries to and exits from all the markets concerned; and (vi) the countervailing power of wholesalers.[861] Rather than assessing the static indicators of competitive strength (such as the relative market shares of the parties), the Commission evaluated the dynamic elements of the futures markets, such as the R&D capabilities of the merging parties and their competitors.[862] Therefore, the Commission ultimately cleared the transaction

---

[854]   *Id.*, paras. 64, 82–101.
[855]   Ciba-Geigy/Sandoz, European Commission Decision 97/469/EC, case IV/M.737 (July 17, 1996).
[856]   *Id.*, para. 53.
[857]   *Id.*, para. 10.
[858]   *Id.*, para. 42.
[859]   *Id.*, para. 44.
[860]   *Id.*, paras. 105, 100–107.
[861]   *Id.*, para. 176.
[862]   Suijkerbuijk, *supra* note 848, at 26.

solely based on the commitments undertaken by the parties with regard to animal health products, which involved granting licenses to third parties with fair terms, to be monitored by the Commission via the submission of quarterly reports with regard to license requests received from third parties, licenses granted/refused and the grounds for such refusals, in order to secure the maintenance of the third parties' presence in the relevant market.[863]

This decision reveals different traits (i.e., a shift) in the Commission's thinking than in earlier examples, where the Commission had focused mainly on the competitive strength that would be gained by the merging parties through their overlapping pipeline products. This trend would continue in the Commission's *Glaxo Wellcome/SmithKline Beecham* decision,[864] in which the Commission put greater emphasis on the potential effects of the transaction on the overall R&D activities in the sector.[865] The relevant decision concerned the establishment of GlaxoSmithKline through the merger between Glaxo Wellcome ("GW") and SmithKline Beecham ("SB"). While both parties were active in human pharmaceuticals, SB was also involved in conducting activities related to vaccines, OTC products, and healthcare-related products. The impact on "R&D markets" was once again evaluated with respect to the defined product markets, which were determined on the basis of overlapping existing and pipeline products, as follows: asthma/chronic obstructive pulmonary disease ("COPD"), anti-migraine (N2C), therapeutic vaccines, and other urological products, including antispasmodics (G4B).[866] The fields in which neither of the parties had an existing product, but only had pipeline products, were diabetes (A10B), oncology (L1), and irritable bowel syndrome. In this case, the Commission analyzed whether there would be a reduction in the "overall R&D potential," specifically in relation to the development of treatments for COPD.[867] However, the Commission decided that a reduction in overall R&D activities in the sector through the removal of R&D activities of the merging parties would not be expected since there was substantial "unmet clinical need in this segment,"[868] which was regarded as a commercial opportunity and thus considered to be attractive for companies. In addition, as the second condition of paragraph 60 of the EU Horizontal Merger Guidelines requires the lack of a significant number of competitors in the market for anti-competitive effects to arise from a merger with a potential competitor, the Commission also took into consideration that the existence of a large number of pipeline products of third parties would serve as a driving force for the parties to continue their R&D activities in the future as well.[869]

Another example of the Commission's traditional approach to the theories of harm related to innovation tied to specific current products and future markets is the *Bayer/Aventis Crop Science*[870] case, which was related to the transaction concerning the acquisition of Aventis by Bayer. In that decision, the Commission's concerns were focused on the diminishment of innovation in the relevant market due to the loss of competition

---

[863]   *Ciba-Geigy/Sandoz*, para. 280.

[864]   Glaxo Wellcome/SmithKline Beecham, European Commission Decision case COMP/M.1846 (May 8, 2000).

[865]   Petit, *supra* note 752, at 37.

[866]   *Glaxo Wellcome/SmithKline Beecham*, para. 150.

[867]   *Id.*, paras. 179–88.

[868]   *Id.*, paras. 187–88.

[869]   Suijkerbuijk, *supra* note 848, at 27.

[870]   Bayer/Aventis Crop Science, European Commission Decision case COMP/M.2547 (Apr. 17, 2000).

between the merging parties, which had robust programs in R&D and innovation.[871] The Commission analyzed the potential impact of the transaction on the "R&D capabilities and incentives" of the parties, regarding "current product markets" and "future product markets," which were determined to be the markets for crop protection, professional pest control, and animal health products, based on the overlapping activities of the parties.[872] The Commission acknowledged that innovation was an essential ingredient for market growth and that extensive capital resources were required due to the costly nature of R&D investments in this sector. The parties would become one of the largest undertakings in the industry, in terms of R&D capabilities, post-merger; therefore, by taking a step further, the Commission decided to evaluate the post-merger R&D conduct, organization, and strategy of the parties in this case.[873] The Commission's concerns were based on the assessment that, due to their successful pipeline products, the potential increase in profits, and the accumulated know-how to be brought about by the transaction, the new entity would emerge as one of the few companies in a leading position for launching new products.[874] Therefore, due to the significance of innovation for enabling players to remain in the market and the high barriers to entry arising from sizable R&D costs, this transaction raised concerns with regard to the potential elimination of future competition in current product markets as well as future markets.[875] Consequently, the Commission decided to approve the transaction based on a set of full commitments from the merging parties, including the divestitures of several businesses and brands, thereby eliminating the competition concerns arising from the overlaps between the parties' activities and products. The Commission considered that these divestitures would result in new entries to the relevant market, thus promoting and enhancing competition.

In its *Syngenta/Monsanto's Sunflower Seed Business* decision,[876] the Commission evaluated the innovation concerns arising from the possible foreclosure effects of the proposed transaction, by defining clear-cut upstream and downstream markets. The decision concerned the transaction related to the acquisition of Monsanto's sunflower seed business by Syngenta, where both of the parties were active in the breeding and trading of new varieties of sunflower (that is, sunflower hybrid seeds and parental lines), as well as the commercialization of sunflower hybrid seeds. Contrary to the parties' stated position regarding the definition of an overall market, the Commission indicated that a distinction should be made between (i) the upstream market for the trading (i.e., the exchange and licensing) of varieties (parental lines and hybrids), and (ii) the downstream market for the commercialization of hybrids.[877]

In line with its decisional practice in the cases discussed above, the Commission evaluated the potential harm to innovation in the relevant market that would arise from (i) the removal of Monsanto, one of the most important innovators with significant R&D

---

[871]   *Id.*, para. 18.
[872]   *Id.*
[873]   Petit, *supra* note 752, at 10.
[874]   *Bayer/Aventis Crop Science*, para. 153.
[875]   *Id.*, para. 18.
[876]   Syngenta/Monsanto's Sunflower Seed Business, European Commission Decision case COMP/5675 (Nov. 17, 2010).
[877]   *Id.*, para. 76.

capabilities in the breeding and trading of new sunflower varieties, and (ii) the removal of the competitive constraint that Monsanto was exerting on Syngenta and on other competitors, which fostered the market players' incentives to compete by launching new and improved products.[878] That said, we observe that this decision also evinced certain different traits (and a shift in the Commission's decisional practice) when compared to the preceding cases. This shift stemmed from the fact that the elimination was based on its adverse effects on prices, innovation, and access to external germplasm in the downstream market.[879] Therefore, since actual and potential competitors would not be able to access Monsanto's important and large germplasm portfolio (which had been developed and expanded through innovative products) in the aftermath of the merger, the Commission assessed that the transaction would lead to a foreclosure in the downstream market due to the loss of innovation. According to the Commission, this foreclosure effect in the downstream market would ensure that Syngenta would have the leading position in that market.[880] Due to the harm to innovation, especially in the downstream market, which would ultimately result in a reduction of options for sunflower seed hybrids for customers,[881] the Commission conditionally cleared the transaction based on a set of commitments from the parties. These commitments concerned (i) the divestment of Monsanto's hybrids commercialized in Hungary and Spain in the previous two years, as well as the hybrids already under official trial for registration in those countries, and (ii) Monsanto's parental lines used to develop these hybrids, as well as the pipeline parental lines currently under development with the aim of producing hybrids for the Spanish and Hungarian markets.[882] The competitive concerns arising from the removal of innovation were thereby eliminated through these commitments since a third player would take over the competitive role exercised by Monsanto before the merger. The commitments, which included the rights to use, cross breed the parent lines, and also commercialize and license the resulting hybrids, would also be extended to the foremost sunflower-growing European countries that were outside the EU such as Russia, Ukraine, and Turkey. This would allow the divested business to be sustainable and competitive in the long term, as well as showing genuine effort on the part of the transaction parties in giving these commitments.

In addition to the assessment of innovation in the relevant markets related to pharmaceutical and crop protection products, the Commission has also evaluated innovation competition in other R&D-driven markets, particularly in its *Seagate/HDD Business of Samsung*[883] and *Western Digital/Viviti Technologies*[884] decisions. In these decisions, the

---

[878]   *Id.*, para. 321.

[879]   Joaquín Almunia, Commission Vice President in charge of Competition Policy, stated that "Syngenta has offered significant remedies to ensure that the transaction will not hamper the development of new sunflower varieties in the EU, or increase prices or reduce customers' choice of sunflower seeds in Spain and Hungary." European Commission Press Release IP/10/1515, Mergers: Commission Clears Syngenta's Acquisition of Monsanto's Sunflower Seed Business, Subject to Conditions (Nov. 17, 2010), para. 2, http://europa.eu/rapid/press-release_IP-10-1515_en.htm.

[880]   *Syngenta/Monsanto's Sunflower Seed Business*, paras. 246, 253.

[881]   European Commission Press Release IP/10/1515, *supra* note 879, para. 4.

[882]   *Id.*, para. 1.

[883]   Seagate/HDD Business of Samsung, European Commission Decision case COMP/M.6214 (Oct. 19, 2011).

[884]   Western Digital Ireland/Vivity Technologies, European Commission Decision case M.6203 (Nov. 23, 2011), paras. 486, 533 & 699.

transactions concerning the acquisition of Samsung's HDD business by Seagate and the acquisition of Hitachi Global Storage Technologies ("HGST") by Western Digital were evaluated. Taken together, after the completion of Seagate's acquisition of Samsung's HDD business and Western Digital's acquisition of HGST, there would only remain three suppliers on the 3.5" desktop market and four suppliers on the 2.5" mobile market, respectively. In the *Seagate/HDD Business of Samsung* decision, the Commission reviewed the parties' positions in the relevant market while evaluating the potential impact of the transaction on innovation. There was no evidence that Samsung was a price leader, nor had it been consistently the first to introduce a new product in the last decade – it was not a significant innovator. As a result, the Commission found that Samsung was not a particularly strong competitor, but rather a "trend follower,"[885] which, in turn, led to the conclusion that innovation would not be harmed.[886]

On the other hand, in the *Western Digital/Viviti Technologies* decision, the Commission did not consider that the merger would produce significant effects on innovation in the market. Instead, it assessed the merger's adverse effects on prices due to the dominant position held by Western Digital through its extensive product and IP-right portfolios.[887] In this respect, the parties to the transaction claimed innovation efficiencies in terms of higher and faster product development, as the combined entity would strengthen and increase its R&D resources. However, the Commission found that the respective dynamic efficiency claims were not verifiable since these claims were not only general and unspecific in nature, but also lacked the quantitative evidence that would allow their credibility to be assessed within the framework of the criteria utilized for efficient defenses.[888] As a result, the Commission conditionally cleared the transaction, subject to the divestiture of essential production assets for the manufacture of 3.5-inch HDDs, including a production plant, the licensing of the IP rights used by the divested business, the transfer of personnel, and the supply of HDD components to the divested business.[889]

4.4.2.2 The Commission's Theories of Harm Related to Innovation Were Traditionally Concerned with the Transaction Parties' Phase III Pipeline Products Rather Than the Pipeline Products at Earlier Stages of Development

The above examples of the Commission's case law aim to demonstrate that its traditional theories of harm related to innovation have been mostly tied to clearly defined (current and future) product markets. It is also evident from specific examples (as provided below) that the theories of harm that were developed in the scope of its merger control assessments were solely limited to the pipeline products at the later

---

[885]   *Seagate/HDD Business of Samsung*, paras. 425, 448.

[886]   *Id.*, para. 427.

[887]   *Id.*, para. 84

[888]   *Id.*, para. 1007.

[889]   European Commission Press Release IP/11/1395, Mergers: Commission clears Western Digital's acquisition of Hitachi's hard disk drive business subject to conditions (Nov. 23, 2011), para. 5, http://europa.eu/rapid/press-release_IP-11-1395_en.htm.

stages of development, meaning that they were on the verge of being released to the relevant market.[890] In this regard, the Commission sought to obtain solid and reliable evidence that would demonstrate that the potential competitor would become a capable, competitive force in the relevant market(s), in order to determine whether there was a "significant likelihood" of entry into the market, as required under paragraph 60 of the EU Horizontal Merger Guidelines. As the scope of this assessment, the Commission considered that the competitors with pipeline products in the earlier stages of development (i.e., Phase I and Phase II) could not potentially exert significant competitive constraints on others since the prospects of success of the new pipeline products remain uncertain.[891] The Commission also noted that, even if the Phase I and Phase II pipeline products indeed turned out to exert a significant competitive force in the future, the theories of harm related to such products cannot possibly be set forth during the time that the transaction is subject to the Commission's review, since any evidence at that stage would be inadequate and inconclusive for determining a significant impediment to competition.[892]

In this regard, the *Medtronic/Covidien* decision, which was related to the merger of two pharmaceutical companies, Medtronic and Covidien, is worth examining. In that case, the Commission evaluated the anti-competitive concerns related to the market for drug-coated balloons to treat vascular diseases, since Medtronic held a leading position in this market and Covidien had a pipeline product at a later stage, which was very likely to pose a significant competitive constraint on Medtronic in the relevant market.[893] Based on this state of affairs, the Commission approved the relevant transaction subject to the commitments relating to the divestiture of the late-stage pipeline product, together with all assets and personnel required for releasing the product to the market.[894] Similarly, in *Pfizer/Hospira*, the Commission approved the transaction based on a commitment that Pfizer would divest certain sterile injectable drugs and its promising infliximab biosimilar pipeline drug.[895]

Some decisions by the Commission, such as *Pasteur Mérieux/Merck* and *Glaxo Wellcome/ SmithKline Beecham*, constitute historical examples in which the theories of harm related to innovation were concerned with the pipeline products at a later stage of development (i.e., Phase III) and did not extend to pipeline products in the earlier stages. The Commission has insisted on the same approach in more recent examples as well, such as *Medtronic/Covidien*[896] and *Pfizer/Hospira*,[897] even though the Commission's assessments therein also embody specific signals and indications of its gradual transition from the traditional theory to the novel theory, which is detailed further below.

---

[890]   Todino et al., *supra* note 841, at 6; Seiler, *supra* note 790.

[891]   Todino et al., *supra* note 841, at 16.

[892]   *Id.* at 16–17.

[893]   Seiler, *supra* note 790, at 33–34.

[894]   European Commission Press Release IP/14/2246, Mergers: Commission approves acquisition of Covidien by Medtronic, subject to conditions (Nov. 28, 2014), para. 4, http://europa.eu/rapid/press-release_IP-14-2246_en.htm.

[895]   Pfizer/Hospira, European Commission Decision case COMP/M.7559 (Aug. 4, 2015).

[896]   Medtronic/Covidien, European Commission Decision case COMP/M.7326 (Nov. 28, 2014).

[897]   Pfizer/Hospira, European Commission Decision case COMP/M.7559 (Aug. 4, 2015).

It is important to note in these cases, as in many others, that the Commission has relied upon the parties' internal documents to assess any potential harm to innovation, especially with regard to their plans on the target's pipeline products. For example, in *GE/Alstom*[898] the evidence garnered from internal documents indicated GE had been planning to forego the Alstom pipeline products[899] and accordingly this was one of the divestment commitments the parties offered to the Commission for the conditional approval.[900] Indubitably, internal documents can provide insight into the parties' strategic plans and post-merger assessments, and also help the Commission "make better decisions, and understand the markets and companies' plans for the future."[901] However, they do have other shortcomings, which makes any strict reliance on them the subject of criticism.[902]

4.4.2.3 In Symmetry with the Evaluation of the Transaction Parties' Phase III Pipeline Products, the Commission's Theories of Harm Related to Innovation Were Also Traditionally Concerned with Third Parties' Phase III Pipeline Products

Under the EU merger control regime, another significant factor in the assessment of whether a proposed transaction would give rise to a significant impediment to competition is the availability of competitors that would be able to exert competitive pressure on the transaction parties. Under the second leg of the assessment provided under paragraph 60 of the EU Horizontal Merger Guidelines, the Commission takes into account whether there is a sufficient number of competitors in the relevant market when developing its theories of harm related to innovation. In this assessment, the Commission also evaluates the competitive pressure exerted by the late-stage pipeline products of third parties, in addition to the transaction parties' late-stage pipeline products. Therefore, arguably, the Commission adopts a symmetric approach in terms of the pipeline products of both the transaction parties and third parties, giving equal footing to the competitive pressure exerted by the third parties' pipeline products.[903]

The *Johnson & Johnson/Guidant*[904] case constitutes one of the most illuminating examples in which the Commission adopted a symmetric approach in terms of the assessment of the competitive pressure exerted by the transaction parties' and third parties' pipeline products. This decision was related to the acquisition of Guidant,

---

[898] GE/Alstom, European Commission Decision case COMP/M.7278 (2015).

[899] Tilman Kuhn, *EC Focus on Internal Documents: Time to Rethink the Architecture of the EU Merger Control Process?* WHITE & CASE, Mar. 8, 2019, https://www.whitecase.com/insight-our-thinking/ec-focus-internal-documents-time-rethink-architecture-eu-merger-control.

[900] European Commission Press Release IP/15/5606, Commission Clears GE's Acquisition of Alstom's Power Generation and Transmission Assets, Subject to Conditions (Sept. 8, 2015), https://ec.europa.eu/commission/presscorner/detail/en/IP_15_5606.

[901] Margrethe Vestager, "Fairness" in Competition Law and Policy: Significance and Implications, Speech at the GCLC Annual Conference (Jan. 25, 2018).

[902] *See* below in Section 5 for an analysis of the Commission's use of internal documents in *Dow/DuPont*.

[903] Todino et al., *supra* note 841, at 7.

[904] Johnson & Johnson/Guidant, European Commission Decision 2006/430/EC, case COMP/M.3687 (Aug. 25, 2005).

a company specializing in cardiovascular medical products, by Johnson & Johnson (J&J), a healthcare group active in the development, production, and sale of vascular medical devices. In line with the parties' overlapping activities and the market conditions, the Commission focused in its examination on the theories of harm related to three major areas: (i) coronary drug-eluting stents ("DES") and accessories, (ii) endovascular stents, and (iii) accessories used in peripheral arteries and devices used in cardiac surgery.[905] The Commission determined that the market for DES was concentrated, with only one other major supplier (namely, Boston Scientific) and several imminent entrants, such as Guidant, Medtronic, and Abbott, which had pipeline products in Phase III of the development stage.[906] In this regard, since Guidant was a significant potential competitor, the Commission evaluated that Guidant's removal from the market would give rise to a substantial loss of competition in the relevant market. The Commission also found that there were equally credible "potential" competitors about to enter the market with their late-stage products, which were expected to act as significant competitive constraints on J&J.[907] This finding enabled the Commission to assess that there were no theories of harm in terms of innovation that were specific to the relevant product market in question. Moreover, the commitments provided by the parties were related to other affected markets that were unrelated to the foregoing assessment.[908]

4.4.2.4 The Commission's Theories of Harm Related to Innovation Were Traditionally Set Forth Based on an Abundance of Evidence, Setting the Standard of Proof Considerably High

Further to the above, the Commission's methods and tactics regarding the standard of proof also show elements of the traditional approach. Initially, the standard of proof is relevant to the quality of the evidence that the Commission needs to adduce when building its case towards a clearance, a conditional clearance, or a prohibition.[909] In the field of merger control, the Commission has traditionally enjoyed a wide margin of discretion, especially due to the role of economic analysis in the assessment of the level of concentration and harm to innovation.[910] To that end, the standard of proof sought out by the Commission is most clearly visible in the *Tetra Laval v. Commission* decision, wherein it was declared that the Commission should be able to show that "[t]he evidence relied on is *factually accurate, reliable and consistent* but also whether that evidence contains all the information which must be taken into account in order to assess a complex situation and whether it is capable of substantiating the conclusions drawn from it."[911]

---

905   European Commission Press Release IP/05/1065, Mergers: Commission approves takeover of Guidant Corporation by Johnson & Johnson, subject to conditions (Aug. 25, 2005), para. 4, http://europa.eu/rapid/press-release_IP-05-1065_en.htm.

906   *Id.*, para. 15.

907   *Johnson & Johnson/Guidant*, paras. 129, 165.

908   European Commission Press Release IP/05/1065, *supra* note 905, para. 7.

909   Todino et al., *supra* note 841, at 29.

910   *Id.* at 38.

911   Case C-12/03 P, Commission v. Tetra Laval, 2005 ECR I-987, para. 328 (emphasis added).

In *Tetra Laval/Sidel*,[912] the Commission prohibited the proposed transaction between Tetra Laval and Sidel, which were both active in the packaging business, due to the competitive advantages that the merged entity would enjoy vis-à-vis its competitors.[913] As for the innovation's harm, the Commission determined that innovation would be diminished in the post-merger market due to the decrease in Tetra Laval's incentives for innovation. After the decision was appealed to the General Court, the General Court indicated that the Commission had not been able to show why the demand would be discontinued in the post-merger market. Considering that the demand in question is the driving force that provides the impetus for future innovation, especially in the aseptic carton markets,[914] the lack of analysis in this respect also taints the Commission's conclusion regarding the diminishing of innovation. Furthermore, the decision was also criticized by the General Court for failing to discuss why the capacity and activities of Tetra Laval's competitors were deemed to be irrelevant, and the General Court found that the contested decision did not establish that the merged entity would be less incentivized to innovate than Tetra Laval currently was.[915] Following the Commission's appeal of the General Court's decision before the European Court of Justice ("ECJ"),[916] the ECJ noted that, since the merger control review relies on (*ex ante*) predictions and forecasts about events that are more or less likely to occur in the future by using the indicators at hand, the prohibition of a proposed concentration should be rendered with more care.[917] Therefore, the ECJ decided that the General Court's position concerning the Commission's failure to demonstrate to the requisite standard of proof that the transaction would cause an impediment to potential competition was, indeed, accurate. Hence, the judiciary's approach, in this case, indicates that, when assessing a concentration, the Commission should effectively establish the potential harm to innovation by utilizing evidence that is factually accurate, complete, abundant, and consistent. Moreover, these judicial decisions seem to indicate that every single fact on which the Commission bases its case is expected to be substantiated and verified by evidence. Advocate General Wahl has stated that the criteria set by the ECJ require the Commission to consider all relevant information and not only the "information in its possession."[918]

In conclusion, within the scope of the traditional approach, shaped by the case law discussed above, the Commission's innovation-based theory of harm is expected to comply with the standard of proof set out in the ECJ's decision. Therefore, the entirety of the relevant information in a merger case needs to be analyzed carefully, which poses a significant challenge to the Commission, considering the already evident complexity of the *ex ante* assessment of innovation concerns, as exemplified by the decisions examined in this section.

---

[912]   Tetra Laval/Sidel, European Commission Decision case COMP/M.2416 (2001).

[913]   *Id.*, para. 385.

[914]   Case T-5/02, Tetra Laval BV v. Commission, 2002 ECR II-4381, para. 329.

[915]   *Id.*, paras. 331–32.

[916]   Case C-12/03 P, Commission v. Tetra Laval, 2005 ECR I-987.

[917]   *Id.*, paras. 42–43; Suijkerbuijk, *supra* note 848, at 29.

[918]   Petit, *supra* note 752, at 39.

4.5 The Gradual Transition to the Novel Theory

Following its use of the traditional methods for assessing innovation in merger cases, as typified by the cases discussed above, the Commission gradually shifted its methodological outlook and began to adopt a new approach to theories of harm surrounding innovation. This approach has been referred to as *"the novel theory of harm"* by various commentators,[919] and it has been criticized from several aspects since it introduces certain ambiguities into the Commission's assessment process that are not yet based on any firm legislative grounds. This gradual transition, ultimately leading up to the seminal *Dow/DuPont* decision, where the novel theory of harm would manifest itself in the most explicit manner, will be elucidated below by way of examining a number of cases that involved the transaction parties taking specific measures in order to eliminate the Commission's concerns relating to the significant impediment to effective innovative competition.

The Commission's traditional theories of harm had been based on the analysis of several key factors and embodied certain principles, including the following (among others):

(I)   The theories of harm in terms of innovation, related to the consummation of a transaction, must be concerned with "late-stage pipeline products."[920] Therefore, the marketing of the innovative product subject to the potential theories of harm generally occurs in a foreseeable and short period of time, i.e., at most within two or three years.[921]

(II)   The theories of harm were concerned with the R&D activities within the product markets that had been concretely defined by the Commission.[922] That is to say, "innovation competition was systematically assessed by reference to current or future downstream product-markets, as opposed to upstream innovation spaces/markets."[923]

(III)   The standard of proof required to establish that the transaction in question raised concerns in terms of inhibiting innovation was set particularly high.[924]

(IV)   The Commission's conduct for assessing potential competitive pressure exerted by third parties and the potential competition stemming from the transaction parties was "symmetrical"[925] – in other words, the same parameters were implemented, rather than using different criteria.

The most prominent and controversial step towards the Commission's transition to the novel theory, in which the Commission visibly abandoned and substantially revised its

---

[919]   Todino et al., *supra* note 841, at 1.
[920]   *Id.* at 2.
[921]   *Id.* at 10.
[922]   Petit, *supra* note 752.
[923]   *Id.*
[924]   Todino et al., *supra* note 841, at 15.
[925]   *Id.* at 7.

earlier approach to its traditional theories of harm, is the *Dow/DuPont*[926] case, which was concerned with the merger of two significant crop protection chemical suppliers. In a nutshell, the Commission's decision showed that "the novelty would come from the fact that the analysis does not relate to markets in the traditional sense. The analysis would also move away from how constraints coming from potential competitors were considered."[927] However, it has also been argued that the transition in the Commission's approach leading up to *Dow/DuPont* and the gradual evolution of its traditional theories of harm were also observable in earlier cases to a certain extent, when some of the Commission's prior decisions are examined. Accordingly, before delving into a detailed assessment of the *Dow/DuPont* case, such examples will be identified and discussed in the sections below.

Medtronic/Covidien (2014)[928]

The *Medtronic/Covidien* decision concerns the merger of two suppliers active in the medical devices sector, in which Medtronic holds a leading position in the market for drug-coated balloons ("DCBs") to treat vascular diseases. The Commission found that few competitors were active in this market and that they exerted limited competitive pressure on Medtronic. The target company, Covidien, had a promising late-stage pipeline product, a drug-coated balloon called "Stellarex."

The Commission considered the promising clinical trial results of Stellarex, and thereby evaluated that Covidien would have competitively constrained Medtronic in the near future. Therefore, the consummation of the transaction was deemed to eliminate a credible competitor and reduce innovation in this area.

In order to address these concerns, Medtronic committed to selling Covidien's worldwide Stellarex business, including, in particular, the relevant manufacturing equipment, related IP rights, and scientific and regulatory materials necessary to complete the Stellarex trials, along with the key personnel. These remedies would provide the purchaser with all the assets required to bring Stellarex to the market. Consequently, in January 2015, Spectranetics Corporation completed the acquisition of Covidien's late-stage pipeline product, Stellarex.

This decision is quite pertinent and illuminating with regard to the gradual transition in the Commission's approach, in the sense that it shows that the Commission relies to a significant extent on the internal documents collected from the parties in order to assess the transaction and set forth its theories of harm, in particular for innovation concerns. This significant reliance on internal documents is an issue in itself. Businesses do, in fact, discuss short to mid-term goals in internal correspondence, but long-term efficiency potential would not be a topic of everyday conversation. Concerns can be flagged through correspondence, but this should not easily switch the burden of proof on the merging parties to prove the potential welfare-maximizing virtues of the transaction. The antitrust authorities should still engage in a balancing effort and analysis of parameters and facts

---

[926]   Dow/DuPont, European Commission Decision case M.7932 (Mar. 27, 2017).

[927]   Pablo Ibáñez Colomo, *Competition Law and Innovation: Where Do We Stand?* 9 J. EUR. COMPETITION L. & PRAC. 561 (2018).

[928]   Medtronic/Covidien, European Commission Decision case COMP/M.7326 (Nov. 28, 2014).

belonging to the complex analysis of the potential consequences of the transaction at hand. Whether a product is considered to be a competitor or a particular product will be withdrawn from the market after the transaction can, of course, be proven through correspondences, provided that they relate to persons authorized to represent the will or influence the decision-making process of the company, on these points. However, whether overall industry-level innovation is going to be impacted cannot be conclusively proven by internal correspondences, in the absence of specific complex economic analysis.

In its decision, the Commission notes that Medtronic treats Bard, who was indicated by the market respondents to have the drug-coated balloon that was the most suitable/similar alternative to Medtronic's product (and therefore, regarded as Medtronic's closest competitor in terms of product characteristics and price),[929] as being the only other competitor with comparable clinical data to Medtronic.[930] Along the same lines, both Bard itself and the target company Covidien believed that Bard had a "good product with strong clinical evidence"[931] and was "a competitor with a sizeable presence on the DCB market." In terms of the target Covidien's product Stellarex, the Commission initially referred to several key opinion leaders' statements, indicating that Covidien's drug-coated balloon and Medtronic's drug-coated balloon could not be subject to any comparison at this stage of development since there was no sufficient clinical data. Subsequently, the Commission also mentioned and took note of the individual opinions of a few surgeons, who indicated that Covidien's product "tends to be a better product as, compared to Medtronic's device, it has a homogenous drug coating on the balloon" and "Stellarex is similar to Medtronic's DCB," and that it "might be the 'best and safest' coming close to Medtronic's DCB."[932]

Finally, the Commission declared that:

> Once Medtronic acquires Covidien, *it appears from Medtronic's internal planning* that it is expected that the development of Covidien's product will be put to an end. This means that the Transaction will have as an effect elimination of a serious future competitor as a result of which DCB patients will be deprived of an innovative and potentially a very effective device.

> Based on the above, the elimination of Covidien's pipeline product following the proposed Transaction will result in the loss of a credible competitor which absent the Transaction would likely have constrained Medtronic on the market for drug-coated balloons in the EEA, where Medtronic is currently the market leader. Furthermore, the Commission considers that the players that are currently on the market would not exert sufficient competitive pressure on the merged entity post-Transaction. In addition, the Transaction will also have a significant effect on innovation in these markets as Covidien had the ability and incentive to continue innovation by further investing in clinical trials and developing Stellarex into a strong contender on the market including for indications for which Medtronic's device is not currently approved.[933]

---

[929] *Id.*, para. 211.
[930] *Id.*, para. 216.
[931] *Id.*, para. 217.
[932] *Id.*, para. 236.
[933] *Id.*, paras. 247–49 (emphasis added).

The Commission's above analysis, which concludes that Covidien's product exerts significant competitive pressure on Medtronic, was based on the opinions of a few surgeons and the parties' internal documents. It has been argued that this position differs significantly from the Commission's approach in the *J&J/Guidant* case (which was also related to cardiovascular devices and exhibited a resemblance to the *Medtronic/Covidien* transaction in terms of the sector), since, in *J&J/Guidant*, "abundant evidence about clinical trials and availability of angiographic parameters proved the prospect of success of the target and the other pipeline products,"[934] and the Commission even disregarded the portion of the opinions that indicated that there was no clinical evidence to prove that the pipeline product of the target company was actually efficient.[935]

Novartis/GSK (2015)[936]

This case demonstrated the first use of innovation theories of harm in its purest sense, as independent from a product market, and analyzing the *effects on competition in innovation* rather than restricting the analysis on actual or potential competition in product markets. It is also the first time the Commission articulated its pipeline concerns for stages before Phase III. Remedies also involved earlier clinical trial stages of products, which would later evolve into the discovery phase concern that was articulated in *Dow/DuPont*.

The *Novartis/Glaxo Smith Kline's Oncology Business* transaction was concerned with the acquisition of a portfolio of GSK's oncology products by Novartis. The Commission noted that, by way of this transaction, Novartis and GSK would be able to combine the clinical research drugs for the same type of cancer, which they had been independently pursuing before the application.[937] In this regard, the Commission found that:

> [B]oth GSK and Novartis have ongoing Phase I and Phase II clinical trials to investigate the potential use of their MEK and B-Raf inhibitors, either as monotherapies or in combination, in a number of other types of cancer, notably colorectal cancer, non-small-cell lung cancer (NSCLC) and advanced melanoma brain metastases. Novartis also has an on-going Phase III clinical trial for the use of its MEK inhibitor in uveal melanoma.[938]

In particular, for B-Raf and MEK inhibitors, which were the focal points for both of the parties' clinical research programs, the Commission's concerns were related to the possibility that (i) the number of companies developing and marketing such products would be reduced from three to two (the other one being Roche), and (ii) innovation in the market would be reduced, since Novartis might be likely to cease its broader clinical program for the development of the relevant inhibitors after the transaction.[939]

---

[934]   Todino et al., *supra* note 841, at 8.

[935]   *Id.*

[936]   Novartis/Glaxo Smith Kline's Oncology Business, European Commission Decision case COMP/M.7275 (Jan. 28, 2015).

[937]   *Id.*, para. 98.

[938]   *Id.*, para. 84.

[939]   Irene Mirabile, Michael Karl Pieber, Lluís Saurí and Arthur Stril, *Protecting the Drugs of Tomorrow: Competition and Innovation in Healthcare*, COMPETITION MERGER BRIEF 1, 2 (July 2015).

This decision has arguably made a significant impact in terms of the development of the Commission's approach to the theories of harm relating to innovation concerns, since its assessments had traditionally been limited to pipeline products in the advanced stages of development, referred to as "Phase III" of the process, as explained in previous sections. However, in the *Novartis/GSK* transaction, the Commission also expressed competition concerns relating to Novartis' pipeline products at earlier stages of development (i.e., Phase I and Phase II), and looked at all phases of clinical research in its assessment of the case. Furthermore, the Commission chose to take this approach despite the parties' statements that Phase I and Phase II of the clinical trials could not provide reliable indicators in terms of the assessment, as they remain uncertain (i) in terms of understanding the future market conditions, and (ii) with respect to the indications or lines of treatment for which the product in question would be granted approval and released to the market.[940] Consequently, the remedies that were submitted to alleviate those concerns also encompassed the relevant products subject to early clinical trials.[941] In this regard:

> Novartis committed (i) to divest Novartis' B-Raf and MEK inhibitors; (ii) to provide transitional support to ensure completion of the phase III clinical studies trialling these drugs in skin and ovarian cancer; and (iii) to ensure the worldwide development and the EEA commercialisation of the broad clinical research programme relating to the drugs, including clinical studies in colorectal and lung cancer.[942]

It can be reasonably argued that this decision was the first instance in which the Commission has set forth its theories of harm related to innovation separately from a specific product market,[943] which planted the seeds of (and ultimately led up to) such an assessment in the *Dow/DuPont* decision,[944] since the Commission explicitly notes in its decision that "a concentration may not only affect competition in existing markets but also competition in innovation and new product-markets,"[945] and also declares that "[i]n principle, the effects of a concentration on competition in innovation in this type of situation may not be sufficiently assessed by restricting the assessment to actual or potential competition in existing product-markets."[946]

Pfizer/Hospira (2015)[947]

The *Pfizer/Hospira* transaction was related to the acquisition of Hospira, which supplies injectable drugs and infusion technologies, by Pfizer, a research-based pharmaceutical company that develops innovative medicines for humans. Pfizer was developing a biosimilar for infliximab, which was regarded as a competitor product to Hospira's Inflectra, the only infliximab biosimilar in the market at the time of the transaction. In addition, only one other undertaking besides Pfizer (namely, Samsung Bioepis) was at

---

[940] *Novartis/Glaxo Smith Kline's Oncology Business*, para. 85.
[941] De Coninck, *supra* note 846, at 41–42.
[942] Todino et al., *supra* note 841, at 9–10.
[943] *Id.*
[944] *Dow/DuPont*, European Commission Decision case M.7932 (Mar. 27, 2017).
[945] *Novartis/Glaxo Smith Kline's Oncology Business*, para. 89.
[946] *Id.*
[947] Pfizer/Hospira, European Commission Decision case COMP/M.7559 (Aug. 4, 2015).

an advanced stage in its R&D in terms of developing a competing biosimilar product. The term "biosimilar" refers to drugs that are developed to have the same therapeutic mechanisms as, although not being the exact copies of, patented biological pharmaceuticals. Since patented biological drugs are often deemed to be rather expensive, the aim of developing biosimilars was to decrease the cost of these treatments through the use of such substitute products.[948] The Commission noted that the parties' activities overlapped in human health pharmaceuticals, particularly in the fields of (i) biosimilars, and (ii) specialty injectable pharmaceuticals ("sterile injectables").[949]

As a result of its investigation, the Commission found serious concerns for the biosimilars market, infliximab and the different types of sterile injectables, in certain countries of the European Economic Area ("EEA").[950] Despite the arguments regarding the limited availability of clinical evidence,[951] the Commission, once again, significantly relied on the parties' internal documents in reaching its conclusions.[952] The Commission was concerned by the possibility that Pfizer could either delay or discontinue its pipeline product, in order to focus on Hospira's product Inflectra, "leading to the net loss of one of only three differentiated biosimilars marketed or in advanced stages of development,"[953] which would, in turn, lead to the diminishment of innovation competition in the relevant market. The Commission was also worried that, upon the consummation of the transaction, Pfizer could potentially give Hospira's biosimilar back to Celltrion,[954] which could, in turn, eliminate the existing price competition between the relevant undertakings.[955] Therefore, the transaction parties committed to fully divesting Pfizer's infliximab biosimilar drug in order to eliminate the Commission's concerns, and Novartis subsequently acquired the biosimilar drug in question in 2016.

This decision was considered to be controversial by commentators, who criticized the Commission for employing a "double standard" in its assessment concerning the potential competition.[956] Critics argued that, in its assessment, the Commission had implemented and applied different standards for the potential competition relating to a third party and the potential competition relating to one of the transaction parties. That is to say, the Commission was accused of utilizing a short time frame (two years, in general, according to the EU Horizontal Merger Guidelines) when evaluating whether any third party would potentially become a viable competitor in the foreseeable future; while the time frame employed to determine the potential competition from Pfizer (i.e., the six to eight years for Pfizer to develop the biosimilar infliximab) had been much longer.[957] Commentators also noted that the foregoing time frames taken into account by the Commission also differed from the time frames used in its analyses of other transactions, since, in *Novartis/GSK*,

---

[948]   Mirabile et al., *supra* note 939, at 1–4.
[949]   *Pfizer/Hospira*, para. 7.
[950]   *Id.*, para. 286.
[951]   Todino et al., *supra* note 841, at 10.
[952]   *Pfizer/Hospira*, para. 57.
[953]   *Id.*, para. 57.
[954]   Inflectra was developed by Celltrion, but co-marketed by Hospira and Celltrion at the time of the assessment.
[955]   European Commission, *supra* note 767.
[956]   Todino et al., *supra* note 841, at 10.
[957]   *Id.*

the Commission used a time frame of "five to seven years" when evaluating the innovative products that could potentially enter the market, whereas the relevant time frame in the *Dow/DuPont* decision was considered to be a period of ten years.

Deutsche Börse AG v. Commission (2015)[958]

The *Deutsche Börse AG v. Commission* decision concerns the judgment in which the Commission's decision regarding the *Deutsche Börse/NYSE*[959] transaction was subject to the review of the General Court. The Commission's decision involved the prohibition of the merger of NYSE Euronext and Deutsche Börse, which were two of the largest exchange platforms on a global scale. The Commission found that the transaction would give rise to a decrease in innovation, due to the fact that the "Notifying Parties compete head-to-head by offering trading services in products which offer identical economic exposure in both the interest rate and single equity derivatives markets,"[960] and that the transaction parties were also in competition with one another in the field of introducing "new and improved" contracts.[961]

The Commission's gradual transition to the novel approach towards theories of harm in terms of innovation was also visible herein, since the theories of harm, in this case, did not concentrate on a specific pipeline product, but were instead evaluated in a broader scope by incorporating the term "innovation spaces,"[962] which was later on frequently referred to in the Commission's subsequent assessments.[963]

The Commission's decision, which found that the merger would reduce third parties' incentives to innovate, was appealed before the General Court. In its appeal, Deutsche Börse argued that the Commission's findings that (i) "the parties constrained each other through innovation competition"[964] and (ii) "the merger could eliminate 'any technological competition' and give rise to a reduction in innovation available for customers"[965] were unsubstantiated. However, the General Court upheld the Commission's prohibition decision by asserting that (i) the Commission was not obliged to evaluate the extent of the reduction in innovation in order to substantiate its conclusion regarding the harm to innovation, and (ii) the elimination of competitive pressure between the parties in the technology market was sufficient for concluding that diminished innovation would harm the consumers' welfare.[966]

Dow/DuPont (2017)[967]

The dramatic shift in terms of the Commission's approach to the theories of harm concerning innovation, and the most obvious step of its transition to the novel theory, occurred in the *Dow/DuPont* case. This case concerned the horizontal merger of two

---

[958] Case T-175/12, Deutsche Börse AG v. Commission, ECLI:EU:T:2015:148.
[959] Deutsche Börse/NYSE Euronext, European Commission Decision case COMP/M.6166 (Feb. 1, 2012).
[960] *Id.*, para. 543.
[961] *Id.*, para. 601.
[962] *Id.*, para. 923.
[963] Petit, *supra* note 752, at 15.
[964] *Id.*
[965] *Id.* at 16.
[966] *Id.* at 15–16.
[967] Dow/DuPont, European Commission Decision case M.7932 (Mar. 27, 2017), §§ V.8.4–V.8.6, recitals 2039–2395.

undertakings conducting activities related to chemicals for crop protection,[968] which would give rise to the creation of the industry leader. More specifically, the consummation of the transaction would bring about the world's largest crop protection and seed company, with a market capitalization of $130 billion, and, as set forth by the Commission in its decision, this industry had already typically been concentrated for decades. The Commission had significant concerns that the merger would reduce price competition and decrease the number of choices for existing pesticides in several markets, as well as reducing innovation.

The Commission considered innovation as a crucial element of competition (to improve existing products and to develop new active ingredients) between the companies in the crop protection industry, where only five players were globally active throughout the entire research and development spectrum. The Commission believed that the transaction would have a substantial impact on innovation competition since it was considered that the merger would result in the loss of competition between crop protection suppliers. In particular, the Commission reflected that such theories of harm would occur as a result of the removal of the parties' incentives (i) to continue to pursue ongoing parallel innovation efforts, (ii) to develop and bring to market new pesticides, and that the transaction would (iii) significantly reduce competition for certain petrochemical products. The parties submitted commitments to address the Commission's concerns by agreeing to divest the entire DuPont pesticide business, including the R&D division. Based on the divestment, the decision also constitutes the first instance in which one of the transaction parties was compelled to divest its R&D division on a global scale, in order to eliminate the Commission's concerns related to innovation competition in the EU jurisdiction.[969] Having DuPont divest its entire R&D division globally is a risky remedy approach. This is much like but even more critical than the remedy of divesting late-stage pipeline product Stellarex in *Medtronic/Covidien*, as it is imperative that the divested unit do not fizzle out after the divestiture, and particularly *because* of the divestiture. In any case, divestiture should not be the only remedy for innovation theories of harm.

It was argued that the Commission's assessment in this decision constituted a novel approach towards theories of harm, referred to as "significant impediment to effective, innovative competition" approach, which was different from the traditional theories of harm under the EU merger control regime, referred to as the "significant impediment to effective competition"[970] approach. The Commission's novel outlook on theories of harm is argued to be discernible from its assertion that "the Commission considers that the Transaction would be likely to *significantly impede effective competition as regards innovation* both in innovation spaces where the Parties lines of research and early pipeline products overlap and overall in innovation in the crop protection industry."[971]

---

[968] The parties also had other overlapping activities; with that said, the focus of the innovation considerations that constitute our subject here is concerned with the crop protection chemicals.

[969] Ben Forbes, Rameet Sangha & Mat Hughes, *Understanding the New Frontier for Merger Control and Innovation – The European Commission's Decision in Dow/DuPont*, in THE INTERNATIONAL COMPARATIVE LEGAL GUIDE TO: MERGER CONTROL 2018 14 (Global Legal Group Ltd 14th ed. 2018), https://www.alixpartners.com/insights-impact/insights/understanding-the-new-frontier-for-merger-control.

[970] Petit, *supra* note 752, at 2.

[971] *Dow/DuPont*, para. 3297 (emphasis added).

In order to assess the effects brought by the transaction on innovation competition, the Commission conducted analyses both at the level of innovation spaces within the crop protection industry and on the innovation competition at the industry level.[972] Annex 4 of the *Dow/DuPont* decision[973] set out more fully how "[a] merger in innovative industries generates standard unilateral effects in innovation."[974] A significant part of Annex 4 is devoted to demonstrating the validity of the economic models that predict a post-merger reduction in an innovation competition. The Commission's role was to identify and evaluate the innovation strength of the players in the industry. For this purpose, it used innovation output measures (such as the number of patents and new active ingredients created in the past) and evaluated the concentration levels in each innovation space based on citation-based patent shares and turnover weighted by new active ingredients shares.[975] Nevertheless, the Commission did not take into account input measures such as R&D spending.[976] I would contend that the standard of proof of innovation theories of harm would need to be higher proportional to how early the R&D stage causing the concern is, and how aggregated (i.e., non-product specific) the harm is, in order to avoid an easy shifting of the burden of proof through speculative futuristic scaremongering, based only on general economic literature adopting an Arrowian view of the relationship between competition and innovation.

The most prominent reason why the *Dow/DuPont* decision is said to mark a significant development in terms of the transition to the "novel theories of harm" is that the Commission's theories of harm, in this case, are not tied to any specific product market in particular, as opposed to previous examples where the Commission had made clear which product markets the competition law concerns were related to. The Commission's analysis herein revolved around R&D activities that were not concerned with any specific product market, but rather "innovation spaces" that extend until the early stages of R&D work, and which "includes the 'discovery stage' where firms fund early 'lines of research' to discover new business areas, concepts, and lines."[977] In this context, the Commission has later on reconfirmed its position that the theories of harm do not necessarily need to be attached to a particular product market, by indicating that "In some cases, you can know in which product the companies are innovating, and you can identify an overlap in the future. But there could be situations where we don't know the outcome of the innovation process, but we nevertheless know the innovation process would be harmed as a result of the merger."[978] When it is alleged by the antitrust agency that it does not know the outcome of the innovation process but still knows the innovation process is harmed, the standards of proof need to be higher, around the question of "how do you know?", which requires a case-specific, factual and concrete parameters-based analysis of the harm on innovation.

---

[972] *Id.*, para. 1956.
[973] Annex 4 is entitled "Implication of the economic theory on mergers, competition and innovation in light of the features of the transaction."
[974] *Dow/DuPont*, Annex 4, § 4.1.1.
[975] *Id.*, recitals 379–402.
[976] *Id.*, recital 384.
[977] Petit, *supra* note 752, at 5.
[978] Matthew Newman, *Dow-DuPont Merger Remedy Reflects EU's Growing Focus on Innovation, Mosso Says*, MLEX MKT. INSIGHT (Mar. 28, 2017).

Both the Commission's approach and the emergence of "innovation spaces" have been criticized because they were not based on a legal framework, thus making its boundaries ambiguous and rendering the determination of its analytical framework speculative. Neither the EU Horizontal Merger Guidelines nor any other piece of legislation incorporate any explanations or provide any guidance on whether (and how) the long-term effects of the theories of harm related to innovation could be assessed independently from any specific relevant product market.[979] In the *Dow/DuPont* decision, the Commission based its theories of harm related to innovation on the possible effects of the transaction in ten years' time, in particular on whether the innovative products may or may not enter the market within the relevant time frame. From an economic standpoint, the Commission's approach can also arguably be claimed to have an "*arbitrary*" nature, since forecasting the success rate of an innovative product and predicting whether it would be marketed in a time frame that is essentially unforeseeable is considered to be impossible.[980] In simpler terms, the intensity of the R&D efforts and investments of an undertaking would not necessarily translate into (or guarantee) the respective product's successful entry into the market. Furthermore, having disregarded defenses based on efficiencies that were deemed not to be specific, quantifiable or verifiable and in its decisions such as the *Western Digital Ireland/Vivity Technologies* case above, as per the Merger Regulations, the Commission's own speculative stance regarding innovation spaces is betraying its own standards in evidentiary basis of assessment and acceptable defenses. This approach hardly follows what the ECJ has also tasked the Commission with, in *Commission v. Tetra Laval*: to be *factually accurate, reliable, and consistent* in its assessments. If the standards of proof have been indeed relaxed in this novel approach, it seems that this was only allowed for the Commission. This asymmetry is what I call the innovation paradox in merger control.

Additionally, the *Dow/DuPont* decision was criticized for the fact that the input for the Commission's assessment and the respective theories of harm was largely based on the information obtained from the parties' internal documents. In particular, "in Dow/DuPont, the EC's document request covered more than 400,000 internal documents, several of which were cited to support the EC's findings that the merging parties were important innovators and that the merger would slow the development of new agrochemicals."[981] The Commission's tendency to rely more and more on the information obtained from the transaction parties' internal documents for the theories of harm related to innovation concerns is another subject of criticism, since the information contained therein could be materially subjective, depending on a particular employee's personal views on the pipeline product, and the chances of success for a product could have been overestimated due to "corporate chest-thumping," commonly seen in any given company.[982] Therefore, it could be argued that such an analysis might be misleading in terms of evaluating whether the early-stage pipeline product would be approved and released to

---

[979] Petit, *supra* note 752, at 13.

[980] Frédéric de Bure & Laurence Bary, *Disruptive Innovation and Merger Remedies: How to Predict the Unpredictable?* CONCURRENCES No. 3-2017, art. No. 84407, para. 17.

[981] Nicholas Levy & Vassilena Karadakova, *The EC's Increasing Reliance on Internal Documents under the EU Merger Regulation: Issues and Implications*, 39 EUR. COMPETITION L. REV. 12 (2018).

[982] Ingrid Vandenborre, *The Importance of the New: Competition Innovation in Life Sciences*, 16 COMPETITION L. INSIGHT (2017); Todino et al., *supra* note 841, at 20.

the market. The internal documents paint a unilateral and usually aggrandized picture of the entity, with various ulterior motives. It is very difficult to filter out the human factor and sentiment in these communications, or the errors made as a result of a limited, single point of view of the market dynamics or restricted access to information on other players. Taken out of context, any number of internal assessments and scenario buildings may be deemed to substantiate the initial theory of harm that the Commission is putting forward. Although internal documents may still be relied upon for identifying a clear breach or intent on the part of the entity, it is imperative that such evidence be consumed with care and by giving the entities the benefit of the doubt. After all, such documents may be merely snapshots of numerous scenarios considered and discarded at one point, or a non-realistic portrayal of forecasts to serve hidden agendas, or even drawn up by persons not in decision-making positions in the entities.[983]

Accordingly, such evidentiary basis should not be deemed as conclusive evidence but merely as a corroborating factor with other objective evidence, to ensure that the Commission's findings are factually accurate and, more importantly, reliable.

4.6 The Implementation of the Novel Approach in the Last Five Years

ChemChina/Syngenta (2017)

After the Commission's decision on conditional clearance of *Dow/DuPont*, there were two other proposed mergers in the seed and agricultural chemical sector, and the Commission employed its novel approach in all these cases.

In *ChemChina/Syngenta*,[984] the Commission evaluated the acquisition of Swiss agrochemical giant Syngenta by ChemChina, which is active in, among others, European pesticide markets through its wholly owned Israel-based subsidiary Adama.[985] Syngenta produces pesticides based on active ingredients it has developed itself, but Adama only makes generic pesticides based on active ingredients developed by third parties when patents have expired and is the world's biggest producer of generic pesticides.[986] Since Adama, a generic player under control of ChemChina, only develops and sells pesticides based on active ingredients that are no longer covered by patents and does not conduct further activities on R&D to discover new active ingredients,[987] the Commission found the transaction at hand would not impact the innovation competition in pesticides, and approved the merger subject to divestitures. Similar to *Dow/DuPont*, the Commission applied its "novel approach" and evaluated the earlier stage pipeline products with respect to the parties' existing R&D activities.[988]

---

[983]   Kuhn, *supra* note 899.

[984]   ChemChina/Syngenta. European Commission Decision case M.7962 (Apr. 5, 2017).

[985]   *Id.*, para. 2.

[986]   *Id.*, para. 3.

[987]   *Id.*, para. 42.

[988]   European Commission Press Release IP/17/882, Mergers: Commission clears ChemChina acquisition of Syngenta, subject to conditions (Apr. 5, 2017), https://ec.europa.eu/commission/presscorner/detail/et/IP_17_882.

Bayer/Monsanto (2018)[989]

The *Bayer/Monsanto* transaction constitutes one of the seminal examples of a case in which the Commission intervened in the transaction based on its novel theories of harm related to innovation. The consummation of the transaction, i.e., the acquisition of Monsanto by Bayer, would create the leading integrated pesticides and seed company on a global scale; furthermore, both of the transaction parties also conducted innovative activities in their respective sectors, which were already concentrated, similar to the characteristics of the relevant product market in the *Dow/DuPont* decision.[990]

In its decision, the Commission's theories of harm related to innovation concerned three industries, in particular, namely, (i) seeds, (ii) pesticides, and (iii) digital agriculture. In this respect, even though the Commission's assessment in *Bayer/Monsanto* proceeded along the same line as its novel approach demonstrated in the *Dow/DuPont* case, in contrast to the *Dow/DuPont* decision, the Commission's assessment herein was more focused on which specific product markets the harm to innovation would actually occur, rather than conducting an assessment that is untied to any specific product market. Therefore, in *Bayer/Monsanto*, the Commission refrained from asserting any theories of harm for several product markets (namely, fungicides, insecticides, microbials, and bee health products) where Bayer and Monsanto were deemed not to be close competitors and in which there was an adequate number of competitors in terms of innovative efforts.[991] That said, the Commission evaluated that, in both cases,[992] the parties were close competitors in several innovation spaces. On this note, the Commission indicated in the *Bayer/Monsanto* decision that "there is evidence that Bayer and Monsanto are important and close innovators in several innovation spaces where few other alternatives are available. In many innovation spaces, the Parties have been in the past, and are likely to continue to be in the future, close and important innovation competitors."[993] Moreover, the Commission found that the early-stage pipeline products being developed by the parties were likely to take revenue from their counterparts in the future, and that there were not enough competitors working on pipeline projects in the "the innovation spaces targeted by these early pipeline products," which were already significantly concentrated and with substantial barriers that rendered entry difficult.[994] In this regard, the Commission found evidence that would suggest that the parties' work related to the pipeline products at the earlier stages of development could be ceased, hindered or reorganized due to cannibalization risks, thereby impeding innovation and preventing the development of new pipeline products. The Commission once again relied heavily on the parties' internal documents: it is indicated that 2.7 million internal documents were reviewed during the evaluation process.[995] On this account, the

---

[989]   Bayer/Monsanto, European Commission Decision case M.8084 (Mar. 21, 2018).

[990]   European Commission Press Release IP/17/2762, Mergers: Commission Opens In-depth Investigation into Proposed Acquisition of Monsanto by Bayer (Aug. 22, 2017), http://europa.eu/rapid/press-release_IP-17-2762_en.htm.

[991]   OECD, Non-price Effects of Mergers – Note by the European Union (DAF/COMP/WD(2018)14, June 1, 2018), para. 31, https://one.oecd.org/document/DAF/COMP/WD(2018)14/en/pdf.

[992]   *Id.*, para. 30.

[993]   *Bayer/Monsanto*, paras. 80–81.

[994]   *Id.*

[995]   European Commission Press Release IP/18/2282, Mergers: Commission Clears Bayer's Acquisition of Monsanto, Subject to Conditions (Mar. 21, 2018), http://europa.eu/rapid/press-release_IP-18-2282_en.

Commission, after its lengthy assessment, determined that the transaction would have significantly impeded both the price competition and the innovation in the markets that were subject to the Commission's theories of harm. This resulted in the conditional approval of the transaction based on the following set of extensive remedies: (i) the overlaps between the parties stemming from the transaction in seeds and pesticides were eliminated through the divestiture of Bayer's seed and trait business on a global scale, including its R&D business organization, as well as a portion of Monsanto's assets, which have been deemed as a future competitor to Bayer's "seed treatment against nematode worms," and (ii) Bayer submitted a commitment to grant "a license to its entire global digital agriculture product portfolio and pipeline products to ensure continued competition on this emerging market."[996]

Johnson & Johnson/Actelion (2017)

In this transaction taking place in the pharmaceutical industry, the Commission conditionally cleared the tie-up in *Johnson & Johnson/Actelion*.[997] Johnson & Johnson ("J&J") and Actelion Pharmaceuticals ("Actelion") both develop and sell innovative pharmaceutical products. Their activities are largely complementary, with Actelion marketing medicines in the EEA primarily for the treatment of pulmonary arterial hypertension, where J&J is not active. The main overlap between J&J's and Actelion's products and activities was regarding two compounds (namely, ACT-541468 and JNJ-7922) under the research and development activities in the treatments for insomnia.[998] These pipeline drugs have an orexin-antagonist base, which reduces the risk of dependency and results in fewer side effects compared to insomnia drugs already available.[999]

The Commission approved the acquisition of Actelion by J&J subject to conditions. There were horizontal overlaps between the activities of the parties to the transaction (i) in the treatments for multiple sclerosis[1000] and (ii) in the development of orexin-antagonist products for insomnia treatments.[1001] For the treatments for multiple sclerosis, considering the existing competitive environment in the market and that Actelion's Phase III pipeline product was not the closest substitute for J&J's already distributed product, the Commission found no concerns.[1002] For the other overlap, parties had competing pipeline medicines for insomnia, both of which were in Phase II of clinical trials.[1003] The Commission decided that, post-transaction, J&J would have the ability and incentive to delay, discontinue or reorient one of these projects for the treatment of insomnia, and since other competing pipeline programs were scarce, abandoning one of them could harm competition on innovation.[1004] In the notification, the parties provided that part of Actelion's research and development activities, including its insomnia research program, would be transferred before the merger

---

[996]   *Id.*

[997]   Johnson & Johnson/Actelion, European Commission Decision case M.8401 (June 9, 2017).

[998]   Lisa Wright, Susan Zhuang & Andrew Gilbert, *Innovation Competition, Economic Dependence and Exceptional Remedies: Three Interesting Aspects of the EC's Decision in Johnson & Johnson/Actelion*, LEXOLOGY, Aug. 29, 2017, https://www.lexology.com/library/detail.aspx?g=528dbd0e-b2ca-445f-afc9-a7941fa3a670.

[999]   *Johnson & Johnson/Actelion*, para. 26.

[1000]   *Id.*, para. 55. The exact market definition was left open, *see* para. 65.

[1001]   *Id.*, paras. 12 & 33.

[1002]   *Id.*, paras. 57, 73 & 76.

[1003]   *Id.*, paras. 13 & 15.

[1004]   *Id.*, paras. 36, 38, 39, 42, 50 & 54.

to Idorsia Ltd ("Idorsia"), a newly created company in which J&J would have a minority shareholding (initially 16% with an additional 16% at J&J's option).[1005] However, the Commission found that J&J could still have influenced Idorsia's strategic decisions due to its economic and structural links with the company.[1006] J&J was developing the overlapped pipeline medicine with a third party, Minerva Neurosciences ("Minerva").[1007]

J&J offered commitments to address the Commission's concerns, which were market-tested by the Commission. Following the feedback received during the market test, J&J amended the commitments by adding that it would cancel its minority shareholding within Minerva and fund 100% of Phase II development costs of its overlapping product.[1008] Accordingly, the final commitments of J&J were as follows: (i) J&J will not influence any of the strategic decisions of Idorsia. To that end, J&J will limit its shareholding to below 10% (or up to 16% provided that it would not be the largest shareholder) in Idorsia, will not nominate any of its board members, and will not receive any information about the overlapping product from Idorsia,[1009] and (ii) J&J will remove its incentives to negatively influence the development of its insomnia research project (by granting Minerva additional independence over the development of the overlapping product and waiving its royalty rights on Minerva's sales), continue funding the project and cancel its shares in Minerva.[1010] The Commission accepted these commitments and approved the transaction.[1011]

Apple/Shazam (2018)

On 6 August 2018, the Commission approved the proposed acquisition of Shazam Entertainment Ltd. ("Shazam") by Apple Inc. ("Apple"). The Commission found that (i) Shazam's data would not materially increase Apple's ability to target listeners, hence would not be able to foreclose the market to Apple's competitors in digital music streaming services, and (ii) restricting access to the Shazam app by Apple could only have limited effect on its competitors. On the transaction's impact on both innovation and competition, the Commission decided that the integration of Shazam's and Apple's datasets on user data (the exclusive use of Shazam's data by Apple) would not provide a unique competitive advantage to the merged entity and is unlikely "to result in a significant price increase or reduction of market incentives to innovate" because Shazam's data was not unique, and Apple's competitors would still have the opportunity to access and use similar databases.[1012]

BMS/Celgene (2019)

The Commission evaluated Bristol Myers Squibb Company's ("BMS") acquisition of Celgene, which gave limited horizontal overlaps related to marketed and/or pipeline

---

[1005]   *Id.*, paras. 43 & 44.
[1006]   J&J would hold up to 32% of the shares, whereas other shareholders would each hold less than 5%, provide a ten-year loan to Idorsia, and be able to appoint one or two board members of Idorsia if some conditions are met. *See Johnson & Johnson/Actelion*, paras. 46, 48 & 49.
[1007]   *Id.*, para. 41.
[1008]   *Id.*, paras. 78 & 95.
[1009]   *Id.*, paras. 98 & 99, Commitments to the European Commission, Section B, paras. 7, 8 & 9.
[1010]   *Id.*, paras. 103 & 106, Commitments to the European Commission, Section B. paras. 2–6.
[1011]   *Id.*, para. 109.
[1012]   Apple/Shazam, European Commission Decision case M.8788 (Sept. 6, 2018).

treatments in autoimmune diseases, fibrotic diseases, and oncology.[1013] The Commission, again taking the "novel approach" by its four-layer competitive assessment from *Dow/DuPont* and *Bayer/Monsanto*,[1014] cleared the acquisition by taking into account the number of actual and potential competitors and its limited impact on the EEA markets,[1015] following only a Phase I review. During the assessment, the Commission took into account and agreed with the defenses of Celgene on the part of oncology for Celgene's marketed drug, Otezla, and BMS's pipeline products. In this instance, the products had different levels of efficacy and safety, the two key elements in the choice of therapy, and therefore were differentiated products. Additionally, there were many already available marketed products and many pipeline projects under development for such treatments. Further, Celgene's marketed drug would probably lose its exclusivity when BMS's pipeline product enters the market, since the Phase I pipeline product would not enter the market for a very long time. Lastly, the merged entity would have no ability and/or no incentive to discontinue (i) the development of BMS' two pipeline projects or (ii) the supply of Celgene's product.[1016]

Google/Fitbit (2020)

In *Google/Fitbit*,[1017] the Commission cleared Google's acquisition of Fitbit, subject to remedies. The commission evaluated Google's incentives to innovate in the future with regard to smartwatches and found that the transaction would not restrict innovation competition since Fitbit was not the only or main source of pressure on Google to innovate in all the assessed markets.[1018] The Commission argued that Google would likely be less incentivized to innovate in the long term due to the lack of contestability resulting from raised barriers to entry and expansion for Google's competitors, even though the quality of its services may increase in the short term because of better ads targeting. Google responded to such an argument that there were no horizontal theories of harm since Google and Fitbit are active in different targeted markets, and that Fitbit has health-related innovation efforts focusing on improving its wearable devices, whereas Google is not active in the wearable devices.[1019] The Commission ruled out such concerns because "the parties are neither actual nor potential competitors in the collection or marketing of user health and fitness data." That said, the parties were neither actual nor potential competitors in online advertising.[1020] Chapter 7 below provides a more detailed analysis and further discussion regarding reverse killer acquisitions in this case.

[1013] BMS/Celgene, European Commission Decision case M.9294 (July 29, 2019).

[1014] *Id.*, para. 22; Marion Provost & Mélanie Thill-Tayara, *At a Glance: Pharmaceutical Merger Review in European Union*, Lexology (2021), https://www.lexology.com/library/detail.aspx?g=5adfdc-dc-63d3-4ce2-9a64-1207fd774ab8.

[1015] European Commission Daily News MEX/19/4849, Mergers: Commission clears acquisition of Celgene by BMS (July 30, 2019), https://ec.europa.eu/commission/presscorner/detail/en/MEX_19_4849.

[1016] *The Commission Unconditionally Approves BM's Acquisition of Celgene*, Cleary Gottlieb, Oct. 10, 2019, https://www.clearyantitrustwatch.com/2019/10/the-commission-unconditionally-approves-bms-acquisition-of-celgene.

[1017] Google/Fitbit, European Commission Decision case M.9660 (Dec. 17, 2020), https://ec.europa.eu/competition/elojade/isef/case_details.cfm?proc_code=2_M_9660.

[1018] *Id.*, para. 398.

[1019] *Id.*, para. 481.

[1020] *Id.*, para. 484.

Johnson & Johnson/Tachosil (2020 – abandoned)

The Commission decided to open an in-depth investigation into Johnson & Johnson's proposed acquisition of Tachosil, where both parties were active in the dual hemostatic patches market, even though Johnson & Johnson was not active in the European market.[1021] In its preliminary view, the Commission argued that the transaction could lead to a significant reduction of competition and innovation in the market for dual hemostatic patches since Johnson & Johnson would eliminate its biggest potential entrant, leading to higher prices, less choice, and reduced incentives to innovate.[1022] The parties decided to abandon the proposed acquisition due to the Commission's preliminary concerns.[1023]

Nvidia/Arm (2021 – abandoned)

The most recent case on innovation before the Commission was the proposed transaction regarding the acquisition of all shares in, and thus sole control of, Arm Limited ("Arm") by NVIDIA Corporation ("NVIDIA").[1024] (The investigation into *Illumina/Grail*[1025] was ongoing at the time, as discussed in more detail in Chapter 7 below.)

NVIDIA and Arm are entities that are both active in the semiconductors industry, albeit at different levels: NVIDIA designs and supplies accelerated computing platforms, including graphics processing units for gaming, data centers, professional visualization, and automotive applications. Through its acquisition of Mellanox in April 2020, NVIDIA also started supplying network interconnect products and solutions. Arm, on the other hand, develops and licenses the intellectual property ("IP") for central processing units ("CPUs") which are used by semiconductor suppliers and systems-on-chip ("SoC").

Due to the extent of the parties' activities, the proposed transaction requires the approval of various competition authorities, including those in Europe, the United States, China, Korea, and the United Kingdom.[1026] At this time, in addition to the Commission, the UK Competition and Markets Authority ("CMA") and the US Federal Trade Commission ("FTC") have also launched in-depth inquiries into the acquisition upon complaints by Google, Microsoft and Qualcomm, which heavily rely on Arm's IP.[1027]

[1021] European Commission Press Release IP/20/529, Mergers: Commission Opens In-depth Investigation into Proposed Acquisition of Tachosil by Johnson & Johnson (Mar. 25, 2020), https://ec.europa.eu/commission/presscorner/detail/en/ip_20_529.

[1022] OECD, *The Concept of Potential Competition – Note by the EU* 9 (DAF/COMP/WD(2021)21, May 25, 2021), https://one.oecd.org/document/DAF/COMP/WD(2021)21/en/pdf.

[1023] *Id.*

[1024] Nvidia/Arm European, Commission case M.9987 (abandoned/withdrawn on Feb. 8, 2022), https://ec.europa.eu/competition/elojade/isef/case_details.cfm?proc_code=2_M_9987.

[1025] *ibid.*

[1026] Baek Byung-Yeul, *Tesla, Amazon oppose Nvidia's acquisition of Arm*, THE KOREA TIMES, Sept. 3, 2021, https://www.koreatimes.co.kr/www/tech/2021/08/133_314738.html.

[1027] David McLaughlin, Ian King & Dina Bass, *Google, Microsoft, Qualcomm Protest Nvidia's Acquisition of Arm Ltd.*, BLOOMBERG, Feb. 12, 2021, https://www.bloomberg.com/news/articles/2021-02-12/google-microsoft-qualcomm-protest-nvidia-s-arm-acquisition.

The Commission was officially notified of the transaction on September 8, 2021,[1028] and announced that it was initiating the Phase II investigation on October 27, 2021.[1029] According to the Commission, competition concerns arise under this proposed transaction not because the two undertakings are close competitors and active in the same product market but because Arm's IP is used in manufacturing the products that compete with the products of NVIDIA in certain sectors, including automotive, the Internet of things ("IoT"), and data centers.

The Commission indicated that the proposed acquisition may lead to more expensive products, fewer alternative products, and reduced innovation in the semiconductor industry. In this regard, Executive Vice-President of the Commission Margrethe Vestager emphasized the semiconductor's prevalence in infrastructure such as data centers, and stated: "Our analysis shows that the acquisition of Arm by NVIDIA could lead to restricted or degraded access to Arm's IP, with distortive effects in many markets where semiconductors are used. Our investigation aims to ensure that companies active in Europe continue having effective access to the technology that is necessary to produce state-of-the-art semiconductor products at competitive prices."

In its press release on the transaction, taking into account Arm's market power for CPU IP, the Commission indicated that the merged entity might have the ability to hinder NVIDIA's rivals' access to Arm's CPU IP. Consequently, the Commission concluded that the proposed acquisition might hinder competition in (i) data center CPUs; (ii) smart network interconnects used in data centers for various purposes such as offload network or storage; (iii) semiconductors used for automotive advanced driver-assistance systems that enable vehicles to assist the driver; (iv) semiconductors used in infotainment applications that include information and entertainment services for drivers and passengers in a vehicle, such as automotive navigation systems, USB and Bluetooth connectivity and Wi-Fi; and (v) SoCs used in high-performance IoT devices, gaming consoles and general-purpose PCs.

In light of the above, the Commission's Phase II review was expected to focus on the effects of the transaction on innovation, particularly whether there would be any stifling of innovation due to the Arm licensees' reluctance to share commercially sensitive information with NVIDIA through the merged entity. The Commission would assess whether Arm's R&D expenditure would be directed towards products with higher profits, to the detriment of players heavily relying on Arm IP in other areas that may not have been as profitable. However, the investigation was aborted/withdrawn on February 8, 2022, as the parties abandoned the transaction due to "significant regulatory challenges preventing the consummation of the transaction."[1030] Considering that the CMA and the FTC, along with other authorities, had also initiated in-depth investigations or lawsuits against this merger, this result is not unexpected.

[1028]   Nvidia/Arm, European Commission case M.9987 (abandoned/withdrawn on Feb. 8, 2022), https://ec.europa.eu/competition/elojade/isef/case_details.cfm?proc_code=2_M_9987.

[1029]   European Commission Press Release IP/21/5624, Mergers: Commission Opens In-depth Investigation into Proposed Acquisition of Arm by NVIDIA (Oct. 27, 2021) https://ec.europa.eu/commission/presscorner/detail/en/ip_21_5624.

[1030]   Nvidia Newsroom Press Release, NVIDIA and SoftBank Group Announce Termination of NVIDIA's Acquisition of Arm Limited (Feb. 7, 2022), https://nvidianews.nvidia.com/news/nvidia-and-softbank-group-announce-termination-of-nvidias-acquisition-of-arm-limited.

Microsoft/Activision (2023)

The proposed acquisition of Activision Blizzard, Inc. ("Activision") by Microsoft was notified to the EU Commission on September 30, 2022.[1031] In terms of the parties' activities, Microsoft sells a gaming console (Xbox) where users download the games they want to play from the Microsoft Xbox Store, and they can also pay to access cloud-based content via Microsoft's multi-game subscription service (Xbox Game Pass). Microsoft is also a game publisher and has (i) a cloud gaming service (Xbox Cloud Gaming); (ii) a network of data centers and cloud computing infrastructure that offers various services, including gaming (Azure); and (iii) the leading PC operating system ("OS") (Windows).[1032] Activision develops and publishes gaming content for consoles, PC, and mobile and distributes PC games.[1033]

The acquisition was approved by the Commission subject to compliance with the commitments offered by Microsoft on May 15, 2023. The Commission's analysis of the effect of the transaction in general[1034] seems to have been similar to the CMA's analysis (as further discussed in Chapter 5, below). However, unlike the CMA, which, as of September 22, 2023, considered that there are reasonable grounds that the restructured transaction (where, among others, Microsoft will not purchase the cloud gaming rights of Activision) might be accepted, the Commission decided that the commitments offered by Microsoft fully addressed its competition concerns. Accordingly, the Commission found that:

- The transaction would not significantly restrict competition in the gaming consoles market since (i) Microsoft would have strong incentives to distribute games to Sony given that Sony is the most popular console game distributor worldwide and in the EEA, and (ii) even if Microsoft refuses to distribute Activision's games to Sony, this would not significantly harm competition in the market, as Sony could leverage its size and market position to preserve its competitive position even without offering the *Call of Duty* game, which is less popular in the EEA than in other regions of the world.

- Activision would not have made its games available for multi-game subscription services since this would affect the sales of individual games; hence, the situation for third-party providers of multi-game subscription services would not change post-transaction.

- The transaction would restrict competition in the distribution of PC and console games via cloud game streaming services because if Microsoft made Activision's games exclusive to its own cloud game streaming service, it would reduce competition in the market. In fact, although cloud game strea-

---

[1031] Microsoft/Activision Blizzard, European Commission Decision case M.10646 (May 5, 2023), https://ec.europa.eu/competition/elojade/isef/case_details.cfm?proc_code=2_M_10646.

[1032] CMA, Anticipated acquisition by Microsoft of Activision Blizzard, Inc. (Final Report) (Apr. 26, 2023), https://assets.publishing.service.gov.uk/media/644939aa529eda000c3b0525/Microsoft_Activision_Final_Report_.pdf ("*Microsoft/Activision* (Final Report)"), para. 2.3.

[1033] *Id.*, paras. 2.11, 2.12 & 2.14.

[1034] European Commission Press Release IP/23/2705, Mergers: Commission Clears Acquisition of Activision Blizzard by Microsoft, Subject to Conditions (May 15, 2023), https://ec.europa.eu/commission/presscorner/detail/en/ip_23_2705.

ming is very limited today, it is an innovative market segment that could transform the way many gamers play video games, and the popularity of Activision's games could promote its growth.

- If Microsoft hinders or degrades the streaming of Activision's games on PCs using OSs other than Windows, this could strengthen the position of Windows in the market for PC OSs.[1035]

In line with the remedies offered to the CMA, Microsoft proposed, for a period of ten years, (i) a free license to consumers in the EEA that would allow them to stream all current and future Activision PC and console games for which they have a license, via any cloud game streaming services of their choice, and (ii) a free license to cloud game streaming service providers to allow EEA-based gamers to stream the said games. The Commission accepted the commitments and noted that they (i) represent a significant improvement for cloud game streaming compared to the current situation (as Activision does not currently license its games to cloud game streaming services); (ii) will empower customers to stream Activision's games using any cloud gaming services operating in the EEA;[1036] (iii) will boost the development of the cloud game streaming technology in the EEA; and (iv) will unlock significant benefits for competition and consumers, making the games available in new platforms and more devices than before.[1037]

The CMA's and the FTC's respective approaches to this transaction are discussed in detail in Chapters 5 and 6 below. The transaction remains under review by the Australian competition authority[1038] despite being approved by the authorities in New Zealand,[1039] Turkey,[1040] Japan, Chile, Brazil, South Africa, Saudi Arabia,[1041] and Serbia.[1042]

The Asymmetry in the Commission's Approach

It is apparent that in the beginning of its "novel approach" (in *Dow/DuPont* and *Bayer/Monsanto*), the Commission ruled out the innovation defenses of the merging parties and conditionally cleared the mergers subject to divestitures. However, the Commission's "novel approach," which takes into account the innovation at such an early stage (by only looking at the early R&D efforts of the merging parties that have not yet gained shape) and the Commission's theory of harm was criticized by some for being speculative and having a narrow point of view.[1043] As such, in *Dow/DuPont*, *ChemChina/Syngenta*,

---

[1035]   *Id.* at 3.

[1036]   If they are purchased in an online store or included in an active multi-game subscription in the EEA.

[1037]   European Commission Press Release IP/23/2705, *supra* note 1034.

[1038]   *See* Australian Competition & Consumer Commission, Microsoft Corporation – Activision Blizzard Inc. (June 16, 2022), https://www.accc.gov.au/public-registers/mergers-registers/public-informal-merger-reviews/microsoft-corporation-activision-blizzard-inc.

[1039]   New Zealand Commerce Commission, Case register, Microsoft Corporation; Activision Blizzard Inc (Aug. 7, 2023), https://comcom.govt.nz/case-register/case-register-entries/microsoft-corporation-activision-blizzard-inc.

[1040]   Microsoft/Activision, Turkish Competition Board Decision No. 23-31/592-202 (July 13, 2023).

[1041]   OECD, *Theories of Harm for Digital Mergers: OECD Competition Policy Roundtable Background Note* (2023), Box 4.1. fn 2.

[1042]   *See* Commission for Protection of Competition Decision (Aug. 12, 2022), https://kzk.gov.rs/kzk/wp-content/uploads/2022/11/Microsoft1.pdf.

[1043]   *See* Silvia Solidoro, *Assessing Innovation Theories of Harm in EU Merger Control* (Policy Briefs, 2019/18, Florence Competition Programme, 2019), https://cadmus.eui.eu/bitstream/handle/1814/64768/PB_2019_18.pdf?sequence=1&isAllowed=y.

and *Bayer/Monsanto*, the Commission does not evaluate the power of future competitors (considering its R&D projects and its pipeline products) and disregards the possibility of success of merging parties' R&D projects. Although the "novel approach" has not significantly changed since *Bayer/Monsanto*, it is still possible to see slight differences in *Johnson & Johnson/Actelion* and *BMS/Celgene*, where the Commission has taken into account the power of future competitors. Moreover, in *Johnson & Johnson/Actelion*, *BMS/Celgene* and *Google/Fitbit*, it can be stated that the Commission evaluated the overlaps in potential innovation markets while taking into account the potential result of the pipeline or R&D products of the parties. However, the "novel approach" still retains its narrow and unpredictable nature, which may also contribute to the abandonment of transactions like *Johnson & Johnson/Tachosil* or *Nvidia/Arm*. The case law of EU courts does not seem to present one single coherent theory of innovation: different parameters of innovation are assessed in similar cases, or innovation is not always given the same weight, and it has been noted that the EU courts have systematically ignored some significant parameters when assessing innovation.[1044] These again highlight the innovation paradox: the transaction parties' burden for efficiency defenses remains almost unattainably high, and yet the Commission can easily rely on literature on general economic theory and internal documents that do not always constitute the most objective or factual evidence, or the courts can pick and choose the relevant parameters. Considering all the tools that are available to the Commission, the novel approach can potentially be wielded much more effectively by considering economic and neutral evidence primarily and only then relying on internal documents as corroborative factors, so that it could actually attain the standard of proof set out in *Tetra Laval*.

4.7 Conclusion

Historically, the theories of harm related to innovation have been based on the underlying principles of the Commission's EU Horizontal Merger Guidelines. The classic framework of the legislation leaves the Commission some room to maneuver for interpretation and case-by-case examination, since the legislation does not provide explicit or detailed guidance on how innovation concerns are to be assessed in merger reviews. This leeway for interpretation is corroborated through the evolving nature of the Commission's approach, as depicted in the scope of the foregoing case law.

The Commission's initial stance towards innovation considerations in merger control was based on utilizing the traditional tools that were available to it. Therefore, its theories of harm were based on SIEC, and the relevant product markets were clearly defined. In the traditional approach, the focus was on developed pipeline products rather than pipeline products in their early stages. Consequently, the Commission assessed the competitive pressure applied by competitors and by the transaction parties themselves to one another. The criteria for assessing

---

[1044] Thibault Schrepel, *A Systematic Content Analysis of Innovation in European Competition Law* (Amsterdam Law & Technology Institute (ALTI) Working Paper 2-2023 // Dynamic Competition Initiative (DCI) Working Paper 1-2023, 2023), https://ssrn.com/abstract=4413584.

these elements were symmetric. Finally, the standard of proof for verifying the assessment of these elements was determined to be meticulously high, incorporating information sources from the field, sector participants, competitors, and the transaction parties, amongst others.

However, the assessment of innovation concerns in competition law has also proved to be as dynamic as innovation's ever-changing nature. The Commission's approach has gradually evolved from the traditional approach into the novel approach, the most significant and easily discernible example of which was the 2017 decision on the merger of Dow and DuPont. The evolved approach of the Commission, as demonstrated in that case, has a number of aspects that differentiate it from the Commission's approach in the traditional era. The most prominent of these differences is the introduction of a novel theory of harm, namely, the assessment of competition for "significant impediment to effective innovative competition." This newly introduced theory of harm is a leap into uncharted territories, considering that its predecessor (namely, "significant impediment to effective competition") was set forth and regulated by the legislative framework itself. This new methodology has also introduced the concept of "innovation spaces" into competition law assessments, rather than the classic and constrained analysis based on the bedrock concept of "relevant market." This new approach considers the terrain on which the competitive analysis takes place to be boundless. Furthermore, the potential subject of such competition law analysis was also extended to encompass early-stage pipeline products, which may lead this new methodological approach to reach conclusions with less predictive ability about products whose futures are more uncertain, if not highly speculative. As for the standard of proof, the novel approach demonstrated in both the *Dow/DuPont* and *Bayer/Monsanto* cases includes a specific focus on using internal documents obtained from the transaction parties. In this context, it is worth remembering that the Commission examined 40,000 internal documents during *Dow/DuPont* and an even more staggering 2.7 million documents during *Bayer/Monsanto*. This methodology was also criticized by commentators, as internal documents may be considered more subjective (due to the potential for corporate chest-thumping), and therefore, considered to fall short of the criteria that one would require neutral evidence material to meet.

All in all, although the current "novel" approach of the Commission could be considered by some to be intrusive or ambiguous, the traditional approach's use of classic tools for assessments might also be deemed to lack the capacity to adapt to the needs of the modern global economy and to assess the dynamism of the evolving market structures. Having said this, the relaxation of boundaries in terms of the markets/products assessed or the standards of proof seem to be flowing only towards one direction and remain asymmetrical, as the transaction parties' efficiency defenses are still required to demonstrate that any efficiencies will be merger-specific, quantifiable and verifiable. Considering the various commercial and cost implications of delaying the transaction until approval, it is very likely that some of the parties may actually choose to divest or provide various commitments, in order to secure the conditional approval as soon as possible, rather than tackle such burden, which conversely could actually harm future innovation. In conclusion, the puzzle of how competition and innovation correlate in the scope of the EU merger control regime is, fundamentally, a question of policy, which may help to foster innovation and strengthen competition or, at times, be overly invasive.

Chapter 5
Innovation Considerations in the Merger Control Regime in the United Kingdom

5.1 Introduction

Since the UK's accession to the EU, the competition law cases affecting businesses and consumers in the United Kingdom were dealt with under EU law, enforced by the Commission and reviewed by the European Court of Justice (and General Court), and this was the case as long as the United Kingdom was a member.[1045] In other words, during that period, if a transaction within the merger control fell within the exclusive jurisdiction of the Commission under the EU Merger Regulation,[1046] then EU law would be applied in reviewing the transaction.

However, when concentrations do not fall under the EU Merger Regulation, they are dealt with the jurisdiction of the Member States. These concentrations are usually evaluated by the national competition authorities of those Member States, such as the competition enforcement authorities in the UK, and known as the "one-stop-shop" regime.[1047] In light of this principle, if the Commission maintains jurisdiction over a merger that has an "EU dimension" (which would be determined on the basis of the turnover of the merging undertakings), then the authorized competition authority in the UK – namely, the Competition and Markets Authority ("CMA") – will not be able to review the case, except in cases where the CMA has a duty to refer such mergers.[1048]

In this regard, the Commission's approach to innovation under the EU merger regime and detailed case analysis is demonstrated in Chapter 4. In this chapter, the author will

---

[1045]   Michael Grenfell, A View from the CMA: Brexit and Beyond, Speech at the Advanced EU Competition Law Conference (May 16, 2018), https://www.gov.uk/government/speeches/a-view-from-the-cma-brexit-and-beyond.

[1046]   Council Regulation (EC) No. 139/2004 of Jan. 20, 2004, on the Control of Concentrations Between Undertakings (the "EC Merger Regulation" or "EUMR"), 2004 OJ (L 24) 1, https://eur-lex.europa.eu/legal-content/EN/TXT/PDF/?uri=CELEX:32004R0139&from=EN.

[1047]   Robert Bell & William Haig, How Will a No-Deal Brexit Effect Merger Control (2019), http://eu-competitionlaw.com/how-will-a-no-deal-brexit-effect-merger-control/

[1048]   Under Chapter 3 of the Enterprise Act 2002, which came into force on June 20, 2003, and the amending Enterprise and Regulatory Reform Act 2013, in case a merger with a Union-dimension has a "principal competitive effect" in the UK, it may be referred back, in whole or in part, for investigation by the CMA. In cases of markets of insufficient importance or the existence of relevant customer benefits that outweigh the expected "substantial lessening of competition" and any adverse effects as a result of the concerned merger, the CMA can exercise its discretion and choose not to make a reference (RICHARD WHISH & DAVID BAILEY, COMPETITION LAW (Oxford Univ. Press 9th ed. 2018)).

attempt to answer the following question: how do the UK's competition authorities, i.e., the CMA and its predecessors, the Office of Fair Trading ("OFT") and the Competition Commission ("CC"), evaluate innovation as a concept or the innovation theories of harm?

The author will also address how these considerations may be affected as a result of "Brexit,"[1049] when the UK's competition law regime broke free from the jurisdiction of the Commission. The CMA became the sole executive authority to tackle all anti-competitive practices that affect the markets in the UK and empowered to review all mergers and acquisitions affecting the UK (assuming the national jurisdictional thresholds are met) once Brexit took effect.[1050] In this regard, we will also discuss whether Brexit has already or is expected to create any effects with regard to innovation considerations in the merger control regime in the UK.

5.2 An Overview of the Merger Regime in the UK

The CMA, which is an independent, non-ministerial government department, is the leading competition and consumer authority in the UK. The CMA acquired its powers on April 1, 2014, and took over the competition enforcement functions of the CC and the OFT. The competition law framework in the UK consists of the Competition Act 1998 ("CA") and the Enterprise Act 2002 ("EA") on mergers and markets. Chapters I and II of

---

[1049] Withdrawal from the EU is a complex negotiation process regulated under article 50 of the Treaty on European Union (TEU). Article 50 requires Member States wishing to withdraw from the EU to take the necessary steps in accordance with their own constitutional requirements for deciding the withdrawal and notify the European Council of such intention. Moreover, as per article 50 TEU, the EU and such Member State(s) that wish to withdraw shall conclude an agreement to set out the arrangements and determine their future relationship with the EU. In light of this provision, the UK's membership to the EU was put to a question on June 23, 2016, with a non-binding national referendum, whereby more than thirty million UK citizens voted on whether the UK should leave or remain in the EU. With 51.9% of the citizens voting in favor of the "leave" option, the political phenomenon known as the "Brexit" has officially commenced. In the aftermath of the referendum, following the agreement by both Houses of Parliament and the Royal Assent, UK Prime Minister Theresa May was authorized to send a letter to the European Council President Donald Tusk on Mar. 29, 2017, in order to notify him of the UK's intention to leave the EU and set out the negotiation goals. After a long and constructive negotiation period, the UK government managed to reach an agreement with the EU officials and set out the terms and conditions for its withdrawal. That being said, the UK Parliament has refused to approve the withdrawal agreement by Mar. 29, 2019, and rejected the agreement three times in total. This led to the postponement of Brexit to Apr. 12, 2019, at first, and Brexit was subsequently postponed a second time with an extension until Oct. 31, 2019. However, on Oct. 17, 2019, the UK and the EU agreed that the UK would leave the UK at midnight on Jan. 31, 2020, with a transition period until Dec. 31, 2020.

[1050] The timing of when the competition authorities would be authorized to exercise their jurisdiction depended on when the withdrawal would take place. Accordingly, the CMA 2020/21 Annual Report provides that "In 2019/20 we have made substantial progress in ensuring that we have the necessary people, skills and infrastructure in place to take on our expanded role outside of the EU from January 2021. We will be ready to launch or take over major international cartel and antitrust cases, merger investigations and (under previously announced Government proposals) potentially enforcement of national subsidy control rules" (para. 3.45, https://assets.publishing.service.gov.uk/government/uploads/system/uploads/attachment_data/file/873689/Annual_Plan_2020-21.pdf).

the Competition Act 1998 mirror articles 101 and 102 of the Treaty on the Functioning of the European Union ("TFEU"), respectively.

The merger control regime in the UK is governed by the Enterprise Act 2002. It promotes competition within and outside the UK, for the benefit of consumers.[1051] As a general rule, mergers that are covered by the EU Merger Regulation ("EUMR") are excluded from review by the CMA.[1052] In this regard, the CMA is tasked with reviewing and investigating mergers that take place within the UK and that raise competition law issues and concerns.[1053]

There are specific structural differences between the EU and UK merger control regimes, which create significant implications for the substantive assessment of mergers.[1054] For instance, under the EUMR, there is a compulsory pre-notification requirement for transactions with an EU dimension, whereas, under the UK competition law rules, there is no duty to pre-notify transactions to the CMA.[1055] Since this is voluntary, it is accepted and acknowledged that not notifying a merger to the CMA does not create negative impacts for the merging undertakings with regard to the CMA's substantive evaluation of the competitive effects of a merger.[1056]

In assessing a particular merger transaction, the CMA considers whether (i) a relevant merger situation has been created (or, for anticipated mergers, will be created) and, if so, (ii) whether or not this situation will lead to a substantial lessening of competition. Here, both elements must be present in order for the CMA to review a transaction on its own initiative.[1057] Therefore, it is essential to analyze first whether a merger can be considered to produce a "relevant merger situation" ("RMS"), and then determine whether there is a realistic prospect of a *substantial lessening of competition.*" This substantive test applied by the CMA is called an "SLC test," which is distinct from the test used by the Commission (i.e., the "SIEC" test, referring to a significant impediment of effective competition, in particular as a result of the creation or strengthening of a dominant position). However, it should be noted here that the underlying economic approaches and analyses in both tests are generally similar.[1058]

Given that a "relevant merger situation" can be defined as "a merger that meets one of the jurisdictional thresholds, and covers several kinds of transactions and arrangements,"[1059] and since this definition, to a great extent, draws the lines of the jurisdictional thresholds for the CMA, we will not go into the details of what constitutes an RMS. For the purposes of this Chapter, it is sufficient to note that the criteria for an RMS include certain formalistic and procedural aspects of the transaction in question, such as whether "two or more enterprises

---

[1051] CMA, Mergers: Guidance on the CMA's Jurisdiction and Procedure (2014), para. 2.4, https://assets.publishing.
service.gov.uk/media/61d45e41e90e07197007de1d/CMA2_guidance.pdf
[1052] *Id.*, para. 3.11.
[1053] *Id.*, para. 3.6.
[1054] *Id.*, para. 1.17.
[1055] WHISH & BAILEY, *supra* note 1048, at 936.
[1056] CMA, *supra* note 1051, para. 6.2.
[1057] *Id.*, para. 3.1.
[1058] CC & OFT, Merger Assessment Guidelines (2010), para. 1.16.
[1059] *Id.*, para. 3.1.1.

(broadly speaking, business activities of any kind) cease to be distinct" and whether there are "arrangements which will lead to enterprises ceasing to be distinct," as well as a turn-over test (i.e., the target company having £70 million or more annual turnover)[1060] and a share of supply test (i.e., the transaction increasing the parties' combined share of supply to at least 25% of the goods or services supplied in the UK or a substantial part of it).[1061]

As competition is viewed as "a process of rivalry between firms seeking to win customers' business over time by offering them a better deal"[1062] under the UK merger regime, the SLC test applied by the CMA includes an analysis of whether the transaction "has a significant effect on rivalry over time, and therefore on the competitive pressure on firms to improve their offer to customers or become more efficient or innovative."[1063] Under this test, the CMA examines and evaluates the unilateral, coordinated and vertical or conglomerate effects of both horizontal and non-horizontal mergers.

In assessing the effects of a merger and applying the SLC test, the CMA resorts to particular theories of harm that address the potential changes arising from the merger, its impact on rivalries in the relevant markets, and the expected harm to customers.[1064] Accordingly, the CMA (i) takes into account the commercial rationale for the transaction, (ii) compares the competitive outlook as a result of the merger with the situation in the absence of the merger,[1065] and (iii) evaluates the competitive offerings of the merging parties and how they may be affected (in terms of both price or non-price aspects, such as the quantity sold, service quality, product range, product quality and innovation) as a result of the transaction.[1066] In this regard, since it is recognized that a merger can give rise to an SLC if it has a significant effect on rivalry in the relevant market over time, the CMA will take into account the competitive pressure to offer improved products and services or to become more efficient or innovative.[1067] Thus, it can be concluded that innovation considerations constitute a vital part of the CMA's SLC test, and are therefore an integral part of the merger control review mechanism in the UK.

[1060]   Under the National Security and Investment Act 2021, the UK government was empowered to review mergers on national security grounds, and a much lower annual turnover merger control threshold (£1 million) was introduced for relevant enterprises active in certain specified sectors (such as quantum and military technology, computer processing units, artificial intelligence, cryptographic authentication, and advanced materials and energy), as well as removing the requirement to increase share of supply. Under its consultation on "Reforming competition and consumer policy," the UK government has, among other notable issues, proposed significant changes to the jurisdictional thresholds to reflect the effect of inflation and enable the review of "killer acquisitions." *See* the government's response to the consultation for more details, https://www.gov.uk/government/consultations/reforming-competition-and-consumer-policy/outcome/reforming-competition-and-consumer-policy-government-response

[1061]   For all criteria, *see* CMA, Mergers: Guidance on the CMA's Jurisdiction and Procedure (2014 as amended Jan. 2022), para. 4.3; Guidance on Changes to the Jurisdictional Thresholds for UK Merger Control (CMA90) (June 11, 2018), para. 3.1, https://assets.publishing.service.gov.uk/government/uploads/system/uploads/attachment_data/file/903147/guidance_on_changes_to_the_jurisdictional_thresholds_for_UK_MC.pdf.

[1062]   CC & OFT, *supra* note 1058, para. 4.1.2.

[1063]   *Id.*, para. 4.1.3.

[1064]   *Id.*, para. 4.2.1.

[1065]   The analytical tool used by the CMA to answer the question of whether the merger gives rise to an SLC is known as the "counterfactual." By way of this tool, the CMA needs to put forth its projection on what would become of the target in the absence of the proposed transaction.

[1066]   CC & OFT, *supra* note 1058, para. 4.2.3.

[1067]   *Id.*, para. 4.1.3.

5.3 Innovation Theory of Harm in the UK Merger Control Regime

Innovation has long been on the agenda of the UK's previous and current competition authorities. Like other counterparts across the globe, the CMA has been showing signs of a growing focus on digital commerce, technology and innovation.[1068] Indeed, there have been a large number of merger cases since 2004 where the UK's competition authorities have included innovation considerations in their evaluations of proposed mergers. This has also been articulated in the CMA's Annual Plan 2019/20,[1069] whereby the CMA has expressed its continuing willingness to maintain "the pressure on companies to innovate." In line with this motivation, the CMA has sent a letter to Her Majesty's Government, following the Digital Competition Expert Panel held by independent academics, in order to call for a number of substantial reforms in the realm of merger control enforcement in digital markets, particularly with respect to amendments to merger control guidelines and the CMA's enforcement tools, such as interim orders, and appeal standards and procedures.[1070]

In its letter, the CMA emphasized that the traditional assessment methods (focusing on price effects) might not be sufficient to accurately determine other indicators and markers of competition, such as quality and innovation, while acknowledging the challenges for post-merger counterfactuals introduced by new and rapidly evolving digital markets.[1071]

As part of its continual evaluation program, the CMA has recently published a commissioned report[1072] (the "Lear Report"), which concerns past merger decisions in the digital sector. The report evaluates the performance of the competition authorities with regard to five cases (namely, *Facebook/Instagram*, *Google/Waze*, *Priceline/Kayak* and *Expedia/Trivago* (analyzed jointly) and *Amazon/The Book Depository*), and extensively scrutinizes the theory of harm they put forward. According to this report, particularly over the last decade, in merger cases involving two important innovators or where the transaction eliminated a firm with new products in the pipeline, the competition authorities assessed the potential effects of these transactions on the incentives to innovate, especially with regard to the merged entities.[1073]

[1068] *See* Andrea Coscelli, Competition in the Digital Age: Reflecting on Digital Merger Investigations, Speech delivered at the OECD/G7 conference on competition and the digital economy (June 3, 2019), https://www.gov.uk/government/speeches/competition-in-the-digital-age-reflecting-on-digital-merger-investigations.

[1069] CMA, Competition and Markets Authority Annual Plan 2019/20 11 (CMA97) (Feb. 2019), https://assets.publishing.service.gov.uk/government/uploads/system/uploads/attachment_data/file/778629/AnnualPlan-201920-FINAL-TRACKED.pdf.

[1070] *Id.*

[1071] Andrea Coscelli, Interim Chief Executive Officer, CMA, Digital Competition Expert Panel recommendations – CMA view (Mar. 21, 2019), https://assets.publishing.service.gov.uk/government/uploads/system/uploads/attachment_data/file/788480/CMA_letter_to_BEIS_-_DCEP_report_and_recommendations_Redacted.pdf.

[1072] Elena Argentesi, Paolo Buccirossi, Emilio Calvano, Tomaso Duso, Alessia Marrazzo & Salvatore Nava, Ex-Post Assessment of Merger Control Decisions in Digital Markets (Final Report prepared by Lear for the Competition Markets Authority, May 9, 2019), https://assets.publishing.service.gov.uk/government/uploads/system/uploads/attachment_data/file/803576/CMA_past_digital_mergers_GOV.UK_version.pdf (the "Lear Report").

[1073] *Id.*

Upon an examination of the decisions discussed in this chapter with respect to their sector category classifications, we also agree with the above findings of the Lear Report. In addition to the Lear Report's findings, our review of these cases in which the competition authorities evaluated innovation-related issues reveals that in certain sectors, such as electronics and online platforms, innovation considerations tend to be given a more pivotal role in merger control cases, and therefore, are examined more thoroughly. The simplest explanation for this phenomenon would be that competition authorities view traditional markets (such as agricultural or clothing industries) as not entailing as many innovative products or processes to the same extent as the electronics industry or online platforms.[1074] As will be explained in detail below, this viewpoint and approach were intentionally adopted by the competition authorities, as they characterize specific industries as requiring constant innovation.

Contrary to numerous other jurisdictions where there is a severe lack of precedents concerning the innovation theory of harm, the UK is a jurisdiction that has dealt with an abundance of innovation cases. This is mostly due to its "market share" test (i.e., the threshold of "one-quarter in the UK," outlined in section 23(3) EA),[1075] which enables the UK to be one of the jurisdictions that handle a large number of merger control cases. By way of this market share test, the competition authorities can review transactions from an innovation aspect, even if the transaction parties do not generate any turnover in the UK.

Revised Merger Guidelines

In line with the above, the CMA has focused more on innovation and non-price factors affecting competition in the recently revised CMA Merger Assessment Guidelines ("Revised Merger Guidelines").[1076] It was also deemed to be more interventionist due to granting the CMA more discretion and flexibility in terms of its assessment on various factors, such as determining what would constitute a substantial lessening of competition and, in certain cases, moving forward with the competitive assessment without a precise market definition and, as indicated above, transitioning to more quantitative non-price factors rather than price-related parameters.[1077] Accordingly, the Revised Merger Guidelines indicate that "substantial" does not always refer to "large" but may transpire into various other meanings that should be evaluated on a case-by-case basis, e.g., whether the transaction would lead to "the merged entity being able to profitably and unilaterally raise its prices, worsen its quality or service and non-price factors of competition, or reduce innovation efforts at one or more of the pre-merger businesses."[1078] Along these lines, it is seen that the CMA now tends to scrutinize more non-price-related factors, such as

---

[1074] That being said, this would not necessarily mean that these traditional markets will never be modernized or introduce innovative products. In fact, in light of the ongoing climate crisis, one of the most important focal points of these markets is providing environmentally friendly products.

[1075] Enterprise Act 2002, as amended by the Enterprise and Regulatory Reform Act 2013, c. 40, § 30.

[1076] CMA, Merger Assessment Guidelines (CMA129) (Mar. 18, 2021), https://assets.publishing.service.gov. uk/government/uploads/system/uploads/attachment_data/file/1051823/MAGs_for_publication_2021_--_.pdf ("Revised Merger Guidelines")

[1077] Greg Olsen & Daniel Schwarz, *The CMA's Revised Merger Assessment Guidelines – Interesting Times and Creative Energy*, 13 J. Eur. Competition L. & Prac. 35 (2022), https://doi.org/10.1093/jeclap/lpab074.

[1078] Revised Merger Guidelines, para. 2.17.

service, quality and innovation, when assessing whether the transaction under review is likely to give rise to a substantial lessening of competition in the said market.[1079]

Similarly, paragraph 2.18 specifies innovation as a key aspect of competition between the transaction parties, noting that any threat to innovative behavior should be especially taken into account within the competitive process. When assessed together with paragraph 2.4, which provides that non-price aspects can even be the primary focus for some cases,[1080] it is considered that both the CMA, the parties to the transaction and interested third parties will be able to put forth new non-price-related theories and arguments, including innovative factors, and these will play a greater role in any given assessment.

Another aspect of the Revised Merger Guidelines is the focus on potential competition, especially in terms of dynamic markets, where competition is fiercer and the evolvement of the market characteristics is less certain.[1081] The CMA has thus taken into account the Furman Report, where it was recommended that the CMA should put more emphasis on theories of harm relating to innovation and potential competition.[1082] Along these lines, the CMA indicates that it could still find that there is a substantial lessening of competition and evaluate that the transaction will have adverse effects, even though the future development of the market is not yet certain.[1083]

Along with the above, the studies and recent reforms undertaken by the CMA are expected to create a more dynamic agency engaged in the current market phenomena; to increase its knowledge, accountability and effectiveness for protecting consumer interest.[1084]

Before delving further into the precedents below, we note, as a general observation, that in their competition analyses of these cases, the competition authorities mainly scrutinized (i) innovation competition between the relevant transaction parties, (ii) the parties' incentive to innovate, and (iii) the number and innovative capabilities of competitors after the completion of the proposed transactions. For instance, in some cases, the competition authorities took into account the number of innovative bidders, as one of the most innovative bidders left the market in which customized services/products were needed due to the characteristics of the downstream markets. Furthermore, the competition authorities also concentrated on whether the parties were motivated to continue to innovate after the

---

[1079] Alex Hazell & Rebecca Saunders, *Bringing the CMA's Merger Assessment Guidelines Up to Date*, CMA BLOG (Apr. 8, 2021), https://competitionandmarkets.blog.gov.uk/2021/04/08/bringing-the-cmas-merger-assessment-guidelines-up-to-date/; Peter Harper, Kate Newman, Nicola Holmes, Annabel Borg, Claire Morgan & Laura Wright, *UK: Merger Control in the Post-Brexit Landscape* GCR (July 14, 2021), https://globalcompetitionreview.com/review/the-european-middle-east-and-african-antitrust-review/2022/article/uk-merger-control-in-the-post-brexit-landscape; Olsen & Schwarz, *supra* note 1077.

[1080] Revised Merger Guidelines, para. 2.4

[1081] Harper et al., *supra* note 1079.

[1082] DIGITAL COMPETITION EXPERT PANEL, UNLOCKING DIGITAL COMPETITION 12 (Mar. 2019). https://assets.publishing.service.gov.uk/government/uploads/system/uploads/attachment_data/file/785547/unlocking_digital_competition_furman_review_web.pdf. Also known as the "Furman Report," it recommended Action 7, where "The CMA should further prioritise scrutiny of mergers in digital markets and closely consider harm to innovation and impacts on potential competition in its case selection and in its assessment of such cases."

[1083] Olsen & Schwarz, *supra* note 1077.

[1084] William E. Kovacic, *The CMA in the 2020s: A Dynamic Regulator for a Dynamic Environment*, Speech delivered at Policy Exchange, London (Feb. 25, 2020), https://www.gov.uk/government/speeches/the-cma-in-the-2020s-a-dynamic-regulator-for-a-dynamic-environment.

merger transaction; in other words, whether they would face any innovation competition in the relevant market. In several cases, the competition authorities also assessed whether one of the parties was able to impose innovative pressure on the other, which is the primary concern in debates surrounding the issue of killer acquisitions. To summarize, the precedents discussed indicate that the competition authorities seem to mainly rely on the continuation and maintenance of innovation competition in granting clearance to the proposed merger transactions.

In this regard, the below precedents of the competition authorities will be assessed as to how the competition authorities approached (i) innovation competition between the parties and (ii) the ability and incentive to innovate in dynamic markets, as the most credible arguments and significant issues in merger control. Furthermore, due to the dynamic nature of such transactions, innovation mergers concerning online platforms will be analyzed separately under section 4.3, as the UK's "market share test" for merger control has culminated in several remarkable precedents in this particular industry.

5.4 Innovation Considerations by UK Competition Authorities: Case Review

5.4.1 Innovation Competition Between the Merger Parties

Getty Images/Digital Vision and Photonica (2006)

The first decision in which the competition authorities endeavored to figure out whether one of the parties to the transaction posed an innovative constraint on the other party was the *Getty Images/Digital Vision and Photonica* decision,[1085] although the two targets were not significantly innovative competitors. In that case, the activities of Getty Images Inc. ("Getty Images") primarily focused on the consolidation and distribution of stock photographs to commercial users through multiple licenses. Similarly, Digital Vision Ltd. ("Digital Vision") consolidated and distributed stock photographs, some film clips and music to commercial users through royalty-free licenses, whereas the other target, Photonica, consisting of three subsidiaries of Amana Inc. (namely, Amana America Inc., Amana Europe Ltd., and Iconica Ltd. – collectively known as "Photonica"), was a photo-library. In its overall assessment, the OFT raised innovation concerns only within the context of horizontal overlaps between the parties and underlined the role of innovation in the parties' ability to compete. In this context, the OFT cited the ratio of customers who viewed

---

[1085]   OFT, Completed Acquisition by Getty Images Inc of Digital Vision Limited and of Amana America Inc, Amana Europe Limited and Iconica Limited trading as Photonica (Feb. 17, 2006), https://assets.publishing.service.gov.uk/media/555de3ece5274a70840000e4/getty.pdf.

an undertaking as their first choice in the relevant product market and linked this to the undertakings' more innovative operations, such as having an e-commerce-enabled website.[1086] Furthermore, during its competitive assessment, the OFT hinted at the possibility of innovations affecting the pricing decisions of a particular undertaking.[1087] While the OFT acknowledged the existence of some evidence regarding Getty Images' innovative nature, it took the activities of its competitors and consumer demand into consideration and found no connection between the undertaking's pricing decisions and its product development.[1088] In this regard, one may deduce that if the OFT were to uncover any evidence of a strong link between the innovative actions of an undertaking and its pricing decisions, then this might lead the OFT to find a competition law violation. Thus, innovative ability could carry tremendous significance for many aspects of a competitive assessment, not all of which are always related to technology or product development.

In this case, the OFT primarily assessed the competitive abilities and qualities of Getty Images and also emphasized the importance of the number of innovative competitors in the relevant market. In relation to Digital Vision and Photonica's positions in the market, the OFT analyzed whether there was sufficient evidence to indicate that their innovative qualities were capable of imposing competitive restraints on other players in the market. The OFT also stated that neither of the other parties "enhanced their competitive ability by innovation," as the OFT observed that Digital Vision did not sufficiently develop its own sales operation but instead relied on Getty Images for 40–50% of its distribution, and that Photonica never developed its e-commerce capabilities.[1089] Therefore, the OFT concluded that none of the targets were innovators. Consequently, the OFT held that, even if Getty Images were to eliminate one of its competitors posing a substantial constraint through the proposed transaction, the impact of the transaction would be negligible. Furthermore, the OFT stated that such a temporary elimination of a significant competitor would be compensated for by substantial entry or expansion in the relevant market.[1090] Therefore, the OFT found that this was not a case that may be expected to result in an SLC.

BBC Worldwide/Channel Four/ITV (2009)

In BBC Worldwide/Channel Four/ITV,[1091] the CC prohibited the formation of a joint venture by the parties, which would operate in the video-on-demand ("VOD") sector. The CC considered that a loss of rivalry at the wholesale level was likely to affect VOD viewers in two ways: (i) third-party VOD retailers would pass on price increases or adverse commercial terms to consumers due to a possible increase in transaction costs

---

[1086] Id., para. 26.
[1087] Id., para. 39.
[1088] Id.
[1089] Id., para. 40.
[1090] Id., para. 41.
[1091] CC, BBC WORLDWIDE LIMITED, CHANNEL FOUR TELEVISION CORPORATION AND ITV PLC (A report on the anticipated joint venture between BBC Worldwide Limited, Channel Four Television Corporation and ITV plc relating to the video on demand sector) (Feb. 4, 2009), https://webarchive.nationalarchives.gov.uk/ukgwa/20140402192408mp_/http://www.competition-commission.org.uk/assets/competitioncommission/docs/pdf/non-inquiry/rep_pub/reports/2009/fulltext/543.pdf.

related to purchasing the content from the parties, and (ii) the content offered would be of lower quality and reduced levels of innovation.[1092] In relation to the latter, the CC detected that a loss of rivalry at the wholesale level would enable the joint venture to foreclose access to retailers, given that the parties were active at both wholesale and retail levels, although the CC also determined that they were unlikely to engage in such actions.[1093]

Concerning the loss of rivalry at the retailer level, the CC held that the concentration of VOD content in a single entity would result in a decrease in developments and prospective initiatives. In this regard, the merger parties raised the argument that three fourths of VOD content (corresponding to 90% of all viewings) would be offered to consumers for free; nevertheless, the CC focused on the possibility that paid transactions in the UK's VOD service market were expected to gain more importance over time, as iTunes (Apple's on-demand video and music service) was starting to successfully charge consumers for access to its content at that time.[1094] With these considerations in mind, the CC blocked the merger, holding that prohibition was the only viable remedy for addressing the SLC and the adverse competitive effects stemming from the proposed transaction.[1095]

Ericsson/Creative (2014)

Following the 2009 prohibition decision in the *BBC Worldwide/Channel Four/ITV* case, the CC evaluated the market for the supply of outsourced linear playout services for channels broadcasting in the UK (such as the BBC, Channel Four, and ITV) in *Ericsson/ Creative*.[1096] In this assessment, linear playout was defined as a process whereby television content is prepared and compiled into a continuous stream for transmission to the audience, in compliance with the broadcaster's program schedule. Due to Ericsson's previous acquisition of Technicolor, which supplied playout services to ITV and NBC Universal at that time, and Creative's ownership of Red Bee Media ("RBM"), with the customers of the BBC, Channel 4, UKTV, BT Sport, Public Broadcasting Service, Japanese Satellite TV and Box TV, the parties were deemed to be the leading players in the sector. Accordingly, the CC assessed the effects of the proposed acquisition on the customers. Firstly, the CC observed that the main factor for some customers in the choice of their supplier was the fact that they had more complex linear playout requirements compared to others, which created an obvious advantage for the incumbent providers (RBM in this case) to win bids for linear playout services.[1097] Noting that the BBC, ITV and Channel 4 were the highest-profile public service broadcasters ("PSBs"), the CC declared that its main concern was whether the PSBs would not be able to benefit from new ideas and innovation in ways that would enable them to best

---

[1092] *Id.*, para. 4.131.

[1093] *Id.*, paras. 4.133–4.134.

[1094] *Id.*, paras. 4.135–4.139.

[1095] *Id.*, paras. 5.87–5.92.

[1096] CC, Telefonaktiebolaget LM Ericsson and Creative Broadcast Services Holdings (2) Limited, (A report on the anticipated acquisition by Telefonaktiebolaget LM Ericsson of Creative Broadcast Services Holdings (2) Limited) (Mar. 27, 2014), https://assets.publishing.service.gov.uk/media/5342bd11ed-915d630e00002f/Final_report__PDF__601_Kb_.pdf (*"Telefonaktiebolaget LM Ericsson and Creative Broadcast Services Holdings (2) Limited"*).

[1097] *Id.*, paras. 8.52–8.65.

meet their requirements as a result of the proposed transaction's elimination of one of the innovative competitors in the market.

Adopting a more optimistic outlook in comparison to the *BBC Worldwide/Channel Four/ ITV* decision above, the CC ultimately found that an increased number of bidders in the PSBs' bidding processes could stimulate new ideas of value for the customers. More specifically, the CC considered that, due to their complex requirements, the transaction would eliminate one of the two most innovative providers to the PSBs, but nevertheless decided to grant a Phase I clearance to the transaction.[1098] In its analysis, the CC concluded that the multistage nature of bids could mitigate the negative outcomes of the transaction to a certain extent by motivating other competitors to take part in the PSBs' bids, enabling providers to bid as forcefully as the lost bidder and to generate ideas during the progress in order to be awarded the bid.[1099] However, Martin Cave, deputy chair of the CC and deputy panel chair of the CMA, expressed his concerns in his dissenting opinion about the loss of innovation competition in BBC bids accounting for 15–25% of industry revenues in the market, due to the fact that one of a few qualifying competitors to the BBC, offering the largest contract concerning playout services, had left the market.[1100]

MasterCard/VocaLink (2017)

Following the CC's evaluation of the number of bidders in the *Ericsson/Creative* case in 2014, the CMA also assessed competitive concerns stemming from the fact that a merger was contemplated between two companies, out of what was already a small number of bidders, in its *MasterCard/VocaLink* decision.[1101] In this case, MasterCard, a provider of financial services with a focus on branded four-party payment credit and debit card schemes, acquired sole control over VocaLink, a provider of central infrastructural services ("CIS") to three UK interbank payment systems (namely, Bacs interbank payment system, Faster Payments Service ("FPS") and the LINK ATM network ("LINK")). As both MasterCard and VocaLink offered ATM switching infrastructure through their proprietary networks, the CMA first observed that VocaLink, Visa and MasterCard were the strongest bidders at LINK's tenders for CIS.[1102] Since the LINK scheme was also a competitor against

---

[1098]   *See* CMA, A Quick Guide to UK Merger Assessment (CMA18) (Mar. 18, 2021)https://assets.publishing.service. gov.uk/government/uploads/system/uploads/attachment_data/file/288677/CMA18_A_quick_guide_to_UK_ merger_assessment.pdf, paras. 2.7–2.8: "Phase one is the initial assessment stage where the CMA determines whether it believes that the merger results in a realistic prospect of a substantial lessening of competition (SLC). If so, the CMA has a duty to launch an in-depth assessment (Phase two), although merging parties may offer to modify aspects of the transaction to 'remedy' any competition concerns identified (known as Undertakings In Lieu (UILs)), thereby obtaining a resolution at Phase one, conditional on acceptance of the remedies. At Phase two, generally limited to twenty-four weeks, a CMA panel of independent members conducts an in-depth investigation to assess if a merger is expected to result in an SLC. If an SLC is expected, the CMA decides upon the remedies required. Such remedies may include prohibiting the merger or requiring the divestiture (sale) of parts of the business."

[1099]   *Telefonaktiebolaget LM Ericsson and Creative Broadcast Services Holdings (2) Limited*, paras. 9.48–9.51.

[1100]   *Id.* at 9–10.

[1101]   CMA, Anticipated Acquisition by Mastercard UK Holdco Limited of VocaLink Holdings Limited (ME/6638/16, Jan. 30, 2017), https://assets.publishing.service.gov.uk/media/588f2c1fed915d4535000041/mastercard-vocalink-ftd.pdf.

[1102]   *Id.* at, para. 10.

MasterCard in the ATM transaction services market, and since VocaLink acted as the provider of ATM switching services to LINK for its ATM transaction services, the CMA evaluated MasterCard's ability and incentive to reduce or prevent innovation through its prospective ownership of the messaging standard known as "LIS5," which was owned by VocaLink at that time and used in the central infrastructure for the LINK scheme.[1103] The CMA found that MasterCard would be able to foreclose LINK from innovative activities through its intellectual property rights on its competitor's messaging standard (LIS5) used in the provision of ATM switching services, amounting to partial input foreclosure, and that LINK's endeavors to innovate may be leaked to MasterCard, since any innovation for LINK users required its submission to VocaLink in advance, and determined that this would probably diminish any competitive advantage of LINK over MasterCard.[1104] On the other hand, the CMA also found that there was no incentive for this strategy, given that the merged entity would still be evaluated and rise or fall on the basis of its innovations, and poor performance on that front would affect both VocaLink and MasterCard, as LINK's members were also MasterCard's customers.[1105]

As VocaLink's "PayPort" product was used in FPS services, the CMA proceeded to evaluate MasterCard's post-transaction measures to prevent or hinder innovation in new FPS services in order to favor its principal products and services. Observing that other providers were available to pose a competitive constraint on MasterCard in the provision of access to FPS services and finding that its contracts substantially limited VocaLink's pre-transaction ability to change the central infrastructure and that any change implemented in the central infrastructure was open to all FPS users without any discrimination, the CMA expressed its view that the merged entity would not have the ability to prevent or impede innovation at the central infrastructure level.[1106]

Aside from these innovation considerations, the CMA accepted undertakings (i.e., commitments) in lieu of reference to the transfer of intellectual property rights relating to Link LIS5 messaging standards to Link Scheme Limited, granting a new supplier of CIS to LINK with access to VocaLink's communication infrastructure, and payment of a confidential amount to LINK members to compensate them for their switching costs.[1107] The CMA finally held that these undertakings were sufficiently comprehensive to mitigate or prevent any SLC arising from the transaction.

Aviagen Group/Hubbard Holding (2018)

In *Aviagen Group/Hubbard Holding*,[1108] the CMA scrutinized the innovation competition between the parties to the transaction, whereby Hubbard Holding SAS, one of the leading chicken parent stock suppliers in the UK, was acquired by Aviagen Group Holding Inc.,

---

[1103] *Id.*, paras. 267–74.
[1104] *Id.*
[1105] *Id.*, paras. 275–79.
[1106] *Id.*, paras. 328–38.
[1107] *Id.*
[1108] CMA, Anticipated Acquisition by Aviagen Group Holding Inc. of Hubbard Holding SAS, Decision on relevant merger situation and substantial lessening of competition (ME/6727-17, Feb. 28, 2018), https://assets.publishing. service.gov.uk/media/5a9592ec40f0b67aa5087b04/aviagen-hubbard-decision.pdf.

which was involved in the same business. The CMA found that the parties' activities overlapped in the supply of chicken parent stock. In its assessment of the relevant product-market definition, the CMA determined that the demand-side substitutability between conventional chicken parent stock and slow-growing chicken parent stock was limited. Therefore, the CMA separated the frames of reference for the product and defined the relevant product markets as (i) "the supply of conventional chicken parent stock" and (ii) "the supply of slow-growing chicken parent stock."[1109]

Evaluating the horizontal unilateral effects in the supply of conventional chicken parent stock, the CMA considered that innovation was an essential element of competition in that market, particularly in terms of the impact of chicken parent stock innovations on the cost of meat production, and determined that such innovation affected the cost of meat manufacturing for suppliers. Accordingly, the CMA determined that customers tended to switch meat sources if the quality of the products changed, and concluded that this state of affairs led to strong competition between the suppliers of conventional chicken parent stock in the UK. Although the CMA observed that Hubbard was able to improve its conventional chicken parent stock product, it conducted further assessments as to whether the level of this activity could exert a constraint on Aviagen through investments in R&D.[1110] In this case, Aviagen submitted that it would be in a position to develop certain technologies through Hubbard, such as CT scanners and genomics, in the post-merger world. Hubbard also contended that the merged entity would be likely to become more innovative in the relevant market.[1111] Some customers also noted that Hubbard needed to increase the competitiveness of its offerings.[1112] In the final part of its assessment of the unilateral effects of the transaction, the CMA appraised Hubbard's innovative constraints on Aviagen and held that Hubbard and its R&D activities would not be able to pose a competitive constraint on Aviagen's innovations in the relevant market in the absence of the acquisition.[1113] The CMA then concluded that the transaction was unlikely to result in an SLC and, accordingly, granted clearance to the proposed transaction.[1114]

5.4.2 Dynamic Markets and the Ability and Incentive to Innovate

Bayard Capital/Landis & GYR (2004)

One of the primary sectors in which the competition authorities have relied upon innovation-related factors was the electronics sector. The competition authorities' precedents, ranging from early 2004 to date, have demonstrated that they have placed considerable importance in their assessments on the weight that innovation carries in

---

[1109]   *Id.*, para. 3.
[1110]   *Id.*, paras. 51–54.
[1111]   *Id.*, paras. 55–56.
[1112]   *Id.*, para. 58.
[1113]   *Id.*, paras. 60–61.
[1114]   *Id.*, para. 86.

this particular sector. Although innovation has been limited to sector-based observations, the competition authorities first assessed the dynamic nature of the electronics sector and innovation in the *Bayard Capital/Landis & GYR* decision.[1115] In that case, the OFT reviewed the acquisition of Landis & Gyr ("Landis") by Bayard Capital Partners Pty Ltd ("Bayard"), where Bayard was the parent company of "Ampy," which was the largest Australian manufacturer of electricity meters. Ampy's activities covered both the sub-assembly and the final assembly of residential electricity meters, including electronic pre-payment meters.[1116] On the other hand, Landis manufactured electromechanical, elec-tronic-credit and pre-payment electricity meters and gas meters, including pre-payment meters, energy data acquisition, processing software, and systems ripple control receiv-ers.[1117] The OFT stated that the activities of the transaction parties overlapped in the market for the manufacture of electricity and gas meters[1118] and, accordingly, defined the relevant product market as "electricity meters." This decision is particularly note-worthy because, when listing the factors that affect the analysis of market shares in the relevant product market, the OFT remarked that "innovation is an important dimension of competition in this sector [electronics]."[1119] Furthermore, under the section entitled "Entry using new technologies," the OFT discussed the role of new innovative technol-ogies in market dynamics. In this context, the OFT first emphasized that "Central to any consideration of the competitive effects of this merger is the role of innovation in the electricity prepayment meter sector."[1120] The OFT also underlined the role of innovation by pointing out that new and innovative technologies facilitated securing larger market shares, and that innovation also had the potential to transform a sector. A crucial point here was that the OFT did not recognize or acknowledge any advantages of the market incumbents in terms of access to or development of technology. Thus, the OFT seemed to consider that, where technology and innovation were strong and formidable factors in a certain relevant product market, all of the players in the market, be they new entrants or long-term players, operate on a level playing field. The OFT then concluded that "past evidence of entry, in particular by a superior new technology offering additional customer benefits, indicates that competition can and has occurred and that entry and the threat thereof will act as a constraint on the merged entity."[1121] While common access to technology and innovation levels the playing field for market players, it may also act as an additional restriction on the parties' activities.

Another aspect of this case in which the OFT assessed the effects of innovation concerned the possible coordinated interaction between the parties. The OFT determined that any coordinated effect would be unlikely to occur when the undertakings in question were

---

[1115] OFT, Completed Acquisition by Bayard Capital Partners Pty Ltd of Landis & GYR (Nov. 15, 2004), https://assets.publishing.service.gov.uk/media/555de461ed915d7ae500011c/bayard.pdf ("*Bayard/Landis*").

[1116] *Id.*, para. 1.

[1117] *Id.*

[1118] *Id.*, para. 6.

[1119] OFT further endorsed this approach in its other decisions as well. *See also* OFT, Completed Acquisition by Francisco Partners L.P. of G International Inc. (Mar. 22, 2005), https://assets.publishing.service.gov.uk/media/555de425e5274a74ca0000f5/francisco.pdf. In this case, the OFT underlined again that the electronics sector was characterized by innovation and technological development.

[1120] *Bayard/Landis*, para. 60.

[1121] *Id.*, para. 65.

found to be at different stages of innovation.[1122] Arguably, the OFT had considered all players to operate on a level playing field before; their levels of innovation were now deemed to constitute a differentiating effect. Having established that the market for electricity meter supply was a dynamic one, and concluded that the emergence of new meter technologies shaped the relevant market, the OFT cleared the transaction after its Phase I assessment.

Similar to this decision on *Bayard Capital/Landis & GYR*, in Adobe's acquisition of Macromedia,[1123] the OFT stated that, for existing players who planned for a change in their market positions or devised product improvements, specific entry barriers (such as R&D costs) might be less relevant. According to the Phase I assessment, the case was cleared.

Research Machines/Sentinel (2004)

In its *Research Machines Plc/Sentinel Products Ltd* decision,[1124] the OFT reviewed the acquisition of Sentinel Products Ltd ("Sentinel") by Research Machines Plc ("RM"), once again in the electronics sector, since the competition authorities categorized software products under the same classification. In this case, RM was a supplier of information and communication technology software, systems and services, providing a wide variety of educational establishments with educational services, and Sentinel also operated as a supplier of computer software. The OFT defined the relevant product market as the network management software ("NMS"), encompassing the supply of education-sector NMS for each category of primary, secondary and tertiary education institutions in the UK.[1125]

While assessing the share of supply, the OFT found that RM would represent nearly half of the total UK supply of the relevant product in both the primary and secondary sectors in question in the post-merger market and close to a quarter of the supply in the tertiary sector. In this context, the evidence on file and the OFT's own findings indicated that "a large proportion of both primary and secondary schools... rely upon OS network tools, providing an incentive to continue to price and innovate at a level that would persuade such customers that dedicated NMS is a value-added proposition." This assessment revealed the two aspects in which the OFT considered and evaluated innovation: (i) the parties' ability to innovate and (ii) the effect of innovation on consumer preferences. Such a two-dimensional approach demonstrated that, even in the early stages of technological development and the evolution of innovation concerns in competition law, the OFT deemed innovation to constitute an essential point of consideration in its merger control regime. Furthermore, it is worth noting that the OFT handled innovation considerations in terms of both horizontal and vertical concerns in this case. In terms of horizontal concerns, the OFT's focus fell upon the assessment of shares of supply, and the OFT examined the distribution of supply shares in terms of prices, functionality,

---

[1122] *Id.*, para. 90.

[1123] OFT, Anticipated Acquisition by Adobe Systems, incorporated of Macromedia, Inc. (Nov. 16, 2005), https://assets.publishing.service.gov.uk/media/555de437e5274a708400110/adobe.pdf.

[1124] OFT, Completed Acquisition by Research Machines plc of Sentinel Products Ltd. (July 23, 2004), https://assets.publishing.service.gov.uk/media/555de442ed915d7ae200011d/researchmachines.pdf ("*Research Machines/Sentinel*").

[1125] *Id.* at 3.

and consumer approach.[1126] Upon concluding that alternative NMS appeared in the market and that RM was likely to be unable to foreclose competition, given that NMS products could emerge very quickly in such a dynamic market, the OFT cleared the transaction according to its Phase I review.[1127]

Thermo Electron/GV (2006)

Building on its previous analyses, in the *Thermo Electron/GV* case, the OFT used innovation considerations as a central element in its competitive assessment.[1128] In this case, Thermo Electron Manufacturing Limited ("Thermo") was active in the markets for various analytical instruments, scientific equipment, services, software solutions and consumables at the global level, while GV Instruments Ltd ("GVI") carried out activities related to the worldwide supply of mass spectrometers. As the parties' activities horizontally overlapped in the market for the supply of mass spectrometers ("MS"), the OFT defined this as the relevant product market, acknowledging that the market in question was global.

For innovation, the OFT first considered it during its assessment of the horizontal overlaps in the case at hand. In this context, the OFT underlined the importance of future product innovation and emphasized that this was one of the areas in which the transaction subject to the assessment could have possible adverse effects. This is evinced in the OFT's decision in this case, where it stated its belief that the relevant transaction could result in the diminishment of the rate of innovation, given that the transaction would create a (near) monopoly in the product segments of both gas isotope ratio mass spectrometers ("IRMS") and thermal ionization mass spectrometers ("TIMS"), a duopoly in the market for multi-collector-inductively coupled plasma-MS ("MC-ICP-MS").[1129] Therefore, the OFT decided to refer the case to the CC.

Contrary to the OFT, the CC defined four separate narrower markets, namely (i) Gas IRMS, (ii) TIMS, (iii) MC-ICP-MS, and (iv) Noble Gas MS. Moreover, the CC determined that product development was a significant driver of competition in the IRMS product segment, due to specific recent innovations, while also acknowledging that this was a mature product market.[1130] Furthermore, the CC established that a new entrant into the markets for gas IRMS, TIMS and MC-ICP-MS would need access to know-how, expertise and investments in R&D, which constituted significant barriers to entry from the CC's perspective.[1131] The CC held that Thermo would have acquired a significantly higher market share in the Gas IRMS market, and a monopoly position in the TIMS market, following the consummation of the transaction.[1132] Therefore, the CC held that the transaction would be likely to result in an SLC, and ordered Thermo to sell either

---

[1126]   *Id.* at 4.

[1127]   Although this section is focused on horizontal concerns, it may be of benefit to mention here that the OFT's evaluation of the vertical and conglomerate issues did not find sufficient evidence to support a foreclosure theory with regard to the said merger. *See Research Machines/Sentinel* at 5.

[1128]   OFT, Completed Acquisition by Thermo Electron Manufacturing Limited of GV Instruments Limited (Dec. 15, 2006), https://assets.publishing.service.gov.uk/media/555de3fbe5274a74ca0000dd/Thermo.pdf.

[1129]   *Id.*, para. 38.

[1130]   *Id.*, para. 4.7.

[1131]   *Id.*, paras. 5.41–5.45.

[1132]   *Id.* at 15–16.

the whole GVI business or those assets relating to the supply of Gas IRMS and TIMS instruments, as the remedies for the expected SLC.

One can assume from this case that the competition authorities consider it very unlikely for monopolies and duopolies to have any incentives to innovate.

Cirrus Logic/Wolfson (2014)

In another decision concerning the electronics sector, the CMA examined a transaction between Cirrus Logic Inc. ("Cirrus"), a developer and supplier of semiconductors, and Wolfson Microelectronics plc ("Microelectronics"), a designer and supplier of semiconductors worldwide. The CMA left the exact market definition open and stated that it would focus its assessment on the level of competition between the parties and their incentives to innovate.[1133] In this context, the *Cirrus Logic/Wolfson* decision emphasized that innovation in product development was a "key feature of the competitive dynamics in the marketplace."[1134] The CMA underlined that the players in the market were driven by the need to innovate in order to be able to conclude contracts for "the next generation of consumer electronic devices."[1135] In this context, the CMA articulated that, since innovation was an important driving factor for parties in their rivalry for securing contracts, it would also examine the merger's possible effects on innovation in the relevant market.[1136] Thus, following these assessments on innovation in terms of product development, the CMA then underlined innovation as one of the primary parameters of competition concerning the transaction, as the parties' activities were related to a rapidly growing market, i.e., a dynamic market. In this context, while making its assessments regarding the shares of supply in the market, the CMA found that, even though the static share of supply data in these types of innovative markets was limited, (i) there were still multiple competitors operating even in markets defined by the narrowest approach to the product definition, and (ii) those competitors, despite having significantly lower supply shares, displayed sufficient expertise in the development and supply of high-end products.[1137] Further, the CMA also conducted its own market research and found that some customers of the parties (with whom they worked closely) were supporting the development of competing products, three to four years into the future.[1138] Accordingly, the CMA granted a Phase I clearance to the transaction.

Akzo Nobel/Metlac (2015)

In the OFT's *Akzo Nobel/Metlac* decision,[1139] which concerned the engineering sector, Akzo Nobel N.V. ("Akzo Nobel"), a global manufacturer and supplier of performance coatings, decorative paints, and specialty chemicals, acquired Metlac Holding S.r.l

---

[1133] CMA, Anticipated Acquisition by Cirrus Logic Inc of Wolfson Microelectronics Plc (ME/6461/14, Nov. 7, 2014), https://assets.publishing.service.gov.uk/media/545ce6f440f0b6130e00001c/Cirrus-Wolfson_decision.pdf, para. 29.

[1134] *Id.*, para. 6.

[1135] *Id.*

[1136] *Id.*, para. 29.

[1137] *Id.*, para. 44.

[1138] *Id.*, para. 48.

[1139] OFT, Anticipated Acquisition by Akzo Nobel NV of Metlac Holding S.R.L (ME/5319/12, May 23, 2012), https://assets.publishing.service.gov.uk/media/555de2f1e5274a74ca00004f/AkzoNobelMetlac.pdf.

("Metlac"), which was active in the manufacture and supply of metal packaging coatings through its subsidiaries. Akzo Nobel's and Metlac's scope of business overlapped in the manufacture and supply of metal packaging coatings, and while the OFT considered defining the relevant product market as "metal packaging coatings worldwide," it nevertheless decided to leave the precise market definition open.[1140] In its assessment, the OFT evaluated Metlac's innovative characteristics, and since the company was considered the most or the second most innovative player in the market from the perspective of third parties, the OFT concluded that Metlac was a strong competitor.[1141] Here, the OFT touched upon several points, including the assessment of Metlac's (i) technological edge in innovative products[1142] and (ii) its innovative capability, interpreted in relation with its research and development capabilities.[1143] In line with its previous assessments, the OFT again evaluated innovation considerations in terms of product characteristics, yet in light of the parties' incentives and ability to innovate. In addition to its previous approaches, the OFT also conducted a slightly more detailed assessment of innovation in terms of new entries into the relevant market. Namely, the OFT declared in this case that a new undertaking was able to enter the market through its ability to utilize innovative technologies.[1144] In light of the high switching costs in the relevant market (due to competition in bids and contracts), the OFT referred the case to the CC upon its Phase I examination.

During the Phase II assessment, the CC's review included an even more detailed examination of innovation considerations.[1145] The CC first acknowledged that innovation was a part of product development,[1146] and noted that one of the likely reasons for loss of competition between competitors was a non-price element, such as innovation.[1147] In this context, some of the consumers that the CC interviewed expressed concern over the adverse effects on innovation that could be caused by the said merger.[1148] The CC, further into its assessment, remarked that since the parties to the transaction were extremely close competitors, a reduction in competition for innovation between the two would result in a similar lessening of innovation.[1149] The CC provided a detailed assessment in Appendix G of its Final Report,[1150] wherein it considered (i) the innovative abilities of Metlac and (ii) the innovation in the relevant market within the context of the significant changes expected in the industry. One can understand, from the CC's references, that the primary reason for its intense focus on the issue was the statements gathered from third parties that expressed the fundamental role of innovation in terms of the relevant products and the parties in question.[1151]

[1140]   *Id.*, paras. 38, 43.
[1141]   *Id.*, paras. 74, 75.
[1142]   *Id.*, paras. 68–75.
[1143]   *Id.*, para. 73.
[1144]   *Id.*, para. 119.
[1145]   *Id.*
[1146]   *Id.* at 29.
[1147]   *Id.*
[1148]   *Id.* at 55.
[1149]   *Id.* at 53.
[1150]   *Id.* Appendix G.
[1151]   *Id.* at 4–9.

In this context, the CC additionally reviewed the statements received from the parties and their internal documents. In its quest to determine the significance of Metlac's level of innovativeness to the competitive dynamics of the market for the supply of metal packaging coatings, the CC found that the quality of the production process was not a decisive factor.[1152] The CC declared that it did not aim to conduct a comparison of the relative innovation levels of Metlac and Akzo Nobel, as the consumers expressed the view that both parties provided high-quality products and that neither was inferior to the other, which could have led the CC to conclude that Metlac would be able to continue its innovative practices in the aftermath of the transaction.[1153] Nonetheless, the CC held that the transaction would result in an SLC within the market for the supply of metal packaging coatings by end use with respect to (i) beer and beverage coatings, (ii) food coatings, (iii) caps and closures coatings, and (iv) general line coatings in the UK, and therefore prohibited the merger, given that Metlac's competitive constraint on Akzo Nobel would be destroyed as a result of the transaction.

BT Group/EE Limited (2016)

The CMA conducted a comprehensive evaluation regarding the ability and incentive of transaction parties to prevent innovation competition in its *BT Group/EE Limited* decision.[1154] This transaction was related to the full acquisition of EE Limited, a joint venture between Orange and Deutsche Telekom, which was one of four mobile network operators ("MNOs") in the UK, by BT Group, which provided telecommunications products and services to retail customers along with local loop or local access network services through its business division named "Openreach." The CMA found that the parties' activities overlapped in the provision of mobile and fixed communications services to retail customers. Defining the relevant product markets in this case as (i) "retail mobile," (ii) "wholesale mobile," (iii) "mobile backhaul," (iv) "wholesale broadband," and (v) "retail broadband,"[1155] the CMA inter alia considered the effects on innovation by examining the question of whether Openreach could foreclose downstream MNOs by frustrating or impeding innovation in the mobile backhaul market.[1156]

The CMA set forth the framework for this competition analysis as discrimination against rival MNOs in relation to the following: (i) the development of small cells, (i) the development of Cloud-RAN, (iii) the development, more generally, of new Openreach products, and (iv) other strategic decisions (i.e., the possibility that BT Group could prioritize the design of its fiber footprint to support its own mobile demand, at the expense of rival communication providers).[1157] With the development of small cells, the CMA acknowledged the presence of alternative suppliers of backhaul solutions for small cells and determined that Openreach was unlikely to impede rival MNOs'

[1152]   *Id.* at 18.

[1153]   *Id.* at 20.

[1154]   CMA, BT GROUP PLC AND EE LIMITED: A REPORT ON THE ANTICIPATED ACQUISITION BY BT GROUP PLC OF EE LIMITED (Jan. 15, 2016), https://assets.publishing.service.gov.uk/media/56992242ed915d4747000026/BT_EE_final_report.pdf.

[1155]   *Id.*, paras. 8.1–8.3.

[1156]   *Id.*, paras. 16.59–16.98.

[1157]   *Id.*, para. 16.64.

deployment of small cells by failing to provide suitable backhaul products.[1158] With respect to the development of Cloud-RAN, the CMA held (i) that Cloud-RAN was just one of the possible evolutions of current architectures, (ii) that the technology upgrades from LTE to LTE-Advanced could also deliver efficiency benefits and capacity uplift, rather than Cloud-RAN, and (iii) that Cloud-RAN was used only in urban areas where alternative providers of backhaul were usually available.[1159] Regarding the development, more generally, of new Openreach products, the CMA found that BT Group would face Ofcom's enforcement actions against discriminatory behavior, as per the Statement of Requirements, which had been undertaken by BT Group before Ofcom, concerning the operation of a new product development process monitored by BT's Equality of Access Board under the regulatory framework introduced by Ofcom.[1160] Concerning other strategic decisions, the CMA determined (i) that there were often competing providers of backhaul alternatives to BT Group in urban areas where 80% of the small cells, which MNOs require connecting to fiber in new radio sites, would be deployed.[1161] Therefore, in light of its in-depth analysis of innovation concerns, the CMA concluded that none of these concerns were sufficient to block the acquisition, and therefore granted a Phase II clearance to the transaction.

In summary, the Ofcom undertakings mentioned above contemplated BT Group's obligation to operate its Openreach division under a separate organization and to provide its new products (and any changes to such products) to all communication providers on fair and equal terms.[1162] These undertakings may very well be the reason why the CMA did not require further undertakings from BT Group, and found sufficient reason to believe that regulation would act as a deterrence to foreclosing competition.

Tobii AB/Smartbox & Sensory (2019)

A critical indicator of the increasing role of innovation considerations in the CMA's competitive assessments arises within the context of the *Tobii AB/Smartbox* case.[1163] In its Issues Statement, the CMA had made the following request in terms of its future assessment: "In particular, we would welcome any new evidence on the drivers of innovation and product development in the industry, and on any competitive constraint that has not been captured at phase 1,"[1164] indicating that innovation would play a further and predominant role in the CMA's final decision on the merger transaction. The expectation was that there would be a focus on the importance of the number of competitors in the market and its effect on product innovation, as the CMA, under its horizontal assessment,

---

[1158]   *Id.*, paras. 16.65–16.81.
[1159]   *Id.*, paras. 16.82–16.85.
[1160]   *Id.*, paras. 16.86–16.93.
[1161]   *Id.*, paras. 16.94–16.98.
[1162]   *Id.*, paras. 4.16–4.45.
[1163]   CMA, Completed Acquisition by Tobii AB of Smartbox Assistive Technologies Limited and Sensory Software International Ltd (Final Report) (Aug. 15, 2019), https://assets.publishing.service.gov.uk/media/5d5d1800e5274a0766482c45/Final_Report2.pdf?_ga=2.117248645.2038125553.1566932195-9236010 75.1560421042 (*"Tobii AB/Smartbox & Sensory* (Final Report)").
[1164]   CMA, Completed Acquisition by Tobii AB of Smartbox Assistive Technology and Sensory Software International Ltd (Issues Statement) (Feb. 26, 2019), para. 26, https://assets.publishing.service.gov.uk/media/5c752294ed915d-3551b9aff9/Tobii_Smartbox_Issues_Statement.pdf.

explicitly stated that the "concern is that the removal of one party as a competitor could allow the Parties to... reduce innovation."[1165]

Following in-depth investigation and assessments, the CMA blocked Tobii AB's acquisition of Smartbox on the grounds that the transaction would lead to higher prices and/or lower quality for relevant communication solutions offered by the parties, as well as upstream and downstream foreclosure of competitors, ordering a full divestiture remedy concerning the sale of Smartbox to a suitable purchaser to be approved by the CMA.

Tobii and Smartbox both supply augmentative and assistive communication ("AAC") solutions globally, which are defined as "communication aids that cater the needs of those who may find communication difficult for a number of reasons... such as cerebral palsy, learning disability or autism."[1166] The CMA found that the parties' activities overlap in the supply of dedicated AAC solutions, which comprise the following four components: (i) dedicated AAC hardware, (ii) AAC software, (iii) access means (in case users cannot control the device solely through the touch screen, an AAC solution includes a means of access, such as a switch or an eye gaze camera) and (iv) customer support such as technical support and training.[1167] Dedicated AAC solutions are generally procured by organizations funding purchases of these devices on behalf of end users, such as national health service authorities, local authorities, and charities. Moreover, the parties also offer individual components of dedicated AAC solutions listed above in the market. In this regard, Tobii sells eye gaze cameras and Smartbox licenses its AAC software, namely Grid, to its components.[1168]

Based on this, the CMA defined the relevant markets as follows: (i) supply of dedicated AAC solutions in the UK; (ii) upstream supply of AAC software worldwide; (iii) upstream supply of eye gaze cameras in AAC applications worldwide.[1169] As the parties offer certain components of dedicated AAC solutions in the market, the CMA also assessed the vertical effects of the transaction along with analyzing horizontal unilateral effects. As to the innovation considerations, the CMA presented its detailed assessments when evaluating the potential vertical effects of the transaction, particularly because of Smartbox's Grid software, which is considered to have a strong position in the AAC software space.[1170] In this regard, the CMA based its vertical theories of harm on three pillars – namely, (i) input foreclosure of Smartbox's Grid software; (ii) customer foreclosure of eye gaze camera competitors; (iii) input foreclosure of Tobii's eye gaze cameras – and for each of them, assessed the ability and incentive of the merged entity to foreclose competitors based on the information submitted by the parties as well as third parties.[1171]

In this regard, in assessing the likelihood of customer foreclosure of Tobii's eye gaze camera competitors, the CMA stated that eye gaze camera suppliers depend on

1165	*Id.*, para. 24.
1166	*Tobii AB/Smartbox & Sensory* (Final Report), para. 2.
1167	*Id.*, para. 2.10.
1168	*Id.*, para. 5.
1169	*Id.*, para. 6.
1170	*Id.*, paras. 6.15, 7.1.
1171	*Id.*, para. 7.2.

compatibility with AAC software, especially Grid, in order to compete in the supply of eye gaze cameras in AAC applications, implying that Grid is an important input for dedicated AAC solutions suppliers.[1172] It also emphasized that there are limited alternatives to Grid. Accordingly, the CMA finds it likely that providers of dedicated AAC solutions may switch to Tobii's eye gaze cameras if Grid's compatibility with other cameras is limited. On that front, the CMA concluded that the effects of weakening Tobii's rivals in the eye gaze camera space are likely to include reduced innovation and higher prices compared to the pre-merger situation. Based on the information obtained from Irisbond, the CMA held that Smartbox's software is considered a catalyzer for eye gaze camera suppliers in allowing product improvement, fair competition and also innovation and that the transaction would result in the loss of a "key partner for innovation and for the development of a wider variety of innovative and affordable AAC solutions."[1173] To that end, the CMA highlighted that partnering with Smartbox is critical for suppliers in enabling innovative solutions in the supply of eye gaze cameras for AAC applications. It also added that the significant investment required for being compatible with alternative AAC software would hamper eye gaze camera suppliers' ability to allocate their sources to other innovation studies for AAC applications. Even though Tobii submitted that innovation in eye gaze cameras is driven by the demand of "mass market" consumer electronics and automotive sectors, the CMA did not find Tobii's argument convincing and stated that companies that are not specialized in AAC applications would ignore the needs of the customer base for AAC solutions, which would hamper innovative efforts for dedicated AAC products and harm customers.[1174] In fact, fundamental difficulties for eye-tracking are ensuring that it operates efficiently in each position of the head and adjusts to the various movements of the eyes.[1175] Since this difficulty concerning the position of the head does not relate to the AAC applications developed for mass use, the developers would not focus on it and innovate dedicated AAC products.[1176]

Regarding the horizontal effects of the transaction, the CMA concluded that both Tobii and Smartbox "*benchmark*" each other and are the main competitors when their products' prices and product range are concerned.[1177] Therefore, the merger would impede "the incentives of the merged entity to engage in R&D and innovate."[1178] On the other hand, Tobii stated innovation incentives are decided at a global level rather than being limited to the UK, where the merged entity has high market shares. Both Smartbox and Tobii engage in global sales and develop their products for customers worldwide.[1179] Moreover, each horizontal merger does not necessarily hinder innovation.[1180] According

---

[1172]   *Id.*, para. 7.133.

[1173]   *Id.*, para. 7.136.

[1174]   *Id.*

[1175]   *Id.*, para. 7.135.

[1176]   *Id.*

[1177]   *Id.*, para. 6.61.

[1178]   *Id.*, para. 6.62.

[1179]   Tobii's Response to Provisional Findings, para. 5(a), https://assets.publishing.service.gov.uk/media/5d10f-5dee5274a065e721726/Tobii_response_.pdf.

[1180]   Vincenzo Denicolò & Michele Polo, *Duplicative Research, Mergers and Innovation*, 166 ECON. LETTERS 56, 59 (2018).

to Tobii, the merger would contribute to customer well-being since, as a result of the merger, it observed "falling prices, low profits, and lots of innovation."[1181]

Tobii also argued that the merged entity would be incentivized to innovate due to the competitive pressure in the mainstream technology companies, as well as the relevant regulations in the EU requiring firms to factor in accessibility considerations. However, the CMA did not find these factors sufficient to eliminate innovation concerns, due to their hypothetical nature.

In terms of efficiencies, Tobii asserted that the merger would combine the research and development capabilities of the merged parties, improve R&D, eliminate duplicative R&D, improve integration between hardware and software, and decrease R&D costs.[1182] It also stated that the fundamental efficiencies of the merger would be observed over time when the merged entity focuses on complementary R&D capabilities of Tobii's hardware, eye-tracking and Smartbox's software.[1183] However, the CMA held that Tobii failed to provide concrete details or evidence supporting its arguments.

As to remedies, the CMA found that a partial divestiture, where Tobii would be able to retain Smartbox's software business, would not address the competitive concerns. Accordingly, the CMA decided that the only remedy to adequately address the competition concerns would be full divestiture.[1184]

After the CMA's decision, Tobii brought the decision before the Competition Appeal Tribunal ("CAT"). The CAT's judgment evaluated both the merits and the procedure of the decision.[1185] The CMA's decision was mostly upheld; however, the CAT quashed part of the CMA decision relating to input foreclosure concerns regarding Smartbox's Grid software, on procedural grounds.[1186] Therefore, the CAT's review showed a high degree of deference to the CMA's factual and economic assessment, including its innovation-related considerations.

Do the UK competition authorities' assessments under *Tobii AB/Smartbox* reflect the EU Commission's novel approach? It seems to be the case. The Commission had introduced its novel theory of harm associated with innovation in the *Dow/DuPont* case.[1187] As discussed in the above chapters in much more detail, in *Dow/DuPont*, the merger was considered to have a considerable influence on innovative competition since it would stifle competition

---

[1181] *Tobii AB/Smartbox & Sensory* (Final Report), para. 6.12.

[1182] *Id.*, para. 8.91. In fact, according to Lofaro et al., a merger may promote innovation by "combining different approaches and best practices" and "complementary assets" of the parties. Andrea Lofaro, Stephen Lewis & Paulo Abecasis, *An Innovation in Merger Assessment: The European Commission's Novel Theory of Harm in the Dow/DuPont Merger*, 32 ANTITRUST 100, 102 (2017).

[1183] *Tobii AB/Smartbox & Sensory* (Final Report), para. 8.92. In support of Tobii's defenses, Lofaro et al. claim that efficiencies related to innovation may occur over time and may be hard to prove. Lofaro et al., *supra* note 1182, at 103.

[1184] *Tobii AB/Smartbox & Sensory* (Final Report), para. 10.9.

[1185] Melissa Healy, Ingrid Vandenborre, Giorgio Motta, Frederic Depoortere & Bill Batchelor, *The UK Competition Appeal Tribunal Confirms a Deferential Standard for the Competition Authority in Its Merger Prohibitions (Tobii / Smartbox)*, E-COMPETITIONS JANUARY 2020, art. No. 93459, 1.

[1186] Tobii AB (Publ) v. Competition and Markets Authority [2020] CAT 1, paras. 11, 22.

[1187] Vincenzo Denicolò & Michele Polo, *The Innovation Theory of Harm: An Appraisal* 2 (2018), https://ssrn.com/abstract=3146731.

among crop protection providers. In this regard, the Commission drew attention to the fact that the transaction involved a merger between two large and independent *innovators* in the crop protection industry. In that case, the Commission set forth cannibalization concerns as there were overlaps between the parties' several lines of research and early pipeline products in innovation spaces. Due to this cannibalization concern, the transaction was found likely to "reduce the incentives for the merged entity to continue with both lines of research and early pipeline products with the same intensity as each of the Party would in the absence of the Transaction."[1188] The Commission noted that in case of such overlaps between the lines of research and early pipeline products, the merged entity would have fewer motives to show the same level of effort on innovation compared to the situation where the parties would individually put, which would eventually result in early pipeline products as well as research being discontinued, deferred or redirected. However, the Commission did not specify which products or research would be discontinued, deferred or redirected as a result of the merger – a hypothetical approach that neither the Commission nor the CMA actually allow transaction parties to employ in their defenses – clearly demonstrating the imbalance and lack of reasoning by the regulators.

In response to the Commission's concerns, the parties argued that their cost-saving plans were planned to eliminate redundant manufacturing capabilities and not pipeline products; however, the Commission did not accept the parties' arguments, based on the documents collected from the parties showing the parties' objective to eliminate duplicative R&D programs. Similar to *Tobii AB/Smartbox*, the parties also stated that competitors would react by increasing or maintaining current levels of innovation due to the intense innovation competition in the market and the impact of regulations and that there was no causal link between concentrations and level of innovation. However, the Commission did not find the parties' arguments convincing and re-emphasized the importance of rivalry as an incentive to innovate in the market. As a result, the transaction was approved conditional on the divestiture of major parts of DuPont's global pesticide business, including its global R&D organization.

Taken together, there are similarities between the arguments set forth by the transaction parties in both cases, on issues such as the impact of regulations, the level of competition, the elimination of duplicative R&D studies, and efficiencies. However, both authorities have put more emphasis on the elimination of rivalry as a factor that would reduce incentives to innovate and did not find the parties' arguments sufficient to eliminate innovation concerns. As the parties are still being held to much more stringent burdens of proof, it is apparent that authorities in the UK[1189] have also yet to embrace innovation wholeheartedly.

[1188]   Dow/DuPont, European Commission Decision case M.7932 (Mar. 27, 2017), para. 3022.

[1189]   As discussed throughout the book, US and EU competition authorities, too, have a similar asymmetric approach to innovation defenses. In the US, the burden of proof regarding innovation defenses/efficiencies lies with the merging parties, both during the investigative process and in potential litigation scenarios. The 2010 Horizontal Merger Guidelines caution that when adverse competitive effects are significant, or there is a merger to monopoly (or near-monopoly), then the efficiencies will not matter. In *FTC v. Heinz*, the court stated that where the competition authority presents a compelling prima facie case indicating potential competitive harm, the parties must provide "proof of extraordinary efficiencies" as a counterargument (OECD, *The Role of Efficiency Claims in Antitrust Proceedings* 192 (Policy Roundtables, DAF/COMP(2012)23, May 2, 2013)). In the EU, burden of proof rested with the parties is a heavy one as the parties must prove that efficiencies

Nvidia/Arm (2021)[1190]

As discussed in Chapter 4 above with regard to the Commission's approach, the proposed *Nvidia/Arm* transaction was one of the most crucial cases recently under scrutiny by the CMA, too, with respect to its potential effects on innovation in the semiconductor industry as well as national security implications.

Similar to the Commission, the CMA also closely examined the acquisition and, in its assessment, which was published in August 2021 as part of its Phase I examination,[1191] emphasized that both NVIDIA and Arm play significant roles in the semiconductor sector. The CMA concluded that the proposed transaction might lead to a "realistic prospect of a substantial lessening of competition ('SLC') and consequently to a stifling of innovation, and more expensive or lower quality products," which would inevitably result in the circumvention and enforcement risks and leave the consumers in a worse-off position with lower quality or overpriced products.[1192] Upon a detailed examination, the CMA has found that the case raises competitive concerns with regard to the supply of central processing units ("CPUs"), interconnect products, graphic processing units ("GPUs") and systems-on-chip ("SoCs"), as well as data center servers, the Internet of things, and automotive and gaming console applications.[1193] The CMA has considered (i) the strength of Arm's software, (ii) the absence of alternative IP suppliers for CPUs, and (iii) restrictions for changing the CPU IP suppliers,[1194] and concluded that given the unique attributes of Arm's CPU IP such as its "technical advantages," it carries crucial importance for these products and services.

With respect to vertical and conglomerate effects in data centers, the CMA has underlined that following the completion of the transaction, the merged entity could impede competition in the supply of data center CPUs and SmartNICs. As for conglomerate effects, the CMA noted that these products offer "key and complementary functions in datacentres"[1195] and that the merged entity would have the ability to impede competition (i) by affecting access to each of these products and their "interoperability," and (ii) by offering these complementary products only as product sets, thereby forcing the customers to buy all of these products.[1196]

In light of CMA's concerns, the parties submitted behavioral undertakings stating that they would apply an open licensing regime and ensure the protection of competitively sensitive

---

are verifiable, merger-specific and beneficial to consumers (EU Horizontal Merger Guidelines, para. 78), and the Commission seems to frequently reject innovation-related efficiency claims for failing to satisfy one or more of these conditions, as demonstrated in *Deutsche Börse/NYSE* and others discussed in Chapter 4.

[1190] Nvidia/Arm Merger Inquiry, CMA Statutory Timetable and Phase I Summary, https://www.gov.uk/cma-cases/nvidia-slash-arm-merger-inquiry.

[1191] NVIDIA – Arm: Summary of the CMA's Report to the Secretary of State for Digital, Culture, Media & Sport on the Anticipated Acquisition by NVIDIA Corporation of Arm Limited, Gov.UK Aug 20, 2021), https://www.gov.uk/government/publications/summary-of-the-cmas-report-to-the-secretary-of-state-for-digital-culture-media-sport-on-the-anticipated-acquisition-by-nvidia-corporation-of-arm/nvidia-arm-summary-of-the-cmas-report-to-the-secretary-of-state-for-digital-culture-media-sport-on-the-anticipated-acquisition-by-nvidia-corpo.

[1192] *Id.*, para. 1.8.

[1193] *Id.*, paras. 1.19 & 1.22.

[1194] *Id.*, para. 1.29.

[1195] *Id.*, para. 1.22.

[1196] *Id.*, para. 1.23.

information after the acquisition.[1197] However, the CMA did not find the parties' explanations sufficient to eliminate its concerns[1198] and noted that the vertical foreclosure concerns raised by customers and competitors that responded to the CMA's investigation could not be assessed fully under the Phase I investigation. According to the CMA, the proposed transaction warranted an in-depth investigation on competition grounds, and the Secretary of State for the Department for Digital, Culture, Media and Sport also announced their concerns regarding the deal on national security grounds.[1199] Nevertheless, faced with such scrutiny from the various regulatory authorities, the parties announced that they had abandoned the proposed acquisition,[1200] and the CMA, therefore, canceled its merger inquiry on February 8, 2022. Considering that approximately 70% of the global population uses products and services that offer or work with technologies developed by Arm,[1201] such as the IP licensed for CPUs that are used in mobile devices, embedded devices, data centers, and automobile applications, it is no wonder that the deal is disconcerting to authorities, competitors and customers alike. Google, Microsoft and Qualcomm, relying heavily on Arm's IP, expressed their concerns to the US antitrust regulators.[1202] Tesla, Amazon and even Samsung Electronics were also said to have strongly opposed the acquisition due to looming antitrust issues.[1203] Chip industry officials and experts have stated that Nvidia's acquisition of Arm would intensify Nvidia's competition with Samsung, Qualcomm and others in self-driving cars and other future technologies, while raising concerns that Arm could increase licensing fees for competitors.[1204]

Microsoft/Activision Blizzard (2023)[1205]

On April 26, 2023, the CMA published its final report on the proposed acquisition of Activision Blizzard, Inc. ("Activision") by Microsoft, which had been notified to the CMA on September 15, 2022. Unlike the EU Commission, which had conditionally approved the transaction, as discussed above,[1206] the CMA had initially chosen to prohibit

---

[1197] *Id.*, para. 1.35.

[1198] *Id.*, para. 1.36.

[1199] CMA Press Release, CMA Finds Competition Concerns with NVIDIA's Purchase of Arm (Aug. 20, 2021), https://www.gov.uk/government/news/cma-finds-competition-concerns-with-nvidia-s-purchase-of-arm.

[1200] Nvidia Newsroom Press Release, NVIDIA and SoftBank Group Announce Termination of NVIDIA's Acquisition of Arm Limited (Feb. 7, 2022), https://nvidianews.nvidia.com/news/nvidia-and-softbank-group-announce-termination-of-nvidias-acquisition-of-arm-limited.

[1201] NVIDIA – Arm: Summary of the CMA's Report to the Secretary of State for Digital, Culture, Media & Sport on the Anticipated Acquisition by NVIDIA Corporation of Arm Limited, *supra* note 1191, para. 1.3.

[1202] David McLaughlin, Ian King & Dina Bass, *Google, Microsoft, Qualcomm Protest Nvidia's Acquisition of Arm Ltd.*, BLOOMBERG (Feb. 12, 2021), https://www.bloomberg.com/news/articles/2021-02-12/google-microsoft-qualcomm-protest-nvidia-s-arm-acquisition

[1203] Baek Byung-Yeul, *Tesla, Amazon oppose Nvidia's acquisition of Arm*, THE KOREA TIMES (Sept. 3, 2021), https://www.koreatimes.co.kr/www/tech/2021/08/133_314738.html.

[1204] Stephen Nellis, Josh Horwitz & Hyunjoo Jin, *Nvidia's Arm Deal Sparks Quick Backlash in Chip Industry*, REUTERS (Sept. 14, 2020), https://www.reuters.com/article/us-arm-holdings-m-a-nvidia-industry-anal/nvidias-arm-deal-sparks-quick-backlash-in-chip-industry-idUKKBN2650GT?edition-redirect=uk.

[1205] CMA, ANTICIPATED ACQUISITION BY MICROSOFT OF ACTIVISION BLIZZARD, INC. (Final Report) (Apr. 26, 2023), https://assets.publishing.service.gov.uk/media/644939aa529eda000c3b0525/Microsoft_Activision_Final_Report_.pdf ("*Microsoft/Activision* (Final Report)"), para. 1.1.

[1206] European Commission Press Release IP/23/2705, Mergers: Commission Clears Acquisition of Activision Blizzard by Microsoft, Subject to Conditions (May 15, 2023), https://ec.europa.eu/commission/presscorner/detail/en/ip_23_2705.

the transaction on the grounds that it would likely result in a substantial lessening of competition in cloud gaming services in the UK. However, in August 2023, Microsoft submitted a restructured transaction to the CMA, where Microsoft will not purchase the cloud gaming rights of Activision, which will instead be sold to Ubisoft, before the deal is completed. After the submission of the restructured transaction, the CMA, as of September 22, 2023, considered that there are reasonable grounds that the restructured version of the transaction (or a modified version of it) might be accepted by the CMA.[1207] As the CMA has diverged from the other competition authorities in this instance, its assessment and concerns merit a more detailed look.

According to the parties' explanations, the rationale for the transaction is to: (i) provide Microsoft with a differentiated gaming content (including Activision's popular franchises such as *Call of Duty* ("CoD"), *World of Warcraft* ("WoW") and *Candy Crush)*, which will help Microsoft to execute a cross-platform strategy (allowing gamers to play games on multiple devices); (ii) improve Microsoft's presence in the mobile segment, where Activision holds an established position; (iii) support Microsoft's investments in Xbox Game Pass and improve user engagement amongst Xbox and PC users; (iv) improve Microsoft's ability to create a "Universal Store" (extending its store in Xbox to non-Xbox platforms); and (v) increase the attractiveness of Microsoft Audience Network.[1208]

In its competitive assessment, the CMA took into account the evidence on concentration and on closeness of competition given that the potential issues under analysis in this case related to how competition between the parties and their competitors would dynamically evolve over time, as opposed to a bright-line definition of the relevant markets.[1209] Accordingly, the CMA decided to assess the effects of the transaction (i) in console gaming services in the UK (despite the transaction parties' view that PCs and consoles are substitutable),[1210] (ii) in the cloud gaming services market in the UK and (iii) on the supply of console game publishing and PC game publishing services globally.[1211]

i. Vertical Theories of Harm

Vertical Effects in Console Gaming Services (i.e., Hardware, Digital Storefronts and Subscription Services)

The CMA noted that (i) for the past twenty years, Microsoft (Xbox), Sony (PlayStation) and Nintendo have been the only significant suppliers of console gaming, and (ii) only

---

[1207] *Microsoft/Activision* (Final Report), paras. 11.307 & 11.311. On August 22, 2023, the CMA published its final order on the matter, prohibiting the transaction. CMA Final Order (Aug. 22, 2023), https://assets.publishing. service.gov.uk/media/64e3764a3309b7000d1c9bd7/Microsoft_Activision_-_Final_Order.pdf. *See also* CMA, Anticipated Acquisition by Microsoft Corporation of Activision Blizzard (Excluding Activision Blizzard's non-EEA Cloud Streaming Rights) (ME/7068/23, Sept. 22, 2023), paras. 8–13.

[1208] *Microsoft/Activision* (Final Report), paras. 2.26–2.28. *See also* Microsoft News Center, Microsoft to Acquire Activision Blizzard to Bring the Joy and Community of Gaming to Everyone, Across Every Device (Jan. 18, 2022), https://news.microsoft.com/2022/01/18/microsoft-to-acquire-activision-blizzard-to-bring-the-joy-and-community-of-gaming-to-everyone-across-every-device.

[1209] *Microsoft/Activision* (Final Report), paras. 5.24 & 5.25.

[1210] *Id.*, para. 5.42.

[1211] *Id.*, paras. 5.74, 5.108 & 5.145.

a handful of AAA games (the term used to refer to most popular games), including CoD, account for the majority of game time and revenues.[1212] The CMA then found that Microsoft's Xbox and Sony's PlayStation closely compete with each other, and Nintendo's consoles (which currently do not offer CoD) compete less closely with Xbox or PlayStation due to different technical specifications, offering and audience.[1213] With respect to the possible foreclosure, the CMA noted the results of a survey conducted on behalf of CMA showed Activision's CoD to be important for PlayStation's users, and found that making CoD exclusive to Xbox would have a material impact on PlayStation's revenue and ability to compete.[1214] The CMA also found that Microsoft would have the ability to engage in total foreclosure of PlayStation, including its distribution storefront and subscription services.[1215] Nevertheless, the CMA decided that Microsoft would not have the incentive to make CoD exclusive to Xbox since it would result in significant financial losses for Microsoft (based on a model to analyze the losses that Microsoft may incur in such case).[1216] Therefore, despite the vertical overlap, the CMA concluded that the transaction is not likely to result in a substantial lessening of competition in console gaming services in the UK.[1217]

Vertical Effects in Cloud Gaming Services

The CMA, before Microsoft submitted in August 2023 the restructured transaction, where, among others, Microsoft will not purchase the cloud gaming rights of Activision, decided that the transaction was likely to result in a substantial lessening of competition in cloud gaming services in the UK as a result of vertical effects in the form of input foreclosure based on the following grounds: (i) Microsoft would have the ability to limit access to Activision's games, multi-homing is unlikely to limit the ability to foreclose, and some of Activision's games are likely to be an important input for the success of rival cloud gaming services;[1218] (ii) Microsoft would have the incentive to make Activision's titles exclusive to its own cloud gaming service because in the cloud gaming market, success is highly uncertain and incumbents such as Microsoft may have the incentive to offer exclusive games on their cloud gaming service to strengthen their market power. This was already part of Microsoft's cloud gaming strategy as it has not made its games available on rival cloud gaming platforms (except for a few Bethesda titles);[1219] (iii) although Microsoft entered into agreements with Nintendo and three other cloud gaming service providers to allow certain Activision content to be made available on their platforms post-transaction, there is uncertainty around the terms of these agreements and they also apply only to a

---

[1212]   *Id.*, paras. 13 & 16.

[1213]   *Id.*, paras. 7.87 & 7.138.

[1214]   *Id.*, paras. 7.149, 7.152, 7.138, 7.235 & 7.304.

[1215]   *Id.*, para. 7.304. With respect to partial foreclosure (e.g., degradation or price increase), the CMA found that PlayStation would not lose the full extent of the range that CoD represents in such case; rather, the partial foreclosure would amount to a deterioration in a small fraction of PlayStation's overall range. *See id.*, para. 7.306.

[1216]   *Id.*, paras. 7.317, 7.398 & 7.399. Regarding the incentives, the CMA noted that Microsoft's past behavior in relation to acquisitions of other gaming studios was inconclusive (e.g., Microsoft did not foreclose other game consoles' access to Minecraft after its acquisition). *See id.*, para. 7.384.

[1217]   *Id.*, para. 7.402.

[1218]   *Id.*, paras. 8.314, 8.346 & 8.347. *See also Microsoft/Activision* (ME/7068/23, Sept. 22, 2023), paras. 8–13.

[1219]   *Microsoft/Activision* (Final Report), paras. 8.384, 8.385 & 8.388.

few existing cloud gaming service providers;[1220] and (iv) considering Microsoft's already strong position in the market due to the ownership of the leading PC OS (Windows), which streams games from Windows servers, cloud infrastructure (Azure and Xbox Cloud Gaming) giving it important advantages in running a cloud gaming service (i.e., without having to pay a fee to third-party cloud platforms), first-party content, its current market share (60%–70%), significant barriers to entry and expansion, including the cost of cloud infrastructure and the cost of acquiring content, and that Microsoft faces only limited competitive constraints from current/potential competitors, Microsoft using Activision's content to foreclose rivals in cloud gaming services would distort the development of the cloud gaming market and result in substantial harm to overall competition in this market.[1221]

It is important to note that, when analyzing the potential foreclosure's impact on cloud gaming services, the CMA took into account Microsoft's power stemming from its wider multi-product ecosystem, and noted the following: "The evidence suggests that the combination of Microsoft's multi-product ecosystem gives it a stronger position in cloud gaming than would be suggested by assessing each of its products and services individually. As described above, this may affect Microsoft's incentive to engage in a foreclosure strategy using Activision's content, and may also magnify the effect of any such foreclosure strategy in the market for cloud gaming services."[1222] Therefore, the CMA focused on how the potential strengthening of Microsoft's integrated offering would affect cloud gaming rivals' ability to compete against Microsoft.[1223] Against this background, the CMA's decision seems to contain elements of ecosystem theory, which is based on the notion that mergers involving a party that controls an ecosystem may have an impact that could be undermined when the parties' products/services are considered individually.[1224]

After the CMA's decision that the transaction was likely to result in a substantial lessening of competition in cloud gaming services in the UK as a result of vertical effects in the form of input foreclosure, Microsoft submitted in August 2023 a restructured transaction to address the CMA's concerns, which will be discussed under a separate chapter below.

ii. Innovation Theory of Harm and the Forward-Looking Assessment

CMA's *Microsoft/Activision* includes several forward-looking analyses on the future behavior of the parties, including with respect to the remedies proposed, and although the CMA explained its concerns under a traditional vertical theory of harm, its assessment also includes elements of an innovation theory of harm.

With respect to the forward-looking analysis, in relation to its finding that Microsoft would have the ability and incentive to limit cloud gaming service providers' access to Activision's games, the CMA, before the submission of the restructured transaction, considered that, in the current state of the market, Activision content has only been

---

[1220]   *Id.*, paras. 8.337, 8.381 & 8.383.
[1221]   *Id.*, paras. 8.434–8.438 & 8.441.
[1222]   *Id.*, para. 198. *See also* Decision, para. 8.96.
[1223]   *See, e.g.*, *Microsoft/Activision* (Final Report), para. 8.359.
[1224]   OECD, *Theories of Harm for Digital Mergers: OECD Competition Policy Roundtable Background Note* (2023), paras. 93–95 & Box 4.1.

available to cloud gaming platforms to a limited extent. Nevertheless, despite the historical evidence[1225] showing that Activision has not yet licensed its content to cloud gaming platforms, the CMA decided that Activision would likely have made its games – including day and date releases – available for cloud gaming in the next five years, taking into account the developments that will tend to increase its incentive to do so (e.g., growth of the market).[1226] The CMA also stated that, as evidence collected from third parties suggests, some of Activision's games are likely to be an important input for the success of rival cloud gaming services as they are today for consoles and PCs.[1227] In analyzing whether Microsoft had an incentive to engage in a foreclosure strategy, the CMA noted that since cloud gaming is a developing market, one should place more emphasis on the long-term objectives as opposed to current positions and margins, and, for this reason, the qualitative evidence based on Microsoft's past behavior and internal documents may be more informative.[1228] Therefore, the CMA considered (i) Microsoft's past behavior of not making its games available on competitor gaming platforms and (ii) Microsoft's internal documents, which reveal a strategy of not making its first-party titles available on rival cloud gaming platforms, to support its finding that Microsoft has an incentive to foreclose access.[1229] The CMA subsequently stated that in the nascent cloud gaming market where success is highly uncertain and there are network effects, incumbents have stronger incentive to offer exclusive games to acquire market power.[1230] These findings provided the basis for the CMA's conclusion in the Final Report that Microsoft using Activision's content to foreclose rivals in cloud gaming services would distort the development of the cloud gaming market.

Overall, the CMA noted, based on Microsoft's internal documents and third-party submissions, that cloud gaming is a growing market and could be transformative for the gaming industry in the next few years, helping to reach new customers and improve choice for existing customers (potentially replacing consoles altogether for some of them).[1231] Accordingly, the CMA stated that (i) absent the transaction, the competition is likely to be intense, dynamic and characterized by innovative competitive strategies given the relative immaturity of the market, its potential for growth, and exogenous factors such as technology advances;[1232] (ii) the transaction could alter the future of gaming by stifling competition in the growing and dynamic market for cloud gaming

---

[1225] With respect to the evidence considered by the CMA, *Microsoft/Activision* (Final Report), para. 8.8, notes that "in the context of sectors that are characterised by fast-moving technological and commercial developments or assessments of potential or dynamic effects that are particularly dependent on the evolution of competitive conditions, the types of evidence that are available to the CMA may be more restricted. In such cases, the CMA may place particular weight on evidence such as internal documents, the expected number of competitors after the merger, similarities between the characteristics of the products or services that are under development, and the views and expansion plans of market participants. As with uncertainty, the absence of certain specific types of evidence such as historical data will not in itself preclude the CMA from concluding that the SLC test is met on the basis of all the other available evidence assessed in the round."

[1226] *Id.*, paras. 8.226, 8.278 & 8.241.

[1227] *Id.*, paras. 8.314, 8.346 & 8.347.

[1228] *Id.*, paras. 8.350 & 8.352.

[1229] *Id.*, paras. 8.385–8.388.

[1230] *Id.*, para. 8.384.

[1231] *Id.*, paras. 8.58, 8.59 & 11.288.

[1232] *Id.*, para. 11.288.

services; (iii) the market for cloud gaming would become an important conduit for playing games, both for new users who are unable or unwilling to buy an expensive console or gaming PC, and for existing gamers looking for an alternative to these devices; (iv) the transaction would make an already strong incumbent in this market even stronger; and (v) this reduction in competition could harm consumers, such as by increasing prices and reducing quality, innovation, and choice over time.[1233]

As a result, the CMA decided that the likely future growth, competitive dynamism and innovation in the cloud gaming market would be substantially reduced as a result of the transaction and this would lead to a significantly greater level of harm to UK consumers than any consumer benefits foregone.[1234] In this regard, the CMA seems to have blocked the transaction considering the possible overall reduction in innovation competition in the relevant nascent cloud gaming market. Therefore, in addition to vertical theories of harm, the CMA seems to have considered an innovation theory of harm.

iii. The CMA's Assessment of the Remedies

Parallel to those offered to the Commission, Microsoft initially offered a behavioral remedy to address the CMA's concerns in cloud gaming services, proposing to license Activision games, including CoD and WoW, royalty-free to certain cloud gaming providers for a period of ten years and to update the consumer licenses on its website, giving the right to any consumer who purchased/obtained a free license to play an Activision game from Microsoft's online stores to stream that game in the cloud gaming services that were covered by the remedy.[1235] The CMA noted that the remedy offered is predominantly behavioral in nature[1236] and that the market in this case is dynamic, which makes it difficult to foresee innovative competitive strategies during the application of a behavioral remedy and to accommodate the changes that may occur in the market within the specification of a behavioral remedy.[1237] The CMA then rejected the initial remedy based on the following grounds, which also portrayed its concerns about limiting innovation:

(i) The scope of the remedy is limited to a model whereby gamers had first to acquire the right to play certain games and stream those games on certain cloud gaming services. However, absent the transaction, cloud gaming service providers may have entered into a different type of commercial relationship with Activision (e.g., through exclusive content or joint marketing arrangements) to access the latter's content, and such relationships are not covered by the remedy. This may risk limiting innovation and competition in buy-to-play and "bring-your-own-game" segments, as there would be extremely limited scope for content exclusives, which are a current feature of the console market, and one would expect, in the absence of the transaction, to be part of the cloud gaming market.[1238]

[1233] *Id.*, para. 72.
[1234] *Id.*, para. 10.
[1235] *Id.*, para. 11.45.
[1236] *Id.*, para. 11.78.
[1237] *Id.*, paras. 11.78, 11.87 & 11.129.
[1238] *Id.*, paras. 11.93–11.102.

(ii) The remedy applies to console and PC versions of Activision games. PC versions are those that are developed to run on a Windows OS. Although Microsoft may produce versions for non-Windows OS after the transaction, it would have limited incentive to do so, given that this may divert demand away from the Microsoft OS. On the other hand, absent the transaction, Activision would make versions of its games compatible with non-Windows PC OSs to maximize profit. Therefore, the remedy may put cloud gaming service providers that wish to use non-Windows OSs at a competitive disadvantage and distort the choice of OSs for new entrants.[1239]

(iii) The remedy has a duration of ten years, but the competitive concerns that may arise in cloud gaming services are not time-limited; thus, it would not be an effective solution due to limited duration.[1240] The remedy may not be suited to future changes that are not currently foreseen given the unpredictability and may give rise to distortion risks relating to business models employed by rival cloud gaming providers since some business models are not covered.[1241] Also, considering the complexity of the remedy and information asymmetry between Microsoft and any monitoring trustee or the CMA, there is a high risk of circumvention, and it would be difficult to monitor effectively.[1242]

Under the Enterprise Act 2022, a remedy must be proportionate considering the benefits resulting from the transaction and the scale of the substantial lessening of competition and its adverse effects.[1243] In this regard, Microsoft asserted that (i) the agreements signed with certain cloud gaming service providers to allow them to make Activision content available on their platforms, (ii) Microsoft's plan for expansion into the mobile gaming market, and (iii) Microsoft's intention to place Activision's content on Game Pass are relevant customer benefits ("RCBs") that would make the prohibition decision disproportionate.[1244] The CMA decided that the first two of these do not quality as RCBs given that (i) Activision's incentives to make its content available in cloud gaming service providers would be higher absent the transaction, and agreements may not lead to material benefits for consumers, and (ii) Microsoft's plans to enter the mobile gaming market is not certain, especially considering that Apple and Google currently prohibit rival mobile gaming app stores or impose strict limits on their ability to monetize content.[1245] As for Microsoft's intention to place Activision's games on Game Pass, the CMA analyzed that it may amount to an RCB considering that (i) it may create a chance to exploit synergies and (ii) Activision's content would be unlikely to be available on Game Pass absent the transaction. However, the CMA decided that this benefit would likely be limited because (i) having Activision's content on Game Pass would represent a new way to pay for the same content that is already available on Xbox, and this would not necessarily be

---

[1239] *Id.*, paras. 11.103–11.111 & 11.131.

[1240] *Id.*, paras. 11.114, 11.115.

[1241] *Id.*, paras. 11.118, 11.125.

[1242] *Id.*, paras. 11.126 & 11.127.

[1243] UK Enterprise Act 2022 § 30.

[1244] *Microsoft/Activision* (Final Report), para. 11.143.

[1245] *Id.*, paras. 11.185, 11.188, 11.189 & 11.220.

cheaper for all consumers, and (ii) Microsoft would have the incentive to increase the price of Game Pass following the addition of Activision's valuable content to it, and this would significantly reduce or eliminate any potential RCB.[1246]

On May 18, 2023, the CMA published its proposed order (draft Final Order) prohibiting the transaction and invited written representations from interested parties.[1247] The statutory period for the CMA to accept final undertakings from the parties or to make a final order would have ended on July 18, 2023, and Microsoft had been ready to appeal the Final Order before the CAT. However, Microsoft argued there were special reasons and a material change of circumstances[1248] as a result of which the CMA should not prohibit the transaction, referring to (i) the Commission's acceptance of Microsoft's commitments as sufficient, (ii) Microsoft and Sony's agreement to keep CoD on PlayStation for ten years, (iii) new evidence that became available under the US litigation, and (iv) new evidence obtained by Microsoft in its UK appeals process.[1249] The CMA, in turn, deemed that none of these developments would constitute a material change of circumstance or special reason to change its initial view[1250] and issued its final order to prohibit the transaction.

It is imperative to highlight here that in light of the above, Microsoft and Activision have submitted a new application to the CMA with revised terms, whereby Activision's non-EEA cloud streaming rights have been excluded from the transaction: instead, Activision's global cloud streaming rights (excluding the EEA) for all games in the next fifteen years will be divested to Ubisoft, which will be able to license these rights to third parties, i.e., other cloud gaming service providers, as well as Microsoft. The terms would also allow Ubisoft to ask Microsoft to adapt the Activision titles to be compatible with non-Windows operating systems. The CMA considered that the restructured transaction would render Ubisoft a key content supplier to cloud gaming services, thereby replicating Activision's role. As a result, Activision would not be able to limit access to the key content, or to withhold the games from its competitors. After the submission of the restructured transaction, the CMA, as of September 22, 2023, considered that there are reasonable grounds that the restructured version of the transaction (or a modified version of it) might be accepted by the CMA.

According to the CMA, the acquisition of Activision's cloud streaming rights by Ubisoft would prevent important contents from being controlled by Microsoft in relation to cloud gaming. It is important to note that the CMA initially established that Microsoft, even in the absence of the transaction, has a strong position in cloud gaming services, which could have been used thanks to its prospective control over the said content to restrict competition.

[1246] *Id.*, paras. 11.249, 11.253–11.259.

[1247] CMA's Draft Order for the Microsoft and Activision Merger Inquiry 2023, https://assets.publishing.service.gov.uk/media/6465ec16e14070000cb6e181/Draft_final_order__.pdf.

[1248] As per the Enterprise Act 2022 § 41.

[1249] CMA Final Decision on Possible Material Change of Circumstances/Special Reasons (Aug. 25, 2023), https://assets.publishing.service.gov.uk/media/64e85b07db1c07000d22b40e/MS_A_-_Final_Decision_on_possible_MCC_and_SR__PUBLICATION_VERSION_.pdf.

[1250] *Id.*, para. 6. *See* CMA Final Order, *supra* note 1207.

Although the CMA considered that the restructured transaction addresses many of the concerns, it still has limited concerns that the sale of cloud streaming rights to Ubisoft could be circumvented, terminated, or not enforced. As such, Microsoft offered remedies, according to which it will be ensured that the terms of the sale are enforceable by the CMA. Accordingly, the CMA, although provisionally, has concluded as of September 22, 2023, that this additional remedy should resolve the concerns.[1251]

5.4.3 Online Platforms

Brightsolid/Friends (2010)

Brightsolid/Friends[1252] constituted the first online platform case, whereby innovation was brought under the scrutiny of the UK's competition authorities. The CC has cleared the acquisition of Friends Reunited Holdings Limited, whose subsidiary (i.e., Genes Reunited Ltd) operated a social networking/family history website, allowing access to family history data, by Brightsolid Group Limited, which operated as an online retailer of data relevant to family history through its subsidiary with the trade name of Find My Past Limited. In defining the relevant product market, the CC observed, first of all, that the UK online genealogy supply chain included four elements, namely, (i) original data holders, which were often public bodies providing private companies acting as digitizers with access to their records; (ii) digitizers, transcribing the records with a short period of practical exclusivity for the use of the relevant data; (iii) retailers, selling the data to end users; and (iv) end users, obtaining information through purchases or publicly available sources, or by sharing information with other end users (constituting "social networking" in the context of this case). As a result of these elements, the CC noted and distinguished between three different aspects of online genealogy services, namely, (i) core data, (ii) non-core data, and (iii) social networking. As a result, the CC found that the parties' activities overlapped only in the provision of core data.[1253] Consequently, the CC defined the relevant market as "supply of online genealogy services in the UK," which included investigations of ancestry and family history online.

As for the unilateral effects of the transaction, the CC compared the innovation capabilities of the merged entity with one of their competitors' offerings, namely, Ancestry.co.uk ("Ancestry"), which was deemed to pose the strongest competitive constraint on the parties, according to the CC's point of view.[1254] As a result of its assessment of the unilateral effects of the transaction, the CC held that the merged entity would

---

[1251] CMA, Microsoft / Activision Blizzard (ex-cloud streaming rights) Merger Inquiry (Aug. 22, 2023), https://www.gov.uk/cma-cases/microsoft-slash-activision-blizzard-ex-cloud-streaming-rights-merger-inquiry. *See also* *Microsoft/Activision* (ME/7068/23, Sept. 22, 2023), paras. 8–13.

[1252] CC, BRIGHTSOLID GROUP LIMITED AND FRIENDS REUNITED HOLDINGS LIMITED: A REPORT ON THE ANTICIPATED ACQUISITION BY BRIGHTSOLID GROUP LIMITED OF FRIENDS REUNITED HOLDINGS LIMITED (Mar. 18, 2010), https://assets.publishing.service.gov.uk/media/55194c73e5274a142b0003be/555final_report_excised.pdf.

[1253] *Id.*, paras. 4.1–4.11.

[1254] *Id.*, paras. 7, 6.1, 6.37.

likely become the biggest innovative competitor against Ancestry, since the transaction would minimize risks stemming from upfront investment costs, and accordingly, trigger a competition in innovation due to the merged entity's product offering emerging as an alternative to Ancestry's offering.[1255] This decision is also noteworthy in the sense that the CC had already decided to identify and separate the different types of data before data-related issues had become a priority in the eyes of competition enforcement authorities around the world.

Google/BeatThatQuote (2011)

Section 23(3) EA triggered the *Google/BeatThatQuote* merger control investigation, whereby Google acquired BeatThatQuote ("BTQ"), and the parties' combined market shares were calculated to be 30–40% in the market for the supply of online advertising in the UK.[1256] Since Google provided a consumer finance tool as a price comparison site ("PCS") called "Google Comparison Ads," and BTQ operated its consumer finance PCS with a particular focus on mortgages and credit cards, the parties' activities were found to overlap in the supply of consumer finance PCSs in the UK. The OFT considered consumer finance PCSs as two-sided platforms because they acted, by their very nature, as intermediaries between two distinct and unrelated types of customers, i.e., users seeking information and prices on products/services and advertisers looking to promote their products and services to users.[1257] Holding that the effects of the transaction (i) on the supply of advertising space on consumer finance PCSs and (ii) on the supply of all online advertising were required to be assessed, the OFT began its examination by observing that the parties' combined shares in the market for the supply of advertising space on consumer finance PCSs were very low (i.e., between 0 and 10%). In relation to the latter market, the OFT found no basis for a prospective SLC, in line with Google's explanations that (i) several types of competitors would continue to offer online advertising services (for example, AOL as a web portal, Ask.com as a search service provider, Facebook as a social network, and Amazon.com as an online commerce site), (ii) new and expanding entrants posed a constraint on online advertising suppliers, and (iii) emerging technologies would bring about new commercial opportunities, such as location-based advertising and online retargeting technologies. For these reasons, the OFT concluded that the transaction was unlikely to result in an SLC.

Amazon/The Book Depository (2011)

Similar to the *Google/BeatThatQuote* case, the market-share threshold under section 23(3) EA granted the OFT jurisdiction over the *Amazon/The Book Depository* transaction.[1258] The OFT did not find it necessary to define a relevant market but instead focused its investigation on the retailing of books. In making this determination, the OFT compared

---

[1255] *Id.*, para. 6.37.
[1256] OFT, Completed Acquisition by Google Inc of BeatThatQuote (July 1, 2011), https://assets.publishing.service. gov.uk/media/555de311ed915d7ae200005f/Google-BeatThatQuote.pdf.
[1257] *Id.* at 10.
[1258] OFT, Anticipated Acquisition by Amazon.com, Inc. of The Book Depository International Limited (ME/5085/11, Oct. 26, 2011), https://assets.publishing.service.gov.uk/media/555de319e5274a708400006e/Amazon.pdf.

the ratio of the parties' sales in different product categories.[1259] The OFT also considered multiple surveys submitted by the transaction parties or consulted *ex officio*, which compared online and offline sales of books and deliberated on their substitutability. The OFT also assessed the activities of the parties, and it was noted that Amazon sold various items online, including books, DVDs, CDs, and consumer electronics, and that The Book Depository was an online book retailer that also sold DVDs, CDs, as well as video and PC games. The OFT evaluated whether the transaction would result in "a realistic prospect of a substantial lessening of competition."[1260]

In its competitive assessment, the OFT conducted its examination under several different headings: (i) prices, (ii) delivery charges, (iii) range of titles, and (iv) potential competition.[1261] In doing so, the OFT found that (i) in light of the parties' pricing models, the merger would not lead to increases in book prices or delivery charges, (ii) as there were several competitors that offered a wide range of titles, the transaction would not significantly reduce the number of titles offered, and (iii) even though there were multiple third-party concerns, there could be new entrants to the market that would be able to do so in a timely manner. The OFT received numerous complaints from third parties, including several from the competitors of the transaction parties.[1262] The OFT addressed these complaints in its decision but did not find them sufficiently persuasive to restrict this transaction. In conclusion, noting that the parties were not close competitors prior to the transaction, the OFT cleared the transaction upon concluding its Phase I assessment and did not choose to refer it to the CC.

Facebook/Instagram (2012)

Section 23(3) EA once again triggered a merger control filing for the *Facebook/Instagram*[1263] transaction in the UK, due to the fact that Facebook's share of supply in the UK with respect to virtual social networking services exceeded the 25% share threshold, even though Instagram had not yet generated any turnover in the UK. The OFT deemed social networks to constitute two-sided markets, owing to the competition between social networks to increase their user numbers and to attract advertisers, even though the OFT declined to provide a precise product-market definition in this case, since it determined that no substantial competition concerns would arise under any plausible market definition. According to the OFT, (i) actual competition in the supply of photo apps and (ii) potential competition in the supply of online display advertising constituted the only theories of harm regarding horizontal issues that needed to be evaluated in this case.[1264]

With respect to the former, the OFT observed that there were other competing photo-sharing apps, including Camera Awesome, Camera+, Flickr, Hipstamatic, Path,

---

[1259]   *Id.*, para. 8.

[1260]   *Id.*, para. 127.

[1261]   *Id.*, paras. 125–53.

[1262]   *Id.*, paras. 118–19.

[1263]   OFT, Anticipated Acquisition by Facebook Inc of Instagram (ME/5525/12, on reference given on Aug. 14, 2012), https://assets.publishing.service.gov.uk/media/555de2e5ed915d7ae200003b/facebook.pdf.

[1264]   *Id.*, paras. 14–29.

and Pixable. Considering that Camera Awesome and Hipstamatic had been downloaded more than three times as much as the Facebook Camera app and that Instagram had been downloaded more than forty-five times as much as the Facebook Camera app, the OFT concluded that the other competitors would pose a much stronger competitive constraint on Instagram than Facebook Camera. In relation to the latter theory relating to online advertising, the OFT expressed its view that Instagram was not likely to compete against Facebook in the short run, given that third-party firms (such as Google, Yahoo, Microsoft, and eBay) appeared to compete against Facebook, especially Google with its 44% market share of expenditures in the global online advertising market.

In the context of vertical issues, the OFT evaluated two distinct theories of harm, namely, (i) the foreclosure of social networks competing with Facebook by limiting Instagram users to uploading their photos to Facebook and (ii) the foreclosure of other photo apps by preventing them from uploading their photos to Facebook.[1265] Since the OFT believed that limiting users and preventing them from uploading their photos to other social networks might negatively affect the value of the app, and as a result, pave the way for pushing users to switch to rival social networks, the OFT did not give any credence to the first theory.[1266] Regarding the second theory, the OFT determined that Facebook was unlikely to adopt this strategy since it would possibly limit the engagement level of Facebook users. In light of this competition analysis, the OFT concluded that the transaction would not give rise to an SLC and thereby decided not to refer the transaction to the CC's review.

In this case, the *ex post* assessment under the Lear Report indicates that the OFT should also have analyzed (i) the exclusivity of the user base and (ii) the platform's size and ability to target ads, in order to accurately assess the competitive harm arising from the transaction.[1267] Given that Facebook and Instagram (i) use information and communication technologies, (ii) collect and use data, (iii) benefit from network effects, (iv) provide services to consumers for free, and (v) pursue advertisement activities, the market definition and the analysis of the closeness of competition, in this case, have been widely criticized, and they have been considered deeply flawed by commentators.[1268]

Priceline/Kayak (2013)

In the *Priceline/Kayak* decision,[1269] section 23(3) EA once again triggered the merger control of a transaction concerning online platforms. In this case, the OFT found that the parties' activities overlapped in the market for the supply of online travel search services to overseas customers searching for UK-based services, with a combined share of 25–35%, even though Kayak's UK turnover did not exceed the thresholds under the turnover test.[1270] Priceline.com Inc. ("Priceline") was a holding company of several

---

[1265]   *Id.*, paras. 30–41.
[1266]   *Id.*, paras. 36–37.
[1267]   Lear Report, *supra* note 1072, paras. II.42–II.43.
[1268]   *Id.*, para. II54; *See also* Tim Wu, *Blind Spot: The Attention Economy and the Law*, 82 ANTITRUST L.J. 771, 5–6 (2019), https://scholarship.law.columbia.edu/cgi/viewcontent.cgi?article=3030&context=faculty_scholarship.
[1269]   OFT, Completed Acquisition by Priceline.com Incorporated of Kayak Software Corporation (ME/5882-12, May 14, 2013), https://assets.publishing.service.gov.uk/media/555de2b6e5274a7084000024/priceline.pdf.
[1270]   *Id.*, para. 6.

online travel agencies ("OTAs"), which worked with travel service providers ("TSPs") to provide travel services, such as booking hotels, airline, and rent-a-cars to consumers. Kayak Software Corporation ("Kayak") was a meta-search site ("MSS") for travel-related needs, which provided a price-comparison service to its customers for hotels, airline tickets, package holidays, and rental cars.[1271]

The OFT examined whether the OTAs were separated from the MSSs in terms of the booking functionality.[1272] The MSSs did not include a booking functionality; instead, they were designed to direct the customers to OTAs or TSPs' websites. Moreover, the OTAs provided a connection between the customers and the TSPs, which had their own booking functionality. In this decision, the parties submitted and argued that the online travel services sector could be considered a two-sided market, owing to the channel between the customers searching for travel services (such as hotels and flight tickets) and the TSPs, which tended to market their travel services.[1273] It should be noted that the MSSs could provide the booking services to the customers through an affiliate service provided by an OTA. Therefore, customers would have a chance to book or use travel services without proceeding to the OTAs' or the TSPs' websites. However, this booking functionality was costly and challenging to set up for hotels. Although Kayak provided this booking functionality, namely "Book Kayak," to its customers as well,[1274] the OFT concluded that there was no horizontal overlap in the booking services.

Even though the OFT did not provide a precise market definition in this case, it referred to two particular markets in its examination: (i) the supply of online travel search services and (ii) the supply of online advertising services.[1275] The OFT stated that there was both a horizontal and a non-horizontal relationship between the MSSs and the OTAs. In its examination of the theories of harm, the OFT determined that the increment in the market for the supply of online travel search services to consumers was minimal.[1276] Moreover, the OFT mentioned that there were more significant and close competitors in this particular market. The OFT also assessed the non-horizontal aspect of the transaction in terms of the foreclosure of rival OTAs from the online travel search services to consumers and the foreclosure of online advertising services to the TSPs for Priceline's ability to use Kayak's website, especially the search results therein. However, the OFT concluded that (i) consumers could have recognized such biased results, so they would have easily declined to use Kayak's website, (ii) biasing Kayak's search results would have caused other OTAs to stop using Kayak's website, and (iii) there were numerous MSSs to generate traffic to their own websites for the OTAs. For these reasons, the OFT concluded that the transaction in question was unlikely to result in an SLC.[1277]

Furthermore, regarding the possible engagement of Priceline in foreclosure activity by raising rivals' costs, the OFT took into account Kayak's small market share and thus

---

[1271]   *Id.*, paras. 1–2.
[1272]   *Id.*, para. 22.
[1273]   *Id.*, para. 14.
[1274]   *Id.*, para. 26.
[1275]   *Id.*, para. 15.
[1276]   *Id.*, para. 64.
[1277]   *Id.*, paras. 89–94.

concluded that the merger did not carry the risk of creating a realistic prospect of an SLC.[1278] For the conglomerate concern involving the ability of Priceline to bundle or tie its other brands, the OFT stated the following: (i) Priceline would have a small increment in market share post-transaction, (ii) there would not be any ability/potential to bundle or tie the OTAs, which comprised the majority of Kayak's customers, and (iii) the TSPs had already signed up to multiple OTAs and MSSs. The OFT, therefore, concluded that there was no realistic prospect of an SLC based on conglomerate effects.[1279] Under this assessment, the OFT decided that the merger was not expected to result in a substantial loss of competition within the UK market.

The author believes that the Lear Report had examined this particular case, along with the *Expedia/Trivago* decision,[1280] to assess the market outcome. However, the main criticism is based on the OFT's failure to provide insights as to whether the relationship between the OTAs and the MSSs was vertical or horizontal, as this could have led to an inaccurate assessment of unilateral effects.[1281] There is also the fact that the OFT relied too much on the consumer's ability to discern possible bias, despite the fact that it could be demonstrated that consumers would – and did in fact – be directed by what was on display. Having said this, the Lear Report also pointed out that while Kayak did show intermediation bias, unlike Trivago, the existence of several other MSSs in the market would help in curbing it.

Motorola/Waze (2013)

As an online service, Google Maps has also been assessed by the OFT from an innovation perspective. In this regard, Google's acquisition of Waze through Motorola (which was owned by Google at the time) triggered the OFT's merger control, once again due to the "share of supply" test under section 23(3) EA. In the *Motorola/Waze* decision,[1282] the OFT did not provide a precise market definition, due to the absence of substantial competition concerns, although the parties submitted that the relevant product market might be broadened from the "provision of turn-by-turn navigation applications for mobile devices" to cover all products and services that offer some form of map-based or navigational service. In light of the parties' activities – namely, (i) Google providing map-based services via its Google Maps application, for which Google licenses an application programming interface ("API") to third parties, and (ii) Waze offering a free map application for mobile devices to enable drivers to build and use live maps, real-time traffic updates and turn-by-turn navigation – the OFT evaluated whether the transaction might cause the loss of Waze's constraint on Google as an innovative competitor, and whether the merger may remove Google's incentives to develop its mapping products further and reduce Google's incentives to innovate.

[1278] *Id.*, paras. 95–98.

[1279] *Id.*, paras. 99–103.

[1280] In this case, the OFT held that the transaction did not qualify for investigation, since none of the UK turnover and market share tests had been satisfied: OFT, Anticipated Acquisition by Expedia of Trivago (ME/5894/13, Mar. 7, 2013), https://assets.publishing.service.gov.uk/media/555de2d2e5274a7084000038/Expedia.pdf.

[1281] Lear Report, *supra* note 1072, paras. II.216–II.220.

[1282] OFT, Completed Acquisition by Motorola Mobility Holding (Google, Inc.) of Waze Mobile Limited (ME/6167/13, Nov. 11, 2013), https://assets.publishing.service.gov.uk/media/555de2cfed915d7ae2000027/motorola.pdf.

In its competitive assessment, the OFT considered the horizontal effects of the merger within the context of (i) the download and usage figures of the parties' applications, (ii) the closeness of competition between the parties, (iii) Waze's future potential as a disruptive force in the market and as a growing competitive constraint on Google, and (iv) constraints from other competitors.[1283]

In relation to these considerations, the OFT ultimately found that (i) other indicators, such as the functionality of the parties' applications, map quality and content, constituted distinctive evidence in the case, (ii) the evidence did not suffice to deem Waze successful in its efforts to attract adequate users for its UK maps and to offer well-developed content in comparison to its competitors, and (iii) Waze would not emerge as a disruptive force in the UK market, as it could not achieve sufficient scale to benefit from significant and insuperable network effects to enable the future growth and acceleration of its application.[1284] In relation to other competitors, the OFT observed that (i) there were a number of competitors to Google in the sector of "turn-by-turn navigation applications for mobile devices," (ii) the portable navigation devices were unable to efficiently constrain turn-by-turn applications in a competition context; however, they could evolve as a competitive constraint on the parties due to the sector-wide shift towards in-car navigation solutions, and (iii) static mobile mapping applications may pose only a limited competitive constraint on the parties.[1285]

For these reasons, designating Apple Maps as the strongest competitor to Google Maps and noting that the parties were not close competitors, the OFT decided not to refer the transaction to the CC. For the market outcome analysis of the case, it is notable that the transaction was not evaluated as detrimental, given that some alternatives exist in the market in question.[1286]

Ladbrokes/Coral (2016)

The CMA considered online betting services in its Ladbrokes/Coral[1287] decision, which was related to the acquisition of Coral, the holding company of a betting and gaming group, by Ladbrokes, which operated betting and gaming business in the UK.

Both Ladbrokes and Coral operated licensed betting offices ("LBOs") in the UK. Ladbrokes and Coral stated that the merger would provide several opportunities (such as faster online growth) and significant synergies with the creation of the UK's largest LBO estate. Ladbrokes and Coral were also two of the largest national LBO operators in the UK, in addition to the other two leading licensed betting shop operators, namely William Hill and Betfred. In paragraph 8 of its final report, the CMA determined that the number of LBOs operated by such leading national LBO operators and their gross gambling yields had remained stable while noting that this industry had shown

---

[1283] *Id.*, paras. 29–73.
[1284] *Id.*, paras. 29–52.
[1285] *Id.*, paras. 53–73.
[1286] Lear Report, *supra* note 1072, paras. II.138–II.142.
[1287] CMA, Ladbrokes and Coral: A Report on the Anticipated Merger between Ladbrokes plc and Certain Businesses of Gala Coral Group Limited (July 26, 2016), https://assets.publishing.service.gov.uk/media/5797818ce5274a27b2000004/ladbrokes-coral-final-report.pdf.

significant improvement in the online channel. The CMA defined the relevant market as (i) the supply of betting and gaming (together referred to as "gambling") products and (ii) the operation of greyhound tracks, in which the parties' activities overlapped.[1288]

During its merger analysis, the CMA examined whether the transaction would create any effects on innovation. In the social theories of harm evaluation, the CMA assessed whether there were any losses of competition relating to innovation. The parties claimed that there were limited innovations in terms of the products in the retail betting industry, and the growth of the online channel had an impact on the retail sector.[1289] However, based on third parties' evidence and documents, the CMA concluded that the innovations were provided by the LBO operators but developed by third parties. The CMA set forth that the sources of innovation were not limited to retail competitors, and also declared that the competitive interaction between the parties was not considered the source of innovation.[1290] Therefore, the CMA assessed the role of innovation in the retail sector along with the effect of the online channel and suppliers. As for the theory of harm involving loss of innovation, the CMA then concluded that the parties were not particularly innovative players and decided that the merger was not expected to result in an SLC at the national level under the loss of innovation.[1291] Consequently, the CMA accepted the undertakings in lieu that had been offered by Ladbrokes and Gala Coral concerning divesture sales of Ladbrokes or Coral LBOs.[1292]

Just Eat/Hungryhouse (2017)

The CMA's review of online platforms in the UK continued with the CMA's decision on *Just Eat/Hungryhouse*,[1293] where both parties operated a food-ordering marketplace in the UK. Hungryhouse was a subsidiary of the German giant Delivery Hero, which owns several food-ordering marketplaces in various jurisdictions, such as Foodpanda, yemeksepeti.com, and Subdelivery.[1294] Holding those food-ordering marketplaces to be two-sided in nature since their services relate to two distinct and unrelated groups of customers (i.e., restaurants on one side and consumers on the other), the CMA defined the relevant market as the "supply of online food platforms in the UK."[1295] In line with the two-sided nature of the market, the CMA evaluated its sole theory of harm on the loss of a supplier of food-ordering platforms in the UK, inter alia on the question of whether customers and restaurants might be harmed through degraded platform functionality

---

[1288] *Id.*, para. 9 (Summary).

[1289] *Id.*, para. 9.54 (Findings).

[1290] *Id.*, para. 44 (Summary).

[1291] *Id.*, paras. 44–45 (Summary).

[1292] CMA, Merger between Ladbrokes Plc and Certain Businesses of Gala Coral Group Limited, Notice of acceptance Final Undertakings pursuant to §§ 41 and 82 of, and Schedule 10 to, the Enterprise Act 2002 (Oct. 11, 2016), https://assets.publishing.service.gov.uk/media/57fdfb66ed915d25be000000/final-undertakings-and-notice-for-publication.pdf.

[1293] CMA, JUST EAT AND HUNGRYHOUSE: A REPORT ON THE ANTICIPATED ACQUISITION BY JUST EAT PLC OF HUNGRYHOUSE HOLDINGS LIMITED (Nov. 16, 2017), https://assets.publishing.service.gov.uk/media/5a0d6521ed-915d0ade60db7e/justeat-hungryhouse-final-report.pdf.

[1294] Delivery Hero SE Annual Report (2018), https://ir.deliveryhero.com/download/companies/delivery/Annual%20 Reports/Final_secured_en.pdf.

[1295] CMA, *supra* note 1293, paras. 7, 4.1–4.36.

and worse user experience, and loss of innovation with respect to the services offered to them.[1296] Having obtained the expansion plans of the parties' competitors – namely, Deliveroo and Uber Eats – which was a candid effort to do a balanced analysis, the CMA stated that the actors in the relevant market regularly sought to implement incremental innovations offered to their customers, based on the evidence in the case.[1297] In line with this finding, the CMA established that the transaction would not raise an SLC concern.[1298] Although the CMA strongly relied on the "failing firm" defense to reach its decision, the approach also reinforces the author's premise that if the agencies are willing to shoulder the evidentiary burden with regard to innovation defenses and adopt a more symmetrical approach by conducting detailed market analysis of innovation, there can be a balanced outcome in competition enforcement.

5.4.3.1 Meta/Giphy (2021)

The *Meta/Giphy* case constitutes one of the prominent examples where the CMA applied the approach under the Revised Merger Guidelines regarding dynamic competition and the preservation of future innovative efforts of the transaction parties. The transaction related to the merger between Facebook, Inc. (now Meta Platforms, Inc.) and GIPHY, Inc. Meta is the largest provider of social media and messaging services in the UK, while GIPHY is considered to be the world's leading provider of free GIFs and GIF stickers.[1299] The acquisition was referred to a Phase II investigation[1300] following Meta's refusal to offer undertakings.

The CMA found serious concerns both horizontally and vertically and explained that the SLC would occur in "the supply of display advertising in the UK due to horizontal unilateral effects from a loss of dynamic competition ('Horizontal SLC')."[1301] While reaching this conclusion, the CMA gave special consideration to potential innovation efforts. By way of carrying out a counterfactual analysis of the likely future competitive situation in the market, the CMA found that absent the merger, GIPHY "would have continued to innovate (and) develop its products and services."[1302] The CMA also evaluated that "GIPHY's efforts to innovate and monetise its services prior to the Merger were valuable" and "[b]y removing GIPHY as an independent competitor, the Merger has eliminated this form of 'dynamic' competition."[1303]

The CMA also stated that although there may be uncertainty regarding the outcome of innovation efforts that would be made absent the merger, this "does not preclude the

---

[1296] *Id.*, paras. 6.96–6.97.

[1297] *Id.*, para. 6.42.

[1298] The CMA also heavily relied on Hungryhouse having incurred losses for the last several years, and on the fact that Hungryhouse was notably unsuccessful in the areas in which neither Deliveroo nor Uber Eats operated, so this decision also appears to be a victory for the "failing firm" defense.

[1299] CMA, Completed Acquisition by Facebook, Inc (Now Meta Platforms, Inc) of Giphy, Inc. (Final Report) (Nov. 30, 2021), para. 4, https://assets.publishing.service.gov.uk/media/61a64a618fa8f5037d67b7b5/Facebook__Meta__GIPHY_-_Final_Report_1221_.pdf.

[1300] CMA, Completed Acquisition by Facebook, Inc. of GIPHY, Inc., Decision to Refer (Apr. 1, 2021), https://assets.publishing.service.gov.uk/media/60659715e90e074e485062e1/Facebook_GIPHY_-_Decision_to_refer.pdf.

[1301] *Id.*, para. 10.2(a).

[1302] *Id.*, para. 31.

[1303] *Id.*, para. 43.

CMA from assessing the impact of a merger on that dynamic process."[1304] Ultimately, in order to address the concerns relating to a substantial lessening of competition, the CMA required Meta to divest GIPHY to a suitable purchaser. Following Meta's appeal, the Competition Authority Tribunal ("CAT") sided with the CMA in its judicial review, stating that the test was correctly applied and that "the CMA acted rationally in order to put itself in a position properly to apply the substantial lessening of competition test in a case of dynamic competition."[1305] The CAT agreed with Meta on a single issue of procedure, noting that certain third-party confidential material was erroneously not disclosed to the parties.[1306] In its reconsideration following appeal, the CMA again concluded that "the only way to avoid the significant impact the deal would have on competition is for Giphy to be sold off in its entirety to an approved buyer."[1307]

The CMA decision requiring to unwind the transaction is a milestone, in terms of both employing structural remedies against a leading technology company and labeling Meta's strategic position within the UK.[1308] The Commission and a large number of national competition authorities around the world have been publicly criticized for allowing big technology companies to acquire their rather smaller competitors in the past,[1309] the most prominent one being Facebook's acquisition of WhatsApp, which was cleared by the Commission back in 2014.[1310] In this regard, the *Meta/Giphy* acquisition was the CMA's first chance to apply a stricter merger control review on significant technology companies without the shadow of the EU rules and case law following Brexit. Whether this was a welfare-enhancing interference happens to be a different debate that needs to be undertaken through the principles discussed in this book, in terms of finding the right balance.

Conclusion on Case Review

As discussed above, the UK's competition authorities tend to evaluate these cases on the basis of the following: (i) innovation competition between the transaction parties, (ii) the parties' incentives to innovate, and (iii) the number and ability of innovative competitors after the completion of the transaction. The competition authorities also take into account the nature of the relevant market, i.e., whether the market in question is a dynamic one. It may also be inferred from the competition authorities' deliberations

---

[1304]   Revised Merger Guidelines, para. 5.2.

[1305]   Meta Platforms, Inc. v. CMA Replace with neutral citation? [2022] CAT 26, https://www.catribunal.org.uk/cases/142941221-meta-platforms-inc.

[1306]   CMA, COMPLETED ACQUISITION BY FACEBOOK, INC (NOW META PLATFORMS, INC) OF GIPHY, INC. (Final Report on the case remitted to the CMA by the Competition Appeal Tribunal) 7(Oct. 18, 2022), https://assets.publishing.service.gov.uk/media/635017428fa8f53463dcb9f2/Final_Report_-_Meta.pdf.

[1307]   CMA Press Release, CMA Orders Meta to Sell Giphy (Oct. 18, 2022), https://www.gov.uk/government/news/cma-orders-meta-to-sell-giphy.

[1308]   Tom Smith, *CMA Blocks the Facebook/GIPHY Merger: You Can't Say They Didn't Warn Us*, THE PLATFORM LAW BLOG (Dec. 7, 2021), https://theplatformlaw.blog/2021/12/07/cma-blocks-the-facebook-giphy-merger-you-cant-say-they-didnt-warn-us.

[1309]   Mark Sullivan, *Facebook Should Never Have Been Allowed to Buy Instagram, Silicon Valley Rep Says*, FAST-COMPANY (Jan. 25, 2019), https://www.fastcompany.com/90297261/facebook-should-never-have-been-allowed-to-buy-instagram-silicon-valley-rep-says.

[1310]   European Commission Press Release IP/14/1088, Mergers: Commission Approves Acquisition of WhatsApp by Facebook (Oct. 3, 2014), https://ec.europa.eu/commission/presscorner/detail/en/IP_14_1088.

in these precedents that third parties generally raise these concerns in the course of the authorities' consultations with the public during an investigation.

In some instances, the competition authorities evaluated the nature of the relevant market in an optimistic manner. For example, in *Ericsson/Creative*, the tendering process appeared as a motivation for other players in the market to place superior bids; therefore, even though there might have been concerns about a lessening of innovation, it was thought that the multistage nature of bids could mitigate the negative outcomes of the transaction. The competition authorities also considered the possibility that IP rights could be used as a tool to restrict innovation competition, as in *MasterCard/VocaLink*. Furthermore, the competition authorities have also assessed the parties' endeavors to invest in R&D activities as an indicator of a robust, innovative competitor in, for instance, the *Getty Images/Digital Vision and Photonica* case and the *Aviagen Group/Hubbard Holding* case.

Concerning dynamic markets, the possibility of a product's rapid emergence is generally assessed as a competitive restraint on incumbent firms, as exemplified in the *Research Machines/Sentinel* and *Cirrus Logic/Wolfson* cases. In other instances, such as *Akzo Nobel/Metlac* and *Thermo Electron/GV*, in markets with high entry barriers, the loss of an innovative competitor led to the elimination of innovation competition, from the competition authorities' perspective – their idea being that a monopoly or duopoly would be unlikely to innovate. In *BT Group/EE Limited*, the CMA also acknowledged that the commitments proffered to a regulatory body could somehow obviate the requirement to provide undertakings in lieu, in cases where an SLC is deemed to be likely to arise. The recent *Facebook/Giphy* case demonstrates that the CMA is going to be taking a stricter view with regard to transactions in dynamic markets, bolstered by the Revised Merger Guidelines.

With respect to online platforms, the competition authorities have a wide range of precedents to pick from, owing to the "share supply test" of section 23(3) EA. As in *Google/BeatThatQuote*, *Priceline/Kayak*, and *Just Eat/Hungryhouse*, the competition authorities also tend to take into account the two-sided nature of online marketplaces in their analysis. Furthermore, they seek alternative online platforms in their assessments of mergers between close innovative competitors, as seen in *Facebook/Instagram*, *Priceline/Kayak*, *Motorola/Waze*, and *Just Eat/Hungryhouse*.

As discussed above, *Just Eat/Hungryhouse* also demonstrates that it is possible for agencies to adopt a more balanced approach when it comes to assessing innovation, notwithstanding the burden required. It is also apparent from a review of the cases that, where there are other defenses available to the parties against the authorities' theory of harm regarding the transaction, the parties have not raised defenses based on innovation efficiencies. Whether this stems from the fact that there were no suitable innovation efficiencies to be raised, or if the transaction parties meant they focused more on non-innovation-related arguments as a cost-effective defense strategy in the limited time granted, is not clear. A more flexible approach to innovation defenses may thus allow more open and balanced debates on innovation concerns.

5.5 What Does Brexit Entail for Innovation Considerations in the UK?

March 29, 2019, which was the initial date proposed by the UK for putting Brexit into effect, has come and gone. The UK and the EU have concluded a withdrawal agreement, but internal conflict remained, with the UK Parliament rejecting the agreement thrice and resulting in a change of prime minister from Theresa May to Boris Johnson on July 24, 2019. After unsuccessful attempts to reach a consensus on the terms, the UK exited the European Union "without a deal," with the transition period ending on December 31, 2020.

Whatever the future of Brexit may be, aiming to provide legal certainty to businesses and to prevent the duplication of regulatory efforts, as well as avoiding potential enforcement gaps,[1311] the CMA has entered into a transition period in order to prepare itself for the consequences of Brexit.[1312] This is because, once Brexit took effect, and the UK left the EU, the Commission's jurisdiction no longer extends to the UK.[1313] According to the withdrawal agreement, the EU and the UK have agreed to follow the fundamental principles of EU competition law. During the transition period, EU competition law rules continued to apply to the UK as if it were still an EU Member State. After the transition period, the UK and the EU will be able to agree to align their evaluation of competition law matters for the long term.[1314]

In this case, under a no-deal Brexit, there were a few scenarios that came into play during the transition period, where the EU retained exclusive jurisdiction upon the "live" cases, i.e., cases that were under review by the European Commission or the CMA during and at the end of the transition period:[1315] where a merger has been formally notified to the Commission so that the "date of notification" falls before the end of the transition period or where the Commission has accepted article 22 or article 4(5) referral requests as per the EUMR, before the end of the transition period 4(5).[1316] As for jurisdiction thresholds regarding merger assessments, the UK turnovers of the transaction parties were included in the calculation of their total EU turnovers, during the transition period.

[1311] European Competition Lawyers Forum (ECLF) prepared a paper with similar concerns in mind. *See* ECLF, *Brexit and Merger Control in the EU: A Proposed Way Forward*, 13 Eur. Competition J. 151 (2017).

[1312] In fact, the CMA has published several guidelines and guidance documents on this matter. *See generally* CMA, Guidance on the Functions of the CMA After a 'No Deal' Exit from the EU (CMA106) (Mar. 2019), https://assets.publishing.service.gov.uk/government/uploads/system/uploads/attachment_data/file/786749/EU_Exit_Guidance_Document_for_No_Deal_final.pdf; CMA, Merger Review and Anti-competitive Activity if There's No Brexit Deal (Sept. 13, 2018), https://www.gov.uk/guidance/merger-review-and-anti-competitive-activity-after-brexit (the earlier version of this document was withdrawn and replaced with a new version on Aug. 8, 2019), CMA, Merger Cases if There's No Brexit Deal (Oct. 30, 2018), https://www.gov.uk/government/publications/cmas-role-in-mergers-if-theres-no-brexit-deal/cmas-role-in-mergers-if-theres-no-brexit-deal.

[1313] John Schmidt, *Hard or Soft Brexit: What Happens to Merger Reviews?* Arnold & Porter (Oct. 2, 2018), https://www.arnoldporter.com/en/perspectives/publications/2018/10/hard-or-soft-brexit-what-happens-to-merger-reviews.

[1314] *Brexit: UK Competition Law in a Deal or No Deal Scenario,* Linklaters Insights (2018),

[1315] CMA, UK Exit from the EU: Guidance on the Functions of the CMA under the Withdrawal Agreement (CMA113) (Jan. 28, 2020), https://www.gov.uk/government/publications/uk-exit-from-the-eu-guidance-on-the-functions-of-the-cma-under-the-withdrawal-agreement.

[1316] *Id.* at 14.

Notwithstanding the above, the UK's relations with the EU post the transition period still remain subject to negotiations, and the CMA emphasizes that there may be future updates and amendments to the guidance.

Accordingly, Brexit caused the UK competition law regime to face notable uncertainty since 2016.[1317] The main practical impact of Brexit on merger control appears to be that the one-stop shop across the 28 Member States provided by the EUMR no longer applies to the UK. As a direct result of that (assuming the transaction triggers the jurisdictional thresholds under both regimes), now merger control clearances are required from both the CMA and the Commission while pre-Brexit, the transition parties could have benefitted from the one-stop-shop principle and would make only one notification.[1318]

Brexit was expected to result in a drastic increase in the number of merger control filings before the CMA.[1319] Such an increase was envisioned for several reasons, such as (i) EU merger control would not be applicable after the transition period,[1320] (ii) the one-stop-shop principle provided in the EUMR[1321] would also not be applicable,[1322] and (iii) the voluntary notification system, which the UK holds might cause detrimental effects on the transactions that are closed without obtaining the CMA's approval, if the CMA were to be alarmed due to the negative effect of the transaction on competition, which might result in legal uncertainty.[1323]

In parallel with the above, the CMA had acknowledged that it expected approximately 30 to 50 more Phase I cases in its written evidence to the Parliament.[1324] As stated in its report, the CMA believed that since many large companies already had to file mergers in multiple jurisdictions, an additional UK filing might not necessarily be a significant additional burden for the companies, and considering many practical similarities between the EU and UK merger review processes, this may mitigate the burden over the companies' shoulders.[1325] Accordingly, the CMA kept its expectations high and planned for an increase of around 50% in the number of merger control cases following the UK's departure from the EU.[1326]

[1317] Maher M. Dabbah, *Brexit and Competition Law: Future Directions of Domestic Enforcement* (2020), 43, WORLD COMPETITION 107 (2020), https://kluwerlawonline.com/journalarticle/World+Competition/43.1/WOCO2020006.

[1318] Vincent Power, *The Implications of Brexit for Competition Law – An Irish Perspective*, 20 IRISH J. EUR. L. 1 (2017), https://ssrn.com/abstract=3833915.

[1319] Sarah Long & Gavin Robert, *Losing the 'One-Stop-Shop': The Real Cost of a Dual UK/EU Merger Process Post Brexit* (Oct. 2, 2018), https://ssrn.com/abstract=3299017.

[1320] European Commission, Notice to the Stakeholders – Withdrawal of the United Kingdom and EU Rules in the Field of Competition (2019), at 4–5.

[1321] Council Regulation No. 139/2004 of Jan. 20, 2004, on the Control of Concentrations Between Undertakings.

[1322] Meaning separate investigations by the European Commission (under the EUMR) and the CMA (under the Enterprise Act 2002). *See* Bruce Lyons, David Reader & Andreas Stephan, *UK Competition Policy Post-Brexit: Taking Back Control While Resisting Siren Calls*, 5 J. ANTITRUST ENFORCEMENT 347 (2017).

[1323] Amanda Persson, Merger Control Post-Brexit – An Analysis of the Future EU-UK Relationship and the Potential Effects on UK Merger Control (2018) (Master thesis, Lund University, Sweden), http://lup.lub.lu.se/student-papers/record/8944192.

[1324] CMA, Written Evidence (CMP0002) (2018), para. 34, http://data.parliament.uk/writtenevidence/committeeevidence.svc/evidencedocument/eu-internal-market-subcommittee/brexit-competition/written/69571.pdf.

[1325] *Id.*, paras. 34–35.

[1326] CMA, COMPETITION AND MARKETS AUTHORITY ANNUAL PLAN 2021/22 7–8 (CMA137) (Mar. 2021), https://assets.publishing.service.gov.uk/government/uploads/system/uploads/attachment_data/file/972070/CMA_Annual_Plan_2021_to_2022_---.pdf.

So, did this increase in the CMA workload come to pass? According to its Annual Report for 2021/22, the CMA expected to enter the new year with a substantial volume of ongoing work and already had 11 competition enforcement cases, 11 consumer enforcement cases, 25 merger investigations (including three Phase II reviews), 2 market studies, and 2 regulatory appeals at the time of publication, i.e., March 2021.[1327] Looking back, the CMA seems to have proven right in its expectations, given that it entered the new year with a substantial caseload, comprising 12 competition enforcement cases, 10 consumer protection cases, 32 merger investigations (including 5 Phase II reviews), 3 market studies and a market investigation as of March 2022,[1328] which is higher in comparison with the previous years, as per the CMA's most recent Annual Report for 2022/23. Consequently, it is fair to expect the authority to be more active in the near future, to handle the drastic increase in the global merger and acquisition activity and corresponding caseload increase before the CMA, especially where post-Brexit jurisdiction and powers of the CMA are taken into account.

Furthermore, looking from the anti-competitive enforcement perspective in terms of jurisdiction, application of articles 101 and 102 TFEU to competition law infringements in the UK will not be possible for the CMA nor for the UK sectoral regulators with concurrent competition law powers, as all such directly applicable EU law will no longer apply in the UK. However, unless agreed otherwise, if anti-competitive conduct has had an effect on trade within the UK and also in other EU Member States, it may be investigated by both the CMA/UK sectoral regulators and the Commission at the same time.[1329] Furthermore, the Commission will be unable to launch new EU competition law investigations into infringements (e.g., pan-European cartels) that affect the UK markets.[1330] As for the regulations that exempt certain types of conduct from the prohibition of anti-competitive agreements (called the block exemption arrangements), these arrangements provide vital predictability for businesses that rely on them, due to their continuity.[1331] Following the end of the Brexit transition period, the parallel exemptions regime ceases to exist, but the beneficiaries of parallel exemptions before the end of the transition period will continue to benefit from the EU block exemptions regulations via the retained exemptions.[1332]

Finally, with respect to the competition principles based on EU State aid, EU State aid rules will remain relevant for those state aids granted before the end of the transition period, but will not otherwise be applicable for the UK.[1333] In its place, the Subsidy

---

[1327] *Id.* For comparison purposes, the CMA reviewed a total of 62 merger reviews (13 referred to Phase II), 4 investigations and 5 market studies between April 1, 2019, and March 31, 2020.

[1328] CMA, COMPETITION AND MARKETS AUTHORITY ANNUAL PLAN 2022/23 (CMA155) (Mar. 24, 2022), https://assets.publishing.service.gov.uk/government/uploads/system/uploads/attachment_data/file/1062414/Final_Annual_Plan_for_2022_23.pdf.

[1329] CMA, Guidance on the Functions of the CMA after the End of the Transition Period (CMA125) (Dec. 1, 2020), https://www.gov.uk/government/publications/guidance-on-the-functions-of-the-cma-after-the-end-of-the-transition-period.

[1330] *See also* European Commission, Directorate-General for Competition (Dec. 2, 2020), https://ec.europa.eu/info/sites/default/files/brexit_files/info_site/eu-competition-law_en_0.pdf.

[1331] CMA, *supra* note 1329, para. 4.32.

[1332] The Competition SI amends section 10 CA98 by substituting "parallel exemptions" with "retained exemptions."

[1333] Ilze Jozepa, *EU State Aid Rules and WTO Subsidies Agreement*, HOUSE OF COMMONS LIBRARY (Aug. 4, 2021), https://researchbriefings.files.parliament.uk/documents/SN06775/SN06775.pdf.

Control Bill (based on the WTO Agreement on Subsidies and Countervailing Measures) has been introduced, as the UK government has expressed a belief that it needs a different state aid regime to protect the British industry after Brexit, and to make it faster and easier for the government to protect jobs in struggling industries.[1334]

Similar to how the future of the merger control regime is yet to be determined, the future of innovation considerations in the UK merger control regime is not entirely clear. Even though the CMA has recognized innovation as a factor in its analysis of SLC, one can argue that the substantial analysis undertaken by the CMA with regard to innovation will continue as before, and increase in number, parallel to the cases following Brexit. In fact, transactions that were previously out of the scope of the jurisdiction of the UK competition authorities, which typically comprise the most significant mergers and acquisitions (such as the well-known recent innovation cases of *Dow/DuPont* and *Bayer/Monsanto* – both of which were reviewed by the Commission), will now find themselves under the microscope of the CMA.[1335] It is yet early to say whether the CMA will still follow the Commission's lead or have a different approach, although there are some indications that not all results will be identical: In 2021, out of the twelve parallel review cases, two had different outcomes,[1336] and the expectation is that this divergence will be a rare occurrence considering that authorities employ similar economic concerns and theories of harm.

Having said that, the UK's approach to the *Illumina/Grail* merger was particularly interesting in terms of procedural boundaries. As discussed in Chapter 7, the Commission had prohibited the implemented acquisition of Grail by Illumina following an in-depth investigation that was initiated upon a complaint dated December 7, 2020. According to the General Court's judgment, the complainant who contacted the Commission had also been in contact with the CMA.[1337] As such, it is understood that the CMA, too, carried out a preliminary examination regarding the concentration at issue in November and December of 2020.[1338] The CMA's decision concluding its preliminary examination with regard to *Illumina/Grail* concentration and not proceeding further is not publicly available; however, it is speculated that the CMA did not conduct an in-depth investigation since the transaction did not exceed the merger control thresholds in the UK (and there was no nexus with the UK).[1339]

While the Commission acted in light of its policy change on article 22 EUMR, which regulates the Commission's ability to review subthreshold transactions at the request

---

[1334] HER MAJESTY'S STATIONERY OFFICE, THE BENEFITS OF BREXIT: HOW THE UK IS TAKING ADVANTAGE OF LEAVING THE EU (Jan. 2022).

[1335] Grenfell, *supra* note 1045.

[1336] Nicole Kar, Jonathan Ford, Lauren O'Brien & Aoife Monaghan, *Divergence Ratios after Brexit. Parallel EU/ UK Merger Reviews One Year on*, LINKLATERS INSIGHTS (Feb. 10, 2022), https://www.linklaters.com/de-de/insights/publications/platypus/platypus-uk-merger-control-analysis/twelfth-platypus-post---divergence-ratios-after-brexit-parallel-eu-uk-merger-reviews-one-year-on.

[1337] Case T-227/21, Illumina Inc. v. Commission, ECLI:EU:T:2022:447, para. 11.

[1338] *Id.*, paras. 186 & 213.

[1339] Jonathan Ford & Nayantara Ravichandran, *When Is a Jurisdictional GOAT Not Good Enough? UK Deal Nexus and the CMA's Expanded Hunt for 'Killer Acquisitions' and Harmful Vertical Mergers*, LINKLATERS INSIGHTS (June 1, 2022), https://www.linklaters.com/en/insights/publications/platypus/platypus-uk-merger-control-analysis/fourteenth-platypus-post---when-is-a-jurisdictional-goat-not-good-enough.

of one or more Member State competition authorities, the UK's current legislation in force does not provide a mechanism for transactions that do not meet the designated thresholds.[1340] As noted above, the merger control regime in the UK has two threshold options (turnover and share of supply) for a notification obligation. Certain scholars deem the share of supply test in the UK merger control regime to be flexible, since the CMA is able to claim jurisdiction over a transaction if the activities of the parties overlap in the supply of goods or services of any description[1341] where they have a combined share of at least 25% in the UK.[1342] CMA's approach to *Illumina/Grail* shows that "the share of supply test does have outer boundaries, elastic though they are" at this time.[1343]

Further to this particular case, the CMA's recent approach in *Microsoft/Activision* is also noteworthy in that the authority did not agree with the Commission (or the other competition authorities) on the sufficiency of remedies initially proposed by Microsoft and prohibited the transaction. With the help of a revised approach (through a new application that excludes Activision's non-EEA cloud streaming rights from the transaction by divesting them to Ubisoft), the CMA considered, as of September 22, 2023, that there are reasonable grounds that the restructured version of the transaction (or a modified version of it) might be accepted by the CMA.[1344]

5.6 Conclusion

As discussed above, the consideration of innovation-related issues in the UK shows much variation, depending on a multitude of factors. These factors include, among others, (i) the market (i.e., sector) characteristics, (ii) the incentives of the transaction parties to innovate, (iii) the number of innovative competitors in the market, and (iv) the general characteristics of the products or services in question. Although the competition authorities in the UK generally appear to have handled theories of harm systematically under both "horizontal and vertical issues" – and in some instances assessed either or both – there were also cases in which the CMA chose not to implement this reasoning. However, it is crucial to note that the most important issues in the view of the UK competition authorities were (i) the parties' motivation to innovate and (ii) the effect of the transaction on the number and capabilities of innovative competitors after the transaction.

The UK competition policy seeks to foster innovation for the benefit of consumers, and deems that the rivalry among undertakings inspires them to improve their own products

---

[1340] The National Security and Investment Act 2021 only lowered the thresholds for certain specific sectors. It came into force on January 4, 2022, applying retrospectively to all transactions completed after November 12, 2020.

[1341] Enterprise Act 2002 § 23(3)

[1342] Sean-Paul Brankin, *They Are Out to Get You. The EU and UK Extend the Scope of Merger Control to Catch More Pharma and Biotech Mergers*, BRISTOWS (Mar. 8, 2022), https://www.bristows.com/news/they-are-out-to-get-you/.

[1343] Kar et al., *supra* note 1336.

[1344] CMA, Microsoft / Activision Blizzard (ex-cloud streaming rights) Merger Inquiry, *supra* note 1251.

as well as innovate new ones, which puts them closer to the Arrowian view.[1345] Innovation is indeed becoming one of the foremost factors and non-price consequences taken into consideration by the CMA. Considering the challenges posed by emerging and fast-developing digital markets for post-merger counterfactuals, the CMA has underlined that the traditional assessment methodologies emphasizing price impacts may not be sufficient to adequately establish other indices of competition, such as quality and innovation.[1346] Having said that, while the CMA generally starts with the premise that increased concentration in the market could reduce innovation, it would still be expected to allow mergers where merger-specific innovation-related efficiencies are likely to outweigh the anti-competitive impact of a transaction. The burden of proof to establish that a merger is anti-competitive remains with the CMA; however, when efficiencies are used as a defense in merger analysis, this burden is reversed and lies with merging parties.[1347] This is because the firms are deemed better positioned to demonstrate the facts relevant to an efficiency claim[1348] or to assess synergies and cost reductions resulting from a transaction.[1349] Also, competition authorities do not wish to take on this burden unnecessarily due to the challenge of identifying and quantifying efficiencies prospectively,[1350] which may unfortunately deprive the firms of defenses based on rival or market-wide innovation incentives that the competition authority's access and analysis may have revealed. As a result, innovation effects are still seen more as a sword than a shield by the authorities, maintaining the asymmetric characteristic of the innovation paradox. There is also asymmetry in terms of what is known to the merging parties (and their defense counsel) and what could be known to the antitrust agency, such as the expansion plans of the competitors. If the burden of proof of efficiencies were to be shifted to the merging parties too quickly, there might be an entirely relevant set of information and data excluded from the whole analysis, avoiding a complex balancing act, and resulting in simplistic labeling.

One may deduce from their decisions that the UK competition authorities tend to focus more on innovation assessments in particular sectors, such as electronics. It is difficult to determine accurately whether the UK competition authorities have adopted this approach intentionally or subconsciously due to the unique characteristics of the markets and products themselves. One could potentially argue that it would not be possible for these competition authorities to review, for instance, the electronics and clothing sectors equally, in terms of the significance of innovation to these industries. Moreover, there are still several cases and precedents in many sectors, indicating that the UK competition authorities did not attribute innovation considerations solely to a couple of sector categories. One can easily argue that this discrepancy was a deliberate choice, as the UK competition authorities did not view innovation considerations as equally crucial for

---

[1345]   Revised Merger Guidelines.

[1346]   Coscelli, *supra* note 1071.

[1347]   CMA, Appendix F: The SMS Regime: A Distinct Merger Control Regime for Firms with SMS (2020), https://assets.publishing.service.gov.uk/media/5fce706ee90e07562d20986f/Appendix_F_-_The_SMS_regime_-_a_distinct_merger_control_regime_for_firms_with_SMS_-_web_-.pdf.

[1348]   OECD, *Competition Policy and Efficiency Claims in Horizontal Agreements* 41, 52 (OCDE/GD(96)65, 1996), https://www.oecd.org/daf/competition/2379526.pdf.

[1349]   CMA, *supra* note 1347.

[1350]   OECD, *supra* note 1348, at 5.

each separate sector category. This is evidenced in one of the earliest decisions, *Bayard Capital/Landis & GYR* (2004), where the OFT deemed innovation a significant dimension of competition in the electronics sector. As more and more transactions in dynamic markets grab the enforcement agencies' attention, and with the flexibility provided under the revised guidelines, these cases will increase in number.

On that note, the effect of Brexit on the UK's merger control regime also bears close watching: To what extent will the CMA apply the mechanisms and theories developed by the Commission in evaluating innovation? Will it diverge or venture to test out new waters regarding innovation assessments in merger control? So far, there have been few clues to conclusively answer this fundamental question, but it seems that the CMA will not be reluctant to challenge a merger, regardless of other competition authorities' assessments on the matter.

Chapter 6
Innovation Considerations in Merger Control in the USA

6.1 Introduction

Innovation embodies a continuous process that is based on cumulative knowledge arising from the interaction of divergent views. In other words, innovation can be appropriately considered a product of society's collective brain[1351] and is one of the most critical drivers of economic growth around the world.[1352] As the economic studies of Nobel laureate Robert Solow have demonstrated, 90% of the per-capita output increase between 1909 and 1949 was generated through technological improvements and innovations.[1353]

Competition enforcement authorities in the US have well recognized the value of innovation.[1354] The United States Department of Justice ("DOJ") officials have made numerous statements emphasizing the importance of innovation, declaring that "the more important that innovation becomes to society, the more important it is to preserve economic incentives to innovate,"[1355] and "as important as price competition is to us, a second major and possibly even greater concern is maintaining competition for innovation."[1356]

Having said that, no unified consensus can be observed on how to achieve more significant innovation in the market. As discussed earlier in Chapter 3, the conflicting views of Joseph Schumpeter and Kenneth Arrow have sparked the debate, with various theoretical and empirical studies trying to reconcile or disprove them. Regardless of their views or preference

---

[1351]   Michael Muthukrishna & Joseph Henrich, *Innovation in the Collective Brain*, 371 PHIL. TRANS. R. SOC. B 1 (2016) https://doi.org/10.1098/rstb.2015.0192.

[1352]   Rana P. Maradana, Rudra P. Pradhan, Saurav Dash, Kunal Gaurav, Manju Jayakumar & Debaleena Chatterjee, *Does Innovation Promote Economic Growth? Evidence from European Countries*, 6 J. INNOVATION & ENTREPRENEURSHIP (2017), art. 1; Michael L. Katz & Howard A. Shelanski, *Merger Policy and Innovation: Must Enforcement Change to Account for Technological Change?* in 5 INNOVATION POLICY AND THE ECONOMY 109, 110 (Adam B. Jaffe, Josh Lerner & Scott Stern eds, MIT Press 2006); Richard Gilbert, *Looking for Mr. Schumpeter: Where Are We in the Competition-Innovation Debate?* in 6 INNOVATION POLICY AND THE ECONOMY 159, 206 (Adam B. Jaffe, Josh Lerner & Scott Stern eds, MIT Press 2006), http://www.nber.org/chapters/c0208.pdf.

[1353]   Vikas Kathuria, *A Conceptual Framework to Identify Dynamic Efficiency*, 11 EUR. COMPETITION J. 319, 232 (2015).

[1354]   Katz & Shelanski, *supra* note 1352.

[1355]   US DEP'T OF JUST., ANNUAL REPORT, ANTITRUST DIVISION 5 (1999), as recalled by Katz & Shelanski, *supra* note 1352.

[1356]   Robert Kramer, Chief, Litigation II Section, Antitrust Div., Dep't of Just., Antitrust Considerations in International Defense Mergers, Address before the American Institute of Aeronautics and Astronautics, Arlington, Virginia 3 (May 4, 1999), as recalled by Katz & Shelanski, *supra* note 1352.

with respect to one of these approaches (i.e., Schumpeterian or Arrowian), competition enforcers will always seek to protect and further promote innovation. It is worth noting that the DOJ's Antitrust Division conducted an average of 107 merger investigations each year from 2000 to 2009, and approximately 70 merger investigations per year between 2010 and 2019.[1357]

Traditional merger policy in the United States mainly relied on conducting static analyses that focused primarily on the impact of the transaction on prices and generally disregarded dynamic considerations such as research and development.[1358] Today, however, innovation as "a force that could make static measures of market structure unreliable or irrelevant"[1359] plays a significant role in merger control assessments.[1360] Indeed, one of the main issues addressed explicitly by the (new) Horizontal Merger Guidelines of 2010, which was issued by the Federal Trade Commission's ("FTC") Bureau of Competition and the DOJ's Antitrust Division, was "restraints on innovation" along with the other substantive merger concerns of exclusion, unilateral effects, and coordinated effects.[1361] Furthermore, the Guidelines also specifically regulate any mergers that may have the effect of limiting innovation and reducing product variety.[1362]

Against this background, this chapter will seek to review the innovation considerations in merger assessments, as adopted by the competition authorities in the United States, in conjunction with the relevant theories of harm.

6.2 An Overview of the Framework for Evaluating Innovation Considerations in Merger Control in the United States

Prior to the Horizontal Merger Guidelines of 2010, innovation considerations in merger control e were addressed in the (i) 1968 Merger Guidelines, (ii) 1982 Merger Guidelines, (iii) 1984 Merger Guidelines (section 4 on vertical integration remained in effect), (iv) Horizontal Merger Guidelines of 1992 (which was also revised in 1997), and (v) 1995 Antitrust Guidelines for the Licensing of Intellectual Property (which was renewed in 2017). However, it was the long-awaited Horizontal Merger Guidelines of 2010 that addressed potential restraints on innovation as one of the substantive anti-competitive unilateral effects that must be assessed by competition enforcement authorities.[1363]

[1357]   US Dep't of Just., Antitrust Division Workload Statistics, 2000–2009, https://www.justice.gov/sites/default/files/atr/legacy/2012/04/04/281484.pdf; Antitrust Division Workload Statistics, 2010–2019, https://www.justice.gov/atr/file/788426/download.

[1358]   Katz & Shelanski, *supra* note 1352.

[1359]   *Id.* at 111.

[1360]   *Id.* at 110.

[1361]   Herbert Hovenkamp, *Harm to Competition Under the 2010 Horizontal Merger Guidelines*, 39 Rev. Indus. Org. 3, 3 (2011), https://www.jstor.org/stable/23885233.

[1362]   *Id.*

[1363]   US Dep't of Just. & Fed. Trade Comm'n, Horizontal Merger Guidelines (2010) § 6.4, https://www.ftc.gov/sites/default/files/attachments/merger-review/100819hmg.pdf.

The 1968 Merger Guidelines had opted for an approach based on *"pure structuralism,"*[1364] noting that those markets that are subject to rapid technological changes might not be defined in line with the traditional market definition criteria. However, the 1968 Merger Guidelines did not include any further explanations on this front. Other than this, the 1968 Merger Guidelines only referred to the concept of innovation within the framework of conglomerate merger assessment, as follows:

> [F]or example, the Department has used Section 7 to prevent mergers which may diminish long-run possibilities of enhanced competition resulting from technological developments that may increase inter-product competition between industries whose products are presently relatively imperfect substitutes.[1365]

Following the 1968 Merger Guidelines, the 1984 Merger Guidelines also touched upon the concept of innovation merely in an indirect manner, i.e., via an example concerning the changing market conditions: "[I]f a new technology that is important to long-term competitive viability is not available to a particular firm, the Department may conclude that the historical market share of the firm overstates the firm's future competitive significance."[1366]

Taking a similar approach, the Horizontal Merger Guidelines of 1992 (which were revised in 1997) also make a single reference to the concept of innovation in a footnote, by stating that "Sellers with market power also may lessen competition on dimensions other than prices, such as product quality, service, or innovation."[1367] Unfortunately, the issue merits no further discussion within the framework of the Horizontal Merger Guidelines of 1992, in line with the trivializing approach of the 1968 and 1984 Merger Guidelines for innovation considerations.

However, the 1995 Antitrust Guidelines for the Licensing of Intellectual Property ("1995 Licensing Guidelines") might be deemed to constitute a turning point on this front due to their policy improvements, most prominently by their creation of the concept of "innovation market."[1368] The 1995 Licensing Guidelines discuss this new concept in comparison with two long-standing views/characterizations of markets that were, indeed, more commonly used within the competition literature – (i) the goods market and (ii) the technology market – whereas the 1995 Licensing Guidelines defined an "innovation market" as "a market for research and development on goods or processes not yet in existence."[1369] However, the innovation markets' concept has been abandoned by antitrust practitioners in favor of returning the focus to produce markets because it has shifted

---

[1364] Hovenkamp, *supra* note 1361, at 7.

[1365] US Dep't of Just., Merger Guidelines (1968), para. 20, https://www.justice.gov/sites/default/files/atr/legacy/2007/07/11/11247.pdf.

[1366] US Dep't of Just., Merger Guidelines (1984), https://www.justice.gov/sites/default/files/atr/legacy/2007/07/11/11249.pdf; *see also* Hovenkamp, *supra* note 1361, at 7.

[1367] US Dep't of Just. & Fed. Trade Comm'n, Horizontal Merger Guidelines (1992, revised 1997), https://www.ftc.gov/sites/default/files/attachments/merger-review/hmg.pdf; *see also* Hovenkamp, *supra* note 1361, at 7.

[1368] Thomas L. Hayslett III, *1995 Antitrust Guidelines for the Licensing of Intellectual Property: Harmonizing the Commercial Use of Legal Monopolies with the Prohibitions of Antitrust Law*, 3 J. INTELL. PROP. L. 375 (1996), https://digitalcommons.law.uga.edu/cgi/viewcontent.cgi?referer=https://www.google.com/&httpsredir=1&article=1117&context=jipl.

[1369] *Id.*

the attention of competition authorities to the actual competition in innovation markets, instead of the potential competition in product markets.[1370]

The 1995 Licensing Guidelines also made significant references to the licensing practices in innovation-intensive markets and even stated that, in situations where the nature of a license or joint venture is related to innovation considerations, the transaction should instead be assessed as a merger.[1371] The 1995 Licensing Guidelines' approach to the concept of innovation in merger control was also observed in the 2017 Antitrust Guidelines for the Licensing of Intellectual Property.

Having said this, the FTC noted in its report on the Competition and IP Law hearings of 2002[1372] that an imbalance between competition and patent law and policy can have a negative impact on innovation. If the enforcement of antitrust laws is too aggressive and limits the use of a valid patent in a manner that fosters competition, it could potentially hinder the innovation that the patent system is designed to encourage.[1373] The report highlights the potential negative impacts of poor-quality patents and legal standards that may unintentionally favor anti-competitive practices. According to the report, poor patent quality could imply that patents are granted for ideas that are not genuinely novel or non-obvious. This could allow certain companies to gain undue control over a market, as they can prevent others from using the patented ideas, even if those ideas are somewhat trivial or obvious in the industry. Also, when patents are granted too easily, companies might find themselves having to pay to license numerous patents, or engage in expensive legal battles to challenge the patents. These costs could eventually be passed on to consumers, raising the prices of products or services. The mentioned factors can stifle competition that would otherwise stimulate innovation. When competition is reduced, companies may feel less pressured to innovate and improve, leading to stagnation in the industry.[1374] The report's emphasis on the need for legal procedures to ensure healthy competition and encourage innovation and criticism of the monopolization of patents approached closer to the Arrowian principles.

Following the 1995 Licensing Guidelines, the Horizontal Merger Guidelines of 2010 addressed restraints on innovation as the main concern of competition authorities in the category of "unilateral effects."[1375] The Guidelines contained a separate section (§ 6.4) on mergers that limit "innovation and product variety," which was concerned with "unilateral effects arising from diminished innovation or reduced product variety":

> [T]he Agencies may consider whether a merger is likely to diminish innovation competition by encouraging the merged firm to curtail its innovative efforts below the level that would prevail in the absence of the merger. That curtailment of innovation

---

[1370]   Michael L. Katz & Howard A. Shelanski, *Mergers and Innovation*, 74 ANTITRUST L.J. 1, 38 & 44 (2007), argued that the exercise of market definition is not able to capture all "the innovation-related effects of a merger."

[1371]   *See* Hovenkamp, *supra* note 1361.

[1372]   FED. TRADE COMM'N, TO PROMOTE INNOVATION: THE PROPER BALANCE OF COMPETITION AND PATENT LAW AND POLICY: A REPORT BY THE FEDERAL TRADE COMMISSION (Oct. 2003), https://www.ftc.gov/sites/default/files/documents/reports/promote-innovation-proper-balance-competition-and-patent-law-and-policy/innovationrpt.pdf.

[1373]   *Id.* at 3.

[1374]   *Id.* at 1.

[1375]   *Id.*

could take the form of reduced incentive to continue with an existing product-development effort or reduced incentive to initiate development of new products.[1376]

The overall historical legislative background of innovation considerations in US merger control has arrived at a point where the "emphasis is on diversion of supply through innovation," which, as Hovenkamp has stated, is a persuasive and cogent antitrust concern that has also been familiar to antitrust law from the very beginning of the 20th century.[1377] Recently, the DOJ and FTC have been working on revising the merger guidelines in order to modernize them to reflect the market realities, such as the effects of the digital transformation, the evolution of relationships and supply paths towards interconnected ecosystems and conglomerates, the rising significance of factors other than market definition, and to respond to the criticisms on their 2020 vertical merger guidelines.[1378] Innovation, intellectual property and digital markets are a few of the many areas that the DOJ and FTC have requested public comment for their review.[1379] It remains to be seen to what extent, if any, these issues will be addressed in the draft regulations.

6.3 Innovation Considerations in Horizontal Mergers

The merger of two competitors generally has two main effects on the market: (i) a decrease in the number of competitors and (ii) an increase in the level of market concentration. This increase in the level of market concentration may hamper competition in the relevant market, and thereby reduce the firms' incentives to innovate.[1380]

The initial approach to merger control in the US consisted of making an assessment based on the market share of the merged undertaking, in order to determine whether the proposed merger would hinder competition. This approach was endorsed and emphasized in the *Brown Shoe* case, where the Supreme Court stated that "the market share which companies may control by merging is one of the most important factors to be considered when determining the probable effects of the combination on effective competition in the relevant market."[1381] In 1967, this approach was once again affirmed by the Supreme Court, which stated that "possible efficiencies cannot be used as a defense to illegality."[1382]

Until 1974, the Supreme Court persisted in its formalistic view and considered "market share" as the primary indicator to be used for assessing whether a proposed merger

---

[1376] Horizontal Merger Guidelines § 6.4.

[1377] Hovenkamp, *supra* note 1361, at 6.

[1378] Jonathan Kanter, Assistant Att'y Gen., Antitrust Div., US Dep't of Just., Remarks to the New York State Bar Association Antitrust Section (Jan. 24, 2022), https://www.justice.gov/opa/speech/assistant-attorney-general-jonathan-kanter-antitrust-division-delivers-remarks-new-york.

[1379] Fraser Tennant, *Crackdown: FTC and DOJ Aim to Rewrite Merger Guidelines*, FINANCIER WORLDWIDE MAG. (Apr. 2022), https://www.financierworldwide.com/crackdown-ftc-and-doj-aim-to-rewrite-merger-guidelines#.Y2-OLnbP02w.

[1380] ROGER VAN DEN BERGH, COMPARATIVE COMPETITION LAW AND ECONOMICS 458 (Edward Elgar Publishing 2017).

[1381] Brown Shoe Co., Inc. v. United States, 370 US 294, 343 (1962).

[1382] FTC v. Procter & Gamble Co., 386 US 568, 580 (1967).

would be likely to hinder competition in the market.[1383] However, in its *United States v. General Dynamics Corporation* decision, the Supreme Court allowed the merger of two coal-mining corporations, by taking into account the non-market share concerns for the first time, stating that the proposed merger would not impede competition in the market since coal was not a resource to be recreated.[1384]

Today, innovation, as a non-market share concern, plays a vital role in merger control assessments in the US. As the above legislative history illustrates, innovation is now even evaluated under a separate section in the 2010 Horizontal Merger Guidelines, which reveals that the competition authorities consider the possibility that the merged undertaking might reduce innovation efforts.[1385] According to the 2010 Horizontal Merger Guidelines, (i) the incentive to continue with an existing product-development effort or (ii) the incentive to initiate the development of new products might decrease as a result of a proposed merger.[1386] The first decline in incentives might occur in the short run, in case a new product developed by one firm captures the revenues generated by the existing product(s) of the other transaction firm.[1387] On the other hand, the second type of reduction in innovation incentives might occur, in the long run, if one firm is likely to be able to develop new products that would capture the other firm's substantial revenues.[1388] The 2010 Horizontal Merger Guidelines further suggest that "combining two of a very small number of firms with the strongest capabilities to successfully innovate in a specific direction" may also harm innovation competition, and thus should not be disregarded by the agencies (the FTC and DOJ).[1389] The approach adopted by the 2010 Horizontal Merger Guidelines is expansive, and not necessarily contrary to Schumpeter's view, as it allows detecting the risk of a decrease in the incentives to innovate resulting from a merger that does not create a monopoly in the market for research and development.[1390]

Antitrust agencies in the US mainly evaluate and challenge horizontal mergers in terms of the "harm to innovation" under two particular theories of harm associated with the emergence of unilateral effects.[1391] Accordingly, a merger may be challenged due to (i) reduced actual competition in research and development, and (ii) harm to future competition.[1392]

The 2010 Horizontal Merger Guidelines do not put forth a specific test for potential competition.[1393] Instead, they provide what might be described as "narrow guidance" to firms

---

[1383] United States v. General Dynamics Corp., 415 US 486 (1974).
[1384] Marleina Paz, *Almost but Not Quite Perfect: The Past, Present and Potential Future of Horizontal Merger Enforcement*, 45 Loy. L.A. L. Rev. 1045, 9 (2012).
[1385] Horizontal Merger Guidelines at 23.
[1386] *Id.*
[1387] *Id.*
[1388] *Id.*
[1389] *Id.*
[1390] Josef Drexl, *Anti-Competitive Stumbling Stones on the Way to a Cleaner World: Protecting Competition in Innovation without a Market*, 8 J. Competition L. & Econ. 507, 520 (2012), as cited in Valeria Dardano, Assessing Innovation in Merger Control 14 (College of Europe 2016).
[1391] Horizontal Merger Guidelines
[1392] Benjamin R. Kern, *Innovation Markets, Future Markets, or Potential Competition: How Should Competition Authorities Account for Innovation Competition in Merger Reviews?* 37 World Competition 173 (2014), https://ssrn.com/abstract=2380130.
[1393] Dardano, *supra* note 1390, at 14.

on the potential approaches taken by the agencies on this front.[1394] It is actually the courts that have clarified through their jurisprudence how a merger could be challenged in terms of the harm to potential competition: (i) "the potential competitor must have an 'available feasible means' for entering the market" and (ii) "those means must 'offer a substantial likelihood of ultimately producing de-concentration… or other significant procompetitive effects.'"[1395]

In this context, the *Steris/Synergy* case[1396] is a relatively recent example illustrating the treatment of innovation considerations associated with the harm to potential competition. In *Steris/Synergy*, the FTC challenged the merger between Steris Corporation ("Steris") and Synergy Health plc ("Synergy"). The FTC argued that Synergy (i.e., the target firm in the transaction) was ready to enter the US market with its X-ray radiation sterilization (a new sterilization technology), and that Steris had abandoned that entry after the merger.[1397] According to the FTC, the merger had anti-competitive effects arising from the "elimination of the likely future competition from Synergy's deployment of X-ray sterilization in the United States."[1398] However, the Court did not accept the FTC's allegations, as it concluded that the evidence submitted by the FTC was insufficient to prove its allegations. The *Steris/Synergy* case is quite significant, as it demonstrates the FTC's sensitivity and responsiveness on the issue of innovation competition, and shows how difficult it is to prove the harm to potential competition before the US courts.

The competition authorities may also challenge mergers relating to markets that do not yet exist (namely, R&D or innovation markets) in the US.[1399] In such mergers, however, the potential competition doctrine does not apply.[1400] Gilbert and Sunshine have introduced a useful methodology and developed the following steps for assessing this type of harm:[1401]

1. Identify overlapping R&D activities of the merging firms
2. Identify alternative sources of R&D
3. Evaluate actual and potential downstream competitors of the merging parties
4. Assess how the increased concentration in R&D would affect investments in R&D
5. Evaluate how the merger would affect the efficiency of R&D[1402]

[1394] M. Sean Royall & Adam J. Di Vincenzo, *Evaluating Mergers Between Potential Competitors Under the New Horizontal Merger Guidelines*, 25 ANTITRUST 33, 33 (2010), https://www.gibsondunn.com/wp-content/uploads/documents/publications/RoyallDiVicenzo-HorizontalMergerGuidelines.pdf.

[1395] *Id.* at 33–38 (quoting the Supreme Court decision in *United States v. Marine Bancorporation*, as cited in DARDANO, *supra* note 1390, at 15).

[1396] In re Steris Corp., FTC File No. 151-0032 (2015), https://www.ftc.gov/enforcement/cases-proceedings/151-0032/sterissynergy-health-matter.

[1397] Maureen K. Ohlhausen, Antitrust Tales in the Tech Sector: Goldilocks and the Three Mergers and Into Muir Woods, Speech at the Antitrust in the Technology Sector: Policy Perspectives and Insights from the Enforcers, Palo Alto, CA (Jan. 26, 2016), https://www.ftc.gov/public-statements/2016/01/antitrust-tales-tech-sector-goldilocks-three-mergers-muir-woods.

[1398] *In re Steris Corp.*, para. 68.

[1399] DARDANO, *supra* note 1390, at 16.

[1400] Kern, *Supra* note 1392. Part II, as cited in DARDANO, *supra* note 1390, at 14.

[1401] DARDANO, *supra* note 1390.

[1402] Richard J. Gilbert & Steven C. Sunshine, *Incorporating Dynamic Efficiency Concerns in Merger Analysis: The Use of Innovation Markets*, 63 ANTITRUST L.J. 569, 595–597 (1995).

In practice, competition authorities first identify the merging parties' research and development efforts and then define a market for the research, development, manufacture, and sale of a particular product, which is, in most such cases, a pharmaceutical product.[1403] However, there have been several cases in which the agencies challenged mergers by way of applying the "innovation markets" theory, without being able to identify the innovation efforts in the relevant geographic market explicitly.[1404]

Agencies, while assessing the level of concentration in the market, do not focus solely on whether there are other undertakings active in the market other than the merging parties, but also consider their respective strengths in order to find out whether the merging parties are the ones that are most capable of undertaking R&D efforts.[1405] In the *Roche/Genentech* case, even though Roche was dealing with the preclinical studies and Genentech was in Phase I review for a particular drug, the FTC nevertheless imposed remedies on Roche with regard to the product that was still in the development phase. However, the drug was not ultimately brought into the market.[1406] This decision was criticized by commentators, including Carrier, who argued that there is no firm evidence of market concentration if the products in question are not at an advanced level of development; therefore, the FTC should not challenge or block the merger in such cases.[1407]

Furthermore, particular innovation-related concerns might arise if a non-existent market is involved.[1408] In the *Nielsen/Arbitron* case, the FTC's concern stemmed from the idea that the merger would lead to unilateral effects through the elimination of future competition in a market that did not yet exist.[1409] Accordingly, the FTC cleared the merger on the condition that the acquirer's assets would be divested.[1410] Although Nielsen and Arbitron were the most capable firms for the research and development of a cross-platform audience measurement service, such a product had not yet been developed or introduced into the relevant product market.[1411] On the other hand, Commissioner J. D. Wright, in his dissenting opinion about the decision, stated that the FTC had challenged the merger under a novel theory, alleging that the competition would be significantly harmed in a non-existent market.[1412] According to Commissioner J. D. Wright's view, predictive merger analysis should be avoided if the evidence at hand is limited or ambiguous, as there exists a risk that the

---

[1403] *See* Complaint, In re Pfizer & Warner-Lambert, No. C-3957 (F.T.C. June. 19, 2000), https://www.ftc.gov/sites/default/files/documents/cases/2000/07/pfizercmp.htm (as cited in DARDANO, *supra* note 1390, at 16).

[1404] *See* ZF/Allison merger, as recalled by Kern, *Supra* note 427 at 12.

[1405] *See* Roche Holdings Ltd, 113 FTC 1086 (1990), as cited in DARDANO, *supra* note 1390, at 17.

[1406] MICHAEL A. CARRIER, INNOVATION FOR THE 21ST CENTURY: HARNESSING THE POWER OF INTELLECTUAL PROPERTY AND ANTITRUST LAW 314 (Oxford Univ. Press 2009): "Firms in preclinical development should not be considered part of the relevant market and the most imminent harm is presented by merging firms in Phase III."

[1407] *Id.* at 322.

[1408] In re Nielsen Holding/Arbitron , FTC Matter No. 131 0058 (2014), https://www.ftc.gov/enforcement/cases-proceedings/131-0058/nielsen-holdings-nv-arbitron-inc-matter (as cited in DARDANO, *supra* note 1390, at 17).

[1409] *Id.,* § 12(b).

[1410] FTC Press Release, FTC Approves Final Order Settling Charges that Nielsen Holdings N.V.'s Acquisition of Arbitron, Inc. Was Anticompetitive (Feb. 28, 2014), https://www.ftc.gov/news-events/press-releases/2014/02/ftc-approves-final-order-settling-charges-nielsen-holdings-nvs.

[1411] Terrell McSweeny, Competition Law: Keeping Pace in a Digital Age, Keynote Remarks at the 16th Annual Loyola Antitrust Colloquium, Chicago Chronicle 5 (Apr. 15, 2016), https://www.ftc.gov/public-statements/2016/04/competition-law-keeping-pace-digital-age.

[1412] *Nielsen Holding/Arbitron* (Wright, J., dissenting), at 1.

results of the case might be affected by non-economic assessments, intuitions, and policy preferences.[1413] I find this fear and self-restraint refreshing, as such doubt helps foster a more complex and holistic look into all parameters of innovation theories of harm.

Several other important cases provide valuable insights concerning innovation considerations in the US merger control regime. For instance, the DOJ, in *United States et al. v. The Dow Chemical Company and E.I. Du Pont De Nemours and Company*,[1414] challenged the merger between Dow and DuPont, which were both leading companies in the markets for crop-protection chemicals and treated seeds. Furthermore, both companies were involved in manufacturing certain types of petrochemicals as well, which included the derivatives of high-pressure ethylene, e.g., the essential input for a significant number of other products and sectors. The DOJ alleged in its complaint that the merger (as proposed) would restrict competition in the relevant product markets for "broadleaf herbicides for winter wheat" and "chewing pest insecticides," and would form a monopoly in the markets for "acid copolymers and ionomers in the U.S." The DOJ arrived at this conclusion by hypothesizing that the proposed merger would lead not only to price increases but also to reduced levels of service and innovation, in these relevant product markets. Having said that, unlike the European Commission, the DOJ's innovation concerns in the case did not expand into "innovation spaces" or early pipeline products and R&D.[1415] As a result, the final judgment of the DOJ required: (i) DuPont to "divest its Finesse-formulated herbicide products and its Rynaxypyr-formulated insecticide products, along with the assets used to develop, manufacture, and sell those products," and (ii) Dow Chemical to "divest its Freeport, Texas, acid copolymers and ionomers manufacturing unit and associated assets."[1416]

In the *EagleView Technology/Verisk Decision*,[1417] the FTC challenged the proposed $650 million acquisition of EagleView Technology Corp. ("EagleView") by Verisk Analytics Inc. ("Verisk"). The FTC claimed that Verisk would "emerge as the only significant firm producing and selling Rooftop Aerial Measurement Products for insurance purposes,"[1418] since EagleView was the leading US provider of rooftop aerial measurement products used by insurance carriers. Although the FTC did not specifically define an "innovation market" regarding the market for "producing and selling rooftop aerial measurement products for insurance purposes," the concept of innovation nevertheless played a vital role in terms of determining the potential result of the proposed merger in the *EagleView Technology/Verisk* case. On that particular matter, the FTC stated that the competition between these two undertakings provided not only lower-priced alternatives for insurance carriers but also more choices, better service and quality, and increased innovation. The FTC referred to the innovative competition for products and services

---

[1413]   *Id.* at 3–4.
[1414]   United States et al. v. The Dow Chemical Co. and E. I. Du Pont De Nemours and Co., FTC No. 1-17-cv-01176 (D.D.C. filed June 15, 2017).
[1415]   The competitive impact assessments in this case do not specifically refer to pipeline products or products in innovation spaces. Coupled with a press release, we understand that, in the end, the DOJ did not advance such claims. *See* DOJ Press Release, Justice Department Requires Divestiture of Certain Herbicides, Insecticides, and Plastics Businesses in Order to Proceed with Dow-DuPont Merger (June 15, 2017), https://www.justice. gov/opa/pr/justice-department-requires-divestiture-certain-herbicides-insecticides-and-plastics.
[1416]   *United States et al. v. The Dow Chemical Co. and E. I. Du Pont De Nemours and Co.*
[1417]   In re Verisk/EagleView, No. 9363 (F.T.C. Dec. 16, 2014)
[1418]   *Id.*, para. 1.

between EagleView and Verisk with a real-world example, stating that "Verisk embarked on a program to capture aerial images with higher resolution imagery to win insurance carrier customers away from Eagle View."[1419] In this context, the FTC remarked that "to the extent there are merger-specific and verifiable efficiencies, they are insufficient to outweigh the Acquisition's likely harm" and arrived at the conclusion that the proposed acquisition agreement would constitute a violation of section 5 of the FTC Act.[1420]

In *Medtronic/Covidien*,[1421] the FTC challenged the proposed $42.9 billion merger between the two undertakings, where Covidien's pipeline product, a drug-coated balloon for the treatment of vascular diseases, was expected to compete with the existing similar products of Medtronic.[1422] The FTC stated that the proposed merger between Medtronic and Covidien in the market for the development, licensing, manufacturing, marketing, distribution, and sale of drug-coated balloon catheters indicated for the femoropopliteal ("fem-pop") artery would eliminate competition for Covidien's innovative product.[1423] The FTC indicated that the proposed merger would hinder competition in the relevant product market by (i) eliminating future competition between Medtronic and Covidien in the US market for drug-coated balloon catheters indicated for the fem-pop artery; (ii) increasing the likelihood that the combined entity would forego or delay the launch of one company's drug-coated balloon catheter indicated for the fem-pop artery; (iii) increasing the likelihood that the combined entity would delay, eliminate, or otherwise reduce the substantial additional price competition that would have resulted from an additional US supplier of drug-coated balloon catheters indicated for the fem-pop artery; and (iv) reducing research and development in the US market for drug-coated balloon catheters indicated for the fem-pop artery.[1424] The merger was eventually cleared by the FTC, subject to the divestiture of Covidien's drug-coated balloon business.[1425]

In the *Broadcom/Brocade Communications Systems* case,[1426] the FTC challenged the acquisition of Brocade Communications Systems Inc. ("Brocade") by Broadcom Limited ("Broadcom") for $5.9 billion. The FTC alleged that the proposed acquisition might be anti-competitive in its effects since it might give Broadcom access to the confidential business information of Cisco Systems, which was a significant competitor of Brocade. This type of information could potentially be used to restrict competition in the relevant product market and also to slow down innovation in "the market for fiber channel switches" globally. As per the FTC's complaint, (i) Cisco and Brocade were the only two rival firms in the market for fiber channel switches worldwide, and (ii) within the manufacturing of fiber channel switches, Broadcom supplied "application-specific integrated circuits" to both companies. The FTC also alleged that Broadcom, as the new owner of Brocade, might use Cisco's confidential business information to exercise market power by itself or

---

[1419]   *Id.*, para. 40.

[1420]   *Id.*, para. 47.

[1421]   Complaint, In Medtronic & Covidien, No. C-4503 (F.T.C. Jan. 13, 2015)https://www.ftc.gov/system/files/documents/cases/150121medtroniccovidiencmpt.pdf.

[1422]   Carles Esteva Mosso, Innovation in EU Merger Control, 66th ABA Section of Antitrust Law Spring Meeting 6 (Apr. 12, 2018), http://ec.europa.eu/competition/speeches/text/sp2018_05_en.pdf.

[1423]   *Id.* at 7.

[1424]   *Medtronic/Covidien.*

[1425]   *Id.*

[1426]   Decision and Order, In re Broadcom Limited/Brocade Communications Systems, No. C-4622 (F.T.C. Aug. 17, 2017).

to engage in coordinative behavior between Brocade and Cisco. The FTC surmised that this would ultimately make it more likely for fiber channel switch prices to increase. To propose a remedy for these concerns, the FTC issued a consent order to prevent Broadcom from using the competitively sensitive information (i.e., the trade secrets of Cisco), except for "designing, manufacturing, and selling fiber channel application-specific integrated circuits" for Cisco. This decision makes a clear reference to the potential harm to the innovative dynamics of the relevant product market, and further states that the proposed acquisition of Brocade by Broadcom might restrict competition.

In *United States et al. v. Comcast Corp., General Electric Co. and NBC Universal Inc.*,[1427] the DOJ filed a complaint against the proposed joint venture between Comcast Corporation ("Comcast"), General Electric Company ("GE"), NBC Universal, Inc. ("NBCU"), and Navy, LLC ("Newco"). The DOJ contended that, as a result of the proposed joint venture, Comcast, which was considered to be the largest US cable company at the time, would have control over the major part of a joint venture that controls a significantly valued video programming product that Comcast's competitors in the distribution of videos needed in order to be able to effectively compete in the relevant market. The DOJ also evaluated that the loss of current and future competition might result in decreases in the quality of the services, with fewer options, increased prices and reduced investments and innovation in the dynamic telecommunications technology sector. On that note, the DOJ explained the potential of online video distributors ("OVDs") by explicitly referring to the dynamic and innovative nature of the market:

> [R]ecognizing the enormous potential of OVDs, dozens of companies are inno-
> vating and experimenting with products and services that either distribute online
> video programming or facilitate such distribution. New developments, products,
> and models are announced on almost a daily basis by companies seeking to
> satisfy consumer demand.[1428]

In other words, the DOJ assessed the anti-competitive effects of the proposed transaction by addressing innovation considerations. The DOJ stated that restraints on innovation are "very likely to produce a far greater amount of economic harm than classical restraints on competition,"[1429] concluding that the proposed joint venture would negatively affect the incentive to innovate.[1430]

In *Pfizer/Hospira*, the FTC challenged the merger of Hospira and Pfizer by claiming that the proposed merger was likely to eliminate the actual, direct, substantial, and also future competition between these two companies.[1431] In order to alleviate the FTC's competition-related concerns, Pfizer Inc. agreed to sell the rights and assets related to four pharmaceutical products for settlement.[1432] While the European Commission had already assessed the possible

---

[1427] United States et al. v. Comcast Corp., General Electric Co. and NBC Universal, Inc., No. 1:11-CV00106 (D.D.C. filed Jan. 18, 2011).

[1428] *Id.*

[1429] *Id.*

[1430] *Id.* at S.3.

[1431] Complaint, In re Pfizer/Hospira, No. C-4537 (F.T.C. Aug. 24, 2015), https://www.ftc.gov/system/files/documents/cases/150824pfizerhospiracmpt.pdf.

[1432] *Id.*

adverse effects of the proposed merger on innovation and had obliged Pfizer to sell its pipeline product, the FTC did not explicitly evaluate the possible adverse effects of the merger on innovation.[1433] To that end, Comanor and Scherer have argued that the FTC might be underestimating the effects of mergers on innovation in the market in its decisional practice.[1434]

In *PowerReviews/Bazaarvoice*, the DOJ challenged the proposed acquisition and argued that the number of companies engaged in "feature-driven one-upmanship" and incentive to innovate in the market would be significantly reduced.[1435] The DOJ further indicated that, as a result of this acquisition, Bazaarvoice would eliminate its most significant rival and effectively insulate itself from the competition in the market.[1436] The Bazaarvoice and PowerReviews competed aggressively on price, resulting in significant savings to customers in the relevant product market of "product ratings and reviews platforms."[1437]

In *AT&T/T-Mobile*, which is one of the most significant cases in terms of the innovation considerations in merger control, the DOJ described the unique nature of telecommunications services before delving into the details of the anti-competitive effects of the proposed merger, and stated that "[i]nnovation in wireless technology drives innovation throughout our 21st-century information economy, helping to increase productivity, create jobs, and improve our daily lives."[1438] In this context, the FTC argued that the proposed merger was likely to reduce innovation and product variety by eliminating T-Mobile's competition in the relevant market. The FTC even provided an example to demonstrate its view of the potential market under a post-merger scenario, where "the innovation that an independent T-Mobile brings to the market – as reflected in the array of industry 'firsts' it has introduced in the past, such as the first Android phone, Blackberry e-mail, and the Sidekick – would also be lost, depriving consumers of important benefits."[1439]

In light of the foregoing considerations, the FTC concluded that the proposed acquisition would eliminate the overall innovation competition that an independent T-Mobile brings to the marketplace,[1440] after highlighting T-Mobile's recent plans to revitalize the company by returning to its roots as an innovation leader.[1441] The FTC also clearly demonstrated its approach towards the incentive to innovate by declaring that "unless this acquisition is enjoined, customers of mobile wireless telecommunications services likely will face

---

[1433]   Margrethe Vestager, Competition: The Mother of Invention, European Competition and Consumer Day (Apr. 18, 2016), https://ec.europa.eu/competition/publications/weekly_news_summary/2016_04_22.html

[1434]   William S. Comanor & F. M. Scherer, *Mergers and Innovation in the Pharmaceutical Industry*, 32 J. HEALTH ECON. 106, 107 (2013).

[1435]   Complaint, United States v. Bazaarvoice, Inc., No. C-13-0133 (JSC) (N.D. Cal. filed Jan. 10, 2013)

[1436]   *Id.*

[1437]   United States v. Bazaarvoice, Inc., Plaintiff United States of America's Post-Trial Proposed Findings of Fact (Oct. 31, 2013), https://www.justice.gov/atr/case-document/plaintiff-united-states-americas-post-trial-proposed-findings-fact-public-version.

[1438]   Complaint, United States v. AT&T, Inc., No. 1:11-cv-01560 (D.D.C. filed Aug. 31, 2011), para. 1.

[1439]   *Id.*, para. 38.

[1440]   *Id.*, para. 33; *see also* para. 40: "As a result, concentration will increase in many local markets and competition likely will be substantially lessened across the nation, resulting in higher prices, diminished investment, and less product variety and innovation than would exist without the merger, both with respect to services provided over today's mobile wireless devices, as well as future innovative devices that have yet to be developed."

[1441]   *Id.*, para. 31: "T-Mobile's future in a Nov./Dec. 2010 document titled 'T-Mobile USA Challenger Strategy: The Path Forward': Our heritage and future [are] as a challenger brand. TMUS will attack incumbents and find innovative ways to overcome scale disadvantages."; para. 36: "Through this proposed merger, AT&T

higher prices, less product variety and innovation, and poorer quality services due to reduced incentives to invest than would exist absent the merger."[1442]

Most recently, with respect to *Microsoft/Activision Blizzard*, the FTC issued an administrative complaint on December 8, 2022, seeking to block the acquisition of Activision by Microsoft, on the grounds that it would enable Microsoft to deny/degrade rival's access to popular gaming content and such conduct would be reasonably likely to substantially lessen competition in the US.[1443] The FTC later applied for a preliminary injunction, which the court denied as the FTC was unable to show it would likely succeed in its assertion that Microsoft would withdraw the game *Call of Duty* from Sony's PlayStation post-transaction or that there would be a substantial decrease in competition in the video game library subscription and cloud gaming markets.[1444] Considering the Commission's conditional approval of the transaction, the CMA's final approval of the restructured transaction submitted in August 2022 remains the only step before the acquisition.[1445]

6.4 Innovation Considerations in Non-Horizontal Mergers

There is a tendency among competition authorities to assume that non-horizontal mergers are less likely to raise competition law concerns, at least compared to horizontal mergers, as the merging firms do not operate in the same product market(s). This explains the fact that the Non-Horizontal Merger Guidelines[1446] in the US had not been revised for thirty-six years, whereas the Horizontal Merger Guidelines have been updated six times over the last fifty-one years.[1447] Accordingly, the treatment of vertical mergers had not been subject to revision until June 2020.[1448]

Competition enforcement authorities are also more prone to consider efficiency defenses for non-horizontal mergers, such as lower transaction costs, cost synergies, and improvement of distribution channels, among others. Non-Horizontal Merger

---

lessens this threat now, and, if the merger is approved, would eliminate it permanently. Its new aggressive and innovative pricing plans, low-priced smartphones, and superior customer service would have been likely to disrupt current industry models and require competitive responses from the other national players."

[1442] *Id.*, para. 3.

[1443] Administrative Complaint, In re Microsoft and Activision Blizzard, No. 9412 (F.T.C. Dec. 8, 2022), https://www.ftc.gov/system/files/ftc_gov/pdf/D09412MicrosoftActivisionAdministrativeComplaintPublicVersionFinal.pdf.

[1444] FTC v. Microsoft Corporation et al., No. 3:23-cv-02880-JSC (N.D. Cal. July 10, 2023).

[1445] Anna Langlois, *Microsoft/Activision Avoids US injunction, as UK Litigation Paused*, GCR (July 11, 2023), https://globalcompetitionreview.com/article/microsoftactivision-avoids-us-injunction-uk-litigation-paused. Microsoft has recently submitted a revised application to address the CMA's concerns, which the CMA will consider under a separate Phase I investigation (*see* Chapter 5 above for further details).

[1446] US Dep't of Just., Merger Guidelines (1984), https://www.justice.gov/sites/default/files/atr/legacy/2007/07/11/11249.pdf.

[1447] James Langenfeld, *The Need to Revise the U.S. Non-Horizontal Merger Guidelines*, in *What is Trump Antitrust?* Concurrences No. 4-2016, art. No. 82309.

[1448] US Dep't of Just. & Fed. Trade Comm'n, Vertical Merger Guidelines (June 30, 2020) ("2020 Guidelines"), https://www.ftc.gov/system/files/documents/reports/us-department-justice-federal-trade-commission-vertical-merger-guidelines/vertical_merger_guidelines_6-30-20.pdf.

Guidelines do, however, pose two conditions under which non-horizontal mergers carry the risk of causing a decrease in the level of competition in the relevant market: (i) entry barriers and (ii) facilitated collusion. Innovation-related concerns are also assessed within the scope of these potential anti-competitive outcomes. Indeed, in sectors where significant amounts of innovation are involved (e.g., digital), the merging parties' capability to innovate similar products in an ecosystem could result in certain anti-competitive concerns in terms of creating innovation, even in conglomerate mergers.[1449]

More commonly accepted theories of harm for vertical mergers would include higher entry barriers and foreclosure that would lead to reduced competitive pressures in the relevant market, which might result in decreased innovation competition. The merging undertakings might, for instance, disappear from the stage as a potential entrant or entry facilitator into the other firm's market.[1450] Some scholars have further argued that vertical mergers could also lead to raises in the costs of downstream rivals, in case the merged entity (i) refuses to sell or degrades the quality of its products in the upstream market, (ii) raises the input price for the downstream rivals, or (iii) restricts their cost-effective ability to expand.[1451] In these instances, vertical mergers might cause higher prices and/or less innovation in the relevant market. The innovation theories of harm regarding conglomerate mergers might emerge in numerous ways, such as reduced research and development incentives of the entrants, especially in cases where the merging parties produce complementary products.[1452]

For instance, in *Comcast Corporation*, the DOJ used its Competitive Impact Statement to address the concern that the transaction would allow Comcast to disadvantage not only its traditional competitors but also the emerging innovative online video distributors. The DOJ noted that the loss of current and future competition in that market would result in "reduced investment and less innovation in this dynamic industry," among others.[1453]

Another (less common) theory of harm would be "facilitated collusion," according to which the non-horizontal merger would lead the merged entity to misuse commercially sensitive information.[1454] So, it is likely to arise, for instance, in case the merged entity takes advantage of its post-merger privileges to access data in order to counter the innovations of competing undertakings.[1455] In addition to pricing information, design specifications are also considered to be among the competitively sensitive information that can be passed on between merging entities in case of vertical

---

[1449] Pierre Régibeau & Ioannis Lianos, *Digital Mergers: A Primer* 12 (2020), https://papers.ssrn.com/sol3/papers.cfm?abstract_id=3837281.

[1450] Steven Salop & Daniel Culley, *Revising the U.S. Vertical Merger Guidelines: Policy Issues and an Interim Guide for Practitioners*, 4 J. Antitrust Enforcement 1 (2015).

[1451] *Id.*

[1452] Frederico Etro, *Conglomerate Mergers and Entry in Innovative Industries* 2–3 (Univ. Ca' Foscari of Venice, Dept. of Econ. Resch., Working Paper Series No. 19/WP/2018, 2018).

[1453] Competitive Impact Statement, DOJ, US & Plaintiff States v. Comcast Corp., et al., No. 1:11-cv-00106, https://www.justice.gov/atr/case-document/competitive-impact-statement-72.

[1454] OECD, *Vertical Mergers in the Technology, Media and Telecom Sector – Background Note by the Secretariat* (DAF/COMP(2019)5, May 2, 2019), https://one.oecd.org/document/DAF/COMP(2019)5/en/pdf.

[1455] *Id.*

integration.[1456] Commentators have argued that this would lead to free-riding practices by the merging undertaking over its rivals' work, which might decrease their incentives to innovate.[1457]

In this regard, the transaction concerning the acquisition by *Silicon Graphics Inc.* of *Alias Research Inc.* and *Wavefront Technologies, Inc.* provides a useful and illustrative example.[1458] The FTC challenged this transaction, which involved the purchase of two of the world's three leading entertainment graphics software firms (Alias Research Inc. and Wavefront Technologies, Inc.) by Silicon Graphics Inc., which had a 90% share of the market for the workstations that run the software in question. The FTC stated that its "goal in bringing the case is to preserve competition on the basis of price and innovation for software and hardware involved in producing sophisticated computer-based graphics for the entertainment industry."[1459]

According to the FTC, the potential post-transaction concerns, in this case, included "foreclosing access by other workstation producers to significant, independent sources of entertainment graphics software" and "giving Silicon Graphics proprietary, competitively sensitive information about other workstation producers."[1460] The FTC further added that, in case other workstation producers were not able to access Alias's and Wavefront's software, this might lead to cost increases for competitors through foreclosing and hinder the access of new entrants, resulting in loss of innovation as well as increased prices.[1461] The FTC reached a Consent Agreement with Silicon Graphics, Inc. to settle these charges, which would require Silicon Graphics to "to take steps to ensure that other companies that develop and sell such software and the workstations to run it can compete with Silicon Graphics" and also contained various reporting provisions that would assist the FTC in monitoring Silicon Graphics' compliance.[1462]

The Long-Awaited (but Short-Lived) 2020 Vertical Merger Guidelines

On June 30, 2020, the agencies (FTC and the DOJ) jointly adopted the 2020 Guidelines in an effort to provide insights on potential anti-competitive harms that arise with vertical mergers, while continuing to recognize that such transactions can be pro-competitive or at least competitively neutral.[1463] However, the 2020 Guidelines received various

---

[1456] Christine A. Varney, *Vertical Merger Enforcement Challenges at the FTC*, The 36th Annual Antitrust Institute, San Francisco, California (July 17, 1995), https://www.ftc.gov/public-statements/1995/07/vertical-merger-enforcement-challenges-ftc.

[1457] *Id.*

[1458] Silicon Graphics, Inc., No. C-3626 (F.T.C. Nov. 14, 1995).

[1459] FTC Press Release, Silicon Graphics, Inc. (June 9, 1995), https://www.ftc.gov/news-events/press-releases/1995/06/silicon-graphics-inc.

[1460] *Id.*

[1461] *Id.*

[1462] *Id.*

[1463] 2020 Guidelines, section 1, para. 6. The Commentary on Vertical Merger Enforcement ("Commentary") set out further explanations to the 2020 Guidelines. *See* FTC Press Release, FTC Issues Commentary on Vertical Merger Enforcement (Dec. 22, 2020), https://www.ftc.gov/news-events/news/press-releases/2020/12/ftc-issues-commentary-vertical-merger-enforcement.

criticisms from different stakeholders.[1464] Despite the DOJ and the FTC seeking opinions from legal professionals, economists, enforcers and academia prior to the adoption of the 2020 guidelines, it seemed almost no substantial changes were made, especially in relation to innovation.[1465] Consequently, on September 15, 2021, the FTC voted to withdraw its approval of the 2020 Guidelines and its support from the related Commentary[1466] since it was evaluated that the 2020 Guidelines had unsound economic theories that were unsupported by the law or market realities.[1467] It was also condemned for being too pro-defendant, with a pro-competitive bias not supported by economic theory.[1468] On the other hand, the removal was also criticized as being part of the FTC's neo-Brandeisian approach towards industry concentrations, namely, against Big Tech.[1469]

The 2020 Guidelines were removed with a majority vote, with two commissioners dissenting.[1470] On the other hand, the DOJ did not remove the 2020 Guidelines and expressed in its statement that the 2020 Guidelines "remain in place at the DOJ" as it was still conducting a careful review of the 2020 Guidelines to ensure they were appropriately skeptical of harmful mergers.[1471] The contradictory approach of the agencies was further criticized for creating uncertainty for the business community.[1472]

Material Changes Brought by the 2020 Guidelines and Critical Assessments

Although now withdrawn, it is worthwhile to briefly review the changes that were brought by the 2020 Guidelines, to demonstrate the evolution of the antitrust enforcement approach and the relevant criticisms. First of all, the 2020 Guidelines, as well as the explanatory

---

[1464] Ryan C. Thomas, Aimee DeFilippo & Lauren Miller Forbes, *What a Difference a Year Makes: FTC Withdraws Vertical Merger Guidelines*, MONDAQ (Dec. 4, 2021), https://www.mondaq.com/unitedstates/antitrust-eu-competition-/1138042/what-a-difference-a-year-makes-ftc-withdraws-vertical-merger-guidelines#:~:text=In%20September%202021%2C%20the%20five,commentary%20on%20vertical%20merger%20enforcement.

[1465] DOJ Press Release, Justice Department Issues Statement on the Vertical Merger Guidelines (Sept. 15, 2021), https://www.justice.gov/opa/pr/justice-department-issues-statement-vertical-merger-guidelines.

[1466] FTC Press Release, Federal Trade Commission Withdraws Vertical Merger Guidelines and Commentary (Sept. 15, 2021), https://www.ftc.gov/news-events/news/press-releases/2021/09/federal-trade-commission-withdraws-vertical-merger-guidelines-commentary.

[1467] *Id.*

[1468] Steven Salop, *The FTC Was Correct to Withdraw the Vertical Merger Guidelines*, PROMARKET (Nov. 22, 2021), https://www.promarket.org/2021/11/22/ftc-vertical-merger-guidelines-economics-withdrawn-lina-khan-salop/#:~:text=The%202020%20Vertical%20Merger%20Guidelines,empirical%20studies%20or%-20economic%20theory.

[1469] James Keyte, *New Merger Guidelines: Are the Agencies on a Collision Course with Case Law?* 36 ANTITRUST MAG. 49 (2021).

[1470] Dissenting Statement of Commissioners Noah Joshua Phillips and Christine S. Wilson (Sept. 15, 2021), https://www.ftc.gov/system/files/documents/public_statements/1596388/p810034phillipswilsonstatementvmgrescission.pdf. The commissioners dissented from the withdrawal decision of the 2020 Guidelines for the following main reasons: (i) the decision will chill pro-competitive deals and hurt consumers; (ii) the decision discards transparency in favor of uncertainty; (iii) the decision leads to unchecked regulatory power over guidance; (iv) the decision lacks any public input; (v) the majority voters' analysis conflates pro-competitive effects of a merger with merger efficiencies and ignore the burden-shifting framework regarding the recognition of pro-competitive effects that may render a competition-eliminating merger pro-competitive overall; and (vi) the analysis of the majority voters lacks the pros and cons of mergers may possibly cause consumer harm.

[1471] FTC Press Release, *supra* note 1466.

[1472] Carl Shapiro & Herbert Hovenkamp, *How Will the FTC Evaluate Vertical Mergers?* PROMARKET (Sept. 23, 2021), https://www.promarket.org/2021/09/23/ftc-vertical-mergers-antitrust-shapiro-hovenkamp/.

Commentary, recognized that vertical mergers often benefit consumers,[1473] yet also set forth non-exhaustive ways in which non-horizontal mergers may substantially lessen competition and require the scrutiny of the agencies.[1474] The primary theories of harm focused on (i) foreclosure and raising rivals' costs, (ii) access to competitively sensitive information, and (iii) facilitating collusion. In addition, the Guidelines explained (i) the harms arising from mergers that potentially increase the cost of entry into a relevant market; (ii) merger and acquisition of complementary products that disadvantage rivals; and (iii) "diagonal" mergers that combine undertakings or assets at different stages of supply chains in competition.[1475]

Elimination of pre-merger double marginalization ("EDM")[1476] was considered an important pro-competitive effect of vertical integration. In this regard, the 2020 Guidelines introduced important changes and replaced the prior language, which read as follows: "[T]he Agencies generally rely on the parties to... demonstrate" with "it is incumbent upon the merging firms to provide substantiation for claims" of EDM.[1477] Accordingly, whereas the word "demonstrate" required the burden of proof to be rested with the agencies, the word "substantiates" referred to the burden of production[1478] rested with the merging parties. To that end, for any effects-based analysis, the 2020 Guidelines suggested that the merging parties were rested with the burden of production, but the agencies had the burden of proof.[1479]

Separately, efficiency of the vertical mergers and EDM's benefit to consumers were highlighted; noting that EDM would indeed ensure an "incentive to set lower downstream prices."[1480] On the other hand, by weighing the pros and cons regarding the efficiency approach, the theory that EDM may possibly "make the market less vulnerable to coordination" as it would create an "incentive to cheat on a tacit agreement" was adopted.[1481]

The 2020 Guidelines further recognized that although horizontal mergers are more likely to be problematic, "vertical mergers are not invariably innocuous" and may comprise possible problematic features such as leading to barriers to market entry and durable market power.[1482]

Following its adoption, a high number of scholars, lawyers, and economists found various flaws and requested a revisit of the Guidelines.[1483] A non-exhaustive list of key arguments in opposition to the Guidelines included the following.

[1473]   2020 Guidelines, section 1, para. 2,

[1474]   *Id.*, section 4, para. 6.

[1475]   *Id.*, section 6.

[1476]   Double marginalization arises when both the upstream and downstream markets exhibit some degree of economic market power, and thus, firms at each level mark up their prices above marginal cost.

[1477]   Koren Wong-Ervin & John David Harkrider, *Assessment of the Vertical Merger Guidelines and Recommendations for the VMGs Commentary* 2 (2020), https://ssrn.com/abstract=3644431.

[1478]   For completeness, the burden of production is a part of the burden of proof; however, it refers to the duty upon a party in a legal proceeding to introduce enough evidence relating to an assertion of a fact to have the issue be considered by the fact finder rather than summarily dismissed or decided.

[1479]   For completeness, in order to ensure the purpose of the Guidelines appropriately, the burden-shifting framework should be applied by the US courts in their review of mergers and determining the net effect of a transaction suggests a deviation from the prevailing legal framework in which the department may establish in court a prima facie case based on evidence of harm alone.

[1480]   2020 Guidelines, Section 4 "Unilateral Effects."

[1481]   2020 Guidelines, Section 5, "Coordinated Effects."

[1482]   Steven Salop, *Invigorating Vertical Merger Enforcement*, 127 YALE L.J. 1962 (2018), https://www.jstor.org/stable/i40225251.

[1483]   Thomas, DeFilippo & Miller Forbes, *supra* note 1464.

i. The 2020 Guidelines do not address the full range of competitive harms

Even though the 2020 Guidelines included various theories of harm, these were deemed insufficient by the critics as some of the crucial anti-competitive presumptions were left out.[1484] The commentators noted that the Guidelines failed to evaluate the full range of potential competitive harms, including higher prices and reduced quality or innovation associated with vertical mergers, and were therefore more permissive.[1485]

Moreover, the 2020 Guidelines attributed minimal importance to innovation harms and quality harms, overlooking their importance to vertical theories of harm.[1486] For example, the 2020 Guidelines did not foresee appropriate scenarios regarding killer acquisitions and the creation of kill zones that are commonly and strategically used by digital platforms to deter innovation in a specific market. Market foreclosure from vertical closures, which can lead to the termination of the innovative product entering the market and ultimately harm innovation, was neglected. Furthermore, the 2020 Guidelines did not address the matter of dominant platforms that avoid the rise of disruptive innovation through individually inconsequential vertical mergers, which may collectively represent a threat to competition.

Indeed, the FTC's majority statement on the withdrawal of the 2020 Guidelines addressed such shortcomings by stating that "the revised guidelines should pay greater attention to the broader set of tactics that firms may use to raise rivals' costs, as well as the impact of an acquisition on competitors' access to capital."[1487]

ii. The 2020 Guidelines do not properly address efficiency benefits (pro-competitive effects)

It is widely known that some commentators and even the enforcers tend to treat vertical mergers more permissively compared to horizontal mergers, based on the presumption that vertical mergers benefit competition regardless of the market structure. However, vertical mergers may create an inherent exclusionary incentive and potential for coordinated effects, just like in horizontal mergers. For this reason, the 2020 Guidelines were criticized for representing an implicit and strong pro-competitive bias, especially in relation to the treatment of EDM, which was criticized for failing to be justified by either economic theory or valid empirical studies.[1488]

[1484] Nathalie Nielson, *An Introspection on the FTC's Withdrawal of 2020 Vertical Merger Guidelines*, COMPETITION F. (2021), art. No. 0028 https://competition-forum.com/an-introspection-on-the-ftcs-withdrawal-of-2020-vertical-merger-guidelines/.

[1485] Jonathan B. Baker, Nancy L. Rose, Steven C. Salop & Fiona Scott Morton, *Five Principles for Vertical Merger Enforcement Policy*, 33 ANTITRUST 12 (2019); Steven C. Salop, *A Suggested Revision of the 2020 Vertical Merger Guidelines*, ANTITRUST BULL. 1 (July 2021), https://ssrn.com/abstract=3839768.

[1486] Nicholas Economides, John Kwoka, Thomas Philippon, Hal Singer & Lawrence J. White, *Comments on the DOJ/FTC Draft Vertical Merger Guidelines* (NET Institute Working Paper No. 20-04, 2020), https://www.ftc.gov/system/files/attachments/798-draft-vertical-merger-guidelines/vmg14_economides_comment.pdf.

[1487] *Id.*

[1488] Salop, *supra* note 1468.

Accordingly, Carl Shapiro stated that "the theory of EDM is that a vertical merger can promote competition by eliminating double markups that occur when two independent firms sell and then resell something."[1489] In some cases, EDM offsets the competitive harms of vertical mergers, but in other cases, it does not.[1490] Accordingly, the Guidelines were concerning for giving little attention to efficiency effects of vertical mergers and limiting such pro-competitive effects only with the EDM.

Another criticism was that the Guidelines did not speak of any burden of proof criteria regarding the efficiencies, which should be demonstrated by the defendant, who has better control over the relevant evidence.[1491]

iii. There is no framework for digital platforms

Digital platforms form a significant part of the current market economy, yet the 2020 Guidelines did not provide any framework for digital platforms. As Nathalie Nielson puts forth, "digital platforms usually follow a pattern of creating a 'core platform service' and then expanding into related markets, creating digital ecosystems 'in which platforms and complementary products work together smoothly'."[1492] However, when the digital ecosystem feature is combined with the rapid fluctuation of markets, there may be uncertainty on the nature of mergers, as mergers that may appear to be vertical or conglomerate may be considered horizontal.[1493] The FTC also alluded to this fact in its majority statement on withdrawal[1494] and included these specifically under the RFI for its current review of the merger regulations.

iv. Further criticisms

It has been emphasized that the 2020 Guidelines should have included more detailed examples of possible scenarios of input foreclosure and customer foreclosure,[1495] as such exclusionary conducts have the potential to harm customers and market prices by raising downstream market prices.[1496]

Last but not least, Salinger has questioned whether the analysis of static pricing incentives should be as central to vertical merger enforcement as it is to horizontal merger enforcement, and criticized the 2020 Guidelines' lack of clarity in identifying the distinguishing features of what would be a vertical merger that would constitute

---

[1489] Shapiro & Hovenkamp, *supra* note 1472.

[1490] *Id. See also* Salop Baker et al., *supra* note 1485.

[1491] Herbert J. Hovenkamp, *Competitive Harm from Vertical Mergers* (Faculty Scholarship at Penn Law. 2218, 2020), https://scholarship.law.upenn.edu/faculty_scholarship/2218.

[1492] Nielson, *supra* note 1484.

[1493] *Id.* at 1–4.

[1494] Statement of Chair Lina M. Khan, Commissioner Rohit Chopra, and Commissioner Rebecca Kelly Slaughter on the Withdrawal of the Vertical Merger Guidelines (Sept. 15, 2021), https://www.ftc.gov/legal-library/browse/cases-proceedings/public-statements/statement-chair-lina-m-khan-commissioner-rohit-chopra-commissioner-rebecca-kelly-slaughter.

[1495] Salop Baker et al., *supra* note 1485, at 3–4.

[1496] Serge Moresi & Steve C. Salop, *Quantifying the Increase in "Effective Concentration" from Vertical Mergers that Raise Input Foreclosure Concerns: Comment on the Draft Vertical Merger Guidelines* 3–5 (Georgetown University Law Center, 2020), https://scholarship.law.georgetown.edu/facpub/2240/.

a threat.[1497] Although the 2020 Guidelines include potential competition as a possible theory for blocking a vertical merger, because challenges that are based on static pricing incentives are going to be difficult to prove, Salinger argues that the 2020 Guidelines are unlikely to have much of an effect on what mergers the agencies successfully block. According to him, the focus on static pricing incentives rather than potential competition has muddied the waters instead of providing clarity to businesses, antitrust practitioners and courts.[1498]

v. What comes next

Following the withdrawal of the 2020 Guidelines, the DOJ noted that it will collaborate with the FTC in relation to a robust public engagement process to seek comment on the improvement of the Vertical Merger Guidelines.[1499] To that end, the DOJ primarily remarked to recount merging parties' burden[1500] to establish that the EDM is verifiable, merger-specific and will likely be passed through to consumers.[1501] Moreover, it was noted that the Guidelines should fully recognize the quantification of price effects and the range of circumstances that can lead to a concern.[1502]

In this regard, on January 19, 2022, the FTC and DOJ released a joint Request for Information on Merger Enforcement ("RFI") seeking public commentary on the extent to which the agencies can "modernize" merger enforcement by way of representing a clear skepticism for the conventional antitrust enforcement tools of analysis.[1503] Overall, the RFI notes that the agencies should explicitly present that the consumer welfare standard should guide the analyses on the anti-competitive effects of mergers, by taking into consideration different perspectives of various stakeholders such as consumers, suppliers, and merging parties.[1504] The RFI[1505] further indicates that the agencies have a particular interest with respect to the aspects of competition that may have been underemphasized or neglected, such as non-price elements of competition like innovation, quality, potential competition, or any trend toward concentration and labor market effects.

While the new Guidelines are under construction, the FTC will analyze mergers in accordance with its statutory mandate – with no presumption of efficiencies for any category of mergers and consideration of all relevant facts.

[1497] Michael A. Salinger, *The New Vertical Merger Guidelines: Muddying the Waters*, 59 REV. INDUS. ORG. 161 (2021).

[1498] *Id.*

[1499] Indeed, the stated goal was to ensure that the Guidelines reflect current features of competition based on modern market realities, and follow the statutory text, legislative history, and established case law around merger enforcement, as well as how the agencies can assess whether a potential competitor could grow into a plausible competitor – and the degree of such probability should be sufficient to condemn the proposed transaction.

[1500] Carl Shapiro, *Vertical Mergers and Input Foreclosure Lessons from the AT&T/Time Warner Case*, 59 REV. INDUS. ORG. 303, 5–6 (2021).

[1501] Salop Baker et al., *supra* note 1485.

[1502] *Id.*

[1503] Request for Information on Merger Enforcement, Document No. FTC-2022-0003 (Jan. 18, 2022), https://www.regulations.gov/document/FTC-2022-0003-0001.

[1504] *Id.*

[1505] *Id.*

6.5 The Significance of R&D in Specific Sectors: The Agencies' Approach to Transactions in the Defense and Pharmaceutical Sectors

6.5.1. The Defense Sector

While most of the proposed mergers and acquisitions in the defense sector have not been challenged by the DOJ's Antitrust Division and the FTC, some of the proposed transactions were subjected to further scrutiny due to competitive concerns in the 1990s.[1506] In *Lockheed Martin/Northrop Grumman*, the DOJ and the Department of Defense decided that the transaction would result in a loss of innovation competition in development of technologies as well as defense programs.[1507] Similarly, the DOJ blocked the proposed acquisition of Newport News Shipbuilding Inc. by General Dynamics on the grounds that the transaction would eliminate all competition and result in General Dynamics enjoying a monopoly in the design, development and construction of nuclear submarines for the US military, which would shield the undertaking from any competition and result in less incentive for R&D for the development of the product.[1508] As highlighted by Robert Kramer, the DOJ's greater concern in both of these transactions was the lessening of competition with respect to innovation due to the decrease in the number of players active in the sector, as it was deemed that competitors of the incumbent entities had often made the most "pathbreaking technological breakthroughs." The DOJ's conclusion in these mergers was that one or even two competitors may not be enough to ensure innovation in such markets.[1509] As for determining the number of competitors, Kramer notes that, although the geographic market was defined as the United States in the previous assessments, considering the internalization of the defense procurement, the DOJ will be asking the Pentagon about the existence of acceptable rivals for the transaction parties (which may include firms from different countries) in future assessments.[1510]

Therefore, in its assessment of mergers, the DOJ (i) finds it sufficient to rely on general economic assumptions set forth in the literature that the decrease in the number of competitors would decrease the incentive to innovate, (ii) mostly focuses on the number of competitors in the market prior to and post-merger, and (iii) finds the elimination of the smaller/second-tier competitors as alarming. The DOJ also takes into account the

---

[1506] Kramer, *supra* note 1356, at 1–3.
[1507] *See* DOJ Complaint against Lockheed Martin Corp. and Northrop Grumman Corp. (Mar. 1998), US District Court for the District of Columbia, https://www.justice.gov/d9/atr/case-documents/attachments/1998/03/23/212680.pdf.
[1508] *See* DOJ Complaint against General Dynamics Corp. and Newport News Shipbuilding Inc. (Oct. 23, 2001), US District Court for the District of Columbia, https://www.justice.gov/atr/case-document/file/497091/download.
[1509] Kramer, *supra* note 1356, at 3–4.
[1510] *Id.* at 7–8.

concerns of the Department of Defense in its merger analysis,[1511] which generally leans towards preserving the rivalry in the defense sector.[1512] Finally, the competition authorities also consider the requirements under the defense legislation, such as the Under Secretary of Defense for Acquisition's provisions in 1993 to maintain the production and R&D capability in case of a national emergency.[1513]

The approach explained above (i.e., the assumption that the lower the number of competitors, the lower the incentives to innovate) and the methods used by the DOJ in the assessment of the above mergers still seem to be relevant for the recent cases of the DOJ, as well as the Commission and the CMA. For instance, the DOJ recently filed a complaint regarding the acquisition of EverWatch Corp. by Booz Allen, which are the two largest rivals providing operational modeling and simulation services to the National Security Agency ("NSA"), and the DOJ set forth that a concentration between these parties will lead to higher prices, lower quality and less innovation, since these undertakings are the only providers for the NSA.[1514]

Looking briefly at the Commission and the CMA's approach, we note that the acquisition of Marconi Electronic Systems Ltd. by British Aerospace PLC., which would create the world's third-largest defense firm, raised concerns about the incentives to innovate and obtained clearance with certain remedies that would promote technological improvements in both the UK and EU.[1515] Furthermore, the Commission blocked the proposed acquisition of Honeywell Inc. by General Electric Co. on the grounds that the concentration would result in the creation or strengthening of a dominant position in several markets (i.e., "the markets for large commercial jet aircraft engines, large regional jet aircraft engines, corporate jet aircraft engines, avionics and non-avionics products, as well as small marine gas turbine").[1516] In its evaluation, the Commission underlined that the merger between these undertakings would significantly hinder their competitors' cash flows, thus depriving them of investing in technological R&D and innovation, and evaluated that General Electric would become the sole innovator for engines and eliminate Honeywell as a potential innovation partner.[1517] The European Competition Commissioner at the time, Mario Monti, stated that the parties had failed to propose remedies that would satisfy the Commission's concerns.[1518]

[1511] Statement of David E. Cooper, Associate Director, Defense Acquisitions Issues, National Security and International Affairs Division before the Subcommittee on Acquisition and Technology, Committee on Armed Services, U.S. Senate, Defense Industry Consolidation: Competitive Effects of Mergers and Acquisitions, https://www.gao.gov/assets/t-nsiad-98-112.pdf.

[1512] William E. Kovacic & Dennis E. Smallwood, *Competition Policy, Rivalries, and Defense Industry Consolidation*, 8 J. ECON. PERSP. 91, 95 (1994).

[1513] Marvin Leibstone, *Corporate Merger-Mania: Good or Bad for US Defence*, 20 MIL. TECH. 174 (1996).

[1514] DOJ Complaint against Booz Allen Hamilton Corp. (June 29, 2022), the US District Court for the District of Maryland https://www.justice.gov/opa/press-release/file/1516576/download.

[1515] British Aerospace/GEC Macroni European Commission Decision case IV/M. 1438 (June 25, 1999). *See also British Aerospace and GEC–Marconi*, 5 STRATEGIC COMMENTS 1 (1999), https://doi.org/10.1080/1356788990514.

[1516] *See* GE (General Electric)/Honeywell, European Commission Decision case COMP/M.2220 (2001).

[1517] *Id.* at, para. 93.

[1518] European Commission Press Release IP/01/939, The Commission prohibits GE's acquisition of Honeywell (July 3, 2001), https://ec.europa.eu/commission/presscorner/detail/en/IP_01_939.

6.5.2. The Pharmaceuticals Sector

In the last twenty years, similar to the Commission, the FTC raised concerns about innovation in pharmaceutical sector mergers. Both authorities analyzed the transactions' impact on innovation by considering the possibility of one party ceasing the research and development efforts for a product that could compete with the other party's current or pipeline products. In their decisions, the authorities relied on the parties' internal documents on plans or intentions to discontinue certain R&D efforts. (Some of the notable decisions of the Commission, such as *Medtronic/Covidien*,[1519] *Novartis/GlaxoSmithKline Oncology Business*,[1520] and *Pfizer/Hospira*,[1521] were discussed in detail above in Chapter 4 above.) Todino et al. criticized the Commission's approach in both *Covidien* and *Hospira* for considering a pipeline product to be an effective competitive substitute to the existing product despite limited clinical evidence, and therefore the Commission's assessment of the likelihood of potential competition between transaction parties.[1522] It is apparent, however, that competition authorities are adamant about keeping a very close eye on the sector, considering the stakes in the matter to be "life or death."[1523]

In *Cytyc/Digene*, the FTC announced on June 24, 2002, that the proposed acquisition of Digene Corporation ("Digene") by Cytyc Corporation ("Cytyc") would lead to decreased competition now and in the future, and that the FTC will seek a federal district court order to block the transaction.[1524] Upon the announcement, Cytyc and Digene abandoned the deal.[1525]

Cytyc was a major player in the market for cervical cancer detection, providing 93% of US liquid-based PAP tests, a tool used for the primary screening of cervical cancer. Digene, on the other hand, was the only company in the US selling a DNA-based test for human papillomavirus ("HPV"), the virus that causes almost all cervical cancer cases. The FTC found that post-transaction, Digene would cease (i) supporting other current liquid PAP test providers (there was only one existing competitor) and potential entrants in obtaining the necessary Food and Drug Administration ("FDA") approval to use Digene's HPV test in conjunction with their products and (ii) commercial access to liquid PAP test providers for Digene's HPV test. The FTC also alleged that, absent the acquisition, Cytyc would face future competition by Digene since, although the HPV test was currently approved by the FDA only as a follow-up test, it would become another primary screening tool for cervical cancer in the future.[1526] Therefore, the FTC

[1519]   Medtronic/Covidien, European Commission Decision case COMP/M.7326 (Nov. 28, 2014).

[1520]   Novartis/Glaxo Smith Kline's Oncology Business, European Commission Decision case COMP/M.7275 (Jan. 28, 2015).

[1521]   Pfizer/Hospira, European Commission Decision case COMP/M.7559 (Aug. 4, 2015).

[1522]   Mario Todino, Geoffroy van de Walle & Lucia Stoican, *EU Merger Control and Harm to Innovation – A Long Walk to Freedom (from the Chains of Causation)*, 64 ANTITRUST BULL. 11, 18 & 20 (2019).

[1523]   FTC Press Release, FTC-DOJ Workshop Summary: The Future of Pharmaceuticals: Examining the Analysis of Pharmaceutical Mergers (June 1, 2023).

[1524]   FTC Press Release, FTC Seeks to Block Cytyc Corp.'s Acquisition of Digene Corp. (June 24, 2002), https://www.ftc.gov/news-events/news/press-releases/2002/06/ftc-seeks-block-cytyc-corps-acquisition-digene-corp.

[1525]   The Associated Press, *Digene Drops Plans for Merger with Cytyc*, N.Y. TIMES (July 2, 2002), https://www.nytimes.com/2002/07/02/business/company-news-digene-drops-plans-for-merger-with-cytyc.html.

[1526]   FTC Press Release *supra* note 1524.

demonstrated a scenario where a merger could potentially manipulate market dynamics and stifle competition, threatening consumer choice and potentially impeding innovations in cervical cancer screening.[1527]

Similar to the Commission, the FTC considers the pipeline products in its merger assessment in this sector and has employed divestment as a remedy to the anti-competitive effects in the market post-transaction.[1528] However, with the increase in mergers and heightened concerns regarding drug prices, the FTC has recently been assessing its approach to the pharmaceutical sector. The Multilateral Pharmaceutical Merger Task Force was launched in March 2021 and culminated in a workshop held in June 2022, where representatives from competition authorities and scholars assessed the pharmaceutical sector in terms of market concentration, merger remedies, innovation concerns and whether previous anti-competitive behavior could be indicative of transaction parties' intentions behind a merger. The sessions' summary highlights the concerns that (i) divestments have not been adequate as remedies; (ii) a stricter approach is required, including the presumption of harm, especially in case of mergers between two large firms and prior anti-competitive behavior of the transaction parties; (iii) authorities should also focus on the role intermediaries play in the market and any supply chain effects, as well as monitoring the parties, their R&D levels and the divested products post-merger.[1529] It remains to be seen whether the FTC shall take these on board in its enforcement practice.

6.6 Innovation Concerns in Non-Merger Competition Cases

The attention to innovation concerns as major – and, sometimes, primary – considerations has also been featured in cases dealing with fields of competition law beyond mergers in the US. One major example of the latter trend is the development, by the DOJ in the 1930s, 1940s, and 1950s, of cases regarding price, quality, and innovation effects of patent licensing arrangements. Another example is the FTC's prosecution of Xerox in the early 1970s for illegal monopolization of the dry paper photocopier sector.

Cases on Patent Licensing Arrangements in 1930–1950

Patents had hardly ever been subjected to scrutiny by competition authorities until the 1930s, when antitrust concerns started to dominate the regulatory actions related to patents.[1530] It is accepted in *General Electric Co. v. Wabash Appliance Corp.* that one of the primary purposes of the patents is to serve as the "notice" function, in order

---

[1527]   Timothy Muris, *More than Law Enforcement: The FTC's Many Tools – A Conversation with Tim Muris and Bob Pitofsky*, 72 ANTITRUST L.J. 773, 823–24 (2005).

[1528]   For example, BMS/Celgene (2021), AbbVie/Allergan (2000). *See also* Robin Feldman, *Pharmaceutical Pipeline Divestitures Study: Preliminary Results* (UC Hastings Rsch. Paper, forthcoming 2021), https://ssrn.com/abstract=3861975.

[1529]   FTC-DOJ Workshop Summary *supra* note 1523, at 13–14.

[1530]   FTC, *supra* note 1372.

"to guard against unreasonable advantages to the patentee and disadvantages to others arising from uncertainty as to their [respective] rights."[1531] During the 1930–1940 period, the US Supreme Court ("Supreme Court") ruled that the scope of the monopoly provided by patents did not exceed antitrust rules.[1532]

Some of these antitrust cases included assessments related to innovation concerns. In *Transparent – Wrap Machine Corp. v. Stokes & Smith Co.*, the DOJ's Antitrust Division analyzed the grant-back provision in the patent licensing agreement and noted that (i) a patentee cannot require a licensee to assign to the patentee any patent that may be issued to the licensee, after the execution of the licensing agreement, (ii) "the logical result of such an assignment grant-back provision is to stifle innovation on the part of the licensee," and (iii) although the patentee may desire to obtain the benefits of commercial embodiments of its invention, this desire can be satisfied by imposing an obligation on the licensee to grant back a non-exclusive license of patents, the licensee may be granted for follow-up improvement.[1533] Therefore, the DOJ seemed to be interested in protecting the licensee's incentive to innovate. Nevertheless, this approach by the DOJ is criticized for disregarding the effect of such prohibition on the patentee's incentive to innovate.[1534] In any case, the Supreme Court disagreed with the DOJ's findings and noted that such grant-back provisions do not extend the limits of the patent monopoly.[1535]

With respect to price fixing through patent licensing agreements and how it relates to incentives for investing in research and development, in the case of *United States v. General Electric*, the Supreme Court held that the license given by the patentee was valid and that the district court was right in dismissing the government's bill, which prohibited the patentee from prosecuting its plan for the distribution and sale of patented electric lamps (on the grounds that it restricts interstate commerce). The Supreme Court assessed that the patentee may limit the licensee's freedom to determine its sales price if the "conditions of sale are normally and reasonably adapted to secure pecuniary reward for the patentee's monopoly."[1536] The Supreme Court seems to have tried to achieve a balance between the objectives of antitrust and patent policies, and, thus, preferred encouraging future investment in research and development by ensuring that patentees are adequately rewarded.[1537]

FTC v. Xerox

The FTC prosecuted Xerox, Corp. ("Xerox") in the early 1970s on the grounds that Xerox engaged in anti-competitive methods in relation to patent misuse, which allowed it to enjoy monopoly in the relevant product market defined as "sale and lease of office

---

[1531]   General Electric Co. v. Wabash Appliance Corp., 304 U.S. 364 (1938).

[1532]   United States v. Line Material Co., 333 U.S. 287 (1948).

[1533]   Willard K. Tom & Joshua A. Newberg, *Antitrust and Intellectual Property: From Separate Spheres to Unified Field*, 66 ANTITRUST L.J. 167, 182 (1997).

[1534]   *Id.* at 182–83.

[1535]   Transparent – Wrap Machine Corp. v. Stokes & Smith Co. 329 U.S. 637 (1947).

[1536]   United States v. General Elec. Co., 272 U.S. 476 (1926).

[1537]   *See* the discussion in Gerald R. Gibbons, *Price Fixing in Patent Licenses and the Antitrust Laws*, 51 VA. L. REV. 273, 276–77 (1965) (arguing that prohibition of price fixing should have little practical effect on the undertaking's incentive to innovate).

copiers" and the relevant submarket "sale and lease of plain paper copiers."[1538] The complaint subjected to the litigation put forth certain allegations, such as monopolizing patents, obstructing competitors' innovation efforts through patent misuse, creating entry barriers, etc.[1539] In more detail, the FTC alleged that Xerox has engaged in "preventing actual and potential competitors from developing plain paper copiers while permitting them to develop coated paper copiers."[1540]

FTC settled with Xerox on the condition that Xerox provide loyalty-free licenses for some of its patents and reasonable royalty licenses for others, to eliminate know-how and entry barriers.[1541] This was one of the first examples of royalty-free compulsory patent licensing used as a remedy for an antitrust violation.[1542]

Other Examples

An earlier example of DOJ's innovation concerns in a patent case can be found in its *Pilkington PLC* case.[1543] The DOJ alleged that licensing arrangements of Pilkington had the potential to violate antitrust laws since the licenses that grant a geographical monopoly to its licensee would deter the licensee from innovating for its own product.[1544] In this regard, the DOJ issued the first Antitrust Guidelines for the Licensing of Intellectual Property in 1995, seeking solutions to protect innovation against anti-competitive conduct related to intellectual property issues.[1545]

In more recent cases, innovation concerns primarily appear in both merger and non-merger cases involving technology companies.[1546] The *U.S. v. Microsoft* case in 2001[1547] focused on the possibility of information technology undertakings to utilize their powers within the relevant markets to harm consumers by way of harming innovation.[1548] Furthermore, in its *Transitions* case, the FTC scrutinized innovation concerns and alleged that Transitions Optical Inc. used its market power to maintain its monopoly in the relevant product market by exclusive dealing practices, "[leading] to higher prices, lower output, reduced innovation and diminished consumer choice."[1549]

These go to show that innovation concerns are one of the major issues that the authorities consider not only in merger cases but also in cases concerning horizontal and vertical restraints and abuse of dominance.

[1538] James McKeown, *The FTC v. Xerox Litigation: Implications for the United States Patent System*, 24 CATH. U. L. REV. 1 (1975).

[1539] *Id.*

[1540] Xerox Corp., No. 8909 (F.T.C. 1975).

[1541] Decision and Order, Xerox Corp., No. 8909 (F.T.C. 1975).

[1542] McKeown, *supra* note 1538

[1543] Gregory Day, *Innovative Antitrust and the Patent System*, 96 NEB. L. REV. 829 (2017).

[1544] United States v. Pilkington plc and Pilkington Holdings, 6 Trade Reg Rep (CCH) (D. Mass. 1994).

[1545] US Dep't of Just. & Fed. Trade Comm'n, Antitrust Guidelines for the Licensing of Intellectual Property (1995).

[1546] DANIEL F. SPULBER, ANTITRUST AND INNOVATION COMPETITION (Oxford Univ. Press 2022).

[1547] United States v. Microsoft Corp., 87 F. Supp. 2d 30, 38 (D.D.C. 2000).

[1548] Daniel L. Rubinfeld, *Competition, Innovation, and Antitrust Enforcement in Dynamic Network Industries* Speech before the Software Publishers Association (1998 Spring Symposium), San Jose, California (Mar. 24, 1998), https://www.justice.gov/atr/speech/competition-innovation-and-antitrust-enforcement-dynamic-network-industries.

[1549] *Id.*

6.7 Conclusion

Increasing levels of interest and a new focus on issues relating to innovation have been observed in US competition law practice, both at the policy and enforcement levels.[1550] In the past, merger policy in the US was mostly based on static analysis, which largely concentrated on how the transaction would influence pricing and often neglected vibrant factors like R&D.[1551] It was much later acknowledged in the 2010 Horizontal Merger Guidelines that "competition often spurs firms to innovate,"[1552] which implies that the US competition authorities steer closer to the idea that competition rather than market concentration fosters innovation and the Arrowian approach, rather than Schumpeter's. A specific section of the guidelines was devoted entirely to the issue of innovation, which provided antitrust agencies improved guidance on how to consider and assess innovation-related matters in merger control cases. This is in contrast to the novel approach that the Commission has recently adopted and the ambiguous concepts such as "innovation spaces" that it has utilized and been criticized for its lack of legislative basis. It may perhaps even be possible to say that such structured guidance has allowed the US antitrust agencies to avoid criticisms of speculative and overly invasive practices, especially in terms of dynamic innovative markets. However, it remains to be seen whether this will be sustained in the upcoming revision of the guidelines. It is also noteworthy that innovation concerns are one of the major issues in certain specific sectors; and if needed, the authorities take innovation into account not just in merger transactions but also in cases regarding horizontal and vertical restraints or abuse of dominance.

Antitrust agencies in the US have examined merger cases under several different theories of harm. Besides their innovation-related evaluations of the potential harm to competition, US antitrust agencies have even considered the protection of competition in non-existing markets.[1553] These innovation considerations, inevitably, have the downside of dearth of information: they cannot always be evaluated based on concrete evidence, or precisely measured with economic tools; thus, there cannot possibly be a single set of standards for the examination of innovation-related issues in merger controls that will apply to every case. To that end, competition enforcement agencies should adopt a case-by-case approach to their analysis in terms of innovation considerations by scrutinizing the specific dynamics of the transaction and the market structure in each investigation. This is especially important in their assessments relating to technology markets, in which the single most important driving force of competition is innovation. Indeed, noting the lack of reliable presumptions in innovation and the challenges this brings, the DOJ conducted a fact-based approach in its assessment of the *Dow/DuPont* merger with respect to the US market, which resulted in a more limited request for the divestiture package as opposed to its European counterpart.[1554] As for the burden of proof, similar

---

[1550] DARDANO, *supra* note 1390, at 14.

[1551] Katz & Shelanski, *supra* note 1352, at 110.

[1552] Horizontal Merger Guidelines at 23.

[1553] *See In re Steris Corp.*

[1554] Charles McConnell, *Innovation Analysis Lacks Reliable Presumptions, Says US DOJ Deputy*, GCR (June 7, 2018), https://globalcompetitionreview.com/article/1170347/innovation-analysis-lacks-reliable-presumptions-says-us-doj-deputy.

to the other jurisdictions, the onus is on the competition authorities to demonstrate the anti-competitive impacts of a merger. However, when it comes to efficiency gains, the 2010 Horizontal Merger Guidelines state that since these are difficult to verify and quantify partly because information related to efficiencies is possessed by merging firms, the burden to substantiate efficiency claims lies with the merging firms.[1555] The transaction entities may indeed have a ready understanding of their own capabilities and even their own expectations regarding the efficiencies of the transaction. However, the author's previous criticisms are still valid, as the relevant entities bear an asymmetrical burden while they lack the breadth of resources and access that agencies have. If deemed necessary, the agencies can request information from rivals and customers to understand the current and potential market structure, collect internal documents from and interview third parties, which is not usually possible for transaction parties. As the agencies themselves are not above wielding their swords and allegations of harm occasionally, even without sufficient proof, as demonstrated by the *Steris/Synergy* case, the innovation paradox is thus perpetuated.

It is worth mentioning that while the 2010 Horizontal Merger Guidelines specifically deal with the concept of innovation, there was no such section devoted to innovation-related concerns in the Vertical Merger Guidelines of 1984, and this does not seem to have substantially changed in the (now withdrawn) 2020 Guidelines. While it did refer to the ability to create innovative products in passing, the lack of reference to pro-competitive effects of efficiencies was one of the criticisms brought, which the agencies may take into account in their in-depth review and reconstruction of the new Merger Guidelines. Even though antitrust agencies were generally less troubled about non-horizontal mergers (as they were deemed unlikely to raise major anti-competitive concerns), in light of the criticisms, it will certainly be worthwhile to consider incorporating a specific section regarding innovation considerations into such merger guidelines as well. If structured guidance has indeed assisted the antitrust agencies in formulating consistent and fair assessments with regard to horizontal mergers, it is very likely that emulating this for vertical mergers will prevent speculative or ambiguous action on the part of the competition authorities.

[1555]   Horizontal Merger Guidelines at 30.

Chapter 7
Creeping and Defensive Acquisitions in Digital Markets of Developed Economies

7.1 Introduction

After examining the difficulties that the competition authorities are facing in developed economies due to the changing nature of the markets and the shift towards more innovative and dynamic structures, we will now focus on the effects of creeping and defensive acquisitions in digital sectors, which comprise one of the most innovative markets in the modern economic system. The principal reason why this study focuses on defensive acquisitions is that although they are almost always branded as "killer acquisitions" due to the argument that they are a means to eradicate competition, the empirical findings do not fully support this view. There are findings that mergers have led to increased innovation or, in certain cases, remain too speculative to say for certain.[1556] Furthermore, an aggressive antitrust enforcement approach by regulatory authorities runs the risk of increasing the exit costs for entrepreneurs, thus diminishing their enthusiasm for investments; what the authorities see as a "killer" acquisition may sometimes be the only exit route for unicorn investors. Not to forget, the efficiency gains that may arise from the acquisition itself and corresponding benefits on consumer welfare should also be taken into account.[1557] Therefore, the discussion in this section will also include approaches that competition enforcement authorities may adopt to handle and cope with these challenges, as well as the recent practices that portray how the authorities are approaching the issue. Firstly, the definitions of (and approaches to) creeping and defensive acquisitions will be set out in Section II of this Chapter. Following this informative background, Section III will provide a general overview of digital markets from the perspective of competition law. In Section IV, the literature on the motivations underlying digital conglomerate mergers will be surveyed, and Section V will offer a discussion on the merger notification thresholds. In

---

[1556]   Anna Rita Bennato, Stephen Davies, Franco Mariuzzo & Peter Ormosi, *Mergers and Innovation: Evidence from the Hard Disk Drive Market*, 77 INT'L J. INDUS. ORG. Elsevier (2021), DOI:10.1016/j.ijindorg.2021.102755. *See also* other views by Wim Holterman and Colleen Cunningham on the strategies of acquiring firms and effects of venture capital in the OECD, *Summary of Discussion of the Roundtable on Start-Ups, Killer Acquisitions and Merger Control* (DAF/COMP/M(2020)1/ANN3/FINAL, Oct. 29, 2021), https://one.oecd.org/document/DAF/COMP/M(2020)1/ANN3/FINAL/en/pdf.

[1557]   *See* Geoffrey A. Manne's Invited Statement to the U.S. House of Representatives Committee on the Judiciary, Subcommittee on Antitrust, Commercial, and Administrative Law, *Correcting Common Misperceptions About the State of Antitrust Law and Enforcement* (Apr. 17, 2020), https://laweconcenter.org/wp-content/uploads/2020/04/Manne_statement_house_antitrust_20200417_FINAL3-POST.pd.

Section VI, the literature on the discussions revolving around the assessment of the competitive effects of pre-emptive mergers in digital markets will be summarized. Finally, Section VII will briefly touch upon the recent cases that give an indication of the authorities' particular assessments.

7.2 Creeping and Defensive Acquisitions

In competition law literature, "creeping acquisitions" are defined as a series of small-scale acquisitions that individually do not substantially lessen competition in a market, but may collectively have that effect over time. In other words, these types of acquisitions usually involve situations where a firm acquires either certain parts of a company or complementary businesses, through a number of consecutive and interrelated transactions.[1558] The crucial point about such creeping acquisitions is that every transaction that is part of such a deal is executed separately, and while they would not meet the criteria for merger notification on their own, they would require merger notification if they were to be considered and treated collectively, as one single transaction.

Currently, at the EU level, the merger notification threshold is based on the monetary turnover of the transaction firms.[1559] Therefore, a concentration involving firms with small monetary turnovers is typically not screened or evaluated by the Commission, even when the value of the transaction itself is very high. For example, the Commission did not examine the acquisition of Instagram (a photo and video-sharing social networking service) by Facebook (an American online social media and networking service), even though the deal itself was valued at $1 billion. Moreover, the acquisition of WhatsApp (a freeware, cross-platform messaging and Voice over Internet Protocol ("VoIP") service) by Facebook[1560] was examined by the Commission, not because the turnover threshold at the EU level had been exceeded, but because of the specific referral by national competition authorities.[1561,1562]

Under normal circumstances, if a transaction does not meet the notification thresholds set by law, it will fall outside the jurisdiction of the relevant competition authority under the merger control rules, and it will not be subject to regulatory scrutiny, leaving the

---

[1558] OECD, *Investigations of Consummated and Non-Notifiable Mergers – Note by the Secretariat* (Working Party No. 3 on Co-operation and Enforcement) (DAF/COMP/WP3(2014)1, Jan. 20, 2015), recital 31, http://www.oecd.org/officialdocuments/publicdisplaydocumentpdf/?cote=DAF/COMP/WP3(2014)1&doclanguage=en.

[1559] European Union, Council Regulation (EC) No. 139/2004 of Jan. 20, 2004, on the Control of Concentrations Between Undertakings (the "EC Merger Regulation" or "EUMR"), 2004 OJ (I 24) 1, art. 1, https://eur-lex.europa.eu/legal-content/EN/TXT/PDF/?uri=CELEX:32004R0139&from=EN.

[1560] Facebook/WhatsApp, European Commission Decision case COMP/M.7217 (Oct. 30, 2014).

[1561] Marc Bourreau & Alexandre de Streel, *Digital Conglomerates and EU Competition Policy* 28 (2019), https://dx.doi.org/10.2139/ssrn.3350512

[1562] The referral mechanism set out in article 22 EUMR allows one or more Member States to request the European Commission to examine a concentration that does not have a Community dimension but affects trade between the Member States and threatens to significantly affect competition within the territory of the Member State or States making the request.

parties free to consummate the transaction without being exposed to regulatory jeopardy. As a rare exception to this general principle, in certain jurisdictions,[1563] the competition authority has jurisdiction to review certain transactions that fall below the notification thresholds.[1564]

Competition authorities worldwide have taken a skeptical approach towards creeping acquisitions. These distrustful attitudes are based on the competition authorities' goal of preventing any possibility of enabling undertakings to structure a large transaction from a series of smaller deals, and thereby circumventing merger review controls, which might result in anti-competitive transactions. There are a variety of methods and models that are used by competition authorities to address and cope with the issue of creeping acquisitions, including the "sectorial method," the "aggregation model," and the "substantial market power model,"[1565] as detailed in Section V below.

A "defensive acquisition," on the other hand, can be understood as a proactive defensive strategy, in which firms acquire other firms or assets as a "defense" against market downturns or possible takeover attempts. A defensive acquisition differs from a regular acquisition in its objective, as the typical impetus for an acquisition is usually the desire for increased market share or revenue. A company will sometimes engage in a defensive acquisition strategy by purchasing smaller firms that are in the same business as itself. By acquiring such firms, the company will aim to protect itself from takeovers by the other firms. In other words, defensive acquisitions can be described as takeovers made by a firm in order to become so large that it becomes unattractive as an acquisition target itself.[1566]

Crémer et al. have observed that, for certain undertakings, buying up successful start-ups within their zone of interest may then act as a barricade for fending off potential attacks on their core market. They further explain that this strategy may be all the more effective in cases in which the position of the acquirer allows it to identify emerging trends in consumer consumption patterns early on and react to them quickly – whether by way of copying new products or services or by acquiring successful start-ups.[1567]

The incentive for the firms holding significant market power to take pre-emptive measures against nascent firms to maintain their profits was pointed out long ago.[1568] These pre-emptive measures include acquisitions of the nascent firms by the incumbents,

---

[1563]   These jurisdictions include Canada, Brazil, Japan, Korea, Mexico, Norway, and Lithuania.

[1564]   OECD, *supra* note 1558, recital 16.

[1565]   OECD Business and Industry Advisory Committee (BIAC) Summary of Discussion Points: "Creeping Acquisitions," Presented to the OECD Competition Committee Working Party No. 3 (WP3) Roundtable (Feb. 15, 2011), recital 5, http://biac.org/wp-content/uploads/2014/05/BIAC_Note_on_creeping_Acquisitions.pdf.

[1566]   Babu G. Baradwaj, David A. Dubofsky & Donald R. Fraser, *Defensive Acquisitions in the Banking Industry: The Takeover Premium Hypothesis*, 20 J. Econ. & Fin. 13, 13 (1996).

[1567]   Jacques Crémer, Yves-Alexandre de Montjoye & Heike Schweitzer, Competition Policy for the Digital Era 121 (Report commissioned by the European Commission, Publications Office of the European Union 2019), http://ec.europa.eu/competition/publications/reports/kd0419345enn.pdf

[1568]   *See* Richard Gilbert & David Newbery, *Preemptive Patenting and the Persistence of Monopoly*, 72 Am. Econ. Rev. 514 (1982), https://www.jstor.org/stable/1831552.

which the entrants view as "entry for buyout."[1569] However, historically, the competition authorities did not find that such acquisition of nascent firms by their rivals was particularly relevant to merger control. This is mainly because, generally speaking, a nascent firm's competitive pressure against its rival acquirer, at the time of the acquisition, is low, and its future competitive pressure cannot be precisely predicted. That is to say, to assess whether the acquisition of a nascent firm restricts competition significantly in a given market, the competition authorities must predict the future competitive pressure of the firm but for the acquisition, i.e., the counterfactual. Establishing the counterfactual is particularly hard as the nascent firms do not have any past data to look into, which could predict the potential of the concerned firm.[1570] Moreover, prohibiting nascent firms' entry by acquisition was argued to be "of little affirmative economic purpose," and shrinking the acquisition market by prohibiting such entries would therefore impair the entrepreneurship incentive.[1571]

A "killer acquisition" describes the type of transaction where the incumbent firm acquires the innovating company and then terminates the innovative efforts of the target company after the merger. In this regard, incumbent firms may acquire innovative targets solely to discontinue the target's innovation projects and to pre-empt and block their future competition.

Crémer et al. point out that "killer acquisitions" are often observed in the pharmaceutical industry, where an incumbent acquires a potential competitor who has an innovative project that is still in the early stages of development, and subsequently terminates the development project of the target's innovation in order to avoid a "replacement effect."[1572] They further explain that, by doing so, the incumbent pre-empts competition from innovating firms that could potentially threaten its market position.[1573] According to some business analysts, a "kill zone" exists for innovative tech firms vis-à-vis the tech giants (such as Google, Facebook, Amazon, and Apple), referring to a zone established by the large digital firms in which start-ups hesitate to invest due to the concern that successful innovations in that zone might either be copied or bought up easily and quickly by the tech giants. Having said this, the typical scenario (in the authors' opinion) would be a situation in which the innovative project of the purchased start-up firm would be integrated into the "ecosystem" of the acquirer or one of its existing products, and such acquisitions should be differentiated from "killer acquisitions" as the integration of innovative complementary services often has a plausible underlying efficiency rationale.[1574]

[1569] Eric Rasmusen, *Entry for Buyout*, 36 J. IND. ECON. 281 (1988), https://www.jstor.org/stable/i336775.

[1570] ELENA ARGENTESI, PAOLO BUCCIROSSI, EMILIO CALVANO, TOMASO DUSO, ALESSIA MARRAZZO & SALVATORE NAVA, EX-POST ASSESSMENT OF MERGER CONTROL DECISIONS IN DIGITAL MARKETS iii (Final Report prepared by Lear for the Competition Markets Authority, May 9, 2019), https://assets.publishing.service.gov.uk/government/uploads/system/uploads/attachment_data/file/803576/CMA_past_digital_mergers_GOV.UK_version.pdf (the "Lear Report").

[1571] Oliver E. Williamson, *The Economics of Antitrust: Transaction Cost Considerations*, 122 U. PA. L. REV. 1492 (1974), https://scholarship.law.upenn.edu/penn_law_review/vol122/iss6/2/.

[1572] CRÉMER ET AL., *supra* note 1567, at 117.

[1573] More precisely, by merging, the acquirer and the acquired firm are able to share the proceeds of monopoly rather than competing with each other. Since monopoly profits are higher than the sum of the profits of two competing firms, this leaves a surplus that they can share.

[1574] CRÉMER ET AL., *supra* note 1567, at 118.

Even though there are slight terminology differences between them, the author will assume in this chapter that "defensive," "pre-emptive," and "killer" types of acquisitions are all elements of a broader set of strategies, as they have close and interrelated meanings. Therefore, by including pre-emptive and killer acquisitions in this discussion, it becomes easier to analyze the literature more comprehensively, as opposed to focusing solely on defensive acquisitions.

Here, we should also point out the more recent terminology of "reverse killer acquisitions": The *"loss of a potential competition"* had already been an established concern in the field of merger control, prior to the current debate of killer acquisitions.[1575] In this regard, a recent paper by Crawford et al., portraying killer acquisitions as a *"loss of a potential competition,"* stated that this concern, in fact, goes beyond the one described by the debate.[1576] The authors argued that large digital platforms have a particular capability to expand rapidly and inorganically, through acquisitions of not-necessarily-rival firms operating in other markets, i.e., expansion through *"buys"* instead of *"builds."*[1577] In these "buys instead of builds," the incumbent acquires an already-well-established product and shuts down the development of its own product, or never starts developing a competing product – the *"reverse killer acquisitions,"* as the authors called them.[1578]

These concerns have given birth to the argument that killer acquisitions and reverse killer acquisitions, by and on their own, are a novel theory of harm that must be addressed by the competition authorities, especially in the digital markets, where the market structure differs from the traditional markets.[1579] As such, the concerns highlighted in the debate on killer acquisitions and reverse killer acquisitions appear to concentrate on the digital markets.

On a relevant note, the Report of the Digital Competition Expert Panel, which was commissioned by the CMA, recognized and acknowledged that most of the acquisitions by large digital companies in recent years have likely been benign or beneficial for consumers. However, the Report also observed that these acquisitions have occurred over a time during which the major digital platforms have grown substantially, consolidated their market positions, and faced close independent rivals. Moreover, the Report explained that some of these acquisitions have targeted platforms (and other companies) that could have provided much-needed competition in these concentrated markets, and that some target companies also appear to have been undertakings in the upstream or downstream markets, whose products have helped to cement the large digital platforms' positions in their core markets, thus enhancing their power

---

[1575] *See* Carl Shapiro, *Antitrust in a Time of Populism*, 61 INT'L J. IND. ORG. 714 (2018), https://faculty.haas.berkeley.edu/shapiro/antitrustpopulism.pdf.

[1576] Gregory Crawford, Tommaso Valletti & Cristina Caffarra, *"How Tech Rolls": Potential Competition and "Reverse" Killer Acquisitions*, VoxEU (May 11, 2020), https://cepr.org/voxeu/blogs-and-reviews/how-tech-rolls-potential-competition-and-reverse-killer-acquisitions

[1577] *Id.*

[1578] *Id.*

[1579] OECD, Directorate for Financial and Enterprise Affairs Competition Committee, *Start-ups, Killer Acquisitions and Merger Control – Background Note for the meeting of the Competition Committee on 10–12 June 2020* 2 (May 2020), http://www.oecd.org/daf/competition/start-ups-killer-acquisitions-and-merger-control.htm.

over their users.[1580] All in all, the Report of the Digital Competition Expert Panel voiced concerns that, in some instances, large digital companies have acquired smaller innovative companies in spaces that were adjacent or overlapping with their main activities, following a so-called *killer acquisition strategy*, which was designed and intended to eliminate potential future rivals in those core markets.

The Report also indicated that some forms of conduct undertaken by large digital platforms towards smaller firms could indirectly lead to consumer harm, such as the practice of *"killer acquisitions,"* where potential rivals to large digital platforms can be removed from the market or absorbed through a strategy of pre-emptive acquisitions, and resisting or evading such acquisitions may be particularly challenging for firms that are dependent on some part of the large platform's ecosystem for their own services.[1581]

Unfortunately, quantitative evidence on the effects of mergers in the digital economy is limited. However, a recent robust analysis of the pharmaceutical sector by Cunningham et al. has estimated that more than 6% of acquisitions in that sector every year are "killer acquisitions," and the authors noted that this estimate was the lower bound for their calculations.[1582] Similar to the digital sectors, the pharmaceutical sector is also characterized by "competition for the market" and the "centrality of innovation." Therefore, in the absence of any detailed analysis of the digital sector, these results can be useful, although it should be kept in mind that they are only roughly informative.[1583] It should also be pointed out that, unlike the digital sector, the pharmaceutical sector is highly regulated, with certain specific and comparable product development milestones and clear product substitutes, which is certainly not the case for digital markets. It would therefore be a stretch to consider the results of this study to be directly applicable in digital markets as well.[1584] Nevertheless, the FTC initiated a study (discussed in more detail below) in February 2020 to analyze the terms of unreported acquisitions in the digital sector by the top five US technology companies, based on similar concerns of killer acquisitions.[1585]

Furthermore, Bourreau and de Streel have argued that one of the primary and most intriguing characteristics of the digital sector is the resurgence of *"conglomerates."* They state that, in recent years, there have been numerous acquisitions in the digital economy in which conglomerates have acquired promising start-ups.[1586] Parallel to this development, over the last ten years, the five largest firms have made over 400 acquisitions globally,

---

[1580] DIGITAL COMPETITION EXPERT PANEL, UNLOCKING DIGITAL COMPETITION 92 (Mar. 2019). https://assets. publishing.service.gov.uk/government/uploads/system/uploads/attachment_data/file/785547/unlocking_digital_ competition_furman_review_web.pdf.

[1581] *Id.* at 45.

[1582] Colleen Cunningham, Florian Ederer & Song Ma, *Killer Acquisitions*, 129 J. POLITICAL ECON. 649 (2021), http://dx.doi.org/10.2139/ssrn.3241707, at 5

[1583] The Digital Competition Expert Panel Report, *supra* note 1580, at 49.

[1584] John M. Yun, Prepared Statement for the US Senate Committee Hearing on "Competition in Digital Technology Markets: Examining Acquisitions of Nascent or Potential Competitors by Digital Platforms" 10 (Sept. 24, 2019), https://www.judiciary.senate.gov/imo/media/doc/Yun%20Testimony.pdf.

[1585] FTC Press Release, FTC Staff Presents Report on Nearly a Decade of Unreported Acquisitions by the Biggest Technology Companies (Sept. 15, 2021), https://www.ftc.gov/news-events/press-releases/2021/09/ftc-report-on-unreported-acquisitions-by-biggest-tech-companies.

[1586] Bourreau & de Streel, *supra* note 1561, at 1–2.

and none of these mergers and acquisitions have been blocked, and very few have had conditions attached to their approval, either in the UK or elsewhere. (A list of the highest value acquisitions by large digital companies for that period is presented in Annex-1 of this Chapter.) Only some of these have been scrutinized by the competition authorities;[1587] however, as the number of high-value acquisitions has increased significantly even in the last year,[1588] what specifically grabbed the attention of the antitrust authorities were the ones realized in the digital markets.[1589] This is not surprising when we consider, as an example, that Google alone acquired about one firm per month between 2001 and 2020.[1590] Therefore, the rising concern of antitrust enforcers all around the world meant they are now focusing their energies specifically on emerging digital markets: e.g., the FTC conducted an in-depth study on "Non-HSR Reported Acquisitions by Select Technology Platforms, 2010–2019"[1591] and published its report in September 2021 ("The Report"). This new focus was also reciprocated by other competition authorities, such as France,[1592] Australia,[1593] and many others.[1594]

There were a total of 819 non-reportable acquisitions under the Hart-Scott-Rodino Antitrust Improvements Act of 1976 ("HSR Act"), and 616 of them had been valued at above $1 million and realized between January 2010 and December 2019 by the five major technology companies, Alphabet Inc. ("Google"), Amazon.com, Inc. ("Amazon"), Facebook, Inc. ("Facebook"), Apple Inc. ("Apple") and Microsoft Corp. ("Microsoft") (together referred to as "GAFAM"). Further, out of these 616 transactions, 94 did, in fact, exceed the HSR transactional thresholds. The Report also finds that GAFAM conducted approximately 60 transactions whose transaction values were below $1 million, and (where data was available) it was noted that the target's age was below five in at least 39.3% of those transactions with a value of over $1 million.

[1587]   The Digital Competition Expert Panel Report, *supra* note 1580, at 12.

[1588]   Looking from the high-value acquisition perspective, 2021 has been a significant year where the value of the total merger and acquisition deals between $1 billion and $5 billion surpassed $1.9 trillion, meaning a considerable surge of 115% compared to 2020. Refinitiv, *Global Mergers & Acquisitions Review: Full Year 2021 | Financial Advisors* 1 (industry report) (2021), https://thesource.refinitiv.com/TheSource/getfile/download/eacef8be-ef5d-4335-b807-5db0db1cf6bc.

[1589]   Ginger Zhe Jin, Mario Leccese & Liad Wagman, *How Do Top Acquirers Compare in Technology Mergers? New Evidence from an S&P Taxonomy* 3 (NBER Working Paper Series No. 29642, 2022).

[1590]   Igor Letina, Armin Schmutzler & Regina Seibel, *Killer Acquisitions and Beyond: Policy Effects on Innovation Strategies* 2 (University of Zurich, Department of Economics, Working Paper No. 358, revised version 2021), https://ssrn.com/abstract=3673150.

[1591]   Fed. Trade Comm'n, Non-HSR Reported Acquisitions by Select Technology Platforms, 2010–2019: An FTC Study (Sept. 2021), https://www.ftc.gov/reports/non-hsr-reported-acquisitions-select-technology-platforms-2010-2019-ftc-study. *See also* US Subcommittee on Antitrust, Commercial and Administrative Law of the Committee on Judiciary, Investigation of Competition in Digital Markets: Majority Staff Report and Recommendations, https://democrats-judiciary.house.gov/uploadedfiles/competition_in_digital_markets.pdf (issued in 2020 concerning the acquisition by GAFAM).

[1592]   The French Competition Authority's Opinion on the Online Advertising Sector (Mar. 2018), https://www.autoritedelaconcurrence.fr/sites/default/files/integral_texts/2019-10/avis18a03_en_.pdf.

[1593]   The Australian Competition & Consumer Commission, Digital Platforms Inquiry: Final Report (July 2019), https://www.accc.gov.au/system/files/Digital%20platforms%20inquiry%20-%20final%20report.pdf.

[1594]   It is also stated in the Stigler Committee's Digital Platforms Final Report that authorities in the United Kingdom, Germany, the European Commission, Israel, and Japan are included. George J. Stigler Center for the Study of the Economy and the State, Stigler Committee on Digital Platforms: Final Report (May 2019) ("Stigler Report"), https://www.chicagobooth.edu/-/media/research/stigler/pdfs/digital-platforms--committee-report---stigler-center.pdf.

This data shows that the concerns about the acquisitions of "nascent competitors"[1595] raised in reports such as the Stigler Center's Committee for the Study of Digital Platforms Market Structure and Antitrust Subcommittee[1596] may indeed be right. As the main concern in the acquisition of a nascent competitor is that, after the consummation of the transaction, the acquirer might terminate the competition, or the potential competition, that the target would constitute in the sector,[1597] the fact that nearly two out of five non-reported cases involved the acquisition of young firms supports the raised concerns.

The Report also highlighted that 36% of the transactions evaluated under the Report would be reportable if the debts and liabilities were included in the purchase price. The FTC announced its finding that target companies take on debts before being acquired, and then the acquirers take on the target's debt, which is not reflected in the deal value; hence, the merging parties avoid notifying their transaction. This finding in the Report turns the spotlight back on the transactional threshold debates all around the world.

The Report also provided that 75% of the 616 transactions included non-compete clauses for founders and key employees of the target, with little variation in the percentage of transactions that had non-compete clauses. This drastic number in the non-compete clauses was also underlined in the FTC's chair Lina Khan's speech, and she remarked on the urgent need to examine digital firms' blockage not only in the assets but also in terms of talent by enforcing non-compete clauses for the target.[1598]

The increased momentum in the global merger activity for high-value acquisitions in the last three years is clearly demonstrated in GAFAM's activities and, accordingly, the approaches in of the competition authorities to these transactions. Very recently, in 2021, one of the notable high-value acquisitions realized by GAFAM was the *Google/Fitbit* case, valued at approximately $2.1 billion, as it marked the Commission's first merger decision that qualifies an acquisition by Google as anti-competitive and puts in place remedies.[1599] As one of the several merger control authorities to which this transaction was notified, the Commission granted its approval to the proposed transaction with remedies.[1600]

[1595]　Nascent competitor refers to an undertaking "with an existing product or technology, whether inside or outside some relevant product market, that could, at some point, be considered a significant competitor, or be developed into a significant competitor," John M. Yun, *Potential Competition, Nascent Competitors, and Killer Acquisitions, in* THE GLOBAL ANTITRUST INSTITUTE REPORT ON THE DIGITAL ECONOMY 651, 655 (Global Antitrust Institute 2020), https://gaidigitalreport.com/wp-content/uploads/2020/11/The-Global-Antitrust-Institute-Report-on-the-Digital-Economy_Final.pdf. *See also* United States v. Microsoft Corp., 253 F.3d 34 (D.C. Cir. 2001), where the consideration of nascent competition was part of the theory of harm established in the case.

[1596]　Stigler Report, *supra* note 1594 at 88. *See also* SUBCOMMITTEE ON ANTITRUST, COMMERCIAL AND ADMINISTRATIVE LAW OF THE COMMITTEE ON JUDICIARY, *supra* note 1591, at 388; C. Scott Hemphill & Tim Wu, *Nascent Competitors*, 168 U. PA. L. REV. 1879 (2020) (NYU Law and Economics Research Paper No. 20-50, Columbia Law and Economics Working Paper No. 645), https://ssrn.com/abstract=3624058.

[1597]　Yun, *supra* note 1584, at 653.

[1598]　FTC Press Release, Remarks of Chair Lina M. Khan Regarding Non-HSR Reported Acquisitions by Select Technology Platforms, Commission File No. P201201 (Sept. 15, 2021), https://www.ftc.gov/system/files/documents/public_statements/1596332/remarks_of_chair_lina_m_khan_regarding_non-hsr_reported_acquisitions_by_select_technology_platforms.pdf.

[1599]　Simon Vande Walle, *The European Commission's Approval of Google / Fitbit – A Case Note and Comment* 2 (2021), https://papers.ssrn.com/sol3/papers.cfm?abstract_id=3893079.

[1600]　Google/Fitbit, European Commission Decision case M.9660 (Dec. 17, 2020).

Another noteworthy transaction that took place in 2021 was the *Amazon/MGM* decision of the Commission, with a total worth of \$8.5 billion. The Commission has approved the proposed high-value acquisition unconditionally and concluded that the transaction would raise no competition concerns within the European Economic Area ("EEA").[1601]

The year 2021 has also witnessed numerous cases where the proposed transactions relating to the digital sectors were challenged and/or called off by the relevant competition authorities.[1602] One of the biggest examples of such a decision was the *NVIDIA/Arm* case discussed in detail above, which concerned the acquisition of Arm Limited's Intellectual Property Group business by chip designer and producer NVIDIA Corporation with a deal worth approximately \$40 billion.[1603] The parties aborted the transaction on February 8, 2022, upon the great resistance from the sector players and detailed reviews and challenges by competition authorities such as the Commission, the CMA, and the FTC.[1604] In the last quarter of 2021, the Commission granted unconditional approval to the transaction on the proposed acquisition of Nuance Communications, Inc. by Microsoft[1605] with a deal value of \$19.7 billion.[1606] In mid-2020, Microsoft publicly announced that it had completed the acquisition of Metaswitch Networks, a provider of virtualized network software and voice, data and communications solutions for operators on its official website.[1607] The transaction was alleged to be \$1.35 billion and was closed swiftly, only two months after its first public release, on May 14, 2020. Another high-value acquisition of 2020 was the *Google/Looker* case, with a total deal value of \$2.6 billion in cash.[1608]

As evident from above, the digital markets have witnessed high numbers of mergers and acquisitions, which were realized regardless of the fact that they were caught under the relevant merger control regimes and have set forth many challenging concepts and flared debate among antitrust experts in recent years.[1609] This has resulted in an even

---

[1601] European Commission Press Release IP/22/1762, Mergers: Commission Approves Acquisition of MGM by Amazon (Mar. 15, 2021), https://ec.europa.eu/commission/presscorner/detail/en/ip_22_1762.

[1602] Please *see* CMA's *Facebook/Giphy* decision, where the CMA directs Facebook to carve the target Giphy out; CMA, COMPLETED ACQUISITION BY FACEBOOK, INC (NOW META PLATFORMS, INC) OF GIPHY, INC. (Final Report) (Nov. 30, 2021).

[1603] CMA Press Release, CMA to Investigate NVIDIA's Takeover of Arm (Jan. 6, 2021), https://www.gov.uk/government/news/cma-to-investigate-nvidia-s-takeover-of-arm.

[1604] CMA, Anticipated Acquisition by NVIDIA Corporation of Arm Limited, Cancellation of Merger Reference (Feb. 8, 2022), https://assets.publishing.service.gov.uk/media/62028f4de90e077f7abdbb4e/Notice_of_cancellation_of_merger_reference_NVIDIA_.pdf.

[1605] European Commission Press Release IP/21/7067, Mergers: Commission Approves Acquisition of Nuance by Microsoft (Dec. 21, 2021), https://ec.europa.eu/commission/presscorner/detail/en/ip_21_7067. In its assessment, the Commission investigated (i) the horizontal overlaps in transcription software, (ii) the vertical link between services the parties provide, as well as (iii) conglomerate links, and ultimately, cleared the transaction in Phase I.

[1606] Microsoft Press release, Microsoft Accelerates Industry Cloud Strategy for Healthcare with the Acquisition of Nuance (Apr. 12, 2021), https://news.microsoft.com/2021/04/12/microsoft-accelerates-industry-cloud-strategy-for-healthcare-with-the-acquisition-of-nuance/.

[1607] Microsoft's public announcement is available at https://blogs.microsoft.com/blog/2020/05/14/microsoft-announces-definitive-agreement-to-acquire-metaswitch-networks-expanding-approach-to-empower-operators-and-partner-with-network-equipment-providers-to-deliver-on-promise-of-5g/#:~:text=Update%20July%2015%2C%202020%3A%20Microsoft,and%20communications%20solutions%20for%20operators.

[1608] The CMA cleared the transaction with a swift unconditional approval in Phase I. CMA, Completed Acquisition by Google LLC of Looker Data Sciences, Inc. (ME/6839/19) (Mar. 16, 2020), para. 24.

[1609] OECD, *OECD Handbook on Competition Policy in the Digital Age* 64 (2022), https://www.oecd.org/daf/competition-policy-in-the-digital-age

more skeptical approach by competition authorities and antitrust experts, advocating new regulations and closer scrutiny as they expect such momentum to be preserved and even grow higher within the next years.

7.3 General Overview of Digital Markets from a Competition Law Perspective

Before delving into the details of creeping acquisitions and defensive acquisitions in digital markets, it would be beneficial to briefly review the digital markets from a competition law perspective, and describe the general approaches of competition authorities to mergers and acquisitions in dynamic markets, specifically in the digital sectors, which present special challenges themselves.[1610] Recognizing challenges is relatively easy, though, compared to adopting legal policy preferences to the requirements of those challenges. There are, of course, many competition law studies attempting to actively propose an entirely different approach to both understanding and regulating these markets with their own dynamics,[1611] but as demonstrated, competition law enforcement on both sides of the Atlantic seems to be more inspired by the threats side of the medallion than the opportunities side, at least as far as the initial enforcement reflexes of the antitrust agencies are concerned, both in terms of rejecting the existence of special circumstances in the form of multi-sided dynamics,[1612] and in terms of a general tendency to use innovation

---

[1610]   *Id. See also* Antonio Capobianco & Anita Nyeso, *Challenges for Competition Law Enforcement and Policy in the Digital Economy*, 9 J. Eur. Competition L. & Prac. 19 (2018).

[1611]   Some examples of such approaches are featured in: Gönenç Gürkaynak, Esra Uçtu & Anıl Acar, *Applying the Dynamic Competition Approach to Zero-Priced Markets*, in Douglas H. Ginsburg, An Antitrust Professor on the Bench – Liber Amicorum, Vol. I 307 (Nicolas Charbit, Carolina Malhado & Ellie Yang eds., Concurrences 2018); D. Daniel Sokol & Ma Jingyuan, *Understanding Online Markets and Antitrust Analysis*, 15 Nw. J. Tech. & Intell. Prop. 43, 46 (2017), http://scholarlycommons.law.northwestern.edu/njtip/vol15/iss1/2; Michal S. Gal & Daniel L. Rubinfeld, *The Hidden Costs of Free Goods: Implications for Antitrust Enforcement*, 80 Antitrust L.J. 521, 522 (2016); David S. Evans, *The Antitrust Economics of Two-Sided Markets*, 20 Yale J. on Regul. 325, 332 (2003); Daniel O'Connor, *Understanding Online Platform Competition: Common Misunderstandings*, Internet Competition and Regulation of Online Platforms Competition Policy Int'l 1, 5 (May 2016), https://papers.ssrn.com/abstract=2760061; Andres V. Lerner, *The Role of "Big Data" in Online Platform Competition* 46 (2014), https://ssrn.com/abstract=2482780; Torsten Körber, *Common Errors Regarding Search Engine Regulation – and How to Avoid Them*, 36 Eur. Competition L. Rev. 239, 241 (2015); and OECD, *The Digital Economy* 5–6 (DAF/COMP(2012)22, Feb. 7, 2013), http://www.oecd.org/officialdocuments/publicdisplaydocumentpdf/?cote=DAF/COMP(2012)22&docLanguage=En; or for an earlier attempt example, Marc Bourreau & Nathalie Sonnac, *Introduction to Competition in Two-Sided Markets: Application to Information and Communication Industries*, 61 Communications & Strategies 11, 12 (2006).

[1612]   Case C-67/13 P, Cartes Bancaires v. European Commission, ECLI:EU:C:2014:2204; Ohio et al. v. American Express Co. et al., 585 U. S.___ (2018). In the European Union, in *Cartes Bancaires*, guiding the Commission and the General Court, the Court of Justice of the European Union concluded that it was necessary to consider the two interlinked sides of the platform in order to properly analyze and evaluate the competitive effects. In the US, in *Ohio*, the Supreme Court concluded that both sides of the two-sided credit card market (i.e., cardholders and merchants) should be taken into consideration when defining the relevant product market , and requiring the effect of Amex's conduct on the (i) number, and (ii) price of credit card transactions, as well as the (iii) competition stifling effects of the provisions to be demonstrated, thereby upholding the anti-steering provisions of Amex.

only as a source of concern and not so much as a counterbalancing factor of traditional distributive efficiency concerns, especially in the merger control analysis.[1613]

Digital markets possess three essential characteristics that might be important in terms of competition law, namely, (i) *extreme returns to scale*, (ii) *network externalities*, and (iii) *the role of data*. Firstly, the cost of production is not proportional to the number of customers served in the case of digital services; in fact, it is much lower, and the marginal cost of production is close to zero. The existence of such *extreme returns to scale* can lead to a significant competitive advantage for incumbents. Secondly, the convenience and utility of using a particular technology or service increase with the number of users that adopt it. These network effects could also prevent a new superior platform from displacing an established incumbent, resulting in yet another *"incumbent advantage."* Finally, the rapid evolution of technology over recent decades has made it possible for companies to collect, store, process, and use large amounts of data. The ability of companies that are working on artificial intelligence projects and creating other online services to employ such data to develop new services and products is an increasingly crucial competitive parameter in the digital sectors.[1614]

The objective of the merger control system is to ensure that proposed merger transactions do not harm competition on the price and quantity of current and new products in the relevant market. If a particular merger is likely to significantly increase the prices or reduce the quantity of the products/services offered in the market, then it would be reasonable to conclude that the merger is anti-competitive in its effects. The virtues of price and quantity as anti-competitive parameters are that they tend to be readily observable and easily lend themselves to empirical analysis. Antitrust practitioners and economists possess a variety of tools to model price and quantity effects, based on sales and diversion data.[1615]

[1613]   For instance, in the European Union, *see* case M.8084 – *Bayer/Monsanto* (2018); case M.7932 – *Dow/DuPont* (2017); case M.7275 – *Novartis/Glaxo Smith Kline's Oncology Business* (2015); case M.7326 – *Medtronic/Covidien* (2014); case M.7559 – *Pfizer/Hospira* (2015); case M.6203 – *Western Digital/Viviti Technologies* (2011); case M.6166 – *Deutsche Börse/NYSE* (2012); case M.7278 – *GE/Alstom* (2015), and in the United States, *see*, for example, *Zillow, Inc./Trulia, Inc.* (2015); and Memorandum Opinion, *U.S. v. Bazaarvoice, Inc.*, C-13-0133 (2012). As discussed in earlier chapters, in *Bayer/Monsanto*, the Commission conditionally approved the acquisition after finding the transaction to be likely to significantly reduce competition on price and innovation, both in Europe and globally, in a number of different markets, relying on a set of remedies to ensure that effective competition and innovation in the markets for seeds, pesticides, and digital agriculture would be preserved and not be harmed as a result of the transaction. In *Dow/DuPont*, the Commission conditionally approved the merger between Dow and DuPont, requiring the divestiture of major parts of DuPont's global pesticide business, including its global R&D organization, so that the transaction would not reduce price competition and innovation in the market for existing pesticides. In *Zillow*, the FTC evaluated innovation claims within the context of two-sided markets and investigated whether the proposed transaction would reduce the merged entity's incentives to innovate (either on the consumer side or the advertiser side of its platform). When deciding unanimously to close its investigation, it cited a lack of evidence suggesting that the combined entity "would have a reduced incentive to innovate either on the consumer side or the advertiser side of its platform."

[1614]   CRÉMER ET AL., *supra* note 1567.

[1615]   Terrell McSweeny & Brian O'Dea, *Data, Innovation, and Potential Competition in Digital Markets – Looking Beyond Short-Term Price Effects in Merger Analysis*, CPI ANTITRUST CHRON. 1, 1 (2018), https://www.competitionpolicyinternational.com/data-innovation-and-potential-competition-in-digital-markets-looking-beyond-short-term-price-effects-in-merger-analysis/.

However, in dynamic markets, merger control's objectives also include preserving the potential for innovation, regardless of who is going to introduce and offer the next innovation to the relevant market. More specifically, in the context of digital markets, the following features must also be considered and taken into account by the merger control authorities in order to achieve the relevant objective: (i) the role of leapfrogging innovation, (ii) network effects that are often strong but short-lived, (iii) the fact that the lines between substitution and complementarity are blurred in such markets, (iv) the characteristics of two-sided markets, and (v) the potential for brand new business models (i.e., the sharing economy).[1616]

Similar to the objectives of merger control, the available methods for analyzing and evaluating possible (anti-)competitive effects also differ for dynamic markets, and specifically in the case of digital markets. In fact, for many digital markets, relying solely on traditional, price-based modeling in merger analysis is likely to be inadequate and ineffective. This is especially true in the case of two-sided markets, which involve two distinct sets of customers and are particularly common in the digital realm.[1617]

It is a common characteristic of two-sided markets that users on one side of the market subsidize the users on the other side. This is often the case in digital markets as well. Indeed, digital products and services are often offered to customers for "free." Well-known examples of such "free" services include Internet search engines, social networks (such as Facebook, WhatsApp, Instagram, and Twitter), booking engines (such as OpenTable and Expedia), and even widely used software products, such as Adobe PDF.[1618]

Modeling the price effects on the "free" side of these digital markets would be of little practical use or analytical value. Therefore, it becomes challenging to employ traditional models to measure the possible effects of a merger in digital markets. On that note, it is not surprising that antitrust practitioners and economists have reached almost the same conclusion in terms of the urgent need for developing alternative approaches and analytical tools for conducting merger reviews in digital markets. An alternative approach has been discussed about the paying side of these markets in merger investigations to focus on the market as a proxy for the overall competition.[1619] However, this approach and analytical method would fail to capture the substantial possibilities for harm to users on the "free" side of the market, since competition can be vigorous even when the products or services are offered to consumers for "free." In many cases, that competition takes the form of innovation to provide customers with quality improvements or new products. Therefore, mergers in digital markets can certainly threaten that sphere of competition, even in situations where users on the "paying" side of the market may be neutral or even in favor of the transactions.

For instance, the section of the US antitrust agencies' 2010 Horizontal Merger Guidelines that deals with innovation issues makes it clear that antitrust enforcement agencies should consider both sides of two-sided markets in the merger enforcement context and

---

[1616] Pascale Déchamps, Dynamic Markets and Dynamic Enforcement: A Focus on Merger Control, 12th Annual Conference of the GCLC 3 (Jan. 26, 2017), https://www2.coleurope.eu/sites/default/files/uploads/event/pascale_dechamps_-_slides.pdf.

[1617] McSweeny & O'Dea, *supra* note 1615.

[1618] *Id.*

[1619] *Id.*

carefully examine the potential for *harm to innovation* and *quality effects* in mergers involving digital markets. McSweeny and O'Dea indicate that antitrust enforcers should also look closely for evidence that mergers in digital markets may eliminate potential competition, and they recommend that enforcement agencies pursue cases aggressively in this area, including under section 2 of the Sherman Act, where appropriate. The authors also suggest that competition enforcement authorities should be sufficiently attuned to the competitive significance of *data*, which can operate as a barrier to entry that may be strengthened by mergers in digital markets.[1620]

All in all, most antitrust practitioners and economists (as well as some competition authorities) agree that merger or acquisition transactions in digital markets should be treated and handled differently than other transactions that are reviewed by using traditional methods. Accordingly, the discussion will now focus on how acquisition transactions in the digital sectors differ and diverge from similar transactions in traditional markets, and examine how they are treated by certain competition enforcement authorities, specifically in cases of *creeping* and *defensive acquisitions*.

7.4 The Motivations Underlying Digital Conglomerate Mergers

Bourreau and de Streel have explained the underlying motivations of conglomerate mergers among digital firms, by utilizing past and current theories that had been developed for analyzing general/traditional conglomerate mergers. In this regard, the *market power theory* in the conglomerate literature asserts that firms expand into neighboring markets because this allows them to increase their market power indirectly. This motivation may also be valid in the case of digital conglomerates. In particular, digital firms may have compelling and rational incentives to create product ecosystems, which increase market differentiation and soften competition.[1621] The authors also point out that the *resource theory* provides another interesting framework to analyze the expansion of digital players into neighboring markets: As digital players possess valuable resources of various types that may be in excess capacity at a particular moment in time, according to this theory, this would incentivize the firms to expand into neighboring markets. Moreover, digital companies also heavily recruit talent, which is considered an essential resource (particularly in technology and software markets), and by doing so, accumulate knowledge and expertise in these same areas. Finally, digital firms use or generate inputs – such as consumer data – that can be used in a variety of products, which may further induce them to consider expanding into neighboring markets.

Another alternative theory put forth by Bourreau and de Streel is that digital conglomerate mergers can also be explained by the *internal capital markets theory*, according to which it is easier for new ventures to obtain funding from internal sources than from external

---

[1620]   *Id.*
[1621]   Bourreau & de Streel, *supra* note 1561, at 6–7.

capital markets. Generally speaking, the digital sector is highly innovative, and firms in this sector mostly engage in product development, which is a risky and uncertain endeavor by its very nature. One could argue that if a particular project fails, the ability to reallocate assets quickly and efficiently may represent an advantage for firms in the digital sector, and the sector may thus favor the conglomerate format. In addition, it can be observed that many digital firms invest in new start-ups through venture funding, which also appears to be consistent with the *internal capital markets theory*.

As for the new theories relating to conglomerate mergers, Bourreau and de Streel explain the rise of digital conglomerates by the presence of substantial economies of scope in the development of digital products and services (on the supply side), and by the consumption synergies derived by consumers when adopting product ecosystems (on the demand side). The authors contend that these two characteristics favor the development of wider product portfolios by digital players.[1622] In this regard, it is worth noting that digital products and services use sharable inputs and thus imply significant economies of scope in product development. Furthermore, modular product design provides a digital output (e.g., a map service) also to be used as an input (e.g., for a navigation system) and some sharable digital inputs (e.g., hardware, software or algorithms) comprise general-purpose technologies, which can be implemented and incorporated into a wide variety of products and services, allowing firms to expand into weakly related markets.[1623] As a consequence, digital firms have broad incentives to expand their product lines, in particular via internal diversification projects. Acquiring new ventures may also allow digital companies to use modules from their targets across their product portfolios, reinforcing the magnitude of the economies of scope gained from such activities. If sharable inputs (e.g., data) and modular design practices facilitate the expansion of a company into a multi-product entity, they can also create opportunities for cooperation in product development between competing firms.[1624]

It has also been argued that synergies can arise from the demand side as well, where, for instance, consumers can positively value and prefer purchasing different products or services from the same seller. Such consumption synergies may be generated by the efficient results of *bundling* or lower transaction costs (e.g., lower search costs for individual products). Consumption synergies can also be endogenous to the decisions of undertakings. Firms can invest in creating ties or linkages between their different products (even possibly unrelated products), in order to increase the complementarity between them (e.g., Apple Watch can only be used together with an Apple iPhone). Therefore, a consumer can derive an additional benefit (i.e., a consumption synergy) when buying complementary products together. The authors refer to such a set of products sold separately by a firm, which generate consumption synergies for consumers when bought together, as a "product ecosystem."[1625] Consequently, such demand-side synergies provide an incentive for firms to expand their product lines (or to create product ecosystems) in order to capture some of the value generated for consumers by consumption synergies, as well as offering an incentive to expand into new markets to develop product ecosystems.[1626]

[1622]   *Id.* at 7.
[1623]   *Id.* at 8.
[1624]   *Id.* at 10.
[1625]   *Id.*
[1626]   *Id.* at 11.

The Report of the Digital Competition Expert Panel provides additional suggestions on the possible motivations underlying acquisitions in digital sectors, as follows: (i) buying companies that could have potentially become competitors to the acquiring company (e.g., Facebook's acquisition of Instagram); (ii) acquiring businesses that have delivered a strong position to a platform in a related market (for example, Google's acquisition of DoubleClick, the advertising technology business); and (iii) purchasing data-driven firms in related markets, which may cement the acquirer's strong position in both markets (e.g., the acquisitions of YouTube by Google and WhatsApp by Facebook).[1627] Nevertheless, these suggestions are criticized and even deemed to feed the various common misconceptions.[1628] Yun also explains that particularly with respect to Instagram, which certainly lacked any substantial income or employee force at the time of its acquisition by Facebook, it may actually be argued that the exponential growth in its users and output following the transaction was *pro*-competitive. This is compared with Google Plus (Google+), which, despite the network effects of the tech giant Google, was scrapped by the company due to its failure to achieve any substantive success.[1629] This just goes to show that it is very difficult to predict market outcomes in the digital sector, and best-laid plans and strategies, even by the mighty big tech with seemingly limitless data analysis capabilities, can topple drastically. Therefore, the overzealous approach by the competition authorities needs more objective and empirical analyses before it can condemn every transaction in this sector as a threat to consumer welfare.

7.5 Discussion on Notification Thresholds: Turnover or Transaction Value?

As stated earlier, the competition authorities worldwide are taking a dim view and skeptical approach towards creeping acquisitions. This skepticism stems from the competition authorities' realization of the possibility of structuring a large transaction as a series of smaller deals, thereby circumventing the merger review process, which might result in anti-competitive transactions. Several different approaches are used by competition enforcement authorities to address and tackle the issue of creeping acquisitions.[1630] The most commonly used methods are (i) the "*sectorial method*," (ii) the "*aggregation model*," and (iii) the "*substantial market power model*,"[1631,1632] which are described in detail below:

  a) Under the "*sectorial method*," transactions that would not usually trigger a merger notification will nevertheless be subject to merger control if they occur in an industry sector in which staggered transactions are identified and perceived as the means for acquiring market power and increasing concentrations. In these cases, implementing specific regulations to handle creeping acquisitions may

---

[1627] The Digital Competition Expert Panel Report, *supra* note 1580, at 11.
[1628] Manne, *supra* note 1557.
[1629] Yun, *supra* note 1584, at 6–8.
[1630] OECD Business and Industry Advisory Committee (BIAC), *supra* note 1565.
[1631] *Id.*
[1632] OECD, *supra* note 1558, recital 33.

be the preferred approach, which would require the notification of transactions that would not usually be subject to a merger filing. For example, in the United Kingdom, acquisitions by any large grocery retailer of any store with grocery sales that is larger than 1,000 square meters must be notified to the Office of Fair Trading by the acquiring party.[1633] Another illustrative example discussed in Chapter 5 was reducing the turnover threshold to ensure jurisdictional authority for mergers in strategic sectors: In 2018, the UK introduced a much lower merger control threshold (£1 million) by an amendment to the Enterprise Act 2002, for "relevant enterprises" (those companies active in sectors such as quantum technology, computer processing units, and military goods) as defined under the Act.

b) Under the "*aggregation model*," a series of transactions that would not ordinarily be subject to notification requirements will be subject to merger control when the acquisitions are carried out by the same parties and in the same or a related market over a specified period.[1634] One illustrative example of this method is the EC Merger Regulation,[1635] which provides that "two or more transactions (within the meaning of the first subparagraph) which take place within a two-year period between the same persons or undertakings shall be treated as one and the same concentration arising on the date of the last transaction."[1636] Similar provisions also apply in both the US[1637] and the UK.[1638,1639]

[1633] *Id.*

[1634] There are three circumstances that may be relevant under the *aggregation model*: (i) when a first transaction not meeting the threshold is followed by a second one requiring notification, then the first transaction must be notified as well; (ii) when a first notifiable transaction is followed by a second transaction falling below the threshold, then the latter transaction is notifiable as well; and (iii) when the same purchaser simultaneously acquires two or more shares of a company from the same vendor, the transactions are treated as constituting a single transaction for determining whether they meet the notification requirements.

[1635] European Union, Council Regulation (EC) No. 139/2004 of Jan. 20, 2004, on the Control of Concentrations Between Undertakings (the "EC Merger Regulation" or "EUMR"), 2004 OJ (I 24) 1, https://eur-lex.europa.eu/legal-content/EN/TXT/PDF/?uri=CELEX:32004R0139&from=EN.

[1636] *See* article 5(2) of the EC Merger Regulation. According to the EC Consolidated Jurisdictional Notice under Council Regulation (EC) No. 139/2004 on the Control of Concentrations Between Undertakings, 2008 OJ (C 95) 1, the purpose of this provision is "to ensure that the same persons do not break a transaction down into series of sales of assets over a period of time, with the aim of avoiding the competence conferred on the Commission by the Merger Regulation." The European courts have supported this interpretation and stated that "a concentration within the meaning of Article 3(1) of Regulation No 4064/89 may be deemed to arise even in the case of a number of formally distinct legal transactions, provided that those transactions are interdependent in such a way that none of them would be carried out without the others and that the result consists in conferring on one or more undertakings direct or indirect economic control over activities of one or more other undertakings" (case T-282/02, Cementbouw v. Commission, 2006 ECR II-319).

[1637] In the United States, the Hart-Scott-Rodino Antitrust Improvements Act of 1976 (Pub. L. No. 94-435, known commonly as the "HSR Act") refers to the aggregation of separate acquisitions of voting securities, assets or other "noncorporate interests" within 180 days (*see* 16 CFR § 801.13 Aggregation of voting securities, assets, and non-corporate interests).

[1638] The OFT has a broader time horizon to treat successive events as having occurred simultaneously. According to subsections 27(5) and 27(6) of the 2002 Enterprise Act, "(5) The decision making authority may, for a reference, treat successive events to which this subsection applies when occurred on the date on which the latest of them occurred. (6) Subsection (5) applies to successive events; (a) which occur within a period of two years under or in consequence of the same arrangements or transaction, or successive arrangements or transactions between the same parties or interests; and (b) by virtue of each of which, under or in consequence of the arrangements or the transaction or transactions concerned, any enterprises cease as between themselves to be distinct enterprises."

[1639] OECD, *supra* note 1558, recital 33.

c) Under the *"substantial market power model,"* an acquisition by a company that has reached a certain level of market power is subject to a merger control filing, irrespective of the size or the market share of the target company. This is, for example, the case in Sweden, where the Swedish Competition Authority may request notification of a merger if (i) the total turnover threshold is met, but the individual turnover threshold is not met, and (ii) the acquirer is a strong undertaking obtaining control over small undertakings one by one.[1640]

Many jurisdictions have provisions that give antitrust authorities an *ex post* control of creeping acquisitions that result in a substantial lessening of competition, or lead to an abuse of dominant position.[1641] On the other hand, some commentators hold divergent views and argue that, regardless of the model used to regulate and prevent creeping acquisitions, a degree of legal uncertainty is incorporated into the merger control system.[1642] This legal uncertainty stems mainly from the fact that a transaction that was considered *de minimis* and not subject to a merger filing can later be "clawed back," and it may have to be undone if it is subsequently found to have had an anti-competitive effect on the relevant market. Rules on creeping acquisitions reflect the need for competition enforcement authorities to be able to challenge situations of a substantial lessening of competition resulting from a series of related transactions, each of which would have failed to meet the notification requirements on a stand-alone basis. This system, however, opens the door to subsequent reviews for those transactions that have already been consummated.[1643]

Moreover, it seems that even a notification threshold based on turnover would not be sufficient to capture some potentially harmful *"killer acquisitions,"* as those acquisitions often happen early in the life cycle of the target firms when they have not yet reached a significant monetary turnover. This is especially true in the case of the digital economy, where many start-ups initially focus much more on growing their customer base than increasing their turnover or profits, as they seek to be the first company to grow sufficiently large to benefit from network effects, so that the market might tip in their favor for the foreseeable future.[1644]

The Monopolies Commission of Germany, in 2015,[1645] recommended that the German government complement the existing merger control thresholds based on turnover by attaching additional notification requirements based on transaction volume. The Monopolies

---

[1640]   *Id.*

[1641]   OECD Business and Industry Advisory Committee (BIAC), *supra* note 1565, recital 12. For instance, in the US, even if the pre-merger notification conditions of the Hart-Scott-Rodino Act are not met, the agencies can intervene against creeping acquisitions, using the more general provisions of section 7 of the Clayton Act and section 5 of the Federal Trade Commission Act. In France, article L. 430-9 of the Commercial Code allows the Competition Authority to issue injunctions (including rescission orders) in respect of concentrations resulting in the abuse of a dominant position or the creation of a "state of economic dependence"; this applies "even if these acts have been subject to the procedure specified in the Code." This prerogative is used in the case of successive acquisitions, which, taken separately, did not breach competition law rules but, in aggregate, resulted in an anti-competitive situation.

[1642]   *Id.*, recital 5; OECD, *supra* note 1558, recital 32, n. 57: "The uncertainty extends to (a) the merging parties' decision on whether to file; (b) the level of supporting work that will be necessary to prepare a filing and ensure clearance; and (c) the competition authority's assessment process."

[1643]   OECD, *supra* note 1558, recital 32.

[1644]   Bourreau & de Streel, *supra* note 1561, at 29.

[1645]   The Monopolies Commission is a permanent, independent expert committee that advises the German government and legislature in the areas of competition policy-making, competition law, and regulation.

Commission reported that the acquisition of a company with low turnover could not be captured or examined by the merger control regime under the current notification requirements of German law, even in cases where the acquired company holds commercially valuable data or possesses considerable market potential for other reasons. According to the Monopolies Commission, in the digital economy, the purchase price often reflects the economic potential of an acquisition target more accurately than its previous turnover.[1646] In 2018, Germany amended its notification thresholds so that transactions exceeding €400 million must obtain an approval from antitrust enforcement authorities even if the target company has substantial operations but little turnover in Germany. By June 2019, the Federal Cartel Office in Germany had reviewed eighteen transactions under this new rule, but did not block any of them. The President of the German competition authority, Andreas Mundt, stated that the new threshold was meant to capture killer acquisitions, and remarked that identifying these deals is still substantively very difficult. He also declared that "It demands an enormous power of prognosis from authorities to say this exact transaction is the one that should be forbidden because it will be a substantial competitor in the future."[1647]

On a relevant note, the Report of the Digital Competition Expert Panel refers to the CMA's merger control review process and asserts that, in contrast to many other competition authorities (which have not been able to assess low-turnover, high-value acquisitions by using their existing turnover or market share thresholds), the CMA has benefited from having the ability to examine any merger or acquisition that results in the supply or purchase of at least 25% of any goods or services in the UK. Furthermore, the panel has observed that this "share of supply" test has provided the CMA with the flexibility and reach to address and evaluate mergers that may not trigger traditional turnover thresholds, but which may nonetheless have a significant impact on competition and innovation.[1648]

Moreover, there is currently a lively debate as to whether the current EU merger control guidelines are capable of identifying the relevant *creeping acquisition* transactions for review.[1649] In fact, in 2016, the European Commission issued its Public Consultation Paper,[1650] which discussed the practice of using turnover-based thresholds for evaluating the effects of mergers. This Public Consultation Paper mainly discussed the effectiveness of the turnover-based jurisdictional thresholds of the EC Merger Regulation and stated that the EC Merger Regulation only applies to concentrations with a European Union dimension, which comprise those transactions where the concerned undertakings meet the relevant turnover thresholds. This paper indicates that debate has recently emerged on the effectiveness of these purely turnover-based jurisdictional thresholds, specifically on whether these thresholds allow antitrust authorities to capture and assess all the transactions that can potentially have an impact on the internal market of the EU. The paper empha-

---

[1646] MONOPOLIES COMMISSION, COMPETITION POLICY: THE CHALLENGE OF DIGITAL MARKET, Special Report by the Monopolies Commission pursuant to Section 44(1)(4) ARC (June 1, 2015), recital S54, https://www.monopolkommission.de/index.php/en/press-releases/52-competition-policy-the-challenge-of-digital-markets.

[1647] Charley Connor, *Vestager: EU Is Considering Value-Based Thresholds*, GCR (June 19, 2019), https://globalcompetitionreview.com/article/1194225/vestager-eu-is-considering-value-based-thresholds.

[1648] The Digital Competition Expert Panel Report, *supra* note 1580, at 120.

[1649] Déchamps, *supra* note 1616, at 4.

[1650] European Commission Public Consultations, Consultation on Evaluation of Procedural and Jurisdictional Aspects of EU Merger Control (2016), http://ec.europa.eu/competition/consultations/2016_merger_control/index_en.html.

sizes that this issue may be particularly significant in specific sectors, such as the digital and pharmaceutical industries, where the acquired company, while having generated little turnover so far, may nevertheless (i) perform a competitive role, (ii) hold commercially valuable data, or (iii) have considerable market potential for other reasons. On that note, the Commission has implied that certain acquisitions in digital sectors might have effects on the relevant market(s), despite not exceeding the turnover thresholds.

A minority of respondents of the above-mentioned Public Consultation Paper, including several national competition authorities and other public bodies, as well as a few companies and associations, have identified and acknowledged the existence of such an enforcement gap, and they have come out in favor of introducing complementary jurisdictional thresholds. On that note, the respondents in question cited the digital sector most frequently as an area where the EC Merger Regulation may fail to capture all of the competitively significant cross-border transactions.[1651] With that said, it should be noted that the majority of public and private stakeholders responding to the questionnaire did not perceive any (significant) enforcement gap with respect to highly valued acquisitions of target companies that do not generate sufficient turnovers to meet the jurisdictional thresholds of article 1 of the EC Merger Regulation, and observed that changing such jurisdictional thresholds would require legislative action. Furthermore, they expressly indicated that, especially for digital transactions, it would be difficult to geographically allocate the value of the transaction (if such an allocation were required as part of a "*deal size*" test).[1652]

Parallel to these discussions, Crémer et al. have assessed the need for an amendment to the merger notification threshold in the European Union, in the 2019 report they prepared on behalf of the Commission regarding competition policy in the digital sectors.[1653] Expressing their personal views, they stated that "[w]hile it is important to ensure that potentially anti-competitive transactions are duly scrutinised by competition authorities, one also has to consider the market need for legal certainty, as well as the need to minimise the additional administrative burden and transaction costs which an extension of jurisdiction would trigger." The authors therefore concluded that it is too early to modify the EC Merger Regulation's jurisdictional thresholds and that it would be better, for the time being, to monitor the performance of the thresholds based on transaction value, which has recently been introduced by certain Member States, as well as the functioning of the referral system. However, they also added that if systematic jurisdictional gaps were to arise in the future, a "smart" amendment to the EC Merger Regulation thresholds might then be justified.

As a counter-argument, Bourreau and de Streel have put forth the view that the current merger notification thresholds should be complemented by a threshold based on the value of the merger transaction, as is now the case in Germany and Austria.[1654] The authors also argue that this complementary threshold would not imply that all concentrations with a transaction value

---

[1651] European Commission, Summary of Replies to the Public Consultation on Evaluation of Procedural and Jurisdictional Aspects of EU Merger Control (July 2017), http://ec.europa.eu/competition/consultations/2016_merger_control/summary_of_replies_en.pdf.

[1652] *Id.*

[1653] CRÉMER ET AL., *supra* note 1567, at 10.

[1654] The European Commission carried out a public consultation on this issue from Oct. 2016 to Jan. 2017, http://ec.europa.eu/competition/consultations/2016_merger_control/index_en.html.

relatively higher than the turnover value should be considered or treated as anti-competitive *killer acquisitions*. Instead, they contend that such a complementary threshold would merely mean that such transactions should be reviewed by the Commission to determine whether the high transaction price reflects the substantial future revenues expected from the innovative target (which would be *welfare-enhancing*) or whether it reflects the insurance premium for achieving market stability and obtaining monopoly rents when the acquired innovation is killed following the merger (which would be *welfare-detrimental*).

Bourreau and de Streel also observe that this change should not substantially increase the number of concentrations to be notified, as the transaction value is aligned with the merging firms' monetary turnovers in most merger cases.[1655]

Several lawyers and consultants have recently expressed concerns about the transaction value being considered as one of the notification criteria in merger cases.[1656] In summary, they are of the view that:

a) High-value deals should not be assumed to be problematic.

b) The value of a deal indicates an expectation about what a business could mean to the future of the purchasing company; it says nothing about possible competition concerns.

c) Hopes and expectations that inform the deal price that one company is willing to pay to acquire another often take years to materialize, and they turn out to be incorrect or inaccurate in many cases. Such uncertainty makes competition analysis rather difficult.

d) Value-based thresholds in the EU could deter investments in the European technology sector. Although the US has high levels of investment despite its value-based notification requirements, US competition authorities require far less information from notifying companies than European authorities do.

e) The merger control process is not necessarily a decisive factor when it comes to investments in innovation; however, adding more complexity to an already challenging investment environment in Europe will not necessarily help increase such investments.

f) Broadly applying a transaction-based threshold would have an effect similar to the abolition of the two-party threshold, and this would capture a huge number of unproblematic transactions in the merger review process.

g) Alternatives to a new notification threshold include (i) expanding the provision that allows Member States to refer deals to the Commission or (ii) allowing the regional antitrust authorities to take up and assess these cases on their own motion(s).

h) The Commission must ensure that national competition authorities are on board with any such proposals, as amendments to the merger control regime will affect the *"carefully balanced distribution of competence"* between national authorities and the regional competition enforcer.

[1655] Bourreau & de Streel, *supra* note 1561, at 30.

[1656] Charley Connor, *Lawyers Warn Against Value-Based Merger Thresholds*, GCR (June 20, 2019), https://global-competitionreview.com/article/1194270/eu-lawyers-warn-against-value-based-merger-thresholds.

The study conducted by the Commission regarding the effectiveness of thresholds[1657] concluded that while the mechanisms in place were able to capture most of the transactions that had a significant impact on competition in the EU internal market, there were still a few transactions, especially in the digital and pharma sectors, which were able to evade the review mechanism of the Commission and Member States. Accordingly, in light of the above-mentioned concerns, the Commission published guidance[1658] regarding the "referral mechanism" set out in article 22 of the EU Merger Regulation, which had been initially designed for Member States without a merger control regime to refer cases to the Commission[1659] and until recently, only used for cases where the referring Member States had jurisdiction.[1660] Now, article 22 has been reappraised as a tool to catch transactions that do not meet the jurisdictional turnover thresholds but are otherwise deemed "competitively significant" by way of the Commission's "Article 22 Guidance" that was introduced following the Commission's examination of the effectiveness of the said thresholds. The first application of this reappraised article 22 referral was used in the proposed *Illumina/Grail* transaction, as explained further below.

7.6 The Assessment of the Competitive Effects of Pre-emptive Mergers in Digital Markets

When reviewing a merger transaction, the European Commission assesses its impacts on all the parameters of competition, such as prices, output, choice, and quality, as well as evaluating its impact on innovation.[1661]

[1657] European Commission, Commission Staff Working Document, *Evaluation of Procedural and Jurisdictional Aspects of EU Merger Control*, SWD(202) 66 final (Mar. 26, 2021), https://ec.europa.eu/competition/consultations/2021_merger_control/SWD_findings_of_evaluation.pdf.

[1658] European Commission, *Commission Guidance on the Application of the Referral Mechanism Set out in Article 22 of the Merger Regulation to Certain Categories of Cases*, C(2021) 1959 final (Mar. 26, 2021) ("Article 22 Guidance"), https://ec.europa.eu/competition/consultations/2021_merger_control/guidance_article_22_referrals.pdf

[1659] Initially discussed in Chapter 4 above. *See also* Sophie Lawrance & Sean-Paul Brankin, *Illumina/GRAIL: Bio-Tech Companies in the Firing Line as the European Commission Expands the Limits of European Merger Control*, BRISTOWS (Oct. 13, 2021), https://www.bristows.com/news/illumina-grail-bio-tech-companies-in-the-firing-line-as-the-european-commission-expands-the-limits-of-european-merger-control.

[1660] Van Bael & Bellis, *Commission Issues Statement of Objections in Illumina/GRAIL Gun-Jumping Investigation as Parties Argue Jurisdictional Overreach*, 2021 VBB ON COMPETITION L. 3 (Sept. 2021), https://www.vbb.com/media/Insights_Newsletters/VBB_on_Competition_Law_Volume_2021_No_8-9.pdf.

[1661] European Commission, Guidelines on the Assessment of Horizontal Mergers Under the Council Regulation on the Control of Concentrations Between Undertakings ("EU Horizontal Merger Guidelines"), 2004 OJ (C 31), recital 38: "In markets where innovation is an important competitive force… effective competition may be significantly impeded by a merger between two important innovators, for instance between two companies with 'pipeline' products related to a specific product-market. Similarly, a firm with a relatively small market share may nevertheless be an important competitive force if it has promising pipeline products."

The US and EU merger guidelines instruct the antitrust agencies to be particularly cautious in authorizing the acquisition of a maverick firm. The US 2010 Horizontal Merger Guidelines declare that:

> A "maverick" firm [is] a firm that plays a disruptive role in the market to the benefit of customers. For example, if one of the merging firms has a strong incumbency position and the other merging firm threatens to disrupt market conditions with a new technology or business model, their merger can involve the loss of actual or potential competition. Likewise, one of the merging firms may have the incentive to take the lead in price cutting or other competitive conduct or to resist increases in industry prices. A firm that may discipline prices based on its ability and incentive to expand production rapidly using available capacity also can be a maverick, as can a firm that has often resisted otherwise prevailing industry norms to cooperate on price setting or other terms of competition.[1662]

The definition of a "*maverick firm*" in the Horizontal Merger Guidelines is broader than the definition of a "*disruptive innovator*," however, the general method of analysis suggested for assessing acquisitions involving maverick firms also applies to disruptive innovators.

For this reason, when a merger is notified, the relevant antitrust agency should determine whether the proposed transaction would increase or decrease consumer welfare. In the context of disruptive innovation, it is argued that the agency should first determine whether the acquired firm is a potential disruptor, and then assess whether the acquisition would slow down or terminate the innovation.[1663] As previously discussed in detail (in Chapter 4), the *Dow/DuPont* transaction is probably the case where the Commission most extensively analyzed the effects of a merger on the incentives of the merging parties to innovate.[1664] In that case, the Commission concluded that the merger was likely to lead to a reduction of innovation due to the discontinuation, delay, or reorientation of the parties' existing overlapping lines of research and pipeline products in the herbicide and insecticide markets and with reduced incentives to start new research projects. For these reasons, the Commission only allowed the merger to proceed after the divestment of a large part of DuPont's herbicide and insecticide businesses and its R&D organization, including pipelines at the discovery stages and its R&D facilities.[1665]

Before further discussing the assessment of the competitive effects of pre-emptive mergers in the context of digital markets, it would be beneficial to remember that, in the EU's merger control policy, conglomerate mergers are generally presumed to have positive welfare effects prior to the transaction, and their negative effects are only analyzed if the merger has potential implications for bundling and tying strategies. However, the specific characteristics of the digital industries may change the effects of conglomerate diversification, and this may very well affect the balance between pro- and anti-competitive effects.[1666]

[1662] US Dep't of Just. & Fed. Trade Comm'n, Horizontal Merger Guidelines (2010) § 2.1.5, https://www.ftc.gov/sites/default/files/attachments/merger-review/100819hmg.pdf.

[1663] OECD, *Disruptive Innovation and Competition Policy Enforcement – Note by Alexandre de Streel and Pierre Larouche* (DAF/COMP/GF(2015)7, Oct. 20, 2015), recital 35, https://ssrn.com/abstract=2678890.

[1664] Dow/DuPont, European Commission Decision case M.7932 (Mar. 27, 2017).

[1665] Bourreau & de Streel, *supra* note 1561, at 29.

[1666] *Id*. at 11.

In this regard, de Streel and Larouche refer to the concept of *"disruptive innovation,"*[1667] arguing that established firms may acquire potential disruptors in order to prevent a scenario in which the potential disruptor's innovation is brought to the market and destroys the established firm's business. The authors set forth that antitrust agencies should prohibit such mergers, which are welfare-detrimental, although it is not easy to determine whether the acquisition of a potential disruptor would decrease consumer welfare. Therefore, de Streel and Larouche assert that a precise test for the theory of harm needs to be applied for this purpose.[1668]

The Report of the Digital Competition Expert Panel (2019) indicates that, in markets where services are increasingly provided to consumers at no direct financial cost (i.e., for "free"), and where the primary focus of many businesses is on growing their user bases rather than concentrating on short-term profits, antitrust authorities will increasingly need to assess non-price effects (such as quality and choice) when reviewing merger and takeover transactions.[1669]

In this context, Shapiro has stated that "one promising way to tighten up on merger enforcement would be to apply tougher standards to mergers that may lessen competition in the future, even if they do not lessen competition right away. In the language of antitrust, these cases involve a loss of potential competition. One common fact pattern that can involve a loss of future competition occurs when a large incumbent firm acquires a highly capable firm operating in an adjacent space. This happens frequently in the technology sector. Prominent examples include Google's acquisition of YouTube in 2006 and DoubleClick in 2007, Facebook's acquisition of Instagram in 2012 and of the virtual reality firm Oculus VR in 2014, and Microsoft's acquisition of LinkedIn in 2016."[1670]

The Report of the Digital Competition Expert Panel put forth the criticism that decisions on whether to approve mergers have often focused on short-term impacts, and argued that, in dynamic digital markets, the long-term effects of a transaction are essential to assess whether a merger will harm competition or consumers.[1671] At present, merger assessments only consider how likely a merger will reduce competition, and this approach can leave a crucial regulatory enforcement gap in the case of digital mergers. On that note, the Report provides the following example: Consider a large platform seeking to acquire a smaller tech company based on an attractive innovation of the target company that gives it a real chance of competing for consumers. For the sake of this example, assume that if the companies were to merge, there would only be a modest efficiency benefit. However, if the smaller company would otherwise have become a serious and innovative competitor to the acquirer, the resulting competition would have generated far more significant consumer benefits. Therefore, the Report is concerned that, under the current merger control system, the relevant competition enforcement authorities could

---

[1667]   OECD, *supra* note 1663, recital 35. The authors refer to Bower and Christensen (1995) for distinguishing between two types of technological innovation: *sustaining innovation* takes place within the value network of the established firms and gives customers something more or better in the attributes they already value; *disruptive innovation* takes place outside the value network of the established firms and introduces a different package of attributes from the one that mainstream customers have historically valued.

[1668]   *Id.* at 9.

[1669]   The Digital Competition Expert Panel Report, *supra* note 1580, at 120.

[1670]   Shapiro, *supra* note 1575.

[1671]   The Digital Competition Expert Panel Report, *supra* note 1580, at 20.

only block the merger if they consider the smaller company more likely than not to be able to succeed as a competitor.[1672]

Colomo's view that restrictions on innovation have been assessed directly or indirectly by competition authorities has also become a subject of intense discussion in anti-trust circles.[1673] According to this framework, in the indirect approach, the competition authorities focus their analysis on market rivalry and foreclosure, which, in turn, influence all the parameters of competition, including innovation. Hence, the effects on innovation are taken into account only indirectly, as a consequence of the change. In the direct approach, however, the authorities focus their analysis directly on the issue of innovation, possibly bypassing the assessment of market foreclosure and its proof to the requisite legal standard. In this regard, Colomo rejects the second alternative and declares that there is no room in EU competition law for the direct introduction/assessment of inno-vation considerations. According to Colomo, the economic theories regarding innovation incentives are not sufficiently robust to meet the convincing high standard of proof set by the European Court of Justice or to ensure a meaningful constraint on the regulatory discretion of antitrust authorities.

Bourreau and de Streel, on the other hand, disagree with Colomo for three reasons. Firstly, they contend that the distinction between the two approaches (i.e., indirect and direct) is not always clear-cut in practice, as the competition authorities always assess the effects of conduct on the market rivalry. For instance, in *Dow/DuPont*, where the European Commission directly determined the effects of the merger on innovation, it also evaluated its effects on the market rivalry. Secondly, the authors argue that the indirect approach assumes that a decrease in the market rivalry is always detrimental to innovation. However, this assumption does not always hold, as demonstrated in several theoretical and empirical studies. Thirdly, and most importantly, there are a number of economic theories (within the industrial organization literature, as well as outside it) on which the antitrust agencies may base their evaluations, which would allow and enable antitrust authorities to directly assess the effects of a merger on innovation. Those economic theories are developing rapidly in the field of industrial organization, notably due to the bombshell *Dow/DuPont* case. In summary, Bourreau and de Streel argue that antitrust authorities should directly assess the effects of a concentration on innovation, by relying on specific but robust tools and useful concepts, such as *innovation markets* (as discussed above) or the *downward innovation pressure* test.

Bourreau and de Streel also assert that the potential anti-competitive effects of conglomerate mergers in digital markets can arise via the following: (i) bundling and envelopment, (ii) economies of scope in product development and product-line expansion, (iii) the emergence of gatekeepers, and (iv) pre-emptive acquisitions.[1674] Our discussion here will focus on the fourth path, as part of our analysis of defensive acquisitions in digital markets.

[1672]   *Id.* at 13.
[1673]   Pablo Ibáñez Colomo, *Restrictions on Innovation in EU Competition Law*, 41 Eur. L. Rev. 201 (2016).
[1674]   Bourreau & de Streel, *supra* note 1561, at 4.

7.6.1. Pre-emptive Acquisitions and Kill Zones

The concept of a *"kill zone"* in digital markets is defined as a range of products or services where incumbent digital players are likely to dominate. It is tough for a start-up firm to survive in the kill zone since the incumbent is likely to dominate either by acquiring its potential rivals or by reacting aggressively to market entries by launching competing products or services.[1675] This market dynamic also makes it very unlikely for potential entrants to obtain funding if their business involves developing products in the kill zone. A kill zone is characterized by the following factors: (i) big-tech companies can collect and process large amounts of data that allow them to predict new trends in the digital markets, (ii) they can also obtain such information from their investments in start-up companies, and finally (iii) many platform markets have tipped[1676] and reached a stable point (e.g., search engines, social networks), leaving little room for potential entrants. Accordingly, as Bourreau and de Streel have noted, a new entrant that wishes to grow as an independent company should avoid the kill zone, even if it possesses a superior technology. On the other hand, if a new entrant's fundamental objective is to be eventually bought out by a big firm, then it may have the opposite incentive, and thus choose to position its products in the kill zone.[1677]

In this context, Cunningham et al. have developed a relevant theory, which aims to analyze the motivation behind a particular type of acquisition known as *"killer acquisitions."* They have also proceeded to analyze the extent of killer acquisitions empirically. In their theoretical model, the project of a target firm is assumed to be still under development, assuming that the project necessitates extra costly investments and that its ultimate success is uncertain. In this framework, an incumbent acquirer would have weaker incentives to continue the development of a project than an entrepreneur if the new project overlaps with (i.e., potentially substitutes for) a product that already exists in the incumbent's portfolio. This is known as "the monopolist's disincentive created by its pre-invention monopoly profits."[1678] The authors demonstrate that this disincentive to innovate can be so strong that an incumbent firm may acquire an innovative entrepreneur to shut down the entrepreneur and its project development. On the other hand, the authors argue that both existing and future product-market competition reduce the disparity in project development decisions (i.e., whether to continue or terminate) between acquirers and independent entrepreneurs. Therefore, this decreases the incentive for making killer acquisitions.[1679]

The authors' empirical findings, gathered from the pharmaceutical industry, support their theoretical hypotheses. Using data regarding 35,000 drug projects that had been

---

[1675]   *Id.* at 19. The authors refer to an article in THE ECONOMIST; *see American Tech Giants Are Making Life Tough for Start-ups*, THE ECONOMIST (Oct. 26, 2018).

[1676]   A market is deemed to be "tipped" when only one platform is active due to all agents opting for a single platform.

[1677]   Bourreau & de Streel, *supra* note 1561, at 19.

[1678]   Kenneth Arrow, Economic Welfare and the Allocation of Resources for Invention, *in* NATIONAL BUREAU OF ECONOMIC RESEARCH, THE RATE AND DIRECTION OF INVENTIVE ACTIVITY: ECONOMIC AND SOCIAL FACTORS 609 (Princeton Univ. Press 1962).

[1679]   Cunningham et al., *supra* note 1582, at 2.

conducted by more than 6,700 pharmaceutical companies in the past two and a half decades, they find evidence indicating that incumbent firms terminate research projects from acquired companies when such projects (threaten to) cannibalize their existing products. In such cases, a project is 39.6% less likely to be continued after the acquisition, compared to drugs that are not acquired (controlling for various factors that could influence the decision to continue or terminate the project). Overall, the authors estimate that 6.4% of the acquisitions in their sample qualified as *killer acquisitions.*[1680] It should be pointed out, however, that despite this finding, Cunningham et al. do acknowledge that the overall effect of killer acquisitions on social welfare is ambiguous, and there may still be increased motivation for innovation.[1681] Furthermore, considering that successful exit opportunities (such as IPOs and acquisitions) are what incentivizes the venture capitalists,[1682] and thus draws investment to innovative start-ups which are prevalent in the digital sector, making "acquisitions" out to be the only villain is counterintuitive. Studies have shown that over-regulating the industry certainly diminishes the appetite and restricts the number of entrepreneurs and, correspondingly, new products and services that could have benefited the consumers.[1683] Nevertheless, authorities try to justify and rigorously defend their approach of increased regulation, claiming that they are not hampering innovation but, in fact, fostering it.[1684]

Some commentators have argued that the conglomeration observed in the digital era is a result of the *"diversification"* strategy, which has a different purpose than it has had in previous eras. In the past, diversification aimed to allocate capital in a way that reduced volatility and decreased the risk in returns for the firm's stakeholders. These commentators believe that, in today's digital era, conglomeration seems to be pursued more in fear of displacement rather than for handling business cyclicality.[1685]

One can argue that the competitive threat from new ventures may be different in the digital sector than it is in the pharmaceutical industry, due to the presence of significant network effects. If consumers switch from one product or service to another more rapidly and easily in the digital sector, the digital incumbent may face the risk of being totally displaced and supplanted by an entrant if consumers all switch to the new rival, thereby increasing the incumbent's pre-emption incentives. Conversely, if consumers face high switching costs due to network effects and coordination problems, then the competition threat faced by established firms will be mild, and hence, the incentives to pre-empt will also be weaker.[1686]

[1680]   Bourreau & de Streel, *supra* note 1561, at 19.

[1681]   Yun, *supra* note 1584, at 8.

[1682]   Devin Reilly, Daniel D. Sokol & David Toniatti, *The Importance of Exit via Acquisition to Venture Capital, Entrepreneurship, and Innovation* 4 (Feb. 8, 2022), https://ssrn.com/abstract=3981970.

[1683]   *Id.* at 22. For analyses on the dynamics of mergers & acquisitions and venture capital ("VC") investments and how stricter competition laws reduce VC activity, *see also* Gordon Phillips & Alexei Zhdanov, *Venture Capital Investments, Merger Activity, and Competition Laws around the World* (Aug. 29, 2021), https://faculty.tuck. dartmouth.edu/images/uploads/faculty/gordon-phillips/VC_Investments_and_Merger_Competition_Laws.pdf.

[1684]   Charles McConnell, *Cracking Down on Big Tech Acquisitions Won't Stifle Innovation, ACCC Official Says*, GCR (Nov. 23, 2021), https://globalcompetitionreview.com/digital-markets/cracking-down-big-tech-acquisitions-wont-stifle-innovation-accc-official-says.

[1685]   Yong Lim, *Tech Wars: Return of the Conglomerate – Throwback or Dawn of a New Series for Competition in the Digital Era?* 10 (2017), https://papers.ssrn.com/sol3/papers.cfm?abstract_id=3051560.

[1686]   Bourreau & de Streel, *supra* note 1561, at 19–20.

In addition to the project by Cunningham et al., the question of whether an incumbent who buys out an entrant will shut down the entrant's project (leading to a *killer acquisition*) has also been analyzed by Denicolò and Polo.[1687] The authors have evaluated the merging firms' incentives not only to stop their projects after the merger but also to avoid cannibalization between their projects. In their model, whether the merged entity keeps both of the research units active (or conversely, decides to shut down one of the research units) hinges on the shape of the function of the probability of success for the project, which depends on the R&D efforts. However, in their model, the acquiring firm decides to close one research unit, not due to *pre-emptive* motives but for reasons that pertain to the *efficiency of R&D*. It is also worth noting that, in Denicolò and Polo's model, if the cost function is not sufficiently convex, a merger to a monopoly can increase investments when, after the merger, one R&D lab is shut down while the other lab innovates with probability one (i.e., guaranteed success).[1688]

On the other hand, acquisitions of start-ups by incumbent firms can be based on valid reasons other than pre-emptive motives. Such acquisitions can be efficient, and they can benefit both parties to the transaction if the start-ups bring innovative new ideas and skills to the table, and the large firms provide the complementary skills and resources that are necessary to develop such ideas commercially.[1689] Indeed, the literature on commercialization strategies analyzes the trade-off for an innovator between selling the innovation and commercializing it on its own. In this regard, Teece[1690] argues that the extent to which complementary assets (such as marketing or after-sales support) are needed for the commercialization of innovation is an important factor as to whether an innovator commercializes its invention. Gans and Stern further contend that if no competitor has control of complementary assets, integrated structures – where the innovators commercialize their own inventions – are more likely to emerge.[1691] By contrast, Bourreau and de Streel indicate that if established firms control complementary assets, then hybrid forms of organization are more likely to emerge, and that it can also be expected that innovators will be more likely to be acquired by incumbents.[1692]

In summary, the acquisition of promising start-ups by large digital firms can be driven by *efficiency motives* or by *pre-emptive motives*, and they can potentially lead to *killer acquisitions*, to the detriment of innovation, although that cannot be a presumptive certainty. As Bourreau and de Streel suggest, competition enforcement authorities should consider the possibility of pre-emptive motives when dealing with mergers and acquisitions in the digital sector, especially in the case of innovative start-ups.

[1687] Vincenzo Denicolò & Michele Polo, *The Innovation Theory of Harm: An Appraisal* (2018), https://ssrn.com/abstract=3146731

[1688] Giulio Federico, Gregor Langus & Tommaso Valletti, *A Simple Model of Mergers and Innovation* 9 n. 15 (CESifo Working Paper No. 6539, June 2017), https://papers.ssrn.com/sol3/papers.cfm?abstract_id=3005163.

[1689] Bourreau & de Streel, *supra* note 1561, at 20.

[1690] David J. Teece, *Profiting from Technological Innovation: Implications for Integration, Collaboration, Licensing and Public Policy*, 15 RSCH. POL'Y 285, 288 (1986).

[1691] Joshua S. Gans & Scott Stern, *The Product Market and the Market for "Ideas": Commercialization Strategies for Technology Entrepreneurs*, 32 RSCH. POL'Y 333 (2003), as referred to in Bourreau & de Streel, *supra* note 1561.

[1692] Bourreau & de Streel, *supra* note 1561.

7.6.2. Possible Methods in Merger Analysis

Downward Innovation Pressure Test

Howard Shelanski has proposed a *"downward innovation pressure"* ("DIP") test, comprising an analysis of how the probabilities of introducing innovation will evolve in the post-merger market.[1693] This analysis is closely linked to the cannibalization effects of the innovation on the acquirer's own products or services. If possible, such an analysis should be carried out based on quantitative economic data and, if not, then on documentary evidence.

Three-Factor Analysis

Carl Shapiro's proposal involved grounding the merger analysis on the examination of three factors: (i) *contestability*, which relates to the nature of *ex post* product-market competition, (ii) *appropriability*, which concerns the possibilities for the successful inventor to capture the social benefits of its invention, and (iii) *synergies*, which involve the capabilities of enhancing innovation by combining the complementary assets of the merging firms. In this regard, it can be observed that the factors of *contestability* and *appropriability* relate to the *incentive* to innovate, while the factor of synergies relates to the *ability* to innovate. According to Shapiro, the antitrust agencies should determine firstly, whether the merger will significantly reduce contestability, i.e., the future rivalry between the merging parties, which is based on the calculation of an *innovation diversion ratio*, and secondly, whether the merger will nonetheless enhance innovation by increasing appropriability or by enabling merger-specific synergies.[1694]

Analysis of Cannibalization Risks and Post-Merger Effects

Similarly, Bourreau and de Streel have suggested that, in practice, the merger review process could occur as follows:

(i) Firstly, the antitrust agency should focus on the risks relating to the cannibalization effects. It could examine whether the acquired firm (i.e., the entrant), using its innovation, could actually "eat into" the market of the acquirer (i.e., incumbent). If the answer is No, then the inquiry need not proceed further.

(ii) If the answer is Yes, then the antitrust agency should ascertain how the post-merger cannibalization effects would influence the incentives of the incumbent to innovate. In this context, the antitrust agency should evaluate, taking uncertainty into account, whether the gains expected from innovating would be more significant than the losses to be incurred. The answer to that question would naturally be correlated to the market position of the incumbent: if the incumbent holds more market power, then its anticipated losses would be more significant.

[1693] Howard Shelanski, *Information, Innovation, and Competition Policy for the Internet*, 161 U. PA. L. REV. 1663 (2013), http://scholarship.law.upenn.edu/cgi/viewcontent.cgi?article=1025&context=penn_law_review.

[1694] Carl Shapiro, *Competition and Innovation: Did Arrow Hit the Bull's Eye? in* THE RATE AND DIRECTION OF INVENTIVE ACTIVITY REVISITED 361 (Josh Lerner & Scott Stern eds., Univ. of Chicago Press 2012), https://www.nber.org/chapters/c12360.pdf.

(iii) Once it becomes clearly apparent to the antitrust agency that the incumbent would have an incentive to delay or terminate the potential innovation, then the agency should inquire directly into the business plans of the incumbent, even if this would be an unusual step under the merger control regime. At that point, the incumbent should be able to explain clearly and convincingly why it would embrace the entrant's potentially disruptive innovation and not shelve or cancel it. Even better, the agency could request a commitment from the incumbent firm along those lines.[1695] In the absence of a convincing explanation or commitment, the merger should be blocked by the antitrust authority. The authors also refer to Schweitzer et al., emphasizing that the agency should also consider whether or not there is an overall strategy on the part of the incumbent to acquire fast-growing potential competitors systematically.[1696]

7.6.3. Discussions on the Need for an Updated Innovation Theory of Harm

Crémer et al. do not believe that the EC Merger Regulation currently requires a legislative update. However, they indicate that the substantive criteria for analyzing defensive acquisitions in digital sectors need to be reconsidered. They explicitly pointed out that the exploration of this competitive concern has been limited to a relatively small group of cases, where a dominant platform that benefits from strong positive network effects acquires a target with currently low turnover, fast-growing user base, and high future market potential. Accordingly, they conclude that it is in the context of such cases that competition law authorities should be particularly concerned about protecting the ability of competitors to enter the market, as competition in the market will typically be reduced. Buying up promising start-ups that offer fringe products or services may, therefore, result in the early elimination of potential competitive threats – which may be particularly problematic if done systematically.[1697]

The central position of the authors is that the SIEC test in general – and the "*strengthening of dominance*" criterion in particular – remains a sound basis for assessing the competitive effects of defensive acquisitions in digital sectors; however, they acknowledge that there exists a regulatory gap in the currently accepted theories of harm. To address this gap, they argue that, in cases involving conglomerate mergers,[1698] competition authorities

---

[1695]   OECD, *supra* note 1663.

[1696]   Heike Schweitzer, Justus Haucap, Wolfgang Kerber & Robert Welker, *Modernizing the Law on Abuse of Market Power. Report for the Federal Ministry for Economic Affairs and Energy of Germany* (2018), https://www.bmwi.de/Redaktion/DE/Downloads/Studien/modernisierung-der-missbrauchsaufsicht-fuer-marktmaechtige-unternehmen-zusammenfassung-englisch.pdf?__blob=publicationFile&v=3.

[1697]   CRÉMER ET AL., *supra* note 1567, at 116.

[1698]   In such conglomerate mergers, the operator of an ecosystem with a dominant position in a core market buys up a firm that is active in a separate but related market, and which has the potential to grow into a competitive threat beyond that market.

should inquire as to whether the acquirer and the target company operate in the same *"technological space"* or *"users' space,"* by asking the following questions:

> *a) Is the target a potential or actual competitive constraint within the techno-logical/users' space or ecosystem?*
>
> *b) Does its elimination increase market power within this space?*
>
> *c) If so, is the merger justified by efficiencies – for which, however, the merging parties bear the burden of proof?*[1699]

The above analysis would broaden the concept of *potential competition* to include all types of products and services that are, on the basis of their current functionalities, not yet close substitutes, but could possibly expand in the future in such a way as to become close competitors – for instance, because they serve similar user groups, their functionalities overlap and the markets are somewhat interlinked – and accordingly, would seem to reflect significant competitive concerns.

Having said this, if the concept of potential competition is expanded in this manner, this could once again lead to the underestimation of the market power of the incumbent in its core market, as the estimate of the number of potential competitors would be vastly increased, which may then make it difficult to show that the number of other potential competitors remaining in the post-merger market would not exert sufficient competitive pressure in the future.[1700]

At this juncture, it is worth noting that, in the pharmaceutical and agrochemical markets, the Commission has addressed the risk of the early elimination of competitive threats by evaluating the competitive relationships in an innovation phase that precedes product-market competition; in other words, by identifying potentially competing research poles.[1701] A similar approach has also been proposed in digital markets: some commentators have argued that *"innovation markets"* should be defined based on analysis of the main capabilities and inputs needed, including the data, engineering skills, high computation power, and risk capital, among others.[1702] However, Crémer et al. argue that the situation in digital markets is frequently different from the circumstances in the pharmaceutical and agrochemical industries. Their view is that, in the pharmaceutical and agrochemical industries, the concept of *"innovation competition"* allows restrictions of competition to be captured at an early point in time, i.e., before an effect on a relevant product market can be predicted with a sufficient degree of certainty, because R&D activities in these sectors typically take the form of distinct and well-structured processes that precede product-market competition. On the other hand, the research projects driving digital innovation are often closer in time to being introduced on the market, and therefore, nearer to the product competition itself. Where identifiable research poles are absent, the concept of *innovation competition* cannot help to reduce the uncertainties relating to the future developments of product markets. Therefore, the authors conclude that the necessary and suitable approach must

---

[1699] CRÉMER ET AL., *supra* note 1567, at 116–17.

[1700] *Id.* at 119.

[1701] Dow/DuPont, European Commission case M.7932 (Mar. 27, 2017). *See also* Bayer/Monsanto, European Commission Decision case M.8084 (Mar. 21, 2018).

[1702] Bourreau & de Streel, *supra* note 1561, at 27–28.

not separate *innovation competition* from *product-market competition*, but rather aim to capture emerging threats to entrenched market power in a conglomerate market setting. Nevertheless, their viewpoint does not exclude the possibility that, in some circumstances, the concept of *innovation competition*, as developed in the pharmaceutical and agrochemical sectors, may be relevant in the digital field as well, in particular to markets where only huge data-rich digital players are able to engage in certain types of research (that is possibly heavily data-driven), or when the markets involve some physical component (e.g., hardware). However, they ultimately believe that this will rarely be relevant for the acquisition of potential competitors at an early stage.[1703]

The authors propose specific modifications to the theories of harm to cases where the acquirer operates a multi-product platform and/or an ecosystem that benefits from strong positive network effects, which act as a significant barrier to entry for potential competitors. However, they also emphasize that this theory of harm should be limited to cases of highly entrenched dominance, where the possibility of entry is limited.[1704]

Crémer et al. are also keenly aware that the risk to competition resulting from an acquisition is not limited to the foreclosure of rivals' access to inputs, but also extends to the strengthening of dominance as the acquisition fortifies the dominance of the ecosystem, in part because the new services provide additional value to the consumers for whom they are complements, and in part because they help retain other users for whom they are partial substitutes.[1705]

7.6.4. Efficiency Considerations

Even if a defensive acquisition in the digital sector leads to a significant impediment of effective competition, it may simultaneously create substantial efficiencies. In this regard, Crémer et al. state that the customers of the dominant ecosystem can be "*leveraged*" to the newly integrated service; in other words, the customers of the target company can be integrated into the incumbent's ecosystem. Therefore, all customers would be less likely to leave the ecosystem afterward due to the stronger network externalities. They further conclude that the acquirer may show that, among other things, the users of its services will benefit from more useful and attractive services after the merger, and that the users of the target firm will benefit from greater network effects as well.[1706] However, it should be noted that these efficiencies would not be considered merger-specific if, for

---

[1703]   CRÉMER ET AL., *supra* note 1567, at 120.
[1704]   *Id.* at 121.
[1705]   *Id.* at 122.
[1706]   For further relevant efficiencies, *see* European Commission, Guidelines on the Assessment of Non-Horizontal Mergers Under the Council Regulation on the Control of Concentrations between Undertakings, 2008 OJ (C 265) 6, recital 118: Conglomerate mergers may "produce cost savings in the form of economies of scope (either on the production or the consumption side), yielding an inherent advantage to supplying the goods together rather than apart. For instance, it may be more efficient that certain components are marketed together as a bundle rather than separately. Value enhancements for the customer can result from better compatibility and quality assurance of complementary components. Such economies of scope, however, are necessary but not sufficient to provide an efficiency justification for bundling or tying. Indeed, benefits from economies of scope frequently can be realized without any need for technical or contractual bundling."

example, they could be achieved via non-exclusive access or interoperability agreements. Moreover, the cumulated efficiencies must be substantial enough to offset the possible long-term anti-competitive effects of the merger.[1707]

7.6.5. Value-based Assessment of Pre-emptive Digital Mergers

Assessment of transaction value

Over the last ten years, the acquisitions that occurred in the digital markets have reflected extremely high transaction values, even though, in most cases, the acquired firms had not generated significant revenue before the transaction. For example, the "big five" tech giants – namely, Alphabet, Amazon, Apple, Facebook, and Microsoft – have made more than 430 acquisitions combined.[1708] In 2017 alone, they bought start-ups for a total amount of $31.6 billion.[1709] More specifically, Facebook acquired WhatsApp for $19 billion in 2014, Google took control of Motorola Mobility in the same year for $12.5 billion, and Microsoft bought LinkedIn for $26 billion in 2016.

This feature of the acquisitions in the digital markets has led some commentators to suggest that the high transaction values may be interpreted as an indicator of the prospect of the acquirer's market power after the merger.

For instance, one commentator posited that since disruption can be very costly in the digital markets, the incumbent firm will be ready and willing to pay a significantly high acquisition price, which represents a premium for market stability. Therefore, paying a high price to buy a firm with low turnover may indicate that the transaction may involve an impediment to the innovation process, which would require and invite antitrust scrutiny. On the other hand, the high acquisition price may also reflect substantial future revenues that are expected from innovation; hence, it may not indicate, on its own, that the merger is welfare-detrimental.[1710]

Other scholars who consider such high purchase prices to be justified claim that by engaging in such a transaction, the incumbent attempts to expand its existing network effects, which make its services more valuable to both its own users and to the users of the target company, and also eliminate the risk that the target firm will attract away (i.e., steal) its users. Accordingly, the high purchase price that is paid for a target firm with no or low turnover (and a product/technology that the incumbent, in principle, possesses itself or could develop on its own) can be rationalized and justified by the

---

[1707]   CRÉMER ET AL., *supra* note 1567, at 122–23.

[1708]   Asher Schechter, *Google and Facebook's "Kill Zone": "We've Taken the Focus Off of Rewarding Genius and Innovation to Rewarding Capital and Scale"*, PROMARKET (May 25, 2018), https://promarket.org/google-facebooks-kill-zone-weve-taken-focus-off-rewarding-genius-innovation-rewarding-capital-scale/.

[1709]   Bourreau & de Streel, *supra* note 1561, at 19.

[1710]   OECD, *supra* note 1663, at 9.

concomitant raising of the barriers to entry, caused by the combination of the acquirer's and the target firm's positive network effects.[1711]

Tommaso Valletti, who serves as chief economist for the EU competition enforcement authority, has recently expressed the view that it makes "economic sense" to look at the transaction value "in some form" when considering the competitive impact of a transaction. In this regard, he has said that the price an acquiring company is willing to pay reveals "relevant market information" that is useful for a merger assessment. For example, large or unexplained payments that are "not in line with evaluation methods of financial analysts" could capture the attention of a competition enforcement authority. Monetization often occurs "into the future" in dynamic markets such as the digital and pharmaceutical sectors; therefore, a company's turnover in recent years would "not be particularly meaningful" for deals in these sectors, unlike in more "traditional and mature industries."[1712]

Assessment of Discounted Cash Flow and Comparator Analysis

Latham et al. have provided a useful overview of valuation analyses that can be utilized to assess whether a given valuation raises competition concerns.[1713] The valuation analyses that are frequently used include discounted cash flow ("DCF") analysis and comparator analysis.[1714] In DCF analysis, the "present value" of the flow of profits expected to be generated over the entire lifetime of a firm is calculated. The additional profits generated by any merger-specific synergies would then be included in the cost or revenue side, depending on the assumptions necessary for calculations performed in a particular case. Theoretically, the value under a "no-synergies" scenario should correspond to the minimum price that the seller would be willing to accept (for any offers that are lower than this price, the seller would be better off keeping the asset for themselves); while the value calculated for the "synergies" case should correspond to the maximum amount that the purchaser is willing to pay (as paying any higher amount would be tantamount to shelling out more than the asset is actually worth).[1715]

In this context, the specific calculations of the seller and the buyer can be different from one another, depending on the various assumptions taken into account,[1716] and

---

[1711]   CRÉMER ET AL., *supra* note 1567.

[1712]   Connor, *supra* note 1656.

[1713]   Oliver Latham, Simon Chisholm & Sam Lynch, *Acquisitions of Potential Rivals in Digital/Tech: Valuation Analysis as Key Economic Tool – PayPal/iZettle*, CRA COMPETITION MEMO (2019), https://ecp.crai.com/wp-content/uploads/2019/06/Use-of-valuation-analysis-in-merger-assessment.pdf.

[1714]   The comparator-based approach is a more straightforward approach than DCF. It involves computing the purchase price for the target firm as a multiple of some other measure (e.g., annual revenue or earnings), and then looking at how these "multiples" compared with other firms. This can be achieved either by considering the equivalent multiples for comparator firms that trade on public markets or by looking at recent transactions. By their nature, comparator-based analyses are less nuanced than DCF analyses. They do not generally allow for judgment calls or explicit assumptions (except with respect to the question of which comparisons are conducted).

[1715]   Latham et al., *supra* note 1713, at 2.

[1716]   DCF models can rely upon multiple assumptions that are specific to the sector and to the companies involved, such as the likely level of growth for the industry and the target firm, the assessment of the progression of prices and margins with and without the transaction, the value that can be placed on increased potential for cross-sale of products, accelerated R&D, or removal of duplicated assets.

the difference between the two would be expected to be analyzed as part of the merger assessment process.[1717]

In assessing the valuation of the transaction, a competition authority can consider whether there is an unexplained factor that might represent a "*market power premium.*" For this analysis, it can inquire as to whether the purchase price can be rationalized and explained with respect to fundamentals – i.e., is the payment amount for the firm consistent with its value under the "*no synergies*" and the "*plausible synergies*" scenarios, and is it in line with the amounts paid for other comparable firms? DCF analysis provides a feasible way of testing this question directly, as it quantifies the fundamental value of the target company. In the context of a merger review, the analysis of this valuation work can provide an assessment of whether a price that is perceived to be "*too high*" is genuinely unexplainable such that it might reflect a "*market power premium*"; in other words, competition authorities can examine whether the incumbent is paying a share of its monopoly profits in order to deter or eliminate a potential market entrant.[1718]

Latham et al. argue that if a purchaser makes significant changes to the valuation initially offered by the target company's management team, this might be indicative of a planned change in strategic direction, which, in turn, might have particular implications for the competitive assessment of the transaction. For example, a competition authority may assess whether there have been dramatic changes in terms of the expected revenue growth or anticipated investment expenditure for specific business units or product lines.[1719] A reduction in assumed revenue growth or a lengthening of the time necessary for a pipeline product to reach the market may be consistent with an anti-competitive intent to eliminate a potential competitor.

In a situation where the transaction price falls somewhere between the value that is calculated without taking into account merger-specific synergies and the calculated value including such synergies, the authors claim that it is reasonable for a competition authority to interrogate situations where a purchaser has been willing to "*payout*" a large proportion of the synergies that it expects to generate from the transaction. This type of payment would signal that the target firm's assets cannot be replicated straightforwardly and might indicate that the purchaser foresees other benefits (such as the elimination of a potential competitor) from the transaction.[1720] However, it should be remembered that the authors emphasize that deal negotiations are complex processes, making it quite difficult to establish or implement a "hard-and-fast" rule. Therefore, the proportion of the expected synergies that are paid out by the acquiring firm needs to be based not only on the overall context of the transaction but also on a case-by-case basis.

[1717]   Latham et al., *supra* note 1713, at 2.
[1718]   *Id.* at 3.
[1719]   *Id.*
[1720]   *Id.*

7.7 Merger Control of Killer Acquisitions in the UK, EU and US

The United Kingdom

Taking into account the findings in the Digital Competition Expert Panel and Lear Reports, the CMA published a policy paper on the digital markets strategy in July 2019 ("Strategy Report") and a study on online platforms and digital advertising ("Study").[1721] The Strategy Report mentions the term "killer acquisitions" only once but acknowledges that the CMA should aim at using its existing tools to a maximum effect in the digital sector and consider the cases and options for regulation. The Study concludes that the UK merger control regime is largely fit for purpose, but the CMA is considering the need for legislative changes to ensure that it has "the right tools to prevent harm to consumers arising from mergers in digital markets." It appears from the CMA's recent case law that it has been taking into account whether the investigated transactions had the risk of loss of potential competition by way of killer acquisitions or reverse killer acquisitions. As such, the CMA's *PayPal/iZettle*,[1722] *Sabre/Farelogix*,[1723] and *Amazon/Deliveroo*[1724] decisions signal that it considered the prospect of future competition in assessing the concerned transactions.

PayPal/iZettle

The CMA cleared PayPal Holdings Inc.'s ("PayPal") acquisition of iZettle AB ("iZettle") on June 12, 2019, following a Phase II inquiry. The US-based PayPal and Swedish iZettle are considered by the CMA as the two largest providers of online payment services to smaller merchants in the UK.[1725] These payment services include the supply of mPOS[1726] services to merchants. The CMA concluded that the combined entity would continue to face significant competition from two rivals (Square Inc. and SumUp Inc.) and, accordingly, no competition concerns were found resulting from the merger regarding the mPOS services.[1727]

That said, the CMA considered whether PayPal's intention was "a tactical elimination of a potentially significant, nascent competitor"[1728] in the omnichannel services.[1729] Such

---

[1721] CMA, Policy paper, *The CMA's Digital Markets Strategy* (July 2019), https://www.gov.uk/government/publications/competition-and-markets-authortys-digital-markets-strategy/the-cmas-digital-markets-strategy; CMA, *Online Platforms and Digital Advertising* (July 2020), https://www.gov.uk/cma-cases/online-platforms-and-digital-advertising-market-study.

[1722] The CMA's PayPal/iZettle decision (June 12, 2019), https://www.gov.uk/cma-cases/paypal-holdings-inc-izettle-ab-merger-inquiry.

[1723] The CMA's Amazon/Deliveroo decision (Aug. 4, 2020), https://www.gov.uk/cma-cases/amazon-deliveroo-merger-inquiry.

[1724] The CMA's Sabre/Farelogix decision (June 19, 2020), https://www.gov.uk/cma-cases/sabre-farelogix-merger-inquiry.

[1725] *PayPal/iZettle* at 11.

[1726] mPOS is a card reader application to be downloaded onto a smartphone or tablet, allowing merchants to accept offline payments by credit cards.

[1727] *PayPal/iZettle* at 13.

[1728] *Id.* at 14.

[1729] Omnichannel services are the provision of integrated payment solutions.

consideration is understood to have resulted from the fact that PayPal was willing to pay \$2.2 billion for the acquisition, although iZettle's recent preliminary initial public offering (pre-IPO) valuation was \$1.1 billion. In assessing whether PayPal attached a considerable value to eliminating a potentially significant competitor, the CMA looked into PayPal's valuation studies and its estimates of the synergies of the acquisition.[1730] As a result, the CMA was convinced that the value attached to iZettle stems not from eliminating a potentially significant competitor, but rather from synergies, including increased sales volume and cost savings.[1731] The CMA has not specifically referred to the terms "killer acquisition" or "reverse killer acquisition."

Amazon/Deliveroo

On August 4, 2020, the CMA cleared the acquisition by Amazon.com, Inc. ("Amazon") of certain rights and 16% shareholding in Roofoods Ltd. ("Deliveroo").[1732] In concluding that the transaction has not and would not be expected to result in a substantial lessening of competition, the CMA looked into the counterfactual of "whether Amazon would re-enter the market for online restaurant platforms,"[1733] among other considerations.

The assessment of the said counterfactual looked into whether the transaction would "kill" Amazon's incentive to re-enter the market for online restaurants, thereby leaving Deliveroo in the market without Amazon's competitive pressure. Such analysis signals that the CMA took into consideration the concerns raised within the scope of the "reverse killer acquisitions."

In light of the extensive data analyzed, the CMA concluded that Amazon would re-enter the supply of online restaurant platforms in the UK, in the absence of the acquisition.[1734] The CMA also found that even if Amazon re-enters the market in addition to the transaction, Amazon may compete less strongly with Deliveroo by worsening its own service, and/or Deliveroo, influenced by Amazon, may compete less strongly with Amazon by worsening its services.[1735] Although the CMA established that the transaction may have a negative impact, to some degree, similar to that of a reverse killer acquisition, it ruled that the concerned impact would not be material.[1736]

Sabre/Farelogix

As opposed to the above, the CMA, on June 19, 2020, decided to prohibit the acquisition by Sabre Corporation ("Sabre") of Farelogix Inc. ("Farelogix") on the grounds that it may result in a substantial lessening of competition within the supply of merchandising solutions and the supply of distribution solutions, on a worldwide basis.[1737]

[1730] *PayPal/iZettle* at 38.

[1731] *Id.*

[1732] The CMA's Amazon/Deliveroo decision (Aug. 4, 2020), https://www.gov.uk/cma-cases/amazon-deliveroo-merger-inquiry.

[1733] *Id.* at 23.

[1734] *Id.* at 131–68.

[1735] *Id.* at 169.

[1736] *Id.* at 189.

[1737] The CMA's Sabre/Farelogix decision 6 (June 19, 2020), https://www.gov.uk/cma-cases/sabre-farelogix-merger-inquiry.

Sabre provides, among others, core and non-core passenger service system ("PSS") IT modules to airlines and operates a global distribution system ("GDS"). The GDS distributes airline content to travel agents for the purpose of booking airline tickets. On the other hand, Farelogix supplies (i) technology solutions for airlines, including non-core PSS modules with a merchandising module as its main product, and (ii) airline content distribution solutions.

The CMA acknowledged Sabre's activities are two-sided in nature, connecting airlines to travel agents.[1738] This is considered to be different from Farelogix's model, where Farelogix supplies distribution solutions to airlines but does not offer any services to manage their relationship with travel agents.[1739] However, the CMA concluded that Sabre faces pricing pressure from Farelogix's channel,[1740] and thereby, a loss of Farelogix's competition in the market would have a significant impact in a relatively concentrated market.[1741] The CMA has put a lot of emphasis on the loss of competition in prohibiting the competition, albeit still refraining from using the term "killer acquisition," despite the parties' specific arguments that the transaction is not a killer acquisition on the grounds of its valuation.[1742]

The European Union

Following up with the findings of the *Competition Policy for the Digital Era* report by Crémer et al., a group of experts[1743] supporting the Commission in monitoring the evolution of the online platform economy published three progress reports in July 2020, wherein they proposed strategies towards the merger control proceedings carried out in the digital sector.[1744]

Having agreed with the findings of the Report regarding the suggested approach towards revisiting the jurisdictional threshold, the progress reports stress that some of the start-ups that bring innovation to the market enter the market with the sole purpose of being acquired by a larger firm operating in the digital sector.[1745] Thus, it may stem from the progress reports that the Commission is also warned against shrinking the acquisition market, which may not benefit the consumers in the long run, as such an approach would also shrink innovation.

[1738]   *Id.* at 8.

[1739]   *Id.*

[1740]   *Id.* at 204.

[1741]   *Id.* at 316.

[1742]   *Id.* at 194, 306.

[1743]   According to the Commission, the experts have been appointed following a competitive selection process. The list of experts can be reached here: EU Observatory on the Online Platform Economy, EUROPEAN COMMISSION, https://ec.europa.eu/digital-single-market/en/expert-group-eu-observatory-online-platform-economy

[1744]   European Commission Shaping Europe's Digital Future (2020) Progress Reports on Online Platform Economy: Work stream on Differentiated treatment; Work stream on Data; Work stream on Measurement and Economic indicators, https://ec.europa.eu/digital-single-market/en/news/commission-expert-group-publishes-progress-reports-online-platform-economy

[1745]   *Id.* at 25.

Google/Fitbit

The Commission announced on August 4, 2020, that it has opened an in-depth investigation to assess the proposed acquisition of Fitbit Inc. ("Fitbit") by Google Inc. ("Google").[1746] According to the announcement, the Commission planned to examine the effects of the combination of Fitbit's and Google's respective databases and capabilities in the digital healthcare sector, which was found to be at the nascent stage in Europe, demonstrating the novel approach as detailed in Chapter 4 above. Despite the loud concerns raised by practitioners and scholars that *Google/Fitbit* might be an example of a so-called reverse killer acquisition[1747] and even explicit calls that the Commission be "very skeptical of this deal,"[1748] the Commission cleared the transaction on December 17, 2020, subject to commitments.[1749] With a view to doing away with the identified potential competition concerns, the Commission reviewed an extensive and long-lasting commitment package submitted by Google.

In its assessment, the Commission identified ten main relevant markets regarding the transaction and expressed concerns with respect to three of them, i.e., the online advertising market, the digital healthcare market, and the wrist-worn wearables market. The Commission noted that the transaction may lead to the following concerns:

(i) With the acquisition, Google would access the data Fitbit collects about its users' health and fitness, and this would further strengthen Google's dominance in the markets for the supply of online search advertising, online display advertising, and "ad tech" services since Google would combine this data with the data that it could already use for the personalization of ads, making it difficult for rivals to compete.

(ii) A number of digital healthcare providers access data provided by Fitbit through a Web application programming interface ("API") to supply services to Fitbit users and collect the users' data in return, and post-transaction, Google might foreclose competitors in the downstream markets for digital healthcare by restricting such access, which may affect the success of the start-ups active in the sector.

(iii) Google could put competing suppliers of wrist-worn wearable devices at a disadvantage by degrading interoperability with Android OS for smartphones. With regard to the online advertising market, the Commission stated that the transaction would raise barriers to entry and prevent Google's

---

[1746] European Commission Press Release IP/20/1446, Mergers: Commission Opens In-depth Investigation into the Proposed Acquisition of Fitbit by Google (Aug. 4, 2020), https://ec.europa.eu/commission/presscorner/detail/en/ip_20_1446.

[1747] *See* Crawford et al., *supra* note 1576.

[1748] Marc Bourreau, Cristina Caffarra, Zhijun Chen Chongwoo Choe, Gregory S. Crawford, Tomaso Duso, Christos Genakos, Paul Heidhues, Martin Peitz, Thomas Rønde, Monika Schnitzer, Nicolas Schutz, Michelle Sovinsky, Giancarlo Spagnolo, Otto Toivanen, Tommaso Valletti & Thibaud Vergé, *Google/Fitbit Will Monetise Health Data and Harm Consumers*, CEPR POL'Y INSIGHT (Sept. 2020), https://cepr.org/system/files/publication-files/103123-policy_insight_107_google_fitbit_will_monetise_health_data_and_harm_consumers.pdf.

[1749] Google/Fitbit, European Commission Decision case M.9660 (Dec. 17, 2020).

competitors from expanding in the market, and therefore gave rise to concerns that the customers (i.e., advertisers) would face higher prices and have less choice, post-transaction.[1750] The Commission's concerns mainly revolved around the possibility that data collected through Fitbit would allow Google to further consolidate its already dominant position in the online search and advertising market. In this regard the Commission determined that with combined dataset, other players would be incapable to compete with Google in the online advertising market.[1751]

Commitments proposed by Google during Phase I and Phase II of the investigation were deemed insufficient to eliminate the identified concerns; as a result of which Google subsequently proposed an additional set of comprehensive commitments characterized as "Final Commitments," which received approval from the Commission.[1752] These final commitments were set out under three distinct categories:

(i) *Ads Commitment:* Google committed not to use the health and wellness data it would collect through Fitbit's devices in search advertising, display advertising, and advertising intermediation products. In order to do so, Google will remain technically separate from Fitbit's user data, which will be stored in a data silo separately from Google's other data used for advertising purposes.[1753] Google will present EEA users with the choice to grant or deny the use of certain data stored in their Google account or Fitbit account by other Google services.[1754,1755]

(ii) *Web API Access Commitments:* Google committed to granting the software applications access to health and fitness data through the Fitbit Web API, without charging for access and subject to user consent.[1756]

(iii) *Android APIs Commitments:* Google committed to maintaining the interoperability between Fitbit's competitors' devices and Android smartphones. To do so, Google will continue to license without any charge to Android OEMs those public APIs covering all current core functionalities that wrist-worn wearable devices need to interoperate with an Android smartphone (e.g., connecting to an Android smartphone via Bluetooth) under the same conditions that apply to other Android APIs made available as part of Android Open Source Project ("AOSP").[1757] Google will not degrade core interoperability APIs by reducing their functionality to third-party wrist-worn wearable devices relative to first-party[1758] wrist-worn wearable

---

[1750] *Id.,* paras. 427–96.
[1751] *Id.,* para. 455.
[1752] *Id.,* para. 1010.
[1753] *Id.,* paras. 964–73.
[1754] For example, Google Search, Google Maps and YouTube. See *Google/Fitbit,* Commitments to the European Commission, Section F.
[1755] *Google/Fitbit,* Commitments to the European Commission, Section A, paras. 1, 2, 3 & 5.
[1756] *Id.,* paras. 974–84.
[1757] Any improvements of those functionalities and updates are also covered. *Google/Fitbit,* Commitments to the European Commission, Section A, para. 10 and *Google/Fitbit,* para. 987.
[1758] Wrist-worn devices developed by Google and Fitbit. See *Google/Fitbit,* Commitments to the European Commission, Section F.

devices.[1759] Google will grant wrist-worn wearable devices OEMs access to all Android APIs that it will make available to Android smartphone app developers.[1760] Google will not circumvent these commitments by degrading users experience with third-party wrist-worn wearable devices in a discriminatory way (e.g., error messages) or by imposing discriminatory conditions to third-party wrist-worn devices on the access of their companion app to the Google Play Store.[1761]

The Commission agreed that the accepted commitments would remain in effect for a period of ten years. However, an extension in the duration of the commitments may also be imposed if the Commission deems it necessary. The commitments also specified that a "Monitoring Trustee" will be appointed throughout the duration of imposed commitments to ensure that commitments set by the notifying party are being fulfilled efficiently.[1762] The commitments also include a fast-track dispute resolution mechanism that can be used by API users or wrist-worn wearable device OEMs.[1763]

This shows that the Commission's approach in *Google/Fitbit* does not seem to be significantly different than the conventional and well-established analysis as to the loss of a potential competitor.[1764] Indeed, the Commission looked into (i) whether Google is already exerting a significant constraining influence or whether it may grow into an effective competitive force, and (ii) whether there is a sufficient number of other wearable manufacturers to maintain sufficient competitive pressure post-transaction.[1765] The Commission concluded that Google would be "unlikely to be able to exert a significant competitive constraint" and that "there is no possible market… where Fitbit is the only or main source of pressure on Google to innovate."[1766]

In light of the above, despite the recent heated debates regarding killer acquisitions and reverse killer acquisitions, it is noteworthy that the Commission apparently saw no reason to change its traditional approach in assessing a loss of potential competition in an acquisition taking place in the digital markets by a large incumbent firm.

As for the discussions on efficiencies, although the Commission, to some extent, weighs the efficiencies stemming from the transaction against its possible anti-competitive effects in the online advertising market, it apparently chooses not to analyze Google's (or any of its competitors') ability to gather the so-called health and wellness data from other sources. On that front, the health data is not particularly scarce,[1767] and Fitbit's users' data, therefore,

---

[1759]   *Google/Fitbit*, Commitments to the European Commission, Section A, para. 11.

[1760]   *Id.*, Section A, para. 12.

[1761]   *Id.*, Section A, para. 13.

[1762]   *Id.* at 5.

[1763]   *Id.*, Annex 5, para. 1.

[1764]   *See, e.g.*, EU Horizontal Merger Guidelines, para. 60; Shapiro, *supra* note 1575; Lars-Hendrik Röller & Miguel de la Mano, *The Impact of the New Substantive Test in European Merger Control*, 2 EUR. COMPETITION J. 9 (2012), https://ec.europa.eu/dgs/competition/economist/merger_control_test.pdf.

[1765]   *Google/Fitbit*, paras. 396–97.

[1766]   *Id.*, paras. 396 & 398.

[1767]   R. Towne, *Data Quality in an Abundance of Electronic Health Information for Electronic Clinical Quality Measures (eCQMs)*, NINJA INSIGHTS (Oct. 2020), https://blog.kpininja.com/data-quality-in-an-abundance-of-electronic-health-information-for-electronic-clinical-quality-measures-ecqms.

does not seem to be significant in affecting in any way Google's ability to do the so-called ads targeting. Taking also into account the existence of many healthcare data analytics companies[1768] (including IBM, Cerner, Health Catalyst), the Commission does not seem to establish clearly that the anti-competitive effects of the synergy between Fitbit's data and Google's online advertising services outweigh the efficiency gains stemming from the transaction, and even if so, indicates that such efficiencies would only be realized in the short-term, and disappear in the long term.[1769] That said, a study conducted by the Spanish Competition Authority on the efficiencies of online advertising demonstrates that online advertising services increase productive efficiency and consequently allocative efficiency.[1770] These improved static efficiencies (productive and allocative efficiencies) would, in turn, generate dynamic efficiencies, which create optimal incentives to compete and invest in the most productive activities. That is, the short-term efficiencies (productive and allocative efficiencies – such as ads targeting of Google) are maintained in the long run, and players in the market are incentivized to innovate and improve constantly.[1771]

The Commission appears to be attaching significant importance to mergers happening in the digital sector. Nevertheless, although the Commission assessed the risk of loss of potential competition in the digital sector following a counterfactual analysis and by measuring how the market would have developed in the absence of such transaction, the heated debate of killer acquisitions (and whether these are novel theories of harm) has not made it into the Commission's review. On the other hand, while accepting long-lasting commitments of ten years, the Commission failed to analyze whether such commitments would negatively affect the dynamic efficiencies that would otherwise stem from the transaction. This is again a reflection of the Commission's reluctance to embrace innovation and consider the dynamic efficiencies as sufficient defenses to a proposed transaction.

Illumina/GRAIL (2022 – appeal pending)

Illumina Inc. ("Illumina"), a global genomics company, announced on August 18, 2021, that it has acquired Grail Inc. ("GRAIL"), a company developing blood-based cancer tests based on genomic sequencing and data science tools.[1772] GRAIL had actually been founded by Illumina in 2016, but it was spun out in the same year as a standalone company, while Illumina retained some 12% ownership stake. Illumina announced on September 21, 2020, that it has entered into a definitive agreement with GRAIL, under which Illumina is to acquire GRAIL back for cash and stock consideration of approx. $8 billion.[1773] The transaction was below the turnover thresholds of the EU Merger

---

[1768] *See Top 10 Healthcare Data Analytics Companies in 2018*, Technavio Blog (Feb. 9, 2018), https://blog.technavio.org/blog/top-10-healthcare-data-analytics-companies.

[1769] *Google/Fitbit*, para. 467.

[1770] Spain, Comisión Nacional de Los Mercados y La Competencia, *Study on the Competition Conditions in the Online Advertising Sector in Spain* 64–66 (July 2021) https://www.cnmc.es/sites/default/files/3696007_1.pdf.

[1771] *Id.*

[1772] Illumina Inc. Press Release, Illumina Acquires GRAIL to Accelerate Patient Access to Life-Saving Multi-Cancer Early-Detection Test (Aug. 18, 2021), https://investor.illumina.com/news/press-release-details/2021/Illumina-Acquires-GRAIL-to-Accelerate-Patient-Access-to-Life-Saving-Multi-Cancer-Early-Detection-Test/default.aspx.

[1773] Illumina Inc. Press Release, Illumina to Acquire GRAIL to Launch New Era of Cancer Detection (Sept. 21, 2020), https://investor.illumina.com/news/press-release-details/2020/Illumina-to-Acquire-GRAIL-to-Launch-New-Era-of-Cancer-Detection/default.aspx.

Regulation; however, competition authorities of some of the EU Member States[1774] and the US Federal Trade Commission raised concerns following the announcement of the acquisition.[1775] The case was referred to the Commission under article 22 of the EU Merger Regulation, and the Commission decided to initiate an in-depth investigation against the concerned transaction, following its preliminary investigation.[1776] It also imposed interim measures[1777] on the parties with a view to restoring and maintaining the conditions of effective competition following Illumina's early acquisition of GRAIL (gun jumping), which means that Illumina held GRAIL as a separate company during the Commission's in-depth investigation.[1778]

This transaction and the Commission's in-depth investigation were closely followed by the competition law practitioners, as they have led to a new practice by the Commission, which decided for the first time in its history to review a transaction where the jurisdictional thresholds were not met, through a reappraisal of article 22 of the EU Merger Regulation.[1779] In addition, the transaction seemed to fall under the recent idea of *"reverse killer acquisitions,"*[1780] which also grabbed a lot of attention.

Following a lengthy and detailed investigation, the Commission announced on September 6, 2022, that it has prohibited the implemented acquisition, as it would have "stifled innovation and reduced choice" for consumers, and the remedies proposed by Illumina were deemed insufficient to address the authority's concerns.[1781] It was noted that this transaction may allow Illumina to do away with the competition in the downstream market by refusing to supply to GRAIL's competitors (i.e., engage in output restriction). The Commission indicated that Illumina may apply vertical input foreclosures by utilizing its leading position in the next-generation sequencing ("NGS") systems, which are required for the development and commercialization of NGS-based cancer

---

[1774] France, Belgium, Greece, the Netherlands, Iceland, and Norway.

[1775] *See* French Competition Authority Press Release, La Commission européenne ouvre une procédure d'examen du rachat de GRAILpar Illumina fondée sur la procédure de l'article 22 du règlement concentrations de 2004 [The European Commission Opens an Examination Procedure for the Takeover of GRAIL by Illumina Based on the Procedure of Article 22 of the 2004 Merger Regulation] (Apr. 20, 2021), https://www.autoritedelaconcurrence. fr/fr/article/la-commission-europeenne-ouvre-une-procedure-dexamen-du-rachat-de-grail-par-illumina-fondee; FTC Press Release, In the Matter of Illumina, Inc., a Corporation and GRAIL, Inc., a Corporation (Aug. 13, 2021), https://www.ftc.gov/enforcement/cases-proceedings/201-0144/illumina-inc-grail-inc-matter.

[1776] European Commission Press Release IP/21/4804, The Commission Adopts a Statement of Objections in View of Adopting Interim Measures Following Illumina's Early Acquisition of GRAIL (Sept. 20, 2021), https://ec.europa.eu/ commission/presscorner/detail/en/ip_21_4804.

[1777] European Commission Press Release IP/21/5661, Commission Adopts Interim Measures to Prevent Harm to Competition Following Illumina's Early Acquisition of GRAIL (Oct. 29, 2021), https://ec.europa.eu/commission/ presscorner/detail/en/ip_21_5661.

[1778] European Commission Press Release IP/21/3844, Commission opens in-depth investigation into proposed acquisition of GRAIL by Illumina (July 22, 2021), https://ec.europa.eu/commission/presscorner/detail/en/IP_21_3844.

[1779] *See Thresholds and Article 22* above in Chapter 4, Section II.2.

[1780] *See* Crawford et al., *supra* note 1576. The authors explain that in cases of "buys instead of builds," the incumbent acquires an already-well-established product and shuts down the development of its own product or never starts developing a competing product, which they call the *"reverse killer acquisitions"* (as opposed to *"killer acquisitions,"* in which the incumbent firm acquires the innovating firm and terminates its innovative efforts, post-merger).

[1781] European Commission Press Release IP/22/5364, Mergers: Commission prohibits acquisition of GRAIL by Illumina (Sept. 6, 2022), https://ec.europa.eu/commission/presscorner/detail/en/ip_22_5364.

detection tests. Furthermore, the Commission also emphasized that Illumina would have the incentive to foreclose GRAIL's rivals, especially considering the market potential and the innovation competition for early cancer detection tests that is currently ongoing. The Commission had already adopted interim measures and certainly pointed out the importance of maintaining GRAIL's innovative activities, by Illumina "to finance additional funds necessary for the operation and development of GRAIL" as a specific interim measure.[1782] Significantly, the Commission has focused on innovation harm in this case, not just in the transaction parties' activities but specifically with respect to the rivals' incentive to innovate: "While there is still uncertainty about the exact results of this innovation race and the future shape of the market for early cancer detection tests, protecting the current innovation competition is crucial to ensure that early cancer detection tests with different features and price points will come to the market."[1783] While Illumina did propose various remedies to address the Commission's concerns (e.g., lowering some of the IP-related barriers to entry for its competitors as well as using a standard contract with GRAIL's rivals until 2033 to ensure GRAIL would not be given preferential treatment), Executive Vice-President Vestager emphasized in her speech that the Commission's in-depth investigation and efficacy tests conducted with market participants had revealed these would fall short of remedying the competition concerns, as the proposals had limited practicality and constituted a challenge to monitor and – if necessary, to enforce – due to their complexity.[1784] In light of the above, the merger was prohibited by the Commission. Illumina has announced its plans to appeal the Commission's decision, arguing that it believes the merger would, in fact, "accelerate innovation."[1785]

Notwithstanding the Commission's stance, remedy proposals constituting a challenge to monitor and to enforce should not be a reason in and of itself to reject that particular remedy proposal when innovation theories of harm are concerned, as otherwise, merger control would be very progressive in its formulation of innovation theories of harm, but extremely conservative in addressing it with remedies, as the only available type of remedy would be reduced to traditional divestitures, where more complex structures of remedy – while creating more burden on the antitrust agency – might be a better candidate to developing a balanced approach and to saving transactions from being prohibited or abandoned. Once again, it should always be kept in mind that merger activities in the field of innovation are not a luxury but a necessity in the long run for systemic innovation.

It is also important to note that although Illumina had objected to the article 22 decision,[1786] the General Court upheld that the Commission had the competence to

---

[1782]   *Id.*

[1783]   *Id.*

[1784]   Margrethe Vestager, Remarks by Executive Vice-President Vestager on the Commission decision to prohibit the acquisition of GRAIL by Illumina (Sept. 6, 2022), https://ec.europa.eu/commission/presscorner/detail/en/speech_22_5371.

[1785]   Illumina Inc. Press Release, Illumina Intends to Appeal European Commission's Decision in GRAIL Deal (Sept. 6, 2022), https://investor.illumina.com/news/press-release-details/2022/Illumina-Intends-to-Appeal-European-Commissions-Decision-in-GRAIL-Deal/default.aspx.

[1786]   Case T-227/21: Action brought on 28 April 2021 – Illumina v. Commission, 2021 OJ (C 252) 27, https://eur-lex.europa.eu/legal-content/EN/TXT/?uri=CELEX%3A62021TN0227.

examine the merger.[1787] The undertaking has further appealed this decision before the Court of Justice of the EU, which, if successful, will annul all the Commission decisions regarding this case. Considering that the Commission may order Illumina, which had closed the transaction in breach of its standstill obligation, to pay fines and also to "dissolve the transaction and restore GRAIL's independence,"[1788] the outcome of this article 22 appeal will be highly significant.

The United States

The Federal Trade Commission has also challenged cases where the acquisition of a nascent company created competitive concerns following the transaction, such as *Össur/ College Park* (concerning medical prosthetics).[1789] However, the criticisms regarding under-enforcement especially in the digital sector transactions incentivized the FTC to launch a market study in February 2020 to see whether there were any killer acquisitions among those unreported past acquisitions by the major tech companies. While the tech sector was the first to be analyzed, FTC officials also point out that healthcare[1790] and other innovative sectors may be the next ones for such a deep dive.

By focusing on the non-reportable acquisitions, this study intended to determine whether the current merger controls were sufficient for this sector or if, indeed, statutory changes would need to be considered to catch potential problems. The inquiry focused on a total of 616 exempted transactions by Google, Amazon.com, Apple, Facebook, and Microsoft during the ten-year period between 2010 and 2019 and analyzed their terms, structure, and purposes.

Discussing the inquiry's findings, FTC Chair Lina M. Khan noted that this study presented a clear picture of the strategies used by big tech firms to avoid the FTC's discerning eye when "buy[ing] their way out of competing."[1791] She highlighted that the FTC would look closely for any reporting loopholes under the Hart-Scott-Rodino Act, and increase its collaboration with other competition authorities and regulators, considering that more than a third of the non-reported transactions were international deals. Khan also drew attention to the significant role of non-compete obligations imposed on founders and key employees of the acquired entities and pointed out that misuse of non-competes would

---

[1787] CJEU Press Release No. 123/22, The General Court Upholds the Decisions of the Commission Accepting a Referral Request from France, as Joined by Other Member States, Asking It to Assess the Proposed Acquisition of GRAIL by Illumina (July 13, 2022), https://curia.europa.eu/jcms/upload/docs/application/pdf/2022-07/cp220123en.pdf.

[1788] Vestager, *supra* note 1784.

[1789] FTC Press Release, FTC Imposes Conditions on Össur Hf's Acquisition of College Park Industries, Inc. (Apr. 7, 2020), https://www.ftc.gov/news-events/press-releases/2020/04/ftc-imposes-conditions-ossurhfs-acquisition-college-park.

[1790] Statement of Commissioner Christine S. Wilson, Joined by Commissioner Rohit Chopra Concerning Non-Reportable Hart-Scott-Rodino Act Filing 6(b) Orders (Feb. 11, 2020), https://www.ftc.gov/system/files/documents/reports/6b-orders-file-special-reports-technology-platform-companies/statement_by_commissioners_wilson_and_chopra_re_hsr_6b_0.pdf.

[1791] FTC Press Release, *supra* note 1598.

be a future consideration for the FTC.[1792] As also noted by Rohit Chopra, it seemed that the big tech firms had also avoided FTC oversight through the use of acquihires (where key employees are kept in and hired by the acquiring firm in exchange for stock share incentives) that would lock up talent and thus potential innovators. The FTC has taken these findings to heart and intends to eradicate any loopholes or avoidance mechanisms that may result in harm to future competition and consumer benefit.

Illumina/Grail – The US Saga

Interestingly, despite a similar beginning to the EU approach, the story unfolded somewhat differently across the pond for this particular acquisition. In 2021, parallel to the EU concerns, the FTC had also emphasized the potential loss of innovation in the US market for multi-cancer early detection tests due to this transaction, as GRAIL is the supplier of the multi-cancer early detection tests and Illumina is the only provider of DNA sequencing. Accordingly, the authority initiated an administrative complaint process and also authorized a federal court lawsuit to block the proposed acquisition.[1793] Once the European Commission commenced its investigation, the FTC dismissed its federal case (as the transaction could not go ahead without EU clearance anyway) and instead preferred to stay with the administrative proceedings. However, on September 1, 2022 (just five days before the Commission's decision), the administrative law judge ("ALJ") ruled in favor of Illumina, noting that the FTC failed to demonstrate that the acquisition would harm competition.[1794] The remedies Illumina proposed, i.e., providing contractual guarantees of access to its sequencing and commitment to significantly reduce prices under the Open Offer,[1795] were thus deemed to be "effective constraints" to prevent foreclosure.[1796] Despite this ruling, however, upon appeal,[1797] the Federal Trade Commission issued an Opinion and Order reversing the ALJ's decision, emphasizing that remedies would not prevent the potential harm to competition and stifling of innovation.[1798] While the ALJ's decision seemed to reiterate the US approach to vertical mergers being pro-competitive, as discussed under Chapter 6, the recent response by the FTC commissioners shows they are clearly not in favor of the deal. The Opinion refers to the difficulties of detecting breaches and enforcing the proposed arbitration process,

---

[1792]   *Id.*

[1793]   FTC Case Summary (Aug. 31, 2021), https://www.ftc.gov/enforcement/cases-proceedings/201-0144/illumina-inc-grail-inc-matter.

[1794]   Illumina Inc. Press Release, Administrative Law Judge Rules in Favor of Illumina in FTC Challenge of GRAIL Deal (Sept. 1, 2022), https://www.illumina.com/company/news-center/press-releases/press-release-details.html?newsid=695f87e8-5d42-4caa-9c9c-4539a2630068.

[1795]   Illumina Inc. Press Release, Illumina Committed to Pursuing GRAIL Acquisition to Accelerate Access to Breakthrough Multi-Cancer Early Detection Blood Test (Mar. 30, 2021), https://www.illumina.com/company/news-center/press-releases/press-release-details.html?newsid=32156cec-c392-4d23-be23-66d7729892db; *see also* the standard contract terms offered and expanded by Illumina, https://www.illumina.com/areas-of-interest/cancer/test-terms.html.

[1796]   Natalie McNelis, *Illumina's Remedy Offer Was Sufficient to Clear FTC's Foreclosure Doubts, Judge Says*, MLEX MKT. INSIGHT (Sep. 2, 2022), https://content.mlex.com/#/content/1406092.

[1797]   *FTC Appeals Judge's Decision on Illumina-GRAIL Deal*, CPI (Sept. 4, 2022), https://www.competitionpolicyinternational.com/ftc-appeals-judges-decision-on-illumina-grail-deal/.

[1798]   Opinion of the Commission, In re Illumina/GRAIL (Mar. 31, 2023), https://www.ftc.gov/legal-library/browse/cases-proceedings/illumina-inc-grail-inc-matter-timeline-item-2023-04-03.

pointing out that Illumina would still be able to cause damage to its rivals and that the remedial measures are inadequate and Open Offer is flawed.[1799]

It is also noteworthy to mention the FTC's approach in the Opinion: "Rather than rely on respondents' self-serving and ultimately vague and unsupported projections of acceleration, we believe the course that Congress clearly enunciated in the antitrust laws is to let competition spur innovation among MCED [multi-cancer early detection] test providers and thereby save lives... When competition is allowed to flourish, consumers benefit."[1800] This indeed points to an Arrowian approach, and in this particular case, it is likely that the Arrowian presumptions were tested and deemed reliable, as the Opinion also refers to the rebuttal reports "estimating that roughly 27,000 more lives would be saved than under Respondents' acceleration scenario," which signal the existence of counterfactual analyses.[1801] This is in keeping with this book's premise, which highlights that the problem lies not in the Arrowian approach itself but in the blind use of Arrowian presumptions. In this most recent development, we note that it will be imperative for the federal courts to assess during the appeal process whether the FTC, instead of relying predominantly on internal company correspondence and general economic theory literature, has chosen a neutral starting point and ran the necessary case-specific complex economic analyses for counterfactual analyses, in line with our arguments hereto.

Illumina is now appealing the decision before the federal courts, which will automatically stay the FTC's order to unwind the transaction.[1802] The decision texts have not been made public yet, but given their recent approaches, it may be that the Commission and/or the FTC reviewed *Illumina/GRAIL* from the perspective of "reverse killer acquisition" in establishing the theory of harm. However, such an approach would be groundbreaking as the competition authorities have so far been very careful and reluctant in using the terms "killer acquisition" or "reverse killer acquisitions" in merger control reviews, even when the case seems suitable for the term.[1803]

The divergence of antitrust agencies in *Illumina/Grail*, *Dow/DuPont*, *Meta/Giphy*, and *Microsoft/Activision* suggests there is work to be done in the innovation theories of harm in merger control.

[1799] *Id.* at 72–73.
[1800] *Id.* at 83.
[1801] *Id.*
[1802] Illumina Inc. Press Release, Illumina Will Appeal FTC Decision in Federal Court, Will Seek US Resolution by Late 2023 or Early 2024 (Apr. 3, 2023), https://investor.illumina.com/news/press-release-details/2023/Illumina-Will-Appeal-FTC-Decision-in-Federal-Court-Will-Seek-US-Resolution-by-Late-2023-or-Early-2024/default.aspx, and Diane Bartz & Mrinmay Dey, *Illumina Appeals FTC Order to Divest Cancer Test Maker GRAIL*, REUTERS (June 6, 2013), https://www.reuters.com/legal/illumina-asks-appeals-court-undo-ftc-ruling-that-it-must-sell-subsidiary-2023-06-06.
[1803] *See* the CMA's *PayPal/iZettle* decision (June 12, 2019), https://www.gov.uk/cma-cases/paypal-holdings-inc-izettle-ab-merger-inquiry; *Amazon/Deliveroo* decision (Aug. 4, 2020), https://www.gov.uk/cma-cases/amazon-deliveroo-merger-inquiry; *Sabre/Farelogix* decision (June 19, 2020), https://www.gov.uk/cma-cases/sabre-farelogix-merger-inquiry; European Commission Press Release IP/20/1446, *supra* note 1746.

Conclusion

The merger notification thresholds in some countries are based on the turnovers of the merging undertakings. Concentrations involving firms with small monetary turnover are typically not screened or assessed by competition authorities, even if the transaction value of the deal is very high. It appears that a notification threshold system based on turnover values is not sufficient to capture some potentially harmful *killer acquisitions*, because such acquisitions often take place early in the life cycle of the target firms when they have not yet reached a large monetary turnover. This is particularly the case in the digital economy, where many start-ups concentrate on growing their customer bases rather than focusing on increasing their turnovers. How this relates to the role of innovation in merger transactions and the approach of the competition authorities lies in the fact that innovative and dynamic markets are now the new engine of economic growth and welfare. The digital economy is the foremost industry that encompasses the concept of continuous and dynamic innovation, almost always without necessitating a high amount of capital or investment in high-tech R&D facilities to bring about new ideas and products, garnering comparatively low turnovers as most services are free for the sake of network effects. This also means that transactions with such entrants run the risk of being overlooked for any restrictions to competition or impediments to innovation, simply by flying below the radar of the legislative thresholds of merger review requirements. It is therefore important for the competition authorities to ensure that the threshold does not actually allow such inflow of innovative entrepreneurship to be curtailed or "killed" by the incumbents, and also to determine the correct methods to assess any restrictive effects and potential efficiencies such a merger may have on consumer welfare.

The European Commission debated whether it might be necessary to use the value of a transaction as a complementary notification threshold for merger transactions. Several commentators have expressed the view that such a complementary measure would be useful; however, some argue that the current system, which is based on referrals by the national competition authorities, functions well for the European Union at this time. The Commission introduced its "Article 22 Guidance" as a response to these concerns, reappraising the referral system to include competitively significant transactions that do not fall under Member State jurisdictions. As *Illumina/GRAIL*, the first case referred to the Commission based on the Article 22 Guidance, is yet under review, it remains to be seen whether this was a correct and sufficient method to address the Commission's concerns on the matter.

Efficiency motives can drive the acquisition of promising start-ups by large digital firms. However, in certain situations, the acquiring firms may also have pre-emptive motives, possibly leading to *killer acquisitions*, to the detriment of innovation. Some scholars contend that the competition authorities should take the possibility of pre-emptive motives into account when handling mergers and acquisitions in the digital sector, in particular for cases involving innovative start-ups.

As for the substantive assessment of the competitive effects of *defensive acquisitions*, the advisors of the European Commission do not believe that the EC Merger Regulation currently requires a legislative update. However, they have also indicated that the substantive criteria for analyzing defensive acquisitions in digital sectors need to be reconsidered. According to these commentators, the *"significant impediment of effective competition"*

("SIEC") test in general – and the "*strengthening of dominance*" criterion in particular – continues to provide a sound basis for assessing defensive acquisitions in digital sectors; nevertheless, they claim that there is currently a regulatory enforcement gap in the accepted theories of harm. In their view, especially in the case of conglomerate mergers, competition authorities should inquire as to whether the acquirer and target firm operate in the same "*technological space*" or "*users' space.*" In addition, they state that the competitive assessment could focus on whether the target firm poses a potential or actual competitive constraint within the technological/users' space or ecosystem, and examine whether the elimination of the target firm would increase market power within this space, and if so, its efficiencies nevertheless justify the merger.

Some other commentators have suggested that, in practice, the merger review process should focus on the risk of cannibalization effects. Accordingly, competition agencies should ascertain how the post-merger cannibalization effects might influence the incentives of the incumbent to innovate. If the incumbent has an incentive to delay or eliminate potential innovation, then the competition agency should inquire directly into the business plans of the incumbent, even if this is an unusual step under the merger control system.

Particular views have been expressed in the relevant literature, which proposes the implementation of an "*innovation markets*" approach in digital markets, similar to the one adopted in the pharmaceutical sector in the recent case law. This view proposes defining "*innovation markets*" by considering the main capabilities and inputs needed in such markets, which include, among other things, data, engineering skills, high computation power, and risk capital.

Some argued that the high transaction values observed in mergers in the digital markets could be interpreted as an indicator of the acquirer's market power prospect in the post-transaction market. According to this approach, it is suggested that competition authorities can evaluate whether there is an unexplained factor in the valuation of the transaction, which might represent a "*market power premium.*" In the context of a merger review, the analysis of this valuation process can provide a means of testing whether a price that is perceived to be "*too high*" is genuinely unexplainable, such that it might, in reality, reflect a "*market power premium.*" In other words, the competition authority can seek to determine whether the incumbent is paying a share of its monopoly profits in order to deter or eliminate a potential entrant. To conduct this assessment, it can inquire as to whether the purchase price can be rationalized and justified with respect to the value of the target company, in a way that would be consistent with its value under both the "*no synergies*" and "*plausible synergies*" scenarios, or by evaluating the transaction price in light of the amounts paid for other comparable firms.

From the analysis of the cases above, it is apparent that since the Report of the Digital Competition Expert Panel, the CMA has been increasingly considering counterfactuals in assessing whether a transaction would result in a significant lessening of competition in the markets. These transactions have been mainly assessed by measuring how the market would have developed but for the transaction. The CMA has not implemented a novel theory of harm but has utilized its counterfactual analysis more effectively in the transactions involving a concern of loss of potential competition. The Commission, on the other hand, is yet to assess, through merger control, the specific concerns raised by the debate of killer acquisitions and reverse killer acquisitions in the digital sector. Having said this, the *Competition Policy for the Digital Era* and subsequent progress reports, as well as the recently published Article 22 Guidance, indicate that the Commission is certainly aware of this recent debate; therefore, it may be just a matter of time, perhaps when the decision regarding the *Illumina/GRAIL* case is issued, that we will see how the Commission will be approaching the issue. On the other side of the pond, the FTC is increasingly focused on killer acquisitions, and any loopholes and avoidance mechanisms that may have allowed the big tech to get away with them. The next few years may see an overzealous approach from both authorities, although such increased antitrust enforcement may prove to be a turn-off for the entrepreneurs, to the detriment of consumer welfare.

Annex-1

Table 1.A: Examples of high-value acquisitions by large digital companies

Year	Acquirer	Company acquired	Transaction value ($ million)
2006	Google	YouTube	1,650
2007	Google	DoubleClick	3,100
2011	Microsoft	Skype Technologies	8,500
2011	Google	Motorola Mobility	12,500
2012	Facebook	Instagram	1,000
2012	Microsoft	Yammer	1,200
2013	Google	Waze	970
2014	Apple	Beats Electronics	3,000
2014	Google	Nest Labs	3,200
2014	Google	DeepMind Technologies	625
2014	Facebook	WhatsApp	19,000
2014	Facebook	Oculus	2,000
2016	Microsoft	LinkedIn	26,200
2017	Apple	Shazam	400
2018	Amazon	Ring	1,000

Source: IG Group[1804]

[1804] *See Interactive Source of Publicly-Known Tech Acquisitions Completed Since 1991*, IG.COM (2019), https://www.ig.com/uk/cfd-trading/research/acquisitive-tech#/acquisitions. Also mentioned in Marc Doucette, *Interactive: Visualizing Major Tech Acquisitions (1991–2018)*, VISUAL CAPITALIST (July 24, 2018),

The effect of COVID-19
and the post-pandemic era

At this point, since the COVID-19 pandemic has permeated all thoughts and plans while this book was being written, we should devote at least a paragraph to the awakening impact of this global phenomenon on antitrust enforcement and regulation in digital markets.

Notwithstanding the above analysis regarding the authorities' approach to the sector, now that COVID-19 is drawing even further attention to the importance of digital markets, this should not be deemed as a convenient excuse to hasten to tighten its regulation, or a reason to think that the innovation concerns discussed here can be discounted in the interest of keeping digital markets under tighter control. On the contrary, the necessity to find a fine balance and proportionality in regulating digital markets is paramount in a post-Covid era: a need for legal certainty and foreseeability in these markets is felt more than ever. Every instance of overregulation will be stifling potential innovative solutions of monetization, market making, and adaptability, which are key to fostering consumer welfare in these extraordinary times. Counterfactual analyses are needed more than ever in antitrust enforcement and regulation in digital markets, as we can no longer be complacent in our ingrained notions of the kinds of impacts that test the viability and sustainability of digital markets. It is true that digital markets will become vital in the post-Covid era. But this also means that any Type II error in antitrust enforcement and regulation will be even more welfare-diminishing for society, while the costs on society will be compounded when regulators fail to show the proper deference to the innate dynamics of these markets. This does not mean that these markets should be left alone: The key here is undertaking a balanced and prudent approach based on counterfactual analyses. The post-pandemic era will need to target and highlight the dynamic efficiencies, by allowing the entrepreneurs in digital markets room for maneuver they will need for creative exercises, in order to secure the adaptability and sustainability of the market-making dynamics of the relevant digital ecosystem.

---

https://www.visualcapitalist.com/interactive-major-tech-acquisitions/.

Chapter 8
Conclusion

The concept of innovation, despite the controversies and negative connotations surrounding it throughout history, has in recent times gained a much more favorable perception. Considering that economic growth stems primarily from innovation, a fact repeatedly demonstrated by economic theorists, it should have been embraced wholeheartedly and incorporated into every facet of public strategies concerning development and economic growth. Nevertheless, there still seems to be a continued skeptical approach, especially by those competition authorities that (despite increasingly recognizing the crucial role played by innovation) are still wary of fully integrating the concept into their assessments, and in particular, of the full potential of innovation efficiencies. Thus, the historical trajectory of the term's negative connotation remains unbroken.

It is true that a uniform approach for innovation cannot be adopted; this might even contravene the goals of competition rules since innovations may lead to different market structures, and therefore a case-by-case and careful analysis must always be conducted for the markets or transactions concerned. The vital role of innovation in the development of economic dynamics, as demonstrated by Schumpeter, can affect local or international, traditional or dynamic markets in very different ways. Accordingly, this author does concede that competition authorities may need to intervene in order to protect the incentives to innovate in the relevant market and ensure that undertakings do not exploit the emphasis put on the concept of innovation (similar to how the emphasis on sustainability and the environment has led certain firms to employ a "greenwashing" strategy). However, this intervention should be almost a measure of last resort, and only after a rigorous case-by-case analysis to make sure that no pro-competitive effects of innovation are disregarded – i.e., competition authorities should not dismiss out of hand the dynamic efficiencies claimed by the parties and (notwithstanding where the burden of proof lies) should conduct full-scale analyses to ascertain what innovative efficiencies could be achieved by the transaction, by employing all available resources at their disposal.

In the research for this book, 76 cases were surveyed from the three jurisdictions (21 from the EU, 20 from the UK, and 35 from the USA) to specifically review innovation concerns, defenses, and the authorities' approach thereto. It has proven to be a challenge to assess whether a different approach to innovation could have changed the outcome, because in a third of the cases (most of them comprising the challenges brought by the FTC), the defendants did not bring forward any specific innovation defenses or respond to the authorities' concerns regarding innovation. One can speculate whether the reason for this was the availability of other defenses to the parties to employ against the authorities' theory of harm regarding the transaction, or a defense strategy that focused more on non-innovation-related arguments as a cost-effective method in the limited time granted, or preferring to settle and/or give commitments to get conditional approval as soon as possible. It is entirely possible that the merging parties might still be feeling that innovation considerations are given a supportive role in cases where the actual issue is unilateral effects. This might frequently be an accurate assumption, and it is also part of the problem. Of the remaining cases, where there have been innovation concerns, it has been very rare that the parties were able to alleviate them through their defenses, and they usually have offered commitments or agreed to divest certain assets to be able to continue commercial transactions. Those commitments typically take the form of standard measures against unilateral effects, as this has been the limits of the willingness of competition authorities in negotiating commitments for innovation so far.

Competition authorities may find it difficult to ascertain precisely at which point intervention would be deemed appropriate and justified. Especially in dynamic markets, circumstances can change rapidly, e.g., a first-comer in a new market can engage in aggressive conduct, which may initially enhance consumer benefit and promote innovation, but once it is entrenched, its abusive behavior towards new entrants down the line may mean that an intervention may be too late to prevent market distortion. Accordingly, running market-specific analyses on a case-by-case basis and conducting the correct assessment of harm and quantification of the detriment creates an important challenge to the authorities in how to put their increased advocacy in support of preserving and promoting innovation into actual practice.

The practices of the competition authorities in the EU, UK, and US, discussed in the above chapters, indicate that competition authorities in these jurisdictions are clearly aware of the link between innovation and competition. That said, they might be relying on assumptions of general economic theory literature too much, where there needs to be a case-specific articulation of the theory of harm for innovation, followed by an *ex officio* exploration of balancing factors by the agency. Concern flagging is not the extent, but just half of the job. In general and specifically with respect to horizontal mergers, competition enforcement authorities' innovation concerns are mainly related to whether the merging parties can internalize the constraint between the rival products and whether this may give the merged entity an incentive to reduce its innovation efforts. In extreme cases, the merged entity can even discontinue one of the products in order to avoid cannibalization of the other product's sales. However, the impact of a merger can also result in dynamic efficiencies by combining the know-how and "brain power" of the undertakings, in addition to its financial capabilities and economies of scale. Thus, the assessment of the impact of a merger on R&D investments requires a complex balancing exercise involving several factors that affect the incentives to innovate. The fact that these factors exert opposing influences on the merged entity's incentives to innovate implies that it would not be accurate to presume that one effect dominates the others. Know-how complementarity, increase in financial capabilities, and potential impact on R&D investments cannot always be assumed to be dominated by the potential loss of innovation incentives due to possible cannibalization. Similarly, a balance between the contestability and appropriability effects should also be found on a case-by-case basis, without assumptions.

The finding in the theoretical models that a horizontal merger reduces innovation incentives is mostly based on the assumption that the merger does not create any efficiency gains.

This finding could be reversed if the synergies resulting from mergers are taken into account properly. Besides, the results can differ when other factors (such as the *demand expansion effect* and *margin expansion effect*) are considered, as well. Competition authorities are also advised to contemplate and incorporate the welfare-increasing effects of information sharing and R&D cooperation between merging firms into their merger assessments. It is not a surprise that the R&D collaboration between competitors during the COVID-19 pandemic, especially during the beginning, to identify the most effective treatment options and development of vaccines had served to benefit consumer welfare and, indeed, perhaps, saved the human race from a bigger catastrophe.

There is not a single overarching general theory on the effects of mergers on innovation, and the findings of current theoretical research papers themselves should be read and interpreted in light of the assumptions underlying a particular study. As for applying the conclusions of a given theoretical research study to a real-life/tangible merger case, one should therefore carefully consider how the assumptions of the relevant research study match up with the particular facts and circumstances of the merger under examination. Otherwise, imprecise assessments would result in overzealous interventions from competition authorities, which would most certainly preclude any efficiencies that may have been gained from the transactions, to the detriment of consumer benefit and economic growth. This means that the theories of harm related to innovation employed by the competition authorities are instrumental in shaping the future of the innovative sectors.

In terms of the practices of the European Commission, the theories of harm related to innovation have historically been based on the underlying principles of the EU Horizontal Merger Guidelines. The classic legislation framework left the Commission some room to maneuver for interpretation and case-by-case examination, since the legislation does not provide explicit or detailed guidance on how innovation concerns are to be assessed in merger reviews. The Commission has availed itself of this leeway, and we observe that its approach to innovation has evolved over time, as demonstrated in the case law. The initial stance towards innovation considerations in merger control had been based on utilizing the traditional tools available to the Commission. Therefore, its theories of harm were based on the SIEC, and the relevant product markets were clearly defined; the focus was on developed pipeline products rather than those in their early stages. The Commission assessed the competitive pressure applied by competitors and by the transaction parties themselves to one another. The criteria for assessing these elements were symmetric. Last but not least, the standard of proof for verifying the assessment of these elements was substantially high, by incorporating information sources from the field, sector participants, competitors, and the transaction parties, amongst others.

Notwithstanding this "traditional" starting point, the Commission's approach gradually evolved into a novel approach, most significantly demonstrated in its decision on the merger of Dow and DuPont in 2017 and continued in the *Bayer/Monsanto* and *ChemChina/Syngenta* cases. The foremost difference from the traditional approach was the introduction of a novel theory of harm, namely, the assessment of competition for "significant impediment to effective *innovative* competition." This new methodology has also introduced the concept of "innovation spaces" into competition law assessments, as opposed to the classic and constrained analysis of "relevant market," which is the bedrock concept of competition law. Furthermore, the potential subject of such competition law analysis was also extended to encompass early-stage pipeline products, which may lead this new methodological approach to reach conclusions with less predictive ability about products whose futures are more uncertain, if not highly speculative. As for the standard of proof, the Commission has examined and relied on internal documents in both the *Dow/DuPont* and *Bayer/Monsanto* cases, despite criticisms of commentators that the subjective nature of such evidence fell short of the evidentiary criteria that they would have expected the Commission to consider.

It may seem that under the novel approach, the Commission builds its assessments of the effects of mergers on innovation competition mainly on (i) the characteristics and structure of the market, (ii) the importance of the merging parties as innovators, (iii) the intensity of innovation rivalry between the merging parties in innovation spaces, (iv) the impact on the incentive to innovate and evidence on the effects of innovation, and (v) the capacity of the remaining competitors in the relevant market to offset the loss in innovation competition as a result of the merger. Having said that, despite recognizing that its traditional tools are inadequate, one wonders whether the replacement has not been intrusive or ambiguous. Furthermore, the relaxation of boundaries in terms of the markets/products assessed or the standards of proof seem to be flowing only towards one direction: The Commission has made proof easier for itself but not for the transaction parties, who are still required to demonstrate in their defenses that any efficiencies will be merger-specific, quantifiable and verifiable. This leads to an asymmetry that would result in wrong legal policy preferences in terms of consumer welfare maximization in the long term.

From our analysis, it is apparent that competition authorities still have to fine-tune their approaches, especially where innovation is being used as a defense, and recognize the opportunities offered with the transaction as a counterbalance to any threats they perceive. Competition regulators recognize the need to move away from static analyses for dynamic markets; however, they still require much convincing in order to embrace and give weight to what may be less concise economic analyses and estimations in terms of dynamic benefits. There has been extensive work by competition authorities, independent experts, and scholars to assess the competitive and regulatory needs of dynamic markets, especially in the context of digital markets. Yet, despite authorities' self-proclaimed stance as proponents of innovation, their first instinct still seems to be one of wariness and skepticism towards the intentions of the transaction parties, and a leaning towards what may turn out to be overzealous intervention. In fact, most recently, the EU has agreed to regulate these markets through the Digital Markets Act, which is designed to limit the market power of big online platforms and ensure fair competition on the Internet, albeit without overregulating small businesses. It remains to be seen whether this regulatory framework shall indeed serve to achieve their intended target of "more competition, more innovation and more choice for users."[1805]

The consideration of innovation-related issues in the UK has shown much variation, depending on, among others, (i) the market (i.e., sector) characteristics, (ii) the incen-

---

[1805] European Parliament Press Release, Deal on Digital Markets Act: EU Rules to Ensure Fair Competition and More Choice for Users (Mar. 24, 2022), https://www.europarl.europa.eu/news/en/press-room/20220315IPR25504/deal-on-digital-markets-act-ensuring-fair-competition-and-more-choice-for-users.

tives of the transaction parties to innovate, (iii) the number of innovative competitors in the market, and (iv) the general characteristics of the products or services in question. The UK competition authorities appear to handle theories of harm under both "horizontal and vertical issues," yet there were cases in which the CMA chose not to implement this reasoning. Nevertheless, the most important issues which the UK competition authorities focused on were the parties' motivation to innovate, and the effect of the transaction on the number and capabilities of innovative competitors after the transaction. Having said that, it is also observed that this approach is not much adopted for traditional sectors, and UK competition authorities – subconsciously or perhaps due to unique market characteristics – tend to focus on innovation assessments in certain particular sectors, such as electronics. This is evinced in one of the earliest decisions, *Bayard Capita/Landis & GYR* (2004), where the OFT deemed innovation as a significant dimension of competition in the electronics sector.

The UK competition authorities' breadth and depth of regulatory approach, which does not rely on a strict methodology or a limited number of guidelines to follow, also leaves more room for further developing their policies and procedures. Similar to the EU, in the last few years, they have directed their attention to effective competition in digital markets, and recently, a Digital Markets Unit has been established within the CMA, "to regulate the most powerful digital firms, promoting greater competition and innovation in these markets, protecting consumers and businesses from unfair practices."[1806] The regulatory structure is planned to be designed with a proportional approach that will avoid over-regulation that would stifle innovation, and instead, create conditions that will incentivize it and also allow new entrants into the various markets to effectively compete with incumbents.[1807] Although this is geared towards digital markets, it may perhaps influence the UK competition authorities to adopt an even more balanced approach for dynamic efficiencies as defenses in other markets, as well.

The UK is trying to set a pro-innovation, pro-technology stance that will attract new start-ups, innovators, and hence investment into the economy, while ensuring a pro-competitive regime. While it is not yet clear to what extent the CMA will apply the mechanisms and theories developed by the Commission in evaluating innovation, the stated intent seems to be to steer away from over-regulating. Having said this, the analysis of the CMA decisional practice in the period following Brexit has shown that in a substantial number of cases, it has acted in unison with the Commission. Yes, there have also been a few cases where the CMA's decision diverged from the Commission (the CMA's lone stance in *Microsoft/Activision* merits a special mention here); however, it remains to be seen whether the CMA will actually venture to test out new waters regarding innovation assessments in merger control, in particular.

In the case of US competition law practice, we have demonstrated there has been an increasing level of interest and a new focus on issues relating to innovation, both at the

---

[1806] Digital Markets Unit (updated on July 20, 2021), CMA, https://www.gov.uk/government/collections/digital-markets-unit.

[1807] Chris Philp, UK Minister for Tech and the Digital Economy, Speech at Digital City Festival (Mar. 9, 2022), https://www.gov.uk/government/speeches/minister-for-tech-and-the-digital-economy-speech-at-digital-city-festival.

policy and enforcement levels. The 2010 Horizontal Merger Guidelines provided guidance to the agencies on how to consider and assess innovation-related matters in merger control cases, in contrast to the Commission's "novel approach" and the ambiguous concepts it has utilized, such as innovation spaces, criticized for lack of legislative basis. It may perhaps even be possible to say that it was such structured guidance that allowed the US antitrust agencies to avoid criticisms of speculative and overly invasive practices, especially in terms of dynamic innovative markets.

Antitrust agencies in the US have employed several different theories of harm when examining merger cases. In addition to evaluating the potential harm to innovation in competition, US antitrust agencies have even considered the effects of the transaction on competition within non-existing markets. Unsurprisingly, the main problem with such innovation considerations is the dearth of information: considering that there is yet no way to measure a potential, non-existing market with economic tools, they cannot always be evaluated based on concrete evidence. This means there cannot possibly be a single set of standards for examining innovation-related issues in merger controls that will apply to every case. As reiterated throughout this work, this demonstrates the need for competition enforcement agencies to adopt a case-by-case approach to their analysis in terms of innovation considerations, by scrutinizing the specific dynamics and effects of the transaction and the market structure in each investigation. This is especially important in their assessments relating to technology markets, where the single most important driving force of competition is innovation.

Although the 2010 Horizontal Merger Guidelines in the US have specifically addressed the concept of innovation, there was no such corresponding section in vertical merger guidelines for a long time. We saw that the 2020 Guidelines, which the FTC and DOJ jointly issued, indeed referred to the ability to create innovative products under the pro-competitive effects, demonstrating at least the intention to recognize innovation as an efficiency defense. But considering that the 2020 Vertical Merger Guidelines were withdrawn in 2021 and are currently undergoing careful scrutiny by the agencies, the final product may turn out to have a whole different view. Structured guidance has indeed assisted antitrust agencies in formulating consistent and fair assessments with regard to horizontal mergers, but whether the revised version of the vertical merger guidelines will still embrace innovation or reflect the other competition agencies' propensity to focus on competition in the market without taking into account future effects and evolution and a more intrusive approach[1808] remains to be seen.

The competition agencies are also focusing more on killer or creeping acquisitions: As the merger notification thresholds in some countries are based on the turnovers of the merging undertakings, concentrations involving firms with small monetary turnover are typically not screened or assessed by competition authorities, even if the transaction value of the deal is very high. This is particularly the case in the digital economy, where many start-ups concentrate on growing their customer bases rather than focusing on increasing

---

[1808] Jonathan Kanter, Assistant Att'y Gen., Antitrust Div., Dep't of Just., Remarks to the New York State Bar Association Antitrust Section (Jan. 24, 2022), https://www.justice.gov/opa/speech/assistant-attorney-general-jonathan-kanter-antitrust-division-delivers-remarks-new-york.

their turnovers, and where the entrepreneurs' motivation largely stems from being able to grab the attention of big firms to sell their shares. It is sometimes the case that such new and innovative products and services are bought up by incumbents to eradicate or "kill" the competition, to the detriment of economic and social welfare. Accordingly, it is important for competition authorities to ensure that any threshold or mechanism adopted does not actually allow such inflow of innovative entrepreneurship to be curtailed, and also to determine the correct methods to assess any restrictive effects and potential efficiencies such a merger may have on consumer welfare.

In light of the above, the European Commission debated whether it might be necessary to use the value of a transaction as a complementary notification threshold for merger transactions. The Commission also introduced its Article 22 Guidance as a response to these concerns, reappraising the referral system to include competitively significant transactions that do not fall under Member State jurisdictions. Considering that creeping/killer acquisitions were prevalent in the digital sectors, the EU has also most recently introduced the Digital Markets Act, to keep the large platforms, i.e., "the gatekeepers" of the digital markets, under scrutiny, with the aim to bring an end to the dominance of Big Tech firms and promote fair competition and innovation.

Parallel to this, the CMA has also announced the creation of a Digital Markets Unit to implement the UK's strategy for a pro-competition regime for digital markets. The CMA has been focused on online platforms and digital advertising, and emphasized the need for creating a pro-competitive approach that would protect consumer welfare. It has worked with Ofcom and the Information Commissioner's Office to ensure a coherent and comprehensive regulatory framework for the UK digital economy. While it does emphasize it is conscious of the need to avoid over-regulation (and perhaps attract those start-ups that may feel the EU has become a bit too constrained for their taste), the proof will be in the enforcement. The CMA's strong stance in *Microsoft/Activision* indicates consumer welfare may trump investor interests. On the other side of the pond, we also see that the FTC is increasingly focused on killer acquisitions in the digital sector, and any loopholes and avoidance mechanisms that may have allowed the big tech to get away with them. The FTC and the DOJ's approach to how the 2020 Vertical Merger Guidelines are to be revised indicates they are ready to take on a much more hands-on view and intervene via injunctions to protect competition in markets, which will be quite a significant change in terms of US competition law.

It is, thus, apparent that we are still seeing a skeptical approach to innovation, despite its incontrovertible role in economic growth and efficiency. The competition authorities' assessment of digital markets may be an indication of how they see any fast-evolving, innovative, future-oriented, and therefore, inherently imprecise market. As they emphasize their role in protecting competition in the market "*as is*" today, they are ignoring their duty to promote innovation, which would expand services, products, and markets, or incentivize efficient processes that would stimulate growth. While we do not and should not condone those utilizing alleged efficiency defenses to whitewash their intentions, it is far too easy for authorities to say "no" outright to any case that presents any innovation concern to be flagged based on general economic theory and literature on innovation. What is crucial to understand here is that, unlike transaction parties, competition authorities have a bird-eye view of the whole market in question, its dynamics and potential efficiencies; they have the power to request data from market players, third parties, even consult with competition agencies in other countries, if they had the inclination to do so. It is therefore even more important that, notwithstanding where the burden of proof lies, the authorities strive to closely assess each case by employing counterfactuals and by using their own information and analytical resources, and not hesitate to step outside the traditional methods that do not address the dynamics of the innovative markets, in order to achieve the maximum potential economic growth. It is discouraging that the above-discussed recent regulations in developed economies indicate that authorities may actually adopt an intensified and more intrusive antitrust enforcement. An overzealous approach is the simpler solution for sure, but it may be more expensive and even damaging, as it may prove to be a turn-off for the entrepreneurs, to the detriment of consumer welfare. Unless this is recognized, maximum potential economic growth may unfortunately never be achieved and, sadly, the counterfactual might not even be known.

BIBLIOGRAPHY

Books

DICTIONARY OF ECONOMICS AND COMMERCE (Stella E. Stiegeler & Glyn Thomas eds., Pan Reference Books 1976)

ENTREPRENEURSHIP, INNOVATION, AND THE GROWTH MECHANISM OF THE FREE-ENTERPRISE ECONOMIES (Eytan Sheshinski, Robert J. Strom, and William J. Baumol eds., Princeton Univ. Press 2007)

THE INTERFACE BETWEEN INTELLECTUAL PROPERTY RIGHTS AND COMPETITION POLICY (Steven D. Anderman ed., Cambridge Univ. Press 2007)

THE LAWS OF PLATO bk. IV (Thomas L. Pangle ed. & trans., Basic Books 1980)

AGHION, PHILIPPE & RACHEL GRIFFITH, COMPETITION AND GROWTH: RECONCILING THEORY AND EVIDENCE (MIT Press 2005)

AGHION, PHILIPPE & PETER HOWITT, THE ECONOMICS OF GROWTH (MIT Press 2008)

Aiken, Howard, *The Future of Automatic Computing Machinery, in* ELEKTRONISCHE RECHENMASCHINEN UND INFORMATIONSVERARBEITUNG [ELECTRONIC DIGITAL COMPUTERS AND INFORMATION PROCESSING] (Alwin Walther & Walter Hoffmann eds., F. Vieweg 1957)

Alexiadis, Peter, *Balancing the Application of Ex Post and Ex Ante Disciplines Under Community Law in Electronic Communications Markets: Square Pegs in Round Holes? in* RIGHTS AND REMEDIES IN A LIBERALISED AND COMPETITIVE INTERNAL MARKET (Eugène Buttigieg ed., University of Malta 2012)

ARISTOTLE, POLITICS bk. II (H. Rackham trans., Harvard Univ. Press 1932)

Arrow, Kenneth, *Economic Welfare and the Allocation of Resources for Invention, in* NATIONAL BUREAU OF ECONOMIC RESEARCH, THE RATE AND DIRECTION OF INVENTIVE ACTIVITY: ECONOMIC AND SOCIAL FACTORS 609–626 (Princeton Univ. Press 1962)

BASALLA, GEORGE, TEKNOLOJININ EVRIMI [THE EVOLUTION OF TECHNOLOGY] (Cen Soydemir trans., Tübitak Publications 2000)

BELLEFLAMME, PAUL & MARTIN PEITZ, INDUSTRIAL ORGANIZATION: MARKETS AND STRATEGIES (Cambridge Univ. Press 2009)

BELLEFLAMME, PAUL & MARTIN PEITZ, INDUSTRIAL ORGANIZATION: MARKETS AND STRATEGIES (Cambridge Univ. Press 2nd ed. 2015)

BESSEN, JAMES & MICHAEL J. MEURER, PATENT FAILURE: HOW JUDGES, BUREAUCRATS, AND LAWYERS PUT INNOVATORS AT RISK (Princeton Univ. Press 2008)

BESSEN, JAMES, LEARNING BY DOING: THE REAL CONNECTION BETWEEN INNOVATION, WAGES, AND WEALTH (Yale Univ. Press 2015)

BOLDRIN, MICHELE & DAVID K. LEVINE, AGAINST INTELLECTUAL MONOPOLY (Cambridge Univ. Press 2008)

BRESSON, ALAIN, THE MAKING OF THE ANCIENT GREEK ECONOMY (Princeton Univ. Press 2016)

BURTON-JONES, ALAN, KNOWLEDGE CAPITALISM: BUSINESS, WORK, AND LEARNING IN THE NEW ECONOMY (Oxford Univ. Press 1999)

Bibliography

CARRIER, MICHAEL A., INNOVATION FOR THE 21ST CENTURY: HARNESSING THE POWER OF INTELLECTUAL PROPERTY AND ANTITRUST LAW 314 (Oxford Univ. Press 2009)

Cohen, Wesley M., *Fifty Years of Empirical Studies of Innovative Activity and Performance*, in 1 HANDBOOK OF ECONOMICS OF INNOVATION 129 (Bronwyn H. Hall & Nathan Rosenberg eds., North Holland 2010)

COMMONS, JOHN R., INSTITUTIONAL ECONOMICS: ITS PLACE IN POLITICAL ECONOMY (Univ. Wisconsin Press 1934)

DARDANO, VALERIA, ASSESSING INNOVATION IN MERGER CONTROL 14 (College of Europe 2016)

ETRO, FREDERICO, COMPETITION, INNOVATION, AND ANTITRUST: A THEORY OF MARKET LEADERS AND ITS POLICY IMPLICATIONS (Springer 2007)

Fagerberg, Jan, Martin Srholec & Bart Verspagen, *Innovation and Economic Development*, in 2 HANDBOOK OF ECONOMICS OF INNOVATION 833 (Bronwyn H. Hall & Nathan Rosenberg eds., Elsevier 2010)

FUMAGALLI, CHIARA, MASSIMO MOTTA & CLAUDIO CALCAGNO, *Introduction*, in EXCLUSIONARY PRACTICES: THE ECONOMICS OF MONOPOLISATION AND ABUSE OF DOMINANCE 1–13 (Cambridge Univ. Press 2018)

GILBERT, RICHARD J., INNOVATION MATTERS: COMPETITION POLICY FOR THE HIGH-TECHNOLOGY ECONOMY (MIT Press 2022)

GODIN, BENOÎT, INNOVATION CONTESTED: THE IDEA OF INNOVATION OVER THE CENTURIES (Routledge 2014)

GORDON, ROBERT, THE RISE AND FALL OF AMERICAN GROWTH 438 (Princeton Univ. Press 2016)

GROSSMAN, GENE M. & ELHANAN HELPMAN, INNOVATION AND GROWTH IN THE GLOBAL ECONOMY (MIT Press 1993)

GROSSMAN, GENE M. & ELHANAN HELPMAN, SPECIAL INTEREST POLITICS (MIT Press 2002)

Hamm, Berndt, *How Innovative was the Reformation?* in ARCHÄOLOGIE DER REFORMATION: STUDIEN ZU DEN AUSWIRKUNGEN DES KONFESSIONSWECHSELS AUF DIE MATERIELLE KULTUR 26 (Carola Jäggi & Jörn Staecker eds., De Gruyter 2007)

Huntington, Hillard G. & John P. Weyant, *Modeling Energy Markets and Climate Change Policy*, in ENCYCLOPAEDIA OF ENERGY 41 (Cutler J. Cleveland ed., Elsevier Science 2004)

Katz, Michael L. & Howard A. Shelanski, *Merger Policy and Innovation: Must Enforcement Change to Account for Technological Change?* in 5 INNOVATION POLICY AND THE ECONOMY 109 (Adam B. Jaffe, Josh Lerner & Scott Stern eds, MIT Press 2006)

Kwoka, John, *The Effects of Mergers on Innovation: Economic Framework and Empirical Evidence*, in THE ROLES OF INNOVATION IN COMPETITION LAW ANALYSIS 13, 23–24 (Paul Nihoul & Pieter Van Cleynenbreugel eds., Edward Elgar Publishing 2008)

LANDES, WILLIAM M. & RICHARD A. POSNER, THE ECONOMIC STRUCTURE OF INTELLECTUAL PROPERTY LAW (Harvard Univ. Press 2009)

Lehmann, Jörg & Francesca Morselli, *Science and Technology in the First World War* (CENDARI Archival Research Guide, 2016)

Lianos, Ioannis & Christos Genakos, *Econometric Evidence in EU Competition Law: An Empirical and Theoretical Analysis* HANDBOOK ON EUROPEAN COMPETITION LAW 64 & 75 (Edward Elgar Publishing 2013), https://EconPapers.repec.org/RePEc:elg:eechap:15373_1

LIANOS, IOANNIS, VALENTINE KORAH & PAOLO SICILIANI, COMPETITION LAW: ANALYSIS, CASES & MATERIALS 1516 (Oxford Univ. Press 2019)

MAY, CHRISTOPHER & SUSAN K. SELL, INTELLECTUAL PROPERTY RIGHTS: A CRITICAL HISTORY 101 (Lynne Rienner Publishers Inc. 2006)

Bibliography

NATIONAL RESEARCH COUNCIL, THE POSITIVE SUM STRATEGY: HARNESSING TECHNOLOGY FOR ECONOMIC GROWTH (Ralph Landau & Nathan Rosenberg eds., The National Academies Press 1986)

NATIONAL RESEARCH COUNCIL, 21ST CENTURY INNOVATION SYSTEMS FOR JAPAN AND THE UNITED STATES: LESSONS FROM A DECADE OF CHANGE: REPORT OF A SYMPOSIUM 206–23 (The National Academies Press 2009) https://doi.org/10.17226/12194

NELSON, RICHARD R., THE RATE AND DIRECTION OF INVENTIVE ACTIVITIES: ECONOMIC AND SOCIAL FACTORS (Princeton Univ. Press 2016)

Nordhaus, William, Integrated Economic and Climate Modeling, in HANDBOOK OF COMPUTABLE GENERAL EQUILIBRIUM MODELING 1069 (Elsevier 2013)

Novelli, Francesco, Detection and Measurement of Sales Cannibalization in Information Technology Markets, Publications of Darmstadt Technical University (Institute for Business Studies (BWL), 2015)

PANOFSKY, ERWIN, RENAISSANCE AND RENASCENCES IN WESTERN ART (Harper & Row 1969)

PHILIPPON, THOMAS, THE GREAT REVERSAL: HOW AMERICA GAVE UP ON FREE MARKETS (Belknap Press 2019)

PLATO, THE SEVENTH LETTER (George Burges trans., 1851) (c. 385 BC)

PORTER, MICHAEL E. & SCOTT STERN, THE NEW CHALLENGE TO AMERICA'S PROSPERITY: FINDINGS FROM THE INNOVATION INDEX (Council on Competitiveness 1999)

Powell, Lynda W. & Clyde Wilcox, Money and American Elections, in THE OXFORD HANDBOOK OF AMERICAN ELECTIONS AND POLITICAL BEHAVIOR (Jan E. Leighley ed., Oxford Univ. Press 2010)

ROGERS, EVERETT M., DIFFUSION OF INNOVATIONS (Free Press 5th ed. 2003)

SCHAFF PHILIP, HISTORY OF THE CHRISTIAN CHURCH, vol. VII: MODERN CHRISTIANITY: THE GERMAN REFORMATION 3–6, 12 (Christian Classics Ethereal Library 2nd ed. 1882)

SCHRAMM, LAURIER L., INNOVATION TECHNOLOGY: A DICTIONARY 1 (De Gruyter 2017)

SCHUMPETER, JOSEPH A., THE THEORY OF ECONOMIC DEVELOPMENT (New Jersey Transaction Publishers 1912)

SCHUMPETER, JOSEPH A., THE THEORY OF ECONOMIC DEVELOPMENT: AN INQUIRY INTO PROFITS, CAPITAL, CREDIT, INTEREST AND THE BUSINESS CYCLE (Redvers Opie trans., Harvard Univ. Press 1934)

SCHUMPETER, JOSEPH A., CAPITALISM, SOCIALISM AND DEMOCRACY (Harper and Brothers 1942), https://periferiaactiva.files.wordpress.com/2015/08/joseph-schumpeter-capitalism-socialism-and-democracy-2006.pdf

SCHUMPETER, JOSEPH A., HISTORY OF ECONOMIC ANALYSIS (Routledge 2nd ed. 1954)

Shapiro, Carl, Competition and Innovation: Did Arrow Hit the Bulls Eye? in THE RATE AND DIRECTION OF INVENTIVE ACTIVITY REVISITED 361 (Josh Lerner & Scott Stern eds., Univ. of Chicago Press 2012), https://www.nber.org/chapters/c12360.pdf

SOLOW, ROBERT M., ON MACROECONOMIC MODELS OF FREE-MARKET INNOVATION AND GROWTH (Princeton Univ. Press, 2007)

SPULBER, DANIEL F., ANTITRUST AND INNOVATION COMPETITION (Oxford Univ. Press 2022)

STUCKE, MAURICE E. & ALLEN P. GRUNES, BIG DATA AND COMPETITION POLICY (Oxford Univ. Press 2016)

TESLA, NIKOLA, MY INVENTIONS: THE AUTOBIOGRAPHY OF NIKOLA TESLA (Wilder Publications Inc. 2014)

Thompson, Peter, Learning by Doing, in HANDBOOK OF THE ECONOMICS OF INNOVATION 220–29 (Bronwyn H. Hall & Nathan Rosenberg eds., Elsevier 2010)

TIROLE, JEAN, THE THEORY OF INDUSTRIAL ORGANIZATION 392 (MIT Press 1997)

VAN DEN BERGH, ROGER, COMPARATIVE COMPETITION LAW AND ECONOMICS 458 (Edward Elgar Publishing 2017)

VAVER, DAVID, INTELLECTUAL PROPERTY RIGHTS: CRITICAL CONCEPTS IN LAW (Taylor & Francis 2006)

Whinston, Michael D., *Competition and Innovation: Did Arrow Hit the Bull's Eye?* in THE RATE AND DIRECTION OF INVENTIVE ACTIVITY REVISITED 404 (Josh Lerner & Scott Stern eds., Univ. of Chicago Press 2012)

WHISH, RICHARD & DAVID BAILEY, COMPETITION LAW (Oxford Univ. Press 9th ed. 2018)

Conference Papers

Déchamps, Pascale, Dynamic Markets and Dynamic Enforcement: A Focus on Merger Control, 12th Annual Conference of the GCLC (Jan. 26, 2017), https://www2.coleurope.eu/sites/default/files/uploads/event/pascale_dechamps_-_slides.pdf

Godin, Benoît, The Spirit of Innovation (Annual Meeting of the Canadian Economics Association, Session on Innovation organized by The Centre for the Study of Living Standards and the Institute for Research in Public Policy, McGill University, June 1–3, 2018), http://www.csiic.ca/wp-content/uploads/2018/06/Spirit.pdf

Graef, Inge, Sih Yuliana Wahyuningtyas & Peggy Valcke, How Google and Others Upset Competition Analysis: Disruptive Innovation and European Competition Law, 25th European Regional Conference of the International Telecommunications Society (ITS), Brussels, Belgium, June 22–25 (2014), https://www.econstor.eu/handle/10419/101378

Gürkaynak, Gönenç, Taking the Lead in Antitrust Enforcement Evaluating Innovation and Technology, 19th Loyola Antitrust Colloquium, Institute for Consumer Antitrust Studies at Loyola University Chicago School of Law (Apr. 26, 2019)

Mosso, Carles Esteva, Innovation in EU Merger Control, 66th ABA Section of Antitrust Law Spring Meeting 5 (Apr. 12, 2018), http://ec.europa.eu/competition/speeches/text/sp2018_05_en.pdf

Novelli, Francesco, *Platform Substitution and Cannibalization: The Case of Portable Navigation Devices*, SOFTWARE BUS. ICSOB 141 (2012)

Rao, Balkrishna C., *Economic Recognition of Innovation*, SINGAPORE ECON. REV. CONF. (SERC) (2007)

Thomond, Peter & Fiona Lettice, Disruptive Innovation Explored, 9th IPSE International Conference on Concurrent Engineering: Research and Applications (CE2002) (July 2002)

Wang, Changtao, The Long-Run Effect of Innovations on Economic Growth, Paper Prepared for the IARIW-UNSW Conference on Productivity: Measurement, Drivers and Trends, Sydney, Australia (Nov. 26–27, 2013), http://www.iariw.org/papers/2013/WangPaper.pdf

Journal Articles

American Tech Giants Are Making Life Tough for Start-ups, THE ECONOMIST (Oct. 26, 2018)

Adner, Ron & Rahul Kapoor, *Innovation Ecosystems and the Pace of Substitution: Re-examining Technology S-curves*, 37 STRATEGIC MGMT. J. 625 (2016)

Agénor, Pierre-Richard & Kyriakos C. Neanidis, *Innovation, Public Capital, and Growth*, J. MACROECONOMICS 252 (2015)

Bibliography

Aghion, Philippe, Nick Bloom, Richard Blundell, Rachel Griffith & Peter Howitt, *Competition and Innovation: An Inverted-U Relationship*, 120 Q. J. Econ. 701 (2005)

Aghion, Philippe, Richard Blundell, Rachel Griffith, Peter Howitt & Susanne Prantl, *The Effects of Entry on Incumbent Innovation and Productivity*, 91 Rev. Econ. & Stat. 20 (2009)

Alexy, Oliver, Paola Criscuolo & Ammon Salter, *Does IP Strategy Have to Cripple Open Innovation?* 51 Sloan Mgmt. Rev. 71 (2009)

Andergassen, Rainer, Franco Nardini & Massimo Ricottilli, *Innovation Diffusion, General Purpose Technologies and Economic Growth*, 40 Structural Change & Econ. Dynamics 72 (2017)

Ang, Edward, *The Positive Effects of Education, Research and Innovation on GDP per Capita* (2012) https://www.researchgate.net/publication/270418934_The_Positive_Effects_of_Education_ Research_ and_Innovation_on_GDP_Per_Capita

Arundel, Anthony & Dorothea Huber, *From Too Little to Too Much Innovation? Issues in Measuring Innovation in the Public Sector*, 27 Structural Change & Econ. Dynamics 146 (2013)

Baker, Jonathan B., *Contemporary Empirical Merger Analysis*, 5 Geo. Mason L. Rev. 347 (1997)

Baker, Jonathan B., *Product Differentiation Through Space and Time: Some Antitrust Policy Issues*, 42 Antitrust Bull. 177 (1997)

Baker, Jonathan B., *Stepping Out in an Old Brown Shoe: In Qualified Praise of Submarkets*, 68 Antitrust L.J. 203 (2000)

Baker, Jonathan B., *Beyond Schumpeter vs. Arrow: How Antitrust Fosters Innovation*, 74 Antitrust L.J. 575 (2007), http://dx.doi.org/10.2139/ssrn.962261

Baker, Jonathan B., *Exclusionary Conduct of Dominant Firms, R&D Competition, and Innovation*, 48 Rev. Indus. Org. 269 (2016)

Baker, Jonathan B., Nancy L. Rose, Steven C. Salop & Fiona Scott Morton, *Five Principles for Vertical Merger Enforcement Policy*, 33 Antitrust 12 (2019)

Baradwaj, Babu G., David A. Dubofsky & Donald R. Fraser, *Defensive Acquisitions in the Banking Industry: The Takeover Premium Hypothesis*, 20 J. Econ. & Fin. 13, 13 (1996)

Bell, Martin & Keith Pavitt, *Technological Accumulation and Industrial Growth: Contrasts Between Developed and Developing Countries*, 2 Indus. & Corp. Change 157 (1993)

Ben-David, Joseph & Awraham Zloczower, *Universities and Academic Systems in Modern Societies* 3 Eur. J. Socio. 45 (1962).

Bennato, Anna Rita, Stephen Davies, Franco Mariuzzo & Peter Ormosi, *Mergers and Innovation: Evidence from the Hard Disk Drive Market*, 77 Int'l J. Indus. Org. Elsevier (2021), DOI: 10.1016/j.ijindorg.2021.102755

Bilbao-Osorio, Beñat & Andrés Rodríguez-Pose, *From R&D to Innovation and Economic Growth in the EU*, 35 Growth & Change 434 (2004)

Bittlingmayer, George, *Property Rights, Progress, and the Aircraft Patent Agreement*, 31 J. L. & Econ. 227 (1988)

Blank, David L., *Socratics Versus Sophists on Payment for Teaching*, 4 Classical Antiquity 1 (1985)

Bloch, Harry & Stan Metcalfe, *Innovation, Creative Destruction and Price Theory*, 27 Indus. & Corp. Change 1 (2018), https://www.researchgate.net/publication/319479740_Innovation_creative_ destruction_and_price_theory

Blundell, Richard, Rachel Griffith & John Van Reenen, *Market Share, Market Value and Innovation in a Panel of British Manufacturing Firms*, 66 Rev. Econ. Stud. 529 (1999)

Boldrin, Michele & David K. Levine, *The Case Against Patents*, 27 J. Econ. Persp. 3 (2013)

Bourreau, Marc & Alexandre de Streel, *Digital Conglomerates and EU Competition Policy* 7–11 (2019), https://dx.doi.org/10.2139/ssrn.3350512

Bourreau, Marc & Nathalie Sonnac, *Introduction to Competition in Two-Sided Markets: Application to Information and Communication Industries*, 61 COMMUNICATIONS & STRATEGIES 11 (2006)

Bower, Joseph L. & Clayton M. Christensen, *Disruptive Technologies: Catching the Wave*, 73 HARV. BUS. REV. 43 (1995)

Bracha, Oren, *The Adventures of the Statute of Anne in the Land of Unlimited Possibilities: The Life of a Legal Transplant*, 25 BERKELEY TECH. L.J. 1427 (2010)

Branstetter, Lee, *Intellectual Property Rights, Innovation and Development: Is Asia Different?* 8 MILLENNIAL ASIA 5 (2017)

Branstetter, Lee G., Raymond Fisman & C. Fritz Foley, *Do Stronger Intellectual Property Rights Increase International Technology Transfer? Empirical Evidence from the United States Firm-Level Panel Data*, 121 Q. J. Econ. 321 (2006)

Brittain, James E., *The International Diffusion of Electrical Power Technology, 1870–1920*, 34 J. ECON. HIS. 108 (1974)

Buehler, Benno & Giulio Federico, *Recent Developments in the Assessment of Efficiencies of Mergers in the EU*, 2 COMPETITION L. & POL'Y DEBATE 64 (2016)

Bure, Frédéric de & Laurence Bary, *Disruptive Innovation and Merger Remedies: How to Predict the Unpredictable?* CONCURRENCES 3-2017, art. No. 84407,

Cameron, Duncan, Mark Glick & David Mangum, *Good Riddance to Market Definition?* 57 ANTITRUST BULL. 719 (2012)

Capobianco, Antonio & Anita Nyeso, *Challenges for Competition Law Enforcement and Policy in the Digital Economy*, 9 J. EUR. COMPETITION L. & PRAC. 19 (2018)

Carlton, Dennis W. & Robert H. Gertner, *Intellectual Property, Antitrust, and Strategic Behavior*, INNOVATION POL'Y & ECON. 29 (2003), https://doi.org/10.1086/ipe.3.25056152

Carrier, Michael A., *Two Puzzles Resolved: Of the Schumpeter–Arrow Stalemate and Pharmaceutical Innovation Markets*, 93 IOWA L. REV. 393 (2008)

Chen, Yongmin & Marius Schwartz, *Product Innovation Incentives: Monopoly vs. Competition*, 22 J. ECON. & MGMT. STRATEGY 513 (2013)

Colino, Sandra Marco, Knut Fournier, Sofia Pais, Derek Ritzmann & Niamh Dunne, *The Lundbeck Case and the Concept of Potential Competition*, CONCURRENCES No 2-2017, art. No. 83827, 24. ww.concurrences.com/83827

Colomo, Pablo Ibáñez, *Restrictions on Innovation in EU Competition Law*, 41 EUR. L. REV. 201 (2016)

Colomo, Pablo Ibáñez, *Competition Law and Innovation: Where Do We Stand?* 9 J. EUR. COMPETITION L. & PRAC. 561 (2018)

Comanor, William S. & F. M. Scherer, *Mergers and Innovation in the Pharmaceutical Industry*, 32 J. HEALTH ECON. 106 (2013)

Comin, Diego & Bart Hobijn, *An Exploration of Technology Diffusion*, 100 AM. ECON. REV. 2031 (2010)

Coppola, Maria & Renato Nazzini, *The European and US Approaches to Antitrust and Tech: Setting the Record Straight – A Reply to Gregory J. Werden and Luke M. Froeb's, Antitrust and Tech: Europe and the United States Differ, and It Matters*, ANTITRUST CHRON. (2020)

Crane, Daniel A., *Ecosystem Competition and the Antitrust Laws*, 95 NEB. L. REV. 412 (2019)

Cunningham, Colleen, Florian Ederer & Song Ma, *Killer Acquisitions*, 129 J. POLITICAL ECON. 649 (2021), http://dx.doi.org/10.2139/ssrn.3241707

Czarnitzki, Dirk & Otto Toivanen, *Innovation Policy and Economic Growth*, 483 ECON. PAPERS (2013)

Dasgupta Partha & Joseph Stiglitz, *Industrial Structure and the Nature of Innovative Activity*, 90 ECON. J. 266 (1980)

Dasgupta, Partha & Joseph Stiglitz, *Learning-by-Doing, Market Structure and Industrial and Trade Policies*, 40 OXFORD ECON. PAPERS 247 (1998)

Day, Gregory, *Innovative Antitrust and the Patent System*, 96 NEB. L. REV. 829 (2017)

De Coninck, Raphaël, *Innovation in EU Merger Control: In Need of a Consistent Framework*, 2 COMPETITION L. & POL'Y DEBATE 41 (2016)

De Loecker, Jan, *Detecting Learning by Exporting*, 5 AM. ECON. J.: MICROECONOMICS 1 (2013)

Denicolò, Vincenzo & Michele Polo, *Duplicative Research, Mergers and Innovation*, 166 ECON. LETTERS 56 (2018)

Denicolò, Vincenzo & Michele Polo, *The Innovation Theory of Harm: An Appraisal* (2018), https://ssrn.com/abstract=3146731

Dewulf, Stéphane, Timo Klein, Andrew Mell & Anastasia Shchepetova, *EU and UK Vertical Merger Control: What's the State of Play?* 14 J. EUR. COMPETITION L. & PRAC 113 (2023)

Dieterlen, Pierre, *Abramovitz (Moses), Resource and Output Trends in the United States Since 1870. Occasional Paper 1952*, 9 REVUE ÉCONOMIQUE 164 (1958).

Dosi, Giovanni, *Technological Paradigms and Technological Trajectories: A Suggested Interpretation of The Determinants and Directions of Technical Change*, 11 RSCH. POL'Y 147 (1982)

Drexl, Josef, *Anti-Competitive Stumbling Stones on the Way to a Cleaner World: Protecting Competition in Innovation without a Market*, 8 J. COMPETITION L. & ECON. 507, 520 (2012); (Max Planck Institute for Intellectual Property & Competition Law Research Paper No. 12-08), https://ssrn.com/abstract=2070099

Dubina, Igor & Elias G. Carayannis, *Potentials of Game Theory for Analysis and Improvement of Innovation Policy and Practice in a Dynamic Socio-Economic Environment*, 3 J. INNOVATION ECON. & MGMT. 165 (2015)

ECLF, *Brexit and Merger Control in the EU: A Proposed Way Forward*, 13 EUR. COMPETITION J. 151 (2017)

Encaoua, David & Abraham Hollander, *Competition Policy and Innovation*, 18 OXFORD REV. ECON. POL'Y 63 (2002), https://doi.org/10.1093/oxrep/18.1.63

Etzkowitz, Henry, *An Innovation Strategy to End the Second Great Depression*, 20 EUR. PLAN. STUD. 1439 (2012)

Evans, David S., *The Antitrust Economics of Multi-Sided Platform Markets*, 20 YALE J. ON REGUL. 325 (2003), https://openyls.law.yale.edu/bitstream/handle/20.500.13051/8032/12_20YaleJonReg325_2003_.pdf?sequence=2&isAllowed=y

Farrell, Joseph & Carl Shapiro, *Antitrust Evaluation of Horizontal Mergers: An Economic Alternative to Market Definition*, 10 B.E. J. THEORETICAL ECON. POLICIES & PERSP. 1 (2010), art. 9, https://faculty.haas.berkeley.edu/shapiro/alternative.pdf

Federico, Giulio, *Horizontal Mergers, Innovation and the Competitive Process*, 8 J. EUR. COMPETITION L. & PRAC. 668 (2017)

Federico, Giulio, Gregor Langus & Tommaso Valletti, *Horizontal Mergers and Product Innovation*, 59 INT'L J. INDUS. ORG. 1 (2018), https://www.researchgate.net/publication/318392882_Horizontal_Mergers_and_Product_Innovation

Ferreira, Joao, Cristina I. Fernandes & Vanessa Ratten, *Entrepreneurship, Innovation and Competitiveness: What Is the Connection?* 18 INT'L J. BUS. & GLOBALISATION 73 (2017)

Bibliography

Finley, M. I., *Technical Innovation and Economic Progress in the Ancient World*, 18 ECON. HISTORY REV. 29 (1965)

Frieden, Rob, *Ex Ante Versus Ex Post Approaches to Network Neutrality: A Cost Benefit Analysis*, 30 BERKELEY TECH. L.J. 1561 (2015)

Furman, Jeffrey L., Michael E. Porter & Scott Stern, *Understanding the Drivers of National Innovative Capacity*, ACAD. MGMT. BEST PAPER PROC. A1 (2000)

Gal, Michal S. & Daniel L. Rubinfeld, *The Hidden Costs of Free Goods: Implications for Antitrust Enforcement*, 80 ANTITRUST L.J. 521 (2016)

Ganguli, Prabuddha, *Intellectual Property Rights: Mothering Innovations to Markets*, 22 WORLD PAT. INFO. 43 (2000)

Gans, Joshua S. & Scott Stern, *The Product Market and the Market for "Ideas": Commercialization Strategies for Technology Entrepreneurs*, 32 RSCH. POL'Y 333 (2003)

Gans, Joshua S., David D. Hsu & Scott Stern, *When Does Start-Up Innovation Spur the Gale of Creative Destruction?* 33 RAND J. ECON. 571 (2002)

Garcés, Eliana & Daniel Gaynor, *Conglomerate Mergers: Developments and a Call for Caution*, 10 J. EUR. COMPETITION L. & PRAC. 457 (2019)

Georgedes, Kimberly, *Religion, Education and the Role of Government in Medieval Universities: Lessons Learned or Lost?* 2 F. PUB. POL'Y 21 (2006)

Gibbons, Gerald R., *Price Fixing in Patent Licenses and the Antitrust Laws*, 51 VA. L. REV. 273 (1965)

Gilbert, Richard, *Looking for Mr. Schumpeter: Where Are We in the Competition-Innovation Debate?* in 6 INNOVATION POLICY AND THE ECONOMY 159 (Adam B. Jaffe, Josh Lerner & Scott Stern eds, MIT Press 2006), http://www.nber.org/chapters/c0208.pdf

Gilbert, Richard & David Newbery, *Preemptive Patenting and the Persistence of Monopoly*, 72 AM. ECON. REV. 514 (1982)

Gilbert, Richard J. & Steven C. Sunshine, *Incorporating Dynamic Efficiency Concerns in Merger Analysis: The Use of Innovation Markets*, 63 ANTITRUST L.J. 569 (1995)

Greenstein, Shane & Garey Ramey, *Market Structure, Innovation and Vertical Product Differentiation*, 16 INT'L J. INDUS. ORG. 285 (1998)

Gurevitch, Michael & Zipora Loevy, *The Diffusion of Television as an Innovation: The Case of the Kibbutz*, 25 HUM. REL. 181 (1972)

Gürkaynak, Gönenç & Naz Topaloglu, *Turkey: Innovation Based Analysis of Mergers*, CONCURRENCES No. 1-2019, art. No. 88891,

Gürkaynak, Gönenç, Esra Uçtu & Anıl Acar, *Applying the Dynamic Competition Approach to Zero-Priced Markets*, in DOUGLAS H. GINSBURG, AN ANTITRUST PROFESSOR ON THE BENCH – LIBER AMICORUM, VOL. I 307 (Nicolas Charbit, Carolina Malhado & Ellie Yang eds., Concurrences 2018)

Hartwell, R. M., *The Causes of the Industrial Revolution: An Essay in Methodology*, 18 ECON. HIST. REV. 164 (1965)

Hayslett III, Thomas L., *1995 Antitrust Guidelines for the Licensing of Intellectual Property: Harmonizing the Commercial Use of Legal Monopolies with the Prohibitions of Antitrust Law*, 3 J. INTELL. PROP. L. 375 (1996), https://digitalcommons.law.uga.edu/cgi/viewcontent.cgi?referer=https://www.google.com/&httpsredir=1&article=1117&context=jipl

Healy, Melissa, Ingrid Vandenborre, Giorgio Motta, Frederic Depoortere & Bill Batchelor, *The UK Competition Appeal Tribunal Confirms a Deferential Standard for the Competition Authority in Its Merger Prohibitions (Tobii / Smartbox)*, E-COMPETITIONS JANUARY 2020, art. No. 93459,

Heller, Michael A. & Rebecca S. Eisenberg, *Can Patents Deter Innovation? The Anticommons in Biomedical Research*, 280 SCIENCE 698 (1998)

Bibliography

Hemphill, C. Scott & Tim Wu, *Nascent Competitors*, 168 U. Pa. L. Rev. 1879 (2020)

Hesse, Carla, *The Rise of Intellectual Property, 700 B.C.-A.D. 2000: An Idea in the Balance*, 131 Daedalus 26 (Spring 2002)

Hirsch-Kreinsen, Hartmut, David Jacobson & Paul L. Robertson, *'Low-tech' Industries: Innovativeness and Development Perspectives – A Summary of a European Research Project*, 24 Prometheus 3 (2006)

Holborn, Louise W., *Printing and the Growth of a Protestant Movement in Germany from 1517 to 1524*, 11 Church Hist. 123 (1942)

Hovenkamp, Herbert, *Harm to Competition Under the 2010 Horizontal Merger Guidelines*, 39 Rev. Indus. Org. 3 (2011), https://www.jstor.org/stable/23885233

Hovenkamp, Herbert & Carl Shapiro, *Horizontal Mergers, Market Structure, and Burdens of Proof*, 127 Yale L.J. 1742, 1996 & 2000 (2018)

Jacobides, Michael G., *Regulating Big Tech in Europe: Why, so What, and How Understanding Their Business Models and Ecosystems Can Make a Difference* 25 (2020), http://dx.doi.org/10.2139/ssrn.3765324

Jacobides, Michael G. & Ioannis Lianos, *Ecosystems and Competition Law in Theory and Practice* 5 (2021) http://dx.doi.org/10.2139/ssrn.3772366

Jacobides, Michael G. & Ioannis Lianos, *Regulating Platforms and Ecosystems: An Introduction*, 30 Ind. Corp. Change 1131 (2021), https://doi.org/10.1093/icc/dtab060

Janger, Jürgen, Torben Schubert, Petra Andries, Christian Rammer & Machteld Hoskens, *The EU 2020 Innovation Indicator: A Step Forward in Measuring Innovation Outputs and Outcomes?* (ZEW Discussion Papers, No. 16-072, 2016)

Jenny, Frederic, Ioannis Lianos, Herbert Hovenkamp, Frances E. Marshall & Sivaramjani Thambisetty Ramakrishna, Competition Law, Intellectual Property Rights and Dynamic Analysis: Towards a New Institutional "Equilibrium?" Concurrences No. 4-2013, art. No. 58808, 13,

Jeon, Doh-Shin & Jay Pil Choi, A Leverage Theory of Tying in Two-Sided Markets with Non-Negative Price Constraints, 13 Am. Econ. J. Microeconomics 283 (2021)

Jullien, Bruno & Yassine Lefouili, *Horizontal Mergers and Innovation* 8–15 (Aug. 1, 2018), https://papers.ssrn.com/sol3/papers.cfm?abstract_id=3135177

Kalkan, Ekrem, *Role of the Economics in the EU's New Vertical Merger Policy: Thoughts on the Merger Between Tomtom and Tele Atlas*, 25 Ekonomik Yaklaşim 55 (2014), https://www.ejmanager.com/mnstemps/94/94-1398808973.pdf?t=1561106271

Kaplow, Louis, *Market Definition and the Merger Guidelines*, 39 Rev. Indus. Org. 107 (2011)

Kappos, David J. & Christopher P. Davis, *Functional Claiming and the Patent Balance*, 18 Stan. Tech. L. Rev. 365 (2015)

Kathuria, Vikas, *A Conceptual Framework to Identify Dynamic Efficiency*, 11 Eur. Competition J. 319, 232 (2015)

Katz, Michael L. & Howard A. Shelanski, *Mergers and Innovation*, 74 Antitrust L. J. 1, 8 (2007)

Kern, Benjamin R., *Innovation Markets, Future Markets, or Potential Competition: How Should Competition Authorities Account for Innovation Competition in Merger Reviews?* 37 World Competition 173 (2014), https://ssrn.com/abstract=2380130

Kern, Benjamin R., Ralf Dewenter & Wolfgang Kerber, *Empirical Analysis of the Assessment of Innovation Effects in U.S. Merger Cases*, 16 J. Indus. Competition & Trade 373 (2016)

Keyte, James, *New Merger Guidelines: Are the Agencies on a Collision Course with Case Law?* 36 Antitrust Mag. 49 (2021)

Bibliography

Kim, Sukkoo, *Industrialization and Urbanization: Did the Steam Engine Contribute to the Growth of Cities in the United States?* 42 EXPL. ECON. HIS. 586 (2005)

Kokkoris, Ioannis & Tommaso Valletti, *Innovation Considerations in Horizontal Merger Control*, 16 J. COMPETITION L. & ECON. 220 (2020)

Körber, Torsten, *Common Errors Regarding Search Engine Regulation – and How to Avoid Them*, 36 EUR. COMPETITION L. REV 239 (2015)

Kovacic, William E. & Dennis E. Smallwood, *Competition Policy, Rivalries, and Defense Industry Consolidation*, 8 J. ECON. PERSP. 91 (1994)

Langenfeld, James, *The Need to Revise the U.S. Non-Horizontal Merger Guidelines*, in *What Is Trump Antitrust?* CONCURRENCES No. 4-2016, art. No. 82309,

Lanjouw, Jean O. & Mark Schankerman, *Patent Quality and Research Productivity: Measuring Innovation with Multiple Indicators*, 114 ECON. J. 441 (2004)

Laskowska, Magdalena, *A Global View of Innovation Analysis in EC Merger Control* 7 (2013), http://dx.doi.org/10.2139/ssrn.2337174

Leibstone, Marvin, *Corporate Merger-Mania: Good or Bad for US Defence*, 20 MIL. TECH. 174 (1996)

Leitner, Karl-Heinz, *Innovation Futures: New Forms of Innovation and Their Implications for Innovation Policy*, 9 INT'L J. FORESIGHT AND INNOVATION POL'Y 269 (2013)

Levina, Marina, *Disrupt or Die: Mobile Health and Disruptive Innovation as Body Politics*, 18 TELEVISION & NEW MEDIA 548 (2017)

Levy, Nicholas & Vassilena Karadakova, *The EC's Increasing Reliance on Internal Documents Under the EU Merger Regulation: Issues and Implications*, 39 EUR. COMPETITION L. REV. 12 (2018)

Leyden, Dennis Patrick & Matthias Menter, *The Legacy and Promise of Vannevar Bush: Rethinking the Model of Innovation and the Role of Public Policy*, 27 ECON. INNOV. NEW TECH. 225 (2018)

Lianos, Ioannis & Bruno Carballa-Smichowski, *A Coat of Many Colours – New Concepts and Metrics of Economic Power in Competition Law and Economics*, 18 J. COMPETITION L. & ECON. 795 (2022), https://doi.org/10.1093/joclec/nhac002

Lim, Yong, *Tech Wars: Return of the Conglomerate – Throwback or Dawn of a New Series for Competition in the Digital Era?* 10 (2017), https://papers.ssrn.com/sol3/papers.cfm?abstract_id=3051560

Loertscher, Simon & Leslie M. Marx, *Merger Review for Markets with Buyer Power*, 127 J. POL. ECON. 2967, 2970 (2019), https://people.duke.edu/~marx/bio/papers/BuyerPower.pdf

Lofaro, Andrea, Stephen Lewis & Paulo Abecasis, *An Innovation in Merger Assessment: The European Commission's Novel Theory of Harm in the Dow/DuPont Merger*, 32 ANTITRUST 100 (2017)

Long, Sarah & Gavin Robert, *Losing the 'One-Stop-Shop': The Real Cost of a Dual UK/EU Merger Process Post Brexit* (Oct. 2, 2018), https://ssrn.com/abstract=3299017

Lugard, Paul & David Cardwell, *Innovation is King. Or is it? Summary Observations on the Application of EU Antitrust and Merger Control Law to Innovation-related Transaction*, ANTITRUST CHRON. 2 (Sep. 2012

Lui, Ariel K. H., Eric W. T. Ngai & Kwan Yu Lo, *Disruptive Information Technology Innovations and the Cost of Equity Capital: The Moderating Effect of CEO Incentives and Institutional Pressures*, 53 INFO. & MGMT. 345 (2016)

Lyons, Bruce, David Reader & Andreas Stephan, *UK Competition Policy Post-Brexit: Taking Back Control While Resisting Siren Calls*, 5 J. ANTITRUST ENFORCEMENT 347 (2017)

Mallet, Joan-Antoine, *War and Peace in Plato's Political Thought*, 1 PHILOSOPHICAL J. CONFLICT & VIOLENCE 87 (2017)

Mansfield, Edwin, *Contribution of R&D to Economic Growth in the United States*, 175 SCIENCE 477 (1972)

Bibliography

Maradana, Rana P., Rudra P. Pradhan, Saurav Dash, Kunal Gaurav, Manju Jayakumar & Debaleena Chatterjee, *Does Innovation Promote Economic Growth? Evidence from European Countries*, 6 J. INNOVATION & ENTREPRENEURSHIP (2017), art. 1

Maurseth, Per Botolf, *The Effect of the Internet on Economic Growth: Counter-Evidence from Cross-Country Panel Data*, 172 ECON. LETTERS 74 (2018)

May, Christopher, *Venise: aux origines de la propriété intellectuelle*, 14 L'ÉCONOMIE POLITIQUE 6 (2002) (Fr.)

McGowan, David, *Innovation, Uncertainty, and Stability in Antitrust Law*, 16 BERKELEY TECH. L. J. 729 (2001)

McKeown, James, *The FTC v. Xerox Litigation: Implications for the United States Patent System*, 24 CATH. U. L. REV. 1 (1975)

McSweeny, Terrell & Brian O'Dea, *Data, Innovation, and Potential Competition in Digital Markets – Looking Beyond Short-Term Price Effects in Merger Analysis*, CPI ANTITRUST CHRON. 1 (2018), https://www.competitionpolicyinternational.com/data-innovation-and-potential-competition-in-digital-markets-looking-beyond-short-term-price-effects-in-merger-analysis

Merges, Robert P., *Contracting Into Liability Rules: Intellectual Property Rights and Collective Rights Organizations*, 84 CAL. L. REV. 1293 (1996)

Mirabile, Irene, Michael Karl Pieber, Lluís Saurí and Arthur Stril, *Protecting the Drugs of Tomorrow: Competition and Innovation in Healthcare*, COMPETITION MERGER BRIEF 1 (July 2015)

Mohammad Hajhashem & Amir Khorasani, *Demystifying the Dynamic of Disruptive Innovations in Markets with Complex Adoption Networks: From Encroachment to Disruption*, 12 INT'L J. INNOVATION & TECH. MGMT. (2015)

Mokyr, Joel, *The Intellectual Origins of Modern Economic Growth*, 65 J. ECON. HIST. 285 (2005)

Moser, Petra, *Patents and Innovation: Evidence from Economic History*, 27 J. ECON. PERSP. 23 (2013)

Muris, Timothy, *More Than Law Enforcement: The FTC's Many Tools – A Conversation with Tim Muris and Bob Pitofsky*, 72 ANTITRUST L.J. 773, 823–24 (2005); (Geo. Mason L. & Econ. Rsch. Paper No. 06-23)

Muthukrishna, Michael & Joseph Henrich, *Innovation in the Collective Brain*, 371 PHIL. TRANS. R. SOC. B 1 (2016) https://doi.org/10.1098/rstb.2015.0192

Nagy, Delmer, Joseph Schuessler & Alan Dubinsky, *Defining and Identifying Disruptive Innovations*, 57 INDUS. MKTG. MGMT. 119 (2016)

Newman, Matthew, *Dow-DuPont Merger Remedy Reflects EU's Growing Focus on Innovation, Mosso Says*, MLEX MKT. INSIGHT (Mar. 28, 2017)

Nickell, Stephen J., *Competition and Corporate Performance*, 104 J. POL. ECON. 724 (1996)

O'Connor, Daniel, *Understanding Online Platform Competition: Common Misunderstandings*, Internet Competition and Regulation of Online Platforms COMPETITION POLICY INT'L (May 2016), https://papers.ssrn.com/abstract=2760061

Odlyzko, Andrew, *Internet Pricing and the History of Communications*, 36 COMPUT. NETWORKS 493 (2001)

Oh, Deog-Seong, Fred Phillips, Sehee Park & Eunghyun Lee, *Innovation Ecosystems: A Critical Examination*, 54 TECHNOVATION 1 (2016)

Olatunji, M. O., *Plato on Political Stability: Some Lessons for Nigeria*, 17 SABARAGAMUWA U. J. 38 (2019)

Olsen, Greg & Daniel Schwarz, *The CMA's Revised Merger Assessment Guidelines – Interesting Times and Creative Energy*, 13 J. EUR. COMPETITION L. & PRAC. 35 (2022), https://doi.org/10.1093/jeclap/lpab074

Bibliography

Ozdemir, Dicle, *A Post-Keynesian Criticism of the Solow Growth Model*, 5 J. ECON. BUS. & MGMT. 134 (2017)

Parkison Hassid, Amanda J., *An Oracle Without Foresight - Plaintiffs' Arduous Burdens Under U.S. v. Oracle*, 58 HASTINGS L.J. 891, 904–05 (2007), https://repository.uchastings.edu/hastings_law_journal/vol58/iss4/6

Paz, Marleina, *Almost but Not Quite Perfect: The Past, Present and Potential Future of Horizontal Merger Enforcement*, 45 LOY. L.A. L. REV. 1045 (2012).

Petit, Nicolas, Innovation Competition, Unilateral Effects and Merger Control Policy, (ICLE Antitrust & Consumer Protection Research Program, White Paper 2018-03), Https://Laweconcenter.Org/Wp-Content/Uploads/2018/06/Icle-Petit-Innovation-Competition-Merger-Control-Policy-Icle-2018.Pdf

Petit, Nicolas, *Innovation Competition, Unilateral Effects, and Merger Policy*, 82 ANTITRUST L.J. 873 (2019), https://papers.ssrn.com/sol3/papers.cfm?abstract_id=3113077

Petit, Nicolas & Thibault Schrepel, *Complexity-Minded Antitrust*, 33 J. EVOLUTIONARY ECON. 541 (2023), https://ssrn.com/abstract=4050536

Petrariu, Ioan Radu, Robert Bumbac & Radu Ciobanu, *Innovation: A Path to Competitiveness and Economic Growth: The Case of CEE Countries*, XX THEORETICAL & APPLIED ECON. 15 (2013)

Pleatsikas, Christopher & David Teece, *The Analysis of Market Definition and Market Power in the Context of Rapid Innovation*, 19 INT'L J. INDUS. ORG. 665 (2001)

Power, Vincent, *The Implications of Brexit for Competition Law – An Irish Perspective*, 20 IRISH J. EUR. L. 1 (2017), https://ssrn.com/abstract=3833915

Pras, Amandine, Catherine Guastavino & Maryse Lavoie, *The Impact of Technological Advances on Recording Studio Practices*, 64 J. AM. SOC'Y INFO. SCI. & TECH. 612 (2013)

Ranchordás, Sofia, *Innovation Experimentalism in the Age of the Sharing Economy*, 19 LEWIS & CLARK L. REV. 871 (2015)

Rasmusen, Eric, *Entry for Buyout*, 36 J. IND. ECON. 281 (1988), https://www.jstor.org/stable/i336775

Régibeau, Pierre & Katharine E. Rockett, *Mergers and Innovation*, 64 ANTITRUST BULL. 31 (2019)

Reinhardt, Ronny & Sebastian Gurtner, *Differences Between Early Adopters of Disruptive and Sustaining Innovations*, 68 J. BUS. RSCH. 137 (2015)

Risch, Michael, *Patent Troll Myths*, 42 SETON HALL L. REV. 457 (2012)

Ritala, Paavo, Vassilis Agouridas, Dimitris Assimakopoulos & Otto Gies, *Value Creation and Capture Mechanisms in Innovation Ecosystems: A Comparative Case Study*, 63 INT'L J. TECH. MGMT. 244 (2013)

Röller, Lars-Hendrik & Miguel de la Mano, *The Impact of the New Substantive Test in European Merger Control*, 2 EUR. COMPETITION J. 9 (2012), https://ec.europa.eu/dgs/competition/economist/merger_control_test.pdf

Romer, Paul M., *Increasing Returns and Long-Run Growth*, 94 J. POL. ECON. 1002 (1986)

Royall, M. Sean & Adam J. Di Vincenzo, *Evaluating Mergers Between Potential Competitors Under the New Horizontal Merger Guidelines*, 25 ANTITRUST 33, 33 (2010), https://www.gibsondunn.com/wp-content/uploads/documents/publications/RoyallDiVicenzo-HorizontalMergerGuidelines.pdf

Salinger, Michael A., *The New Vertical Merger Guidelines: Muddying the Waters*, 59 REV. INDUS. ORG. 161 (2021)

Salop, Steven, *Invigorating Vertical Merger Enforcement*, 127 YALE L.J. 1962 (2018), https://www.jstor.org/stable/i40225251

Salop, Steven & Daniel Culley, *Revising the U.S. Vertical Merger Guidelines: Policy Issues and an Interim Guide for Practitioners*, 4 J. ANTITRUST ENFORCEMENT 1 (2015)

Bibliography

Schildkraut, Marc G., *Oracle and the Future of Unilateral Effects*, 19 ANTITRUST 20 (2005)

Schultz, Jason & Jennifer Urban, *Protecting Open Innovation: The Defensive Patent License as a New Approach to Patent Threats, Transaction Costs, and Tactical Disarmament*, 26 HARV. J.L. & TECH. 1 (2012)

Schumpeter, Joseph A., *Business Cycles: A Theoretical, Historical, and Statistical Analysis of the Capitalist Process*, 6 CAN. J. ECON. POL. & SCI. 90 (1940)

Shapiro, Carl, *Antitrust in a Time of Populism*, 61 INT'L J. IND. ORG. 714 (2018), https://faculty. haas.berkeley.edu/shapiro/antitrustpopulism.pdf

Shapiro, Carl, *Vertical Mergers and Input Foreclosure Lessons from the AT&T/Time Warner Case*, 59 REV. INDUS. ORG. 303 (2021), https://doi.org/10.1007/s11151-021-09826-x

Shelanski, Howard, *Information, Innovation, and Competition Policy for the Internet*, 161 U. PA. L. REV. 1663 (2013), http://scholarship.law.upenn.edu/cgi/viewcontent.cgi?article=1025&context=penn_law_review

Si, Steven & Hui Chen, *A Literature Review of Disruptive Innovation: What It Is, How It Works and Where It Goes*, 56 J. ENG'G & TECH. MGMT. (2020)

Sidak, Gregory J. & David J. Teece, *Dynamic Competition in Antitrust Law*, 5 J. COMPETITION L. & ECON. 581 (2009)

Sokol, D. Daniel & Ma Jingyuan, *Understanding Online Markets and Antitrust Analysis*, 15 NW. J. TECH. & INTELL. PROP. 43, 46 (2017), http://scholarlycommons.law.northwestern.edu/njtip/vol15/iss1/2

Solow, Robert M., *A Contribution to the Theory of Economic Growth*, 70 Q. J. ECON. 70 65 (1956)

Solow, Robert M., *Technical Change and the Aggregate Production Function*, 39 REV. ECON. & STAT. 312 (1957)

Stiglitz, Joseph, *Economic Foundations of Intellectual Property Rights*, 57 DUKE L.J. 1693 (2008)

Suseno, Yuliani, *Disruptive Innovation and the Creation of Social Capital in Indonesia's Urban Communities*, 24 ASIA PACIFIC BUS. REV. 174 (2018)

Suseno, Yuliani, Christofer Laurell & Nathalie Sick, *Assessing Value Creation in Digital Innovation Ecosystems: A Social Media Analytics Approach*, 27 J. STRATEGIC INFO. SYS. 335 (2018)

Taques, Fernando Henrique, Manuel G. López, Leonardo Fernando Cruz Basso, Nelson Areal, *Indicators Used to Measure Service Innovation and Manufacturing Innovation*, 6 J. INNOVATION & KNOWLEDGE 11 (2021)

Teece, David J., *Profiting from Technological Innovation: Implications for Integration, Collaboration, Licensing and Public Policy*, 15 RSCH. POL'Y 285 (1986)

Teece, David J., *Next Generation Competition: New Concepts for Understanding How Innovation Shapes Competition and Policy in the Digital Economy*, 9 J.L. ECON. & POL'Y 97, 100 (2012)

Thatchenkery, Sruthi & Riitta Katila, *Innovation and Profitability Following Antitrust Intervention Against a Dominant Platform: The Wild, Wild West?* 44 STRATEGIC MGMT. J. 943 (2023)

Todino, Mario, Geoffroy van de Walle & Lucia Stoican, *EU Merger Control and Harm to Innovation – A Long Walk to Freedom (from the Chains of Causation)*, 64 ANTITRUST BULL. 11 (2019)

Tom, Willard K. & Joshua A. Newberg, *Antitrust and Intellectual Property: From Separate Spheres to Unified Field*, 66 ANTITRUST L.J. 167, 182 (1997)

Valletti, Tommaso M. & Hans Zenger, *Should Profit Margins Play a More Decisive Role in Merger Control?* 9 J. EUR. COMPETITION L. 336 (2018)

Vande Walle, Simon, *The European Commission's Approval of Google / Fitbit – A Case Note and Comment* (2021), https://papers.ssrn.com/sol3/papers.cfm?abstract_id=3893079

Vandenborre, Ingrid, *The Importance of the New: Competition Innovation in Life Sciences*, 16 COMPETITION L. INSIGHT (2017)

Vertinsky, Liza A., *Responding to the Challenges of "Against Intellectual Monopoly*, 5 REV. L. & ECON. 1115 (2009)

Vives, Xavier, *Innovation and Competitive Pressure*, 56 J. INDUS. ECON. 419 (2008)

Werden, Gregory, *Why (Ever) Define Markets? An Answer to Professor Kaplow*, 18 ANTITRUST L.J. 729 (2013)

Werden, Gregory J. & Luke M. Froeb, *Antitrust and Tech: Europe and the United States Differ, and It Matters*, ANTITRUST CHRON. (2019)

Williamson, Oliver E., *The Economics of Antitrust: Transaction Cost Considerations*, 122 U. PA. L. REV. 1492 (1974), https://scholarship.law.upenn.edu/penn_law_review/vol122/iss6/2/

Witt, Ulrich, *How Evolutionary Is Schumpeter's Theory of Economic Development?* 9 INDUS. & INNOVATION 7 (2002)

Wu, Qiang & Qile He, *DIY Laboratories and Business Innovation Ecosystems: The Case of Pharmaceutical Industry*, 161 TECH. FORECASTING & SOC. CHANGE 1 (2020)

Wu, Tim, *Taking Innovation Seriously: Antitrust Enforcement If Innovation Mattered Most*, 78 ANTITRUST L.J. 313 (2012)

Wu, Tim, *Blind Spot: The Attention Economy and the Law*, 82 ANTITRUST L. J. 771 (2019), https://scholarship.law.columbia.edu/cgi/viewcontent.cgi?article=3030&context=faculty_scholarship

Xu, Min, Jeanne M. David & Suk Hi Kim, *The Fourth Industrial Revolution: Opportunities and Challenges*, 9 INT'L J. FIN. RSCH. 90 (2018)

Zhang, Yufei, G. Tomas M. Hult, David J. Ketchen Jr. & Roger J. Calantone, *Effects of Firm-, Industry-, and Country-Level Innovation on Firm Performance*, 31 MKTG. LETTERS 231 (2020), https://doi.org/10.1007/s11002-020-09530-y

Zhao, Rui, *Technology and Economic Growth: From Robert Solow to Paul Romer*, 1 HUM. BEHAV. & EMERGING TECH. 62 (2019)

Online Resources

Book of Common Prayer, ENCYCLOPAEDIA BRITANNICA, https://www.britannica.com/topic/Book-of-Common-Prayer

Brexit: UK Competition Law in a Deal or No Deal Scenario, LINKLATERS INSIGHTS (2018),

British Aerospace and GEC–Marconi, 5 STRATEGIC COMMENTS 1 (1999), https://doi.org/10.1080/1356788990514

The Commission Unconditionally Approves BM's Acquisition of Celgene, CLEARY GOTTLIEB (Oct. 10, 2019), https://www.clearyantitrustwatch.com/2019/10/the-commission-unconditionally-approves-bms-acquisition-of-celgene

Ex Post v. Ex Ante Regulatory Remedies Must Consider Consumer Benefits and Costs, ACI (May 14, 2008), https://www.theamericanconsumer.org/2008/05/ex-post-v-ex-Ante-regulatory-remedies-must-consider-consumer-benefits-and-costs/ (last visited May 10, 2021)

FTC Appeals Judge's Decision on Illumina-Grail Deal, CPI (Sept. 4, 2022), https://www.competitionpolicyinternational.com/ftc-appeals-judges-decision-on-illumina-grail-deal/

How Does Innovation Lead to Growth? EUROPEAN CENTRAL BANK (June 27, 2017), https://www.ecb.europa.eu/explainers/tell-me-more/html/growth.en.html

Bibliography

Interactive Source of Publicly-Known Tech Acquisitions Completed Since 1991, IG.COM (2019), https://www.ig.com/uk/cfd-trading/research/acquisitive-tech#/acquisitions

ONLINE ETYMOLOGY DICTIONARY, https://www.etymonline.com

Open Internet Policy, EUROPEAN COMMISSION (2021), https://ec.europa.eu/digital-single-market/en/open-internet

Top 10 Healthcare Data Analytics Companies in 2018, TECHNAVIO BLOG (Feb. 9, 2018), https://blog.technavio.org/blog/top-10-healthcare-data-analytics-companies

Ali, Agha, *How Many Websites Are There?* DIGITAL INFORMATION WORLD (2019), https://www.digitalinformationworld.com/2019/09/how-many-websites-exist-today-on-the-internet.html

Atluri, Venkat, Miklós Dietz & Nicolaus Henke, *Competing in a World of Sectors Without Borders*, MCKINSEY QUARTERLY (July 12, 2017), https://www.mckinsey.com/business-functions/mckinsey-analytics/our-insights/competing-in-a-world-of-sectors-without-borders

Bailly, Marion, *The EU Commission Clears the Acquisition of a Pharmaceutical Company by a Global Conglomerate Subject to a Commitment That Clinical Development of Innovative Insomnia Drugs Will Not Be Adversely Affected by the Merger (Johnson & Johnson / Actelion)*, E-COMPETITIONS JUNE 2017, art. No. 86509,

Bartz, Diane & Mrinmay Dey, *Illumina Appeals FTC Order to Divest Cancer Test Maker Grail*, REUTERS (June 6, 2013), https://www.reuters.com/legal/illumina-asks-appeals-court-undo-ftc-ruling-that-it-must-sell-subsidiary-2023-06-06

Bell, Robert. & William Haig, *How Will a No-Deal Brexit Effect Merger Control* (2019), http://eu-competitionlaw.com/how-will-a-no-deal-brexit-effect-merger-control/

Bon, Julie, San Sau Fung, Alan Reilly, Terry Ridout, Robert Ryan & Mike Walker, *Recent Developments at the CMA: 2020–2021*, 59 REV. INDUS. ORG. 665 (2021), doi: 10.1007/s11151-021-09848-5

Bourreau, Marc & Alexandre de Streel, *Big Tech Acquisitions: Competition and Innovation Effects and EU Merger Control* (CERRE Issue Paper, Feb. 2020), https://cerre.eu/publications/big-tech-acquisitions-competition-and-innovation-effects-eu-merger-control

Bourreau, Marc, Cristina Caffarra, Zhijun Chen Chongwoo Choe, Gregory S. Crawford, Tomaso Duso, Christos Genakos, Paul Heidhues, Martin Peitz, Thomas Rønde, Monika Schnitzer, Nicolas Schutz, Michelle Sovinsky, Giancarlo Spagnolo, Otto Toivanen, Tommaso Valletti & Thibaud Vergé, *Google/Fitbit Will Monetise Health Data and Harm Consumers*, CEPR POL'Y INSIGHT (Sept. 2020), https://cepr.org/system/files/publication-files/103123-policy_insight_107_google_fitbit_will_monetise_health_data_and_harm_consumers.pdf

Brankin, Sean-Paul, *They Are Out to Get You. The EU and UK Extend the Scope of Merger Control to Catch More Pharma and Biotech Mergers*, BRISTOWS (Mar. 8, 2022), https://www.bristows.com/news/they-are-out-to-get-you/

Bruland, Kristine & David Mowery, *Innovation Through Time* (Feb. 22, 2004), http://hdl.handle.net/1853/43162

Bundeskartellamt, *Innovations – Challenges for Competition Law Practice, Series of Papers on Competition and Consumer Protection in the Digital Economy* 8–29 (2017), https://www.bundeskartellamt.de/SharedDocs/Publikation/EN/Schriftenreihe_Digitales_II.pdf?__blob=publicationFile&v=3

Byung-Yeul, Baek, *Tesla, Amazon Oppose Nvidia's Acquisition of Arm*, THE KOREA TIMES (Sept. 3, 2021), https://www.koreatimes.co.kr/www/tech/2021/08/133_314738.html

Connor, Charley, *Vestager: EU Is Considering Value-Based Thresholds*, GCR (June 19, 2019), https://globalcompetitionreview.com/article/1194225/vestager-eu-is-considering-value-based-thresholds

Connor, Charley, *Lawyers Warn Against Value-Based Merger Thresholds*, GCR (June 20, 2019), https://globalcompetitionreview.com/article/1194270/eu-lawyers-warn-against-value-based-merger-thresholds.

Bibliography

Consumer Federation of America, *Microsoft Monopoly Caused Consumer Harm*, https://consumerfed.org/pdfs/antitrustpr.pdf

Cook, Nigel B., *Review of H.G. Barnett's Book, Innovation: The Basis of Cultural Change* (2014), http://rxiv.org/pdf/1405.0301v1.pdf

Coyle, Diane, *Rethinking GDP*, 54 Fin. & Dev. 16 (2017), https://www.imf.org/external/pubs/ft/fandd/2017/03/coyle.htm

Crawford, Gregory, Tommaso Valletti & Cristina Caffarra, *"How Tech Rolls": Potential Competition and "Reverse" Killer Acquisitions*, VoxEU (May 11, 2020), https://cepr.org/voxeu/blogs-and-reviews/how-tech-rolls-potential-competition-and-reverse-killer-acquisitions

Dabbah, Maher M., *Brexit and Competition Law: Future Directions of Domestic Enforcement* (2020), 43, World Competition 107 (2020), https://kluwerlawonline.com/journalarticle/World+Competition/43.1/WOCO2020006

Deazley, Ronana, *Commentary on the Statute of Monopolies 1624*, in Primary Sources on Copyright (1450–1900) (L. Bently & M. Kretschmer eds., 2008), www.copyrighthistory.org

Delivery Hero SE (2019) Annual Report (2018), https://ir.deliveryhero.com/download/companies/delivery/Annual%20Reports/Final_secured_en.pdf.

Devin Reilly, Daniel D. Sokol & David Toniatti, *The Importance of Exit via Acquisition to Venture Capital, Entrepreneurship, and Innovation* (Feb. 8, 2022), https://ssrn.com/abstract=3981970

Donovan, Paul, *Why Do Some Economies Grow Faster Than Others?* UBS Nobel Perspectives (2020), https://www.ubs.com/microsites/nobel-perspectives/en/laureates/robert-solow.html

Doucette, Marc, *Interactive: Visualizing Major Tech Acquisitions (1991–2018)*, Visual Capitalist (July 24, 2018), https://www.visualcapitalist.com/interactive-major-tech-acquisitions/

Etzkowitz, Henry & Loet Leydesdorff, *Universities and the Global Knowledge Economy: A Triple Helix of University-Industry-Government Relations* (Jan. 2002), https://www.researchgate.net/publication/239066835_Universities_and_the_global_knowledge_economy_A_triple_helix_of_university-industry-government_relations

European Commission, Commission Staff Working Document, SEC(2007) 1472 (Nov. 12, 2007), https://ec.europa.eu/transparency/documents-register/detail?ref=SEC(2007)1472&lang=en

Forbes, Ben, Rameet Sangha & Mat Hughes, *Understanding the New Frontier for Merger Control and Innovation – The European Commission's Decision in Dow/DuPont*, in The International Comparative Legal Guide to: Merger Control 2018 (Global Legal Group Ltd 14th ed. 2018), https://www.alixpartners.com/insights-impact/insights/understanding-the-new-frontier-for-merger-control

Ford, Jonathan & Nayantara Ravichandran, *When Is a Jurisdictional GOAT Not Good Enough? UK Deal Nexus and the CMA's Expanded Hunt for 'Killer Acquisitions' and Harmful Vertical Mergers*, Linklaters Insights (June 1, 2022), https://www.linklaters.com/en/insights/publications/platypus/platypus-uk-merger-control-analysis/fourteenth-platypus-post---when-is-a-jurisdictional-goat-not-good-enough

Gilbert, Richard, Christian Riis & Erlend S. Riis, *Stepwise Innovation by an Oligopoly*, 61 Int'l J. Indus. Org. 413 (2018), https://eml.berkeley.edu/~gilbert/Selected%20Papers/Stepwise%20innovation%20by%20oligopoly_IJIO.pdf

GSMA, *Resetting Competition Policy Frameworks for the Digital Ecosystem* (2016), https://www.gsma.com/publicpolicy/wp-content/uploads/2016/10/GSMA_Resetting-Competition_Report_Oct-2016_60pp_WEBv2.pdf

Harper, Peter, Kate Newman, Nicola Holmes, Annabel Borg, Claire Morgan & Laura Wright, *UK: Merger Control in the Post-Brexit Landscape* GCR (July 14, 2021), https://globalcompetitionreview.com/review/the-european-middle-east-and-african-antitrust-review/2022/article/uk-merger-control-in-the-post-brexit-landscape

Bibliography

Hazell, Alex & Rebecca Saunders, *Bringing the CMA's Merger Assessment Guidelines Up to Date*, CMA BLOG (Apr. 8, 2021), https://competitionandmarkets.blog.gov.uk/2021/04/08/bringing-the-cmas-merger-assessment-guidelines-up-to-date/

Hoffmann, Linus J., Anouk van der Veer, Friso Bostoen, Bowman Heiden & Nicolas Petit, *Dell – A Case Study of Dynamic Competition* 6 (DCI Case Study, Oct. 27, 2022), https://www.dynamiccompetition.com/wp-content/uploads/2022/10/DCI-CS2-Hoffmann-et-al-compressed.pdf

Hovenkamp, Herbert J., *Competitive Harm from Vertical Mergers* (Faculty Scholarship at Penn Law. 2218, 2020), https://scholarship.law.upenn.edu/faculty_scholarship/2218

Illumina Inc. Press Release, Illumina to Acquire GRAIL to Launch New Era of Cancer Detection (Sept. 21, 2020), https://investor.illumina.com/news/press-release-details/2020/Illumina-to-Acquire-GRAIL-to-Launch-New-Era-of-Cancer-Detection/default.aspx

Illumina Inc. Press Release, Illumina Committed to Pursuing GRAIL Acquisition to Accelerate Access to Breakthrough Multi-Cancer Early Detection Blood Test (Mar. 30, 2021), https://www.illumina.com/company/news-center/press-releases/press-release-details.html?newsid=32156cec-c392-4d23-be23-66d7729892db

Illumina Inc. Press Release, Illumina Acquires GRAIL to Accelerate Patient Access to Life-Saving Multi-Cancer Early-Detection Test (Aug. 18, 2021), https://investor.illumina.com/news/press-release-details/2021/Illumina-Acquires-GRAIL-to-Accelerate-Patient-Access-to-Life-Saving-Multi-Cancer-Early-Detection-Test/default.aspx

Illumina Inc. Press Release, Administrative Law Judge Rules in Favor of Illumina in FTC Challenge of GRAIL Deal (Sept. 1, 2022), https://www.illumina.com/company/news-center/press-releases/press-release-details.html?newsid=695f87e8-5d42-4caa-9c9c-4539a2630068

Illumina Inc. Press Release, Illumina Intends to Appeal European Commission's Decision in GRAIL Deal (Sept. 6, 2022), https://investor.illumina.com/news/press-release-details/2022/Illumina-Intends-to-Appeal-European-Commissions-Decision-in-GRAIL-Deal/default.aspx

Illumina Inc. Press Release, Illumina Will Appeal FTC Decision in Federal Court, Will Seek US Resolution by Late 2023 or Early 2024 (Apr. 3, 2023), https://investor.illumina.com/news/press-release-details/2023/Illumina-Will-Appeal-FTC-Decision-in-Federal-Court-Will-Seek-US-Resolution-by-Late-2023-or-Early-2024/default.aspx

Illumina Inc., Test Terms for US oncology Customers, https://www.illumina.com/areas-of-interest/cancer/test-terms.html

J&J Media Center, Johnson & Johnson to Acquire Actelion for $30 Billion with Spin-Out of New R&D Company, https://www.jnj.com/media-center/press-releases/johnson-johnson-to-acquire-actelion

Johnson, Matthew, *Mergers and Innovation: Fewer Players, More Ideas?* OXERA (Feb. 27, 2017), https://www.oxera.com/agenda/mergers-and-innovation-fewer-players-more-ideas

Kar, Nicole, Jonathan Ford, Lauren O'Brien & Aoife Monaghan, *Divergence Ratios After Brexit. Parallel EU/UK Merger Reviews One Year on*, LINKLATERS INSIGHTS (Feb. 10, 2022), https://www.linklaters.com/de-de/insights/publications/platypus/platypus-uk-merger-control-analysis/twelfth-platypus-post---divergence-ratios-after-brexit-parallel-eu-uk-merger-reviews-one-year-on

Kuhn, Tilman, *EC Focus on Internal Documents: Time to Rethink the Architecture of the EU Merger Control Process?* WHITE & CASE, Mar. 8, 2019, https://www.whitecase.com/insight-our-thinking/ec-focus-internal-documents-time-rethink-architecture-eu-merger-control

Langlois, Anna, *Microsoft/Activision Avoids US Injunction, as UK Litigation Paused*, GCR (July 11, 2023), https://globalcompetitionreview.com/article/microsoftactivision-avoids-us-injunction-uk-litigation-paused

Bibliography

Latham, Oliver, Simon Chisholm & Sam Lynch, *Acquisitions of Potential Rivals in Digital/Tech: Valuation Analysis as Key Economic Tool – PayPal/iZettle*, CRA COMPETITION MEMO (2019), https://ecp.crai.com/wp-content/uploads/2019/06/Use-of-valuation-analysis-in-merger-assessment.pdf

Lawrance, Sophie & Sean-Paul Brankin, *Illumina/Grail: Bio-Tech Companies in the Firing Line as the European Commission Expands the Limits of European Merger Control*, BRISTOWS (Oct. 13, 2021), https://www.bristows.com/news/illumina-grail-bio-tech-companies-in-the-firing-line-as-the-european-commission-expands-the-limits-of-european-merger-control

Lerner, Andres V., *The Role of "Big Data" in Online Platform Competition* (2014), https://ssrn.com/abstract=2482780

Manne, Geoffrey A., Invited Statement to the U.S. House of Representatives Committee on the Judiciary, Subcommittee on Antitrust, Commercial, and Administrative Law, *Correcting Common Misperceptions About the State of Antitrust Law and Enforcement* (Apr. 17, 2020), https://laweconcenter.org/wp-content/uploads/2020/04/Manne_statement_house_antitrust_20200417_FINAL3-POST.pdf

Marchant, Jo, *Decoding the Antikythera Mechanism, the First Computer*, SMITHSONIAN MAG. (Feb. 2015), https://www.smithsonianmag.com/history/decoding-antikythera-mechanism-first-computer-180953979.

McConnell, Charles, *Innovation Analysis Lacks Reliable Presumptions, Says US DOJ Deputy*, GCR (June 7, 2018), https://globalcompetitionreview.com/article/1170347/innovation-analysis-lacks-reliable-presumptions-says-us-doj-deputy

McConnell, Charles, *Cracking Down on Big Tech Acquisitions Won't Stifle Innovation, ACCC Official Says* GCR (Nov. 23, 2021), https://globalcompetitionreview.com/digital-markets/cracking-down-big-tech-acquisitions-wont-stifle-innovation-accc-official-says

McLaughlin, David, Ian King & Dina Bass, *Google, Microsoft, Qualcomm Protest Nvidia's Acquisition of Arm Ltd.*, BLOOMBERG (Feb. 12, 2021), https://www.bloomberg.com/news/articles/2021-02-12/google-microsoft-qualcomm-protest-nvidia-s-arm-acquisition

McNelis, Natalie, *Illumina's Remedy Offer Was Sufficient to Clear FTC's Foreclosure Doubts, Judge Says*, MLEX MKT. INSIGHT (Sep. 2, 2022), https://content.mlex.com/#/content/1406092

Mee, Simon, *Joseph Schumpeter and the Business Cycle: An Historical Synthesis* 87 (2015), https://www.tcd.ie/Economics/assets/pdf/SER/2009/simon_mee.pdf

Microsoft Public announcement, OFFICIAL MICROSOFT BLOG (May 14, 2020), https://blogs.microsoft.com/blog/2020/05/14/microsoft-announces-definitive-agreement-to-acquire-metaswitch-networks-expanding-approach-to-empower-operators-and-partner-with-network-equipment-providers-to-deliver-on-promise-of-5g/#:~:text=Update%20July%2015%2C%202020%3A%20Microsoft,and%20communications%20solutions%20for%20operators

Microsoft Press release, Microsoft Accelerates Industry Cloud Strategy for Healthcare with the Acquisition of Nuance (Apr. 12, 2021), https://news.microsoft.com/2021/04/12/microsoft-accelerates-industry-cloud-strategy-for-healthcare-with-the-acquisition-of-nuance/

Microsoft News Center, Microsoft to Acquire Activision Blizzard to Bring the Joy and Community of Gaming to Everyone, Across Every Device (Jan. 18, 2022), https://news.microsoft.com/2022/01/18/microsoft-to-acquire-activision-blizzard-to-bring-the-joy-and-community-of-gaming-to-everyone-across-every-device/

Moresi, Serge & Steve C. Salop, *Quantifying the Increase in "Effective Concentration" from Vertical Mergers That Raise Input Foreclosure Concerns: Comment on the Draft Vertical Merger Guidelines* 3–5 (Georgetown University Law Center, 2020), https://scholarship.law.georgetown.edu/facpub/2240

Mowery, David, *Technological Change and the Evolution of the U.S. National Innovation System 1880–1990, in* INNOVATION: PERSPECTIVES FOR THE 21ST CENTURY (BBVA 2011), https://www.

Bibliography

bbvaopenmind.com/en/articles/technological-change-and-the-evolution-of-the-u-s-national-innovation-system-1880-1990

Nellis, Stephen, Josh Horwitz & Hyunjoo Jin, *Nvidia's Arm Deal Sparks Quick Backlash in Chip Industry*, REUTERS (Sept. 14, 2020), https://www.reuters.com/article/us-arm-holdings-m-a-nvidia-industry-anal/nvidias-arm-deal-sparks-quick-backlash-in-chip-industry-idUKKBN2650GT?edition-redirect=uk

Newman, John M., *Regulating Attention Markets* (University of Miami Legal Studies Research Paper, 2020), https://papers.ssrn.com/sol3/papers.cfm?abstract_id=3423487

Nielson, Nathalie, *An Introspection on the FTC's Withdrawal of 2020 Vertical Merger Guidelines*, COMPETITION F. (2021), art. No. 0028, https://competition-forum.com/an-introspection-on-the-ftcs-withdrawal-of-2020-vertical-merger-guidelines/

Nvidia Newsroom Press Release, NVIDIA and SoftBank Group Announce Termination of NVIDIA's Acquisition of Arm Limited (Feb. 7, 2022), https://nvidianews.nvidia.com/news/nvidia-and-softbank-group-announce-termination-of-nvidias-acquisition-of-arm-limited

OECD, *Considering Non-Price Effects in Merger Control – Background Note by the Secretariat* (DAF/COMP(2018)2, May 4, 2018), https://one.oecd.org/document/DAF/COMP(2018)2/en/pdf

OECD, *Digital Competition Policy: Are Ecosystems Different? – Note by Amelia Fletcher* (DAF/COMP/WD(2020)96, Nov. 9, 2020), https://one.oecd.org/document/DAF/COMP/WD(2020)96/En/pdf

Pencheva, Rositsa, Noa Laguna-Goya & Marion Bailly, *Johnson&Johnson/Actelion – Falling Asleep Fast and Deeply While Staying Fully Awake on Innovation*, COMPETITION MERGER BRIEF (2017), https://www.researchgate.net/publication/323757930_Competition_merger_brief_JJActelion-falling_asleep_fast_and_deeply_while_staying_fully_awake_on_innovation

Petit, Nicolas, *Significant Impediment to Industry Innovation: A Novel Theory of Harm in EU Merger Control?* (ICLE Antitrust & Consumer Protection Research Program, White Paper 2017-1, 2017), https://orbi.uliege.be/bitstream/2268/207345/1/SSRN-id2911597.pdf

Petit, Nicolas, *A Framework for Antitrust Retrospectives: Illustrated by the 1993 Antitrust Case Against General Motors' Sale of Allison Transmission Roundtable Takeaways* (DCI Roundtable Takeaways, 2022), https://www.dynamiccompetition.com/wp-content/uploads/2022/11/DCI-RT2-GM-ZF-Complaint-FINAL-1.pdf

Phillips, Gordon & Alexei Zhdanov, *Venture Capital Investments, Merger Activity, and Competition Laws Around the World* (Aug. 29, 2021), https://faculty.tuck.dartmouth.edu/images/uploads/faculty/gordon-phillips/VC_Investments_and_Merger_Competition_Laws.pdf

Provost, Marion & Mélanie Thill-Tayara, *At a Glance: Pharmaceutical Merger Review in European Union*, LEXOLOGY (2021), https://www.lexology.com/library/detail.aspx?g=5adfdcdc-63d3-4ce2-9a64-1207fd774ab8

Rai, Arti, Stuart Graham & Mark Doms, *Patent Reform: Unleashing Innovation, Promoting Economic Growth & Producing High-Paying Jobs* (A White Paper from the US Department of Commerce, Apr. 13, 2010), https://www.commerce.gov/sites/default/files/migrated/reports/patentreform_0.pdf

RBB Economics, *An Innovative Leap Into the Theoretical Abyss: Dow/Dupont and the Commission's Novel Theory of Harm* (2017), https://www.datocms-assets.com/79198/1667304872-rbb-brief-54.pdf

Refinitiv, *Global Mergers & Acquisitions Review: Full Year 2021 | Financial Advisors* (industry report) (2021), https://thesource.refinitiv.com/TheSource/getfile/download/eacef8be-ef5d-4335-b807-5db0db1cf6bc

Régibeau, Pierre & Ioannis Lianos, *Digital Mergers: A Primer* (2020), https://papers.ssrn.com/sol3/papers.cfm?abstract_id=3837281

Reuters, *US Drops Appeal of UnitedHealth Acquisition of Change Healthcare* (Mar. 21, 2023), https://www.reuters.com/legal/us-drops-appeal-unitedhealth-acquisition-change-healthcare-2023-03-21

ROGERS, EVERETT M., DIFFUSION OF INNOVATIONS (Free Press 3d ed. 1983), https://teddykw2.files.wordpress.com/2012/07/everett-m-rogers-diffusion-of-innovations.pdf

Rosenberg, Nathan, *Innovation and Economic Growth* (OECD, 2004), https://www.oecd.org/cfe/tourism/34267902.pdf

Salop, Steven C., *A Suggested Revision of the 2020 Vertical Merger Guidelines*, ANTITRUST BULL. 1 (July 2021), https://ssrn.com/abstract=3839768

Salop, Steven, *The FTC Was Correct to Withdraw the Vertical Merger Guidelines*, PROMARKET (Nov. 22, 2021), https://www.promarket.org/2021/11/22/ftc-vertical-merger-guidelines-economics-withdrawn-lina-khan-salop/#:~:text=The%202020%20Vertical%20Merger%20Guidelines,empirical%20studies%20or%20economic%20theory

Schechter, Asher, *Google and Facebook's "Kill Zone": "We've Taken the Focus Off of Rewarding Genius and Innovation to Rewarding Capital and Scale"*, PROMARKET (May 25, 2018), https://promarket.org/google-facebooks-kill-zone-weve-taken-focus-off-rewarding-genius-innovation-rewarding-capital-scale/

Schilirò, Daniele, *A Glance at Solow's Growth Theory* (MPRA Paper No. 84531, Feb. 13, 2018), https://mpra.ub.uni-muenchen.de/84531/1/MPRA_paper_84531.pdf

Schmidt, John, *Hard or Soft Brexit: What Happens to Merger Reviews?* ARNOLD & PORTER (Oct. 2, 2018), https://www.arnoldporter.com/en/perspectives/publications/2018/10/hard-or-soft-brexit-what-happens-to-merger-reviews

Schrage, Michael & Marshall Van Alstyne, *Life of IP*, 58 COMMC'N ACM 20 (2015), https://cacm.acm.org/magazines/2015/5/186009-life-of-ip/fulltext

Schwab, Klaus, *The Fourth Industrial Revolution: What It Means, How to Respond*, WORLD ECONOMIC FORUM (Jan. 14, 2016), https://www.weforum.org/agenda/2016/01/the-fourth-industrial-revolution-what-it-means-and-how-to-respond

Shapiro, Carl & Herbert Hovenkamp, *How Will the FTC Evaluate Vertical Mergers?* PROMARKET (Sept. 23, 2021), https://www.promarket.org/2021/09/23/ftc-vertical-mergers-antitrust-shapiro-hovenkamp/

Smith, Gary N. & Jeffrey Funk, *Why We Need to Stop Relying on Patents to Measure Innovation*, PROMARKET (Mar. 19, 2021), https://www.promarket.org/2021/03/19/patents-bad-measure-innovation-new-metric

Smith, Tom, *CMA Blocks the Facebook/GIPHY Merger: You Can't Say They Didn't Warn Us*, THE PLATFORM LAW BLOG (Dec. 7, 2021), https://theplatformlaw.blog/2021/12/07/cma-blocks-the-facebook-giphy-merger-you-cant-say-they-didnt-warn-us

Solidoro, Silvia, *Assessing Innovation Theories of Harm in EU Merger Control* (Policy Briefs, 2019/18, Florence Competition Programme, 2019), https://cadmus.eui.eu/bitstream/handle/1814/64768/PB_2019_18.pdf?sequence=1&isAllowed=y

Solomon, Brian, *Yahoo Sells to Verizon in Saddest $5 Billion Deal in Tech History*, FORBES (July 25, 2016), https://www.forbes.com/sites/briansolomon/2016/07/25/yahoo-sells-to-verizon-for-5-billion-marissa-mayer/#46fc9051450f

Sullivan, Mark, *Facebook Should Never Have Been Allowed to Buy Instagram, Silicon Valley Rep Says*, FASTCOMPANY (Jan. 25, 2019), https://www.fastcompany.com/90297261/facebook-should-never-have-been-allowed-to-buy-instagram-silicon-valley-rep-says

Tennant, Fraser, *Crackdown: FTC and DOJ Aim to Rewrite Merger Guidelines*, FINANCIER WORLDWIDE MAG. (Apr. 2022), https://www.financierworldwide.com/crackdown-ftc-and-doj-aim-to-rewrite-merger-guidelines#.Y2-OLnbP02w

The Associated Press, *Digene Drops Plans for Merger with Cytyc*, N.Y. TIMES (July 2, 2002), https://www.nytimes.com/2002/07/02/business/company-news-digene-drops-plans-for-merger-with-cytyc.html

The Legal 500, *The Legal 500 Webinars: A Contemporary Analysis of the Prime Objective(s) of Competition Law*, YOUTUBE (Sept. 29, 2022), https://www.youtube.com/watch?v=S3RuEJFOUkk (last visited Feb. 26, 2023)

The Legal 500, *Innovation and Competition Law* (webinar moderated by Jorge Padilla, Rachel Brandenburger and Gönenç Gürkaynak (June 15, 2023)), YOUTUBE, https://www.youtube.com/watch?v=Dw23C-7UYoM (last visited Aug. 19, 2023)

Thomas, Ryan C., Aimee DeFilippo & Lauren Miller Forbes, *What a Difference a Year Makes: FTC Withdraws Vertical Merger Guidelines*, MONDAQ (Dec. 4, 2021), https://www.mondaq.com/unitedstates/antitrust-eu-competition-/1138042/what-a-difference-a-year-makes-ftc-withdraws-vertical-merger-guidelines#:~:text=In%20September%202021%2C%20the%20five,commentary%20on%20vertical%20merger%20enforcement

Towne, R., *Data Quality in an Abundance of Electronic Health Information for Electronic Clinical Quality Measures (eCQMs)*, NINJA INSIGHTS (Oct. 2020), https://blog.kpininja.com/data-quality-in-an-abundance-of-electronic-health-information-for-electronic-clinical-quality-measures-ecqms/

Van Bael & Bellis, *Commission Issues Statement of Objections in Illumina/Grail Gun-Jumping Investigation as Parties Argue Jurisdictional Overreach*, 2021 VBB ON COMPETITION L. 3 (Sept. 2021), https://www.vbb.com/media/Insights_Newsletters/VBB_on_Competition_Law_Volume_2021_No_8-9.pdf

Vickers, Brian, *The Idea of the Renaissance* 74–90 (2019), https://www.researchgate.net/publication/268396324_THE_IDEA_OF_THE_RENAISSANCE_REVISITED

Wong-Ervin, Koren & John David Harkrider, *Assessment of the Vertical Merger Guidelines and Recommendations for the VMGs Commentary* (2020), https://ssrn.com/abstract=3644431

Wright, Lisa, Susan Zhuang & Andrew Gilbert, *Innovation Competition, Economic Dependence and Exceptional Remedies: Three Interesting Aspects of the EC's Decision in Johnson & Johnson/Actelion*, LEXOLOGY, Aug. 29, 2017, https://www.lexology.com/library/detail.aspx?g=528dbd0e-b2ca-445f-afc9-a7941fa3a670

Yun, John M., Prepared Statement for the US Senate Committee Hearing on "Competition in Digital Technology Markets: Examining Acquisitions of Nascent or Potential Competitors by Digital Platforms" (Sept. 24, 2019), https://www.judiciary.senate.gov/imo/media/doc/Yun%20Testimony.pdf

Yun, John M., *Potential Competition, Nascent Competitors, and Killer Acquisitions*, in THE GLOBAL ANTITRUST INSTITUTE REPORT ON THE DIGITAL ECONOMY 651 (Global Antitrust Institute 2020), https://gaidigitalreport.com/wp-content/uploads/2020/11/The-Global-Antitrust-Institute-Report-on-the-Digital-Economy_Final.pdf

Reports

ARGENTESI, ELENA, PAOLO BUCCIROSSI, EMILIO CALVANO, TOMASO DUSO, ALESSIA MARRAZZO & SALVATORE NAVA, EX-POST ASSESSMENT OF MERGER CONTROL DECISIONS IN DIGITAL MARKETS (Final Report prepared by Lear for the Competition Markets Authority, May 9, 2019), https://assets.publishing.service.gov.uk/government/uploads/system/uploads/attachment_data/file/803576/CMA_past_digital_mergers_GOV.UK_version.pdf

CRÉMER, JACQUES, YVES-ALEXANDRE DE MONTJOYE & HEIKE SCHWEITZER, COMPETITION POLICY FOR THE DIGITAL ERA (Report commissioned by the European Commission, Publications Office of the European Union 2019), http://ec.europa.eu/competition/publications/reports/kd0419345enn.pdf

EU Observatory on the Online Platform Economy, EUROPEAN COMMISSION, https://ec.europa.eu/digital-single-market/en/expert-group-eu-observatory-online-platform-economy

European Commission Public Consultations, Consultation on Evaluation of Procedural and Jurisdictional Aspects of EU Merger Control (2016), http://ec.europa.eu/competition/consultations/2016_merger_control/index_en.html

European Commission Shaping Europe's Digital Future (2020) Progress reports on Online Platform Economy: Work stream on Differentiated treatment; Work stream on Data; Work stream on Measurement and Economic indicators, https://ec.europa.eu/digital-single-market/en/news/commission-expert-group-publishes-progress-reports-online-platform-economy

European Commission, Commission Staff Working Document, *Evaluation of Procedural and Jurisdictional Aspects of EU Merger Control* (SWD(202) 66 final, Mar. 26, 2021), https://ec.europa.eu/competition/consultations/2021_merger_control/SWD_findings_of_evaluation.pdf

EUROPEAN COMMISSION, DIRECTORATE-GENERAL FOR COMPETITION, THE IMPACT OF VERTICAL AND CONGLOMERATE MERGERS ON COMPETITION (Publications Office of the European Union 2004).

European Commission, Study for DG Enterprise and Industry, *Impact of EU Competition Legislation on Innovation* (2000)

GEORGE J. STIGLER CENTER FOR THE STUDY OF THE ECONOMY AND THE STATE, STIGLER COMMITTEE ON DIGITAL PLATFORMS: FINAL REPORT (May 2019) ("Stigler Report"), https://www.chicagobooth.edu/-/media/research/stigler/pdfs/digital-platforms---committee-report---stigler-center.pdf

ILZKOVITZ, FABIENNE & ADRIAAN DIERX, EX-POST ECONOMIC EVALUATION OF COMPETITION POLICY ENFORCEMENT: A REVIEW OF THE LITERATURE (Publications Office of the European Union 2015), https://ec.europa.eu/competition/publications/reports/expost_evaluation_competition_policy_en.pdf

OECD Business and Industry Advisory Committee (BIAC) Summary of Discussion Points: "Creeping Acquisitions", Presented to the OECD Competition Committee Working Party No. 3 (WP3) Roundtable (Feb. 15, 2011), http://biac.org/wp-content/uploads/2014/05/BIAC_Note_on_creeping_Acquisitions.pdf

OECD, *Investigations of Consummated and Non-Notifiable Mergers – Note by the Secretariat* (Working Party No. 3 on Co-operation and Enforcement) (DAF/COMP/WP3(2014)1, Jan. 20, 2015), http://www.oecd.org/officialdocuments/publicdisplaydocumentpdf/?cote=DAF/COMP/WP3(2014)1&doclanguage=en

SCHWEITZER, HEIKE, JUSTUS HAUCAP, WOLFGANG KERBER & ROBERT WELKER, MODERNIZING THE LAW ON ABUSE OF MARKET POWER. REPORT FOR THE FEDERAL MINISTRY FOR ECONOMIC AFFAIRS AND ENERGY OF GERMANY (2018), https://www.bmwi.de/Redaktion/DE/Downloads/Studien/modernisierung-der-missbrauchsaufsicht-fuer-marktmaechtige-unternehmen-zusammenfassung-englisch.pdf?__blob=publicationFile&v=3

UK, Reforming Competition and Consumer Policy: Government Response (Apr. 2022), https://www.gov.uk/government/consultations/reforming-competition-and-consumer-policy/outcome/reforming-competition-and-consumer-policy-government-response

UK, DIGITAL COMPETITION EXPERT PANEL, UNLOCKING DIGITAL COMPETITION ("Furman Report") (Mar. 2019), https://assets.publishing.service.gov.uk/government/uploads/system/uploads/attachment_data/file/785547/unlocking_digital_competition_furman_review_web.pdf

Speeches

Coscelli, Andrea, Competition in the Digital Age: Reflecting on Digital Merger Investigations, Speech delivered at the OECD/G7 conference on competition and the digital economy (June 3, 2019), https://www.gov.uk/government/speeches/competition-in-the-digital-age-reflecting-on-digital-merger-investigations

Creighton, Susan, OECD, Summary of the Roundtable Discussion on the Non-Price Effects of Mergers (DAF/COMP/M(2018)1/ANN2/FINAL, May 14, 2019)

Currie, David, On the Role of Competition in Stimulating Innovation, Speech at the Concurrences Innovation Economics Conference (Feb. 3, 2017), https://www.gov.uk/government/speeches/david-currie-on-the-role-of-competition-in-stimulating-innovation

Furman, Jason, Trade, Innovation, and Economic Growth, Remarks at The Brookings Institution (Apr. 8, 2015), https://obamawhitehouse.archives.gov/sites/default/files/docs/20150408_trade_innovation_growth_brookings.pdf

Grenfell, Michael, A View from the CMA: Brexit and Beyond, Speech at the Advanced EU Competition Law Conference (May 16, 2018), https://www.gov.uk/government/speeches/a-view-from-the-cma-brexit-and-beyond

Kanter, Jonathan, Assistant Att'y Gen., Antitrust Div., US Dep't of Just., Remarks to the New York State Bar Association Antitrust Section (Jan. 24, 2022), https://www.justice.gov/opa/speech/assistant-attorney-general-jonathan-kanter-antitrust-division-delivers-remarks-new-york

Khan, Lina, Remarks of Chair Lina Khan at the Charles River Associates Conference, Competition & Regulation in Disrupted Times in Brussels, Belgium (Mar. 31, 2022), https://www.ftc.gov/news-events/news/speeches/remarks-chair-lina-m-khan-charles-river-associates-conference-competition-regulation-disrupted-times

Kovacic, William E., The CMA in the 2020s: A Dynamic Regulator for a Dynamic Environment, Speech delivered at Policy Exchange, London (Feb. 25, 2020), https://www.gov.uk/government/speeches/the-cma-in-the-2020s-a-dynamic-regulator-for-a-dynamic-environment

Kramer Robert, Chief, Litigation II Section, Antitrust Div., US Dep't of Jus., Antitrust Considerations in International Defense Mergers, Address before the American Institute of Aeronautics and Astronautics, Arlington, Virginia (May 4, 1999)

McSweeny, Terrell, Competition Law: Keeping Pace in a Digital Age, Keynote Remarks at the 16th Annual Loyola Antitrust Colloquium, Chicago Chronicle (Apr. 15, 2016), https://www.ftc.gov/public-statements/2016/04/competition-law-keeping-pace-digital-age

Ohlhausen, Maureen K., Antitrust Tales in the Tech Sector: Goldilocks and the Three Mergers and Into Muir Woods, Speech at the Antitrust in the Technology Sector: Policy Perspectives and Insights from the Enforcers, Palo Alto, CA (Jan. 26, 2016), https://www.ftc.gov/public-statements/2016/01/antitrust-tales-tech-sector-goldilocks-three-mergers-muir-woods

Parolini, Giuditta, 'The Commission Would Have Been Definitely Appointed If the War Had Not Supervened': The International Meteorological Organisation and Its Commission for Agricultural Meteorology after WWI, The First World War: The Aftermath, The Royal Society, London (Sept. 13, 2018)

Philp, Chris, UK Minister for Tech and the Digital Economy, Speech at Digital City Festival (Mar. 9, 2022), https://www.gov.uk/government/speeches/minister-for-tech-and-the-digital-economy-speech-at-digital-city-festival

Rubinfeld, Daniel L., Competition, Innovation, and Antitrust Enforcement in Dynamic Network Industries, Speech before the Software Publishers Association (1998 Spring Symposium), San Jose, California (Mar. 24, 1998), https://www.justice.gov/atr/speech/competition-innovation-and-antitrust-enforcement-dynamic-network-industries

Varney, Christine A., Promoting Innovation Through Patent and Antitrust Law and Policy, Remarks as Prepared for the Joint Workshop of the United States Patent and Trademark Office, the Federal Trade Commission, and the Department of Justice on the Intersection of Patent Policy and Competition Policy: Implications for Promoting Innovation, Alexandria, Virginia (May 26, 2010), https://www.justice.gov/atr/speech/promoting-innovation-through-patent-and-antitrust-law-and-policy

Varney, Christine A., Vertical Merger Enforcement Challenges at the FTC, The 36th Annual Antitrust Institute, San Francisco, California (July 17, 1995), https://www.ftc.gov/public-statements/1995/07/vertical-merger-enforcement-challenges-ftc

Vestager, Margrethe, Competition: The Mother of Invention, European Competition and Consumer Day (Apr. 18, 2016), https://ec.europa.eu/competition/publications/weekly_news_summary/2016_04_22.html

Vestager, Margrethe, "Fairness" in Competition Law and Policy: Significance and Implications, Speech at the GCLC Annual Conference (Jan. 25, 2018)

Vestager, Margrethe, Remarks by Executive Vice-President Vestager on the Commission decision to prohibit the acquisition of GRAIL by Illumina (Sept. 6, 2022), https://ec.europa.eu/commission/presscorner/detail/en/speech_22_5371

Wang, Ping, *Theorizing Digital Innovation Ecosystems: A Multilevel Ecological Framework*, *in* PROCEEDINGS OF THE 27TH EUROPEAN CONFERENCE ON INFORMATION SYSTEMS (ECIS) 6 (Stockholm & Uppsala, Sweden, June 8–14, 2019)

Statutes, Legislative and Administrative Materials

Australian Competition & Consumer Commission, DIGITAL PLATFORMS INQUIRY: FINAL REPORT (July 2019), https://www.accc.gov.au/system/files/Digital%20platforms%20inquiry%20-%20final%20report.pdf

CJEU Press Release No. 123/22, The General Court Upholds the Decisions of the Commission Accepting a Referral Request from France, as Joined by Other Member States, Asking It to Assess the Proposed Acquisition of Grail by Illumina (July 13, 2022), https://curia.europa.eu/jcms/upload/docs/application/pdf/2022-07/cp220123en.pdf

DOJ Complaint against Lockheed Martin Corp. and Northrop Grumman Corp. (Mar. 1998), in the US District Court for the District of Columbia, https://www.justice.gov/d9/atr/case-documents/attachments/1998/03/23/212680.pdf

DOJ Complaint against General Dynamics Corp. and Newport News Shipbuilding Inc. (Oct. 23, 2001), https://www.justice.gov/atr/case-document/file/497091/download

DOJ Complaint against Unitedhealth Group and Change Healthcare (Feb. 24, 2022), in the US District Court for the District of Columbia, https://www.justice.gov/media/1208936/dl?inline

DOJ Complaint against Booz Allen Hamilton Corp. (June 29, 2022), US District Court for the District of Maryland https://www.justice.gov/opa/press-release/file/1516576/download

DOJ Press Release, Justice Department Requires Divestiture of Certain Herbicides, Insecticides, and Plastics Businesses in Order to Proceed with Dow-Dupont Merger (June 15, 2017), https://www.justice.gov/opa/pr/justice-department-requires-divestiture-certain-herbicides-insecticides-and-plastics

European Commission, Commission Notice on the Definition of the Relevant Market for the Purposes of Community Competition Law, 1997 OJ (C 372) 5

European Commission, Guidelines on the Assessment of Horizontal Mergers Under the Council Regulation on the Control of Concentrations Between Undertakings, 2004 OJ (C 31) 5 ("Horizontal Merger Control Guidelines"), https://eur-lex.europa.eu/legal-content/EN/TXT/HTML/?uri=CELEX:52004XC0205(02)&from=EN

European Commission, Commission Notice on Remedies Acceptable under Council Regulation (EC) No. 139/2004 and under Commission Regulation (EC) No. 802/2004, 2008 OJ (C 267) 1

European Commission, Guidelines on the Assessment of Non-Horizontal Mergers Under the Council Regulation on the Control of Concentrations Between Undertakings, 2008 OJ (C 265) 6

Bibliography

European Commission, Consolidated Jurisdictional Notice Under Council Regulation (EC) No. 139/2004 on the Control of Concentrations Between Undertakings, 2008 OJ (C 95) 1

European Commission, Guidelines on the Applicability of Article 101 of the Treaty on the Functioning of the European Union to Horizontal Co-operation Agreements, 2011 OJ (C 11)

European Commission, Guidelines on the Application of Article 101 of the Treaty on the Functioning of the European Union to Technology Transfer Agreements, 2014 OJ (C 89) 3

European Commission, *EU Merger Control and Innovation*, COMPETITION POLICY BRIEF (Apr. 2016), http://ec.europa.eu/competition/publications/cpb/2016/2016_001_en.pdf

European Commission, COMPETITION MERGER BRIEF (May 2017), http://ec.europa.eu/competition/publications/cmb/2017/kdal17001enn.pdf

European Commission, *Industry Concentration and Competition Policy*, COMPETITION POLICY BRIEF (Nov. 2021), https://op.europa.eu/en/publication-detail/-/publication/e2e54d72-5cbf-11ec-91ac-01aa75ed71a1/language-en

European Commission, Summary of Replies to the Public Consultation on Evaluation of Procedural and Jurisdictional Aspects of EU Merger Control (July 2017), http://ec.europa.eu/competition/consultations/2016_merger_control/summary_of_replies_en.pdf

European Commission, Notice to the Stakeholders – Withdrawal of the United Kingdom and EU Rules in the Field of Competition (2019)

European Commission, Directorate-General for Competition (Dec. 2, 2020), https://ec.europa.eu/info/sites/default/files/brexit_files/info_site/eu-competition-law_en_0.pdf

European Commission, Commission Staff Working Document, *Evaluation of the Commission Notice on the Definition of Relevant Market for the Purposes of Community Competition Law of 9 December 1997* 62, SWD(2021) 199 final (July 12, 2021), https://competition-policy.ec.europa.eu/system/files/2021-07/evaluation_market-definition-notice_en.pdf

European Commission, Commission Staff Working Document, *Evaluation of Procedural and Jurisdictional Aspects of EU Merger Control*, SWD(202) 66 final (Mar. 26, 2021)

European Commission, *Commission Guidance on the Application of the Referral Mechanism Set Out in Article 22 of the Merger Regulation to Certain Categories of Cases*, C(2021) 1959 final (Mar. 26, 2021) ("Article 22 Guidance"), https://ec.europa.eu/competition/consultations/2021_merger_control/guidance_article_22_referrals.pdf

European Commission Press Release IP/01/939, The Commission prohibits GE's acquisition of Honeywell (July 3, 2001), https://ec.europa.eu/commission/presscorner/detail/en/IP_01_939

European Commission Press Release IP/05/1065, Mergers: Commission approves takeover of Guidant Corporation by Johnson & Johnson, subject to conditions (Aug. 25, 2005), http://europa.eu/rapid/press-release_IP-05-1065_en.htm

European Commission Press Release IP/10/1515, Mergers: Commission Clears Syngenta's Acquisition of Monsanto's Sunflower Seed Business, Subject to Conditions (Nov. 17, 2010), http://europa.eu/rapid/press-release_IP-10-1515_en.htm

European Commission Press Release IP/11/1395, Mergers: Commission clears Western Digital's acquisition of Hitachi's hard disk drive business subject to conditions (Nov. 23, 2011), http://europa.eu/rapid/press-release_IP-11-1395_en.htm

European Commission Press Release IP/14/489, Antitrust: Commission Finds that Motorola Mobility infringed EU Competition Rules by Misusing Standard Essential Patents (Apr. 29, 2014), http://europa.eu/rapid/press-release_IP-14-489_en.htm

European Commission Press Release IP/14/1088, Mergers: Commission Approves Acquisition of WhatsApp by Facebook (Oct. 3, 2014), https://ec.europa.eu/commission/presscorner/detail/en/IP_14_1088

European Commission Press Release IP/14/2246, Mergers: Commission approves acquisition of Covidien by Medtronic, subject to conditions (Nov. 28, 2014), http://europa.eu/rapid/press-release_IP-14-2246_en.htm

European Commission Press Release IP/15/5606, Commission Clears GE's Acquisition of Alstom's Power Generation and Transmission Assets, Subject to Conditions (Sept. 8, 2015), https://ec.europa.eu/commission/presscorner/detail/en/IP_15_5606

European Commission Press Release IP/17/882, Mergers: Commission Clears ChemChina Acquisition of Syngenta, Subject to Conditions (Apr. 5, 2017) https://ec.europa.eu/commission/presscorner/detail/et/IP_17_882

European Commission Press Release IP/17/2762, Mergers: Commission Opens In-depth Investigation into Proposed Acquisition of Monsanto by Bayer (Aug. 22, 2017), http://europa.eu/rapid/press-release_IP-17-2762_en.htm

European Commission Press Release IP/18/2282, Mergers: Commission Clears Bayer's Acquisition of Monsanto, Subject to Conditions (Mar. 21, 2018), http://europa.eu/rapid/press-release_IP-18-2282_en

European Commission Daily News MEX/19/4849, Mergers: Commission clears acquisition of Celgene by BMS (July 30, 2019), https://ec.europa.eu/commission/presscorner/detail/en/MEX_19_4849

European Commission Press Release IP/20/529, Mergers: Commission Opens In-depth Investigation into Proposed Acquisition of Tachosil by Johnson & Johnson (Mar. 25, 2020), https://ec.europa.eu/commission/presscorner/detail/en/ip_20_529

European Commission Press Release IP/20/1446, Mergers: Commission Opens In-depth Investigation into the Proposed Acquisition of Fitbit by Google (Aug. 4, 2020), https://ec.europa.eu/commission/presscorner/detail/en/ip_20_1446

European Commission Press Release IP/20/2077, Antitrust: Commission Sends Statement of Objections to Amazon for the Use of Non-Public Independent Seller Data and Opens Second Investigation into its E-commerce Business Practices (Nov. 10, 2020), https://ec.europa.eu/commission/presscorner/detail/en/ip_20_2077

European Commission Press Release IP/22/1762, Mergers: Commission Approves Acquisition of MGM by Amazon (Mar. 15, 2021), https://ec.europa.eu/commission/presscorner/detail/en/ip_22_1762.

European Commission Press Release IP/21/3844, Commission opens in-depth investigation into proposed acquisition of GRAIL by Illumina (July 22, 2021), https://ec.europa.eu/commission/presscorner/detail/en/IP_21_3844

European Commission Press Release IP/21/4804, The Commission Adopts a Statement of Objections in View of Adopting Interim Measures Following Illumina's Early Acquisition of GRAIL (Sept. 20, 2021), https://ec.europa.eu/commission/presscorner/detail/en/ip_21_4804

European Commission Press Release IP/21/5624, Mergers: Commission Opens In-depth Investigation into Proposed Acquisition of Arm by NVIDIA (Oct. 27, 2021) https://ec.europa.eu/commission/presscorner/detail/en/ip_21_5624

European Commission Press Release IP/21/5661, Commission Adopts Interim Measures to Prevent Harm to Competition Following Illumina's Early Acquisition of GRAIL (Oct. 29, 2021), https://ec.europa.eu/commission/presscorner/detail/en/ip_21_5661

European Commission Press Release IP/21/7067, Mergers: Commission Approves Acquisition of Nuance by Microsoft (Dec. 21, 2021), https://ec.europa.eu/commission/presscorner/detail/en/ip_21_7067

European Commission Press Release IP/22/5364, Mergers: Commission prohibits acquisition of GRAIL by Illumina (Sept. 6, 2022), https://ec.europa.eu/commission/presscorner/detail/en/ip_22_5364

European Commission Press Release IP/23/2705, Mergers: Commission Clears Acquisition of Activision Blizzard by Microsoft, Subject to Conditions (May 15, 2023), https://ec.europa.eu/commission/presscorner/detail/en/ip_23_2705

European Parliament Press Release, Deal on Digital Markets Act: EU Rules to Ensure Fair Competition and More Choice for Users (Mar. 24, 2022), https://www.europarl.europa.eu/news/en/press-room/20220315IPR25504/deal-on-digital-markets-act-ensuring-fair-competition-and-more-choice-for-users

European Union, Council Regulation (EC) No. 139/2004 of Jan. 20, 2004, on the Control of Concentrations Between Undertakings (the "EC Merger Regulation" or "EUMR"), 2004 OJ (I 24) 1, https://eur-lex.europa.eu/legal-content/EN/TXT/PDF/?uri=CELEX:32004R0139&from=EN

France, French Competition Authority Press Release, La Commission européenne ouvre une procédure d'examen du rachat de Grail par Illumina fondée sur la procédure de l'article 22 du règlement concentrations de 2004 [The European Commission Opens an Examination Procedure for the Takeover of Grail by Illumina Based on the Procedure of Article 22 of the 2004 Merger Regulation] (Apr. 20, 2021), https://www.autoritedelaconcurrence.fr/fr/article/la-commission-europeenne-ouvre-une-procedure-dexamen-du-rachat-de-grail-par-illumina-fondee

France, French Competition Authority's Opinion on the Online Advertising Sector (Mar. 2018), https://www.autoritedelaconcurrence.fr/sites/default/files/integral_texts/2019-10/avis18a03_en_.pdf

France, The Commercial Code

FTC, Administrative Complaint, In re Microsoft and Activision Blizzard (Dec. 8, 2022), https://www.ftc.gov/system/files/ftc_gov/pdf/D09412MicrosoftActivisionAdministrativeComplaintPublicVersionFinal.pdf

FTC, Administrative Complaint, FTC v. Facebook, Inc., case No. 1:20-cv-03590 (Dec. 9. 2020), https://www.ftc.gov/system/files/documents/cases/051_2021.01.21_revised_partially_redacted_complaint.pdf

FTC, Administrative Complaint, In re Illumina and Grail (Mar. 30, 2021), https://www.ftc.gov/system/files/documents/cases/redacted_administrative_part_3_complaint_redacted.pdf

FTC, Opinion of the Commission, In re Illumina/Grail (Mar. 31, 2023), https://www.ftc.gov/legal-library/browse/cases-proceedings/illumina-inc-grail-inc-matter-timeline-item-2023-04-03

FTC Press Release, FTC Approves Final Order Settling Charges that Nielsen Holdings N.V.'s Acquisition of Arbitron, Inc. Was Anticompetitive (Feb. 28, 2014), https://www.ftc.gov/news-events/press-releases/2014/02/ftc-approves-final-order-settling-charges-nielsen-holdings-nvs

FTC Press Release, FTC Imposes Conditions on Össur Hf's Acquisition of College Park Industries, Inc. (Apr. 7, 2020), https://www.ftc.gov/news-events/press-releases/2020/04/ftc-imposes-conditions-ossurhfs-acquisition-college-park

FTC Press Release, FTC Issues Commentary on Vertical Merger Enforcement (Dec. 22, 2020), https://www.ftc.gov/news-events/news/press-releases/2020/12/ftc-issues-commentary-vertical-merger-enforcement

FTC Press Release, In the Matter of Illumina, Inc., a Corporation and GRAIL, Inc., a Corporation (Aug. 13, 2021), https://www.ftc.gov/enforcement/cases-proceedings/201-0144/illumina-inc-grail-inc-matter

FTC Press Release, FTC Staff Presents Report on Nearly a Decade of Unreported Acquisitions by the Biggest Technology Companies (Sept. 15, 2021), https://www.ftc.gov/news-events/press-releases/2021/09/ftc-report-on-unreported-acquisitions-by-biggest-tech-companies

FTC Press Release, Federal Trade Commission Withdraws Vertical Merger Guidelines and Commentary (Sept. 15, 2021), https://www.ftc.gov/news-events/news/press-releases/2021/09/federal-trade-commission-withdraws-vertical-merger-guidelines-commentary

FTC Press Release, Remarks of Chair Lina M. Khan Regarding Non-HSR Reported Acquisitions by Select Technology Platforms Commission File No. P201201 (Sept. 15, 2021), https://www.ftc.gov/

system/files/documents/public_statements/1596332/remarks_of_chair_lina_m_khan_regarding_non-hsr_reported_acquisitions_by_select_technology_platforms.pdf

FTC Press Release, FTC-DOJ Workshop Summary: The Future of Pharmaceuticals: Examining the Analysis of Pharmaceutical Mergers (June 1, 2023), https://www.ftc.gov/system/files/ftc_gov/pdf/Future%20of%20Pharma%20Workshop%20--%20Summary.pdf

FTC Press Release, FTC Seeks to Block Cytyc Corp.'s Acquisition of Digene Corp. (June 24, 2002), https://www.ftc.gov/news-events/news/press-releases/2002/06/ftc-seeks-block-cytyc-corps-acquisition-digene-corp

FTC, Statement of Chairman Timothy J. Muris in the matter of Genzyme Corporation / Novazyme Pharmaceuticals, Inc. (2004), https://www.ftc.gov/system/files/attachments/press-releases/ftc-closes-its-investigation-genzyme-corporations-2001-acquisition-novazyme-pharmaceuticals-inc./murisgenzymestmt.pdf

FTC, Dissenting Statement of Commissioner Mozelle W. Thompson Genzyme Corporation's Acquisition of Novazyme Pharmaceuticals Inc., https://www.ftc.gov/system/files/attachments/press-releases/ftc-closes-its-investigation-genzyme-corporations-2001-acquisition-novazyme-pharmaceuticals-inc./thompsongenzymestmt.pdf

FTC, Statement of Commissioner Christine S. Wilson, Joined by Commissioner Rohit Chopra Concerning Non-Reportable Hart-Scott-Rodino Act Filing 6(b) Orders (Feb. 11, 2020), https://www.ftc.gov/system/files/documents/reports/6b-orders-file-special-reports-technology-platform-companies/statement_by_commissioners_wilson_and_chopra_re_hsr_6b_0.pdf

FTC, Statement of Chair Lina M. Khan, Commissioner Rohit Chopra, and Commissioner Rebecca Kelly Slaughter on the Withdrawal of the Vertical Merger Guidelines (Sept. 15, 2021), https://www.ftc.gov/legal-library/browse/cases-proceedings/public-statements/statement-chair-lina-m-khan-commissioner-rohit-chopra-commissioner-rebecca-kelly-slaughter

FED. TRADE COMM'N, TO PROMOTE INNOVATION: THE PROPER BALANCE OF COMPETITION AND PATENT LAW AND POLICY: A REPORT BY THE FEDERAL TRADE COMMISSION (Oct. 2003), https://www.ftc.gov/sites/default/files/documents/reports/promote-innovation-proper-balance-competition-and-patent-law-and-policy/innovationrpt.pdf

MONOPOLIES COMMISSION, COMPETITION POLICY: THE CHALLENGE OF DIGITAL MARKET, Special Report by the Monopolies Commission pursuant to Section 44(1)(4) ARC (June 1, 2015), https://www.monopolkommission.de/index.php/en/press-releases/52-competition-policy-the-challenge-of-digital-markets

Netherlands, SCIENCE, TECHNOLOGY AND INNOVATION IN THE NETHERLANDS (Ministry of Economic Affairs, The Hague 2006)

OECD, *Theories of Harm for Digital Mergers: OECD Competition Policy Roundtable Background Note* (2023), https://www.oecd.org/daf/competition/theories-of-harm-for-digital-mergers-2023.pdf

OECD, *Vertical Mergers in the Technology, Media and Telecom Sector – Background Note by the Secretariat* (DAF/COMP(2019)5, May 2, 2019), https://one.oecd.org/document/DAF/COMP(2019)5/en/pdf

OECD, Directorate for Financial and Enterprise Affairs Competition Committee, *Start-ups, Killer Acquisitions and Merger Control – Background Note for the Meeting of the Competition Committee on 10–12 June 2020* 2 (May 2020), http://www.oecd.org/daf/competition/start-ups-killer-acquisitions-and-merger-control.htm

OECD, *Dynamic Efficiencies in Merger Analysis* (Policy Roundtables, DAF/COMP(2007)41, May 15, 2008), https://www.oecd.org/daf/competition/mergers/40623561.pdf

OECD, *Innovation and Growth: Rationale for an Innovation Strategy* (2007), https://www.oecd.org/science/inno/39374789.pdf

OECD, *Key Points of the Hearing on Disruptive Innovation* (DAF/COMP/M(2015)1/ANN8/FINAL, May 11, 2017), https://one.oecd.org/document/DAF/COMP/M(2015)1/ANN8/FINAL/en/pdf

OECD, *Competition Policy and Efficiency Claims in Horizontal Agreements* 41 & 52 (OCDE/ GD(96)65, 1996), https://www.oecd.org/daf/competition/2379526.pdf

OECD, *Merger Review in Emerging High Innovation Markets* (Policy Roundtable, DAFFE/ COMP(2002)20, Jan. 24, 2003)

OECD, Non-price Effects of Mergers – Note by the European Union (DAF/COMP/WD(2018)14, June 1, 2018), para. 31, https://one.oecd.org/document/DAF/COMP/WD(2018)14/en/pdf

OECD/Eurostat, Oslo Manual 2018: Guidelines for Collecting, Reporting and Using Data on Innovation, 4th edition (The Measurement of Scientific, Technological and Innovation Activities, OECD Publishing/Eurostat 2018).

OECD, *OECD Handbook on Competition Policy in the Digital Age* (2022), https://www.oecd.org/ daf/competition-policy-in-the-digital-age

OECD, *Summary of Discussion of the Roundtable on Start-Ups, Killer Acquisitions and Merger Control* (DAF/COMP/M(2020)1/ANN3/FINAL, Oct. 29, 2021), https://one.oecd.org/document/ DAF/COMP/M(2020)1/ANN3/FINAL/en/pdf

OECD, *Lobbyists, Governments and Public Trust, Volume 3: Implementing the OECD Principles for Transparency and Integrity in Lobbying* (2014), https://www.oecd.org/gov/ethics/lobbyists-governments-trust-vol-3-highlights.pdf

OECD, *Rethinking Antitrust Tools for Multi-Sided Platforms* (2018), https://www.oecd.org/ competition/rethinking-antitrust-tools-for-multi-sided-platforms.htm

OECD, *The Concept of Potential Competition – Note by the EU* 9 (DAF/COMP/WD(2021)21, May 25, 2021), https://one.oecd.org/document/DAF/COMP/WD(2021)21/en/pdf

OECD, *The Evolving Concept of Market Power in the Digital Economy, OECD Competition Policy Roundtable Background Note* (2022), https://www.oecd.org/daf/competition/the-evolving-concept-of-market-power-in-the-digital-economy-2022.pdf

OECD, *The Digital Economy* (DAF/COMP(2012)22, Feb. 7, 2013), http://www.oecd.org/ officialdocuments/publicdisplaydocumentpdf/?cote=DAF/COMP(2012)22&docLanguage=En

OECD, *The Role of Efficiency Claims in Antitrust Proceedings* (Policy Roundtables, DAF/ COMP(2012)23, May 2, 2013), https://www.oecd.org/competition/EfficiencyClaims2012.pdf

Spain, Comisión Nacional de Los Mercados y La Competencia, *Study on the Competition Conditions in the Online Advertising Sector in Spain* (July 2021) https://www.cnmc.es/sites/default/ files/3696007_1.pdf

UK, CMA, A Quick Guide to UK Merger Assessment (CMA18) (Mar. 18, 2021) https://assets. publishing.service.gov.uk/government/uploads/system/uploads/attachment_data/file/288677/ CMA18_A_quick_guide_to_UK_merger_assessment.pdf

UK, CMA, Mergers: Guidance on the CMA's Jurisdiction and Procedure (2014), https://www.gov. uk/government/publications/mergers-guidance-on-the-cmas-jurisdiction-and-procedure UK, CMA, UK Exit from the EU: Guidance on the Functions of the CMA under the Withdrawal Agreement (CMA113) (Jan. 28, 2020), https://www.gov.uk/government/publications/uk-exit-from-the-eu-guidance-on-the-functions-of-the-cma-under-the-withdrawal-agreement

UK, CMA, Ladbrokes and Coral: A Report on the Anticipated Merger between Ladbrokes plc and Certain Businesses of Gala Coral Group Limited (July 26, 2016), https://assets. publishing.service.gov.uk/media/5797818ce5274a27b2000004/ladbrokes-coral-final-report.pdf

UK, CMA: Annual Plan Consultation 2019/20 (CMA97con) (Dec. 2018), https://assets. publishing.service.gov.uk/government/uploads/system/uploads/attachment_data/file/761071/annual_ plan_consultation.pdf.

UK, CMA, Guidance on Changes to the Jurisdictional Thresholds for UK Merger Control (CMA90) (June 11, 2018), https://assets.publishing.service.gov.uk/government/uploads/system/uploads/attachment_data/file/903147/guidance_on_changes_to_the_jurisdictional_thresholds_for_UK_MC.pdf

UK, CMA, Merger Cases if There's No Brexit Deal (Oct. 30, 2018), https://www.gov.uk/government/publications/cmas-role-in-mergers-if-theres-no-brexit-deal/cmas-role-in-mergers-if-theres-no-brexit-deal

UK, CMA COMPETITION AND MARKETS AUTHORITY ANNUAL PLAN 2019/20 (CMA97) (Feb. 2019), https://assets.publishing.service.gov.uk/government/uploads/system/uploads/attachment_data/file/778629/AnnualPlan-201920-FINAL-TRACKED.pdf

UK, CMA, COMPETITION AND MARKETS AUTHORITY ANNUAL PLAN 2020/21 (CMA112) (Mar. 2020), https://assets.publishing.service.gov.uk/government/uploads/system/uploads/attachment_data/file/873689/Annual_Plan_2020-21.pdf

UK, CMA, COMPETITION AND MARKETS AUTHORITY ANNUAL PLAN 2021/22 (CMA137) (Mar. 2021), https://assets.publishing.service.gov.uk/government/uploads/system/uploads/attachment_data/file/972070/CMA_Annual_Plan_2021_to_2022_---.pdf

UK, CMA, COMPETITION AND MARKETS AUTHORITY, ANNUAL PLAN 2022/23 (CMA155) (Mar. 24, 2022), https://assets.publishing.service.gov.uk/government/uploads/system/uploads/attachment_data/file/1062414/Final_Annual_Plan_for_2022_23.pdf

UK, CMA, Guidance on the Functions of the CMA After a 'No Deal' Exit from the EU (CMA106) (Mar. 2019), https://assets.publishing.service.gov.uk/government/uploads/system/uploads/attachment_data/file/786749/EU_Exit_Guidance_Document_for_No_Deal_final.pdf

UK, CMA, Guidance on the Functions of the CMA after the End of the Transition Period (CMA125) (Dec. 1, 2020), https://www.gov.uk/government/publications/guidance-on-the-functions-of-the-cma-after-the-end-of-the-transition-period

UK, CMA, Anticipated Acquisition by NVIDIA Corporation of Arm Limited, Cancellation of Merger Reference (Feb. 8, 2022), https://assets.publishing.service.gov.uk/media/62028f4de90e077f7abdbb4e/Notice_of_cancellation_of_merger_reference_NVIDIA_.pdf

UK, Digital Markets Unit (updated on July 20, 2021), CMA, https://www.gov.uk/government/collections/digital-markets-unit

UK, CMA, JUST EAT AND HUNGRYHOUSE: A REPORT ON THE ANTICIPATED ACQUISITION BY JUST EAT PLC OF HUNGRYHOUSE HOLDINGS LIMITED (Nov. 16, 2017), https://assets.publishing.service.gov.uk/media/5a0d6521ed915d0ade60db7e/justeat-hungryhouse-final-report.pdf

UK, CMA, Merger Review and Anti-competitive Activity if There's No Brexit Deal (Sept. 13, 2018), https://www.gov.uk/guidance/merger-review-and-anti-competitive-activity-after-brexit

UK, CMA, Written Evidence (CMP0002) (2018), http://data.parliament.uk/writtenevidence/committeeevidence.svc/evidencedocument/eu-internal-market-subcommittee/brexit-competition/written/69571.pdf

UK, Competition Commission and Office of Fair Trading, Merger Assessment Guidelines (2010),

UK, CMA, Merger Assessment Guidelines (CMA129) (Mar. 18, 2021), https://assets.publishing.service.gov.uk/government/uploads/system/uploads/attachment_data/file/1051823/MAGs_for_publication_2021_--_.pdf

UK, CMA, Digital Competition Expert Panel recommendations – CMA view (Mar. 21, 2019), https://assets.publishing.service.gov.uk/government/uploads/system/uploads/attachment_data/file/788480/CMA_letter_to_BEIS_-_DCEP_report_and_recommendations__Redacted.pdf

CMA, Policy paper, The CMA's Digital Markets Strategy (July 2019), https://www.gov.uk/government/publications/competition-and-markets-authoritys-digital-markets-strategy/the-cmas-digital-markets-strategy

UK CMA, Online Platforms and Digital Advertising: Market Study Interim Report (2019), https://assets.publishing.service.gov.uk/media/5ed0f75bd3bf7f4602e98330/Interim_report_---_web.pdf.

UK, CMA, Online Platforms and Digital Advertising (July 2020), https://www.gov.uk/cma-cases/online-platforms-and-digital-advertising-market-study

UK, NVIDIA – Arm: Summary of the CMA's Report to the Secretary of State for Digital, Culture, Media & Sport on the Anticipated Acquisition by NVIDIA Corporation of Arm Limited, Gov.UK (Aug. 20. 6, 2021), https://www.gov.uk/government/publications/summary-of-the-cmas-report-to-the-secretary-of-state-for-digital-culture-media-sport-on-the-anticipated-acquisition-by-nvidia-corporation-of-arm/nvidia-arm-summary-of-the-cmas-report-to-the-secretary-of-state-for-digital-culture-media-sport-on-the-anticipated-acquisition-by-nvidia-corpo

UK, CMA Press Release, CMA Finds Competition Concerns with NVIDIA's Purchase of Arm (Aug. 20, 2021), https://www.gov.uk/government/news/cma-finds-competition-concerns-with-nvidia-s-purchase-of-arm

UK, CMA Press Release, CMA to Investigate NVIDIA's Takeover of Arm (Jan. 6, 2021), https://www.gov.uk/government/news/cma-to-investigate-nvidia-s-takeover-of-arm

UK, CMA Press Release, CMA Orders Meta to Sell Giphy (Oct. 18, 2022), https://www.gov.uk/government/news/cma-orders-meta-to-sell-giphy

UK, CMA, Submission from the Competition and Markets Authority to the Business, Innovation and Skills Committee's inquiry into the Government's industrial strategy (Sept. 28, 2016), https://www.gov.uk/government/publications/governments-industrial-strategy-cma-submission-to-bis-committee

UK, CMA, Appendix F: The SMS Regime: A Distinct Merger Control Regime for Firms with *SMS* (2020), https://assets.publishing.service.gov.uk/media/5fce706ee90e07562d20986f/Appendix_F_-_The_SMS_regime_-_a_distinct_merger_control_regime_for_firms_with_SMS_-_web_-.pdf

UK, Department for Business, Energy and Industrial Strategy (BEIS) June 2020 guidance, https://assets.publishing.service.gov.uk/government/uploads/system/uploads/attachment_data/file/902531/Enterprise_Act_2002_guidance_on_changes_to_the_turnover_and_share_of_supply_tests_for_mergers__Orders_2020_.pdf

UK, HER MAJESTY'S STATIONERY OFFICE, THE BENEFITS OF BREXIT: HOW THE UK IS TAKING ADVANTAGE OF LEAVING THE EU (Jan. 2022)

UK, Ilze, Jozepa, EU State Aid Rules and WTO Subsidies Agreement, HOUSE OF COMMONS LIBRARY (Aug. 4, 2021), https://researchbriefings.files.parliament.uk/documents/SN06775/SN06775.pdf

UK, Enterprise Act 2002 as amended by the Enterprise and Regulatory Reform Act 2013.

UK, REPORT OF THE DIGITAL COMPETITION EXPERT PANEL, UNLOCKING DIGITAL COMPETITION (2019), https://assets.publishing.service.gov.uk/government/uploads/system/uploads/attachment_data/file/785547/unlocking_digital_competition_furman_review_web.pdf.

UK, Statute of Monopolies 1623

UK, National Security and Investment Act 2021

US, Dep't of Just., Merger Guidelines (1968), https://www.justice.gov/sites/default/files/atr/legacy/2007/07/11/11247.pdf.

US, America COMPETES Reauthorization Act of 2010 (2010)

US, Dep't of Just. & Fed. Trade Comm'n, Horizontal Merger Guidelines (1992, revised 1997), https://www.ftc.gov/sites/default/files/attachments/merger-review/hmg.pdf

US, Dep't of Just. & Fed. Trade Comm'n, Horizontal Merger Guidelines (2010), https://www.ftc.gov/sites/default/files/attachments/merger-review/100819hmg.pdf

US, Dep't of Just. & Fed. Trade Comm'n, Antitrust Guidelines for the Licensing of Intellectual Property (1995)

US, Dep't of Just., Merger Guidelines (1984), https://www.justice.gov/sites/default/files/atr/legacy/2007/07/11/11249.pdf

US, Dep't of Just. & Fed. Trade Comm'n, Vertical Merger Guidelines (June 30, 2020) ("2020 Guidelines"), https://www.ftc.gov/system/files/documents/reports/us-department-justice-federal-trade-commission-vertical-merger-guidelines/vertical_merger_guidelines_6-30-20.pdf

US, Dep't of Just., Antitrust Division Workload Statistics, 2000–2009, https://www.justice.gov/sites/default/files/atr/legacy/2012/04/04/281484.pdf

US, Dep't of Just., Antitrust Division Workload Statistics, 2010–2019, https://www.justice.gov/atr/file/788426/download.

US, Dep't of Just., Press Release, Justice Department Issues Statement on the Vertical Merger Guidelines (Sept. 15, 2021), https://www.justice.gov/opa/pr/justice-department-issues-statement-vertical-merger-guidelines

US, The Clayton Antitrust Act (1914)

US, The Federal Trade Commission Act (1914)

US, The Hart-Scott-Rodino Antitrust Improvements Act of 1976

US, Fed. Trade Comm'n, Dissenting Statement of Commissioners Noah Joshua Phillips and Christine S. Wilson (Sept. 15, 2021), https://www.ftc.gov/system/files/documents/public_statements/1596388/p810034phillipswilsonstatementvmgrescission.pdf

US, Fed. Trade Comm'n, Request for Information on Merger Enforcement, Document No. FTC-2022-0003 (Jan. 18, 2022), https://www.regulations.gov/document/FTC-2022-0003-0001

US, General Accounting Office, Statement of David E. Cooper, Associate Director, Defense Acquisitions Issues, National Security and International Affairs Division before the Subcommittee on Acquisition and Technology, Committee on Armed Services, U.S. Senate, Defense Industry Consolidation: Competitive Effects of Mergers and Acquisitions, https://www.gao.gov/assets/t-nsiad-98-112.pdf

US, Subcommittee on Antitrust, Commercial and Administrative Law of the Committee on Judiciary, Investigation of Competition in Digital Markets: Majority Staff Report and Recommendations (2020), https://democrats-judiciary.house.gov/uploadedfiles/competition_in_digital_markets.pdf

US, Fed. Trade Comm'n, Non-HSR Reported Acquisitions by Select Technology Platforms, 2010–2019: An FTC Study (Sept. 2021), https://www.ftc.gov/reports/non-hsr-reported-acquisitions-select-technology-platforms-2010-2019-ftc-study

Theses and Research Papers

Easterly, William, *The Ghost of Financing Gap: How the Harrod-Domar Growth Model Still Haunts Development Economics* (World Bank Policy Research Working Paper No. 1807, 1997), https://ssrn.com/abstract=11020

Feldman, Robin, *Pharmaceutical Pipeline Divestitures Study: Preliminary Results* (UC Hastings Rsch. Paper, forthcoming 2021), https://ssrn.com/abstract=3861975

Fox, Eleanor M. & Deborah Healey, *When the State Harms Competition – The Role for Competition Law* (NYU Law and Economics Research Paper No. 13-11, UNSW Law Research Paper No. 2013-312013), https://ssrn.com/abstract=2248059

Hauptmann, Stefan, Empirical Research in Evolutionary Economics. The Potential of the "Social World Perspective" (2004) (M.Sc. thesis, University of Manchester) (on file with the University of Manchester), https://epub.uni-regensburg.de/25312/1/Hauptmann_MSc_Empirical_Research_in_Evolutionary_Economics.pdf

Lianos, Ioannis, *Competition Law for the Digital Era: A Complex Systems' Perspective* (CLES Research Paper Series 6/2019, 2019), https://www.ucl.ac.uk/cles/sites/cles/files/cles_6-2019_final.pdf

Lianos, Ioannis & Rochelle C. Dreyfuss, *New Challenges in the Intersection of Intellectual Property Rights with Competition Law: A View from Europe and the United States* (CLES Working Paper Series 4/2013, 2013), https://discovery.ucl.ac.uk/id/eprint/10045063

Lianos, Ioannis, Abel Mateus & Azza Raslan, *Development Economics and Competition: A Parallel Intellectual History* (CLES Working Paper Series 1/2012, 2012), https://discovery.ucl.ac.uk/id/eprint/10045074

Parker, Geoffrey, Georgios Petropoulos & Marshall W. Van Alstyne, *Platform Mergers and Antitrust* (Boston University Questrom School of Business Research Paper No. 376351, 2021)

Persson, Amanda, Merger Control post-Brexit – An Analysis of the Future EU-UK Relationship and the Potential Effects on UK Merger Control (2018) (Master thesis, Lund University, Sweden), http://lup.lub.lu.se/student-papers/record/8944192

Seiler, Markus, Innovation Competition in EU Merger Control (2018) (on file with the University of St. Gallen), http://www.mbl.unisg.ch/sites/default/files/Seiler_Markus_Read_Full_Thesis_0.pdf. (abstract available at https://mbl.ch/wp-content/uploads/2022/02/Abstract-Seiler-Markus.pdf)

Shi, Mengmeng, The Divestiture Remedies Under Merger Control in the US, the EU and China: A Comparative Law and Economics Perspective (2019) (doctoral thesis, Maastricht University) (on file with the Maastricht University)

Suijkerbuijk, L. I. M., Innovation, Competition in EU Merger Control (2018) (on file with the Tilburg University), http://arno.uvt.nl/show.cgi?fid=145944

Telfer, Robert Thomas Currie, Forum Shopping and the Private Enforcement of EU Competition Law: Is Forum Shopping a Dead Letter? 264 (2017) (Ph.D. thesis, University of Glasgow) (on file with the University of Glasgow)

Torfason, Ólafur Páll, Appropriability Mechanisms and Strategies for Innovations: The Case of Rotulus (2011) (master thesis, Copenhagen Business School) (on file with the Copenhagen Business School), https://research.cbs.dk/files/58427580/olafur_pall_torfason.pdf

Torun, Hasan & Cumhur Çiçekçi, *Innovation: Is the Engine for the Economic Growth* (Ege University, Faculty of Economics and Administrative Sciences 2007), http://citeseerx.ist.psu.edu/viewdoc/download?doi=10.1.1.452.4897&rep=rep1&type=pdf

Vincent, E. J. A., The Impact of Regulation on Innovation: A Case Study on Small Biscuit Producers in The Netherlands (2017) (bachelor thesis, University of Twente) (on file with the University of Twente)

Working and Discussion Papers

Bottomley, Sean, *Patents and the First Industrial Revolution in the United States, France and Britain, 1700–1850* (Institute for Advanced Study in Toulouse (IAST) Working Papers 14-14, 2014), https://ideas.repec.org/p/tse/iastwp/28752.html

Bourreau, Marc, Bruno Jullien & Yassine Lefouili, *Mergers and Demand-Enhancing Innovation* (Toulouse School of Economics, Working Paper No. 18-907, Mar. 2018, Revised July 2018), https://www.tse-fr.eu/sites/default/files/TSE/documents/doc/wp/2018/wp_tse_907.pdf

Colomo, Pablo Ibáñez, *Restrictions on Innovation in EU Competition Law* (LSE Law, Society and Economy Working Papers 22/2015, 2015), http://ssrn.com/abstract=2699395

Costa-Cabral, Francisco, *Innovation in EU Competition Law: The Resource-Based View and Disruption* (NYU School of Law, Jean Monnet Working Paper 2/17, 2018)

Dellis, Konstantinos & David Sondermann, *Lobbying in Europe: New Firm-Level Evidence* 2 (European Central Bank, Working Paper No. 2071, 2017)

Economides, Nicholas, John Kwoka, Thomas Philippon, Hal Singer & Lawrence J. White, *Comments on the DOJ/FTC Draft Vertical Merger Guidelines* (NET Institute Working Paper No. 20-04, 2020), https://www.ftc.gov/system/files/attachments/798-draft-vertical-merger-guidelines/vmg14_economides_comment.pdf

Encaoua, David & Abraham Hollander, *Competition Policy and Innovation* (Université Paris1 Panthéon-Sorbonne Post-Print and Working Papers, 2002) https://ideas.repec.org/p/hal/cesptp/halshs-00185360.html

Etro, Frederico, *Conglomerate Mergers and Entry in Innovative Industries* (Univ. Ca' Foscari of Venice, Dep't of Econ. Resch., Working Paper Series No. 19/WP/2018, 2018)

Federico, Giulio, Gregor Langus & Tommaso Valletti, *A Simple Model of Mergers and Innovation* (CESifo Working Paper No. 6539, June 2017), https://papers.ssrn.com/sol3/papers.cfm?abstract_id=3005163

Fumagalli, Chiara, Massimo Motta & Emanuele Tarantino, *Shelving or Developing? The Acquisition of Potential Competitors under Financial Constraints* (Universitat Pompeu Fabra, Department of Economics and Business, Economics Working Papers No. 1735, 2020)

Gault, Fred & Eric A. von Hippel, *The Prevalence of User Innovation and Free Innovation Transfers: Implications for Statistical Indicators and Innovation Policy* (MIT Sloan School Working Paper No. 4722-09, 2009), https://papers.ssrn.com/sol3/papers.cfm?abstract_id=1337232

Gautier, Axel & Joe Lamesch, *Mergers in the Digital Economy* (CESifo Working Paper No. 8056, 2020)

Godin, Benoît, *Innovation: History of a Category* (Project on the Intellectual History of Innovation, Working Paper No. 1, 2008), http://www.csiic.ca/PDF/IntellectualNo1.pdf

Godin, Benoît, καινοτομία: *An Old Word for a New World, or, The De-Contestation of a Political and Contested Concept* (Project on the Intellectual History of Innovation, Working Paper No. 9, 2011), http://www.csiic.ca/PDF/Old-New.pdf.

Godin, Benoît, *Innovation and Conceptual Innovation in Ancient Greece* (Project on the Intellectual History of Innovation, Working Paper No. 12, 2012), http://www.csiic.ca/PDF/Antiquity.pdf

Godin, Benoît, *The Vocabulary of Innovation: A Lexicon* (Project on the Intellectual History of Innovation, Working Paper No. 20, 2014), http://www.csiic.ca/PDF/LexiconPaperNo20.pdf.

Godin, Benoît, *Innovation: A Conceptual History of an Anonymous Concept* (Project on the Intellectual History of Innovation, Working Paper, No. 21, 2015), http://www.csiic.ca/PDF/WorkingPaper21.pdf

Gregor, Martin, *Corporate Lobbying: A Review of the Recent Literature* 29 (Charles University, Inst. of Econ. Stud. Working Paper, No. 32/2011, 2011)

Grossman, Gene M. & Elhanan Helpman, *Protection for Sale*, 84 AM. ECON. REV. 833 (1994)

Gutiérrez, Germán & Thomas Philippon, *How EU Markets Became More Competitive Than US Markets: A Study of Institutional Drift* 25–29 (NBER Working Paper No. 24700, 2018)

Haucap, Justus, *Merger Effects on Innovation: A Rationale for Stricter Merger Control?* (University of Düsseldorf, Düsseldorf Institute for Competition Economics, Discussion Paper No. 268, Sep. 2017), http://www.dice.hhu.de/fileadmin/redaktion/Fakultaeten/Wirtschaftswissenschaftliche_Fakultaet/DICE/Discussion_Paper/268_Haucap.pdf

Helpman, Elhanan & Manuel Trajtenberg, *Diffusion of General Purpose Technologies* (NBER Working Paper Series, 117, 1998) also in GENERAL PURPOSE TECHNOLOGIES AND ECONOMIC GROWTH 85–119 (Elhanan Helpman ed., MIT Press 1998)

Hemphill, C. Scott & Tim Wu, *Nascent Competitors*, 168 U. Pa. L. Rev. 1879 (2020) (NYU Law and Economics Research Paper No. 20-50, Columbia Law and Economics Working Paper No. 645), https://ssrn.com/abstract=3624058

Hoover, Kevin D., *Was Harrod Right?* (CHOPE Working Paper No. 2012-01, 2012), https://ssrn.com/abstract=2001452

Hüschelrath, Kai & Sebastian Peyer, *Public and Private Enforcement of Competition Law: A Differentiated Approach* (Centre for Competition Policy (CCP) Working Paper 13-5, Apr. 2013)

Jin, Ginger Zhe, Mario Leccese & Liad Wagman, *How Do Top Acquirers Compare in Technology Mergers? New Evidence from an S&P Taxonomy* (NBER Working Paper Series No. 29642, 2022)

Jullien, Bruno & Yassine Lefouili, *Horizontal Mergers and Innovation* 5 (Toulouse School of Economics, Working Papers No. 18-892, 2018) https://www.tse-fr.eu/sites/default/files/TSE/documents/doc/wp/2018/wp_tse_892.pdf

Kamepalli, Sai Krishna, Raghuram Rajan & Luigi Zingales, *Kill Zone* (NBER Working Paper 27146, 2019)

Kerber, Wolfgang, *Competition, Innovation, and Competition Law: Dissecting the Interplay* (MAGKS Joint Discussion Paper Series in Economics, No. 42-2017, 2017)

Koski, Heli, Otto Kässi & Fabian Braesemann, *Killers on the Road of Emerging Start-ups – Implications for Market Entry and Venture Capital Financing* (ETLA Working Papers 81, 2020).

Letina, Igor, Armin Schmutzler & Regina Seibel, *Killer Acquisitions and Beyond: Policy Effects on Innovation Strategies* (University of Zurich, Department of Economics, Working Paper No. 358, revised version 2021), https://ssrn.com/abstract=3673150

MacLeod Christine & Alessandro Nuvolari, *Patents and Industrialization: An Historical Overview of the British Case* (Laboratory of Economics and Management (LEM), Working Paper Series No. 1624-1907, 2010)

Motta, Massimo & Emanuele Tarantino, *The Effect of a Merger on Investments* (Centre for Economic Policy Research (CEPR) Discussion Paper Series No. DP11550, 2016), https://papers.ssrn.com/sol3/papers.cfm?abstract_id=2850392

Motta, Massimo & Emanuele Tarantino, *The Effect of Horizontal Mergers, When Firms Compete in Prices and Investments* (University of Mannheim, Department of Economics, Working Paper No. 17-01, Sept. 2017), https://ub-madoc.bib.uni-mannheim.de/42805/1/17-01_Motta%2C%20Tarantino.pdf

OECD, *Disruptive Innovation and Competition Policy Enforcement – Note by Alexandre de Streel and Pierre Larouche* (DAF/COMP/GF(2015)7, Oct. 20, 2015)

Petit, Nicolas & David J. Teece, *Innovating Big Tech Firms and Competition Policy: Favouring Dynamic Over Static Competition* 9 (DCI Working Paper, 2021), https://www.dynamiccompetition.com/wp-content/uploads/2022/08/DCI-WP2-Petit-and-Teece-2021.pdf

Schrepel, Thibault, *A Systematic Content Analysis of Innovation in European Competition Law* (Amsterdam Law & Technology Institute (ALTI) Working Paper 2-2023 // Dynamic Competition Initiative (DCI) Working Paper 1-2023, 2023), https://ssrn.com/abstract=4413584

Schulz, Norbert, *Review of the Literature on the Impact of Mergers on Innovation* 8 (ZEW Discussion Paper No. 07-061, 2007), https://www.econstor.eu/bitstream/10419/24635/1/dp07061.pdf

Vancraybex, Eline, *Innovation in the EU Merger Control Battlefield: In Search for Best Practices* (Maastricht Centre for European Law, Working Paper No. 1, 2018)

Table of Cases

Australia

Microsoft/Activision Blizzard

Australian Competition & Consumer Commission, Microsoft Corporation – Activision Blizzard Inc. (June 16, 2022), https://www.accc.gov.au/public-registers/mergers-registers/public-informal-merger-reviews/microsoft-corporation-activision-blizzard-inc

European Union

Court of Justice and General Court

Case C-67/13 P, Cartes Bancaires v. European Commission, ECLI:EU:C:2014:2204

Case T-282/02, Cementbouw v. Commission, 2006 ECR II-319

Case C-12/03 P, Commission v. Tetra Laval, 2005 ECR I-987

Case T-175/12, Deutsche Börse AG v. Commission, ECLI:EU:T:2015:148

Joined Cases T-374/94, T-375/94, T-384/94 and T-388/94, European Night Services and Others v. Commission, 1998 ECR II-03141

Case T-227/21, Illumina Inc. v. Commission, ECLI:EU:T:2022:447

Case T-227/21: Action brought on 28 April 2021 – Illumina v. Commission, 2021 OJ (C 252) 27, https://eur-lex.europa.eu/legal-content/EN/TXT/?uri=CELEX%3A62021TN0227

Case T-5/02, Tetra Laval BV v. Commission, 2002 ECR II-4381

Case T-83/91, Tetra Pak International SA v. Commission, 1994 ECR II-755

Case C-333/94 P, Tetra Pak International SA v. Commission, 1996 ECR I-5951

Case T-194/13: Action brought on 5 April 2013 – United Parcel Service v. Commission, 2013 OJ (C 147) 30, https://eur-lex.europa.eu/legal-content/en/TXT/PDF/?uri=uriserv%3AOJ.C_.2013.147.01.0030.01.ENG

European Commission

Abbvie/Allergan, European Commission Decision case COMP/M.9461 (2020)

Amazon.com Inc., European Commission Decision case AT.40153 (May 4, 2017)

Apple/Shazam, European Commission Decision case M.8788 (Sept. 6, 2018)

Bayer/Aventis Crop Science, European Commission Decision case COMP/M.2547 (Apr. 17, 2000)

Bayer/Monsanto, European Commission Decision case M.8084 (Mar. 21, 2018)

BMS/Celgene, European Commission Decision case M.9294 (July 29, 2019)

British Aerospace/GEC Macroni European Commission Decision case IV/M. 1438 (June 25, 1999)

ChemChina/Syngenta, European Commission Decision case M. 7962 (Apr. 5, 2017)

Ciba-Geigy/Sandoz, European Commission Decision 97/469/EC, case IV/M.737 (July 17, 1996)

Deutsche Börse/NYSE Euronext, European Commission Decision case COMP/M.6166 (Feb. 1, 2012)

Dow/DuPont, European Commission Decision case M.7932 (Mar. 27, 2017)

DuPont/ICI, European Commission Decision case IV/M.214 (1992)

Facebook/WhatsApp, European Commission Decision case COMP/M.7217 (Oct. 30, 2014)

GE(General Electric)/Alstom, European Commission Decision case COMP/M.7278 (2015)

GE(General Electric)/Honeywell, European Commission Decision case COMP/M.2220 (2001)

Glaxo Wellcome/SmithKline Beecham, European Commission Decision case COMP/M.1846 (May 8, 2000)

Google/Fitbit, European Commission Decision case M.9660 (Dec. 17, 2020), https://ec.europa.eu/competition/elojade/isef/case_details.cfm?proc_code=2_M_9660

Google Search (Shopping), European Commission Decision case AT.39740 (June 27, 2017).

Hutchison 3G UK/Telefónica Ireland, European Commission Decision case M.6992 (May 28, 2014)

Illumina/Grail, European Commission Decision case M.10188 (Sept. 6, 2022)

Inco/Falconbridge, European Commission Decision case COMP/M.4000 (July 4, 2006), https://ec.europa.eu/competition/mergers/cases/decisions/m4000_20060704_20600_en.pdf

Intel/McAfee, European Commission Decision case COMP/M.5984 (Jan. 26, 2011)

Johnson&Johnson/Actelion, European Commission Decision case M.8401 (June 9, 2017)

Johnson & Johnson/Guidant, European Commission Decision 2006/430/EC, case COMP/M.3687 (Aug. 25, 2005)

Johnson & Johnson/Tachosil European Commission case M.9547 (2020)

Medtronic/Covidien, European Commission Decision case COMP/M.7326 (Nov. 28, 2014)

Microsoft Corporation, European Commission Decision case C –3/37.792 (Mar. 24, 2004)

Microsoft, European Commission Decision case COMP/C –3/39.530 (Dec. 16, 2009)

Microsoft/Activision Blizzard, European Commission Decision case M.10646 (May 5, 2023), https://ec.europa.eu/competition/elojade/isef/case_details.cfm?proc_code=2_M_10646

Microsoft/LinkedIn, European Commission Decision case M.8124 (Dec. 6, 2016)

Novartis/Glaxo Smith Kline's Oncology Business, European Commission Decision case COMP M.7275 (Jan. 28, 2015).

Nvidia/Arm, European, Commission case M.9987 (abandoned/withdrawn on Feb. 8, 2022), https://ec.europa.eu/competition/elojade/isef/case_details.cfm?proc_code=2_M_9987

Pasteur Mérieux/Merck, European Commission Decision 94/770/EC, case IV/34.776 (Oct. 6, 1994)

Pfizer/Hospira, European Commission Decision case COMP/M.7559 (Aug. 4, 2015)

Ryanair/Aer Lingus III, European Commission Decision case COMP/M.6663 (Feb. 27, 2013)

Seagate/HDD Business of Samsung, European Commission Decision case COMP/M.6214 (Oct. 19, 2011)

Siemens/Alstom, European Commission Decision case M.8677 (Feb. 6, 2019)

Syngenta/Monsanto's Sunflower Seed Business, European Commission Decision case COMP/5675 (Nov. 17, 2010)

Telefónica Deutschland/E-Plus, European Commission Decision case M.7018 (July 2, 2014)

Tetra Laval/Sidel, European Commission Decision case COMP/M.2416 (2001)

TomTom/Tele Atlas, European Commission Decision case M.4854 (May 14, 2008)

UPS/TNT Express, European Commission Decision case M.6570 (Jan. 1, 2013)

Western Digital Ireland/Vivity Technologies, European Commission Decision case M.6203 (Nov. 23, 2011)

New Zealand

Microsoft/Activision Blizzard

New Zealand Commerce Commission, Case register, Microsoft Corporation; Activision Blizzard Inc (Aug. 7, 2023) , https://comcom.govt.nz/case-register/case-register-entries/microsoft-corporation-activision-blizzard-inc

Serbia

Microsoft/Activision, Serbian Commission for Protection of Competition, Decision (Aug. 12, 2022), https://kzk.gov.rs/kzk/wp-content/uploads/2022/11/Microsoft1.pdf

Turkey

Gemplus/Exalto, Turkish Competition Board Decision No. 06-33/410-107 (May 11, 2006)

Legrand/Schneider, Turkish Competition Board Decision No. 01-48/486-121 (Oct. 8, 2001)

Microsoft/Activision, Turkish Competition Board Decision No. 23-31/592-202 (July 13, 2023)

United Kingdom

Competition Appeal Tribunal

Merck and Generics UK v. CMA [2021] CAT 9

Meta Platforms, Inc. v. CMA, [2022] CAT 26. https://www.catribunal.org.uk/cases/142941221-meta-platforms-inc

Sabre Corporation v. CMA [2021] CAT 11

Tobii AB (Publ) v. CMA ([2020] CAT 1

Competition Authorities

Adobe/Macromedia

OFT, Anticipated Acquisition by Adobe Systems, incorporated of Macromedia, Inc. (Nov. 16, 2005), https://assets.publishing.service.gov.uk/media/555de437e5274a7084000110/adobe.pdf

Akzo Nobel N.V./Metlac Holding S. R. L

OFT, Anticipated acquisition by Akzo Nobel NV of Metlac Holding S.R.L (ME/5319/12, May 23, 2012), https://assets.publishing.service.gov.uk/media/555de2f1e5274a74ca00004f/AkzoNobelMetlac.pdf

CC, Akzo Nobel N.V./Metlac Holding S. R. L. (Dec. 21, 2012), https://assets.digital.cabinet-office.gov.uk/media/5329e008e5274a226b0002ef/main_report.pdf

Amazon/Book Depository

OFT, Anticipated Acquisition by Amazon.com, Inc. of The Book Depository International Limited (ME/5085/11, Oct. 26, 2011), https://assets.publishing.service.gov.uk/media/555de319e5274a708400006e/Amazon.pdf

Amazon/Deliveroo

CMA (Aug. 4, 2020), https://www.gov.uk/cma-cases/amazon-deliveroo-merger-inquiry

Aviagen /Hubbard

CMA, Anticipated acquisition by Aviagen Group Holding Inc. of Hubbard Holding SAS, Decision on relevant merger situation and substantial lessening of competition (ME/6727-17, Feb. 28, 2018), https://assets.publishing.service.gov.uk/media/5a9592ec40f0b67aa5087b04/aviagen-hubbard-decision.pdf

Bayard/Landis

OFT, Completed acquisition by Bayard Capital Partners Pty Ltd of Landis & GYR (Nov. 15, 2004), https://assets.publishing.service.gov.uk/media/555de461ed915d7ae500011c/bayard.pdf

BBC Worldwide Limited

CC, BBC WORLDWIDE LIMITED, CHANNEL FOUR TELEVISION CORPORATION AND ITV PLC (A report on the anticipated joint venture between BBC Worldwide Limited, Channel Four Television Corporation and ITV plc relating to the video on demand sector) (Feb. 4, 2009)

Brightsolid Group Limited and Friends Reunited Holdings Limited

CC, Brightsolid Group Limited and Friends Reunited Holdings Limited: A Report on the Anticipated Acquisition by Brightsolid Group Limited of Friends Reunited Holdings Limited (Mar. 18, 2010), https://assets.publishing.service.gov.uk/media/55194c73e5274a142b0003be/555final_report_excised.pdf.

BT Group plc and EE Limited

CMA, BT Group plc and EE Limited: A Report on the Anticipated Acquisition by BT Group plc of EE Limited (Jan. 15, 2016), https://assets.publishing.service.gov.uk/media/56992242ed915d4747000026/BT_EE_final_report.pdf

Cirrus Logic Inc/Wolfson Microelectronics Plc

CMA, Anticipated acquisition by Cirrus Logic Inc of Wolfson Microelectronics Plc (ME/6461/14, Nov. 7, 2014), https://assets.publishing.service.gov.uk/media/545ce6f440f0b6130e00001c/Cirrus-Wolfson_decision.pdf

Expedia/Trivago

OFT, Anticipated Acquisition by Expedia of Trivago (ME/5894/13, Mar. 7, 2013), https://assets.publishing.service.gov.uk/media/555de2d2e5274a7084000038/Expedia.pdf

Facebook (Meta Platform)/Giphy

CMA, Completed Acquisition by Facebook, Inc (Now Meta Platforms, Inc) of Giphy, Inc. (Final Report) (Nov. 30, 2021), https://assets.publishing.service.gov.uk/media/61a64a618fa8f5037d67b7b5/Facebook__Meta__GIPHY_-_Final_Report_1221_.pdf

CMA, Completed Acquisition by Facebook, Inc. of GIPHY, Inc., Decision to Refer (Apr. 1, 2021), https://assets.publishing.service.gov.uk/media/60659715e90e074e485062e1/Facebook_GIPHY_-_Decision_to_refer.pdf

CMA, Completed Acquisition by Facebook, Inc (now Meta Platforms, Inc) of Giphy, Inc. (Final Report on the case remitted to the CMA by the Competition Appeal Tribunal) (Oct. 18, 2022), https://assets.publishing.service.gov.uk/media/635017428fa8f53463dcb9f2/Final_Report_-_Meta.pdf

Facebook/Instagram

OFT, Anticipated Acquisition by Facebook Inc of Instagram (ME/5525/12, on reference given on Aug. 14, 2012), https://assets.publishing.service.gov.uk/media/555de2e5ed915d7ae200003b/facebook.pdf

Francisco/G International

OFT, Completed acquisition by Francisco Partners L.P. of G International Inc. (Mar. 22, 2005), https://assets.publishing.service.gov.uk/media/555de425e5274a74ca0000f5/francisco.pdf

Getty/Digital Vision/Photonica

OFT, Completed Acquisition by Getty Images Inc of Digital Vision Limited and of Amana America Inc, Amana Europe Limited and Iconica Limited trading as Photonica (Feb. 17, 2006), https://assets.publishing.service.gov.uk/media/555de3ece5274a70840000e4/getty.pdf

Google/Beattthatquote

OFT, Completed Acquisition by Google Inc of BeatThatQuote (July 1, 2011), https://assets.publishing.service.gov.uk/media/555de311ed915d7ae200005f/Google-BeatThatQuote.pdf

Google/Looker

CMA, Completed Acquisition by Google LLC of Looker Data Sciences, Inc. (ME/6839/19) (Mar. 16, 2020)

Ladbrokes/Gala Coral

CMA, Merger between Ladbrokes Plc and Certain Businesses of Gala Coral Group Limited, Notice of acceptance Final Undertakings pursuant to §§ 41 and 82 of, and Schedule 10 to, the Enterprise

Act 2002 (Oct. 11, 2016), https://assets.publishing.service.gov.uk/media/57fdfb66ed915d25be000000/final-undertakings-and-notice-for-publication.pdf

Mastercard UK Holdco Limited/VocaLink Holdings

CMA, Anticipated Acquisition by Mastercard UK Holdco Limited of VocaLink Holdings Limited (ME/6638/16, Jan. 30, 2017), https://assets.publishing.service.gov.uk/media/588f2c1fed915d4535000041/mastercard-vocalink-ftd.pdf

Microsoft/Activision Blizzard

CMA, ANTICIPATED ACQUISITION BY MICROSOFT OF ACTIVISION BLIZZARD, INC. (Final Report) (Apr. 26, 2023), https://assets.publishing.service.gov.uk/media/644939aa529eda000c3b0525/Microsoft_Activision_Final_Report_.pdf

CMA, Anticipated Acquisition by Microsoft Corporation of Activision Blizzard (Excluding Activision Blizzard's non-EEA Cloud Streaming Rights) (ME/7068/23, Sept. 22, 2023)

CAT conditional decision (Jul 17, 2023), https://www.catribunal.org.uk/sites/cat/files/2023-07/2023.07.18_1590_Ruling%20%28Second%20Adjournment%20Application%29.pdf

CMA's Draft Order for the Microsoft and Activision Merger Inquiry 2023, https://assets.publishing.service.gov.uk/media/6465ec16e14070000cb6e181/Draft_final_order__.pdf

CMA Final Order (Aug. 22, 2023), https://assets.publishing.service.gov.uk/media/64e3764a3309b7000d1c9bd7/Microsoft_Activision_-_Final_Order.pdf

CMA Final Decision on Possible Material Change of Circumstances/Special Reasons (Aug. 25, 2023), https://assets.publishing.service.gov.uk/media/64e85b07db1c07000d22b40e/MS_A_-_Final_Decision_on_possible_MCC_and_SR__PUBLICATION_VERSION_.pdf

Microsoft/Activision (ex-cloud streaming rights)

CMA, Microsoft / Activision Blizzard (ex-cloud streaming rights) Merger Inquiry (Aug. 22, 2023), https://www.gov.uk/cma-cases/microsoft-slash-activision-blizzard-ex-cloud-streaming-rights-merger-inquiry

Motorola/Waze

OFT, Completed Acquisition by Motorola Mobility Holding (Google, Inc.) of Waze Mobile Limited (ME/6167/13, Nov. 11, 2013), https://assets.publishing.service.gov.uk/media/555de2cfed915d7ae2000027/motorola.pdf

Nvidia/Arm

CMA, Merger Inquiry Statutory Timetable and Phase I Summary, https://www.gov.uk/cma-cases/nvidia-slash-arm-merger-inquiry

PayPal/iZettle

CMA (June 12, 2019), https://www.gov.uk/cma-cases/paypal-holdings-inc-izettle-ab-merger-inquiry

Priceline/Kayak

OFT, Completed Acquisition by Priceline.com Incorporated of Kayak Software Corporation (ME/5882-12, May 14, 2013), https://assets.publishing.service.gov.uk/media/555de2b6e5274a7084000024/priceline.pdf

Research Machines/Sentinel

OFT, Completed Acquisition by Research Machines plc of Sentinel Products Ltd. (July 23, 2004), https://assets.publishing.service.gov.uk/media/555de442ed915d7ae200011d/researchmachines.pdf

Roche/Spark Therapeutics, CMA, Anticipated acquisition by Roche Holdings, Inc. of Spark Therapeutics, Inc. (ME/6831/19, Dec. 16, 2019)

Sabre/Farelogix

CMA, Sabre / Farelogix Merger Inquiry (June 19, 2020), https://www.gov.uk/cma-cases/sabre-farelogix-merger-inquiry

Telefonaktiebolaget LM Ericsson and Creative Broadcast Services Holdings (2) Limited

CC, TELEFONAKTIEBOLAGET LM ERICSSON AND CREATIVE BROADCAST SERVICES HOLDINGS (2) LIMITED (A report on the anticipated acquisition by Telefonaktiebolaget LM Ericsson of Creative Broadcast Services Holdings (2) Limited) (Mar. 27, 2014), https://assets.publishing.service.gov. uk/media/5342bd11ed915d630e00002f/Final_report__PDF__601_Kb_.pdf

Thermo/GVI

OFT, Completed Acquisition by Thermo Electron Manufacturing Limited of GV Instruments Limited (Dec. 15, 2006), https://assets.publishing.service.gov.uk/media/555de3fbe5274a74ca0000dd/Thermo.pdf

CC, Thermo Electron Manufacturing Limited and GV Instruments Limited Merger Inquiry (May 30, 2007)

Tobii AB/Smartbox & Sensory

CMA, COMPLETED ACQUISITION BY TOBII AB OF SMARTBOX ASSISTIVE TECHNOLOGIES LIMITED AND SENSORY SOFTWARE INTERNATIONAL LTD (Final Report) (Aug. 15, 2019), https://assets. publishing.service.gov.uk/media/5d5d1800e5274a0766482c45/Final_Report2.pdf?_ga=2.1172486 45.2038125553.1566932195-923601075.1560421042.

CMA, Completed Acquisition by Tobii AB of Smartbox Assistive Technology and Sensory Software International Ltd (Issues Statement) (Feb. 26, 2019), https://assets.publishing.service. gov.uk/media/5c752294ed915d3551b9aff9/Tobii_Smartbox_Issues_Statement.pdf

Tobii's Response to Provisional Findings, https://assets.publishing.service.gov.uk/ media/5d10f5dee5274a065e721726/Tobii_response_.pdf

United States

Courts

Brown Shoe Co., Inc. v. United States, 370 U.S. 294 (1962)

Ohio et al. v. American Express Co. et al., 585 U.S.___ (2018)

FTC v. Microsoft Corporation et al., No. 3:23-cv-02880-JSC (N.D. Cal. July 10, 2023), https:// storage.courtlistener.com/recap/gov.uscourts.cand.413969/gov.uscourts.cand.413969.305.0_32.pdf

FTC v. Procter & Gamble Co., 386 U.S. 568 (1967)

General Electric Co. v. Wabash Appliance Corp., 304 U.S. 364 (1938)

Transparent – Wrap Machine Corp. v. Stokes & Smith Co. 329 U.S. 637 (1947)

United States v. Am. Tel. & Tel. Co., 552 F. Supp. 131, 195 (D.D.C.1982), aff'd sub nom. Maryland v. United States, 460 U.S. 1001, 103 S. Ct. 1240, 75 L. Ed. 2d 472 (1983)

United States v. Bazaarvoice, Inc., Case No. 13-cv-00133-WHO (N.D. Cal. Jan. 8, 2014)

United States et al. v. Comcast Corp., General Electric Co. and NBC Universal, Inc., No. 1:11-CV00106 (D.D.C. filed Jan. 18, 2011)

United States et al. v. The Dow Chemical Co. and E. I. Du Pont De Nemours and Co., FTC No. 1-17-cv-01176 (D.D.C. filed June 15, 2017)

United States v. General Dynamics Corp., 415 US 486 (1974)

United States v. General Elec. Co., 272 U.S. 476 (1926)

United States v. Line Material Co., 333 U.S. 287 (1948)

United States v. Microsoft Corp., 253 F.3d 34 (D.C. Cir. 2001)

United States v. Microsoft Corp., 87 F. Supp. 2d 30 (D.D.C. 2000)

United States v. Pilkington plc and Pilkington Holdings, 6 Trade Reg Rep (CCH) (D. Mass. 1994)

United States v. Sabre Corp. et al., case 19-1548 (D. Del. 2020)

Competition Authorities

AbbVie/Allergan, FTC Matter No. 191 0169 (2000)

United States v. AT&T, Inc., No. 1:11-cv-01560 (D.D.C. filed Aug. 31, 2011) BMS/Celgene, No. C-4690 (F.T.C. 2021)

Broadcom Ltd. and Brocade Communications Systems, Inc., No. C-4622 (F.T.C. Aug. 17, 2017) (Decision and Order)

Danaher Corp., No. C-4710 (F.T.C. 2021)

DOJ, US & Plaintiff States v. Comcast Corp., et al., No. 1:11-cv-00106 (Competitive Impact Statement)

EagleView Technology/Verisk, No. 9363 (F.T.C. Dec. 16, 2014) (Final Order issued)

FTC v. Facebook, Memorandum Opinion Civil Action No. 20-3590 (JEB), https://s3.documentcloud.org/documents/21177063/memorandum-opinion.pdf

FTC v. Steris/Synergy Health, FTC File No. 151 0032, (2015)

Genzyme/Novazyme, FTC File No. 021-0026 (2004) iRobot/Amazon, FTC File No. 001-36414 (2022)

Medtronic/Covidien, No. C-4503 (F.T.C. Jan. 13, 2015) (Complaint), https://www.ftc.gov/system/files/documents/cases/150121medtroniccovidiencmpt.pdf

Nielsen Holding/Arbitron, FTC Matter No. 131 0058 (2014)

Pfizer Inc./Hospira, Inc., FTC No. 151 0074, No. C-4537 (Oct. 15, 2015)

Pfizer/Hospira, No. C-4537 (F.T.C. Aug. 24, 2015) (Complaint)

Pfizer/Warner-Lambert, No. C-3957 (F.T.C. June. 19, 2000) (Complaint)

Roche Holdings Ltd., 113 FTC 1086 (1990)

Silicon Graphics, Inc., FTC Press Release (June 9, 1995), at https://www.ftc.gov/news-events/press-releases/1995/06/silicon-graphics-inc

Silicon Graphics, Inc. No. C-3626 (F.T.C. Nov. 14, 1995)

Steris/Synergy, No. 9365 (F.T.C. May 28, 2015) (Final Order)

United States v. Bazaarvoice, Inc., No. C-13-0133 (JSC) (N.D. Cal. filed Jan. 10, 2013)United States v. Bazaarvoice, Inc., Plaintiff United States of America's Post-Trial Proposed Findings of Fact (Oct. 31, 2013), https://www.justice.gov/atr/case-document/plaintiff-united-states-americas-post-trial-proposed-findings-fact-public-version

Xerox Corp., FTC Docket No. 8909 (1975)

Zillow, Inc./Trulia, Inc. FTC File No. 141-0214 (2015)

The Institute of Competition Law

The Institute of Competition Law is a publishing company, founded in 2004 by Dr. Nicolas Charbit, based in Paris, London and New York. The Institute cultivates scholarship and discussion about antitrust issues though publications and conferences. Each publication and event is supervised by editorial boards and scientific or steering committees to ensure independence, objectivity, and academic rigor. Thanks to this management, the Institute has become one of the few think tanks in Europe to have significant influence on antitrust policies.

AIM

The Institute focuses government, business and academic attention on a broad range of subjects which concern competition laws, regulations and related economics.

BOARDS

To maintain its unique focus, the Institute relies upon highly distinguished editors, all leading experts in national or international antitrust: Bill Kovacic, Mario Monti, Eleanor Fox, Laurence Idot, Frédéric Jenny, Ioannis Lianos, Richard Whish, etc.

AUTHORS

4,000 authors, from 85 jurisdictions.

PARTNERS

- Universities: University College London, King's College London, Queen Mary University, Paris Sorbonne Panthéon-Assas, etc.

- Law firms: Allen & Overy, Cleary Gottlieb Steen & Hamilton, Baker McKenzie, Hogan Lovells, Jones Day, Norton Rose Fulbright, Skadden Arps, White & Case, etc.

EVENTS

Brussels, Dusseldorf, Hong Kong, London, Milan, New York, Paris, Singapore, Warsaw and Washington DC.

ONLINE VERSION

Concurrences website provides all articles published since its inception.

PUBLICATIONS

The Institute publishes Concurrences Review, a print and online quarterly peer-reviewed journal dedicated to EU and national competitions laws. e-Competitions is a bi-monthly antitrust news bulletin covering 85 countries. The e-Competitions database contains over 24,000 case summaries from 4,000 authors.

Concurrences Review

Concurrences is a print and online quarterly peer reviewed journal dedicated to EU and national competitions laws. It has been launched in 2004 as the flagship of the Institute of Competition Law in order to provide a forum for academics, practitioners and enforcers. Concurrences'influence and expertise has garnered contributions or interviews with such figures as Christine Lagarde, Bill Kovacic, Emmanuel Macron, Antonin Scalia and Magrethe Vestager.

CONTENTS

More than 14,000 articles, print and/or online. Quarterly issues provide current coverage with contributions from the EU or national or foreign countries thanks to more than 2,500 authors in Europe and abroad.

FORMAT

In order to balance academic contributions with opinions or legal practice notes, Concurrences provides its insight and analysis in a number of formats:

- Forewords: Opinions by leading academics or enforcers
- Interviews: Interviews of antitrust experts
- On-Topics: 4 to 6 short papers on hot issues
- Law & Economics: Short papers written by economists for a legal audience
- Articles: Long academic papers
- Case Summaries: Case commentary on EU and French case law
- Legal Practice: Short papers for in-house counsels
- International: Medium size papers on international policies
- Books Review: Summaries of recent antitrust books
- Articles Review: Summaries of leading articles published in 45 antitrust journals

BOARDS

The Scientific Committee is headed by Laurence Idot, Professor at Panthéon Assas University. The International Committee is headed by Frederic Jenny, OECD Competition Comitteee Chairman. Boards members include Douglas Ginsburg, Benoît Cœuré, Howard Shelanski, Richard Whish, Wouter Wils, Joshua Wright, etc.

ONLINE VERSION

Concurrences website provides all articles published since its inception, in addition to selected articles published online only in the electronic supplement.

WRITE FOR CONCURRENCES

Concurrences welcome spontaneous contributions. Except in rare circumstances, the journal accepts only unpublished articles, whatever the form and nature of the contribution. The Editorial Board checks the form of the proposals, and then submits these to the Scientific Committee. Selection of the papers is conditional to a peer review by at least two members of the Committee. Within a month, the Committee assesses whether the draft article can be published and notifies the author.

e-Competitions Bulletin

Case Law Database

e-Competitions is the only online resource that provides consistent coverage of antitrust cases from 85 jurisdictions, organized into a searchable database structure. e-Competitions concentrates on cases summaries taking into account that in the context of a continuing growing number of sources there is a need for factual information, i.e., case law.

- 24,000 case summaries
- 4,000 authors
- 85 countries covered
- 30,000 subscribers

Sophisticated Editorial and IT Enrichment

e-Competitions is structured as a database. The editors make a sophisticated technical and legal work on all articles by tagging these with key words, drafting abstracts and writing html code to increase Google ranking. There is a team of antitrust lawyers – PhD and judges clerks – and a team of IT experts. e-Competitions makes comparative law possible. Thanks to this expert editorial work, it is possible to search and compare cases by jurisdiction, legal topics or business sectors.

Prestigious Boards

e-Competitions draws upon highly distinguished editors, all leading experts in national or international antitrust. Advisory Board Members include: Sir Christopher Bellamy, Ioanis Lianos (UCL), Eleanor Fox (NYU), Frédéric Jenny (OECD), Jacqueline Riffault-Silk (Cour de cassation), Wouter Wils (King's College London), etc.

Leading Partners

- Association of European Competition Law Judges: The AECLJ is a forum for judges of national Courts specializing in antitrust case law. Members timely feed e-Competitions with just released cases.

- Academics partners: Antitrust research centres from leading universities write regularly in e-Competitions: University College London, King's College London, Queen Mary University, etc.

- Law firms: Global law firms and antitrust niche firms write detailed cases summaries specifically for e-Competitions: Allen & Overy, Baker McKenzie, Cleary Gottlieb Steen & Hamilton, Jones Day, Norton Rose Fulbright, Skadden, White & Case, etc.

19 years of archives
30,000 articles

4 DATABASES

Concurrences
Access to latest issue and archives

- 14,000 articles from 2004 to the present

- European and national doctrine and case law

e-Competitions
Access to latest issue and archives

- 24,000 case summaries from 1911 to the present

- Case law of 85 jurisdictions

Books
Access to all Concurrences books

- 70 e-Books available

- PDF version

Conferences
**Access to the documentation
of all Concurrences events**

- 600 conferences (Brussels, Hong Kong, London,
  New York, Paris, Singapore and Washington, DC)

- 350 PowerPoint presentations, proceedings and
  syntheses

- 550 videos

- Verbatim reports

NEW

New search engine
Optimized results to save time

- Search results sorted by date, jurisdiction,
  keyword, economic sector, author, etc.

New modes of access
IP address recognition

- No need to enter codes: immediate access

- No need to change codes when your team changes:
  offers increased security and saves time

Mobility

- Responsive design: site optimized for tablets
  and smartphones